Lecture Notes of the Institute for Computer Sciences, Social Informatics and Telecommunications Engineering

460

More information about this series at https://link.springer.com/bookseries/8197

Honghao Gao · Xinheng Wang · Wei Wei ·
Tasos Dagiuklas (Eds.)

Collaborative Computing: Networking, Applications and Worksharing

18th EAI International Conference, CollaborateCom 2022
Hangzhou, China, October 15–16, 2022
Proceedings, Part I

 Springer

Editors
Honghao Gao
Shanghai University
Shanghai, China

Xinheng Wang
Xi'an Jiaotong-Liverpool University
Suzhou, China

Wei Wei
Zhejiang University City College
Hangzhou, China

Tasos Dagiuklas
London South Bank University
London, UK

ISSN 1867-8211 ISSN 1867-822X (electronic)
Lecture Notes of the Institute for Computer Sciences, Social Informatics
and Telecommunications Engineering
ISBN 978-3-031-24382-0 ISBN 978-3-031-24383-7 (eBook)
https://doi.org/10.1007/978-3-031-24383-7

This Springer imprint is published by the registered company Springer Nature Switzerland AG
The registered company address is: Gewerbestrasse 11, 6330 Cham, Switzerland

Preface

We are delighted to introduce the proceedings of the 18th European Alliance for Innovation (EAI) International Conference on Collaborative Computing: Networking, Applications and Worksharing (CollaborateCom 2022). This conference has brought together researchers, developers and practitioners from around the world who are interested in fully realizing the promises of electronic collaboration from the aspects of networking, technology and systems, user interfaces and interaction paradigms, and interoperation with application-specific components and tools.

This year's conference attracted 171 submissions. Each submission was reviewed by an average of 3 reviewers. After a rigorous review process, 57 papers were accepted. The conference sessions were: Session 1, Federated Learning and Applications; Sessions 2, 3 and 8, Edge Computing and Collaborative Working; Session 4, Recommendation Systems and Collaborative Working; Session 5, Blockchain Applications; Sessions 6 and 7, Security and Privacy Protection; Session 9, Deep Learning and Applications; Sessions 10 and 11, Collaborative Working; Session 12, Image Processing and Recognition. Apart from high quality technical paper presentations, the technical program also featured one keynote speech that was delivered by Prof. Kun Yang from the University of Essex, UK.

Coordination with the steering chair, Imrich Chlamtac, and steering committee members Song Guo, Bo Li, Xiaofei Liao, Xinheng Wang, Honghao Gao, was essential for the success of the conference. We sincerely appreciate the constant support and guidance. It was also a great pleasure to work with such an excellent organizing committee team, we thank them for their hard work in organizing and supporting the conference. In particular, we thank the Technical Program Committee, led by our General Chairs and TPC Co-Chairs, Xinheng Wang, Honghao Gao, Wei Wei, Tasos Dagiuklas, Yuyu Yin, Tun Lu, Minghui Wu, and Lqbal Muddesar, who completed the peer-review process on the technical papers and put together a high-quality technical program. We are also gratefulto the conference manager, Lucia Sedlárová, for her support and all the authors who submitted their papers to the CollaborateCom 2022 conference and workshops.

We strongly believe that the CollaborateCom conference provides a good forum for all researchers, developers and practitioners to discuss all science and technology aspects that are relevant to collaborative computing. We also expect that the future CollaborateCom conferences will be as successful and stimulating, as indicated by the contributions presented in this volume.

December 2022

Honghao Gao
Xinheng Wang
Wei Wei
Tasos Dagiuklas

Conference Organization

Steering Committee

Chair

Imrich Chlamtac — Bruno Kessler Professor, University of Trento, Italy

Members

Bo Li	The Hong Kong University of Science and Technology, China
Honghao Gao	Shanghai University, China
Ning Gu	Fudan University, China
Song Guo	University of Aizu, Japan
Xiaofei Liao	Huazhong University of Science and Technology, China
Xinheng Wang	Xi'an Jiaotong-Liverpool University, China

Organizing Committee

General Chairs

Honghao Gao	Shanghai University, China
Xinheng Wang	Xi'an Jiaotong-Liverpool University, China
Wei Wei	Zhejiang University City College, China
Tasos Dagiuklas	London South Bank University, UK

TPC Chair and Co-chairs

Yuyu Yin	Hangzhou Dianzi University, China
Tun Lu	Fudan University, China
Minghui Wu	Zhejiang University City College, China
Lqbal Muddesar	London South Bank University, UK

Web Chair

Hanghao Gao — Shanghai University, China

Publicity and Social Media Chairs

Rui Li   Xidian University, China
Yucong Duan   Hainan University, China

Workshops Chair

Yuyu Yin   Hangzhou Dianzi University, China

Sponsorship and Exhibit Chair

Hanghao Gao   Shanghai University, China

Publications Chair

Youhuizi Li   Hangzhou Dianzi University, China

Local Chairs

Shuoping Wang   Zhejiang University City College, China
Yuan-yi Chen   Zhejiang University City College, China
Jin Canghong   Zhejiang University City College, China

Technical Program Committee

Zhongqin Bi   Shanghai University of Electric Power, China
Shizhan Chen   Tianjing University, China
Lizhen Cui   Shandong University, China
Weilong Ding   North China University of Technology, China
Yucong Duan   Hainan University, China
Honghao Gao   Shanghai University, China
Fan Guisheng   East China University of Science and Technology,
                                China
Haiping Huang   Nanjing University of Posts and
                                Telecommunications, China
Li Kuang   Central South University, China
Youhuizi Li   Hangzhou Dianzi University, China
Rui Li   Xidian University, China
Xuan Liu   Yangzhou University, China
Tong Liu   Shanghai University, China
Xiaobing Sun   Yangzhou University, China
Haiyan Wang   Nanjing University of Posts &
                                Telecommunications, China
Xinheng Wang   Xi'an Jiaotong-Liverpool University, China
Xiaoxian Yang   SSPU, China

Yuyu Yin   Hangzhou Dianzi University, China
Jun Zeng   Chongqing University, China
Zijian Zhang   University of Shanghai for Science and
                               Technology, China
Li Yu   Hangzhou Dianzi University, China
Yueshen Xu   Xidian University, China
Yunni Xia   Chongqing University, China
Huang Jiwei   China University of Petroleum, China
Tong Liu   Shanghai University, China
Ding Xu   Hefei University of Technology, China
Ruihui Ma   Shanghai Jiao Tong University, China
Ying Chen   Beijing Information Science and Technology
                               University, China
Kong Linghe   Shanghai Jiao Tong University, China
Bin Cao   Zhejiang University of Technology, China
Hongyue Wu   Tianjin University, China
Gangyong Jia   Hangzhou Dianzi University, China
Zigui Jiang   Sun Yat-Sen University, China
Xuan Liu   Yangzhou University, China

Contents – Part I

Edge Computing and Collaborative Working

Blockchain Applications

Contents – Part II

Deep Learning and Application

Collaborative Working

Images Processing and Recognition

Recommendation System

A Negative Sampling-Based Service Recommendation Method

Ziming Xie[1], Buqing Cao[1(✉)], Xinwen Liyan[2], Bing Tang[1], Yueying Qing[1], Xiang Xie[1], and Siyuan Wang[1]

[1] School of Computer Science and Engineering and Hunan Key Laboratory of Service Computing and New Software Service Technology, Hunan University of Science and Technology, Xiangtan, Hunan, China
buqingcao@gmail.com

[2] School of Software and Big Data, Changzhou College of Information Technology, Changzhou, Jiangsu, China

Abstract. As the number of services has increased dramatically in recent years, it has become a challenge to provide users with high quality services. At present, the collaborative filtering technology based on graph neural network has achieved good results in service recommendation. However, these methods ignore the influence of negative sample neighbor nodes. Therefore, we propose a service recommendation method based on negative sampling, which uses the information of neighbor nodes of non-interacted services to generate negative samples to improve the recommendation accuracy. In this method, firstly, we construct the dataset for training based on the interaction records between users and services; second, we use the interpolation mixing technique to pollute the negative samples, and generate synthetic hard negative samples by fusing the negative samples selected by the hard negative selection strategy through the pooling operation; then, the samples are used in GNN-based recommender systems to obtain more accurate user and service embedding representations; next, calculate the inner product score embedded by the user and the service, and recommend high inner product score services to user. Finally, experiments were conducted on three real datasets, Shopify, Programmable, and 360Apps, and the experimental results demonstrate that the proposed method can achieve better recommendation results such as average relative increase of 30% for LightGCN and 8% for NGCF in terms of NDCG@20.

Keywords: Service recommendation · Negative sampling · Graph neural networks

1 Introduction

With the rapid development of technologies such as the internet of things and cloud computing, the number and types of services continue to increase, bringing convenience and information overload to users. It is difficult for users to select the desirable services for them. Therefore, how to select the satisfying services from numerous services and make personalized service recommendations has become a major challenge.

© ICST Institute for Computer Sciences, Social Informatics and Telecommunications Engineering 2022
Published by Springer Nature Switzerland AG 2022. All Rights Reserved
H. Gao et al. (Eds.): CollaborateCom 2022, LNICST 460, pp. 3–19, 2022.
https://doi.org/10.1007/978-3-031-24383-7_1

According to our survey, collaborative filtering-based recommender systems perform better in addressing the above challenges [1]. It recommends items to users according to the preferences of groups with common interests. At present, model-based collaborative filtering is the most popular, and it predicts users' ratings of non-interacted items from their interaction data and recommend highly-rated items to users. For example, collaborative filtering based on matrix factorization [2] is a typical method of model-based collaborative filtering, which decomposes the user-item interaction matrix into a user matrix and an item matrix, and then uses the product of the user matrix and the item matrix as the user's rating for the item. Moreover, collaborative filtering based on neural networks [3], which learns a score function from hidden feedback information through neural networks. In order to provide more accurate recommendations to users, some researchers consider modeling the user-item graph structure and utilize the idea of recursively aggregating neighbor information in GNNs to obtain the final embedding of the target node. Currently, NGCF [4] and LightGCN [5] have achieved better results in this work. In general, GNN-based recommender systems first aggregate and propagate neighborhood information through an embedding aggregation layer and an embedding propagation layer, and then obtain the final embedding of users (items) through pooling operations. Finally, the inner product score is used to predict the user's preference for the item. It is generally believed that users prefer interacted items (positive samples) to non-interacted items (negative samples). Taking the classic BPR loss [6] as an example, for each user and each positive sample, we select one of the items that the user has not interact with as a negative sample.

Negative samples largely affect the performance of GNN-based recommender systems. A good negative sampling method can not only improve the calculation efficiency of the model, but also enhance the training effect of the model. Typically, negative sampling uses a uniform distribution [6, 7]. In order to improve the quality of negative samples, some researchers consider using the user's score on the negative samples during model training [8, 9], and use the negative samples with high scores as negative samples. Others researchers consider using GAN to select negative samples [10, 11], but the model is too complicated, the training effect is not good, and the application scenarios are not widely used. Another researcher considers negative sampling combined with graph structure information. For example, PinSage [12] uses PageRank score to select hard negative examples based on the random walk strategy. MCNs [13] proposes to sample negative samples according to an approximate distribution of positive samples, and accelerates negative sampling by Metropolis-Hastings. However, they only consider negative sampling from the perspective of discrete space, ignoring the process of neighborhood aggregation in GNNs.

Inspired by the work of Huang et al. [14], We consider combining the user-item graph structure with a GNN-based aggregation process to synthesize hard negative samples, and propose a negative sampling-based service recommendation method (NSSR). Specifically, the method uses interpolation mixing technology to pollute the negative samples, and fuses the negative samples selected by the hard negative selection strategy through the pooling operation to generate synthetic hard negative samples, which are used in the GNN-based recommendation system. Thus, a more accu rate embedded representation of users and services can be obtained, and finally services are recommended through the inner product of users and services. In summary, the contributions of this paper are as follows:

- This paper proposes a negative sampling-based service recommendation method. The method utilizes the information of non-interacted service's neighbor nodes to generate hard negative samples, and the samples is used for the training of the recommendation system based on graph neural network, which improve the accuracy of service recommendation.
- We inject the information of the interactive services into the negative samples to make the negative samples closer to the positive samples, and use the pooling operation to fuse the information of the hard negative samples of different layers to synthesize high-quality hard negative samples, and improve the recommendation model's ability to distinguish between positive and negative samples.
- We conduct corresponding experiments on the proposed method on real datasets from Kaggle. The experimental results verify the effectiveness of the service recommendation method proposed in this paper, which can better improve the recommendation result of the GNN-based recommendation system.

The rest of this paper is organized as follows. Section 2 is related work on negative sampling methods. Section 3 is the basic process of GNN-based recommender systems. Section 4 details the steps of the method. Section 5 is experimental evaluation and analysis. Section 6 is the conclusion and outlook of this paper.

2   Related Work

2.1   GNN-Based Recommender System

In recent years, with the rapid increase in the number of services, it is difficult for users to find the services they are interested in from a wide variety of services. Therefore, relevant researchers have explored collaborative filtering-based recommendation, usually assuming that users with a similar history of interactions may have the same preferences for the same services.

At present, GNN-based recommender systems have attracted much attention. It models users and services as a bipartite graph, and exploits graph higher-order connectivity to capture collaborative signals from user and service interactions to obtain better latent representations of users and services. Among them, the neighborhood aggregation module affects the quality of the transmitted neighbor information, which largely determines the accuracy of the recommender system. Therefore, NGCF [4] aggregates neighbor information recursively to capture cooperative signals in higher-order connectivity. Specifically, each node obtains its high-order representation by recursively aggregating its neighbor information. When LightGCN [5] does not retain the target node's own information when updating node information through neighbor aggregation and only uses neighbor information as to its representation. It is also found that feature transformation and non-linear activation operations do not contribute to GNN-based collaborative filtering recommendation.

2.2 Negative Sampling Method

The negative sampling method will greatly affect the training quality of the model. Negative samples with better effect can not only improve the training speed of the model, but also provide more valuable information to the model for better training effect. At present, the negative sampling methods mainly fall into the following categories:

Static Negative Sampling. Items are usually selected as negative examples in non-interacted datasets, and by setting different strategies, the corresponding negative samples can be obtained as training data. For example, Rendle et al. [6] propose RNS (Random Negative Sampling) to select a negative example from the negative sample candidate set through a uniform distribution. The PNS (popularity-based negative sampling) proposed by He et al. [16] uses the number of occurrences of items in the training set as the weight for selection, that is, it prefers items with a high frequency of occurrence as negative samples. However, the static negative sampling method does not change with the training, does not adjust well to the training results and makes it difficult to mine negative samples that are more useful to the model.

Hard Negative Sampling. Static negative sampling cannot be adjusted according to the results of training, which may result in some negative samples containing useless information, and making it difficult to mine negative samples that are more effective for the model. Therefore, it is suggested that the discriminative ability of the model can be improved if those samples that are misclassified can be utilized. For example: Zhang et al. [8] consider that the negative examples with high prediction scores can improve the quality of model training, so they propose dynamic negative sampling (DSN), which can dynamically extract the highest scoring negative samples in each training. Kalantidis et al. [9] propose the MoCHi model, which does not directly obtain negative samples from the data, and synthesizes the negative samples directly in contrastive learning. However, hard negative sampling only utilizes the semantic information of the samples in the embedding space, and does not utilize the structural information on the user-item graph.

Graph-Based Negative Sampling. The above studies consider negative sampling using the semantic information of samples in the embedding space, but negative sampling techniques based on graph structure have not been widely explored. Hamilton et al. [16] propose a recommendation model (i.e.SamWalker) that utilizes social network information to obtain negative samples through random wandering at target nodes. Ying et al. [12] proposed the PinSage model based on the random wandering strategy, which further leverages the structural information of the graph to select hard negative examples through PageRank scores. Yang et al. [13] propose Markov Chain Monte Carlo Negative Sampling (MCNs), which proposes to sample negative samples according to the approximate distribution of positive samples, and redesign the sample distribution of positive and negative samples according to the structural correlation on the graph.

Adversarial Sampling. In recent years, generative adversarial networks have gradually become a popular neural network algorithm. The key to the adversarial sampling method lies in the adversarial sampler, which is used to mine the data for negative information.

Wang et al. [10] propose IRGAN, which selects negative examples through GAN, and the generator acts as a negative sample, making it impossible for the discriminator to distinguish positive examples from those selected by the generator. Park et al. [11] propose AdvIR, which is based on GAN, with adversarial training in which adversarial perturbations are imposed. However, the adversarial negative sampling model framework is too complex, the training time is too long, and the training effect is unstable.

3 Preliminaries

Now, we introduce the collaborative filtering recommendation model based on graph neural network (GNN).

When given a set of users $U = \{u\}$, item $V = \{v\}$, positive sample $R^+ = \{(u, v^+) | u \in U, v^+ \in V\}$, The recommender system predicts the user's preference for unknown items through the user's historical interaction records in the positive sample.

Recent studies have shown that The CF model based on GNN has obvious advantages in solving the above problems [4, 5, 12]. The main idea is to use the high-order connectivity of the graph to capture the high-order neighbor node information of the user (item) target node to generate the final latent representation, and then express its preference degree through the inner product score. That is, $\hat{y} = e_u^T \cdot e_v$. Next, we'll give a brief introduction to aggregation, pooling, and negative sampling optimizations.

Aggregation. Each user and item have an initial embedding vector e_u and e_v. In the propagation process, by aggregating neighbor information, the cooperative signals of neighbors can be captured. For example, the aggregation process of LightGCN is:

$$e_u^{(l+1)} = \sum_{i \in N_u} \frac{1}{\sqrt{|N_u||N_i|}} e_i^l, \; e_i^{(l+1)} = \sum_{i \in N_i} \frac{1}{\sqrt{|N_u||N_i|}} e_u^l \tag{1}$$

where e_u^l, e_i^l represent the embeddings of user u and item i in the l-th layer of GNN, respectively. $\frac{1}{\sqrt{|N_u||N_i|}}$ is a symmetric normalization term, and $|N_u|, |N_i|$ represent the number of first hop neighbors of user u and item i.

Pooling. GNNs for recommendation are different from GNNs [17, 18] for node classification, which directly use the representation of the last layer, and the former adopt a pooling operation to generate the final representations of users and items. According to [19], adopting a pooling operation helps avoid transition smoothing and determines the degree of validity of node subgraph information.

Specifically, for an L-layer GNN, the pooling operation is used to generate the final representations of users and items. For example, LightGCN uses a sum-based pooling operation:

$$e_u^* = \sum_{l=0}^{L} \lambda_l e_u^{(l)}, \; e_i^* = \sum_{l=1}^{L} \lambda_l e_i^{(l)} \tag{2}$$

NGCF uses a sum-based pooling operation:

$$e_u^* = e_u^{(0)} \cdots e_u^{(l)}, \; e_u^* = e_u^{(0)} \cdots e_u^{(l)} \tag{3}$$

Negative Sampling Optimization. The purpose of learning to rank is to rank users' scores according to items. Items that users like are generally considered to have higher scores than others. However, we usually only get implicit feedback information from users. Therefore, we assume that users prefer interacted items to non-interacted items. Since the user interacted items are only a small fraction, the BPR loss is used to represent the learning objective:

$$\max \prod_{v^+, v^- \sim f_n(u)} P_u(v^+ > v^- | \Theta) \tag{4}$$

where v^+ and v^- represent positive and negative samples respectively, $P_u(x > y)$ represents that user u prefers x to y, and Θ is a parameter of the model. $f_n(u)$ is the distribution of negative sampling, and most recommended methods use uniformly distributed negative sampling [4–6, 20].

4   Method

The overall framework of the NSSR model proposed in this paper is shown in Fig. 1, including: (1) data preprocessing; (2) synthetic hard negative samples; (3) graph neural network; (4) service recommendation.

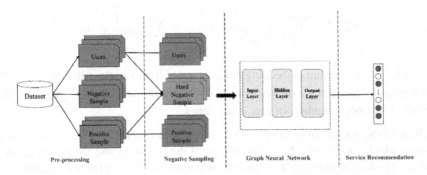

Fig. 1. Service recommendation framework

4.1   Data Preprocessing

This article uses three datasets, Shopify, 360Apps, and ProgrammableWeb respectively, and do the following operations for these three datasets:

Eliminate Invalid Information. In all three datasets, there are some services with incomplete interaction information, and the interaction objects of these services cannot be judged, which will affect the generation of negative samples and the training of neural networks. So, we delete these incomplete interaction records.

Generate the Final Dataset. Since most users only have three or less interaction data, in order to facilitate the training and testing of the neural network, we only retain user data with more than four interaction records. For the Shopify and 360Apps datasets, it still has a lot of interaction data after the above operation. In order to facilitate the training of the model, we randomly extract part of the interaction data according to the proportion of its application categories to generate the final dataset.

Take Raw Negative Samples. Following the convention [15], we adopt the same method to select negative examples from the services that the user has not interacted with to form the candidate set M.

4.2 Synthetic Hard Negative Samples

Positive Mixing. For an l layer GNN, each service v has $L + 1$ layers embedding vector, and each vector $e_v^{(l)}$ contains the previous l layer information. For the candidate set M. These N negative examples have a total of $N \times (L + 1)$ vectors, which constitute a negative sample candidate set $\varepsilon = \{e_{v_i}^{(l)}\}$.

Inspired by the technology of mixup [9, 21], we inject the service information e_{v+} that the user has interacted with into the negative sample vector in ε, which can improves the model's discrimination ability. For each negative sample vector $e_{v_i}^{(l)}$ in the candidate set, the operation of positive mixing is as follows:

$$e_{v_i}'^{(l)} = \alpha^{(l)} e_{v+}^{(l)} + \left(1 - \alpha^{(l)}\right) e_{v_i}^{(l)}, \alpha \in (0, 1) \tag{5}$$

where $\alpha^{(l)}$ is the l-th layer mixing coefficient uniformly sampled from (0,1), which is used to control the amount of information injected into positive samples and enhance the model's adaptability to different data. And ε' r represents the set of hard negative samples after positive mixing, and $\varepsilon' = \{e_{v_i}'^{(l)}\}$.

Hop Mixing. Positive mixing generates synthetic negative samples v^- and their embeddings e_{v^-} according to the idea of aggregation in GNNs. For the hard negative sample set $\varepsilon' = \{e_{v_i}'^{(l)}\}$ obtained in the positive mixture, we extract a hard negative example $e_{v_i}'^{(l)}$ $(1 \le i \le M)$ from each layer $l(0 \le l \le L)$ in the set. For example, when $L = 2$, we can sample $e_{v_1}'^{(0)}$, $e_{v_2}'^{(1)}$ and $e_{v_3}'^{(2)}$, where v_1, v_2, v_3 can be the same service or different services. Finally, the hard negative samples sampled in each layer are aggregated through the pooling operation, and get the representation e_{v^-} of the synthetic negative sample v^-. The form is as follow:

$$e_{v^-} = f_{pool}\left(e_{v_1}'^{(0)}, \cdots, e_{v_n}'^{(L)}\right) \tag{6}$$

where f_{pool} is the pooling operation, and its operation is the same as the recommended pooling operation of GNN, $e_{v_1}'^{(l)}$ is the l-th layer embedding vector of v_1.

About how to select a valid $e_{v_i}'^{(l)}$ from each layer of ε'. A recent study on negative sampling for link prediction (MCNS)[13] showed that the expected risk of optimal parameters between expected and empirical losses satisfies:

$$E\left[\|(\theta_T - \theta^*)_u\|^2\right] = \frac{1}{T}\left(\frac{1}{P_d(v|u)} - 1 + \frac{1}{P_n(v|u)} - \frac{1}{K}\right) \tag{7}$$

where $P_d(v|u)$ and $P_n(v|u)$) represent the estimated positive and negative distributions, respectively, and T is the number of user-item node pairs, K is the number of negatives for each user recruiting in the loss. By analyzing the above formula, we can conclude that when the positive distribution is proportional to the negative distribution, the expected risk is only affected by the positive distribution. And the higher the internal score of the user and the item, the more accurate the interaction probability predicted by the recommender system.

Based on the above theory, the problem then becomes how to select negative samples according to the distribution of positive samples. Inspired by the idea that the inner product approximates the positive distribution in the hard negative selection strategy [22, 8], We calculate the inner product of the user vector and the negative sample vector, and select the hard negative sample with the largest inner product. The hard negative sample selection strategy of the l-th layer is of the following form:

$$e'^{(l)}_{v_i} = \text{argmax} f_M(u, l) \cdot e^{(l)}_{v_j} \tag{8}$$

where $e^{(l)}_{v_j} \in \varepsilon^{(l)}$, $f_M(u, l)$ is the mapping function, which represents the user's embedding in the l-th layer, and $\cdot$ is the inner product operation.

The mapping function in Eq. (7) depends on the pooling operation in Eq. (6). At present, the mainstream pooling operations include sum-based and concat-based pooling operations. Therefore, the inner product form of user embedding e_u and negative sample embedding e_{v^-} can be divided into two types:

- Sum-based pooling: $e_u \cdot e_{v^-} = \sum_{l=0}^{L} \lambda_l e_u \cdot e^{(l)}_{v^-}$
- Concat-based pooling: $e_u \cdot e_{v^-} = \sum_{l=0}^{L} \lambda_l e^{(l)}_u \cdot e^{(l)}_{v^-}$

In order to make $f_M(u, l)$ in Eq. (3) consistent with the pooling operation for GNN recommendation, we set $f_M(u, l) = e_u$ for sum-based pooling and $f_M(u, l) = e^{(l)}_u$ for concat-based pooling.

Loss Function. Through the above modeling process, we replace the negative sampling method $f_n(u)$ in Eq. (4) with the NSSR model, and the BPR loss function is updated as:

$$L_{BPR} = - \sum_{\substack{(u, v^+) \in R^+ \\ e_{v^-} \sim f_{WR(u,v^+)}}} \ln\sigma(e_u \cdot e_{v^+} - e_u \cdot e_{v^-}) \tag{9}$$

where $\sigma()$ is the sigmoid activation function, R^+ is the interaction set between the user and the service, and $e_{v^-} \sim f_{WR(u,v^+)}$ means that e_{v^-} is obtained through the NSSR model.

4.3 Graph Neural Network

This paper adopts two graph neural network models, NGCF and LightGCN, for final recommendation prediction. They aggregate the information of neighbors to the target node, which can usually be expressed as:

$$e_u^{(l+1)} = AGG(e_u^{(l)}, \{e_i^{(l)} : i \epsilon N_u\}) \tag{10}$$

where AGG is an aggregation function that aggregates the information of the target node and its neighbors in the l-th layer to obtain a higher-order representation.

This paper uses user feature sampling, positive sample data and strong negative samples generated by the NSSR module as the input data of the graph neural network, and uses the recommendation relationship as the label to train the graph neural network, so that the graph neural network can achieve the ideal recommendation effect. The model uses the inner product of the embedding vectors of users and services as the ranking score of service recommendations. The calculation formula is as follows:

$$\hat{y}_{ui} = e_u^T e_i \tag{11}$$

4.4 Service Recommendation

In the process of recommending services to users, we take the information of users, positive samples and negative samples as input to generate synthetic difficult negative samples, and it is used in the training process based on the GNN recommendation model, so that users can more accurately recommend services of interest. The specific process is as follows:

First, the dataset is preprocessed, according to the convention [15], we select some of the non-interacted services as the negative sample candidate set.

Then, we inject positive sample information into the negative samples, and then fuse the hard negative samples selected by the hard negative selection strategy through the pooling operation to generate synthetic hard negative samples.

Next, we apply the synthesized hard-negative samples to a GNN-based recommendation model which can make model more difficult to distinguish between positive and negative samples and obtain a more accurate final embedding representation of users and services, thereby improving model recommendation quality.

Finally, we obtain user and service embedding representations from model training, and recommend high scoring services to users based on their inner product scores.

5 Experiments

5.1 Dataset Description

The datasets in this paper are the public datasets Shopify app store, Programma-bleWeb, and 360Apps from Kaggle. The Shopify and 360Apps datasets contain user-App inter-action data. The Shopify dataset contains 292,029 interaction records, and 360Apps contains 24,631,734 interaction records. To facilitate model training, we first preprocess the data to remove incomplete interaction records and user data with less than 4 interaction records. According to the app category ratio, the data is randomly selected as the final data set. The ProgrammableWeb dataset contains records of different Mashup calling APIs, and we also remove the incomplete interaction records. Finally, we randomly select 30% of the interaction records from the processed dataset as the test set and 70% of the interaction records as the training set. The detailed information is shown in Table 1.

Table 1. Statistics of the dataset

Dataset	User	Item	Interactions	Density
Shopify	5969	2831	44478	0.00263
ProgrammableWeb	6156	1550	12970	0.00136
360Apps	8724	1720	46026	0.00307

5.2 Evaluation Metrics

In this experiment, we use Recall@K, and NDCG@K (default setting K = 20) to evaluate the effectiveness of users' service preference ranking. Where Recall is the proportion of correctly classified services to all the services of this category, and the Normalized Depreciation Cumulative Gain (NDCG), which is used to evaluate the gap between the ranking list of the recommender system and the real user interaction list. The formula and meaning are as follows:

$$Recall = \frac{TP}{TP + FN} \tag{12}$$

$$DCG = \sum_{i=1}^{p} \frac{2^{rel_i} - 1}{log_2(i + 1)} \tag{13}$$

$$IDCG = \sum_{i=1}^{|REL|} \frac{2^{rel_i} - 1}{log_2(i + 1)} \tag{14}$$

$$NDCG = \frac{DCG}{IDCG} \tag{15}$$

5.3 Baseline Methods

In order to verify the effectiveness of the experimental model, we conduct comparative experiments on the recommendation module and the negative sampling module respectively:

Recommendation Model. To verify the effectiveness of the recommendation module in this paper, we conduct comparative experiments on two GNN-based recommender systems, LightGCN and NGCF.

a) LightGCN[5]: It is a state-of-the-art CF method. LightGCN believes that directly using GCN for collaborative filtering recommendation would make the model too complex, because each node in the user-item graph of CF does not contain any attributes. LightGCN adopts a simple weighted sum aggregator and abandons feature transformation and nonlinear activation to achieve better performance.
b) NGCF[4]: Inspired by graph convolutional networks, NGCF exploits the bipartite graph structure by propagating embeddings. Cooperative signals are explicitly encoded with high-order connectivity. Specifically, each node obtains its high-order representation by recursively aggregating its neighbor information.

Negative Sampling Model. The proposed NSSR negative sampling method is compared with RNS.

a) RNS[6]: Also called uniform negative sampling. During the training process, the probability of each negative sample being selected remains unchanged, that is, one is randomly selected as a negative example from the negative example candidate set.

5.4 Experimental Performance

Table 2. Service recommendation performance comparison

	Shopify		ProgrammableWeb		360Apps	
	Recall	NDCG	Recall	NDCG	Recall	NDCG
LightGCN + RNS	0.0517	0.0293	0.3977	0.2619	0.4952	0.2916
LightGCN + NSSR	**0.1019**	**0.0514**	**0.4185**	**0.2902**	**0.5163**	**0.3069**
NGCF + RNS	0.0824	0.0424	0.2256	0.1171	0.5082	0.2994
NGCF + NSSR	0.0845	0.0443	0.2523	0.1531	0.4407	0.2611

In this section, we cross comparison the recommendation module and the negative sampling module to analyze the experimental results. From Table 2, Fig. 2 and Fig. 3 we can analyze that:

- LightGCN + NSSR consistently maintains the best performance among all comparison methods. LightGCN has an average improvement of 50% for Recall@20, 30% for NDCG@20.
- In most cases, LightGCN performs better than NGCF, indicating that feature transformation and non-linear activation operations can indeed increase the training burden of collaborative filtering recommendation, which will reduce the accuracy of recommendation.

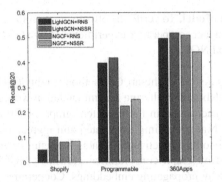

Fig. 2. Comparison of Recall@20 values of different models

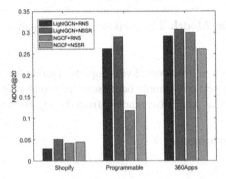

Fig. 3. Comparison of NDCG@20 values of different models

- For both NGCF and LightGCN, NSSR outperforms RNS in almost all cases. We analyze the following reasons: (1) The negative samples are enhanced by the skipmixing technique, which improves the generalization ability of the recommender system. (2) The synthesized hard negative samples are obtained by aggregating multiple hard negative samples from different layers, making the negative samples more informative. The generation of hard negative samples combines semantic information from different samples, thereby providing the model with information-rich gradients.

Table 3. The number of user-App pairs in training and test sets with different sparsity

Shopify	Train	Test
0.26	30282	14196
0.20	22981	10815
0.15	17235	8112
0.10	11490	5408

Table 4. Comparison of service recommendation under different densities in Shopify dataset

	Density	Recall	NDCG
LightGCN + NSSR	0.0026	0.1019	0.0514
	0.0020	0.0903	0.0417
	0.0015	0.0753	0.0341
	0.0010	0.0627	0.0262
LightGCN + RNS	0.0026	0.0517	0.0293
	0.0020	0.0485	0.0259
	0.0015	0.0444	0.0237
	0.0010	0.0357	0.0176

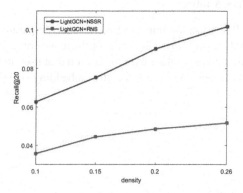

Fig. 4. Recall@20 variation curve under different densities

In order to further explore the performance of different negative sampling methods for different density datasets. We select the above mentioned LightGCN with the best recommendation effect as the recommendation system, and conduct comparative experiments on the Shopify dataset. Without changing the number of users and apps, we vary the sparsity of the dataset by keeping the ratio of its training set to its test set constant and only changing the number of interactions. The number of user-App pairs in the final Shopify dataset for the training and test sets at different densities is set as shown in Table 3.

By comparing Table 4 and Fig. 4 and Fig. 5. We find that both the Recall and NDCG values of NSSR and RNS increase as the dataset density increases, but the Recall and NDCG values of NSSR increase by a larger margin compared to RNS. We analyze that due to the increase of user interaction data, the NSSR model can better capture information from the RNS, enhancing the expression of difficult samples in the positive mixture, while obtaining a better representation of the final negative sample embedding by aggregating richer neighbor information, making it more difficult to distinguish between positive and negative samples, improving the discriminative power of the model and obtaining more accurate recommendations.

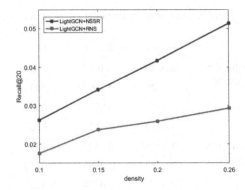

Fig. 5. NDCG@20 variation curve under different densities

5.5 Hyperparameters Analysis

In this section, we will analyze the impact of the three hyperparameters of embedding size, node loss rate, and message loss rate on the performance of recommender systems. The essence of embedding is to replace high dimensional of user and service with a low dimensional vector, the dimension of which is the embedding size (Fig. 6).

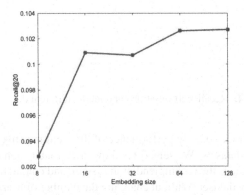

Fig. 6. Recall@20 variation with different embedding sizes

We test the effect of different embedding dimensions of the service on the results of the experiment. As the embedding dimension of the user with the service increases, it effectively improves the results of the experiment. Embedding size increases significantly from 8 to 16, increases slowly from 16 to 64, and flattens out when it is greater than 64. When the embedding dimension is 8, it can be seen that the effect is not ideal, which means that when the embedding dimension is very low, the result will be unsatisfactory because the number of features after embedding of users and services is too small. As the embedding dimension increases, the model becomes more complex, causing the training process to be too slow. When the embedding dimension is 128, it is not much different from the experimental results with the embedding dimension 64, but it is much longer than the time it takes, so we do not conduct relevant experiments on the subsequent embedding dimensions (Fig. 7).

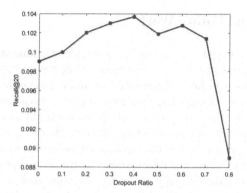

Fig. 7. Variation of Recall@20 in the loss rate of different nodes

We then test the change in Recall@20 for different node loss rates. When the node loss rate changes from 0.0 to 0.4, Recall@20 gradually increases, indicating that the node loss rate within a certain range can make the training effect of the model better. When the node loss rate is greater than 0.6, the training decreases, and when it is greater than 0.7, the effect decreases sharply, indicating that too many nodes loss makes the model obtain too little information, making it difficult for the model to make accurate predictions (Fig. 8).

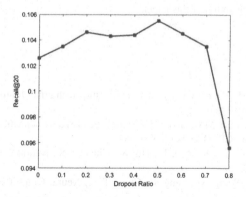

Fig. 8. Variation of Recall@20 with different message loss rates

We also test the variation of Recall@20 for different message loss rates. When the message loss rate changes from 0 to 0.5, the experimental effect is slowly improved, and when the message loss rate is around 0.5, the model accuracy will reach the best. It shows that losing some messages can make model recommendation more effective. When the message loss rate is between 0.5 and 0.7, Reeall@20 decreases slowly, and when the message loss rate is greater than 0.7, Recall@20 decreases significantly, which again shows that too much message loss will greatly affect the model's recommendation performance.

6 Conclusion and Future Work

This paper proposes a negative sampling-based service recommendation method. This method firstly use interpolation mixing technique to inject positive sample information into negative samples, and fuses the negative samples selected by the hard negative selection strategy through the pooling operation to generate synthetic difficult negative samples, which are used in the GNN-based recommendation system to obtain more accurate user and service embedding representation. Finally, according to the inner product score of the user and the service, recommend the service with high inner product score to the user. The experimental results show that the method proposed in this paper can effectively improve the accuracy of service recommendation. In future work, we will consider reducing the number of false negatives, that is, we do not want the model to regard services that users may be interested in as negatives. In future work, we will consider the impact of the selection of negative sampling ratio on the model, and will also consider reducing the number of false negative examples, that is, we do not want the model to regard the services that users may be interested in as negative examples in the future.

Acknowledgment. Our work is supported by the National Natural Science Foundation of China (No. 61873316, 61872139, 61832014, and 61702181), the National Key R&D Program of China (No.2018YFB1402800), Hunan Provincial Natural Science Foundation of China under grant No. 2021JJ30274, and the Educational Commission of Hunan Province of China (No.20B244). Buqing Cao is the corresponding author of this paper.

References

1. Koren, Y., Bell, R.M., Volinsky, C.: Matrix factorization techniques for recommender systems. Computer **42**(8), 30–37 (2009)
2. Ma, H., Yang, H., Lyu, M.R., King, I.: Sorec: social recommendation using probabilistic matrix factorization, CIKM2008, pp. 931–940
3. He, X., Liao, L., Zhang, H., Nie, L., Hu, X., Chua, T.-S.: Neural Collaborative Filtering, WWW2017, pp. 173–182
4. Wang, X., He, X., Wang, M., Feng, F., Chua, T.-S.: Neural Graph Collaborative Filtering, SIGIR2019
5. He, X., Deng, K., Wang, X., Li, Y., Zhang, Y., Wang, M.: LightGCN: Simplifying and Powering Graph Convolution Network for Recommendation, SIGIR2020
6. Rendle, S., Freudenthaler, C., Gantner, Z., Schmidt-Thieme, L.: BPR: Bayesian Personalized Ranking from Implicit Feedback, UAI2009, pp. 452–461
7. He, X., et al.: Fast matrix factorization for online recommendation with implicit feedback, SIGIR2016
8. Zhang, W., Chen, T., Wang, J., Yu, Y.: Optimizing top-n collaborative filtering via dynamic negative item sampling, SIGIR2013, pp. 785–788

9. Kalantidis, Y., Sariyildiz, M.B., Pion, N., Weinzaepfel, P., Larlus, D.: Hard Negative Mixing for Contrastive Learning, NeurIPS2020
10. Wang, J., et al.: IRGAN: A Minimax Game for Unifying Generative and Discriminative Information Retrieval Models, SIGIR2017, pp. 515–524
11. Park, D.H., Chang, Y.: Adversarial Sampling and Training for Semi-Supervised Information Retrieval, WWW2019, pp. 1443–1453
12. Ying, R., He, R., Chen, K., Eksombatchai, P., Hamilton, W.L., Leskovec, J.: Graph convolutional neural networks for -scale recommender systems, KDD2018, pp. 974–983
13. Yang, Z., Ding, M., Zhou, C., Yang, H., Zhou, J., Tang, J.: Understanding Negative Sampling in Graph Representation Learning, KDD2020
14. Huang, T., et al.: MixGCF: An Improved Training Method for Graph Neural Network-based Recommender Systems, KDD2021
15. Huang, J.-T., et al.: Embedding-based Retrieval in Facebook Search, KDD2020
16. Chen, J., Wang, C., Zhou, S., et al.: Samwalker: Social recommendation with informative sampling strategy, WWW2019, pp.228–239
17. Hamilton, W.L., Ying, R., Leskovec, J.: Inductive Representation Learning on Large Graphs, NeurIPS2017, pp.1025–1035
18. Kipf, T.N., Welling, M.: Semi-Supervised Classification with Graph Convolutional Networks. ICLR2017
19. Xu, K., Li, C., Tian, Y., Sonobe, T., Kawarabayashi, K.I., Jegelka, S.: Representation Learning on Graphs with Jumping Knowledge Networks. ICML2018
20. Qiu, J., Tang, J., Ma, H., Dong, Y., Wang, K., Tang, J.: DeepInf: Social Influence Prediction with Deep Learning, KDD2018, pp. 2110–2119
21. Zhang, H., Cisse, M., Dauphin, Y.N., Lopez-Paz, D.: Mixup: Beyond empirical risk minimization, ICLR2018
22. Rendle, S., Freudenthaler, C.: Improving pairwise learning for item recommendation from implicit feedback, WSDM2014, pp.273–282

Knowledge Graph Enhanced Web API Recommendation via Neighbor Information Propagation for Multi-service Application Development

Zhen Chen[1,3]([✉]), Yujie Li[1], Yuying Wang[1], Xiaowei Liu[1], Yifan Xing[1], Linlin Liu[2], Dianlong You[1,3], and Limin Shen[1,3]

[1] College of Information Science and Engineering, Yanshan University, Qinhuangdao 066004, China
[2] National Science Libraries, Chinese Academy of Sciences, Beijing 100864, China
[3] The Key Laboratory for Computer Virtual Technology and System Integration of Hebei Province, Qinhuangdao 066004, China
zhenchen@ysu.edu.cn

Abstract. In cloud era, Web APIs have been the best carrier for service delivery, capability replication and data output in multi-service application development. Currently, the number of Web APIs on the Internet is huge and growing exponentially. To enable accurate and fast Web API selection for developers, researchers have proposed a variety of Web API recommendation methods. However, existing methods cannot solve the inherent data sparsity problem well. In addition, existing methods use context information indirectly by finding neighbors or discretely through embedding techniques, while rich semantic information in the Web API ecosystem is ignored. To solve the above problems, we firstly crawl and analyze Web API data to construct a Web API knowledge graph, which laid a data foundation for alleviating the data sparsity problem. Then, we propose a knowledge graph-enhanced Web API recommendation model, so as to improve recommendation accuracy by capturing high-order structural information and semantic information. Typically, multivariate representations of user and Web API are made by the neighbor information propagation in Web API knowledge graph. The proposed model supports end-to-end learning for beneficial feature extraction. Finally, experiments results demonstrate the proposed model outperforms baselines significantly, thereby promoting the development of Web API economy.

Keywords: Multi-service application development · Web API recommendation · Knowledge graph · Neighbor information propagation

Supported by National Natural Science Foundation of China, No. 62102348, 62276226. Natural Science Foundation of Hebei Province, China, No. F2022203012, F2021203038. Science and Technology Research Project of Hebei University, No. QN2020183. Innovation Capability Improvement Plan Project of Hebei Province, No. 22567626H.

H. Gao et al. (Eds.): CollaborateCom 2022, LNICST 460, pp. 20–40, 2022.
https://doi.org/10.1007/978-3-031-24383-7_2

1   Introduction

Service-oriented architecture (SOA) is an enterprise-wide approach to agile application development as well as a collection of design principles that support loose coupling and reusability of different components in distributed applications [1]. Nowadays, SOA is changing the way of software development, which enables software development through the cloud by seamlessly composing readily interoperable service components [2], with each service component being responsible for a small subset of the application's functionality. On one hand, developers are able to invoke existing services for many required functionalities rather than write one start-to-finish set of codes after another, avoiding repeated wheel reinventing, long development cycles, and improving application elasticity. On the other hand, enterprises release their core business capabilities and valuable data in the form of services, realizing the maximum utilization of their legacy assets. Therefore, with the rise of SOA, software development has currently started undergoing a major shift from monolithic applications, to graphs of hundreds of loosely-coupled service components, and multi-service applications have become the de-facto standard for delivering today's enterprise IT applications [3].

Currently, Web API is the mainstream technology to realize SOA. Different from the traditional SOAP based Web services, Web API is based on a simpler REST architecture and has attracted great attention due to the advantages of easy access, easy composition and lightweight [4]. Web APIs serve as the fundamental building blocks of modern software that provide direct and indirect cloud services and data to developers. Hence, developers can combine different kinds of existing Web APIs to achieve required functions in almost any distributed multi-service application today [5], which greatly reduces the burden of developers and improves developer agility and productivity. For instance, developers only need to focus on their key business process of the check-in system, rather than designing and training a complex face recognition algorithm for the implementation of identity authentication module. Hence, with the increasing complexity of distributed application system, learning and invoking Web API has become a common activity and a key challenge in modern multi-service application development.

In recent years, multi-service application drives the formation and the increasing prosperity of Web API economy. As a result of such a driving force, the number of Web APIs on the Web is huge and growing exponentially [6]. Many Web API sharing platforms appear on the Internet, such as ProgrammableWeb, RapidAPI and APIList. Although rich Web API resources provide users with more choices, it is difficult for developers lacking expertise to quickly choose appropriate Web APIs that meet their personalized needs, due to the fact that there are a large number of Web APIs with similar functionalities on the Web. We note that ProgrammableWeb and other platforms provide the way of keyword and tag search, but the returned results through keyword or tag search are not satisfactory. This passive retrieval method is not conducive to meeting the needs of developers for Web APIs, thereby hindering the efficient software development. Therefore, the active and personalized Web API recommendation has become an urgent problem to be addressed.

Among some methods that have been proposed to solve the personalized recommendation of Web API, neighborhood-based recommendation method has been widely understood and applied in the field of recommendation. Neighborhood-based recommendation is one line of collaborative filtering method [7], which works by searching a group neighbors for the target user or Web API based on the calculated similarity using the historical interaction data between user and Web API, user's preference to the target Web API can be predicted by these selected neighbors, and the final Web API recommendation list is generated based on the predicted preferences [8]. Noting that the number of available Web APIs on the Internet is huge, a single user only used a few of them, and thus the user-Web API interaction matrix is usually sparse in real Web API ecosystem. In such data sparse situations, the similarity between users in neighborhood-based methods may be exaggerated. Faced with the unavoidable problem of data sparsity, neighborhood-based method has the disadvantages of low accuracy. Model-based methods use some machine learning algorithms to train the vector of items, and then build a model to predict the probability that a user will have a demand for a Web API [9]. Although data sparsity is alleviated by avoiding similarity calculation, the interaction between users and Web APIs in real scenarios is complex and nonlinear, the simple linear dot product calculation in model-based recommendation methods limits the prediction accuracy [10]. In recent years, with the strong representational learning ability of deep learning, deep learning is able to establish the complex interaction relationship between user and Web API, which provides promising opportunities to advance Web API recommendation.

However, there are still some challenges on the research road of realizing accurate Web API recommendation. Specifically, there are the following challenges:

(1) *The widely used embedding technology in deep learning method only produces single user and API representation, which makes the inevitable data sparsity still not resolved effectively.* Existing deep learning based Web API recommendation methods usually use embedding technology to transform users, Web APIs and their attribute features into dense vectors. The interactive relationship between users and Web APIs attempts to be captured by the complex and deep network structure. However, it is easy to produce over fitting problem when the deep learning model is complex with small amount of training data, which makes the sparsity problem still unresolved and even more serious.

(2) *High-order structural information and semantic information are ignored in many existing Web API recommendation methods, which make the accuracy of Web API recommendation results still unsatisfactory.* There is a lot of contextual information in the interaction between users and APIs, but they are not fully exploited. However, in practical scenario, user, API, and contextual information are not independent of each other, but have rich

semantic and associated relationships. Using these relationships can effectively enrich and enhance the intrinsic feature representation of the user and Web API, thus providing a promising solution to solve the sparsity problem and improve accuracy.

(3) *Existing feature representation methods strongly rely on the use of feature engineering for beneficial feature extraction, which cannot achieve end-to-end training and reduce the scalability of the model.* Many existing studies believe that contextual information between user and API interaction can effectively solve the sparsity problem, but not all contextual information is beneficial. Therefore, identifying beneficial contexts is the key to improve the accuracy of recommendation. Existing methods mostly depend on the tedious manual features engineering for beneficial feature extraction. However, this method cannot be generalized to the patterns in untrained samples and cannot realize end-to-end training, and thus reducing the scalability of recommendation model.

To further improve the accuracy of recommendation, we consider introducing knowledge graph into Web API recommendation. Knowledge graph is a semantic network graph that describes various entities and their relationships in the objective world, which can be used as an effective tool to describe the entities and their relationships in Web API ecosystem. With structured Web API knowledge, knowledge graph provides the ability to analyze problem from a "relation" perspective, and provides a new way to solve the above challenges. In this paper, we introduce a knowledge graph enhanced Web API recommendation approach, named KGWARec, which makes full use of the multivariate representation of user and Web API to mimic a decision-making process where the multivariate representation is determined by the high-order structural and semantic information through neighbor information propagation in our established Web API knowledge graph. Specifically, a user/Web API as a node in knowledge graph is represented by his/her multi-hop neighbors in our constructed Web API knowledge graph through information propagation, so as to realize the multivariate representation of user and Web API. Through estimating the preference of user on the target Web API, we can generate effective Web API recommendation list for multi-service application developers. Since our embedding representation of user and Web API is a multivariate representation, which can automatically discover users' hierarchical potential interests and capture Web APIs' potential multivariate representation by iteratively propagating information in a knowledge graph, generating accurate Web API recombination results.

In conclusion, the contributions of this paper are as follows:

(1) We construct a Web API knowledge graph based on the crawled data from real-world Web API platform ProgrammableWeb, which provides a new perspective of mining potential interest of users and multivariate representation of Web APIs from the perspective of semantic relations.

(2) We develop a multivariate representation method for users and Web APIs based on knowledge graph, wherein high-order structural information and

semantic information are captured, which has a better capability to predict accurate preference of user on the target Web API in the data sparse case.

(3) We propose a knowledge graph enhanced Web API recommendation model via neighbor information propagation with an end-to-end training manner, wherein no prior knowledge of feature representation is needed in the training.

The reminder of this paper is organized as follows. We review works related to our approach in Sect. 2. We describe the Web API knowledge graph construction and formulate our recommendation task in Sect. 3. In Sect. 4, we introduce the details of the proposed approach. We through extensive experiments prove the effectiveness and superiority of our approach in Sect. 5. Finally, we conclude this paper and discuss our future works.

2   Related Works

2.1   Collaborative Filtering Based Web API Recommendation

Collaborative filtering based Web API recommendation method is a traditional recommendation method that appeared earlier and has a wider range of uses. Because the idea of collaborative filtering method is easy to understand and accept, many researchers improve the accuracy of Web API recommendation by improving collaborative filtering method. Tang et al. [11] integrate the spatial information of users and Web services in the traditional similarity calculation process. Chen et al. [12] use the user's credit and spatial context information to improve the accuracy of similarity calculation. Collaborative filtering based Web API recommendation method still mainly relies on the user's historical usage records. However, it can be noticed from observation that among the platforms that provide Web API, the number of Web APIs is very large, but the number of Web APIs used by users is small, and the user-Web API historical interaction matrix is very sparse. Satisfactory recommendation results cannot be obtained under such conditions.

2.2   Model Based Web API Recommendation

Different from neighborhood based methods that only use neighbors for prediction, model based methods usually use the overall data to learn a prediction model to solve the high sparsity problem. The most representative matrix factorization (MF) method projects the high-dimensional sparse matrix into two low-dimensional dense matrices, and uses the obtained matrices to discover the user's preference for Web API [13]. Fletcher [14] propose a MF method that considers the quality features of Web APIs, which enhances the quality and the diversity of Web API recommendations. Chen et al. [15] assume that similar neighbors have similar latent feature, and a MF model that considers the neighborhood is proposed by integrating the diversified neighbors of the API.

Although model-based methods can effectively alleviate the problem of data sparsity and improve the accuracy of recommendations by introducing similar relationships and contextual information, model-based Web API recommendation methods still have the problem that the performance decreases as the sparsity and dimensionality of the input data increase. And it is also difficult to accurately determine the optimal dimension of the low-dimensional dense matrices in practical applications. In addition, Web API recommendation systems often lack explicit scoring data and usually need to use implicit interaction data. However, researchers have found that MF is more suitable for explicit feedback matrices, while the results of the feedback matrix for implicit behavior are not ideal [16]. Therefore, model-based methods still have great limitations in Web API recommendation.

2.3   Deep Learning Based Web API Recommendation

Deep learning method integrate heterogeneous side information such as feedback data, social networks, attributes and so on to optimize the recommendation results. In recent years, there have been many applications of deep learning in Web API recommendation: Xiong et al. [17] propose a deep hybrid service recommendation (DHSR) model that integrates MLP and text similarity calculations to learn the nonlinear relationship between mashups and Web APIs. Cao et al. [18] use Doc2Vec and attention factorization machine (AFM)to extract and identify the importance of each feature of Web API and then realize the modeling of multi-dimensional information. Zhao et al. [19] propose a Web API recommendation method using feature integration and learning ranking. This method uses the text, nearest neighbor, Web API specific feature and tag of Web APIs to estimate the correlation between Web APIs. Web API recommendation based on deep learning converts information such as attributes and context into a single feature vector input model, and there are still a large number of potential associated semantic information between various information that does not play a role. Knowledge graph can show the complete ecology of a field in the real world, mainly through the relationship to complete the connection between things. Therefore, consider introducing knowledge graphs to further improve the performance of Web API recommendation methods.

2.4   Knowledge Graph Based Web API Recommendation

Recently, researchers began to pay attention to how to make full and in-depth use of the information in the knowledge graph for knowledge perception recommendation [20]. Due to the existence of a large number of potential users, association information and attribute information between various individuals in Web API ecosystem, the recommendation method based on knowledge graph has also begun to emerge in the field of Web API recommendation. Kwapong et al. [21] presented a knowledge graph based framework for Web API recommendation, and show how to use knowledge graph to improve Web API recommendation with side information. Based on the above framework, a method for mashup tag recommendation is further proposed [22]. Wang et al. [23] designed a knowledge graph schema to encode the mashup-specific contexts and model the mashup requirement with graphic entities, and then exploit random walks with restart to assess the potential relevance between the mashup requirement and the Web APIs according to the knowledge graph. Geng [24] used KGCN to mine the high-order relationship between Web services and mashup preference, and adopt Doc2Vec model to get the semantics of mashups. Inspired by the above work, this paper uses the knowledge graph neighbor information propagation method to obtain the neighbors of the Web API and the user, and makes full use of the attribute information and colorful relationship information of various entities in the Web API knowledge graph to generate multiple representations of the user and the Web API, and then achieve accurate recommendation.

3 Preliminaries

3.1 Web API Knowledge Graph Construction

Knowledge graph provides the ability to make Web API recommendation from a "relation" perspective. We construct a Web API knowledge graph according to the following steps: data acquisition, knowledge extraction and knowledge integration.

Stage 1: *Data acquisition.* We collect data from ProgrammableWeb, which contains name, category, label and other detailed information of Web APIs, mashups, users and so on.

Stage 2: *Knowledge extraction.* We propose a Web API knowledge extraction method based on top-down analysis. Specifically, we first use graph mapping to define the top-level entity relationship pattern, and then extract the entity and relation knowledge according to the relationship pattern. Finally, seven types of entities and eight types relations are extracted.

Stage 3: *Knowledge integration.* Based on the crawled data and the extracted entity and relation knowledge, we form the knowledge of Web API ecology in the form of triple (head entity-relationship-tail entity).

Based on the above process, the statistics of the Web API knowledge graph we built are shown in Table 1.

3.2 Problem Formulation

For the Web API ecosystem in real world, we have a set of users $U = \{u_1, u_2, ...\}$, a set of Web APIs $A = \{a_1, a_2, ...\}$ and the user-Web API interaction matrix $Y = \{y_{ua} \mid u \in U, a \in A\}$. The user-Web API interaction matrix Y is defined by whether a user has used a Web API. The multi-service application Mashup consists of Web APIs with various functions, which builds usage relationship between Web APIs invoked by the Mashup and the Mashup developer. Specifically, if user u has used the Web API a, then $y_{ua} = 1$, otherwise, $y_{ua} = 0$. Web API knowledge graph is a semantic network and can be expressed as a collection

Table 1. Statistics of the built Web API knowledge graph

Name	Knowledge type	Count
Web API	Entity	21,126
User	Entity	147,566
Web API Category	Entity	421
Web API Secondary Category	Entity	925
Web API Tag	Entity	7,617
Mashup	Entity	7,621
Provider	Entity	6,529
(Web API, belong, Category)	Triple relation	21,070
(Web API, belong, SCategory)	Triple relation	49,120
(Web API, has, Tag)	Triple relation	50,878
(User, follow, Web API)	Triple relation	567,044
(Provider, provide, Web API)	Triple relation	26,048
(User, follow, Mashup)	Triple relation	15,180
(User, develop, Mashup)	Triple relation	5,516
(Mashup, invoke, Web API)	Triple relation	13,138

of triples $G\{(h, r, t)\}$, where (h, r, t) denotes the knowledge triple, $h \in \epsilon$, $r \in R$, $t \in \epsilon$ are the head entity, relation and tail entity of a knowledge triple respectively, and the symbol ϵ and R represent the entity set and relation set in the Web API knowledge graph respectively.

The knowledge graph enhanced Web API recommendation problem can be formulated as: given user-Web API interaction matrix Y and Web API knowledge graph G, our goal is to predict whether user u has potential interest to the Web API a that user u has not used before. Specifically, our task is to learn a prediction model

$$\hat{y}_{u,a} = \mathcal{F}(u, a \,|\, Y, \mathcal{G}) \tag{1}$$

where $\hat{y}_{u,a}$ denotes the preference probability that user u may use Web API a in the future.

4 Methodology

In this section, we describe the proposed KGWARec in detail. We first introduce the overall framework of KGWARec. Then, we present the modeling process of KGWARec from three aspects: preprocessing layer, multivariate representation layer and prediction layer. Finally, the learning algorithm of KGWARec is described.

4.1 Framework

Figure 1 shows the framework of KGWARec, consisting of preprocessing layer, multivariate representation layer and prediction layer.

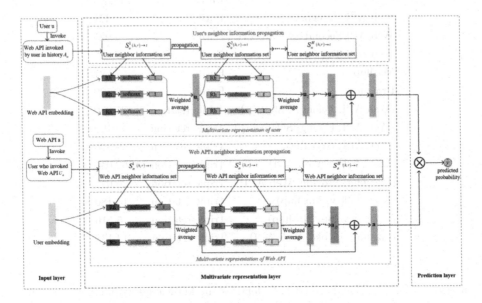

Fig. 1. Overview of the proposed KGWARec.

(1) *Preprocessing layer.* The goal of this layer is to generate an initial embedding vector for a given user and a given Web API. The preprocessing layer makes sufficient preparation for the following multivariate representation layer.

(2) *Multivariate representation layer.* This layer is mainly applied to iteratively calculate the feature representation of users and Web APIs after each layer of propagation through the neighbor information obtained at each hop, so as to propagate and expand the initial neighbor information.

(3) *Prediction layer.* This layer uses the multivariate representations of users and Web APIs learned in the previous layer to predict the probability of users using candidate Web APIs.

4.2 Modeling

Preprocessing Layer

The preprocessing layer mainly uses the user-Web API interaction records to make initial preparation for propagation and calculation of the multi-representation layer. For the input user and Web API, they are initialized by the dense embedding technique. These embedded feature vectors are later sent to the multivariate representation layer for iterative interaction. Combining all Web APIs used by the user before into a collection, we define the user history usage collection, which can be expressed as: $A_u = \{a \mid Web\ API\ \ used\ \ by\ \ user\ u\}$. The characteristics of Web APIs used by users in history contain the needs of users. Using these Web APIs as initial neighbor nodes can expand and propagate users' interests and explore users' deep intentions.

Similarly, all users who have used the candidate Web API constitute the historical user set of the Web API, $U_a = \{u \mid user\ \ who\ \ used\ \ Web\ API\}$. On the knowledge graph of Web APIs, the neighbors of one Web API can describe the characteristics of the Web API from a certain point of view, and the propagation of neighbor information also starts from the user entity node. The initial neighbor node is also the head entity in the one hop neighbor information set.

Multivariate Representation Layer

Neighbor Information Propagation Based on Knowledge Graph. In the Web API knowledge graph, various types of neighbor entities of users or Web APIs can be found through different kinds of relationships. These relationships and entities contain rich information, which can be used to describe users' interests and the characteristics of Web APIs. We can get the neighbor entities and neighbor information set of each hop by continuously propagating along the relation edges on the knowledge graph. The elements in the neighbor information set are in the form of triples, which contain the relation information between entities. Neighbor entities can be regarded as the natural extension of users' historical interests and Web APIs' characteristics, and contain personalized information of users and Web APIs. Therefore, through the propagation of neighbor information, we can mine users' potential preferences and interests, and capture the semantic association between Web APIs.

In order to explore users' needs through the propagation of neighbor information in the Web API knowledge graph, we recursively define the set of k-hop neighbor entities and k-hop neighbor information set for user u as follows:

Definition 1: *Given user-Web API interaction matrix Y and Web API knowledge graph G, the set of k-hop neighbor entities for user u is defined as:*

$$\mathcal{E}_u^k = \{t \mid (h, r, t) \in \mathcal{G} \quad and \quad h \in \mathcal{E}_u^{k-1}\} \tag{2}$$

where $k = 1,\ 2,\ ...H$, $\epsilon_u^0 = A_u\{y_{ua} = 1\}$ is the set of user u's used Web APIs in the past, which can be seen as the initial neighbor set of user u in Web API knowledge graph G.

Definition 2: *The k-hop neighbor information set of user u is defined as the set of knowledge triples starting from ϵ_u^{k-1}:*

$$S_u^k = \{(h, r, t) \mid (h, r, t) \in \mathcal{G}, \quad h \in \mathcal{E}_u^{k-1}\} \tag{3}$$

where $k = 1,\ 2,\ ...H$.

Just as exploring the deep needs of users through the propagation of neighbor information in the knowledge graph, Web APIs can also find their corresponding neighbors through the connection with other entities in the knowledge graph, and use neighbor information to accurately describe the characteristics of them. The initial neighbors of one Web API are the users who have used the Web API before. Similarly, we give the definitions of the set of k-hop neighbor entities and k-hop neighbor information set of the Web API:

Definition 3: *Given user-Web API interaction matrix Y and Web API knowledge graph G, the set of k-hop neighbor entities for Web API a is defined as:*

$$\mathcal{E}_a^k = \left\{ t \mid (h, r, t) \in \mathcal{G} \quad and \quad h \in \mathcal{E}_a^{k-1} \right\} \tag{4}$$

where k = 1, 2, ...H, $\epsilon_u^0 = A_u\{y_{ua} = 1\}$ is the set of user's used Web APIs in the past, which can be seen as the initial neighbor set of user u in Web API knowledge graph.

Definition 4: *The k-hop neighbor information set of Web API a is defined as the set of knowledge triples starting from ϵ_a^{k-1}:*

$$S_a^k = \left\{ (h, r, t) \mid (h, r, t) \in \mathcal{G}, h \in \mathcal{E}_a^{k-1} \right\} \tag{5}$$

where k = 1, 2, ...H.

The size of the neighbor information set refers to the number of neighbor information in the neighbor information set. As the number of hops k increases, the size of the neighbor information set may become too large, which may bring some noisy data, and the influence of the noisy data is greater than that of the valid data. Because the distance between entities after multiple hops is too far from the initial node, the similarity between them decreases, and their features play a relatively small role in users' potential interest exploration and Web APIs' characterization. Therefore, it's necessary to select an appropriate number of hops first, while fixing the size of the neighbor information set to avoid errors and reduce the amount of computation. The selection of specific hop number and neighbor information set size (neighbor size for short) will be discussed in the experiment section.

User Multivariate Representation. The following is a detailed discussion on how to mine users' deep potential interests through knowledge graph neighbor information propagation and obtain users' multivariate representation. As shown in Fig. 1, each Web API a is associated with a d-dimensional embedding $\mathbf{q} \in \mathbf{R}^d$. Given the Web API embedding $\mathbf{q}$ and the one-hop neighbor information set S_u^1 of user u, for each triple (h_i, r_i, t_i) in S_u^1, we compare head h_i and relation r_i with Web API a, and the correlation probability w_i is calculated as follows:

$$w_i = \mathrm{softmax}\left(\mathbf{q}^{\mathrm{T}}\mathbf{R}_i\mathbf{h}_i\right) = \frac{\exp\left(\mathbf{q}^{\mathrm{T}}\mathbf{R}_i\mathbf{h}_i\right)}{\sum_{(h,r,t)\in S_u^1} \exp\left(\mathbf{q}^{\mathrm{T}}\mathbf{R}\mathbf{h}\right)} \tag{6}$$

where $\mathbf{R}_i \in \mathbf{R}^{d \times d}$ is the embedding of relation r_i, $\mathbf{h}_i \in \mathbf{R}^d$ is the embedding of head h_i, w_i represents the similarity between the neighbor entity $\mathbf{h}_i$ and Web API $\mathbf{a}$ measured in the space of relation $\mathbf{R}_i$. Because different relationships will also lead to different similarity between neighbor entity h_i and Web API $\mathbf{q}$, the relationship embedding matrix $\mathbf{R}_i$ should be considered in calculation. Such as Twitter API and Facebook API, if measured by their primary category relation, they are more similar, but when measured by their secondary categories or tags, they are less similar. For all triples in S_u^1, user's potential interest propagates from the head entity h_i to the tail entity t_i along the relation r_i, and take the calculated w_i as the weight to weighted sum of all tail entities. Then the one-order multivariate representation of user u after one-hop propagation is obtained as follows:

$$\mathbf{u_1} = \sum_{(h_i r_i t_i) \in S_u^1} w_i \mathbf{t}_i \qquad (7)$$

where $\mathbf{t}_i \in \mathbf{R}^d$ is the d-dimensional vector embedding of t_i. The user u is represented by his neighbor information in the knowledge graph, rather than an independent feature vector.

Then, the neighbor information of user u continues to propagate. When calculating the two-hop user multivariate representation, we need to replace the $\mathbf{q}$ in (6) with $\mathbf{u_1}$ calculated by (7) and recalculate w_i. For further propagation, $S_u^i, i = 1, 2, ..., H$ for each hop, we repeat the above iterative operation to calculate $\mathbf{u_1}, \mathbf{u_2}, ... \mathbf{u_H}$. Combined with the user multivariate representation obtained by each hop propagation, the final multivariate representation of user u is obtained as:

$$\mathbf{u} = \mathbf{u_1} + \mathbf{u_2} + ... + \mathbf{u_H}. \qquad (8)$$

Web API Multivariate Representation. Similar to the method of obtaining multivariate representation, for the multivariate representation of Web APIs, we first obtain the d-dimensional embedded representation vector of each user, and then define the user embeddings and the one-hop neighbor information set S_a^1 with users who have used Web API a as head nodes. For each triple (h'_i, r'_i, t'_i) in S_a^1, we compare head h'_i and relation r'_i with user u to calculate the correlation probability w'_i, which is the similarity between each neighbor node h'_i and user u under relation R'_i:

$$w'_i = \text{softmax}\left(\mathbf{p}^T \mathbf{R'}_i \mathbf{h'}_i\right) = \frac{\exp\left(\mathbf{p}^T \mathbf{R'}_i \mathbf{h'}_i\right)}{\sum_{(h', r', t') \in S_a^1} \exp\left(\mathbf{p}^T \mathbf{R'} \mathbf{h'}\right)} \qquad (9)$$

where $\mathbf{p}$ is the embedding of user u, $\mathbf{R'}_i \in \mathbf{R}^{d \times d}$ is the embedding of relation r'_i, $\mathbf{h'}_i \in \mathbf{R}^d$ is the embedding of head h'_i.

Web APIs obtain various types of neighbors through the triple propagation in KG. The information of neighbors arriving at each layer is aggregated to enrich the feature representation of Web APIs. After one-hop propagation, the multivariate representation of Web API a is:

$$\mathbf{a_1} = \sum_{(h'_i r'_i t_i') \in S_a^1} w'_i \mathbf{t}'_i \tag{10}$$

where $\mathbf{t}'_i \in \mathbf{R}^d$ is the d-dimensional vector expression.

Continuing to propagate along the relation edges in the Web API knowledge graph to obtain the neighbor characteristics of the next layer of Web API a, we use $\mathbf{a_1}$ to replace $\mathbf{u}$ in (9), recalculate according to the above steps and repeat the iterative process to obtain Web API a's multivariate representation $\mathbf{a_1}, \mathbf{a_2}, \dots \mathbf{a_H}$ of each layer through H-hops. Finally, by overlaying the results of each layer, we get Web API a's multivariate representation obtained through the propagation of the knowledge graph's neighbor information:

$$\mathbf{a} = \mathbf{a_1} + \mathbf{a_2} + \dots + \mathbf{a_H} \tag{11}$$

Prediction Layer

According to multivariate representation layer, we get the final multivariate representation $\mathbf{u}$ and $\mathbf{a}$ of user u and Web API a. The user multivariate representation $\mathbf{u}$ contains the history information of user u and its neighbor information in the knowledge graph. The Web API multivariate representation $\mathbf{a}$ contains the API itself and its neighbor information in the knowledge graph. Then we use the inner product of user embedding and Web API embedding to get the predicted probability value:

$$\hat{y}_{ua} = \sigma \left(\mathbf{u}^T \mathbf{a} \right) \tag{12}$$

The loss function for KGWARec is as follows:

$$\min \mathcal{L} = \sum_{(u,a) \in \mathbf{Y}} \mathcal{T} \left(\hat{y}_{ua}, y_{ua} \right) + \frac{\lambda_2}{2} \sum_{r \in \mathcal{R}} \left\| \mathbf{I}_r - \mathbf{E}^T \mathbf{R} \mathbf{E} \right\|_2^2 +$$
$$\frac{\lambda_1}{2} \left(\|\mathbf{A}\|_2^2 + \|\mathbf{U}\|_2^2 + \|\mathbf{E}\|_2^2 + \sum_{r \in \mathcal{R}} \|\mathbf{R}\|_2^2 \right) \tag{13}$$

where $\mathbf{A}$ and $\mathbf{E}$ are the embedding matrices for all Web APIs and entities respectively, and $\mathbf{I}_r$ is the slice of the indicator tensor $\mathbf{I}$ in KG for relation r. In (13), the first term is the cross entropy-loss function, which measures the difference between the real value of the interaction matrix $\mathbf{Y}$ and the predicted value by KGWARec, the second term is the loss for knowledge graph feature representation, and the third term is the parameter regularization loss, which is to prevent over-fitting.

5   Experiments

5.1   Preparation

Datasets. We crawl Web API-related data from the ProgrammableWeb platform, and use historical interaction records between users and Web APIs as the experimental dataset. The statistics of the experimental dataset are shown in Table 2. In addition, under the premise of ensuring that the historical needs of users are not changed, negative sampling is performed to reduce the imbalance of positive and negative samples. This specific method is to randomly select a set of Web APIs with no user behavior from all Web APIs, whose amount is equal to the amount of data marked as 1, and mark the records composed of APIs from the set and the users as 0 as negative samples.

All experiments are conducted using python-3.6.5 in Windows 10 OS. The configuration is CPU i7-7700 @ 3.60 GHz, 8G RAM. The ratio of training set, evaluation set, and test set is 6:2:2.

Table 2. Statistics for experimental dataset

Item	Count
Web API	1,163
User	2,701
Interaction	15,184
Sparsity	0.9953

5.2   Comparison

The following methods are selected as the baselines:

FM [25], considers the interaction between features and models the interaction of all nested variables. It can estimate reliable parameters in the case of sparse data, so as to obtain the interaction prediction probability of user items.

AFM [26], introduces the attention mechanism into the feature crossover module to learn the importance of different crossover features. The attention score calculated by the attention network is used to weighted sum the interactive features, and the FM model is extended.

NFM [27], is a neural network attempt of FM model. It combines the linear intersection of FM to second-order features with the nonlinear intersection of neural network to higher-order features to strengthen the expression ability of the model.

MKR [28], automatically learns the high-order feature interaction between the items in the recommendation system and the entities in the knowledge graph through the cross-compression unit, and uses the multi task learning framework for alternating learning to improve the recommendation quality.

KGCN [29], combines the features of knowledge graph with graph convolution neural network, enriches the embedded representation of items by aggregating neighbor information, catch local neighborhood structure, and obtains the personalized preferences of user.

KGNN-LS [30], develops a method based on label smoothness, designs a loss function for label propagation, regularizes the edge weight in the process of learning, and realizes better generalization.

The compared results are presented in Table 3.

Table 3. AUC and ACC results of different models

Model	AUC	ACC
FM	0.8460	0.7621
AFM	0.8438	0.7663
NFM	0.8467	0.7370
MKR	0.7849	0.7906
KGCN	0.8502	0.8143
KGNN-LS	0.8779	0.8277
KGWARec	0.9372	0.8763

(1) It can be seen from Table 3, our KGWARec model achieves the best results on the evaluation metrics AUC and ACC. Compared with the KGNN-LS model with the best performance in the baseline model, the AUC and ACC improvements of KGWARec is 5.7% and 4.9% respectively, indicating the utilization of structural information and semantic information of knowledge graph can achieve more accurate predictions under sparse scenarios.

(2) By observing the results of ACC in the table, it can be seen that the performance of MKR, KGCN, KGNN-LS and KGWARec, that is, models integrated with the knowledge graph, perform better than the FM, AFM and NFM without knowledge graph. This indicates that leveraging knowledge graph as auxiliary information to recommendation can indeed provide richer auxiliary information for recommendation tasks, optimize feature representation, and improve recommendation accuracy.

(3) FM, AFM and NFM models also achieve better results in the case of sparse interaction data, but the performance is not as good as the proposed KGWARec model. The reason is that although models such as FM take into account the intersection between features, but these models ignore the semantic information of the relationship between features, while KGWARec focuses on the role of different relational spaces.

(4) KGCN, KGNN-LS and KGWARec have better performance than MKR, which can show that mining knowledge graph by capturing neighbor information in knowledge graph is effective. In addition, KGWARec utilizes the

method of neighbor information propagation on the knowledge graph, and enriches the multiple representations of users and Web APIs, which further improves the recommendation performance.

(5) Figure 2 shows the performance of each model under the evaluation Recall@K. K is the number of selected Web APIs with the highest predicted value, and the value of K is 1, 10, 20, 30, 40, 50. It can be seen that KGWARec also shows the best performance under the Recall@K indicator.

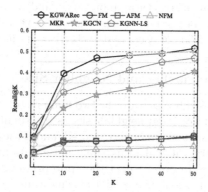

Fig. 2. The results of Recall@K.

5.3   Ablation Study

In this experiment, we study the impact of knowledge graph on Web API recommendation. KGWARec-None indicates not using knowledge graph, KGWARec-U and KGWARec-A indicate multi-representation of user and Web API using knowledge graph, respectively. Experimental results are shown in Table 4.

Table 4. AUC and ACC results with different ablation strategy

Model	AUC	ACC
KGWARec-None	0.7121	0.4529
KGWARec-U	0.8166	0.6580
KGWARec-A	0.8701	0.7597
KGWARec	0.9372	0.8763

It can be seen from Table 4 that the performance of KGWARec-None is the worst, ACC has not reached 0.5, which means that the classifier is unqualified.

The reason is that user Web API interaction data is very sparse, KGWARec-None do not use any auxiliary information of the knowledge graph, it is difficult to characterize user's interest or Web API's feature through the sparse interaction. Compared with KGWARec-None, the AUC and ACC results obtained by KGWARec-U and KGWARec-A are significantly higher, which well proves that the neighbor information propagation method introduced into the knowledge graph can effectively improve the data sparsity problem. KGWARec obtains the best results, compared with KGWARec-A, the AUC is increased by 7.7%, and the ACC is increased by 15.3%, which further proves the theoretical validity of this model. The addition of structural information and semantic information will have a positive impact on the recommendation, it is very meaningful to enrich the multiple representations of users and Web APIs at the same time.

5.4   Impact of Hop Number and Neighbor Size

The hop number and neighbor size are the two main factors of our model. Specifically, if the number of hops and neighbor size is too small, the correlation and dependency between entities cannot be explored, and if the hop number and and neighbor size is too large, it will bring some noise data and affect the performance of the algorithm. In order to get the appropriate hop and neighbor size, we change the hop and neighbor size at the same time to observe the changes of evaluation indicators AUC and ACC, which not only ensures the best representation of the characteristics of Web API and users' interests, but also avoids the influence of too much noise information.

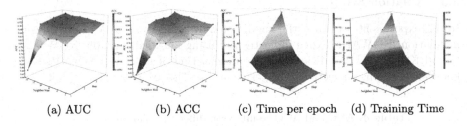

(a) AUC   (b) ACC   (c) Time per epoch   (d) Training Time

Fig. 3. Impact of hop number and neighbor size

By observing Fig. 3(a), it can be seen that when the number of hops is selected as 1, the value of AUC is low, and then it first increases and then decreases with the increase of the number of hops. The change trend of AUC with the size of neighbors also increases first and then decreases. At the same time, it can be observed that the AUC results are better when the hop count is 2, the neighbor size is 16, the hop count is 3, the neighbor size is 32, and the hop count is 4, and the neighbor size is 64. It can be clearly observed in Fig. 3(b) that the ACC reaches a maximum of 0.8749 when the hop count is set to 2 and the neighbor size is set to 16. Therefore, although the AUC values obtained at 3 hops of 32 neighbors and 4 hops of 64 neighbors increase slightly for 2 hops of 16 neighbors, the magnitude is very small, while the ACC is at 3 hops of 32 neighbors and 4 hops of 64 neighbors. There is a significant decrease in neighbors, so the performance of AUC and ACC is comprehensive, and it is believed that setting the number of hops to 2 and the size of neighbors to 16 can make the model reach the optimum.

Figure 3(c) and Fig. 3(d) shows the effect of the hop and neighbor size on training time per epoch and the total training time. It can be obviously observed that the training time is increased with the rising of hops and neighbor size, which demonstrates that the efficiency of KGWARec is affected by hop and neighbor size.

5.5   Impact of Embedding Size

In this section, we study the effect of embedding size on the performance of our model KGWARec. We adjusted the embedding size from 2 to 32, while keeping the other parameters unchanged. The values of AUC and ACC are shown in Fig. 4(a) and Fig. 4(b).

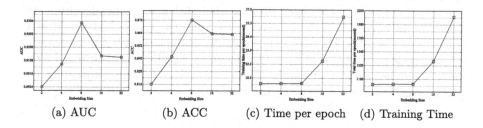

(a) AUC   (b) ACC   (c) Time per epoch   (d) Training Time

Fig. 4. Impact of hop embedding size

It can be observed from the research results that the accuracy of our KGWARec model has been improved at the beginning, because more useful information can be obtained by appropriately increasing the embedded dimension. When the embedding size approach 8, the best experimental results are reached, and then it begins to decline. Figure 4(c) and Fig. 4(d) show the values of training time per epoch and total training time under different embedding sizes. We can clearly see that training time is linear with the increasing of embedding size, illustrating the efficient of our KGWARec model related to embedding size.

5.6   Convergence of KGWARec

To evaluate the efficiency and convergence of KGWARec, we observe the training time of KGWARec and investigate whether the prediction results converge through the increasing of training epoch. Figure 5(a) and (b) report the training time of each epoch and the total training time of KGWARec respectively. Figure 5(c) and (d) present the values of AUC and ACC for each epoch, and the training loss as the epoch grows, respectively.

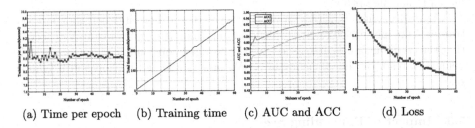

(a) Time per epoch   (b) Training time   (c) AUC and ACC   (d) Loss

Fig. 5. Convergence of KGWARec

As can be seen in Fig. 5(a), the training time of each epoch fluctuates in a small range, which show that our algorithm is stable. In Fig. 5(b), the total training time increases linearly with the training epoch, showing that the training epoch is also one of the factors affecting the efficiency of our algorithm. By observing the curve in Fig. 5(c), it can be see that, the value of AUC and ACC first increase significantly and then gradually stabilized with the increase of epoch. The loss curve in Fig. 5(d) first decreases rapidly and then tends to be stable with the increase of epoch. These results can strongly prove that our method has good convergence within the effective training times.

6   Conclusion

In this paper, we presented a knowledge graph-enhanced Web API recommendation model based on neighborhood information propagation method. To this end, we first use the crawled real-world Web API data to build a Web API knowledge graph, and then propose a neighbor information propagation method to make full use of the higher-order structural information and contextual semantic information in the knowledge graph for obtaining the multivariate representation of users and Web APIs. The probability of users' interest to the target Web API is predicted through the multivariate representation of users and Web API. KGWARec uses an end-to-end joint training method to update parameters, no manual feature extraction is needed. Finally, experimental results demonstrate the superiority and effectiveness of our KGWARec model. And it proves that improving Web API recommendation performance by incorporating with knowledge graph neighbor information is a correct research route. In the near future, we plan to further improve the accuracy of Web API recommendation from the perspective of API complementarity by using knowledge graph.

References

1. Zhang, L., Zhang, J., Cai, H.: Services Computing. Springer, Heidelberg (2007). https://doi.org/10.1007/978-3-540-38284-3
2. Niknejad, N., Ismail, W., Ghani, I., Nazari, B., Bahari, M., et al.: Understanding Service-Oriented Architecture (SOA): a systematic literature review and directions for further investigation. Inf. Syst. **91**, 101491 (2022)
3. Hustad, E., Olsen, D.: Service-oriented architecture. Creating a sustainable digital infrastructure: the role of service-oriented architecture. Procedia Comput. Sci. **181**, 597–604 (2021)
4. Tang, B., Yan, M., Zhang, N., et al.: Co-attentive representation learning for web services classification. Expert Syst. Appl. **180**, 115070 (2021)
5. Qi, L., Song, H., Zhang, X., et al.: Compatibility-aware web API recommendation for mashup creation via textual description mining. ACM Trans. Multimedia Comput. Commun. Appl. **17**(1s), 1–19 (2021)
6. Adeleye, O., Yu, J., Wang, G., et al.: Constructing and evaluating evolving web-API networks-a complex network perspective. IEEE Trans. Serv. Comput. (2021)
7. Ebesu, T., Shen, B., Fang, Y.: The 41st International ACM SIGIR Conference on Research & Development in Information Retrieval, pp. 515–524 (2018)
8. Cui, Z., Xu, X., Fei, X., Cai, X., et al.: Personalized recommendation system based on collaborative filtering for IoT scenarios. IEEE Trans. Serv. Comput. **13**(4), 685–695 (2020)
9. Yi, B., Shen, X., Liu, H., et al.: Deep matrix factorization with implicit feedback embedding for recommendation system. IEEE Trans. Industr. Inf. **15**(8), 4591–4601 (2019)
10. Chen, C., Zhang, M., Ma, W., et al.: Efficient non-sampling factorization machines for optimal context-aware recommendation. In: Proceedings of the Web Conference 2020, pp. 2400–2410 (2020)
11. Tang, M., Jiang, Y., Liu, J., et al.: Location-aware collaborative filtering for QoS-based service recommendation. In: 2012 IEEE 19th International Conference on Web Services, pp. 202–209(2012)
12. Chen, K., Mao, H., Shi, X., et al.: Trust-aware and location-based collaborative filtering for Web service QoS prediction. In: 2017 IEEE 41st Annual Computer Software and Applications Conference (COMPSAC), vol. 2, pp. 143–148 (2017)
13. Zhang, Y., Wang, K., He, Q., et al.: Covering-based web service quality prediction via neighborhood-aware matrix factorization. IEEE Trans. Serv. Comput. **14**(5), 1333–1344 (2019)
14. Fletcher, K.K.: A quality-aware web API recommender system for mashup development. In: Ferreira, J.E., Musaev, A., Zhang, L.-J. (eds.) SCC 2019. LNCS, vol. 11515, pp. 1–15. Springer, Cham (2019). https://doi.org/10.1007/978-3-030-23554-3_1
15. Chen, Z., Shen, L., Li, F.: Your neighbors are misunderstood: on modeling accurate similarity driven by data range to collaborative web service QoS prediction. Futur. Gener. Comput. Syst. **95**, 404–419 (2019)
16. Jannach, D., Lerche, L., Zanker, M.: Recommending based on implicit feedback. In: Brusilovsky, P., He, D. (eds.) Social Information Access. LNCS, vol. 10100, pp. 510–569. Springer, Cham (2018). https://doi.org/10.1007/978-3-319-90092-6_14
17. Xiong, R., Wang, J., Zhang, N., et al.: Deep hybrid collaborative filtering for web service recommendation. Expert Syst. Appl. **110**, 191–205 (2018)

18. Cao, Y., Liu, J., Shi, M., et al.: Service recommendation based on attentional factorization machine. In: 2019 IEEE International Conference on Services Computing (SCC), pp. 189–196 (2019)
19. Zhao, H., Wang, J., Zhou, Q., Wang, X., Wu, H.: Web API recommendation with features ensemble and learning-to-rank. In: Jin, H., Lin, X., Cheng, X., Shi, X., Xiao, N., Huang, Y. (eds.) BigData 2019. CCIS, vol. 1120, pp. 406–419. Springer, Singapore (2019). https://doi.org/10.1007/978-981-15-1899-7_29
20. Huang, J., Zhao, W.X., Dou, H., et al.: Improving sequential recommendation with knowledge-enhanced memory networks. In: The 41st International ACM SIGIR Conference on Research & Development in Information Retrieval, pp. 505–514 (2018)
21. Kwapong, B., Fletcher, K.: A knowledge graph based framework for web API recommendation. In: 2019 IEEE World Congress on Services (SERVICES), vol. 2642, pp. 115–120 (2019)
22. Kwapong, B., Anarfi, R., Fletcher, K.K.: A knowledge graph approach to mashup tag recommendation. In: 2020 IEEE International Conference on Services Computing (SCC), pp. 92–99 (2020)
23. Wang, X., Wu, H., Hsu, C.H.: Mashup-oriented API recommendation via random walk on knowledge graph. IEEE Access **7**, 7651–7662 (2018)
24. Geng, J., Cao, B., Ye, H., et al.: Web service recommendation based on knowledge graph convolutional network and Doc2Vec. In: 2020 IEEE World Congress on Services (SERVICES), pp. 95–100 (2020)
25. Rendle, S.: Factorization machines. In: 2010 IEEE International Conference on Data Mining, pp. 995–1000 (2010)
26. Xiao, J., Ye, H., He, X., et al.: Attentional factorization machines: learning the weight of feature interactions via attention networks. arXiv preprint arXiv:1708.04617 (2017)
27. He, X., Chua, T.S.: Neural factorization machines for sparse predictive analytics. In: Proceedings of the 40th International ACM SIGIR Conference on Research and Development in Information Retrieval, pp. 355–364 (2017)
28. Wang, H., Zhang, F., Zhao, M., et al.: Multi-task feature learning for knowledge graph enhanced recommendation. In: The World Wide Web Conference, pp. 2000–2010 (2019)
29. Wang, H., Zhao, M., Xie, X., et al.: Knowledge graph convolutional networks for recommender systems. In: The World Wide Web Conference, pp. 3307–3313 (2019)
30. Wang, H., Zhang, F., Zhang, M., et al.: Knowledge-aware graph neural networks with label smoothness regularization for recommender systems. In: Proceedings of the 25th ACM SIGKDD International Conference on Knowledge Discovery & Data Mining, pp. 968–977 (2019)

Expertise-Oriented Explainable Question Routing

Yulu Li[1], Wenjun Wang[1,5], Qiyao Peng[2], Hongtao Liu[3], Minglai Shao[2(✉)], and Pengfei Jiao[4]

[1] College of Intelligence and Computing, Tianjin University, Tianjin, China
{liyulu,wjwang}@tju.edu.cn
[2] School of New Media and Communication, Tianjin University, Tianjin, China
{qypeng,shaoml}@tju.edu.cn
[3] Du Xiaoman Financial, Beijing, China
htliu@tju.edu.cn
[4] School of Cyberspace, Hangzhou Dianzi University, Hangzhou, China
pjiao@hdu.edu.cn
[5] College of Information Science and Technology, Shihezi University, Xinjiang, China

Abstract. Question routing aims at routing questions to the most suitable expert with relevant expertise for answering, which is a fundamental issue in Community Question Answering (CQA) websites. Most existing question routing methods usually learn representation of the expert's interest based on his/her historical answered questions, which will be used to match the target question. However, they always ignore the modeling of expert's ability to answer questions, and in fact, precisely modeling both expert answering interest and expertise is crucial to the question routing. In this paper, we design a novel Expertise-oriented Modeling explainable Question Routing (EMQR) model based on a multi-task learning framework. In our approach, we propose to learn expert representation by fully capturing the expert's ability and interest from his/her historical answered questions and the corresponding received vote scores respectively. Furthermore, based on the representations of expert and target question, a multi-task learning model is adopted to predict the most suitable expert and his/her potential vote score, which could provide the intuitive explanation that why routes the question to the expert. Experimental results on six real-world CQA datasets demonstrate the superiority of EMQR, which significantly outperforms existing state-of-the-art methods.

Keywords: Question routing · Community question answering · Recommender systems

1 Introduction

Community Question Answering (CQA) websites have become popular web service which could share and spread knowledge, having drawn much more attention

H. Gao et al. (Eds.): CollaborateCom 2022, LNICST 460, pp. 41–57, 2022.
https://doi.org/10.1007/978-3-031-24383-7_3

recently, such as StackOverflow[1] and Quora[2]. A large volume of questions are daily raised on the CQA websites. There are usually low user responses for the majority questions and question raisers need to wait long time to obtain satisfactory answers. Hence, the need for question routing arises in CQA websites. And the question routing aims to recommend suitable experts in the community to answer questions, which could help the question raisers receive satisfactory answers.

Existing approaches for question routing can be categorized into two aspects, including traditional methods and deep learning-based methods respectively. In the traditional approaches, Zhou et al. [34] captures local and global features to explore the possible respondents via a classification task. Liu et al. [18] designs a topic-sensitive probabilistic model to rank user authority, which extracts the topics applying LDA method [1]. However, traditional methods rely on massive labor cost which expend lots of time selecting handcrafted features and are not effective enough to learn complex semantic information. The deep learning-based approaches commonly concentrate on modeling user's expertise by the semantic feature extraction of historical records [8,32].

Despite effectiveness, current deep learning-based methods suffer from the following two key challenges:

- **Expertise Modeling Implicitly.** The great majority of users answering the questions would receive the vote scores from others in the community, which reflect the quality of answers. However, existing deep learning-based methods don't take the score information into account, which could be not comprehensive enough to measure user's expertise. For instance, Fu et al. [8] retrieves similar information between expert historical questions and a raised question to recommend the experts, exploring implicit relevance from the question content.
- **Question Routing Explainablely.** The question routing approaches based on the deep learning usually learn the user representation from his/her historical answered questions to predict the most suitable expert. Although previous methods have achieved great performance, most of them haven't made a reasonable explanation for the routing results. As mentioned above, the answer vote scores could be intuitive explanations whether the users are able to answer questions. Nevertheless, current approaches haven't explored explainable question routing, which would affect the routing credibility.

In order to alleviate the mentioned challenges, we present a novel Expertise-oriented Modeling explainable representation learning approach for the Question Routing (**EMQR**). The core of our approach is to learn expertise-oriented expert representation and utilize the predicted vote scores to enhance the explainability of question routing. To be specific, the question titles and answer scores are encoded into expertise-oriented user representation entangled in the context of semantic and score information of the questions. Moreover, we utilize a

---

[1] https://www.stackoverflow.com.

[2] https://www.quora.com.

multi-task model to realize the fusion of question routing and recommendation explainability, which not only predicts whether to route new questions to the suitable experts, but also forecasts the answer score to illustrate the explainability of question routing.

The main contributions of our work are summarized as follows:

- We propose an expertise-oriented modeling approach (EMQR) to learn user representation, which is exploited to model expertise explicitly and make explainable question routing effectively. Compared with existing models, EMQR achieves the explainability of routing in addition to question routing.
- We design the multi-task framework that incorporates score encoding into user representation to predict the most suitable expert, which facilitates to learn more appropriate representations for experts. This is a novel attempt to adopt the multi-task learning-based approach to question routing in CQA websites.
- We perform extensive experiments on six real-world datasets from different domains to evaluate the performances of baselines, where EMQR significantly outperforms existing methods over multiple metrics. The experimental results also show that the multi-task framework improves the routing performance.

2   Related Works

In this section, we fall the related works into three aspects, including question routing, multi-task learning and explainable recommendation.

2.1   Question Routing

The question routing aims to recommend suitable experts for the raised questions in CQA websites. And the existing methods can be categorized into traditional methods and deep learning-based methods: **(i) Traditional methods** Traditional methods [2,3,11,15,24,31] have been popular to realize question routing during the earlier periods. Chang et al. [3] proposes a collaborative framework to route the question for a group of users, which introduces the user-user compatibility to build topical expertise via the Linear Regression [27]. Yang et at. [31] designs CQARank model to jointly model textual information and user expertise under different topics. **(ii) Deep Learning-based Methods.** Deep Learning-based methods [9,16,22,23,32] evaluate user expertise via the extraction of semantic information and user features in the neural network. Qiu et al. [23] matches similar questions to route satisfactory experts through a tensor layer, which integrates question representation and semantic retrieval to capture the interaction between different question sentences. Li et al. [16] establishes a heterogeneous information network to incorporate user's profile and utilizes the metapath-based method to learn personalized expert representation in the community. Fu et al. [8] focuses on similar historical information related to new questions and explores the latent relevance between different questions in semantic space.

2.2 Multi-task Learning

The objective of multi-task learning is to improve the generalization by sharing multiple parameters in related tasks [17,28], which has been widely leveraged in recommender systems. And recent approaches [17,19,20,33] primarily introduce deep neural network into the multi-task model. For instance, Ma et al. [20] devises an entire space modeling approach to estimate post-click conversion rate (pCVR) and post-view click-through rate (pCTR) simultaneously for the recommender system. Lin et al. [17] proposes HMTGIN model to concurrently learn the embedding of CQA forum graph on the multi-relational graph, which explicitly models the relationship between question askers and answerers by sharing features. Zhao et al. [33] presents MMoE framework that captures multiple user behavior to optimize engagement objective and satisfaction objective, significantly improving the quality of video watching recommendation.

2.3 Explainable Recommendation

The explainable recommendation attempts to provide the reason why could recommend a particular item to users. And explainable recommender system could improve the acceptance of target items, persuade users to choose the recommended items, and even enhance the overall credibility of system [12]. Many works with respect to the explainable recommendation has been proposed recently [4,5,13,21,30]. For instance, MTER [30] exploits a multi-task learning strategy which integrates two companion tasks via a joint tensor factorization, including user preference modeling for recommendation and opinionated content modeling for explanation. NARRE [4] introduces a novel attention mechanism which could obtain the highly-useful reviews regarded as review-level explanations. RUM [5] introduces memory-augmented neural networks to learn item-level and feature-level representations at a finer granularity, providing reasonable explanations by applying attention mechanism in memory networks.

2.4 Compared with Existing Methods

Although existing methods have achieved great performance, they neglect to model the answer ability of expert for question routing, which would degrade the quality of expert modeling. In this paper, our proposed EMQR aims to model the ability of experts to answer different questions under the influence of score characteristics, which could achieve expertise-oriented explainable representation learning. Furthermore, to enhance the question routing explanation, a multi-task learning framework is employed to perform question routing and provide intuitive explanations for the routing results.

3   Methods

In this section, we first introduce the problem definition for question routing in CQA websites. Next, we present the expertise-oriented explainable question routing approach with multi-task framework (EMQR). The overall architecture is shown in Fig. 1, consisting of three major modules: a *Question Title Encoder* to extract semantic features from the question titles, an *Expertise-oriented Expert Encoder* to capture the expert's interest and expertise with respect to different questions from his/her historical records. Finally, based on the learned expert and target question representations, we employ a *Multi-task Framework* to compute question-expert relevance scores, and simultaneously predict expert potential vote scores for the target question.

3.1   Problem Definition

In this paper, the question routing aims to predict the most suitable expert who can provide an "accepted answer" for the target question in CQA websites. Suppose that the target question is q^t and the candidate expert set is $U = \{u_1, ..., u_m\}$ respectively, where m represents the quantity of candidate experts. For an expert $u_i \in U$, he/she has answered a series of questions denoted as $Q_u^i = \{q_1, ..., q_n\}$, where n represents the size of historical answered question set. And the answers of expert u_i are associated with the vote scores denoted as $V_u^i = \{v_1, ..., v_n\}$. Moreover, the title of j-th answered question q_j is denoted as $W_j = \{w_1, ..., w_l\}$, $j \in [1, n]$, where l is the length of question title. It is notable that the expert who provides the "accepted answer" for target question is regarded as the ground truth.

3.2   Question Title Encoder

In this section, we propose the *Question Title Encoder* to capture the title semantic features of each question. We utilize token embedding layer to project the word sequence of title to a low-dimensional vector sequence. Given a question title q, denoted as $W = \{w_1, ..., w_l\}$, the Byte Pair Encoding [26] is applied to convert the title to token sequence $W' = \{w_1', ..., w_{l+}'\}$, where $l+$ is the length of token sequence. Then we transform each token in the sequence into a vector, which is denoted as $\mathbf{t} \in \mathcal{R}^{d_w}$ with d_w as dimension. Thus, we can obtain the token embedding matrix $\mathbf{T} = \{\mathbf{t}_1, ..., \mathbf{t}_{l+}\}$, where the dimension of title token sequence is $\mathbf{T} \in \mathcal{R}^{(l+) \times d_w}$. The semantic features of title are extracted through the Convolution Neural Network (CNN) from the token matrix $\mathbf{T}$. Afterwards, we stack the convolution results of K filters denoted as $\mathbf{C}$ and employ a dense layer to convert the dimension from $\mathcal{R}^K$ to $\mathcal{R}^t$:

$$\mathbf{c}_i = \text{ReLU}(\mathbf{W_i T} + \mathbf{b_i}), i \in [1, ..., K], \tag{1}$$

$$\mathbf{C} = [\mathbf{c}_1, ..., \mathbf{c}_K], \tag{2}$$

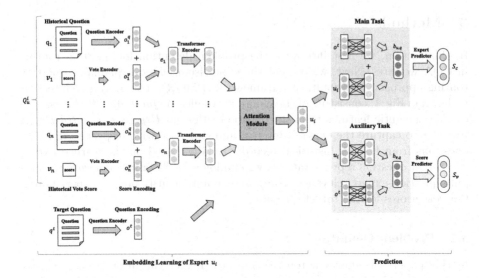

Fig. 1. General architecture of EMQR method.

where $\mathbf{W}_i$ and $\mathbf{b}_i \in \mathcal{R}^{l+}$ are the parameter of i-th filter, $\mathbf{c}_i \in \mathcal{R}^{l+}$ is the i-th convolution result, $\mathbf{C}$ represents the stacked features of a question title and K is the quantity of filters.

In this way, our model could learn the title representation $\mathbf{o} \in \mathcal{R}^t$ via the Question Title Encoder. To distinguish the representations of historical answered questions and target question, we denote the former as $\mathbf{o}_j^q$ and the latter is $\mathbf{o}^t$.

3.3   Expertise-Oriented Expert Encoder

As mentioned above, the expert historical questions and corresponding vote scores could measure his/her interest and expertise in a specific field. The *Expertise-oriented Expert Encoder* aims to model the expert's interest and expertise from his/her historical answered questions. The encoder contains two important modules: (1) a *Transformer Encoder* to unify question title information and vote score features for learning expert's ability to answer different questions; (2) an *Attention Module* to concentrate on more essential and relevant histories for modeling the expert.

Transformer Encoder. For an expert $u_i \in U$, he/she is associated with vote scores which implicitly represent his/her domain ability to answer different questions. Given a vote score $v_j \in V_u^i$ of j-th historical answered question, we encode the score feature and convert it to a low-dimensional vector $\mathbf{o}_j^v \in \mathcal{R}^t$. As shown in Fig. 1, we further combine $\mathbf{o}_j^q$ and $\mathbf{o}_j^v$ of j-th historical question feature by sum operation, denoted as $\mathbf{e}_j$:

$$\mathbf{e}_j = \mathbf{o}_j^q + \mathbf{o}_j^v, j \in [1, n], \tag{3}$$

where $e_j \in \mathcal{R}^t$ is the representation of j-th historical answered question, which is used as the input of following module.

So as to acquire complex relationship in the long sequence, we take full advantage of the Transformer [29] encoder to learn the aggregated representation of a user's all historical questions, which is utilized to obtain the embedding of j-th historical question feature:

$$e_j = \text{Trm}(e_j + (e_j)_p), \tag{4}$$

where $e_j, (e_j)_p \in \mathcal{R}^t$ are semantic features and position embedding of j-th historical question, $\text{Trm}(\cdot)$ represents the Transformer encoder as in [29], which includes two sub-layers: a Multi-head Self-attention (MS) layer and a Position-wise fully connected Feed-forward (PF) layer respectively. In order to transmit the information more deeply and enhance the fitting capability of model, the residual connection is utilized in the Transformer layer:

$$\text{Trm}(e_j) = \text{LN}(m_j + \text{D}(\text{PF}(m_j))), \tag{5}$$

$$m_j = \text{LN}(e_j + \text{D}(\text{MS}(e_j))), \tag{6}$$

where $\text{LN}(\cdot)$ is the normalization layer and $\text{D}(\cdot)$ is the dropout layer. Through the MS layer, we acquire expertise features of the user by h attention heads. Afterwards, the multi-head representations are concatenated to obtain the matrix of all historical questions features denoted as $\mathbf{H}_u^i$:

$$\mathbf{H}_u^i = [\text{MS}(e_1), ..., \text{MS}(e_n)], \tag{7}$$

$$\text{MS}(e_j) = \text{Concat}(\mathbf{h}_1, ..., \mathbf{h}_h)\mathbf{W}_m, \tag{8}$$

$$\mathbf{h}_i = \text{Att}(e_j \mathbf{W}_Q^i, e_j \mathbf{W}_K^i, e_j \mathbf{W}_V^i), \tag{9}$$

$$\text{Att}(\mathbf{Q}, \mathbf{K}, \mathbf{V}) = \text{Softmax}\left(\frac{\mathbf{Q}\mathbf{K}^T}{\sqrt{t/h}}\right)\mathbf{V}, \tag{10}$$

where $\mathbf{H}_u^i \in \mathcal{R}^{t \times n}$ is the feature matrix of expert u_i all historical questions, $\text{MS}(\cdot) \in \mathcal{R}^t$ is the concatenation of representations, $\mathbf{W}_m \in \mathcal{R}^{t \times t}$ is the weight parameter, $\mathbf{W}_Q^i, \mathbf{W}_K^i, \mathbf{W}_V^i \in \mathcal{R}^{t \times t/h}$ are the trainable transformation matrix for the i-th attention head respectively, and $\mathbf{Q}, \mathbf{K}, \mathbf{V}$ are both the parameter of attention.

Attention Module. Considering that different historical records have distinct relevances to the target question, we employ the *Attention Module* to pay attention to more essential historical questions under the guidance of target question.

As mentioned above, we have acquired the representation of target question o^t via the Question Title Encoder. Given the j-th historical feature $\mathbf{h}_j$ in $\mathbf{H}_u^i$, we incorporate target question o^t into the concatenate feature matrix as follows:

$$\mathbf{a}_u^j = [\mathbf{h}_j \otimes o^t; \mathbf{h}_j; o^t], j \in [1, n], \tag{11}$$

where $\mathbf{a}_u^j \in \mathcal{R}^{3 \times t}$ is the aggregated representation with respect to concatenate feature matrix and target question, and $\otimes$ represents the element-wise product operation. Afterwards, we adopt the linear layer to project l_j as a vector and calculate the attention weight α_u^j which is computed as:

$$l_j = \mathbf{W}_{j\mathbf{a}_u^j} + b_j, j \in [1, n], \tag{12}$$

$$\alpha_u^j = \frac{\exp(l_j)}{\sum_{i=1}^n \exp(l_i)}, \alpha_u^j \in (0, 1), j \in [1, n], \tag{13}$$

where $\mathbf{W}_j$ is the weight parameter, b_j is the bias and α_u^j is the normalized attention weight. Furthermore, we stack all historical questions features and aggregate them with different weights via the sum-pooling operation to obtain final representation $\mathbf{u}_i$ of expert u_i:

$$\mathbf{u}_i = \sum_{i=1}^n \alpha^{j_u} \mathbf{h}_j, \tag{14}$$

To sum up, we acquire the final user representation $\mathbf{u}_i$ under the guidance of target question, which will be used for decoding in the following multi-task learning framework to route target question to the most suitable expert.

3.4   Multi-task Learning Framework

In this section, we report the *Multi-task Learning Framework* to decode user representation in order to locate the most suitable expert and acquire expert potential vote score, which includes two types of predictors: the *Expert Predictor* and the *Score Predictor* respectively.

Expert Predictor. For the main task, we first utilize different dense layers to project the expert representation $\mathbf{u}_i$ and target question encoding $\mathbf{o}^t$ separately. And we concatenate them as the input of Expert Predictor. Then we adopt another dense layer to compute the relevance score S_c between the expert and the target question, which is computed as:

$$\mathbf{b}_{u,q} = \mathbf{u}_i \oplus \mathbf{o}^t, S_c = \mathbf{W}_c^T (\mathbf{b}_{u,q}) + \mu_c, \tag{15}$$

where $\oplus$ is the concatenation operation, $\mathbf{b}_{u,q} \in \mathcal{R}^{2 \times t}$ is the concatenate representation of expert and target question, $\mathbf{W}_c$ and μ_c are the parameters. Afterwards, the candidate answerer who obtains the highest relevance score will be recommended as the most suitable expert, and the answer provided by him/her will be regarded as the "accepted answer" for target question.

Score Predictor. With respect to the auxiliary task, we conduct potential vote score prediction based on the features of historical records and target question. Analogously, we convert above features to different dense layers and concatenate them as the input of Score Predictor. Then we employ another dense layer to predict the answer score as follows:

$$\mathbf{b}_{v,q} = \mathbf{u}_i \oplus \mathbf{o}^t, S_v = \mathbf{W}_v^T(\mathbf{b}_{v,q}) + \mu_v, \tag{16}$$

where $\mathbf{b}_{v,q} \in \mathcal{R}^{2 \times t}$ is the concatenate feature matrix of expert and target question, S_v is the predicted score label, $\mathbf{W}_v$ and μ_v are the parameters. Then the potential vote score provides an intuitive explanation that why recommends the candidate expert to target question. And the higher the potential vote score, the higher the probability which the answer provided by candidate expert will be accepted.

Model Training. In this section, we train our model based on the negative sampling method [14]. And we adopt two loss functions during the train process. Pointing at the main task training, the expert who provides the "accepted answer" is regraded as the positive sample for each question. And other K experts are sampled as negative samples, including answerers who didn't respond this question and who didn't provide acceptable answers. So as to minimize the cross-entropy loss between predicted labels and true labels, the training objective of main task is defined as:

$$\mathcal{L}_{main} = -\sum_{c=1}^{K+1} \hat{S}_c log(S_c), \tag{17}$$

where $\hat{S}_c$ represents the ground truth of user label, and S_c is the probability of expert prediction.

Meanwhile, we also sample N vote score labels for training the auxiliary task. Our purpose in the auxiliary task training is to minimize the cross-entropy loss between predicted score labels and true vote score labels as follows:

$$\mathcal{L}_{aux} = -\sum_{v=1}^{N} \hat{S}_v log(S_v), \tag{18}$$

where $\hat{S}_v$ is the ground truth of vote score label and S_v is the probability for score prediction.

Finally, we unify the expert prediction task with potential vote score prediction task and simultaneously optimize above two tasks with the weight λ, and the total loss of proposed model is defined as follows:

$$\mathcal{L} = \mathcal{L}_{main} + \lambda \mathcal{L}_{aux}. \tag{19}$$

3.5   Differences with Existing Techniques

In this section, we highlight the key differences between the proposed method and existing techniques.

RMRN. RMRN [8], a recent deep learning-based method for the question routing, exploits recurrent memory reasoning network to explore the relevance between user historical records and target question. Both our proposal and RMRN learn expert representations from his/her historical answered questions, which recommend suitable experts for raised questions. For the expertise modeling, RMRN couldn't explicitly measure expert's ability to answer questions. Unlike RMRN, our approach leverages expertise-oriented expert encoder to model expert's interest and expertise, instead of a complex recurrent structure equipped with cascading reasoning memory cells, control and memory units.

NeRank. NeRank [16], a recently proposed method to achieve personalized question routing, utilizes heterogeneous information network embedding algorithm to learn user representation which takes question raiser's profile into account. Compared with NeRank, EMQR provides intuitive explanations for routing results via the multi-task learning framework. Thus, our model not only recommends experts precisely when new questions are raised, but also makes the explanations for recommended experts improving user credibility for CQA websites. Moreover, our method adopts a score prediction module to forecast the answer score corresponding to target question.

4 Experiments

In this section, we further conduct experiments on six real-world datasets to evaluate the performance of proposed method, EMQR. First, we introduce the datasets and experiment settings successively. Then the performance is evaluated against several existing methods in terms of three metrics. And we dissect the impact of vote score features on the model performance with an ablation study. In addition, the parameter sensitivity experiment is performed to explore the effect of auxiliary hyper-parameter. Finally, in order to make it suitable for the question routing, we demonstrate the explainability of our proposed EMQR via a case study.

4.1 Datasets and Experimental Settings

Datasets. Six real-world datasets related to the CQA are applied to conduct the experiments, including six domains, i.e., Print, History, Bioinformatics, AI, Biology and English. Each dataset contains a question set where each question includes its title and a vote score, which indicates how satisfied other users in the community are with the answer. Following the work [16], we reserve the experts who have answered at least 5 questions to avoid cold start problem. Table 1 shows the statistics of six datasets in details.

In chronological order, each dataset is divided into a training set (80%), a validation set (10%) and a testing set (10%) respectively. For each question, a candidate expert set is built with 20 experts which includes respondents whose answers were not accepted and others who didn't answer the question. In addition, the expert who provides the "accepted answer" for target question is the ground truth.

Table 1. Statistics of the datasets.

Dataset	#question	#answerer	#answer	#avg.title length	#avg.vote	#vote range
AI	1,205	195	1,719	1097	7.20	$-3\sim136$
Print	1,033	112	1,686	9.51	9.24	$-6\sim44$
Biology	8,704	630	11,411	9.84	9.59	$-7\sim241$
English	46,692	4,781	104,453	9.68	16.34	$-69\sim828$
History	4,904	471	9,452	12.38	29.57	$-14\sim292$
Bioinformatics	958	113	1,489	9.93	7.72	$-5\sim142$

Hyper-parameter Setting. In our experiment, the dimensions of token embedding and question features are set to 100. And the quantity of Transformer heads and Transformer encoder layers are both 2 respectively. We employ truncate or pad operations to fix the length of historical answered question to 30. For each question, the length of question title is fixed to 15. In order to balance two tasks in our model, we set the auxiliary weight λ as 0.9.

Evaluation Metrics. We adopt common recommendation ranking metrics to evaluate our approach following the literature [32], which include MRR [7], Precision@K where $K = 1$ and $K = 3$.

Baselines. We compare the proposed EMQR with eight competitive methods: **(1) Score:** A feature engineering-based approach selects the answerer who has greater quantities of "accepted answer" as the recommended expert. **(2) BM25** [25]: A text-retrieval algorithm calculates the short-text similarity between historical document collection and a given document. **(3) Doc2Vec:** A document representation method learns semantic encoding from historical answered questions to obtain the relevance in regard to target question, which predicts a vector to represent different documents. **(4) CNTN** [23]: The CNTN approach extracts semantic information of the question by integrating question representation and word token matching. **(5) RMRN** [8]: The RMRN method adopts a recurrent memory reasoning network to retrieve historical information as to the target question, exploring implicit relevance of textual content. **(6) TCQR** [32]: The model considers temporal characteristics to acquire the expert's expertise dynamically under the multi-shift and multi-resolution. **(7) NeRank** [16]: NeRank constructs heterogeneous information network to learn three representations of questions, raisers and answerers, and designs a convolutional scoring function to calculate the ranking score. **(8) UserEmb** [9]: The approach explores text and node similarity to model expert's interest in social network, which applies word2vec [6] to obtain semantic encoding of the question and node2vec [10] for learning the node representation.

4.2 Performance Comparison

Table 2 reports the results compared our model EMQR with above baselines on six real-world datasets. We observe that the proposed model (EMQR) achieves more excellent performance than all baselines, which demonstrates that our approach can effectively recommend the most suitable expert for target question.

MRR metric in each dataset indicates a huge improvement for all baselines in terms of the overall ranking performance.

Specifically, our model achieves 37.16% P@1 on History dataset, meaning that around 37.16% of the results where correct candidate experts have 37.16% probability to be ranked first, which is significantly better than 5.26% P@1 of the best baseline method, RMRN.

In addition, EMQR outperforms the best baseline over P@3 metric on all datasets, which demonstrates our proposed method can effectively recommend the expert who provides the "accepted answer" when new question is raised.

From the comparison results of all baselines, we can also conclude as follows: 1) We observe that the models (RMRN, NeRank and EMQR) which capture the interaction under the guidance of target question consistently outperform than those not (Doc2Vec, CNTN, TCQR and UserEmb). The reason is the methods pay attention to capturing expert's interest from historical records which are more similar to target question under the finer granularity. 2) Our proposal achieves obvious improvement compared to all baselines, since we integrate vote score features into user expertise to achieve expert representation learning for distinct expertise. EMQR describes expert's ability to answer the questions from different domains, while other methods don't take vote score features into account for question routing. For instance, RMRN discovers the latent relevance of semantic information related to a new question over the historical records, and NeRank recommends the expert which regards user ID as a personalized characteristic in heterogeneous network. 3) We demonstrates that our proposed EMQR based on multi-task framework improves the explainability of recommended experts, which routes the questions to answerers with higher vote scores in related domains.

4.3 Ablation Study

Since the vote scores play a critical role on modeling the user expertise, we further study the effectiveness of score features in this section. We conduct an ablation experiment in the absence of vote score features denoted as *w/o Score*.

As shown as in Table 3, removing score information obviously reduces the model performance across three metrics, due to w/o Score variant is insufficient to represent user's expertise for question routing. The results indicate that our modeling choice of score features for each question is appropriate to tackle the expertise integration challenge involved in question routing task. In addition, we can conclude that the vote score features have significant impact on modeling expert representation.

Table 2. Performances (%) of the baselines on six datasets.

Dataset	Print			History			Bioinformatics		
Method	Metric								
	MRR	P@1	P@3	MRR	P@1	P@3	MRR	P@1	P@3
Score	19.32	10.67	19.36	18.97	6.411	19.76	17.89	10.23	23.39
BM25	35.68	18.72	40.11	25.91	15.41	26.74	28.73	15.16	39.27
Doc2Vec	39.77	19.62	39.22	28.43	17.43	29.87	32.64	18.13	44.23
CNTN	47.32	29.11	58.05	39.31	25.34	43.05	43.37	25.31	50.62
RMRN	48.44	29.79	<u>59.57</u>	<u>52.21</u>	<u>33.51</u>	<u>68.86</u>	44.44	26.58	53.16
TCQR	44.25	26.67	51.11	40.21	27.37	47.02	39.46	26.01	43.18
NeRank	<u>51.33</u>	<u>31.65</u>	59.37	46.75	27.73	56.67	<u>45.01</u>	<u>28.11</u>	<u>54.68</u>
UserEmb	36.39	28.34	48.31	40.39	26.39	47.42	37.89	25.05	43.03
EMQR	**52.96**	**35.17**	**60.09**	**55.59**	**37.16**	**69.11**	**47.96**	**33.28**	**58.23**
Dataset	AI			Biology			English		
Method	Metric								
	MRR	P@1	P@3	MRR	P@1	P@3	MRR	P@1	P@3
Score	22.32	9.851	24.29	19.73	10.17	13.76	17.21	7.761	19.74
BM25	35.64	15.47	40.15	27.12	14.86	25.76	20.13	14.21	28.77
Doc2Vec	38.21	17.78	43.32	29.12	16.08	28.73	23.26	15.23	29.46
CNTN	45.06	27.78	54.44	33.58	20.17	33.69	29.68	18.37	36.39
RMRN	45.24	27.83	<u>62.22</u>	<u>43.62</u>	<u>24.53</u>	<u>55.62</u>	46.77	25.22	<u>61.62</u>
TCQR	41.96	27.78	45.59	39.62	24.06	44.22	34.25	19.27	49.87
NeRank	<u>49.89</u>	<u>33.03</u>	62.04	41.71	23.86	47.61	<u>48.95</u>	<u>27.16</u>	61.43
UserEmb	41.01	23.35	44.57	32.23	19.87	32.75	31.73	19.56	42.36
EMQR	**50.96**	**34.44**	**64.38**	**48.19**	**30.31**	**58.44**	**51.35**	**31.85**	**62.73**

Table 3. Effectiveness of vote score features.

Dataset	Print			Biology			Bioinformatics		
Method	Metric								
	MRR	P@1	P@3	MRR	P@1	P@3	MRR	P@1	P@3
w/o Score	37.99	25.83	52.13	45.16	27.49	54.85	40.15	31.52	53.80
EMQR	**52.96**	**35.17**	**60.09**	**48.19**	**30.31**	**58.44**	**47.96**	**33.28**	**58.23**

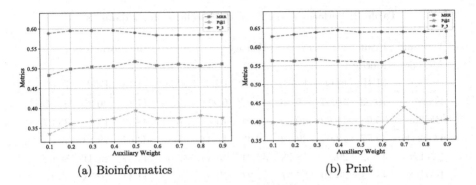

Fig. 2. The impact of hyper-parameter.

4.4   Parameter Sensitivity Analysis

To investigate the impact of auxiliary task on the performance of EMQR, in this section, we conduct parameter sensitivity analysis for the hyper-parameter λ. Figure 2 shows the results of hyper-parameter experiment with the auxiliary weight λ ranging from 0.1 to 0.9 in Bioinformatics and Print datasets. As shown in Fig. 2, we observe that the performance continues to improve with the increase of auxiliary weight. If the auxiliary weight exceeds a turning point, the performance begins to decrease gradually due to the over fitting. For example, the performance of Bioinformatics dataset starts to decline when the auxiliary weight is greater than 0.5. And the results in Print dataset indicate EMQR performance achieves the best when the auxiliary weight is set to 0.7.

4.5   Case Study

In order to verify that EMQR can enhance the explainability of question routing, we show a case study about experts receiving scores for the "accepted answer". We randomly select several questions over three datasets (AI, Bioinformatics and Biology), showing the title of question (i.e., Question), the answerer of question (i.e., Answerer), the potential vote score predicted by Score Predictor (i.e., Score) and the reception of answer (i.e., Reception) in Table 4. Each question receives numerous answers provided by the experts from different fields, however, only one candidate expert who acquires the higher score is accepted as the most suitable expert. From the results, we can observe that the experts obtaining higher scores are respectively recommended to target questions. For instance, the question "why is turner syndrome a problem?" in Biology dataset is separately answered by the Answerer c and the Answerer d. And the answer provided by the former gains 6 points with a higher score, while the answer of the latter receives 4 points with a lower score. Hence, our proposed EMQR not only precisely routes questions to the experts, but also makes the routing results explainable in CQA websites.

Table 4. The case study of vote scores with respect to the "accepted answer" in different datasets.

Dataset	Question	Answerer	Score	Reception
AI	is fuzzy logic invalid?	a	4	Accepted
		b	1	No
Biology	why is turner syndrome a problem?	c	6	Accepted
		d	4	No
Bioinformatics	cds length for each human gene?	e	4	Accepted
		f	0	No
	what does pca mean on gwas?	g	3	Accepted
		h	2	dejkfvcNo

5   Conclusion

In this paper, we propose an expertise-oriented explainable question routing model with a multi-task framework, EMQR, which can precisely recommend suitable experts for questions in CQA websites. Our approach learns the expert representation by combining semantic information and score characteristics, which reflects the expert's interest and expertise for answering different questions. Afterwards, we leverage the multi-task framework to realize expert prediction and potential vote score prediction, which could route target question to the most suitable expert and provide the reason why routing. Compared to existing state-of-art methods, the proposed EMQR achieves more remarkable performance in extensive experiments and enhances the explainability of question routing.

Acknowledgments. This work was supported by the China Postdoctoral Science Foundation (2022T150470, 2021M702448), the Sustainable Development Project of Shenzhen (KCXFZ20201221173013036).

References

1. Blei, D.M., Ng, A.Y., Jordan, M.I.: Latent dirichlet allocation. J. Mach. Learn. Res. **3**, 993–1022 (2003)
2. Cao, X., Cong, G., Cui, B., Jensen, C.S., Yuan, Q.: Approaches to exploring category information for question retrieval in community question-answer archives. ACM Trans. Inf. Syst. (TOIS) **30**(2), 1–38 (2012)
3. Chang, S., Pal, A.: Routing questions for collaborative answering in community question answering. In: Proceedings of the International Conference on Advances in Social Networks Analysis and Mining, pp. 494–501. IEEE (2013)
4. Chen, C., Zhang, M., Liu, Y., Ma, S.: Neural attentional rating regression with review-level explanations. In: Proceedings of the 2018 World Wide Web Conference, pp. 1583–1592 (2018)

5. Chen, X., et al.: Sequential recommendation with user memory networks. In: Proceedings of the Eleventh ACM International Conference on Web Search and Data Mining, pp. 108–116 (2018)
6. Church, K.W.: Word2vec. Nat. Lang. Eng. **23**(1), 155–162 (2017)
7. Craswell, N.: Mean reciprocal rank. Encyclopedia of Database Systems, vol. 1703 (2009)
8. Fu, J., et al.: Recurrent memory reasoning network for expert finding in community question answering. In: WSDM, pp. 187–195 (2020)
9. Ghasemi, N., Fatourechi, R., Momtazi, S.: User embedding for expert finding in community question answering. ACM Trans. Knowl. Discov. Data **15**(4), 1–16 (2021)
10. Grover, A., Leskovec, J.: node2vec: scalable feature learning for networks. In: Proceedings of the ACM SIGKDD International Conference on Knowledge Discovery and Data Mining, pp. 855–864 (2016)
11. Guo, J., Xu, S., Bao, S., Yu, Y.: Tapping on the potential of Q&A community by recommending answer providers. In: Proceedings of the ACM Conference on Information and Knowledge Management, pp. 921–930 (2008)
12. Herlocker, J.L., Konstan, J.A., Riedl, J.: Explaining collaborative filtering recommendations. In: Proceedings of the 2000 ACM Conference on Computer Supported Cooperative Work, pp. 241–250 (2000)
13. Hou, Y., Yang, N., Wu, Y., Yu, P.S.: Explainable recommendation with fusion of aspect information. World Wide Web **22**(1), 221–240 (2019)
14. Huang, P.S., He, X., Gao, J., Deng, L., Acero, A., Heck, L.: Learning deep structured semantic models for web search using click through data. In: Proceedings of the Conference on Information and Knowledge Management, pp. 2333–2338 (2013)
15. Ji, Z., Wang, B.: Learning to rank for question routing in community question answering. In: Proceedings of the ACM International Conference on Information & Knowledge Management, pp. 2363–2368 (2013)
16. Li, Z., Jiang, J.Y., Sun, Y., Wang, W.: Personalized question routing via heterogeneous network embedding. In: Proceedings of the International Conference on Artificial Intelligence, vol. 33, pp. 192–199 (2019)
17. Lin, Z., et al.: Multi-relational graph based heterogeneous multi-task learning in community question answering. In: Proceedings of the 30th ACM International Conference on Information & Knowledge Management, pp. 1038–1047 (2021)
18. Liu, X., Ye, S., Li, X., Luo, Y., Rao, Y.: ZhihuRank: a topic-sensitive expert finding algorithm in community question answering websites. In: Li, F.W.B., Klamma, R., Laanpere, M., Zhang, J., Manjón, B.F., Lau, R.W.H. (eds.) ICWL 2015. LNCS, vol. 9412, pp. 165–173. Springer, Cham (2015). https://doi.org/10.1007/978-3-319-25515-6_15
19. Ma, J., Zhao, Z., Yi, X., Chen, J., Hong, L., Chi, E.H.: Modeling task relationships in multi-task learning with multi-gate mixture-of-experts. In: Proceedings of the 24th ACM SIGKDD International Conference on Knowledge Discovery & Data Mining, pp. 1930–1939 (2018)
20. Ma, X., et al.: Entire space multi-task model: an effective approach for estimating post-click conversion rate. In: The 41st International ACM SIGIR Conference on Research & Development in Information Retrieval, pp. 1137–1140 (2018)
21. Peake, G., Wang, J.: Explanation mining: Post hoc interpretability of latent factor models for recommendation systems. In: Proceedings of the 24th ACM SIGKDD International Conference on Knowledge Discovery & Data Mining, pp. 2060–2069 (2018)

22. Qian, Y., Tang, J., Wu, K.: Weakly learning to match experts in online community (2016)
23. Qiu, X., Huang, X.: Convolutional neural tensor network architecture for community-based question answering. In: Proceedings of the International Joint Conference on Artificial Intelligence (2015)
24. Riahi, F., Zolaktaf, Z., Shafiei, M., Milios, E.: Finding expert users in community question answering. In: Proceedings of the International Conference on World Wide Web, pp. 791–798 (2012)
25. Robertson, S., Zaragoza, H.: The probabilistic relevance framework: BM25 and beyond. Found. Trends Inf. Retr. **3**(4), 333–389 (2009)
26. Sennrich, R., Haddow, B., Birch, A.: Neural machine translation of rare words with subword units. In: Proceedings of the International Conference on Association for Computational Linguistics (2016)
27. Su, X., Yan, X., Tsai, C.L.: Linear regression. Wiley Interdiscip. Rev. Comput. Stat. **4**(3), 275–294 (2012)
28. Vandenhende, S., Georgoulis, S., Van Gansbeke, W., Proesmans, M., Dai, D., Van Gool, L.: Multi-task learning for dense prediction tasks: a survey. IEEE Trans. Pattern Anal. Mach. Intell. (2021)
29. Vaswani, A., et al.: Attention is all you need. In: Proceedings of the International Conference of Neural Information Processing Systems, pp. 5998–6008 (2017)
30. Wang, N., Wang, H., Jia, Y., Yin, Y.: Explainable recommendation via multi-task learning in opinionated text data. In: The 41st International ACM SIGIR Conference on Research & Development in Information Retrieval, pp. 165–174 (2018)
31. Yang, L., et al.: CQARank: jointly model topics and expertise in community question answering. In: Proceedings of the ACM International Conference on Information & Knowledge Management, pp. 99–108 (2013)
32. Zhang, X., et al.: Temporal context-aware representation learning for question routing. In: WSDM, pp. 753–761 (2020)
33. Zhao, Z., et al.: Recommending what video to watch next: a multitask ranking system. In: Proceedings of the 13th ACM Conference on Recommender Systems, pp. 43–51 (2019)
34. Zhou, T.C., Lyu, M.R., King, I.: A classification-based approach to question routing in community question answering. In: Proceedings of the International Conference on World Wide Web, pp. 783–790 (2012)

An API Recommendation Method Based on Beneficial Interaction

Siyuan Wang, Buqing Cao$^{(\boxtimes)}$, Xiang Xie, Lulu Zhang, Guosheng Kang,
and Jianxun Liu

School of Computer Science and Engineering and Hunan Key Laboratory of Service Computing
and New Software Service Technology, Hunan University of Science and Technology, Xiangtan,
Hunan, China
buqingcao@gmail.com

Abstract. With the wide application of Mashup technology, it has become one of
the hot and challenging problems in the field of service computing that how to recommend the API to developers to satisfy their Mashup requirements. The existing
service recommendation methods based on Graph Neural Network (GNN) usually construct feature interaction graph by the interactions of service features, and
regard it as the input of GNN to achieve service prediction and recommendation.
In fact, there are some distinctions in the interactions between service features, and
the importance of interactions is also different. To address this problem, this paper
proposes an API recommendation method based on beneficial feature interaction,
which can distinguish and extract beneficial feature interaction pairs from a large
number of service feature interaction relationships. Firstly, feature extraction of
Mashup requirements and API services is performed, and the correlation between
API services is calculated based on the label and description document of the API
services and used as a basis for recommending API services to Mashup requirements. Secondly, edge prediction component is used to extract beneficial feature
pairs from input features of Mashup requirements and API services to generate
beneficial feature interaction diagram between features. Thirdly, the beneficial
feature interaction diagram is used as input of the graph neural network to predict
and generate the API services set of recommendations for the Mashup requirements. Finally, the experiment on ProgrammableWeb dataset shows that the AUC
of the proposed method has increased 20%, 24%, 27%, 13% and 21% respectively
than that of AFM, NFM, DeepFM, FLEN and DCN, which means the proposed
method improves the accuracy and quality of service recommendation.

Keywords: Recommendation · Beneficial feature interaction · L0-Predictin ·
GNN

1 Introduction

An API is an application programming interface that performs a specific function and
allows software developers to call the API according to their requirements. Due to the

H. Gao et al. (Eds.): CollaborateCom 2022, LNICST 460, pp. 58–72, 2022.
https://doi.org/10.1007/978-3-031-24383-7_4

diversity and complexity of requirements, software developers often need to look up and call the API many times, which undoubtedly increases the time cost and complexity of software development. Mashups help software developers to achieve the functionality they need more easily and quickly by combining multiple APIs with different functionalities. The number of APIs has increased rapidly in recent years. As of 2021, for example, there were more than 24,073 APIs available on the Programmable Web platform. It is a challenge to quickly and effectively find the API services from such a large-scale service collection that meet the needs of Mashup for developer users.

To solve above problems, some researchers exploit service recommendation technology to improve the accuracy of service discovery. There is no doubt that how to recommend appropriate APIs to Mashup developers in the process of Mashup construction or update has become a hot topic in the field of service computing. In recent years, with the rapid development of neural network, some researchers begin to use graph neural network technology to carry on the recommendation process. For example, Zheng et al. [1] proposed a kind of deep cooperative neural network model, two parallel neural network models are used to learn the hidden features of users and items, and then an interaction layer is constructed on the two neural networks to predict the users' scores of items. Liu et al. [2] studied the problem of behavior prediction in location-based social networks, by using recurrent neural networks to grasp the dependence of sequential behavior, and to predict the behavior of the next moment based on the user's historical behavior sequence. When using graph neural network to make recommendation, because of the subjectivity of constructing input graph, graph neural network may not achieve the best effect, thus affecting the performance of recommendation. To solve this problem, this paper proposes a module to generate input graph automatically, so as to improve the accuracy and applicability of graph neural network.

According to our survey, there is no clear standard definition of how Mashups and APIs interact with each other in the existing research on Mashup-oriented API recommendations, whereas in previous research on graph neural networks, feature interactions are usually constructed based on relevant experience or personal judgment. This paper holds that the interaction between features can be divided into beneficial feature interaction and unbeneficial feature interaction. When extracting the beneficial feature interaction correctly, it is beneficial to improve the training accuracy of graph neural networks, when extracting the unbeneficial feature interaction, the feature relation graph based on this will adversely affect the training accuracy of the graph neural network. For example, in Mashups and APIs data sets, Mashup_category and API_category are a pair of beneficial features, while Mashup_Name and API_Name are a pair of unbeneficial features. Obviously, it is reasonable to recommend the relevant type of API to a Mashup based on its type, while it is not reasonable to recommend an API based on the name of the Mashup and API. In order to improve the accuracy of the recommendation model, this paper proposes an API recommendation method based on the beneficial feature interaction pair, which uses the edge prediction component to extract the beneficial feature interaction and removes the unbeneficial feature interaction. Specifically, the main contributions of this paper are as follows:

- Construct interactive graph of beneficial features exploiting edge prediction components. By using an edge prediction component L0, the beneficial feature interactions between the input features of Mashup requirement and API services are extracted to progressively generate a graph structure suitable for graph neural network inputs and improve the accuracy of graph neural network training.

- Propose a method based on graph neural network to predict and recommend API services. The beneficial feature interaction graph is used as the input of the graph neural network, and the node vector representation of the graph neural network is updated to predict and get the recommendation set of the Mashup requirement- oriented APIs.
- Perform the comparative experiments based on the data crawled from ProgrammableWeb platform. The experimental results show that this proposed method has better recommendation quality than other state-of-art methods.

2   Related Work

The related work consists of two parts, i.e., traditional Web service recommendation method and deep learning-based Web service recommendation method. The traditional Web service recommendation methods usually explore features from users and items, and design recommendation system according to the similarity calculated by these features. Deep learning-based Web service recommendation methods exploit deep learning model and technology, such as LSTM, GCN, FNN, to devise recommendation system.

2.1   Traditional Web Service Recommendation Method

The traditional Web service recommendation methods mainly explore the functional feature, non-functional feature and hybrid feature for recommendation. Some researchers have developed the recommendation method by using a document topic generation model to improve the accuracy of service similarity matching [3, 4]. The document topic generation model trains Web service description documents to obtain the distribution of potential topics that represent the semantic information of their functions, and from this, the similarity between Mashup requirements and API description documents can be calculated. Web service recommendation considering non-functional features usually exploits users' activity and historical interaction information to learn users' preferences and uses collaborative filtering, matrix factorization and other techniques to predict missing QoS values, achieving the goal of recommending high-quality Web services. Collaborative filtering-based Web services recommendation [5–7]. Yao et al. [7] incorporated users, topics, and service- related latent features into service discovery and recommendation. QoS-based Web service recommendation methods [8–10] are more likely to predict missing QoS values and then recommend high-quality services to users. Rendle et al. [11, 12] devised a factorization model to alleviate the data sparsity problem. The model can handle any length and any number of eigenvectors. This means that the feature information fused by the model is multi-dimensional, which can reduce the influence of sparse data on recommendation performance. In the process of Web service recommendation, the combination of service functional characteristics and nonfunctional characteristics can comprehensively describe the association relationship between services. Therefore, Web service recommendation based on hybrid features has become more and more popular [13–18]. Lu et al. [13] raised a novel Web service recommendation method based on the functional characteristics and QoS information. Cao et al. [14] explored a two-layer topic model, which aggregates the text information and network information of services to enhance the effect of service clustering, and then improve the recommendation accuracy of Web APIs. Gao et al. [15] first developed an API recommendation method based on diverse learning, and then proposed a service recommendation method by integrating the user's preference, service, Mashup, and topic [16].

2.2 Deep Learning-Based Web Service Recommendation

With the rapid development of deep learning technology, Web service recommendation based on deep learning has become a hot topic in recommendation system. In recent years, the use of GNNs for service recommendation has become a new direction. Zheng et al. [8] designed a deep cooperative neural network model, which uses two parallel neural network models to learn the hidden features of users and items, then an interaction layer is built on the two neural networks to predict the user's score on the items. Liu et al. [18] studied the problem of behavior prediction in location-based social networks, by using recurrent neural networks to capture the dependence of sequential behavior and predict the behavior of the next moment based on the user ' s historical behavior sequence. He et al. [19] designed the common framework of neural CF (NCF) based on the classical deep learning model. Sun et al. [20] developed a recommendation system based on long and short-term network which collects user preferences. In recent years, some studies focus on combination of neural network and knowledge graph for recommendation. Zhu et al. [21] developed a knowledge-aware attentional reasoning network for recommendation. Consequently, there are many studies has been conducted about deep learning-based Web service recommendation. Some representative studies of them include Web service recommendation based on deep neural network, graph neural network, knowledge graph and some other model. In the study of this paper, we believe that the structure of input graph has an influence on the accuracy of graph neural network. So, we use an edge prediction module to generate input graph automatically to make the graph neural network achieve more better recommendation quality.

3   Method

The framework of the proposed approach is shown in Fig 1, which consists of four components, i.e., data pre-processing, API similarity computation, L0-SIGN model construction, and API recommendation.

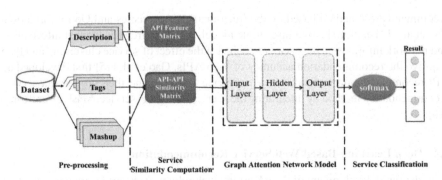

Fig. 1. The framework of service classification

3.1 Pre-processing

We use a dataset on mashups and APIs crawled from the ProgrammableWeb platform, and perform data pre-processing as follows:

Text normalization. Uniform case formatting of all words in the dataset, and remove all punctuation from the API description text.

Eliminate stop words. Remove function words and stop words from the API description text, leaving only the meaningful words for later processing.

Word stemming. Remove inflections or suffixes from the same word in the API description text. The same word may have different forms of expression because of its tense or part of speech. For example, the words "manage", "managed", and "management" appear in the description text, but all of their roots are "manage". We only extract their stems that can improve their computational accuracy in subsequent similarity calculations.

Invalid message culling. In the dataset, there are some APIs lack of function annotation and description document, which makes these APIs hard to calculate their similarity with other APIs, and also leads to the missing of input features. Therefore, we regard these APIs as invalid APIs information and cull them.

3.2 API Similarity Calculation

An API usually includes two important attributes, i.e., function annotation and description text. They can be used as a measure of API similarity. Specifically, (1) With API function annotation, each API adds labels according to its functions, and the similarity between APIs can be calculated through the labels of APIs. If two APIs share more tags, we determine that the two APIs have a higher similarity; (2) With API description text, each API adds a description text according to its function. The description text usually introduces the functions realized by the API in detail. We can measure the similarity of the corresponding API by comparing the similarity of the description text. The more similar the description texts are, the higher the similarity of the corresponding API. In order to express the similarity between APIs as accurately as possible, we designed a weighted similarity based on tag similarity and description similarity to express the similarity between APIs.

3.2.1 Functional Annotation Similarity of API

Tag refers to some descriptive words specified by users for various resources on the Internet, such as web services, music, video, and so on. Similar to keywords, tags also reflect the description and generalization of resources. However, keywords usually come from the resource content itself. They are keywords extracted from resources and can summarize and describe the content of resources to a certain extent. Tags are descriptive words specified by users for resources according to their understanding. They are unconstrained and subjective. Therefore, the tag may come from the content of the resource, or it may be a general word that does not appear in the resource.

The tags of API services usually summarize the functional attributes of services. For this reason, when two services have a shared annotation relationship, they can be considered to have a certain degree of similarity in functionality. In the API dataset, most APIs have at least three tags, so we use the Jaccard similarity coefficient to calculate the tag similarity between each two APIs. For example, the Jaccard similarity coefficient of service i and service j is shown in formula (1):

$$Jac(a_i, a_j) = \frac{|T_i \cap T_j|}{|T_i \cup T_j|} \tag{1}$$

where T_i, T_j are the tags owned by service a_i and a_j, $|T_i \cap T_j|$ represents the number
of common tags owned by two services, $|T_i \cup T_j|$ represents the union of the number of tags owned by two services respectively.

3.2.2 Description Text Similarity of API

In data preprocessing, we make all cases in the description documents uniform, and remove the stop words in advance, while only meaningful word information is retained, to calculate the text-similarity of description documents between APIs more accurately. After completing the preprocessing, we use the doc2vec model to convert the API description text into the corresponding vector, and then use the cosine similarity to calculate the description text similarity between APIs, which can be denoted as below:

$$Dsim(a_i, a_j) = \frac{v(a_i) * v(a_j)}{|v(a_i)| * |v(a_j)|} \tag{2}$$

where $Dsim(a_i, a_j)$ represents the text-similarity of the description document of a_i and a_j, and $v(a_n)$ represents the generation vector of the description text of the n-th API.

3.2.3 Overall Similarity of API

By integrating the functional annotation similarity and description text similarity between APIs, the overall similarity between APIs will be obtained as:

$$sim(a_i, a_j) = w_1 * Jac(a_i, a_j) + w_2 * Dsim(a_i, a_j) \tag{3}$$

where $sim(a_i, a_j)$ represents the overall similarity between a_i and a_j, w_1, $w_2 \in (0,1)$, $w_1 + w_2 = 1$. To ensure the accuracy of overall similarity calculation between APIs, this paper will set different weight combinations for experiments to determine their optimal values.

3.3 L$_0$-sign Model Construction

The core idea of the L$_0$-sign model is to eliminate the unnecessary information between input features by exploiting information bottleneck theory, to retain only the beneficial interaction between features. In the L$_0$-sign model, firstly, an edge prediction component is used to automatically extract useful feature interaction pairs, and based on this, an appropriate feature interaction graph is generated as the input of the sign module. Then, the sign module updates the feature vector representation based on the structure of the feature interaction graph. Finally, a softmax function is used to generate a binary value to represent the recommendation relationship of the API [22].

3.3.1 Information Bottleneck Theory

Information bottleneck theory states that when facing a problem, people will try to use the least information to complete it [23]. The information bottleneck theory holds that the neural network will squeeze the information out of a bottleneck, to remove the input data containing noise, and retain only the characteristic data most related to the prediction target.

Information bottleneck theory aims to extract the most relevant information that input random variables X contains output variables Y by considering a trade-off between the accuracy and complexity of the process. The relevant part of X over Y denotes S. Information bottleneck theory can be represented as:

$$\min(I(X; S) - \beta I(S; Y)) \tag{4}$$

where I is a function to denote mutual information between two variables and β is a weight factor.

A neural network often contains multiple functional layers with different functions. For instance, a simple convolutional neural network often includes a convolution layer, pooling layer, and full connection layer. When the neural network is trained with specific input x and label y, the training process can be understood as a process of weight combination. In the training process, the neural network constantly adjusts the weight of each functional layer, so that the information mostly related to the input x and the corresponding label y can be retained. According to the information bottleneck constraint, through multiple iterative training processes, the neural network can gradually squeeze out the information related to input x but not related to prediction y, to retain only the information related to input x and prediction value y, so that the neural network can complete the prediction function [24].

3.3.2 Edge Prediction Module

According to the constraints of information bottleneck theory, this paper chooses to use a neural network to construct an edge extraction module L0, to remove the feature interaction including noise that will lead to the decline of prediction effect, that is, useless feature interaction. At the same time, a model based on matrix factorization is used to extract useful feature interaction pairs. The module will determine the edge extraction according to the final prediction accuracy of the GNN. For example, if <

Mashup_Name, API_Name > is a pair of useless feature interactions. When inputting the set of feature interactions, the final test accuracy of GNN will decline, and the model effect will be affected. Therefore, the module will automatically eliminate < *Mashup_Name, API_Name* >. To achieve this, in the L0 edge prediction module, we first represent each feature as a k-dimensional vector, and then judge the interaction relationship of each group of features to determine whether it belongs to a beneficial feature interaction relationship or useless feature interaction relationship. For a set of feature interaction relations P, an edge prediction function based on matrix factorization is used to judge their interaction relation, i.e., $Z_{ij} = f_{ep}(v_i, v_j)$, where $(v_i, v_j) \in P$. The prediction function takes two b-dimensional vectors as inputs and outputs a binary value to indicate whether the feature interaction relationship belongs to beneficial feature interaction relationship. The input vectors in the prediction function is $v_i = O_i * W$, where O_i is the embedding vector of node i, and is a matrix parameter. During the process of model training, we reduce the number of useless feature interaction pairs through L0 edge prediction module, so as to generate an effective feature relationship graph for graph neural network as input to improve its accuracy.

We leverage activation regularization to link model with Information bottleneck theory to ensure the success of the interaction detection, which is shown as the below formula (4):

$$R(\theta, \omega) = \frac{1}{N} \sum_{n=1}^{N} (L(F_{LS}(G_n(X_n); \omega, \theta), y_n)) + \lambda_1 \sum_{i,j \in X_n} (\pi_n)_{ij} + \lambda_2 z_n \quad (5)$$

where θ and ω are the parameters in model, π_n is the probability of *(en)ij* being 1 (which means feature i and j is beneficial interaction feature pairs), $\lambda 1$ and $\lambda 2$ are the weight factors, and L corresponds to a loss function which minimizes loss and adjusts θ, ω.

3.3.3 SIGN Module

In the L0 edge prediction module, this paper takes the features of Mashup and API as the input, and extracts the beneficial feature interaction pairs as the input of sign module. In the sign module, firstly, each node is represented as a d-dimensional node embedding vector. The interaction of each pair of beneficial features is analyzed. The edge analysis function $h(u_i, u_j)$, is used to analyze node i and node j, where $= u_i = x_i * v_i$, v_i is the d-dimensional embedded vector of node i. The analysis result of the function is defined as, and the node embedding vector is updated with the result. Then, for each node, the embedded vector value of the node is updated by aggregating all the analysis result values z of its neighbor node. Finally, a linear function is used to generate a binary value as the final output of the sign module according to the finally updated node embedding vector, namely:

$$Y = f_{LS}(G(X_n, \varnothing); \theta, \omega) = f_S(G_n(X_n, F_{ep}(X_n; \omega); \theta)) \quad (6)$$

where, Y indicates the final prediction result of SIGN and it is calculated by a softmax function. We use a softmax function to calculate the possibility of each category, so as to complete the classification. When its value is 1, it indicates that the API is recommended to the Mashup, and when its value is 0, it is the opposite. X_n represents all input feature nodes of Mashup and API, ω and θ is the relevant parameters of the model. f_{LS} means L0-SIGN which is able to extract edges and it should perform as well as the SIGN whose input is an appropriate graph which represented by f_S.

3.3.4 API Recommendation

In the process of Mashup-oriented APIs recommendation, the features of Mashup and API will be used as input, and a large number of feature data and interactive relationships are used to train the L0-SIGN model, so that the model can accurately predict the results of API recommendation. The specific process is as follows:

Firstly, Mashups are classified according to their characteristics, and the number of Mashups under each category is counted. On top of this, the number of Mashups under each category is sorted, and the Top-k Mashup categories are selected as Mashup classification data.

Secondly, according to the calling relationship between Mashup and API and the similarity between APIs, the recommendation relationship between Mashup and API is jointly mined and considered. According to experience, the API called by each Mashup is selected and the API with the strongest correlation is recommended, and the negative samples in other APIs are randomly generated, to build experimental data with recommendation relationship and train the L0-SIGN model.

Then, in the training process of the L0-SIGN model, the Mashup and API features are used as input, and the recommendation relationship is constructed as labels to train the L0 edge prediction module, so that the L0 edge prediction module can correctly extract the beneficial interaction between features and generate the beneficial feature interaction graph.

Finally, the beneficial feature interaction graph is used as the input of the SIGN module. In the SIGN module, the GNN iteratively updates the vector embedding of each feature according to the graph structure relationship. The softmax function is used to output a binary value y', which represents the recommendation relationship between the Mashup and the API, to achieve the API recommendation for Mashup requirements.

4 Experiment

4.1 Dataset Description and Experimental Setup

We crawl 17,783 Web APIs from ProgrammableWeb platform as the dataset source of service classification. For each Web API, its information includes service name, description text, category, tags and other information. Because the experimental dataset is too large, the top 10, 15, 20, 25 and 30 categories with the largest number of Web APIs are selected as the experimental dataset. The distribution of the top 30 categories with the largest number is shown in Table 1. During training, we randomly reorganized the experimental data, and then 60% of the dataset is selected as the training set, 20% as the verification set and 20% as the test set. Adam [26] method is used as the optimizer of the model. The learning rate is equal to 0.005, the batch size is 1, the number of attention heads is 8, and service similarity threshold is set to 0.8.

Table 1. Top 30 categories order by number

Category	Number	Category	Number	Category	Number
Tools	850	Telephony	338	Games	240
Financial	758	Reference	308	Photos	228
Messaging	601	Security	305	Music	221
eCommerce	546	Search	301	Stocks	200
Payments	526	Email	291	Cloud	195
Social	501	Video	289	Data	187
Enterprise	472	Travel	284	Bitcoin	173
Mapping	437	Education	275	Other	165
Government	369	Transportation	259	Project Management	165
Science	368	Advertising	254	Weather	164

4.2 Baselines

AFM [25]. An improved model designed by Jun Xiao [25] based on the deficiency that FM uses the same weight for different cross features. AFM model uses an attention network to better learn the feature interaction relationship, to improve the accuracy of the model prediction.

NFM [26]: A model presented by Xiangnan He by improving the FM model based on the intersection problem of sparse features. Its main feature is that after the embedding layer, a Bi-interaction operation is innovatively proposed to cross-process the features, to reduce the network complexity and accelerate the network training process.

DeepFM[27]: A model combining a deep neural network and factor decomposition machine. It uses the deep neural network part to do the high-order combination between features, exploits FM to do the low-order combination between features and combines the two methods in parallel..

FLEN [28]: A Spatio-temporal and efficient large-scale prediction model that uses field information to alleviate gradient coupling. It applies the field-wise Biinteraction pooling technology to solve the dilemma of time complexity and space complexity in the large-scale application of feature field information. At the same time, a method dice-factor to alleviate the gradient coupling problem is proposed.

DCN [29]: A model for Ad-click prediction proposed by Google and Stanford University in 2017 [29]. It is very efficient in learning specific order combinations, does not need feature engineering, and the additional complexity introduced is quite small.

4.3 Expriment Results and Analysis

4.3.1 API Recommendation Performance

Experimental results of API recommendation under different Mashup categories (i.e., 5, 10, 15, 20) are shown in Table 2. The best results are marked in bold. We draw Figure 2 clearly shows an improvement in the recommendation performance of the proposed method compared with the baseline methods under different mashup categories. The overall experimental results show that the proposed method is superior to other baseline methods in terms of ACC and AUC, and generally, AUC improvements are better than ACC.

The improvement in ACC is the most obvious in the case of 20 categories, and the AUC is improved when the number of categories is 15. Compared with AFM, NFM, DeepFM, FLEN, and DCN, the proposed method improves ACC by 12%, 19%, 21%, 9%, and 16%, respectively. Similarly, our proposed method improves AUC by 20%, 24%, 27%, 13%, and 21% on these same baselines. We attribute the performance of our proposed method to the fact that it considers the interaction relationship between features, which makes it easy to deeply mine the implicit information between features, resulting in better recommendation performance. The proposed method uses the beneficial interaction relationship between features to construct the feature interaction graph so that the neural network can deeply mine the implicit relationship between features. Doing so significantly improves the recommendation performance.

Table 2. Experimental results of different recommendation methods

Method	Number of Categories							
	5		10		15		20	
	ACC	AUC	ACC	AUC	ACC	AUC	ACC	AUC
AFM	0.85	0.90	0.90	0.92	0.84	0.81	0.83	0.88
NFM	0.86	0.82	0.86	0.82	0.82	0.78	0.78	0.85
DeepFM	0.85	0.84	0.87	0.85	0.79	0.82	0.77	0.77
FLEN	0.87	0.89	0.88	0.89	0.85	0.86	0.85	0.87
DCN	0.85	0.82	0.84	0.83	0.82	0.82	0.80	0.86
L0-SIGN	**0.95**	**0.99**	**0.94**	**0.98**	**0.93**	**0.97**	**0.93**	**0.98**

As shown in Table 2, when the number of Mashup categories is 5, the recommendation performance of the proposed method is the best. Most baseline methods can achieve the best recommendation effect when the number of Mashup categories is 10. The increase shown in the Fig. 2. Mashup categories, in turn, increases the number of individual services it contains so that the proposed method can mine more implicit information and improve its recommendation performance. However, continuously increasing the number of Mashup categories further increases the interference between Mashups, resulting in the decline in the recommendation performance of the proposed method.

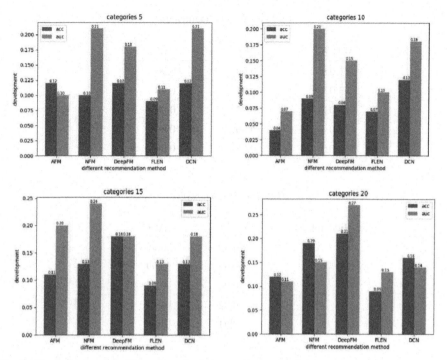

Fig. 2. The improvement of the recommendation performance of the proposed method compared with the baseline methods

Therefore, the recommendation performance of most baseline methods shows an overall trend of rising first and then declining, among which that of DeepFM decreases the fastest. The proposed method in this paper can eliminate the noise between features, and so reduce the decline of recommendation performance caused by the increase of Mashup categories to a certain extent.

4.3.2 Parameter Analysis

In this section, we analyze the influences of the weight coefficient w_1, w_2 in the overall similarity calculation between APIs and hidden layers of the model on recommendation performance in the proposed method (Table 3).

Influence of Different Weight Coefficient on API Recommendation. The different weight combinations in the calculation process of overall similarity indicate the proportion of functional annotation similarity and description text similarity. It can be seen from Table 3 that with the increase of the proportion of functional annotation similarity, the recommendation performance first increases and then decreases. When the proportion of functional annotation similarity is 0.7, the recommendation performance reaches the best. This is because the functional annotation or tag attribute of API can better represent its implied information than the description text, when the functional annotation accounts for a larger proportion, it can achieve a more recommendation effect. In addition, more

Table 3. Weight coefficient

W1: W2	ACC	AUC
0.1:0.9	0.90	0.96
0.3:0.7	0.95	0.98
0.5:0.5	0.95	0.99
0.7:0.3	0.96	0.99
0.9:0.1	0.95	0.98

Table 4. Hidden layers

Hidden Layer	ACC	AUC
8	0.89	0.96
16	0.95	0.99
32	0.94	0.99
64	0.92	0.97
128	0.91	0.96

importantly, the overall recommendation performance is relatively excellent and stable, which indicates that different weight coefficient of overall similarity calculation has a small impact on the proposed method.

Influence of Different Hidden Layers of the Model on API Recommendation. It can be seen from Table 4 that with the increase of the number of hidden layers in the model, its recommendation performance first increases and then decreases. When the number of hidden layers is 16, the proposed model and method can obtain the best recommendation performance, while when the number of hidden layers is 8, its recommendation performance is poor. Meanwhile, when the number of hidden layers is too large, the complexity of the model increases, making the model prone to over-fitting and resulting in a downward trend in the recommendation performance.

5   Conclusion and Future Work

Focusing on the problems existing in the service recommendation method using GNN, this paper proposes an API recommendation method based on the extraction of beneficial feature interaction pairs. Compared with the state-of-art recommendation methods based on GNN, this method firstly uses the edge prediction module to capture the interaction relationship between features. Then objectively constructs edges for beneficial feature interaction pairs and finally builds the input graph structure of GNN. The experimental results verify the effectiveness and advantage of the proposed method. In future work, we will consider exploring other neural networks such as graph convolutional networks, to further improve the performance of Web API recommendations.

Acknowledgment. Our work is supported by the National Natural Science Foundation of China (No. 61873316, 61872139, 61832014, and 61702181), the National Key R&D Program of China (No.2018YFB1402800), Hunan Provincial Natural Science Foundation of China under grant No. 2021JJ30274, and the Educational Commission of Hunan Province of China (No.20B244). Buqing Cao is the corresponding author of this paper.

References

1. Zheng, L., Noroozi, V., Philip, S.Y.: Joint deep modeling of users and items using reviews for recommendation. In: Proceedings of the Tenth ACM International Conference on Web Search and Data Mining, pp. 425–434 (2017)
2. Liu, Q., Wu, S., Wang, L., et al.: Predicting the next location: a recurrent model with spatial and temporal contexts. In: Proceedings of the Thirtieth AAAI Conference on Artificial Intelligence, pp. 194–200 (2016)
3. Fan, W., Ma, Y., Li, Q., et al.: Graph neural networks for social recommendation. The World Wide Web Conference, pp. 417–426 (2019)
4. Cao, B., Liu, J., Tang, M., et al.: Mashup service recommendation based on usage history and service network. Int. J. Web Services Res. (IJWSR) **10**(4), 82–101 (2013)
5. Klusch, M., Fries, B., Sycara, K.: OWLS-MX: a hybrid semantic web service matchmaker for OWL-S services. Web Semantics Science Services & Agents on the World Wide Web **7**(2), 121–133 (2009)
6. Xu, S., Raahemi, B.: A semantic-based service discovery framework for collaborative environments. Int. J. Simulation Modelling (IJSIMM) **15**(1), 83–96 (2016)
7. Yao, L., Sheng, Q.: Unified collaborative and content-based web service recommendation. IEEE Trans. Serv. Comput. **8**(3), 453–466 (2015)
8. Zheng, Z., Ma, H., Michael, R., et al.: Collaborative web service QoS prediction via neighborhood integrated matrix factorization. IEEE Trans. Serv. Comput. **6**(3), 289–299 (2013)
9. Chen, X., Zheng, Z., Yu, Q., et al.: Web service recommendation via exploiting location and QoS information. IEEE Trans. Parallel and Distributed Syst. **25**(7), 1913–1924 (2014)
10. Wang, X., Zhu, J., Zheng, Z., et al.: A spatial-temporal QoS prediction approach for time-aware web service recommendation. ACM Trans. Web **10**(1), 1–25 (2016)
11. Rendle, S.: Factorization machines. In: 2010 IEEE International Conference on Data Mining. Dec. 13- 17, pp. 995–1000 (2010)
12. Rendle, S.: Factorization machines with LibFM. ACM Trans. Intelligent Syst. Technol. (TIST) **3**(3), 1–22 (2012)
13. Lu, A.: Web service reputation evaluation model based on QoS and user recommendation. Yanshan University, pp. 18–26 (2010)
14. Cao, B., Liu, X., Rahman, M., et al.: Integrated content and network-based service clustering and web APIs recommendation for mashup development. IEEE Trans. Serv. Comput. **13**(1), 99–113 (2017)
15. Gao, W., Chen, L., Wu, J., et al.: Manifold-learning based API recommendation for mashup creation. In: 2015 IEEE International Conference on Web Services, June. 27-July. 2, pp. 432–439 (2015)
16. Gao, W., Chen, J.W., et al.: Joint modeling users, services, mashups, and topics for service recommendation. In: 2016 IEEE International Conference on Web Services (ICWS), June. 27-July. 2, pp. 260–267 (2016)

17. Xia, B., Fan, Y., Tan, W., et al.: Category-aware API clustering and distributed recommendation for automatic mashup creation. IEEE Trans. Serv. Comput. **8**(5), 674–687 (2015)
18. Liu, X., Fulia, I.: Incorporating user, topic, and service-related latent factors into web service recommendation. In: 2015 IEEE International Conference on Web Services (ICWS), June 27-July 2, pp. 185–192 (2015)
19. He, X.N., Liao, L.Z., Zhang, H.W., et al.: Neural collaborative filtering. In: Proceedings 26th International Conference on World Wide Web, pp. 173–182 (2017)
20. Sun, K., Qian, T., Chen, T., et al.: Where to go next: modeling long- and short-term user preferences for point-of-interest recommendation. In: National Conference on Artificial Intelligence Association for the Advancement of Artificial Intelligence (2020)
21. Zhu, Q., Zhou, X., Wu, J., et al.: A knowledge-aware attentional reasoning network for recommendation. In: National Conference on Artificial Intelligence Association for the Advancement of Artificial Intelligence (2020)
22. Su, Y., Zhang, R., Erfani, S., Xu, Z.: Detecting beneficial feature interactions for recommender systems. In: Proceedings of the 34th AAAI Conference on Artificial Intelligence (AAAI) (2021)
23. Tishby, N., Pereira, F., Bialek, W.: The Information Bottleneck Method. arXiv preprint physics/0004057
24. Louizos, C., Welling, M., Kingma, D.: Learning Sparse Neural Networks through L_0 Regularization. arXiv preprint/1712 01312
25. Xiao, J., Ye, H., He, X., et al.: Attentional factorization machines: learning the weight of feature interactions via attention networks. In: proceedings of the Twenty-Sixth International Joint Conference on Artificial Intelligence (IJCAI), pp. 3120–3125 (2017)
26. He, X., Chua, T.: Neural factorization machines for sparse predictive analytics. In: Proceedings of the 40th International ACM SIGIR conference on Research and Development in Information Retrieval, Aug, pp. 355–364 (2017)
27. Guo, H., Tang, R., Ye, Y., Li, Z., He, X.: DeepFM: A Factorization-Machine based Neural Network for CTR Prediction. arXiv preprint arXiv:1703 04247
28. Chen, W., Zhan, L., Ci, Y., et al.: FLEN: Leveraging Field for Scalable CTR Prediction. arXiv preprint arXiv:1911 04690
29. Wang, R., Fu, B., Fu, G., et al.: Deep&Cross Network for Ad Click Predictions. In: Proceedings of the ADKDD'17, August, pp. 1–7 (2017)

A Flow Prediction Model of Bike-Sharing Based on Cycling Context

Yizhu Zhao, Jun Zeng$^{(\boxtimes)}$, Min Gao, Wei Zhou, and Junhao Wen

School of Big Data and Software Engineering, Chongqing University, Chongqing, China
{zhaoyizhu,zengjun,gaomin,zhouwei,jhwen}@cqu.edu.cn

Abstract. The prediction of the number of bike-sharing is of great significance to maintain the balance of the number of bikes at each station. The cycling trajectory of users is dynamically changing and different in different districts of a city. This has caused the problem of no bikes at some stations, while others have accumulated bikes. However, most of the research work adds contexts such as spatiotemporal and weather features to the bike flow prediction, but ignores the problem of the imbalance of the number of bikes at each station. Therefore, we predict the number of bikes at the station based on the context features. To this end, we study the context features based on user's cycling data, and consider the features of time and climate. Along this line, we first analyze the features of time and climate to find the user's cycling habits. Then, we introduce the Long Short-Term Memory (LSTM) to capture the dependence relationship between time series. Using the Attention Mechanism to obtain key features can reduce prediction errors. We propose the context-based prediction model of the number of bike-sharing on the station with LSTM and Attention Mechanism (C-LSTMAM). This model can specifically capture more important context feature for the prediction. Finally, extensive experiments on real-world datasets demonstrate the effectiveness of the C-LSTMAM.

Keywords: Prediction of the number of bike-sharing · Context analysis · Long Short-Term Memory · Attention mechanism

1 Introduction

With the construction of Smart City and the increment of people's trips, bike-sharing is widely used in cities [1, 2]. According to Statista's estimation, as of May 2018, more than 1,600 bike-sharing programs were in operation worldwide, providing more than 18 million bikes for public use. With the increase of the number of bikes and users, bike-sharing companies can collect a great scale of cycling information [3, 4], which includes the user's cycling time, starting place, single cycling time and whether to buy a cycling card. However, because everyone's travel path is different, there will be a phenomenon of stacking bikes at some stations [5]. This phenomenon makes the use of bike-sharing become very unbalanced, leading to the situation that some stations have no bikes, while others have abundant bikes [6]. Therefore, it is necessary to predict the

H. Gao et al. (Eds.): CollaborateCom 2022, LNICST 460, pp. 73–92, 2022.
https://doi.org/10.1007/978-3-031-24383-7_5

number of bike-sharing on the station to balance the number of bikes at each station in real life.

The existing bike-sharing systems have comprehensive functions [7], but it is still challenging to effectively predict the number of bike-sharing each station so as to balance the bike demand of each station. Researchers use data mining related technologies to analyze user behavior from user historical cycling data [4, 8]. According to the user's cycling trajectory predict the number of bike on the station, so as to assist bike managers to allocate bikes reasonably [3, 9]. The number of bike-sharing prediction problem of bike-sharing is to predict the number of bike-sharing at each bike station in the future, which is based on the user's historical cycling data. Many scholars have solved the problem [5, 6, 10, 11], but the prediction accuracy still needs to be improved. Due to the mature development of deep learning and its good feature extraction ability and robustness, researchers generally use deep learning to study the flow prediction problem of bike-sharing [12, 13]. Although machine learning or neural network models can capture the features of time series, they often lack the ability to extract features dynamically. Therefore, some researchers [14–16] propose that the flow association pattern which can be abstracted into a graph structure. Chai et al. [15] expresses the bike-sharing system with a weighted graph, where the nodes are the stations, the edges are the relationships between the stations, and the weights of the edges represent the strength of the relationship between the stations. This method ignores the factors of the riding environment. Deng et al. [17] use Convolutional Neural Network (CNN) to extract temporal and spatial features of the grid, and model the time dependence between any two regions. The construction of dynamic time series models to extract effective features plays the important role in the prediction of the number of bikes.

In prediction problem of the number of bike-sharing, the user's cycling at any time always be affected by the previous moment, and there is a strong correlation between these effects. The Long Short-Term Memory (LSTM) can deal with long sequences of data and time series processing. What's more, LSTM can mine these connections, including information about the current node and important information at the previous moment. However, the results of each step of LSTM are dependent on the results of the previous step, so parallel computing is not possible. There is no result dependence in Attention Mechanism, so it can be processed in parallel and retain the previous information of LSTM. In addition, Attention Mechanism can grasp the key content of text or other information and assign different weights according to the importance of the information, so as to obtain more effective information. We introduce the Attention Mechanism to LSTM, which can help the model to retain the connection between time series, and it can also capture the more important context feature information for the prediction moment.

We analyze the features of the context information of users' historical cycling data, including the features of time and climate. The LSTM is used to capture the dependence between time series, and combine the Attention Mechanism to build a dynamic the number of bike-sharing prediction model. By analyzing the time context features of the datasets, it is found that the fluctuation of the data presents certain regularities. These regularities are called trend, periodicity, and proximity according to their internal relationships. Further analysis of these regularities, we found that weekends and weekdays, morning and evening rush hours have different effects on cycling demand. Therefore, when predicting the number of bike-sharing, we construct weekends and weekdays, morning and evening rush hours as new features to assist the model to learn users' cycling habits, and further improve the prediction accuracy. We also statistical analyze the climate context feature of the datasets such as weather, wind speed, pressure, temperature and humidity. The analysis results show that weather, wind speed, pressure and temperature have an effect on users' riding times. Besides, the linear relationship between humidity and user riding times is irregular. After analyzing the average filtering of the data, the linear relationship between humidity and user riding times is still irregular, so we regard humidity as redundant features.

The main contributions of this paper are summarized as follows:

- In order to balance the number of bikes at each station, we fully explore features such as climate and user riding habits to predict the number of bikes parked at station in the future. In context analysis, we extract the features of time and climate, and exclude the redundant feature humidity.
- In order to predict the number of bikes at station, the main work of the research is to mine the relationship between these features and the number of rides by users based on the time context and climate context.
- Compared with the problem of bike flow prediction, we are more concerned about balancing the number of bikes at each station in the future by predicting the number of bikes, so as to solve the situation of users without bikes at station.

The rest of the paper is organized as follows. Section 2 summarizes the related work, which is highly relevant to the research. Section 3 describes the analysis of context features. Section 4 provides detailed methodology of we proposed model. Section 5 presents experiments and the results, and Sect. 6 concludes this paper and outlines prospects for future study.

2 Related Work

Bike-sharing has become a necessary transportation tool for urban residents. The huge users produce hundreds of millions of behavioral data, and the value hidden behind the data has attracted wide attention from both academia and industry [18–21]. Lihua et al. [22] make prediction based on the features of non-linearity and different time and space in the cycling data, and used the good linear fitting ability of the Auto-regressive Integrated Moving Average model to process the data. However, ARIMA model can only consider the features of time level, which makes the prediction ability relatively weak. To solve this problem, Zhang et al. [23] propose a hybrid model based on Seasonal Auto-regressive Integrated Moving Average model (SARIMA) and Support Vector Machine (SVM) model by using the periodicity, non-linearity, uncertainty and complexity of short-term traffic flow prediction to predict time series. SARIMA model can find the correlation between time series, especially suitable for the modeling of seasonal and random time series. SVM has strong nonlinear mapping ability for input and output data. They mixed the two models and combined their advantages. Compared with the traditional ARIMA model, this model takes into account the influence of different seasons on the flow prediction, and the accuracy has been greatly improved.

With the development of machine learning, researchers have gradually weakened the use of time series modeling methods. Ahn et al. [24] propose a real-time flow prediction method based on Bayesian Classifier and Support Vector Regression (SVR). They use 3D Markov to model the flow of road traffic and its relationship in time and space, and divide the regions with close relationship together. Multiple Linear Regression and SVR are used to estimate the dependence between regions, so as to predict the traffic flow. Although the relationship between regions is considered in this method, the correlation of traffic flow between different roads in the same region is not considered. Traditional machine learning methods generally focus on the modeling of time and space, which are two kinds of features in the dataset. However, without other features, the accuracy is limited.

Compared with traditional machine learning, deep learning is favored by researchers for its ability to solve complex problems. Lv et al. [12] not only consider the temporal and spatial features of traffic flow prediction involved in traditional methods, but also used stacked Auto-Encoder to reduce the dimension of the data so as to complete the feature extraction. Finally, the output of the last layer of the Auto-Encoder is taken as the input of a regression network for supervised learning to complete flow prediction. Compared with the traditional machine learning, the prediction accuracy is improved. But like the traditional methods, it only considers the temporal features covered in the data, and does not do additional feature engineering. Zhang et al. [13] divide the urban area into large and small grids, and used Convolutional Neural Network (CNN) to extract temporal and spatial features in the grid. However, the author did not conduct a comprehensive and detailed analysis of the dataset or select the features, resulting in the problem of feature redundancy, which affected the final prediction results. Besides, users' travel rules and cycling preferences change over time. Machine learning or neural network models can capture temporal features, but they often lack the ability to extract features dynamically. The Attention Mechanism can grasp the feature factors corresponding to each moment. Therefore, the introduction of Attention Mechanism on the basis of sufficient feature engineering can construct dynamic time series model. The more important features are captured from the historical data, while the unimportant features are selectively ignored. Therefore, we focus on analyzing the historical data of user's cycling habits to find out the main features that affect the flow prediction of bike-sharing. In a word, we propose a prediction of the number of bikes model based on LSTM and Attention Mechanism.

3   Analysis of Context Features

In this section, we conduct contexts analysis of users' cycling data. The user's riding data includes the riding records of the bike and the climate features of the day of riding. According to experience in life, users choose bike-sharing as a way to travel in a suitable climate. The suitable or bad weather affects users' cycling behaviors, which also affects users' demands for bike-sharing. Therefore, we analyze the time context and climate context respectively to study their influences on users' cycling behavior. The datasets include cycling records of Citi Bike [25] and climate data obtained from the website of Weather Spark[1].

3.1 Analysis of Time Context

We analyze the period of the dataset in March 2017 by hour, which consist of 15 features, 114,698 rows of data and 619 bike stations. The analysis result is shown in Fig. 1. The tendency of a broken line to move up or down over a continuous period of time is called trend. A period of one week is called periodicity when the same period has a similar trend in the direction of the broken line. On the other hand, a period of one day is called proximity.

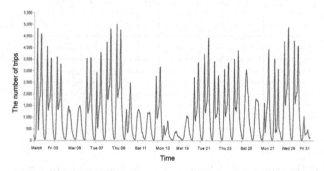

Fig. 1. The trend chart of the number of trips with time

We conduct further analysis on the datasets. The data for March 2017 was aggregated in hours, and the total number of rides by users in March was counted. According to hourly clustering, the periodic features of the number of bikes on the site can be counted, which are the number of bikes that we predict at a certain moment in the previous hour, at the same time in the previous day, and at the same time in the previous week. Besides, the weather data is based on hourly statistics, and the hourly data is different. Therefore, the user's riding habits features can be analyzed, morning peak and evening peak from the context of time and climate. The data distribution of the top 5 stations in the total number of rides is shown in Fig. 2. There are two obvious peaks, which are 7 am to 9 am and 5 pm to 6 pm. The phenomenon is consistent with the user's daily routine, the commuting time, which is called rush hours. Based on this data analysis, the main users of bike-sharing may be commuters. Commuters' travel has obvious regularity, which can be used to construct features advantageously. In order to verify this conclusion, we use Baidu Map API to analyze users' cycling heat map. Figure 3 (a) shows the heat map in the morning rush hour, and Fig. 3 (b) shows the heat map in the evening rush hour. After converting the number of rides to space, commuters mostly work in the city center, while they often live around the city. At different times, users have different travel patterns and demand for bike-sharing, which fully shows that it is correct to conclude that the main users of bike-sharing are commuters.

---

[1] https://zh.weatherspark.com/.

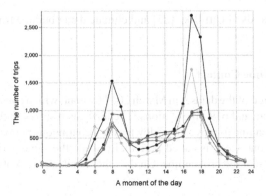

Fig. 2. The ridership of the top 5 stations in one day

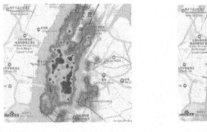

(a) The morning rush hour   (b) The evening rush hour

Fig. 3. The heat map of the top 5 stations in one day

According to experience in life, commuters' demands for bike-sharing vary in time. Therefore, we analyze the dataset based on weekends and weekdays, as shown in Fig. 4. The number of trips at each station varies greatly on weekends and weekdays. This data distribution is consistent with experience in life, which is that commuters go to

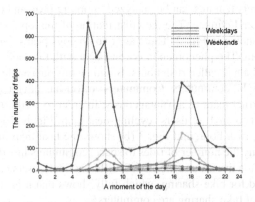

Fig. 4. The trips number of top 5 stations on weekdays and weekends

work from Monday to Friday, and the demand for bike-sharing peaks in the morning and evening from Monday to Friday. However, commuters take a rest on weekends, and there is no obvious peak on weekends. Based on these data analysis, when predicting the number of bike-sharing, we construct new features on weekends and weekdays, as well as morning and evening rush hours. This can help the model learn users' cycling habits and further improve the prediction accuracy of the model.

3.2   Analysis of Climate Context

We crawled the weather data corresponding to the user's riding time from the Weather Spark website. The data contains weather data for New York from June 1st to September 30th, 2017. The weather data has 16 types of weather, which we map into 6 types of weather.

The influence of different weather on cycling demand is shown in Fig. 5, and it shows that users have a great demand for bike-sharing in sunny day. In addition, we also analyze the two features of wind speed and pressure. Figure 6 shows that the wind speed is most suitable for cycling when the wind speed is level 1 to level 4. With the increase of wind speed after Level 4, the cycling demand decreases to varying degrees. Figure 7 shows a great difference in the impact of 1014 kPa and 1015 kPa on the user's cycling demand, even though the pressure difference is only 1 kPa. Therefore, the two features of wind speed and pressure is added to the feature analysis of bike-sharing number prediction. The relationship between the temperature and the number of trips by the user is shown in the Fig. 8. When the temperature is between 27 and 32 °C, the number of rides is the largest, and when the temperature is lower than 25 °C, the number of rides is lower. Among them, when the temperature is 23 °C, there are more riding times, because in addition to weather features, there are other factors such as pressure and wind speed.

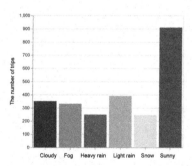

Fig. 5. The influence of weather on the trips number

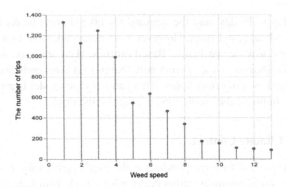

Fig. 6. The influence of wind speed on the trips number

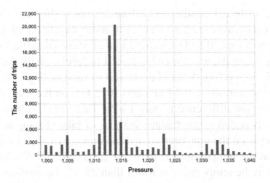

Fig. 7. The influence of pressure on the trips number

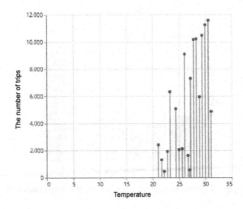

Fig. 8. The ridership of the top 5 stations in one day

We also analyze the feature of humidity, but the influence of humidity on the number of trips is not regular, and the results are shown in Fig. 9. Humidity is directly affected by weather, so the humidity is considered as redundant features. In order to verify the rationality of removing redundant features, we analyze the influence of features on the

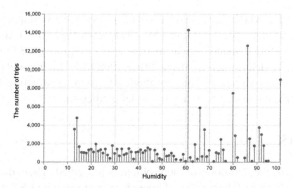

Fig. 9. The influence of humidity on the trips number

number of rides, namely weather and humidity. This experiment is to compare the effects of weather and humidity on ridership by filtering out the data that are lower than the average the number of trips.

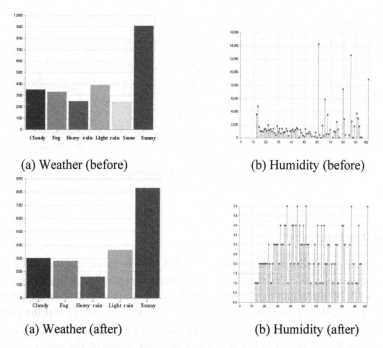

(a) Weather (before)	(b) Humidity (before)
(a) Weather (after)	(b) Humidity (after)

Fig. 10. The influence of weather and humidity on the trips number

In the dataset with humidity features, the average number of trips in the user's historical cycling data is 3602, and the data is filtered based on the average number. Figure 10 shows the influence of weather and humidity on the cycling demand of bike-sharing. Comparing Fig. 10 (a) with Fig. 10 (c), the snow type of weather disappeared after filtering the data, which shows that bad weather has a negative impact on the cycling demand of bike-sharing. By comparing Fig. 10 (b) with Fig. 10 (d), the influence of humidity on the cycling demand of bike sharing is still irregular after filtering the data. Humidity is directly determined by the weather, therefore, the humidity as redundant features. Deleting the redundant feature of humidity when constructing features of the model can further improve the accuracy of model prediction.

4 Framework

In this section, first, the definition of the problem is presented. Then, the details of the context-based prediction of the number of bike-sharing model with LSTM and Attention Mechanism (C-LSTMAM) is introduced. The Long Short-Term Memory (LSTM) is used to capture the dependence between time series, and a dynamic prediction model is constructed by combining Attention Mechanism. The model structure is shown in Fig. 11.

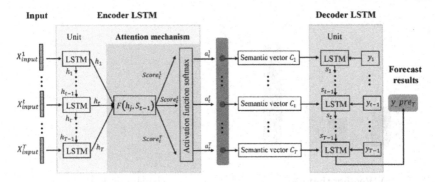

Fig. 11. The model structure diagram

4.1 Problem Definition

First, the notations of this paper are shown in Table 1. Next, the definitions are described.

For any station, x_t is called the observation value corresponding to time t in this paper. The number of bike prediction problem includes the historical observation sequence $X = \{x_1, x_2, \cdots, x_T\}$, the target flow sequence $Y = \{y_1, y_2, \cdots, y_{T-1}\}$ and the predicted value $\tilde{y}_T$, where T is the time step size. The number of bike prediction is to use the observed data of the first T hours to predict the flow value of the next one hour. y_1 represents the station flow corresponding to the historical observation sequence value x_1.

According to the previous analysis, all historical observations are divided into three parts: $S_{hour}, S_{day}, S_{week}$. The difference between the three parts lies in the different feature window w. When the feature window w is 1 h, and the time step T = 3, the unit is w. T is the length of sampling to obtain historical data as feature. When the value of w is 24 h

Table 1. The notations of this paper.

Notation	Definition	Notation	Definition
x_t	The observed the number of bike-sharing value at time T	y_t	The target the number of bike-sharing value at time T
X	Historical the number of bike-sharing observation sequence	Y	Target the number of bike-sharing sequence
T	Time step	w	The feature window
S	The historical observations	E	The context features
h_t	The hidden layer state in the encoder at time T	s_t	The hidden layer state in the decoder at time T
b	The offset vector	U	The weight matrices
V	The weight matrices	W	The weight matrices
$\widetilde{y_T}$	The predicted the number of bike-sharing value at time T	C_t	The semantic vector at time T
a_t^i	The attention weight of the i-th input at time T	$Score_t^i$	The attention score of the i-th input at time T
X_t^i	The corresponding input features at time T		

and T = 3, it means that the historical the number bike of three days before the forecast period is used as feature. When the value of w is 148 h and T = 3, it means that the historical bike of three weeks before the forecast period is used as feature. Equation (1) is expressed as follows:

$$S = \left[X_{t-Tw}, X_{t-(T_w)}, \cdots, X_{t-1} \right] \tag{1}$$

When w is 1 h, 24 h and 148 h, S is recorded as $S_{hour}, S_{day}, S_{week}$. The context features introduced in this paper include time, weather, weekends and weekdays. The forecast period refers to the time period of the day or the day of the week. The context feature is represented by E, as shown in Eq. (2).

$$E = \{weather, windspeed, pressure, dayofweek, hourofday\} \tag{2}$$

Then the input feature corresponding to time t is $X_{input}^t = \{S_{hour}^t, S_{day}^t, S_{week}^t, E_t\}$. Finally, the prediction problem of bike-sharing is defined as: input all X and part of the observation sequence $\{y_1, y_2, \cdots, y_{T-1}\}$ within the time step T, and calculate the number of bikes $\widetilde{y_t}$ corresponding to the time T, as shown in Eq. (3).

$$\widetilde{y_T} = F\left(X_{input}^1, X_{input}^2 \ldots X_{input}^T, y_1, y_2 \ldots y_{T-1} \right) \tag{3}$$

where E_t is the context feature corresponding to time t. F is a nonlinear mapping relation to be learned.

4.2 Feature Extraction of Time Series Based on LSTM

The essence of the number of bike-sharing prediction is to deal with the problem of seq2seq. The seq2seq problem refers to that both input and output are sequences, such as machine translation [26], question answering system, document abstract, etc. The Encoder- Decoder model [27] is suitable for the seq2seq sequence problem. In the study of the number of bike-sharing prediction, we use the encoder to convert the input historical sequence and corresponding features into a fixed-length semantic vector C, and the decoder is responsible for converting the semantic vector C generated by the encoder into the output of prediction results, as shown in Fig. 13.

We use the LSTM [28] model based on the framework of encoder and decoder, which uses the classic three-layer gate structure for each neuron, namely forget gate, input gate and output gate. LSTM retains the advantages of Recurrent Neural Network in time series processing, and the structure of gate can delete or add information to the cell, which overcomes the problem that RNN cannot capture the long term dependence. The input of encoder is $\{X_{input}^1, X_{input}^2 \ldots X_{input}^T\}$, in LSTM, the hidden state of current time t is determined by the state h_{t-1} of the previous time and the input x_t of the current time. Then according to Eq. (4), the hidden state in the encoder can be obtained.

$$h_t = f_1(h_{t-1}, x_t) \tag{4}$$

The encoder reads the input data of historical $\{X_{input}^1, X_{input}^2 \ldots X_{input}^T\}$ one by one and encodes them as a hidden state sequence $\{h_1, h_2 \ldots h_T\}$. These hidden states contain the feature of the original input data. The semantic vector C is formed by the rule of q, which is used by the decoder. A simple method is to generate semantic vector C by obtaining the final hidden layer directly, as shown in Eq. (5). However, the feature of the T−1 moments of last time is ignored. The final prediction result is only related to the state of hidden layer at the last moment, which leads to large prediction error.

$$C = q(\{h_1, h_2 \ldots h_T\}) = h_T \tag{5}$$

Decoder can be regarded as the inverse process of encoder. The decoder is used to combine the semantic vector C and the part of the observation sequence $\{y_1, y_2 \ldots y_{T-1}\}$ to predict the next output value $\tilde{y}_T$. The LSTM is still used in the decoder section, and The formula for predicting $\tilde{y}_T$ is shown in Eq. (6).

$$\tilde{y}_T = g(s_t, y_{T-1}, C) \tag{6}$$

where s_t is the state of hidden layer corresponding to time t in LSTM. The semantic vector C is the output of the encoder, which contains the input information after encoding. y_{T-1} is the output of time T−1, and it's also the input at time T. g is LSTM in the decoder.

Although the Encoder-Decoder model is classical and can solve the seq2seq problem well, it also has certain limitations. Because the only connection between encoder and decoder is a fixed length semantic vector C, which requires the encoder compresses the entire input data of historical sequence into a fixed-length vector. There are two disadvantages. First, the length of the semantic vector C is limited. In other words, only part of the features is encoded and the semantic vector C cannot completely represent the information of the whole sequence. Secondly, the information in the front of the time node will be diluted or even overwritten by the information in the back. The input sequence is sometimes very long in the number of bike-sharing prediction problem, and the semantic vector C cannot obtain a lot of useful information from the input sequence due to the limitation of the encoder. Therefore, the accuracy will be reduced when decoding. In order to solve this problem, attention mechanism is added to the encoder, which can retain the features more related to the prediction results while ignoring the relatively unimportant features.

4.3 Computation of Important Features Based on Attention Mechanism

Attention mechanism [29] is a technology that can make the model focus on important information and fully learn. In the prediction of bike-sharing, $\{X_{input}^1, X_{input}^2 \ldots X_{input}^T\}$ are taken as the input, which are not all important to the result of the moment t. Some of the input sequences of features have great influence on the prediction results, while others have little influence.

The traditional LSTM model assigns the same weight to all input features. In the problem of the number of bike-sharing prediction, if predict the number of bike-sharing at 6 pm, the data at 5 pm is more important for the prediction at 6 pm, but the data at 3 pm is relatively weak effect on the results. In order to distinguish the importance, the semantic vector C in the encoder can obtain the feature information of the input sequence more effectively and completely, and we introduced the Attention Mechanism into the encoder. We use LSTM model to encode the input time series $\{X_{input}^1, X_{input}^2 \ldots X_{input}^T\}$ to the hidden layer state corresponding to each input feature, and accumulate the hidden vector sequence $\{h_1, h_2 \ldots h_T\}$ by weighting, as shown in Eq. (7).

$$C_t = \sum_{i=1}^{T} a_t^i h_i \tag{7}$$

Then, the encoder encode the input information into a semantic vector sequence $\{C_1, C_2 \ldots C_T\}$, which contains feature information that is more important to the prediction results at the corresponding time. The LSTM model is used when encoding, where h_i contains the i-th input sequence and some of the previous sequence information in the input sequence of features. The hidden layer vectors are added according to the weights, which means that the attention distribution is different when the output at time t is generated. The larger the value of a_t^i, the more attention is allocated to the output corresponding to the time t on the $i - th$ input sequence. And a_t^i is jointly determined by the corresponding output hidden state s_{t-1} at time t−1 the hidden layer states in the input, as shown in Eq. (9). In order to distinguish the state of hidden layer between encoder and decoder, the state of the hidden layer in the encoder is h_t and the state of the hidden layer in the decoder is s_t at time t. *tanh* is activation function.

$$Score_t^i = V^T tanh(W[h_i, s_{t-1}]) \tag{8}$$

$$a_t^i = softmax(Score_t^i) = \exp(Score_t^i)/\sum_{j=1}^{T} \exp(Score_t^j) \tag{9}$$

The above equation represents a nonlinear mapping relation, which can make s_{t-1} and the hidden layer state h_i corresponding to the input vectors of feature calculate to get a value, and then use softmax to get the attention weight at time t. Each influence factor is given a certain weight to represent the importance of the input features. During decoding, the corresponding semantic vector C_t is used for decoding. C_t contains the most important part of the information and ignores the unimportant feature, which makes the prediction errors more less.

4.4 The Model Based on LSTM and Attention Mechanism

As discussed above, the Encoder-Decoder model can deal with the seq2seq problem such as the number of bike-sharing prediction. Due to the limitation of encoder, semantic vector C cannot obtain enough useful information of input sequence. The Attention Mechanism enables the model to focus on important information and fully learn, which is no longer limited to encode all input information $\{X_{input}^1, X_{input}^2 \ldots X_{input}^T\}$ into a fixed length semantic vector C, but to encode the input information into semantic vector sequence $\{C_1, C_2 \ldots C_T\}$. Each semantic vector contains more important feature information for the results of prediction at corresponding time, which makes up for the deficiency of Encoder-Decoder model, LSTM decodes the semantic vector sequence to get the final prediction result is shown in Eq. (10).

$$s_t = f_2(s_{t-1}, U[y_{t-1}; C_{t-1}] + b) \tag{10}$$

where y_{t-1} is the observed value corresponding to time t−1, which is the number of bike-sharing prediction corresponding to time t−1. C_{t-1} is the semantic vector corresponding to time t−1, which contains the input feature information most relevant to the value of prediction at time t-1. $[y_{t-1}; C_{t-1}]$ is to connect the two algorithms and use them as the input of LSTM network together with the hidden layer state corresponding to time t−1. f_2 is calculated by the LSTM model, and U and b are the learning parameter in the network.

The final results of prediction can be obtained by using Eq. (11). Where $\tilde{y}_T$ is the value of prediction corresponding to time T. V, W, b_w and b_v are all parameters that need to be learned in the network. s_T is the hidden layer state of decoder at time T, and C_T is the semantic vector obtained by encoding corresponding to time T.

$$\tilde{y}_T = V(W[s_T; C_T] + b_w) + b_v \tag{11}$$

5 Experiments

In this section, the effectiveness of proposed method is demonstrated by utilizing the datasets of Citi Bike. We compare model with other baseline methods, analyze the generalization of our approach, and evaluate the accuracy of the model prediction.

5.1 Datasets

Citi Bike [25] has collected user history ride data since 2013. Following other researcher, we use 114,698 rows of data from June 1st to September 30th, 2017. The climate data of the same period is added, and the details of the final experimental dataset including the context features are shown in Table 2. In the experiment, 70% of the total data is selected as the training set and the remaining 30% as the test set.

Table 2. The details of the dataset.

Details of dataset	Information	Details of dataset	Information
Place	New York	Number of Stations	621
Time Span	2017/06/01–2017/09/30	Weather	6 types (light rain, snow…)
Data Field	15 species	Temperature	[31.1, 21.1]
Missing Value	Age (missing rate 0.5%, mean filling)	Wind Speed	[0, 12]
Number of Data	114,698	Pressure	[995, 1040]

5.2 Setting

In our method, we use encoder and decoder base on attention and LSTM to predict the number of bikes on the station. We use the deep learning framework Pytorch to perform experiments on NVIDIA GeForce GTX 1650 (with 12G RAM). The model is trained by using the Adam optimizer with a learning rate of 0.001. The batch size is 128 and the dimension of encoder and decoder is 128. The parameters of the baselines are the default values. In experiment, loss gradually decreases with epoch. When the epoch is 47, the model loss is the smallest. Therefore, the epoch is set to 50 and take the parameters when the model is optimal. In the process of data processing, we count the number of bikes used by all users of station in hour. The number of times the bike is used is counted by the starting station when the user uses the car, divided by hourly clusters and stations. Whether it is a weekend or not, it is divided according to the fact that Monday to Friday is set to 0 for the week, and Saturday to Sunday is set to 1 for the weekend. Similarly, whether the peak period is divided into 1 and 0 according to the above time period analysis, 1 refers to the peak period, and 0 refers to the off-peak period.

5.3 Evaluation Metrics

In this paper, Mean Absolute Error (MAE) and Root Mean Squared Error (RMSE) are used as the evaluation metric. The Mean Absolute Error can reflect the fitting effect of the model, as shown in Eq. (12). MAE accumulates the error between each predicted value and the real value. The larger the MAE, the greater the prediction error. So a model with good predictive power should ensure that the MAE is as small as possible. However, RMSE can magnify the value with large prediction error and compare the robustness of different models. As shown in Eq. (13). Where n is the number of test samples, y_i is the true value, and $\tilde{y}_i$ is the predicted value. In the same way, a model with good predictive power should ensure that the RMSE is as small as possible.

$$MAE = 1/n \sum_{i=1}^{n} |y_i - \tilde{y}_i| \tag{12}$$

$$RMSE = \sqrt{1/n \sum_{i=1}^{n} (y_i - \tilde{y}_i)^2} \tag{13}$$

5.4 Results

Analysis of Prediction Results
The downtown station has a greater demand for bikes than the suburban station. It can be seen from the Fig. 12 that the model can fit the trend of the number of bikes at each station over time. Figure 12 shows the number of bikes predicted to have a site ID of 223 in the next week. The value of the number of bikes predicted by the model is close to the true value and fits the trend of the true value. This shows the effectiveness of the model for the number of bikes prediction. Similarly, the model can only fit the trend of the true value very well, and cannot accurately predict the specific number of bikes. This is because the number of bikes is related to other features such as geographic and location features. C-LSTMAM cannot predict the maximum peak value because the maximum peak value is an abnormal value in a continuous period of time.

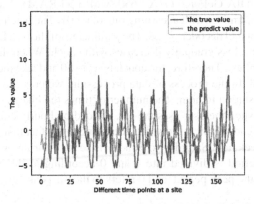

Fig. 12. Predict the number of bikes with a station ID of 223 in the next week (ID = 223)

Comparison to Baselines
We compare the performances of the proposed method against the following baseline algorithms.

RNN [30]: Recurrent Neural Network is used to capture the correlation between time series data to predict future values.

LSTM [31]: The recurrent neural network with gating mechanism is used to mine the long-term dependence of sequence data to predict future values.

XGBoost [32]: XGBoost has good learning effect and fast training speed. It is a machine learning library that focuses on gradient boosting algorithms.

Figure 13 shows the performance results of our proposed C-LSTMAM as compared to all the baselines. MAE and RMSE are all the smaller the equivalent value, the better the performance of the model. Although the recurrent neural network RNN and LSTM are effective in processing time series data, they have poor performance compared to the LSTM model with attention. This is because the attention mechanism can assign different weights to each feature according to the relationship between the data feature and the result, and strengthen the importance of certain features. Compared with RNN, LSTM adds a gating mechanism to mine the long-term dependence between sequence data, so the results on the three evaluation indicators are better. XGBoost is an optimized distributed gradient boosting library that implements decision tree boosting in parallel. It has a stronger performance than LSTM. Similarly, because of the lack of attention mechanism distribution and the inability to mine important features, the performance is lower than the model based on combination of LSTM and Attention. Considering MAE and RMSE indicators, the C-LSTMAM is better than others.

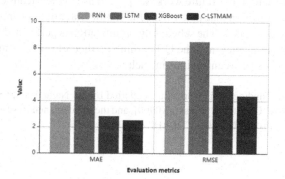

Fig. 13. The comparison with baselines

Context Feature Verification

In order to verify the feature importance analysis, we select the temperature in the feature for an ablation experiment. C-LSTMAM + temp considers the temperature features, while C-LSTMAM-temp removes the temperature features. The results are shown in the Table 3, and the performance of the model taking into account the temperature features is obviously better. This shows that the temperature feature has an impact on predicting the number of bikes on the station, which verifies the importance of considering the riding context.

Table 3. Temperature importance analysis

Methods	MAE	RMSE
C-LSTMAM+temp	2.516	4.368
C-LSTMAM-temp	2.958	4.880

6 Conclusion

In this paper, we analyze the historical cycling dataset of users. Then, select and construct the relevant features. The number of bike-sharing prediction method based on LSTM and Attention mechanism was proposed. The algorithm proposed in this paper not only considers the temporal features, but also introduces the context features of climate related to cycling data. Through the combination of LSTM and Attention Mechanism, the dynamic to predict the number of bike-sharing model is constructed. In other words, this model can extract features dynamically. The proposed model is verified by using Citi Bike dataset, and the experimental results show that the model can reduce prediction errors well. The performance of MAE and RMSE shows the effectiveness of the proposed algorithm, and the rationality of feature selection is verified by experiments. The C-LSTMAM model can predict the number of bikes at station, thereby balancing the number of bikes at station. For future work, we plan to use the K-Means clustering algorithm based on the transition matrix to divide the station into different areas according to the predicted number of bikes. The scheduling optimization is performed by considering the local maximum efficiency, and the Q-Learning method of reinforcement learning is used to schedule bikes between stations in each area.

Acknowledgement. Funding: This work was supported by the Natural Science Foundation of Chongqing, China [No. Cstc2020jcyj-msxmX0900]; and the Fundamental Research Funds for the Central Universities [Project No. 2020CDJ-LHZZ-040].

References

1. Yang, X.-H., et al.: The impact of a public bicycle-sharing system on urban public transport networks. Transp. Res. Part Policy Pract.**107**, 246–256 (2018)
2. Jiang, W., Luo, J.: Graph neural network for traffic forecasting: a survey. 117921 (2022)
3. Chemla, D., Meunier, F., Calvo, R.W.: Bike sharing systems: solving the static rebalancing problem. Disc. Optim. **10**(2), 120–146 (2013)
4. O'Mahony, E., Shmoys, D.B.: Data analysis and optimization for (citi) bike sharing. In: Twenty-Ninth AAAI Conference on Artificial Intelligence, Citeseer (2015)
5. Yang, Z., Hu, J., Shu, Y., Cheng, P., Chen, J., Moscibroda, T.: Mobility modeling and prediction in bike-sharing systems. In: International Conference on Mobile Systems, Applications, and Services (2016)
6. Y. Tang, H. Pan, and Y. J. T. R. P. Fei, "Research on Users' Frequency of Ride in Shanghai Minhang Bike-sharing System," vol. 25, pp. 4983–4991, 2017
7. Wang, B., Vu, H.L., Kim, I., Cai, C.: Short-term traffic flow prediction in bike-sharing networks. J. Transp. Syst. **26**(4), 461–475 (2022)

8. Chang, X., Feng, Z., Wu, J., Sun, H., Wang, G., Bao, X.: Understanding and predicting the short-term passenger flow of station-free shared bikes: a spatiotemporal deep learning approach. IEEE Intell. Transp. Syst. Mag. **14**(4), 73–85 (2021)
9. Hua, M, Chen, X., Chen, J., Jiang, Y.: Minimizing fleet size and improving vehicle allocation of shared mobility under future uncertainty: a case study of bike sharing. J. Clean. Prod. **370**, 133434 (2022)
10. Wang, B., Kim, I.: Short-term prediction for bike-sharing service using machine learning. Transp. Res. Proc. **34**, 171–178 (2018)
11. Singhvi, D., et al.: Predicting bike usage for New York City's bike sharing system. In: National Conference on Artificial Intelligence (2015)
12. Lv, Y., Duan, Y., Kang, W., Li, Z., Wang, F.-Y.: Traffic flow prediction with big data: a deep learning approach. IEEE Trans. Intell. Transp. Syst. **16**(2), 865–873 (2014)
13. Zhang, J., Zheng, Y., Qi, D.: Deep spatio-temporal residual networks for citywide crowd flows prediction (2016)
14. Xie, M., Yin, H., Wang, H., Xu, F., Chen, W., Wang, S.: Learning graph-based poi embedding for location-based recommendation. In: Proceedings of the 25th ACM International on Conference on Information and Knowledge Management, pp. 15–24 (2016)
15. Chai, D., Wang, L., Yang, Q.: Bike flow prediction with multi-graph convolutional networks. In: Proceedings of the 26th ACM SIGSPATIAL international conference on advances in geographic information systems, pp. 397–400 (2018)
16. Chen, K., et al.: Dynamic spatio-temporal graph-based cnns for traffic prediction (2018)
17. Deng, S., Jia, S., Chen, J.: Exploring spatial–temporal relations via deep convolutional neural networks for traffic flow prediction with incomplete data. Appl. Soft Comput. **78**, 712–721 (2019)
18. Bargar, A., Gupta, A., Gupta, S., Ma, D.: Interactive visual analytics for multi-city bikeshare data analysis. In: The 3rd International Workshop on Urban Computing (UrbComp 2014), New York, USA, vol. 45 (2014)
19. Dell'Amico, M., Iori, M., Novellani, S., Subramanian, A.: The bike sharing rebalancing problem with stochastic demands. Transp. Res. Part B Methodol. **118**(DEC), 362–380 (2018)
20. Vogel, P., Greiser, T., Mattfeld, D., Sciences, B.: Understanding bike-sharing systems using data mining: exploring activity patterns. Proc. Soc. Behav. Sci. **20**(6), 514–523 (2011)
21. Yan, Y., Tao, Y., Jin, X., Ren, S., Lin, H.: Visual analytics of bike-sharing data based on tensor factorization. J. Visual. **21**(3), 495–509 (2018). https://doi.org/10.1007/s12650-017-0463-1
22. Lihua, N., Xiaorong, C., Qian, H.: ARIMA model for traffic flow prediction based on wavelet analysis. In: The 2nd International Conference on Information Science and Engineering (2011)
23. Zhang, N., Zhang, Y., Lu, H.: Seasonal autoregressive integrated moving average and support vector machine models: prediction of short-term traffic flow on freeways. Transp. Res. Record. **2215**(1), 85–92 (2011)
24. Ahn, J.Y., Ko, E., Kim, E.Y.: Predicting spatiotemporal traffic flow based on support vector regression and Bayesian classifier. In: IEEE Fifth International Conference on Big Data & Cloud Computing (2015)
25. Xie, P., Li, T., Liu, J., Du, S., Zhang, J.: Urban flow prediction from spatiotemporal data using machine learning: a survey. Inform. Fusion. **59**, 1–2 (2020)
26. Cho, K., et al.: Learning Phrase Representations using RNN Encoder-Decoder for Statistical Machine Translation (2014)
27. Cho, K., Merrienboer, B.V., Bahdanau, D., Bengio, Y.: On the Properties of Neural Machine Translation: Encoder-Decoder Approaches (2014)
28. Hochreiter, S., Schmidhuber, J.: Long short-term memory. Neural Comput. **9**(8), 1735–1780 (1997)

29. Bahdanau, D., Cho, K., Bengio, Y.: Neural Machine Translation by Jointly Learning to Align and Translate (2014)
30. Fu, R., Zhang, Z., Li, L.: Using LSTM and GRU neural network methods for traffic flow prediction. In: 2016 31st Youth Academic Annual Conference of Chinese Association of Automation (YAC), pp. 324–328. IEEE (2016)
31. Greff, K., Srivastava, R.K., Koutník, J., Steunebrink, B.R., Schmidhuber, N.: LSTM: a search space Odyssey. IEEE Trans. Neural Netw. Learn. Syst. **28**(10), 2222–2232 (2016)
32. Chen, T., Guestrin, C.: XGBoost: a scalable tree boosting system. In: the 22nd ACM SIGKDD International Conference (2016)

Federated Learning and Application

FedFR: Evaluation and Selection of Loss Functions for Federated Face Recognition

Ertong Shang, Zhuo Yang, Hui Liu[✉], Junzhao Du, and Xingyu Wang

Xidian University, Xi'an 710126, Shaanxi, China
{etshang,zhuo_yang}@stu.xidian.edu.cn, {liuhui,dujz}@xidian.edu.cn

Abstract. With growing concerns about data privacy and the boom in mobile and ubiquitous computing, federated learning, as an emerging privacy-preserving collaborative computing approach, has been receiving widespread attention recently. In this context, many clients collaboratively train a shared global model under the orchestration of a remote server, while keeping the training data localized. To achieve better federated learning performance, the majority of existing works have focused on designing advanced learning algorithms, such as server-side parameter aggregation policies. However, the local optimization on client devices, especially selecting an appropriate loss function for local training, has not been well studied. To fill this gap, we construct a federated face recognition prototype system and test five classical metric learning methods(i.e. loss functions) in this system, comparing their practical performance in terms of the global model accuracy, communication cost, convergence rate, and resource occupancy. Extensive empirical studies demonstrate that the relative performance between these approaches varies greatly in different federated scenarios. Specifically, when the number of categories to recognize on each client is large, using the classification-based loss function can make a better global model faster with less communication cost; while when there are only a few classes on each client, using the pair-based method can be more communication-efficient and obtain higher accuracy. Finally, we interpret this phenomenon from the perspective of similarity optimization and offer some suggestions on making suitable choices amongst various loss functions.

Keywords: Federated learning · Face recognition · Loss function · Metric learning

1 Introduction

In the last few years, fueled by advances in big data, processing power, and algorithms, Artificial Intelligence (AI), especially Deep Learning (DL), has achieved great breakthroughs in a wide range of applications. However, conventional single-machine model training requires the great amount of data to be centralized in a cloud server or a data center to produce effective inference models, which is facing unprecedented challenges for the following reasons. On the one

© ICST Institute for Computer Sciences, Social Informatics and Telecommunications Engineering 2022
Published by Springer Nature Switzerland AG 2022. All Rights Reserved
H. Gao et al. (Eds.): CollaborateCom 2022, LNICST 460, pp. 95–114, 2022.
https://doi.org/10.1007/978-3-031-24383-7_6

hand, nations across the world are strengthening laws to protect users' privacy and data security, posing new challenges to the data-transaction procedures commonly used today in AI [38]. On the other hand, the popularity of networked devices has led to an exponential increase in data generated at the edge of networks. As a consequence, existing cloud-based AI is gradually unable to manage such massively distributed computing power and analyze these data.

Thanks to the rapid advancement of computational and storage capabilities of edge smart devices and wireless communication technologies such as 5G, federated learning provides a potential solution to this dilemma. Federated Learning (FL), first proposed by Google [19], is a privacy-preserving distributed machine learning setting where many clients (e.g. resource-constrained edge devices or whole organizations) collaboratively train a model under the orchestration of a central server(e.g. a service provider) while keeping the training data decentralized [12]. Since the data never leave the data owners' devices, FL not only mitigates potential privacy leakage risks but also relieves computation and storage burden on servers. Other advantages of FL, as described in [40], include: reducing communication overhead by avoiding massive data uploads; enabling a global model that applies to different scenarios.

Because of the aforementioned great benefits, FL has attracted widespread attention recently. Among the existing researches, a large number of works focused on improving the performance and generalization capabilities of federated learning models by designing advanced learning algorithms [11,35,36], reducing communication costs [27] and enhancing privacy security of federated learning [22]. However, only a few works dealt with its implementation to real-world large-scale applications since the majority of existing works are carried out on small-scale datasets, e.g. MNIST, CIFAR, and their variants [8]. More importantly, the local optimization on client devices, especially selecting an appropriate loss function for local training, which determines the fundamental performance of the FL system, remain unexplored.

On the other hand, although a range of loss functions have been compared and studied on different tasks [3,23,28], they are all conducted in the traditional centralized training scenario, whose data characteristics are different from those in FL. For example, millions of images composed of tens of thousands of individuals are gathered together in the traditional face recognition task which thus can be regarded as a very large-scale classification problem. But in federated face recognition, each client may only contain images of dozens of people. The performance of these loss functions on such small-scale data is still unknown, which is also the motivation of this work.

Accordingly, in this paper, we focus on the implementation and evaluation of FL in a real large-scale application, face recognition. Meanwhile, we introduce the latest progress of metric learning into FL and explore the system performance in detail when different loss functions are used for local training. Interestingly, we observed large differences in relative performance between these loss functions in different FL scenarios. In other words, the loss function should be carefully selected according to the data characteristics of application scenarios when using

FL. To the best of our knowledge, this is the first time to study and evaluate the performance of different loss functions in FL settings. The main contributions of this research are as follows.

- Firstly, we construct a large-scale FL prototype system for face recognition, Federated Face Recognition (FedFR), and consider various application scenarios for it.
- Further, we evaluate and compare the performance of five classical loss functions in our federated face recognition system. The abundant experiments not only prove that the advances in metric learning are still effective in FL but also show that the performance of these methods varies greatly in different federated settings.
- Finally, we provide a similarity optimization-based interpretation for the observed results and draw important conclusions that would help the researchers in making suitable choices amongst various loss functions for federated face recognition.

2 Related Works

2.1 Face Recognition

Face recognition technology is a biometric technology, which is based on the identification of facial features of a person and is also one of the most important topics in computer vision and pattern recognition [14]. It can be categorized into closed-set or open-set settings. For the closed-set setting, all testing identities are predefined in the training set, thus can be addressed as a classification problem. For the open-set setting, the testing identities are not seen during training. Therefore it is usually seen as a metric learning problem in which faces must be mapped to a discriminative embedding space. In the past, traditional machine learning algorithms were mainly used for face recognition, such as the Eigenfaces [31], Bayesian face [20], support vector machine based [6], etc. Recently, with the development of deep neural networks, there have been significant advances in deep learning-based face recognition technology [25,29,34]. However, deep learning-based approaches need to collect a large number of high-quality face image centrally for training, which is very difficult now due to the emphasis on data privacy and security. Fortunately, FL is suitable to cope with this dilemma.

Besides the advances in deep model architectures and the appearance of some public face datasets, the design of powerful loss functions [4,17,25,29,32–34] is another major factor for the great success of face recognition and is also a research hotspot in recent years. In general, loss functions in metric learning can be divided into classification-based and pair-based types. Classification-based methods train an efficient feature extractor by correctly classifying samples with class-level labels, while pair-based ones learn embeddings directly via optimizing the similarity between samples with pair-wise labels. Although both the types of approaches have been extensively studied in metric learning, their performance in federated settings is still unknown, which is the focus of this work.

2.2   Federated Learning

Federated Learning is a distributed machine learning approach for training models from decentralized data residing on remote devices. In recent years, many efforts have been made to address various challenges in it, such as statistical heterogeneity, expensive communication, and poisoning attacks [12,16]. For statistical heterogeneity, FedProx proposed adding a proximal term to the local objective to help ensure convergence in statistically heterogeneous settings [24], while MOON introduced model-contrastive federated learning, correcting the local updates by maximizing the similarity of representation learned by the local model and the representation learned by the global model [15]. For efficient communication, McMahan et al. [18] proposed the federated averaging algorithm (FedAvg) to reduce the number of communication rounds, which is the most commonly used method for FL now. On the other hand, Konecny et al. [13] focused on communication compression techniques to lower the amount of data traffic in a single round. Finally, for privacy protection, Bonawitz et al. introduced a secure multiparty computation protocol to protect individual model updates [1]. Geyer et al. proposed an algorithm for client-sided differential privacy-preserving federated optimization to tackle differential attacks [5]. However, the core of this paper is the local optimization on client devices, especially the selection of loss functions in different federated settings, which is compatible with and complementary to these techniques.

3   Classical Loss Functions

As shown in Sect. 2.1, many excellent loss functions have been proposed, which made great advances in recognition accuracy. However, the performance of these methods in federated settings is still unknown, so we decide to study them in detail in FedFR. Next, we will introduce the five loss functions studied in this paper, namely, Softmax Loss [29], Large Margin Cosine Loss(CosFace Loss) [34], ArcFace Loss [4], Triplet Loss [25] and Multi-Similarity Loss(MS Loss) [37]. Softmax Loss and its latest variants, ArcFace and CosFace Loss, are classification-based methods. Triplet Loss is usually regarded as the baseline of pair-based methods, and MS Loss is one of the latest developments in this category.

3.1   Classification-Based Loss Functions

Softmax Loss. Softmax Loss is the most widely used classification loss function in deep learning. In particular, it consists of a classifier layer followed by a multi-class cross-entropy loss. It is presented as follows:

$$L = -\frac{1}{N} \sum_{i=1}^{N} log \frac{e^{W_{y_i}^T x_i + b_{y_i}}}{\sum_{j=1}^{n} e^{W_j^T x_i + b_j}} \qquad (1)$$

where W and b are the weight matrix and bias vector of the last layer, that is, the classifier layer. x_i and y_i denote the deep feature and the ground-truth label of the i-th training sample respectively. N is the batch size, n is the total class number. W_j and b_j are the j-th column of W and the j-th item of b respectively, which correspond to the j-th class.

By simply fixing the bias $b = 0$ and further normalizing the deep feature as well as the columns of the weight matrix, NormFace [33] reformulate Eq. (1) as:

$$L = -\frac{1}{N} \sum_{i=1}^{N} log \frac{e^{s \, cos(\theta_{y_i,i})}}{\sum_{j=1}^{n} e^{s \, cos(\theta_{j,i})}} \tag{2}$$

where $\theta_{j,i}$ is the angle between W_j and x_i, and s is a large constant to prevent the gradient from getting too small in the training phase.

CosFace Loss. However, the embedding features learned by Softmax Loss and its normalized version are not sufficiently discriminative because they only penalize classification errors. To address this issue, CosFace Loss introduces an additive cosine margin $m(m \geq 0)$ to the classification boundary, described by:

$$L = -\frac{1}{N} \sum_{i=1}^{N} log \frac{e^{s \, (cos(\theta_{y_i,i})-m)}}{e^{s \, (cos(\theta_{y_i,i})-m)} + \sum_{j \neq y_i} e^{s \, cos(\theta_{j,i})}} \tag{3}$$

ArcFace Loss. Similarly, ArcFace Loss adds an additive angular margin penalty $m(m \geq 0)$ between x_i and W_{y_i} to simultaneously enhance the intra-class compactness and inter-class discrepancy. It is presented as follows:

$$L = -\frac{1}{N} \sum_{i=1}^{N} log \frac{e^{s \, (cos(\theta_{y_i,i}+m))}}{e^{s \, (cos(\theta_{y_i,i}+m))} + \sum_{j \neq y_i} e^{s \, cos(\theta_{j,i})}} \tag{4}$$

3.2 Pair-Based Loss Functions

Triplet Loss. Triplet Loss aims to learn discriminative feature embeddings using embedding triplets. A triplet consists of an anchor, a positive sample, and a negative one, where the positive shares the same label as the anchor while the negative comes from other classes. Each triplet tries to tries to enforce the anchor-positive distance to be smaller than the anchor-negative distance by a predefined margin m. It can be described as follows:

$$L = \sum_{i=1}^{N} \left[\|x_i^a - x_i^p\|_2^2 - \|x_i^a - x_i^n\|_2^2 + m \right]_+ \tag{5}$$

where N is the number of triplets constructed in a mini-batch, x_i^a, x_i^p and x_i^n denote the feature embedding of the anchor, positive and negative sample in the i-th triplet, respectively.

MS Loss. How to improve sampling schemes to construct pairs with more information is the key to embedding-based methods. To meet this challenge, [37] casts the sampling problem into a general pair weighting formulation and considers three similarities, defined as self-similarity, positive relative similarity, and negative relative similarity, for pair mining and weighting. Where the positive relative similarity is used for pair mining, while the self-similarity and negative relative similarity are jointly used for weighting the selected pairs. On this basis, they proposes MS loss:

$$L = \frac{1}{N} \sum_{i=1}^{N} \left\{ \frac{1}{\alpha} log \left[1 + \sum_{k \in \mathcal{P}_i} e^{-\alpha(S_{ik}-\lambda)} \right] + \frac{1}{\beta} log \left[1 + \sum_{k \in \mathcal{N}_i} e^{\beta(S_{ik}-\lambda)} \right] \right\} \quad (6)$$

where N is the number of samples in a mini-batch, S_{ik} denotes the similarity between x_i and x_k. $\mathcal{P}_i$ and $\mathcal{N}_i$ denote the index set of selected positive pairs and negative pairs for an anchor x_i. λ, α, β are fixed hyper-parameters.

4   System Design and Performance Metrics

In this section, we will introduce our federated face recognition system, FedFR. Specifically, we start with the architecture and learning protocol of FedFR before introducing its application scenarios. Next, we show the performance metrics we defined to evaluate the performance of different loss functions, including effectiveness, communication efficiency, convergence rate, and memory usage.

4.1   System Overview

As shown in Fig. 1, the federated face recognition prototype system, FedFR, is designed based on the Client-Server architecture implementing the FedAvg [18] algorithm. In this system, K participants, called clients, collaboratively learn a global face recognition model under the coordination of a central server. Clients are data owners and they train local models using their own data and computation resources. The server maintains a global model and updates it by aggregating the local models periodically. It is worth noting that each client's raw data is stored locally and not exchanged or transferred. Correspondingly, there is no data stored and no training performed in the central server.

We use FedAvg as the learning protocol of FedFR. Its main process is as follows:

(1) Global Parameter Broadcasting: Server selects some clients and broadcasts the global model parameters to them.
(2) Local Model Training: Each selected client independently trains its local model using the local data.
(3) Local Parameter Backing: Clients send back their updated local parameters to the server.
(4) Model Aggregation: Server aggregates the received parameters using a certain aggregation algorithm and updates the global model.

The four main steps are iterated until the global model achieves the desired performance or completes a specified number of iterations.

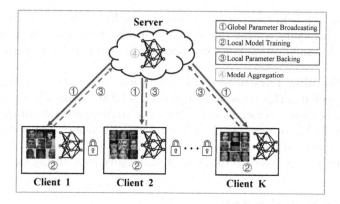

Fig. 1. The architecture of FedFR.

4.2 Application Scenarios

We consider two typical application scenarios for FedFR: Federated-by-organizations and Federated-by-devices. The main differences between them lie in the number of clients, the hardware capacity of a single client, and the amount of data stored on each client.

Federated-by-Organizations Scenario. In this scenario, clients are companies or organizations with massive data. The number of clients is usually relatively small and each client has great computational and communication powers. For example, several companies in a building can use this system to jointly learn a face recognition model for the building's access control.

Federated-by-Devices Scenario. In this scenario, clients are usually defined as mobile devices or embedded devices. Contrary to the Federated-by-organizations scenario, each device usually has a relatively small amount of data as well as limited computational and communication powers in this setting, so the devices cannot afford to perform much computation to train a huge model. Moreover, due to a large number of clients, only a small fraction of devices perform computation during each round of training. For example, a large number of cameras in different locations can be viewed as clients to build an intelligent safe-guard system that uses face recognition technology, without uploading their privacy sensitive images.

4.3 Performance Metrics

Test Accuracy is used to evaluate the effectiveness of each method. By following the standard face recognition evaluation protocol, we test the face verification accuracy of the global model at intervals and record all results during training. And then, we report the highest test accuracy.

Communication Rounds. Communication cost can be calculated by multiplying the number of communication rounds and the amount of data traffic in a single round. While in this paper, we use the number of communication rounds when the global model reaches the desired accuracy (**A**) for the first time (**R@A**) to measure communication efficiency because the data traffic in each round is the same.

Local Training Time of each global iteration refers to the time required for all clients selected in this round to complete their local training. It, together with the number of global iterations determines the convergence rate of the system. In a real-world FL system, Local Training Time depends on the slowest one of all clients selected in that iteration.

Memory Usage refers to the amount of memory used during local training.

5   Experimental Setup

In this section, we describe the experimental setup in detail, including the simulation environment (Sect. 5.1), datasets and data preprocessing (Sect. 5.2), network architectures we used (Sect. 5.3), and some implementation details (Sect. 5.4).

5.1   Simulation Environment

We simulate the FL setup (one server and K clients) on a commodity machine with Intel Xeon Silver 4214 CPU @ 2.2 GHz and 3 NVIDIA GeForce RTX 2080Ti GPUs. All experiments are implemented using Pytorch with Python 3.6. We select a number of parameters to control the federated settings in our experiments. These parameters are: 1) K - number of devices, 2) C - clients' participation percentage in each round, 3) S - number of online clients in each round (i.e., $S = K \times C$), 4) R - number of communication rounds, 5) E - number of local training epochs per round, 6) N - number of individuals (training classes) on each client.

5.2   Datasets and Preprocessing

Training Data. CASIA-WebFace [39] and MS-Celeb-1M (MS1M) [7] are the most widely used public datasets for face recognition, containing 0.49M face images from 10,575 different subjects and about 10M images from 100K celebrities, respectively. So we use the two datasets as our training sets. In this work, we take 10K individuals from CASIA-WebFace and 50K individuals from MS1M clean version respectively, and divide them into many small subsets according to their identities, where each subset represents the private dataset of one client in FedFR. According to the characteristics of the Federated-by-organizations scenario and Federated-by-devices scenario described in Sect. 3.2, we partition these individuals into multiple subsets in two manners, which is shown in Table 1. To eliminate the impact of unbalanced data distribution, each client simply has the same number of identities(i.e., classes) in this paper, and there is no identity overlap among clients.

Table 1. Characteristics of two different federated face recognition scenarios. **Ids/client** and **Imgs/client** represents the number of identities and the number of image samples per client, respectively. **Clients** indicates the number of clients in the corresponding scenario.

Dataset	Scenarios	Ids/client	Imgs/client	Clients
CASIA-WebFace	Federated-by-organizations	1,000	~50K	10
	Federated-by-devices	20	~1K	500
MS1M	Federated-by-organizations	1,000	~53K	50
	Federated-by-devices	20	~1.1K	2500

Test Data. During training, we use an efficient face verification dataset, Labeled Faces in the Wild (LFW) [10], to test the accuracy and to analyze the convergence of the global model on the server. The LFW dataset consists of 13,233 face images from 5749 persons from uncontrolled conditions. We use the standard verification protocol mentioned in [10] to evaluate 6,000 image pairs.

In addition, we also use CFP-FP [26] as well as AgeDB-30 [21], two more difficult test protocols, to evaluate the model accuracy. Celebrities in Frontal-Profile data set (CFP) [26] contains 12,557 face images of 500 celebrities in front and profile views. It contains two verification protocols: one comparing only frontal faces (CFP-FF), the other comparing frontal and profile faces (CFP-FP). Each protocol consists of 7000 comparisons, and we consider the more challenging verification protocols, CFP-FP, in our experiments. AgeDB [21] is a manually collected in-the-wild age database, containing 16,488 images of 568 various famous people. It is a more challenging face verification dataset since it with large range of ages for each subject. Generally, the original AgeDB contains four verification schemes, where the compared faces have an age difference of 5, 10, 20 and 30 years, respectively. In our experiments, we select the most challenging scheme(AgeDB-30) for evaluation, which also contains 6,000 comparisons.

For data prepossessing, we follow the most common treatment to generate the face crops (112 × 112) by utilizing five facial points. Each pixel ([0, 255]) in the RGB images is then normalized by subtracting 127.5 and divided by 128, without any other data augmentation.

5.3   Network Architectures

For the trunk network, we employ two widely used CNN architectures, ResNet and MobileFaceNet. It is worth noting that the classification-based method requires an additional classifier layer, which is always maintained in clients and does not need to be uploaded for aggregation because each column of the parameter matrix of the classifier layer represents the proxy of its corresponding class.

ResNet. The ResNet architecture was first proposed by He et al. in 2015 [9]. It has proven to be an effective network architecture for a wide variety of vision tasks. In this paper, we adopt the ResNet50 model used in ArcFace to get a 512-D feature embedding for each image. This model contains 43 million parameters and has a computational cost of 6,309 million MAdds(the number of operations measured by multiply-adds) in total. Given limited computation resources, we only train ResNet-50 model on CASIA-WebFace.

MobileFaceNet. Chen et al. [2] presented a light face feature embedding CNN, MobileFaceNet, which aims to improve the efficiency for real-time face verification on mobile and embedded devices. It learns a more compact face embedding of 128 dimensions, using only about 1 million parameters and 227 million MAdds.

5.4   Implementation Details

We conduct abundant experiments in different federated settings to comprehensively compare the system performance with different loss functions. For the sake of fair comparison, we use the same hyper-parameter settings as their authors for all loss functions except ArcFace Loss, because the original setting(s is 64, m is 0.5) for ArcFace Loss can not converge well in our federated settings. After several attempts, we eventually set the feature scale s to 30 and choose the angular margin m of 0.3 for ArcFace Loss. For classification-based methods, the batch size is set to 64. For pair-based methods, we first randomly choose 16 classes and then randomly sample 4 instances from each class selected to form a mini-batch. As a comparison, we also train a model in the traditional centralized way using the loss functions described above. For all settings, the stochastic gradient descent(SGD) algorithm with momentum set to 0.9 and weight decay of 5e-4 is used as an optimizer. Starting from 0.1, the learning rate decreases by 10% every 5 rounds for all federated settings.

For centralized training, the number of training epochs is set to 20 for both datasets. For Federated-by-organizations scenario, we set $R = 80, E = 1, S = 10$ (i.e., $K = 10, C = 1.0$ for CASIA-WebFace; $K = 50, C = 0.2$ for MS1M). For Federated-by-devices scenario, we set $R = 200, E = 10$ for both dataset, $S = 25$ (i.e., $K = 500, C = 0.05$) for CASIA-WebFace; $S = 50$ (i.e., $K = 2500, C = 0.02$) for MS1M.

6   Performance Evaluation and Summary

In this section, we conduct a series of experiments in different federated settings to compare the loss functions mentioned above according to the performance metrics we defined. By analyzing the abundant results, we gain some meaningful conclusions. More importantly, some suggestions are given for selecting appropriate loss functions in federated face recognition.

6.1   Comparison of Test Accuracy

Table 2 and Table 3 show the test accuracy of the models trained with CASIA-WebFace and MS1M dataset, respectively. We can see that for each loss function, the accuracy achieved in federated settings is very close to that in the centralized setting. That is to say, the federated training protocol we adopted can obtain satisfactory results, which proves the effectiveness of FL for large-scale face recognition tasks.

Table 2. Highest test accuracy for both models trained with CASIA-Webface dataset. **Cent**, **Fed_O** and **Fed_D** represents centralized training, Federated-by-organizations scenario and Federated-by-devices scenario, respectively.

Model	Loss	LFW			CFP-FP			AgeDB-30		
		Cent	Fed_O	Fed_D	Cent	Fed_O	Fed_D	Cent	Fed_O	Fed_D
ResNet	CosFace	99.25	99.05	94.40	94.51	93.77	83.30	92.73	91.23	75.55
	ArcFace	99.17	99.12	93.58	94.34	93.67	82.43	92.63	91.03	76.12
	Softmax	98.82	96.93	91.53	92.51	88.00	78.80	89.65	86.13	74.17
	MS	98.40	98.31	95.40	92.24	91.73	85.31	89.08	88.28	79.28
	Triplet	97.98	97.78	94.33	91.20	90.74	83.57	86.25	84.90	76.00
MobileFaceNet	CosFace	99.00	98.70	92.57	92.73	92.00	80.03	91.43	89.87	74.00
	ArcFace	98.88	98.68	92.38	93.07	91.94	80.31	90.97	89.82	74.27
	Softmax	97.90	96.37	91.83	90.04	87.29	79.27	87.00	84.08	74.75
	MS	98.28	97.38	94.40	90.33	89.60	82.84	87.15	85.37	77.18
	Triplet	97.65	97.02	92.57	90.59	89.25	81.79	84.57	82.88	73.65

Table 3. Highest test accuracy for MobileFaceNet trained with MS1M dataset.

Model	Loss	LFW			AgeDB-30			CFP-FP		
		Cent	Fed_O	Fed_D	Cent	Fed_O	Fed_D	Cent	Fed_O	Fed_D
MobileFaceNet	CosFace	99.25	98.85	95.05	95.18	92.87	79.57	87.20	85.10	74.89
	ArcFace	99.28	98.77	94.57	95.45	91.70	79.68	88.39	84.37	74.30
	Softmax	98.97	96.30	93.65	92.93	85.42	78.55	85.56	77.11	73.46
	MS	98.82	97.93	96.43	92.20	88.97	83.85	87.17	83.36	78.75
	Triplet	98.57	97.78	95.97	90.67	87.20	82.67	86.73	83.35	78.20

We also compare the performance of different loss functions in FedFR. First of all, it can be seen that for classification-based loss functions, ArcFace and CosFace loss consistently outperform Softmax loss. Similarly, for pair-based ones, MS loss is always better than Triplet loss too. This is entirely in accord with the observation in the centralized setting. In other words, it demonstrates that the progress made in centralized metric learning is also applicable in FL.

Another phenomenon is that the model trained in Federated_by_organizations scenario outperform its counterpart in Federated_by_devices scenario, which is true for all loss functions. However, what's surprising is that the performance of classification-based methods and pair-based ones varies greatly in these two scenarios. Specifically, in the Federated-by-organizations scenario, ArcFace and

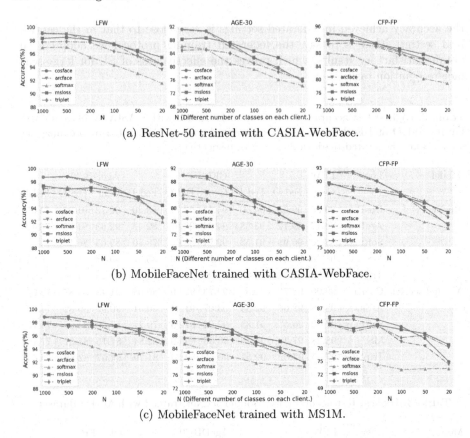

(a) ResNet-50 trained with CASIA-WebFace.

(b) MobileFaceNet trained with CASIA-WebFace.

(c) MobileFaceNet trained with MS1M.

Fig. 2. Comparison of the highest test accuracies for both model using different loss functions in different federated settings. N on the horizontal axis indicates that the number of individuals on each client is N.

CosFace loss completely beat MS loss, while in the Federated-by-devices scenario, the opposite is true. Similarly, Triplet Loss, the baseline of pair-based methods, is also superior to its rival, Softmax loss, in the Federated-by-devices scenario. To further explore these observations, we conduct additional experiments, where the training set is divided into different number of subsets. Specifically, the training dataset is more exhaustively divided according to the number of classes (individuals) on each client which varies within the range of {1000, 500, 200, 100, 50, 20}. The results in all federated settings are shown in Fig. 2.

From Fig. 2, we can clearly observe a trend that as the amount of data on each client decreases, the test accuracy of the global model decreases, which is consistent on all three test sets. The reason is that the decrease in the amount of local data on each client increases the over-fitting degree of local models as well as the variance between local models, making model aggregation difficult. It is worth mentioning that the negative impact on the performance can be alleviated by some federated optimization techniques, such as using a more robust

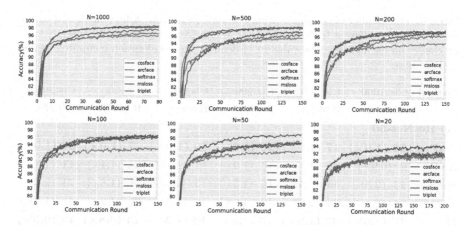

Fig. 3. Test accuracy of MobiFaceNet on LFW test set vs. number of communication rounds for the above five loss functions in different federated settings.

aggregation mechanism [36], introducing a proximal term to the local objective to reduce local bias [24], reducing the number of local epochs and etc., while it's not the point of this work. At the same time, we see that in the case of more data on each client, the performance of the classification-based loss function is better than that of the pair-based one, while the situation is just on the contrary in the case of less local data. To be specific, when each client contains 1000 or 500 individuals, the model accuracy using CosFace Loss and ArcFace Loss is completely superior to MS Loss. As the number of individuals decreased to 200 or 100, the three methods attain close results. Nevertheless, Ms Loss has a great advantage over CosFace and ArcFace Loss when the number of individuals is further reduced to 20. That is to say, with the decrease of the amount of local data on each client, the performance degradation of classification-based methods is more severe than that of pair-based ones.

6.2   Comparison of Communication Efficiency

As mentioned above, we measure communication efficiency in terms of **R@A**, i.e., the number of communication rounds when the global model reaches the desired accuracy (**A**) for the first time. For each federated setting, we set the values for (**A**) based on the lowest accuracy achieved among these loss functions. Table 4 reports the test results on LFW for the MobileFaceNet and ResNet-50 trained with CASIA-WebFace dataset. Moreover, Fig. 3 visualizes the training dynamics of MobileFaceNet using the five methods in different federated settings.

From the recorded results, we observe a similar trend in the communication cost comparison among these methods with the test accuracy comparison among them. First, in almost all settings, Cosface and ArcFace Loss have similar communication cost, which is less than Softmax, and the communication cost of MS Loss is less than that of Triplet Loss. Morever, it can be seen from the test accuracy curves with varing epochs in Fig. 3, in Cls_1000 (i.e., a thousand

Table 4. The number of communication rounds for first-time achievement of a certain test accuracy in different federated settings, where Cls_N represents there are N training classes on each client. The value in () denotes the deceleration computed against CosFace Loss.

Method	Cls_1000	Cls_500	Cls_200	Cls_100	Cls_50	Cls_20
	R@95%	R@95%	R@90%	R@90%	R@90%	R@90%
(1) ResNet-50						
CosFace	**10 (1.0×)**	**17 (1.0×)**	**10 (1.0×)**	**10 (1.0×)**	**17 (1.0×)**	**33 (1.0×)**
ArcFace	9 (0.9×)	19 (1.1×)	10 (1.0×)	11 (1.1×)	24 (1.4×)	43 (1.3×)
Softmax	23 (2.3×)	56 (3.3×)	15 (1.5×)	12 (1.2×)	31 (1.8×)	70 (2.3×)
Triplet	24 (2.4×)	48 (2.8×)	19 (1.9×)	16 (1.6×)	21 (1.2×)	41 (1.2×)
MS	**16 (1.6×)**	**32 (1.9×)**	**15 (1.5×)**	**12 (1.2×)**	**13 (0.8×)**	**19 (0.6×)**
(2) MobileFaceNet						
CosFace	**11 (1.0×)**	**21 (1.0×)**	**10 (1.0×)**	**11 (1.0×)**	**20 (1.0×)**	**60 (1.0×)**
ArcFace	12 (1.1×)	19 (0.9×)	9 (0.9×)	11 (1.0×)	20 (1.0×)	51 (0.9×)
Softmax	22 (2.0×)	61 (2.9×)	10 (1.0×)	15 (1.4×)	21 (1.0×)	66 (1.1×)
Triplet	26 (2.4×)	76 (3.6×)	17 (1.7×)	16 (1.5×)	19 (1.0×)	61 (1.0×)
MS	**21 (1.9×)**	**82 (4.3×)**	**19 (1.9×)**	**17 (1.5×)**	**13 (0.6×)**	**26 (0.4×)**

training classes per client), Cls_500, Cls_200 and Cls_100 federated settings, the classification-based approaches required fewer communication rounds (i.e. have more efficient communication) than the pair-based approaches to reach the same accuracy, whereas the reverse is true as the number of training classes per client decreased. For example, in the Cls_1000 setting, the communication cost of MS Loss is 1.9× compared to that of CosFace Loss. But in the Cls_20 setting, the communication cost of MS Loss is only 0.4× compared to that of CosFace Loss.

6.3   Comparison of Local Training Time

For all the loss functions, we also record the time required for all clients to complete their local training in each global iteration, called Local Training Time. In a real-world FL system, it is the time consumed by the slowest one of the all clients selected in each iteration. In this work, all the clients are simulated using the same desktop computer, thus we report the average time of all the clients completing a global iteration as the Local Training Time. Specifically, we compare the Local Training Time of MobileFaceNet and ResNet-50 model trained on different computing platforms (i.e., GPU or CPU).

Firstly, Fig. 4 demonstrates that for the same model, Local Training Time for classification-based loss functions is usually less than that for pair-based ones because the latter requires extra time to construct effective sample pairs or triplets. For example, when MobileFaceNet is used as the backbone network and trained on GPUs, Softmax, ArcFace, and CosFace loss functions have almost the same Local Training Time, while in all federated settings, Local Training Time for Triplet and MS Loss are roughly its 2X and 4X, respectively. However, by comparing the results in Fig. 4(a) and Fig. 4(b), we find that as the network architecture changes, so do the exact ratio between the Local Training Time for these loss functions. More precisely, Local Training Time for Triplet and MS Loss is only about 1.2X and 1.7X what it is for classification-based loss functions when using ResNet50 and trained on GPUs. In addition, similar phenomenon can be observed when the same model is trained on different computing platforms. Specially, for both models, the Local Training Time required for these five loss functions is relatively close when trained on the CPU. In other words, Local Training Time is not only related to the selected loss function but also closely related to the model architecture and the hardware resources used.

6.4   Comparison of Memory Usage

As described in Sect. 5.1, the classification-based method requires an additional classifier layer whose number of parameters is dependent on the size of the embedding and the number of classes contained on the client. For the Federated-by-devices scenario, each client contains only 20 different subjects, so there are only $20 * 128 = 2560$ and $20 * 512 = 10240$ additional parameters when using MobileFaceNet and ResNet50 respectively. Compared with the number of parameters of the backbone network(1M for MobileFaceNet and 43M for ResNet50), these additional parameters are completely negligible. Similarly, even for the Federated-by-organizations scenario that each client contains more individuals, the number of additional parameters introduced by the classifier layer is still insignificant. That is to say, for the two application scenarios we described, these loss functions are almost identical in terms of memory usage.

6.5   Summary and Suggestion

To sum up, based on the above observations, we first confirm the effectiveness of FedFR. Besides, we find a valuable rule that when the amount of data, especially the number of classes, is large on each client, using the classification-based loss function results in a more accurate global model faster with less communication cost. But when there is only a small number of classes on each client, using the pair-based one yields higher global accuracy with less communication cost instead, while the local training time of each iteration is longer than that of their rivals. In particular, in our federated face recognition experiment, this change occurs when the number of subjects on each client is about 100.

On this basis, some suggestions are given here for selecting appropriate loss functions in federated face recognition. When each client participating in feder-ated training can collect large amounts of training data, the classification-based loss function, especially its latest developments, is the best choice. On the contrary, when there is only limited training data on each client, we should make choices based on the actual performance requirements. If the focus is on the final

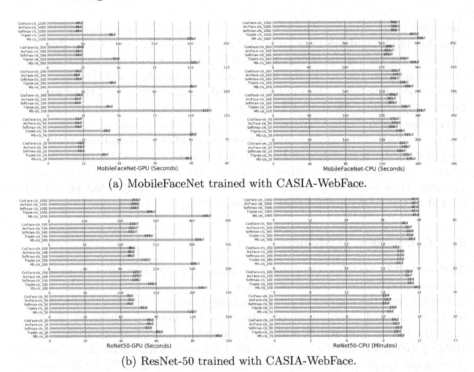

(a) MobileFaceNet trained with CASIA-WebFace.

(b) ResNet-50 trained with CASIA-WebFace.

Fig. 4. Comparison of Local Training Time for models trained on CPU and GPU using different loss functions. The naming convention is as follows: Loss function-federated setting. **Cls_1000**: Each client performs $E = 1$ local epochs; **Cls_500**: Each client performs $E = 1$ local epochs; **Cls_200**: Each client performs $E = 2$ local epochs; **Cls_100**: Each client performs $E = 5$ local epochs; **Cls_50**: Each client performs $E = 5$ local epoch; **Cls_20**: Each client performs $E = 10$ local epoch.

accuracy and communication cost during training, the latest pair-based methods are preferred. If the model owner wants to get a usable model faster, which loss function to choose should be considered in conjunction with the computing power of the client and the network model they used.

7   Similarity Optimization Based Interpretation

Our evaluation reported above shows that the classification-based method and the pair-based method vary greatly in performance in different federated settings. This section attempts to provide a theoretical interpretation for this meaningful phenomenon.

According to [30], there is no intrinsic difference between the two methods from the perspective of similarity optimization. Specifically, they both aim to minimize between-class similarity S_n as well as to maximize within-class similarity S_p by embedding S_n and S_p into similarity pairs and seeking to reduce

$(S_n - S_p)$. But during the optimization process, the way they construct positive pairs and negative pairs which are used to calculate S_p and S_n respectively is completely different. For the classification-based method, similarity scores are calculated between the deep feature x and each weight vector of the classifier layer, w_i(also called the proxy for class i). Thus, 1 positive pair and $N - 1(N$ is the number of training classes) negative pairs can be built for each sample regardless of the size of mini-batches. While for the pair-based method, similarity scores between x and the other features in the same mini-batch are calculated, so the number of positive and negative pairs depend entirely on the number of samples contained in a mini-batch. For instance, if a mini-batch consists of M classes in which each class contains K samples, then $K - 1$ positive pairs and $(M - 1)K$ negative pairs can be formed for each sample. Therefore, for both the optimization approaches, the number of $(S_n - S_p)$ pairs in mini-batches of the same size may vary greatly.

More importantly, the classification-based method can obtain more global information in each optimization iteration because the similarity scores between x and all classes' proxies are calculated. But for the pair-based one, only limited local information can be seen since only similarity scores between x and other samples contained in the same mini-batch are calculated, which is a serious drawback for large-scale classification tasks. In general, when the total number of training classes is far greater than the number of classes contained in a mini-batch, using the classification-based loss function can not only yield more global information but also construct more $(S_n - S_p)$ pairs than the pair-based one. That is why it can converge faster and achieve higher accuracy in this case. However, when the number of training classes is not much larger than the number of classes contained in a mini-batch, the pair-based approach may outperform its counterpart because it can build more diverse sample pairs in a mini-batch, which becomes the decisive factor of performance.

8   Conclusion

In this paper, we construct a federated face recognition prototype system to evaluate and compare five commonly used metric learning methods in different federated settings. The abundant results not only demonstrate the effectiveness of FL for large-scale face recognition task but also show that the performance of these loss functions varies greatly in different federated settings. Finally, we explain this phenomenon from the perspective of similarity optimization and give some suggestions on the selection of loss functions in federated face recognition task. This work can serve as a useful reference for the researchers and practitioners working in federated metric learning.

For future work, we will deploy our FedFR in real-world environments that involve more challenges to be addressed, such as stricter privacy protection and system heterogeneity. In addition, a broader range of metric learning tasks and methods in FL can be further investigated in the future.

Acknowledgment. This work is partially supported by a grant from the National Natural Science Foundation of China (No. 62032017), the Fundamental Research Funds for the Central Universities, the Innovation Fund of Xidian University, the Key Industrial Innovation Chain Project in Industrial Domain of Shaanxi Province (No. 2021ZDLGY03-09, No. 2021ZDLGY07-02, No. 2021ZDLGY07-03) and The Youth Innovation Team of Shaanxi Universities.

References

1. Bonawitz, K., et al.: Practical secure aggregation for federated learning on user-held data. arXiv preprint arXiv:1611.04482 (2016)
2. Chen, S., Liu, Y., Gao, X., Han, Z.: MobileFaceNets: efficient CNNs for accurate real-time face verification on mobile devices. In: Zhou, J., et al. (eds.) CCBR 2018. LNCS, vol. 10996, pp. 428–438. Springer, Cham (2018). https://doi.org/10.1007/978-3-319-97909-0_46
3. Chung, J.S., et al.: In defence of metric learning for speaker recognition. arXiv preprint arXiv:2003.11982 (2020)
4. Deng, J., Guo, J., Xue, N., Zafeiriou, S.: Arcface: additive angular margin loss for deep face recognition. In: Proceedings of the IEEE Conference on Computer Vision and Pattern Recognition, pp. 4690–4699 (2019)
5. Geyer, R.C., Klein, T., Nabi, M.: Differentially private federated learning: a client level perspective. arXiv preprint arXiv:1712.07557 (2017)
6. Guo, G., Li, S.Z., Chan, K.: Face recognition by support vector machines. In: Proceedings fourth IEEE International Conference on Automatic Face and Gesture Recognition (cat. no. PR00580), pp. 196–201. IEEE (2000)
7. Guo, Y., Zhang, L., Hu, Y., He, X., Gao, J.: MS-Celeb-1M: a dataset and benchmark for large-scale face recognition. In: Leibe, B., Matas, J., Sebe, N., Welling, M. (eds.) ECCV 2016. LNCS, vol. 9907, pp. 87–102. Springer, Cham (2016). https://doi.org/10.1007/978-3-319-46487-9_6
8. He, C., et al.: FedML: a research library and benchmark for federated machine learning. arXiv preprint arXiv:2007.13518 (2020)
9. He, K., Zhang, X., Ren, S., Sun, J.: Deep residual learning for image recognition. In: Proceedings of the IEEE Conference on Computer Vision and Pattern Recognition, pp. 770–778 (2016)
10. Huang, G.B., Mattar, M., Berg, T., Learned-Miller, E.: Labeled faces in the wild: a database for studying face recognition in unconstrained environments. In: Workshop on faces in Real-Life Images: Detection, Alignment, and Recognition (2008)
11. Jiang, J., Ji, S., Long, G.: Decentralized knowledge acquisition for mobile internet applications. World Wide Web 23(5), 2653–2669 (2020)
12. Kairouz, P., et al.: Advances and open problems in federated learning. Found. Trends® Mach. Learn. 14(1–2), 1–210 (2021)
13. Konečnỳ, J., McMahan, H.B., Yu, F.X., Richtárik, P., Suresh, A.T., Bacon, D.: Federated learning: strategies for improving communication efficiency. arXiv preprint arXiv:1610.05492 (2016)
14. Li, L., Mu, X., Li, S., Peng, H.: A review of face recognition technology. IEEE Access 8, 139110–139120 (2020)
15. Li, Q., He, B., Song, D.: Model-contrastive federated learning. In: Proceedings of the IEEE/CVF Conference on Computer Vision and Pattern Recognition, pp. 10713–10722 (2021)

16. Li, T., Sahu, A.K., Talwalkar, A., Smith, V.: Federated learning: challenges, methods, and future directions. IEEE Signal Process. Mag. **37**(3), 50–60 (2020)
17. Liu, W., Wen, Y., Yu, Z., Li, M., Raj, B., Song, L.: Sphereface: deep hypersphere embedding for face recognition. In: Proceedings of the IEEE Conference on Computer Vision and Pattern Recognition, pp. 212–220 (2017)
18. McMahan, B., Moore, E., Ramage, D., Hampson, S., Arcas, B.A.: Communication-efficient learning of deep networks from decentralized data. In: Artificial Intelligence and Statistics, pp. 1273–1282. PMLR (2017)
19. McMahan, H.B., Moore, E., Ramage, D., Arcas, B.A.: Federated learning of deep networks using model averaging (2016)
20. Moghaddam, B., Jebara, T., Pentland, A.: Bayesian face recognition. Pattern Recogn. **33**(11), 1771–1782 (2000)
21. Moschoglou, S., Papaioannou, A., Sagonas, C., Deng, J., Kotsia, I., Zafeiriou, S.: AgeDB: the first manually collected, in-the-wild age database. In: Proceedings of the IEEE Conference on Computer Vision and Pattern Recognition Workshops, pp. 51–59 (2017)
22. Mothukuri, V., Parizi, R.M., Pouriyeh, S., Huang, Y., Dehghantanha, A., Srivastava, G.: A survey on security and privacy of federated learning. Futur. Gener. Comput. Syst. **115**, 619–640 (2021)
23. Musgrave, K., Belongie, S., Lim, S.-N.: A metric learning reality check. In: Vedaldi, A., Bischof, H., Brox, T., Frahm, J.-M. (eds.) ECCV 2020. LNCS, vol. 12370, pp. 681–699. Springer, Cham (2020). https://doi.org/10.1007/978-3-030-58595-2_41
24. Sahu, A.K., Li, T., Sanjabi, M., Zaheer, M., Talwalkar, A., Smith, V.: On the convergence of federated optimization in heterogeneous networks. arXiv preprint arXiv:1812.06127 (2018)
25. Schroff, F., Kalenichenko, D., Philbin, J.: Facenet: a unified embedding for face recognition and clustering. In: Proceedings of the IEEE Conference on Computer Vision and Pattern Recognition, pp. 815–823 (2015)
26. Sengupta, S., Chen, J.C., Castillo, C., Patel, V.M., Chellappa, R., Jacobs, D.W.: Frontal to profile face verification in the wild. In: 2016 IEEE Winter Conference on Applications of Computer Vision (WACV), pp. 1–9. IEEE (2016)
27. Shahid, O., Pouriyeh, S., Parizi, R.M., Sheng, Q.Z., Srivastava, G., Zhao, L.: Communication efficiency in federated learning: achievements and challenges. arXiv preprint arXiv:2107.10996 (2021)
28. Srivastava, Y., Murali, V., Dubey, S.R.: A performance evaluation of loss functions for deep face recognition. In: Babu, R.V., Prasanna, M., Namboodiri, V.P. (eds.) NCVPRIPG 2019. CCIS, vol. 1249, pp. 322–332. Springer, Singapore (2020). https://doi.org/10.1007/978-981-15-8697-2_30
29. Sun, Y., Chen, Y., Wang, X., Tang, X.: Deep learning face representation by joint identification-verification. Adv. Neural. Inf. Process. Syst. **27**, 1988–1996 (2014)
30. Sun, Y., et al.: Circle loss: a unified perspective of pair similarity optimization. In: Proceedings of the IEEE/CVF Conference on Computer Vision and Pattern Recognition, pp. 6398–6407 (2020)
31. Turk, M., Pentland, A.: Eigenfaces for recognition. J. Cogn. Neurosci. **3**(1), 71–86 (1991)
32. Wang, F., Cheng, J., Liu, W., Liu, H.: Additive margin softmax for face verification. IEEE Signal Process. Lett. **25**(7), 926–930 (2018)
33. Wang, F., Xiang, X., Cheng, J., Yuille, A.L.: Normface: L2 hypersphere embedding for face verification. In: Proceedings of the 25th ACM International Conference on Multimedia, pp. 1041–1049 (2017)

34. Wang, H., et al.: Cosface: large margin cosine loss for deep face recognition. In: Proceedings of the IEEE Conference on Computer Vision and Pattern Recognition, pp. 5265–5274 (2018)
35. Wang, H., Yurochkin, M., Sun, Y., Papailiopoulos, D., Khazaeni, Y.: Federated learning with matched averaging. In: International Conference on Learning Representations (ICLR) (2020)
36. Wang, J., Liu, Q., Liang, H., Joshi, G., Poor, H.V.: Tackling the objective inconsistency problem in heterogeneous federated optimization. Adv. Neural. Inf. Process. Syst. **33**, 7611–7623 (2020)
37. Wang, X., Han, X., Huang, W., Dong, D., Scott, M.R.: Multi-similarity loss with general pair weighting for deep metric learning. In: Proceedings of the IEEE/CVF Conference on Computer Vision and Pattern Recognition, pp. 5022–5030 (2019)
38. Yang, Q., Liu, Y., Chen, T., Tong, Y.: Federated machine learning: concept and applications. ACM Trans. Intell. Syst. Technol. (TIST) **10**(2), 1–19 (2019)
39. Yi, D., Lei, Z., Liao, S., Li, S.Z.: Learning face representation from scratch. arXiv preprint arXiv:1411.7923 (2014)
40. Zhuang, W., et al.: Performance optimization of federated person re-identification via benchmark analysis. In: Proceedings of the 28th ACM International Conference on Multimedia, pp. 955–963 (2020)

FedCL: An Efficient Federated Unsupervised Learning for Model Sharing in IoT

Chen Zhao[1], Zhipeng Gao[1(✉)], Qian Wang[2], Zijia Mo[1], and Xinlei Yu[1]

[1] State Key Laboratory of Networking and Switching Technology,
Beijing University of Posts and Telecommunications, Beijing, China
gaozhipeng@bupt.edu.cn
[2] Beijing University of Technology, Beijing, China

Abstract. Federated Learning (FL) continues to make significant advances, solving model sharing under privacy-preserving. However, these existing methods are only of limited utility in the Internet of Things (IoT) scenarios, as they either heavily depend on high-quality labeled data or only perform well under idealized conditions, which typically cannot be found in practical applications. As such, a natural problem is how to leverage unlabeled data among multiple clients to optimize sharing model. To address this shortcoming, we propose Federated Contrastive Learning (FedCL), an efficient federated learning method for unsupervised image classification. The proposed FedCL can be summarized in three steps: distributed federated pretraining of the local model using contrastive learning, supervised fine-tuning on a server with few labeled data, and distillation with unlabeled examples on each client for refining and transferring the personalized-specific knowledge. Extensive experiments show that our method outperforms all baseline methods by large margins, including 69.32% top-1 accuracy on CIFAR-10, 85.75% on SVHN, and 74.64% on Mini-ImageNet with the only use of 1% labels.

Keywords: Federated learning · Internet of things · Self-supervised learning · Unsupervised learning

1 Introduction

With the ubiquity of smart devices, federated learning [1] has become one of the most-used types of privacy-preserving model sharing method, and has been popularly applied in many scenarios, such as user habits prediction [2], personalized recommendation [3] and wireless network optimization [4]. Existing federated learning methods typically only consider supervised training settings, where the client data are fully labeled. Yet local data including sophisticated annotations is not realistic for IoT applications since users always have different habits and usage frequencies, which inspires the recent work to combine semi-supervised learning with federated learning to optimize sharing model [3,5,6]. However,

© ICST Institute for Computer Sciences, Social Informatics and Telecommunications Engineering 2022
Published by Springer Nature Switzerland AG 2022. All Rights Reserved
H. Gao et al. (Eds.): CollaborateCom 2022, LNICST 460, pp. 115–134, 2022.
https://doi.org/10.1007/978-3-031-24383-7_7

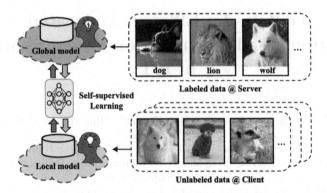

Fig. 1. Illustration of practical IoT scenario in federated unsupervised learning. Many unlabeled data are available at clients, few labeled data are available at the server.

these works normally adopt knowledge transfer techniques between labeled and unlabeled data, which limits the applications when clients are complete without available labeled data. For example, suppose that we have a photo classifier app that automatically categorizes pictures in albums. In this case, the app users may reluctant to annotate these private and sensitive pictures by themself, this leads the service providers can only use limited public on the central server. Thus, in many realistic IoT scenarios, clients' data may completely *unlabeled* and with few labeled data only available at the server. This leads to practical challenges of FL with deficiency of labels, namely, *Federated Unsupervised Learning* (FUL).

Therefore, a universal FL method should work in both supervised and unsupervised scenarios, which inspired the recent work to integrate semi-supervised techniques into the FL framework [5,7] (i.e. employing domain confusion technique to train labeled and unlabeled data). Such research directions are extremely active and have been shown to yield significant accuracy improvements in semi-supervised settings, which can be crucial when making such techniques available in realistic applications. However, different from idealized distribution conditions, data among IoT devices are normally non-independent and identically distributed (non-IID), leading to sharing model performance degradation.

There have been some studies trying to address these issues and provide convergence guarantees for sharing model. To achieve this, researchers use dissimilarity measurement [8], move distance [9], model-contrastive learning [10], and so on. Despite these efforts, these methods fail to achieve good performance when ground-truth annotations are absent. Although some works both address the unsupervised and non-IID problems, such as FedCA [11] and FedU [12], they fail to consider personalization requirements for each client.

In this paper, employing the self-supervised learning technique, we propose an efficient method, named *Federated Contrastive Learning (FedCL)*, to optimize sharing model using unlabeled data among multiple clients, as shown in Fig. 1. Although the recent Federated Self-Supervised Learning (FSSL) works (e.g. [13,14]) have made great progress on label-limited problems, however, for model sharing in an unsupervised setting, due to the different behavior preferences (e.g., some user like take pet pictures, while others prefer to take life pictures), a big extra challenge is to guarantee local models are personalized after collaboration training, these existing methods are only of limited utility as they either heavily depends on high quality labeled data on clients or ignore the personalized requirement for optimizing sharing models.

By contrast, our FedCL is an effective method that optimizes sharing model when clients come without available labeled data while preserving clients' model personalized. Motivated by recent advances in unsupervised learning [15,16] and self-supervised learning [5,7], we follow unsupervised pre-train at client and supervised fine-tune at server for model training at IoT scenarios. Specifically, we employ RandAugment as data augmentation on each client and compute cosine similarity to learning visual representations on distributed unlabeled data. Then, fine-tuning the sharing model using supervised data at the server to adapt a task-agnostically model for a specific task. Finally, we distill sharing model at each client on local unlabeled data for personalized-preserved and lightweight use.

In summary, our main contributions are three-fold:

- We propose a novel federated self-supervised learning method to pre-train sharing model from clients' unlabeled data, which follows the pretext task of unsupervised learning and can learn distributed network representations by maximizing agreement between augmented images.
- We propose a central fine-tune and personalized distillation in network optimization, which can balance the sharing model consensus and personalization respectively.
- Based on the above two contributions, we propose FedCL, an efficient method to collaborate optimize sharing model under unsupervised settings, where clients' data is completely unlabeled and only a few labeled at the server. Experiments prove that FedCL significantly outperforms related works under both semi-supervised and unsupervised settings.

The remaining of this article is organized as follows. In Sect. 2, we introduce the related work. The design details of the FedCL method, especially the federated self-supervised learning, supervised fine-tuning and personalized distillation are described in Sect. 3. In Sect. 4, we present the experimental results on several commonly used semi-supervised benchmarks. Finally, conclusions are drawn in Sect. 6.

2 Related Work

Below we summarize the related work that involves three main topics, federated semi-supervised learning, federated self-supervised learning, and federated unsupervised learning.

Federated Semi-supervised Learning. Recently, interests of tackling scarcity of labels are discussed [3,17,18]. The motivation of federated semi-supervised learning methods is to optimize a sharing model iteratively by knowledge transfer between devices. One family of highly relevant methods is based on knowledge transfer [3,5,6] or inter-client consistency [19,20], which is followed by supervised fine-tuning on a few labeled datasets. Aside from the transfer learning paradigm, there is a large and diverse set of approaches for practical federated learning. Another family of methods are based on contrast learning [21] or self-learning [15,16]. The main difference between these methods and ours is that FedCL can efficiently optimize sharing model when clients are without available labels.

Federated Self-supervised Learning. The idea of methods based on self-supervised learning is first to pre-train distributed local model using contrastive learning, and then fine-tune sharing model for the downstream task, where the representative works are FCL [22] and FLESD [14]. FCL [22] proposes a two-staged method, i.e., each client exchanges the features of its local data with other clients and then leverage structural similarity of image examples to align similar features among clients for better model performance. FLESD [14] gathers a fraction of the clients' inferred similarity matrices on a public dataset, and then ensembles the similarity matrices via similarity distillation. Although these methods can optimize a generalized model, the local model personalization cannot be well preserved due to there is no developed personalized model for each client.

Federated Unsupervised Learning. the motivation of federated unsupervised learning methods is to learn a generic representation from decentralized data. Jin et al. [23] first point out the advantages that leverage unlabeled data for unsupervised training. Then, researchers propose a series of unsupervised works to improve the performance on data privacy [24], specific application [25,26], and non-IID distribution [11]. Zhuang et al. [12] present a new framework to leverage unlabeled data while dynamically updating network predictors. Although these works study federated learning in unsupervised scenarios, they bypass the non-IID problems.

Unlike the above methods, our work combines representation learning and knowledge distillation, considering the model personalized requirement caused by data non-IID, and can automatically classify image samples when clients without labels.

3   Method

3.1   Federated Unsupervised Problem Definition

Given a set of IoT clients $C = \{c_1, c_2, ..., c_n\}$ and a global server G, each client possesses a local unlabeled dataset x_U^n. Our method is modeled as a function Φ to optimize a sharing model $N_G = \Phi(x_U, x_L)$, where $x_U = \{x_U^1, x_U^2, ..., x_U^n\}$ are clients' local unlabeled data that used to learn model representation and specific-task, x_L is server's labeled data that are used to fine-turn the sharing model. The total objective function $\mathcal{L}_\Phi$ of N_G can be represented as

$$\mathcal{L}_\Phi = \mathcal{L}_{self}(x_U) + \mathcal{L}_{fine}(x_L) + \mathcal{L}_{distill}(x_U), \tag{1}$$

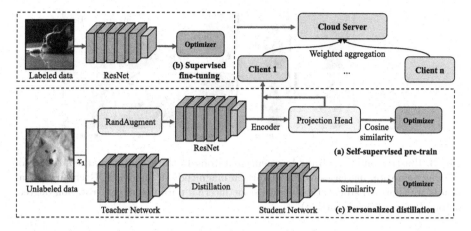

Fig. 2. Overall pipeline. Given a set of IoT clients $C = \{c_1, c_2, ..., c_n\}$ and a cloud server G, each client possesses a local unlabeled dataset $\mathbf{x}_U^n$. Our method is modeled as a function Φ to optimize a sharing model $N_G = \Phi(\mathbf{x}_U, \mathbf{x}_L)$. Our method can be summarized in three steps: federated self-supervised learning, supervised fine-tuning, and personalized distillation.

where self-supervised loss $\mathcal{L}_{self}$ and distillation loss $\mathcal{L}_{fine}$ are used for self-supervised learning and fine-tuning model respectively, and network distillation loss $\mathcal{L}_{distill}$ are used to improve the network for local specific-task.

A key challenge of federated unsupervised learning is that data among clients are always non-IID since users always have different habits and usage frequencies, both data size and distribution may also vary heavily on different devices [27]. These independent distributions are almost unable to be learned and optimized by a simple weight average and could result in a poor representation. In this work, we aim to leverage these unlabeled data from clients to learn a generic representation and personalized model without violating users' privacy.

3.2 FedCL Overview

Inspired by the recent successes of SimCLRv2 [16], the proposed FedCL leverages local unlabeled data in both sharing model optimization and the local model distillation process. As shown in Fig. 2, the first time the local unlabeled data is used for learning visual representations via federated unsupervised pretraining. Then the general sharing model is adapted for the downstream task via central labeled data fine-tuning, to further improve classification performance. To this end, we train the student model from the fine-tuned model with unlabeled data on each client to further improve the model for clients specific-task. Our method can be summarized in three steps: federated self-supervised learning, supervised fine-tuning, and personalized distillation.

Before presenting technique details, we introduce the training pipeline of FedCL with the following steps: (a) Self-supervised pre-train: each client conducts a pretext task through representation learning that can be used to obtain

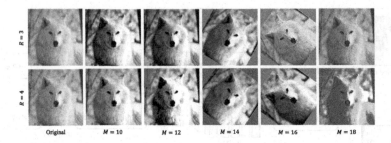

Fig. 3. Illustration of the RandAugment operators. In these examples, the strength of the augmentation increases as the distortion magnitude M increases. Each augmentation is transformed stochastically with some internal parameters (e.g. rotation degree, cutout region, color distortion).

semantically meaningful features. (b) Supervised fine-tuning: the server fine-tunes the sharing model to further improve model performance and then aggregates the client's model parameters to update sharing model. (c) Personalized distillation: to improve the local model for specific tasks, we train the student model for each client based on sharing model. We will detail the three steps in Sect. 3.3 and Sect. 3.4, respectively.

3.3 Federated Self-supervised Learning

Inspired by contrastive learning [28,29], FedCL learns distributed model representations by maximizing agreement between augmented image examples on each client, as shown in Fig. 2 (a), and we will detail the two components as follows.

Data RandAugment. The goal of data augmentation is to constrain model predictions to be invariant to noise and through the similarity between augmentation data to learn visual representation. However, one obstacle of existing augmentation methods is a separate search of optimal parameters which significantly increases the clients' training complexity and is computationally expensive. Considering the limited computing and storage resources of the clients. We use a data augmentation called RandAugment [21] which removes the search phase and requires no labeled data.

Specifically, in clients data augmentation phase, we consider several common augmentation including {*identity, rotate, posterize, sharpness, translate-x, translate-y, shear-x, shear-y, autoContrast, solarize, contrast, equalize, color, brightness*} and stochastically choosing $T = 14$ available transformations to apply each augmentation. To reduce the parameter space while still preserving image diversity, we replace the learned policies for applying each transformation with a parameter-free procedure of selecting a transformation with probability $1/T$ [30]. As shown in Fig. 3, Randaugment contains two parameters R and M, which are used to control the transformation numbers and distortion magnitudes, we observe that the larger values of R and M will increase regularization strength

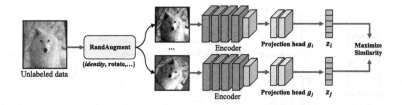

Fig. 4. Pipeline of self-supervised pre-train.

and the two hyperparameters may suffice for parameterizing all transformations. The goal of the pretext task is to minimize the distance between image samples x and their augmentations $T[x]$, expressed as $\min d(f(x), T(f(x)))$, we observe that the samples with similar features are assigned to semantically similar [31], any pretext task that satisfies the equation above can be used for representation learning. We refer to Sect. 4.2 for a concrete experiment.

Self-supervised Pre-train. Inspired by the SimCLR [15,16] which introduces a learnable nonlinear transformation between the representation and the contrastive loss. The local pre-train is shown in Fig. 4, Our self-supervised pre-train is designed according to each client's unlabeled dataset. Specifically, given a set of local data $\mathbf{x}_U^n$, each image examples $x \in \mathbf{x}_U^n$ is augmented twice using RandAugment, creating two views x_{2k} and x_{2k-1}, and encode two images via encoder network ResNet to generate representations g_{2k} and g_{2k-1}. Then we transform the representation via a non-linear function to generate z_{2k} and z_{2k-1} that are used to compute the contrastive loss. We adopt the normalized temperature-scaled cross-entropy loss instead of cross-entropy loss as contrastive loss, represent as

$$\mathcal{L}(i,j) = -\log \frac{\exp(\mathrm{sim}(z_i, z_j)/\tau)}{\sum_{k=1}^{2K} \mathbb{1}_{[k \neq i]} \exp(\mathrm{sim}(z_i, z_j)/\tau)}, \tag{2}$$

where i, j is the augmented examples from the same image, $\mathrm{sim}(z_i, z_j) = \frac{z_i^{\mathrm{T}} z_j}{\tau \|z_i\| \|z_j\|}$ is cosine similarity between two images, $\mathbb{1}_{[k \neq i]}$ is indicator function evaluating to 1 if $k \neq i$ and τ is a temperature scalar.

Finally, the self-supervised loss of client n can be represented as

$$\mathcal{L}_{self}^n = \frac{1}{2K} \sum_{k=1}^{K} [\mathcal{L}(2k-1, 2k) + \mathcal{L}(2k, 2k-1)], \tag{3}$$

where K is the local batch size. In each communication round, we choose p fraction of clients to train local unsupervised networks and then update model parameters to the server for weighted aggregation. Accordingly, the sharing model parameters can be updated as

$$\omega_{t+1} \leftarrow \sum_{i=1}^{S_t} \frac{|\mathbf{x}_U^n|}{|\mathbf{x}_U|} \omega_t^i, \tag{4}$$

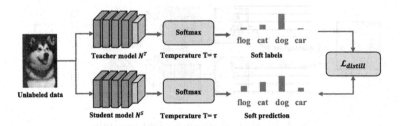

Fig. 5. Pipeline of personalized distillation.

where $|\mathbf{x}_U|$ is unlabeled data size, ω is model parameters, $S_t = n * p$ is the collection of clients participating in this round of training, and t is the current communication round.

3.4 Fine-Tuning and Distillation

To further improve the sharing model performance with central labeled data and local unlabeled data, we adopt supervised fine-tuning and unsupervised distillation to optimize sharing model and preserve local models personalized respectively.

Supervised Fine-Tuning. Fine-tuning is widely used to adapt task-agnostically model for a downstream task. When the self-supervised sharing model is converged, we fine-tuned the sharing model on the server to improve the accuracy of the model. In FedCL, we incorporate the second layer of MLP projection heads into ResNet during fine-tuning, instead of throwing it all away. Then we fine-tuned the network with a few labeled data examples for a specific task. The fine-tuning loss $\mathcal{L}_{fine}$ are not the key points of our work, thus we roughly use the definition in [16,32].

Personalized Distillation. To further improve the network for local specific-task, here we use personalized distillation to train the local model for the target task. As shown in Fig. 5, we fixed the teacher network and only train the student network with local unlabeled data in this procedure. Inspired by [33–36], we use the sharing network as teacher model to classify impute labels for training a student network. Therefore, the distillation loss of client n can be represent as

$$\mathcal{L}_{distill}^n = - \sum_{x_i \in \mathbf{x_U}} [\sum_y p_T(y|x_i; \tau) \log p_S(y|x_i; \tau)], \tag{5}$$

where $p(y|x_i; \tau) = \exp(f(x_i, y)/\tau)/\sum_y \exp(f(x_i, y)/\tau)$, p_T and p_S is the data distribution of teacher network and student network respectively. According to the practical IoT applications, the architecture of the student network and teacher network can be the same or smaller.

Considering that the server may contain a large amount of labeled and unlabeled data in the realistic IoT scenarios, we further extend the self-distillation procedure to the semi-supervised scenario [16]. While Eq. 5 only focuses on the distillation using unlabeled examples, when there are a significant amount of labeled examples, we can also use a weighted combination to compute the distillation loss with the ground truth labeled examples, the distillation loss can be represent as

$$\mathcal{L}_{distill}^n = -(1-\alpha) \sum_{x_i \in \mathbf{x_U}, \mathbf{x_L}} [\log p_S(y|x_i; \tau)] - \sum_{x_i \in \mathbf{x_U}} [\sum_y p_T(y|x_i; \tau) \log p_S(y|x_i; \tau)],$$

(6)

This procedure can be performed to improve the task-specific performance of each client.

4 Experiment

In experiments, we detail the implementation settings of FedCL, and then we mainly evaluate the performance of our method in two aspects, accuracy and scalability.

4.1 Implementation Details

Datasets. Following the semi-supervised setting in [15,37], we evaluate the efficacy of FedGAN on several commonly used SSL image benchmarks. Specifically, we perform experiments with varying amounts of labeled data on three real-world datasets, including CIFAR-10 [38], SVHN [39], and Mini-ImageNet [40], with a randomly sub-sampled 1% or 10% of labeled images on the server and the rest are distributed on clients, which are widely used for evaluating image-processing deep learning algorithms. We use these datasets in the form of unstructured and low-pixel images, which is similar to the unprocessed fragmented data collected in the IoT scenario, such as image recognition and classification in the smart devices usage process.

CIFAR-10 constitute the proof of experiment since it is a well-established benchmark, CIFAR-10 is an image recognition dataset for machine learning, that contains 60000 color images covering 10 categories.

SVHN is a real-world image dataset for developing machine learning and object recognition algorithms. It can be seen as similar in flavor to MNIST, but incorporates an order of magnitude more labeled data (over 600,000 digit images) and comes from a significantly harder, unsolved real-world problem, which is commonly used in semi-supervised learning evaluation.

Mini-ImageNet is selected from the Imagenet dataset, which is a very famous large-scale visual data set established to promote the research of visual recognition. The mini-ImageNet dataset contains 60000 RGB images with 100 categories, including 600 samples in each category, and the specification of each picture is 84 × 84. Compared with the CIFAR-10 dataset, the mini-ImageNet dataset is more complex, but it is more suitable for prototype design and experimental research.

We follow the most used linear evaluation protocol [28] to fine-tune the local model. Beyond linear evaluation and fine-tuned, we also compare against SOTA on federated semi-supervised and unsupervised learning. The previous works were almost performed with a uniform distribution of data in which every client was assigned the same data size. In realistic IoT scenarios, however, the data on different clients will typically vary heavily in category and size. To simulate different degrees of unbalancedness, we split the data according to [27] as non-IID settings, and the data size of each client is assigned a fraction:

$$\varphi_c(\delta, \gamma) = \frac{\delta}{n} + (1 - \delta)\frac{\gamma^c}{\sum_{j=1}^{n} \gamma^j}, \tag{7}$$

where δ controls the minimum data size on each client, and γ controls the data concentration.

Experiment Setting. Our program is implemented by PyTorch and all experiments are performed on a server with four NVIDIA Geforce RTX 3090 GPUs. For all experiments, the sharing model has the same network architecture as the local model, for a fair comparison, we take the same neural network architecture as SimCLRv2 [16]. By default, we set client number $n = 20$ and $R = 3$, $M = 19$ in Sect. 3.3, $\tau = 0.9$ in Eq. (2), $K = 256$ in Eq. (3), $p = 0.4$ in Eq. (4). We use ResNet-50 as the base encoder, a 3-layer MLP as the projection head and select the second layer as optimal classifier layer, the optimizer is Adam, the learning rate is 0.001 and momentum parameters $\beta_1 = 0.5$, $\beta_2 = 0.999$. To evaluate the impact of data distribution on model performance, we set $\delta = 0.1$ and $\gamma = 0.9$ as our non-IID data partition settings. We train the self-supervised local model, fine-tuning and unsupervised distillation for 100, 400 and 200 epochs respectively, and the communication round is 200 in federated self-supervised learning.

4.2   Ablation Study

In the following, we analyze the effects of several components in our model.

Influence of RandAugment. In Sect. 3.3, the data augmentation is used to learn the visual representation of the network. We evaluate the CIFAR-10 dataset ten times and reach between 66.48% and 70.34% average Top-1 test accuracy with a median of 69.32%. Then we replace the RandAugment with random crop and color distortion and compare it with default components, experimental results in Table 1 show that the model performance has slightly dropped around 2.64%, which means the RandAugment component can effectively improve self-supervised learning performance from unlabeled data.

Influences of Central Fine-Tuning and Personalized Distillation. To further analyze the improvements of FedCL, we removed the central fine-tuning and personalized distillation respectively. Experimental as shown in Table 1, we can observe that average model performance has dropped (2.56%–11.84%). This gap

Table 1. Personalized accuracy of FedCL on CIFAR-10 dataset with different components

Methods	Label fraction	
	1%	10%
W/O RandAugment	66.68	70.59
W/O central fine-tuning	57.48	65.82
W/O personalized distillation	66.76	76.44
FedCL (with default settings)	**69.32**	**74.35**

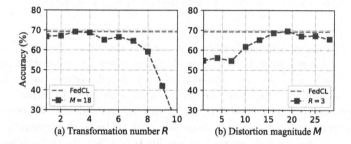

(a) Transformation number R   (b) Distortion magnitude M

Fig. 6. Optimal data augmentation parameters. All results report CIFAR-10 test validation for ResNet-50 model architecture averaged 10 random initializations. (a) Varying the transformation number. (b) Measuring the effect of augmentation while varying the distortion magnitude. The accuracy of FedCL with default hyperparameters is in the red dotted line. (Color figure online)

tells us that our FedCL improves model optimization while keeping reliable classification knowledge. This effective separation of pretext task and downstream task enhances the overall performance of our methods even without available labeled data on clients.

4.3   Performance Analysis

Below we conduct a series of experiments to evaluate the role of hyperparameters (including transformation number R, distortion magnitude M, training batch size K, and projection head) in FedCL to tease apart the experimental factors that are important to FedCL's improvement.

Influence of Transformation Number and Distortion Magnitude. To explore the influence of parameters in data augmentation, we experiment with different RandAugment hyperparameters on the CIFAR-10 dataset since it is a baseline and well-studied dataset. Our goal is to demonstrate the relative benefits of employing this method over previous random augmentation methods.

We systematically measure the effects of transformation number R and distortion magnitude M with Top-1 model accuracy. We train local models with unlabeled data and measure the average accuracy compared to a baseline model

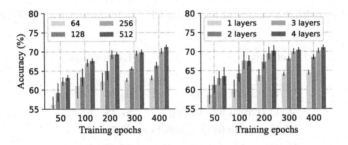

Fig. 7. Evaluation of the different batch sizes and layers of projection head. (a) Results with different batch sizes. (b) Results with different projection heads.

trained with random augmentations (i.e. rotate and color). We fix $M = 18$, the experimental results in Fig. 6(a) show that too much augmentation algorithm fusion will lead to the system underfitting, which will reduce the performance of the shared model. Therefore, we set $R = 3$ as our default value. As shown in Fig. 6(b), we vary M between 1 and 29 in our experiments. We observe that the model accuracy increases monotonically with distortion magnitude. We conjecture that aggressive data augmentation leads to a low single-to-noise ratio in clients' data. Regardless, This experiment trend highlights the benefits of the RandAugment method, here, we set $M = 19$ as our default value.

Influences of Batch Size and Projection Head. We increase the batch size in a range of 64, 128, 256, and 512 on the CIFAR-10 task, Our method shows consistent performance improvement as the batch size increases. Note that the model accuracy shown in Fig. 7(a) can be improved if we allow a larger batch size, however, the improvement is small when batch sizes are larger than 256, considering the limited computing resources of the client, we set batch size is 256 as our default value.

To further evaluate the effect of projection head, we pre-train ResNet using federated self-supervised learning with different numbers of projection heads (from 1 to 4 fully connected layers) and examine average model Top-1 accuracy after fine-tuning local models. The experimental results are shown in Fig. 7(b), we find that using a deeper projection head during local self-supervised training is better when fine-tuning from the optimal layer of the projection head, here, we set the number of layers in the projection head as 3 as our default value.

4.4 Comparison with Related Methods

We compare our method with other related federated semi-supervised learning methods and naive combination of federated learning and semi-supervised learning, that have the potential to optimize sharing model in unsupervised settings. We evaluate the classification ability learned on CIFAR-10 datasets, following the most used linear evaluation protocol [28] and testing the sharing model accuracy. We first train a visual representation with unlabeled data using FedCL and

Table 2. Averaged local performance on semi-supervised and unsupervised task

Methods	Model	Label fraction	
		1%	10%
Supervised baseline [37]	ResNet-50	36.63	51.94
Semi-supervised learning methods			
FL Pseudo Label [41]	ResNet-50	–	56.73
FL UDA [21]	ResNet-50	–	60.15
DS-FL [5]	VGG-16	55.38	62.71
FL FM-GAN [42]	GAN	58.34	64.28
FedMatch (labels-at-client) [7]	ResNet-9	62.47	70.88
Unsupervised learning methods			
FedMatch (labels-at-server) [7]	ResNet-9	56.35	62.35
FedMatch (labels-at-server) [7]	ResNet-50	62.84	71.21
FCL [22]	U-Net	61.26	66.47
FL SimCLR [15]	ResNet-50	64.17	71.75
Our methods with different network architecture			
FedCL (self-distilled)	ResNet-50	69.32	74.35
FedCL (distilled)	ResNet-50($2\times$)	70.83	75.19
FedCL (distilled)	ResNet-152($3\times$)	**72.41**	**78.73**

other baseline methods for 200 epochs; Next, we fix the representation parameters and train a new classifier at the output layer. The following are baselines and training details. (1) *Federated semi-supervised learning methods:* we compare our method with semi-supervised learning methods, including FL Pseudo Label [41], FL UDA [21], DS-FL [5], FL FM-GAN [42], and FedMatch [7] that only have labels at clients. (2) *Federated unsupervised learning methods:* we compare our method with unsupervised learning methods, including FedMatch [7] that have labels at server, FCL [22], and FL SimCLR [15]. Besides, we also compare FedCL with different network architectures. For the compared supervised and semi-supervised baselines, we evenly split labeled data for each client. We find this setting to be realistic as IoT scenarios, since the user may not have willing and skills that would label the examples collected by smart devices.

Table 2 shows the performance comparison of our FedCL and related methods on 1% and 10% label fraction tasks with default network architecture, our method consistently outperforms these baseline methods with large margins (about 6%–13%) in both label fractions. In particular, compared with supervised baselines in fine-tuning settings, we observe that our model achieves significant improvements in model performance, which means our method can effectively address the issues of lack labeled caused by requirements of various application scenarios.

To further study the effect of network architecture on our method, we train ResNet by varying width and depth. We can see that increasing network architecture can improve model performance (about 4%). While even the smallest model can offer decent or even competitive performances compared to the related works. We believe that these comparison experimental results further strengthen our paper.

4.5   Analysis of Scalability

Performance Under Different Label Fraction. To study the effects of label fraction and number of clients. We conduct experiments with our methods and two baselines (containing supervised methods FedAvg and semi-supervised FedMatch). As shown in Fig. 8(a), our FedCL has good scalability when the label fraction is changing and shows much performance improvement when the label fraction increases. Interestingly, we observe that our method improves most when there are fewer label data, which implies that our FedCL has the effectiveness of contrastive learning and preserves reliable knowledge in the novel federated unsupervised scenarios.

Performance Under Different Number of Clients. With the increase of clients, the data will become more scattered, leading to model performance degradation. To evaluate the scalability of our method, we conduct a comparative experiment on related works and our method. We train on CIFAR-10 datasets with 10% labeled examples for each work (including FedAvg, FedMatch, and our results under different clients number). Then we train each client for 50 epochs in parallel and take the average accuracy in 100 communication rounds as model performance.

The comparison results in Fig. 8(b) show that with the increase of clients, our method achieves better performance compared with the baselines (15%–25.41%). We conjecture that this is because, for the unsupervised pretext task, the model may not sufficiently be learned by local data, while the FedCL method overcomes it by utilizing the data augmentation and contrastive learning. Due to the huge amount of IoT clients in the actual application scenario, our method obviously has strong advantages.

Performance Under Different Distillation Methods. To analyze the influence of different distillation methods on model performance, we trained distributed model with local unlabeled data to preserve personalized in two ways: (a) student model has the same structure as the teacher model (excluding projection heads); (b) student model has relative small structure than the teacher model. Here, we set ResNet-152 as our teacher model.

The evaluation results as shown in Fig. 9, for both personalized methods, distillation improves the average model performance by transferring task-specific knowledge to a client model. For FedCL, even though it reduced model parameters amount, our method still significantly improves the semi-supervised learning performance, which indicates our FedCL is meaningful for lightweight applications in the IoT scenarios.

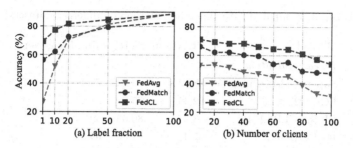

Fig. 8. Evaluation on label fraction and number of clients. (a) Model performance with different label fractions. (b) Model performance with a different number of clients.

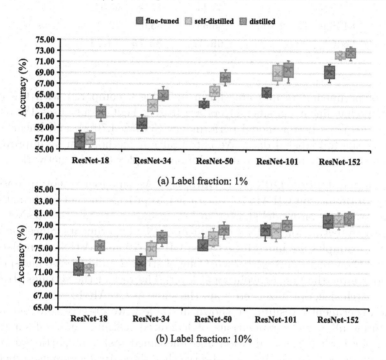

Fig. 9. Top-1 accuracy of FedCL method compared to the fine-tuned model. (a) The self-distilled model has the same structure as the teacher model. (b) The distilled model is trained by the ResNet-152 model.

Performance on Fine-Tuning and Linear Evaluation. For fine-tuning, after federated self-supervised training on clients, we add a full-connected layer after encoder as a linear classifier and use 1% labeled data to train the whole network, we do not use any regularization algorithm. For linear evaluation, we take the same training steps as fine-tuning, except we train the linear classifier on full labeled data.

Table 3. Compared with supervised method on different datasets

Methods	CIFAR-10	SVHN	Mini-ImageNet
Linear evaluation			
Supervised Learning [1]	88.53	89.73	79.42
FCL [22]	62.49	75.72	51.24
FL SimCLRv2 [16]	63.27	80.05	69.71
FedCL (ours)	67.41	81.88	69.94
Fine-tuned (default setting)			
Supervised Learning [1]	92.52	94.18	87.36
FCL [22]	63.44	77.68	65.44
FL SimCLRv2 [16]	66.59	83.68	72.79
FedCL (ours)	**69.32**	**85.75**	**74.64**

The experimental results are shown in Table 3, compared with the linear evaluation that linear classifier layers are frozen, FedCL only uses 1% labeled data and achieves better model performance (3.87%–4.70%), and linear evaluation uses the full labeled data. We note that our method can be improved by incorporating extra unlabeled data and more complex encoder network.

Performance Under Different Datasets. As our goal is not to optimize model performance on CIFAR-10, but rather to provide further confirmation of our improvements on model sharing in IoT scenarios, we use the ResNet-50 as the base architecture for SVHN and Mini-ImageNet experiments. Since the Mini-ImageNet examples are much bigger than CIFAR-10 and SVHN, we replace the first 3×3 Conv of stride 1 with 7×7 Conv of stride 2 and increase max-pooling operations after the first convolutional layer. The rest of the settings (training rounds, batch size, optimizer, etc.) are the same as CIFAR-10.

The experimental results are shown in Table 3, we observe that our model outperforms all naive combinations of federated learning and self-supervised learning for both linear evaluation and fine-tuned tasks. In particular, under the unsupervised IoT scenario, we observe that the naive combination methods significantly suffer from the so-called catastrophic forgetting [43] and their performances keeps deteriorating after sharing model converged. This phenomenon is mainly caused by fine-tuned model failing to properly preserve local personalization, in which case the learned sharing model from the central labeled data causes inter-task interference. Contrarily, our methods adapt to the optimized personalized target to integrate new knowledge (plasticity) without significant interference of new unsupervised examples on existing knowledge (stability). In addition, we observe that our best model trained with batch size 256 can achieve 69.32%, 85.75%, and 74.64% top-1 on three datasets. Although model performance is worse than the supervised method (8.43%–23.2%), consider that we only use 1% labeled data, and the supervised baseline achieves 87.36% need full-labeled datasets, which implies our method has the scalability and strength on commonly used semi-supervised datasets.

5 Advantage and Limitation

According to the advantages of representation learning and self-supervised learning afore-mentioned in Sect. 1, our federated unsupervised learning method can leverage unlabeled data from multiple clients to learn image classification, and can dynamically balance the sharing model consensus and personalization.

However, our FedCL is a three-step method that combines improved techniques and requires a manual search for the optimal parameter combination, which is time-consuming and error-prone. This is much different from other methods that mainly used representation learning and supervised fine-tuning (e.g., [12,16,24]). Therefore, in future work, we plan to examine the potential of reinforcement learning to discover the structure of the unsupervised model for the best performance given a set of clients and datasets.

6 Conclusion

In this paper, we propose FedCL, an efficient federated learning method for unsupervised image classification. To guarantee the sharing method are efficient and scalable, we designed a local self-supervised pre-train mechanism, a central supervised fine-tuning, and a personalized distillation mechanism.

Our experimental results demonstrate that FedCL can effectively optimize sharing model on commonly used semi-supervised and real-world datasets while preserving locally personalized. At the same time, we note that FedCL also provides good scalability, our analysis in Sect. 3.4 suggests that because it preserves the local knowledge for each client, and is optimized for specific-task.

In our experimental process, we performed a manual search for the encoder network architecture, which is time-consuming and error-prone. In future work, we plan to examine the potential of reinforcement learning to discover the structure of the sharing model and optimal hyperparameters for the best performance given a set of clients and datasets.

Acknowledgement. This work is supported by the National Natural Science Foundation of China (62072049).

References

1. McMahan, B., Moore, E., Ramage, D., Hampson, S., Arcas, B.A.: Communication-efficient learning of deep networks from decentralized data. In: Proceedings of Machine Learning Research, Fort Lauderdale, FL, USA, vol. 54, pp. 1273–1282 (2017)
2. Hard, A., et al.: Federated learning for mobile keyboard prediction. arXiv preprint arXiv:1811.03604 (2018)

3. Zhu, Y., Liu, Y., Yu, J.J.Q., Yuan, X.: Semi-supervised federated learning for travel mode identification from GPS trajectories. IEEE Trans. Intell. Transp. Syst. 1–12 (2021). https://doi.org/10.1109/TITS.2021.3092015

4. Tran, N.H., Bao, W., Zomaya, A., Nguyen, M.N.H., Hong, C.S.: Federated learning over wireless networks: optimization model design and analysis. In: IEEE INFOCOM 2019 - IEEE Conference on Computer Communications, pp. 1387–1395 (2019). https://doi.org/10.1109/INFOCOM.2019.8737464

5. Itahara, S., Nishio, T., Koda, Y., Morikura, M., Yamamoto, K.: Distillation-based semi-supervised federated learning for communication-efficient collaborative training with non-iid private data. arXiv preprint arXiv:2008.06180 (2020)

6. Nandury, K., Mohan, A., Weber, F.: Cross-silo federated training in the cloud with diversity scaling and semi-supervised learning. In: ICASSP 2021–2021 IEEE International Conference on Acoustics, Speech and Signal Processing (ICASSP), pp. 3085–3089 (2021). https://doi.org/10.1109/ICASSP39728.2021.9413428

7. Jeong, W., Yoon, J., Yang, E., Hwang, S.J.: Federated semi-supervised learning with inter-client consistency & disjoint learning. arXiv preprint arXiv:2006.12097 (2020)

8. Sahu, A.K., Li, T., Sanjabi, M., Zaheer, M., Talwalkar, A., Smith, V.: Federated optimization in heterogeneous networks. CoRR abs/1812.06127 (2018). http://arxiv.org/abs/1812.06127

9. Zhao, Y., Li, M., Lai, L., Suda, N., Civin, D., Chandra, V.: Federated learning with non-IID data. CoRR abs/1806.00582 (2018). http://arxiv.org/abs/1806.00582

10. Li, Q., He, B., Song, D.: Model-contrastive federated learning. In: 2021 IEEE/CVF Conference on Computer Vision and Pattern Recognition (CVPR), pp. 10708–10717 (2021). https://doi.org/10.1109/CVPR46437.2021.01057

11. Zhang, F., et al.: Federated unsupervised representation learning. arXiv preprint arXiv:2010.08982 (2020)

12. Zhuang, W., Gan, X., Wen, Y., Zhang, S., Yi, S.: Collaborative unsupervised visual representation learning from decentralized data. CoRR abs/2108.06492 (2021). https://arxiv.org/abs/2108.06492

13. Saeed, A., Salim, F.D., Ozcelebi, T., Lukkien, J.: Federated self-supervised learning of multisensor representations for embedded intelligence. IEEE Internet Things J. 8(2), 1030–1040 (2021). https://doi.org/10.1109/JIOT.2020.3009358

14. Shi, H., Zhang, Y., Shen, Z., Tang, S., Li, Y., Guo, Y., Zhuang, Y.: Federated self-supervised contrastive learning via ensemble similarity distillation. CoRR abs/2109.14611 (2021). https://arxiv.org/abs/2109.14611

15. Chen, T., Kornblith, S., Norouzi, M., Hinton, G.: A simple framework for contrastive learning of visual representations. In: International Conference on Machine Learning, pp. 1597–1607. PMLR (2020)

16. Chen, T., Kornblith, S., Swersky, K., Norouzi, M., Hinton, G.: Big self-supervised models are strong semi-supervised learners. arXiv preprint arXiv:2006.10029 (2020)

17. Zhang, C., Zhu, Y., Markos, C., Yu, S., Yu, J.J.: Towards crowdsourced transportation mode identification: a semi-supervised federated learning approach. IEEE Internet Things J. (2021). https://doi.org/10.1109/JIOT.2021.3132056

18. Thakur, A., Sharma, P., Clifton, D.A.: Dynamic neural graphs based federated reptile for semi-supervised multi-tasking in healthcare applications. IEEE J. Biomed. Health Inform. (2021). https://doi.org/10.1109/JBHI.2021.3134835

19. Verma, V., Kawaguchi, K., Lamb, A., Kannala, J., Bengio, Y., Lopez-Paz, D.: Interpolation consistency training for semi-supervised learning. arXiv preprint arXiv:1903.03825 (2019)

20. Sohn, K., et al.: Fixmatch: simplifying semi-supervised learning with consistency and confidence. arXiv preprint arXiv:2001.07685 (2020)
21. Xie, Q., Dai, Z., Hovy, E.H., Luong, M.T., Le, Q.V.: Unsupervised data augmentation. CoRR abs/1904.12848 (2019). http://arxiv.org/abs/1904.12848
22. Wu, Y., Zeng, D., Wang, Z., Shi, Y., Hu, J.: Federated contrastive learning for volumetric medical image segmentation. In: de Bruijne, M., et al. (eds.) MICCAI 2021. LNCS, vol. 12903, pp. 367–377. Springer, Cham (2021). https://doi.org/10.1007/978-3-030-87199-4_35
23. Jin, Y., Wei, X., Liu, Y., Yang, Q.: Towards utilizing unlabeled data in federated learning: a survey and prospective. arXiv preprint arXiv:2002.11545 (2020)
24. Berlo, B., Saeed, A., Ozcelebi, T.: Towards federated unsupervised representation learning. In: Proceedings of the Third ACM International Workshop on Edge Systems, Analytics and Networking, pp. 31–36 (2020)
25. Zhuang, W., Gan, X., Wen, Y., Zhang, X., Zhang, S., Yi, S.: Towards unsupervised domain adaptation for deep face recognition under privacy constraints via federated learning. arXiv preprint arXiv:2105.07606 (2021)
26. Zhuang, W., Wen, Y., Zhang, S.: Joint optimization in edge-cloud continuum for federated unsupervised person re-identification. In: Proceedings of the 29th ACM International Conference on Multimedia, pp. 433–441 (2021)
27. Sattler, F., Wiedemann, S., Müller, K.R., Samek, W.: Robust and communication-efficient federated learning from non-IID data. IEEE Trans. Neural Netw. Learn. Syst. 31(9), 3400–3413 (2019)
28. Bachman, P., Hjelm, R.D., Buchwalter, W.: Learning representations by maximizing mutual information across views. arXiv preprint arXiv:1906.00910 (2019)
29. Tschannen, M., Djolonga, J., Rubenstein, P.K., Gelly, S., Lucic, M.: On mutual information maximization for representation learning. arXiv preprint arXiv:1907.13625 (2019)
30. Cubuk, E.D., Zoph, B., Shlens, J., Le, Q.V.: Randaugment: practical data augmentation with no separate search. CoRR abs/1909.13719 (2019). http://arxiv.org/abs/1909.13719
31. Van Gansbeke, W., Vandenhende, S., Georgoulis, S., Proesmans, M., Van Gool, L.: SCAN: learning to classify images without labels. In: Vedaldi, A., Bischof, H., Brox, T., Frahm, J.-M. (eds.) ECCV 2020. LNCS, vol. 12355, pp. 268–285. Springer, Cham (2020). https://doi.org/10.1007/978-3-030-58607-2_16
32. Yosinski, J., Clune, J., Bengio, Y., Lipson, H.: How transferable are features in deep neural networks? arXiv preprint arXiv:1411.1792 (2014)
33. Hinton, G., Vinyals, O., Dean, J.: Distilling the knowledge in a neural network. arXiv preprint arXiv:1503.02531 (2015)
34. Bucilua, C., Caruana, R., Niculescu-Mizil, A.: Model compression. In: Proceedings of the 12th ACM SIGKDD International Conference on Knowledge Discovery and Data Mining, New York, NY, USA (2006)
35. Yalniz, I.Z., Jégou, H., Chen, K., Paluri, M., Mahajan, D.: Billion-scale semi-supervised learning for image classification. arXiv preprint arXiv:1905.00546 (2019)
36. Xie, Q., Luong, M.T., Hovy, E., Le, Q.V.: Self-training with noisy student improves imagenet classification. In: Proceedings of the IEEE/CVF Conference on Computer Vision and Pattern Recognition, pp. 10687–10698 (2020)
37. Zhai, X., Oliver, A., Kolesnikov, A., Beyer, L.: S4L: self-supervised semi-supervised learning. In: Proceedings of the IEEE/CVF International Conference on Computer Vision, pp. 1476–1485 (2019)
38. Krizhevsky, A.: Learning multiple layers of features from tiny images (2009)

39. Netzer, Y., Wang, T., Coates, A., Bissacco, A., Wu, B., Ng, A.: Reading digits in natural images with unsupervised feature learning (2011)
40. Deng, J., Dong, W., Socher, R., Li, L.J., Li, K., Fei-Fei, L.: ImageNet: a large-scale hierarchical image database. In: CVPR 2009 (2009)
41. Lee, D.H., et al.: Pseudo-label: the simple and efficient semi-supervised learning method for deep neural networks. In: Workshop on Challenges in Representation Learning, ICML, vol. 3, p. 896 (2013)
42. Salimans, T., Goodfellow, I., Zaremba, W., Cheung, V., Radford, A., Chen, X.: Improved techniques for training GANs. Adv. Neural. Inf. Process. Syst. **29**, 2234–2242 (2016)
43. French, R.M.: Catastrophic forgetting in connectionist networks. Trends Cogn. Sci. **3**(4), 128–135 (1999). https://doi.org/10.1016/S1364-6613(99)01294-2

Edge Federated Learning for Social Profit Optimality: A Cooperative Game Approach

Wenyuan Zhang[1,2], Guangjun Wu[1(✉)], Yongfei Liu[1,2], Binbin Li[1], and Jiawei Sun[1,2]

[1] Institute of Information Engineering, Chinese Academy of Sciences, Beijing 100093, China
{zhangwenyuan,wuguangjun,liuyongfei,libinbin,sunjiawei}@iie.ac.cn
[2] School of Cyber Security, University of Chinese Academy of Sciences, Beijing 100049, China

Abstract. As an emerging machine learning paradigm, federated learning satisfies people's privacy protection for private data properties to a certain extent. Especially in the field of Internet of Things (IoT), edge federated learning (EFL) allows edge devices to save private data locally when collaborative training. Most studies regard edge devices as rational and independent individuals, and use non-cooperative game methods to motivate devices to participate in training and maximize individual interests. But few studies have considered the fact that devices belonging to government or social construction agencies are more concerned with overall benefits than individual ones. In this paper, we propose an incentive mechanism for edge cooperative federated learning: ECFL. From the perspective of overall benefit, ECFL will fairly identify the contribution of edge devices and ensure the overall social benefit of the cooperative system. First, we propose a method of Shapley Value contribution degree estimated by Integrated Gradients based on the method of cooperative game (IG-Shapley Value). This method can quantitatively evaluate the contribution that edge devices provide to the model at each round of training in a fine-grained manner. At the same time, based on IG-Shapley Value, we design a collaborative contribution-aware aggregation algorithm IG-Fedavg. In order to maximize the overall social benefit, we consider the communication, storage and computing overhead of edge devices, and make joint optimization with reference to the contribution of edge devices. Extensive experimental results show that our proposed method can still make the model converge faster and achieve better performance when the overall profit is improved by more than 30%.

Keywords: Federated learning · Cooperative game · Internet of Things · Contribution evaluation

1 Introduction

With the rapid development of the Internet of Things (IoT), a large amount of data is collected by IoT devices, which contains a wealth of information valuable

H. Gao et al. (Eds.): CollaborateCom 2022, LNICST 460, pp. 135–153, 2022.
https://doi.org/10.1007/978-3-031-24383-7_8

to society. The emerging federated learning [2,11] paradigm allows collaborative training of distributed clients to extract value from edge data. This training mode avoids the client transmitting its own data to the cloud, thereby reducing the data security problems caused by centralized learning [12,20]. In edge scenarios where a large number of IoT devices are deployed, this training paradigm is called Edge Federated Learning (EFL). The edge devices save their own private data (such as facial recognition images), and only need to upload the training parameters to the edge server for collaborative training.

A great deal of works [4,8,10,15] treat edge devices as independent and rational individuals who do not cooperate but consider how to maximize their own benefits in federated learning. The quality of an individual dataset often determines the benchmark for edge device revenue, as this quantifies the device's contribution to overall training. However, since the incentive goals are selfish and independent, the contribution of equipment is often jointly modeled with heterogeneous resources in order to maximize the individual benefits without considering the overall benefits. [23] considers the multi-dimensional resource differences of mobile edge devices, a lightweight incentive framework FMore is designed. But the incentive of this paper is based on the multi-dimensional auction of individual selfishness. The federated learning incentive mechanism based on reputation and reverse auction theory mentioned by [24] also treats devices as rational and independent individuals.

The reality is that many social infrastructures with unified ownership, such as edge devices deployed by government departments or social service-oriented groups, are not independent and selfish. At this time, a cooperative group is formed between edge devices for collaborative learning. This kind of research based on collective interests is relatively few and incomplete. [14] designed the S-Fedavg aggregation algorithm to optimize the selection of clients, considering the cooperative game between clients. But this work ignores the overall social benefits of participating clients. [13] designed a Contribution-Aware Federated Learning (CAreFL) framework to provide a fair and interpretable quantification of FL participants' contributions to the problem of collaborative learning by collaborating medical institutions in the healthcare domain. However, in resource-constrained edge scenarios, the multi-faceted overhead of edge devices cannot be ignored. [3] proposes a collaborative learning framework for CFL in order to optimize the overall communication performance. But this work does not take into account the overall social profit, nor does it provide a fair contribution quantification mechanism for edge devices with Non-IID data.

Shapley Value is a classic cooperative game contribution evaluation method, which is widely used in machine learning feature selection [22] and model interpretation [1,5,7,18]. At the same time, the cooperating edge devices are actually playing a static cooperative game, which is relative to the non-cooperative game of similar work. In order to solve the problem of fair quantification of the contribution of cooperative devices, we consider using the powerful properties of Shapley Value for data quality evaluation of collaborative learning of edge devices. However, due to its exponential computational complexity [17], when the number of edge devices grows linearly, the computational load of Shapley Value will not be tolerated. We propose the fringe federation cooperation incentive mechanism ECFL to solve the above problems. First, we innovatively introduced the Integrated Gradients method to approximate Shapley Value. The Shapley Value method based on Integrated Gradients (IG-Shapley Value) can not only reduce the computational complexity of Shapley Value, but also fairly determine the contribution of each client in each round of training in the deep learning process. At the same time, we design a quality-aware federated learning aggregation algorithm IG-Fedavg based on IG-Shapley Value to achieve fair selection of cooperative edge devices. In addition, we fully consider the resource consumption of heterogeneous edge devices, including storage cost, computing overhead and communication overhead. In order to maximize the overall social benefit of co-trained edge devices, we build a joint revenue maximization model based on the IG-Shapley Value method.

The main contributions of this paper are summarized as follows:

- We propose a edge federation cooperation incentive mechanism ECFL. It ensures that in edge collaborative training, the contribution of edge devices in each round of training can be quantified fairly. In addition, ECFL can ensure that the overall social benefit of collaborative training is maximized.
- We model the contribution evaluation problem of edge devices as a static cooperative game problem, and propose the Shapley Value estimated by the method based on Integrated Gradients (IG-Shapley Value) to reduce the computational complexity and ensure fairness. At the same time, based on IG-Shapley Value, we design a collaborative contribution-aware aggregation algorithm IG-Fedavg.
- We conduct extensive experiments with a two-layer CNN model as an example. The experimental results show that the selection of edge devices based on IG-Shapley Value can make the model converge faster and obtain better performance while increasing the overall profit by more than 30%.

The rest of this paper is organized as follows. Section 2 gives an overview of the system and gives some background. In Sect. 3, we propose IG-Shapley Value and IG-Fedavg. In Sect. 4, we propose a social benefit optimization model based on IG-Shapley Value, and then give the experimental analysis results in Sect. 5. Section 6 presents related work, and Sect. 7 summarizes the entire paper.

2 Preliminary

2.1 System Overview

The Edge Federated Learning (EFL) architecture is composed of edge devices and edge parameter servers. We denote edge devices as $D = \{d_1, d_2, \ldots, d_n\}$ and edge parameter servers as S. As social infrastructure, edge devices and edge parameter servers jointly train valuable global models, such as face recognition, etc. This model has commercial value and social value, and also provides better basic services for the people. We assume that the edge devices participating in the training belong to the same or cooperative institutions, such as government functions or a consortium of enterprises that provide basic urban services. Specifically, edge devices use local datasets to collaboratively train specific tasks specified by the edge parameter server. In the communication round t, the set of participating edge devices is denoted as D^t, and the edge device d_i^t will send the local parameter ω_i^t to the edge server. After the parameter server performs model aggregation, it returns the aggregation parameter ω^{t+1} to the edge devices.

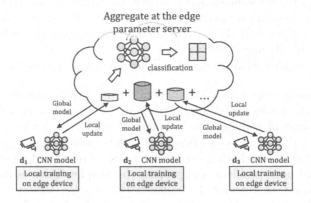

Fig. 1. The process of edge federated learning.

However, as shown in Fig. 1, datasets in edge devices are often Non-IID, and the training results of each round are skewed with different data distributions. This results in slower model convergence and lower accuracy. Considering the Non-IID data of heterogeneous devices, we abstract this problem as the contribution of edge devices. The local parameters provided by each edge device in one round of training have different effects on the overall model, that is, they have different contributions in each round. Because the edge server cannot directly collect the raw data of the edge device, it can only infer different contribution values through parameters. We use the Shapley Value to describe the contribution of edge device training to be able to quantify the cost and benefit of each round of the model.

In addition, heterogeneous edge devices have great differences in communication overhead, storage costs, and computing costs. In order to maximize social benefits, edge devices need to be selected during each round of training. This enables the model with the greatest social value to be trained with the least cost.

For better understanding, Table 1 shows the symbols that appear frequently below.

Table 1. Notation and their explanation

Notation	Explanation
$\phi(\cdot)$	The profit function
$\varepsilon(\cdot)$	Model Approximation Error
δ_i	Contribution ratio of edge device d_i
ω_k	Global aggregation parameters composed of k devices
R_k	Data transfer rate between edge device d_k and edge parameter server
T_{tr}	Transmission delay between edge device d_k and edge parameter server
T_s, T_k	Edge parameter server and edge device d_k training delay
W_{test}, W_{Sh}, W_k	Calculations required for testing, computing Shapley Value and d_k
E_k^s	Energy consumption per unit of communication between d_k and the edge parameter server
E_k^{store}	Storage cost of d_k
E_k^W	Local computation cost of d_k
E_s^W	Edge parameter server computing cost
$\sigma, r, \epsilon, \varphi, \gamma, \varpi_1, \varpi_2$	Positive scalar parameter

2.2 Cooperative Games

Cooperative games are an independent research system relative to non-cooperative games. The players involved in the game coordinate with each other to advance their own interests by forming alliances. This is a game method that emphasizes overall rationality.

We denote the cooperative game as $[N, val]$, where $N = \{N_1, N_2, \ldots, N_n\}$ is a set of n players. $C \subseteq N$ is any subset of N, represented as a alliance. $val(C)$ is expressed as the characteristic function of n-players cooperative game, which reflects the benefit of the alliance.

2.3 Shapley Value

The Shapley Value is derived from cooperative game theory and is a method created by Shapley in 1953 [16] to describe the players' contribution to the total payout to allocate payouts. The cooperating players can earn a payoff based on the sum of their contribution margins after the game is over. In recent work, the Shapley Value has been deeply used to explain machine learning. Usually the total payout represents the predicted value of an instance, and the player represents the feature value. The payoff is the difference between the actual prediction for that instance and the average prediction for all instances. Shapley Value is usually defined as follows:

$$Sh_i(val) = \sum_{\mathcal{C} \subseteq \mathcal{N} \setminus \{x_i\}} \frac{|\mathcal{C}|!(|\mathcal{N}| - |\mathcal{C}| - 1)!}{|\mathcal{N}|!} (val(\mathcal{C} \cup \{x_i\}) - val(\mathcal{C})), \qquad (1)$$

where $\mathcal{C}$ is the subset of model features, $|\mathcal{N}|$ is the number of features, $\frac{|\mathcal{C}|!(|\mathcal{N}| - |\mathcal{C}| - 1)!}{|\mathcal{N}|!}$ is the weight of $\mathcal{C}$, and x is the eigenvalue vector. Shapley Value is the only attribution method that satisfies the four properties of cooperative games, which ensures the fairness of the method. The four properties are:

Efficiency: The accumulation of features contributions is equal to the difference between the predicted and predicted mean of x, where $\hat{f}(\cdot)$ is a prediction model:

$$\sum_{j=1}^{|\mathcal{N}|} Sh_j = \hat{f}(x) - E_X(\hat{f}(X)), \qquad (2)$$

Symmetry: The features j and k contribute the same if and only if they contribute the same to all possible alliance:

$$\begin{aligned} if \quad & val(C \cup x_j) = val(C \cup x_k) \\ for\ all \quad & C \subseteq \{x_1, \ldots, x_{|N|}\}\{x_j, x_k\} \\ then \quad & Sh_j = Sh_k, \end{aligned} \qquad (3)$$

Dummy: The feature j that does not change the predicted value, no matter it is added to any feature alliance, the Shapley Value is always 0:

$$\begin{aligned} if \quad & val(C \cup \{x_j\}) = val(C) \\ for\ all \quad & C \subseteq \{x_1, \ldots, x_{|N|}\} \\ then \quad & Sh_j = 0, \end{aligned} \qquad (4)$$

Additivity: For games with combined payouts, the corresponding Shapley Value is as follows:

$$Sh_j = Sh_j^+. \qquad (5)$$

2.4 Shapley Value in EFL

To maximize the overall profit of Edge Federated Learning, we need to quantify the contribution of local models provided by edge devices. We use the rigorously proven Shapley Value as a quantification method. Specifically, the edge devices participating in the t round form a cooperative game alliance, which can be defined as $[\omega_{local}^t, val]$, where $\omega_{local}^t = \{\omega_d^t\}_{d \in D^t}$, val is defined as contributions for computing D^t subset alliance.

The method for estimating Shapley Value is detailed in Sect. 3.1. After obtaining the contribution of different edge devices, joint modeling is carried out according to the contribution and the operating cost of the target device, which can ultimately maximize the overall social benefit.

3 Contribution and Aggregation Algorithms

In this section, we introduce our proposed IG-Shapley Value and the aggregation algorithm designed based on the contribution of edge devices.

3.1 Estimate of Shapley Value

Since the exact Shapley Value needs to face exponentially increasing computation, such time overhead is intolerable in Edge Federated Learning. We use the Integrated Gradients (IG) method [19] to estimate the contribution of each edge device to a training round. We extend the Shapley Value to IG-Shapley Value based on IG, predicting the gradient to reformulate the integral as the expectation of player behavior. The method is shown to conform to *Sensitivity* and *Implementation Invariance*, and satisfy:

$$\sum_{i=1}^{n} IG_i(x) = F(x) - F(x'), \tag{6}$$

The integral expression is as follows:

$$IG_i(x) ::= (x_i - x_i') \times \int_{\alpha=0}^{1} \frac{\partial F(x' + \alpha \times (x - x'))}{\partial x_i} d\alpha, \tag{7}$$

In a real edge environment, the result of the integral can be approximated to reduce the computational complexity:

$$IG_i^{approx}(x) ::= (x_i - x_i') \times \sum_{k=1}^{m} \frac{\partial F(x' + \frac{k}{m} \times (x - x'))}{\partial x_i} \times \frac{1}{m}, \tag{8}$$

where x' is the baseline input, and x' can be set to an all-zero vector according to [19]. This paper takes the validation set $V = \{x_1, x_2, \ldots, x_n\}$ in the edge server as the input x_i vector. The respective Shapley Values are approximately estimated based on the locally trained models of different edge devices. The Shapley Value can be expressed as the quantitative contribution of an edge device to the final trained global model in a certain round. $F(\cdot)$ represents a neural network model.

In this paper, we take a two-layer CNN network as an example. $F(\cdot)$ is a CNN network whose input vector is image data. m represents the samples generated within the algorithm based on the input to estimate the final Shapley Value. Eigen roots with larger absolute Shapley Values are important. Since global contribution is required, we average the absolute values of the IG-Shapley Values of all validation vectors for each model:

$$Sh_i^t = \sum_{j=1}^{|V|} \sum_{i=1}^{n} |IG_i^j|, \tag{9}$$

where $|V|$ represents the validation set size. Then Sh_i^t is the final estimated Shapley Value of device d_i in round t, that is, its contribution in this round.

3.2 IG-Shapley Value Based Federated Averaging (IG-Fedavg)

Based on IG-Shapley Value, we innovatively propose a federated learning aggregation algorithm IG-Fedavg. Details of the algorithm refer to Algorithm 1. Initially, the edge server randomly initializes the global parameter ω_0 and broadcasts it to all edge devices. After the edge device performs local computation, it returns the parameter ω_i^t of this round of training to the edge server within a certain delay limit. The edge server executes IG-Shapley Value according to the local test set, and calculates the contribution of each client in this round of aggregation. After obtaining the contribution set Sh^t, sort according to the size of the contribution from small to large, and select the appropriate edge device parameters according to the optimization result k (see Sect. 4 for the calculation method of k). At this time, the set of edge devices D^t is determined, and a signal is sent to them to update and share.

For each edge device, after receiving the update request, it performs local training according to the parameters sent by the edge server and the local data set, and fits the local model of E *epochs*. After the edge device calculates the new model parameters, it sends an update to the edge server. After the edge server collects these updated parameters, it aggregates the parameters to obtain the global parameters of a new round of communication. The aggregation process can also refer to the flow shown in Fig. 1.

4 System Model

This section models the overall architecture of federated learning at the edge. The purpose of modeling is to maximize the social benefit of the system. Our model takes into account modeling the benefits of each round of training, as well as modeling the energy costs of heterogeneous edge devices in terms of communication, storage, and computing.

4.1 Income Model Based on IG-Shapley Value

The overall income of the system comes from the revenue of model training. In this section, we design a income model based on IG-Shapley Value considering the profit changes at the model communication round level.

Let the overall profit function be:

$$\phi^t(F) = \frac{\kappa}{1 + e^{r\varepsilon^t(F)-\epsilon}}, \tag{10}$$

where κ, r, ϵ are positive scalars, $\varepsilon^t(F)$ is the approximate error of the model in round t, when $\varepsilon^t(F) \to 0$, the current round profit $\phi^t(F)$ reaches the maximum value. A large $\varepsilon^t(F)$ results in a small profit $\phi^t(F)$.

Algorithm 1: IG-Shapley Value based Federated Averaging (IG-Fedavg)

Input: k^t: optimal number of edge device selections in round t; ω: parameter of the edge server model; η_i: learning rate of edge device i; B: minibatch size; T: maximum number of communication rounds; E: number of local epochs; D: set of edge devices;

Output: parameter ω^T of the edge server model;

1 **for** *each round t=1,2,...,T* **do**
2   edge server executes:
3     $Sh^t = \sum_{j=1}^{|V|} \sum_{i=1}^{n} |IG_i^j|$;
4     $Sh_{sort}^t \leftarrow sort(Sh^t)$;
5     $D^t \leftarrow choose(Sh_{sort}^t, k^t)$;
6   clients (D^t) execute:
7
8   **for** *each client $i \in D^t$* **do**
9        $\omega_i \leftarrow \omega^t$ **for** *each local epoch e* **do**
10   **for** *batch $b \in B$* **do**
11             $\omega_i^{t+1} \leftarrow \omega_i^t - \eta_i \nabla l(\omega_i^t; b)$;
12   **end**
13   **end**
14   **return** ω_i^{t+1};
15   **end**
16
17   edge server executes:
18     $\omega_k^{t+1} = \frac{\sum_{i=1}^{k} |\mathbb{D}_i| \omega_i^{t+1}}{\sum_{i=1}^{k} |\mathbb{D}_i|}$;
19 **end**

Through the method described in Sect. 3.2, we obtain the candidate set D^t of t rounds of training within the specified time delay, and obtain all the Shapley Values calculated by the set:

$$Sh^t = \{Sh_1^t, Sh_2^t, \ldots, Sh_K^t\}, \tag{11}$$

where $K = |D^t|$. $\varepsilon^t(F)$ is expressed as:

$$\varepsilon^t(F) = \varphi(\sum_{i=1}^{k} \delta_i^t |\mathbb{D}_i|)^\gamma, \quad k \in K, \tag{12}$$

where φ and γ are positive scalars, and $|\mathbb{D}_i|$ is the dataset size local to d_i. δ_i^t represents the proportion of parameter contribution:

$$\delta_i^t = \frac{Sh_i^t}{\sum_{j=1}^{k} Sh_j^t}, \tag{13}$$

where $\delta_i^t \in [0, 1)$.

4.2   System Latency of EFL

We take into account that edge devices and servers incur system delays in transmitting model parameters. Specifically, the latency of edge parameter servers includes data loading latency and computation latency. Assuming that the parameters of k edge devices are received in round t, their communication links are orthogonal. The data transmission rate between the edge device d_k and the edge parameter server is:

$$R_k^t = B \log_2(1 + \frac{P_k^t h_k}{\sigma^2}), \tag{14}$$

where B is the channel bandwidth and P_k is the transmission power of d_k to the edge server. h_k is the channel gain and σ^2 is the noise power.

The transmission delay between d_k^t and the edge server is:

$$T_{tr}^t = \frac{|\omega_k^t|}{R_k^t}, \tag{15}$$

where $|\omega_k^t|$ is the parameter size uploaded by d_k^t in round t. The maximum tolerated waiting time of the edge parameter server is T, so the constraint condition is obtained:

$$T_{tr}^t \leq T, \quad t \in T. \tag{16}$$

The training delay of the parameter server in round t is:

$$T_s^t = \frac{W^t}{e_s}, \tag{17}$$

where W^t is the total amount of edge server computing in round t. The amount of computation can be thought of as the number of CPU cycles. e_s is the CPU frequency of the edge server. W^t is expressed as:

$$W^t = W_{test}^t + W_{Sh}^t, \tag{18}$$

where W_{test}^t is the amount of computation required to test the accuracy of the model, which is proportional to the size of the test datasets:

$$\begin{aligned} W_{test}^t &= \tau_{test} E_n C_s E_s \\ &= \tau_{test}(\frac{|\mathbb{D}_{test}|}{E_s}) C_s E_s \\ &= \tau_{test} C_s |\mathbb{D}_{test}|, \end{aligned} \tag{19}$$

where τ_{test} is the total number of epochs tested, E_n is the number of batches in the epoch, E_s is the batch size, C_s is the number of edge server CPU, and $|\mathbb{D}_{test}|$ is the size of test dataset.

W_{Sh}^t is the amount of computation required to estimate Shapley Value for each parameter aggregation process:

$$W_{Sh}^t = C_s|\mathbb{D}_{val}| + m|\mathbb{D}_{val}|, \tag{20}$$

where m is the number of generated samples set in IG, and $|\mathbb{D}_{val}|$ is the size of validation dataset.

W^t can be simplified to:

$$W^t = \tau_{test}C_s|\mathbb{D}_{test}| + (C_s + m)|\mathbb{D}_{val}|, \tag{21}$$

$$W^t \leq \mathcal{W}, \quad t \in T, \tag{22}$$

where $\mathcal{W}$ is the maximum computing load of the edge server.

For the edge server d_k, the training delay in round t is:

$$T_k^t = \frac{W_k^t}{e_k}, \tag{23}$$

where W_k^t is the local calculation amount of d_k, and e_k is the CPU frequency of d_k.

W_k^t is denoted as:

$$\begin{aligned}
W_k^t &= \tau_k E_n^k C_k E_s^k \\
&= \tau_k(\frac{|\mathbb{D}_k|}{E_s})C_k E_s^k \\
&= \tau_k C_k|\mathbb{D}_k|,
\end{aligned} \tag{24}$$

where τ_k is the number of epochs set by device d_k, E_n^k is the number of batches in the epoch of d_k, E_s^k is the size of d_k batches, C_k is the number of CPU in d_k, and $|\mathbb{D}_k|$ is the size of local training datasets in d_k.

4.3   EFL Costs and Cooperation Benefits

Since edge devices incur communication overhead when broadcasting local parameters, this brings communication costs to the system. The unit communication energy consumption between the edge server d_k and the edge parameter server in round t is:

$$E_k^{s,t} = P_k^t T_{tr}^t, \tag{25}$$

where P_k^t represents the transmission power of d_k uploading local parameters to the edge server in round t, denoted as:

$$p_k^t = \frac{\sigma^2}{h_k}(2^{\frac{R_k^t}{B}} - 1), \tag{26}$$

Assuming that the storage unit price of the edge server is e_0, the storage cost for the device d_k is:

$$E_k^{store,t} = e_0(|\mathbb{D}_k| + |\omega_k^t|). \tag{27}$$

We suppose the rated power of the edge device d_k is p_k, then its unit calculation cost in round t is:

$$E_k^{W,t} = p_k T_k^t. \tag{28}$$

Assuming that the rated power of the edge parameter server is p_S, its unit calculation cost in round t is:

$$E_s^{W,t} = p_s T_s^t. \tag{29}$$

The total cost of training in round t is:

$$E^{total,t} = \sum_{k=1}^{|D|} a_k(E_s^{W,t} + E_k^{s,t}) + E_k^{store,t} + E_k^{W,t}, \tag{30}$$

where a_k is the cooperative decision value, and $|D|$ is the number of edge devices. When $a_k = 1$, d_k transmits the parameters to the edge parameter server within the specified delay, and $a_k = 0$ indicates that the parameters are not received.

Maximizing system utility is expressed as:

$$\max \quad \Phi^t = \sum_{t=1}^{T} \varpi_1 \phi^t(F) - \varpi_2(1 - \varpi_1)E^{total,t}$$

$$s.t. \quad \begin{cases} W^t \leq \mathcal{W}, \quad t \in T \\ T_{tr}^t \leq \mathcal{T}, \quad t \in T. \end{cases} \tag{31}$$

where ϖ_1 is the weighting factor and ϖ_2 is the mapping factor.

5   Experiments

5.1   Simulation Setting

In system simulations, we validate the proposed method using the MNIST dataset and perform classification tasks based on the FedML framework. Our codes are based on the widely used pytorch-1.11.0 software environment, with Intel(R) Xeon(R) CPU E5-2609 v4 @ 1.70GHz, memory of 128G, and OS of centos7. The MNIST dataset is a ten-class dataset of handwritten digit images widely used for testing federated learning evaluations, which contains 60,000 training examples and 10,000 test examples. The edge parameter server publishes a Convolutional Neural Network (CNN) model that edge devices collaborate to train for classification tasks.

We set up 1000 edge devices distributed in an area of 3×3 km^2, and they have pre-divided Non-IID datasets to simulate the difference data collected by devices in different environments. The transmission power of the edge device is uniformly distributed in $[0.1, 2] W$, $e_s = e_k = 5$, $C_s = 4$, $C_k = 2$. The local dataset size is distributed in $[2, 2000]$, the size of the IG generated sample is 50, and the validation set is sampled from the test set with a size of 1000. The epoch of edge devices and edge parameter server is 1, and batch size is 50. The maximum transmission delay is 600, and the maximum calculation amount of the edge server is 150,000. The scalar parameters κ, r, ϵ, φ, γ are 1.25, 9, 5.5, 0.39 and 0.03.

5.2 Performance Analysis of Shapley Value Based Training

In order to verify the training effect of selecting the edge devices through Shapley Value, we conduct comparative experiments. Specifically, for the same number of edge devices, we assume that parameters such as system latency, device power range, and model hyperparameters are the same. As shown in Fig. 2, we compare the overall training accuracy with Shapley Value selection and without this method. In the 200 rounds of communication, we set the Shapley Value selection to not apply for the first 20 rounds. The reason for this setting is that the datasets referenced in the initial stage of model construction are too small, and edge devices that are important to the classification results but have a small amount of data may be deleted through screening, thus affecting the training accuracy.

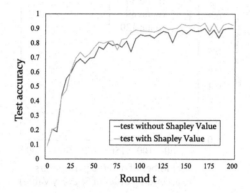

Fig. 2. Test accuracy with or without Shapley Value.

The experimental results show that the model selected by Shapley Value can not only converge, but also the performance of model accuracy and convergence speed are better than the random selection of random edge device parameters.

We choose the round 30, 80 and 120 of the 200 rounds as examples for comparative experiments. They represent the three stages of the rate of increase in model accuracy. Figure 3 shows the distribution of Shapley Value in different rounds.

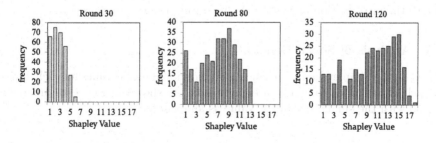

Fig. 3. Shapley Value histograms at 30, 80, 120 rounds.

The experimental results show that with the increase of rounds, the overall distribution of Shapley Value becomes larger and larger. This reflects that as the model is trained, the contribution of edge device data that meets certain characteristics to model training increases. At the same time, the minimum value range of Shapley Value does not increase, indicating that the contribution of these device data to the model is not much different from that in the early training stage.

We sort Shapley Value in ascending order, and delete the corresponding edge device parameters one by one. After testing on the test set, the training error is shown in Fig. 4.

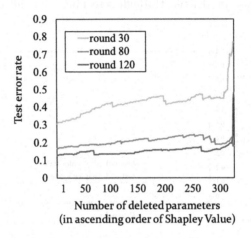

Fig. 4. The effect of deleting parameters in ascending order of Shapley Value on accuracy.

The abscissa in the figure is the Shapley Value of the first 300 edge device parameters collected within the delay range. In the round 30, the error rate increases rapidly with the reduction of edge devices participating in the training, while in the round 80 and 120, the error does not increase much when reducing a small number of device parameters, but decreases at some moments. This is also the reason why the model convergence speed and accuracy will be improved due to the introduction of Shapley Value during the training process.

5.3   Analysis of Social Benefit

Based on the Shapley Value, we calculated individual profit values for each device in each of the three comparison experiments. As shown in Fig. 5, we intercept the 50 with the smallest Shapley Value as an example.

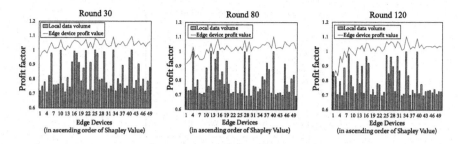

Fig. 5. The relationship between edge device profit value and Shapley Value.

In order to facilitate comparative analysis, we normalized the local data volume of edge devices. For device d_k, the amount of processed data is:

$$|\mathbb{D}_k|_{normal} = \frac{1}{1 + e^{-\frac{|\mathbb{D}_k|\sum_{i=1}^{K}|\mathbb{D}_i|}{K}}} \tag{32}$$

According to the experimental results, we can see that the profit value of edge devices with a large amount of data is relatively high, but the Shapley Value will affect the overall revenue. As the number of rounds increases, the profit of edge devices with smaller Shapley values declines as a whole, which verifies the decrease in the contribution of these nodes to the model accuracy.

Fig. 6. The total income value for alliances.

As shown in Fig. 6, observe the change of the total revenue of the system in a single round with the deletion of the edge device parameters with a smaller value of Shapley Value.

As training progresses, the range of maximum profit points remains roughly constant, and reducing a small number of edge device parameters will improve the overall profit margin. The highest profit is increased by 12.26%, 19.05% and 29.21% respectively compared with the absence of Shapley Value. In addition, as the number of rounds increases, the profitable range becomes larger and larger, which shows that the Shapley Value in the later stage of training can better represent the contribution to the parameters of the edge devices in this training.

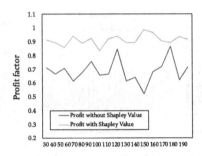

Fig. 7. Profit factor with or without Shapley Value.

Figure 7 shows the difference between the global profit of using IG-Shapley Value and the profit of normal training during a complete training process. The experimental results clearly demonstrate that our proposed method can greatly improve the social benefits. Compared with the baseline, the average profit of the overall training has increased by 32.77%, of which the profit factor of the baseline is 0.6821, and the profit factor of the optimized profit is 0.9045. This strongly validates the effectiveness of our proposed method.

6   Related Work

In recent years, edge federated learning has received extensive attention. Wang et al. [20] focused on a generic class of machine learning models that were trained using gradientdescent based approaches. They analyzed the convergence bound of distributed gradient descent from a theoretical point of view, based on which they proposed a control algorithm that determines the best trade-off between local update and global parameter aggregation to minimize the loss function under a given resource budget. Wang et al. [21] designed the "In-Edge AI" framework in order to intelligently utilize the collaboration among devices and edge nodes to exchange the learning parameters for a better training and inference of the models, and thus to carry out dynamic system-level optimization and application-level enhancement while reducing the unnecessary system communication load. To address the resource-constrained reality of edge devices, he et al. [6] reformulated FL as a group knowledge transfer training algorithm, called FedGKT. FedGKT designed a variant of the alternating minimization approach to train small CNNs on edge nodes and periodically transfer their knowledge by knowledge distillation to a large server-side CNN. Zhang et al. [25] formulated the first faithful implementation problem of federated learning and designed two faithful federated learning mechanisms which satisfy economic properties, scalability, and privacy.

There are many research results in the client incentive direction of edge federated learning. Khan et al. [9] modeled the incentive-based interaction between a global server and participating devices for federated learning via a Stackelberg game to motivate the participation of the devices in the federated learning process. Zeng et al. [23] proposed FMore as multi-dimensional incentive framework for federated learning. FMore covered a range of scoring functions and was Pareto efficient for some specific cases. It used game theory to derive optimal policies for marginal players and used expected utility theory to guide aggregators to efficiently obtain required resources. Jiao et al. [8] proposed an auction-based market model for incentivizing data owners to participate in federated learning. They designed two auction mechanisms for the federated learning platform to maximize the social welfare of the federated learning service market.

However, in edge devices under government agencies and other departments, the assumption of rational independence of devices does not apply. [13,14] consider the client selection problem, which can solve the fairness problem of contribution to a certain extent, but do not study how to maximize the profit of cooperative equipment. In addition, [3] studied the overhead of optimizing communication and other aspects, but did not propose how to fairly calculate the contribution of heterogeneous devices.

7 Conclusions

For edge federated learning with edge devices as a community of interests in IoT scenarios, we propose an edge federation cooperation incentive mechanism ECFL. We introduce the Shapley Value estimated by Integrated Gradients to fairly compute the contribution of edge devices in each round of training. Furthermore, we design a quality-aware federated learning aggregation algorithm IG-Fedavg based on IG-Shapley Value to achieve fair selection of cooperative edge devices. Taking into account the overall profit and the storage, communication and computing costs of edge parameter servers and edge devices, we optimize social benefits. Extensive experiments show that our proposed method can still make the model converge faster and achieve better performance when the overall profit is improved by more than 30%. In the future, we can further study how to better measure contributions and how to design models when edge devices are dynamic.

Acknowledgements. This work is supported by the National Key Research and Development Program of China (Grant No. 2021YFB3101305), National Natural Science Foundation of China (Grant No. 61931019).

References

1. Aas, K., Jullum, M., Løland, A.: Explaining individual predictions when features are dependent: more accurate approximations to shapley values. Artif. Intell. **298**, 103502 (2021)
2. Bonawitz, K., et al.: Towards federated learning at scale: system design. Proc. Mach. Learn. Syst. **1**, 374–388 (2019)
3. Chen, M., Poor, H.V., Saad, W., Cui, S.: Wireless communications for collaborative federated learning. IEEE Commun. Mag. **58**(12), 48–54 (2020)

4. Ding, N., Fang, Z., Huang, J.: Optimal contract design for efficient federated learning with multi-dimensional private information. IEEE J. Sel. Areas Commun. **39**(1), 186–200 (2020)
5. Ghorbani, A., Zou, J.Y.: Neuron shapley: discovering the responsible neurons. Adv. Neural. Inf. Process. Syst. **33**, 5922–5932 (2020)
6. He, C., Annavaram, M., Avestimehr, S.: Group knowledge transfer: federated learning of large CNNs at the edge. Adv. Neural. Inf. Process. Syst. **33**, 14068–14080 (2020)
7. Heskes, T., Sijben, E., Bucur, I.G., Claassen, T.: Causal shapley values: exploiting causal knowledge to explain individual predictions of complex models. Adv. Neural. Inf. Process. Syst. **33**, 4778–4789 (2020)
8. Jiao, Y., Wang, P., Niyato, D., Lin, B., Kim, D.I.: Toward an automated auction framework for wireless federated learning services market. IEEE Trans. Mob. Comput. **20**(10), 3034–3048 (2020)
9. Khan, L.U., et al.: Federated learning for edge networks: resource optimization and incentive mechanism. IEEE Commun. Mag. **58**(10), 88–93 (2020)
10. LE, T.H.T., et al.: An incentive mechanism for federated learning in wireless cellular networks: an auction approach. IEEE Trans. Wireless Commun. **20**(8), 4874–4887 (2021)
11. Li, T., Sahu, A.K., Talwalkar, A., Smith, V.: Federated learning: challenges, methods, and future directions. IEEE Signal Process. Mag. **37**(3), 50–60 (2020)
12. Lim, W.Y.B., et al.: Federated learning in mobile edge networks: a comprehensive survey. IEEE Commun. Surv. Tutor. **22**(3), 2031–2063 (2020)
13. Liu, Z., et al.: Contribution-aware federated learning for smart healthcare. In: Proceedings of the 34th Annual Conference on Innovative Applications of Artificial Intelligence (IAAI-22) (2022)
14. Nagalapatti, L., Narayanam, R.: Game of gradients: mitigating irrelevant clients in federated learning. arXiv preprint arXiv:2110.12257 (2021)
15. Pandey, S.R., Tran, N.H., Bennis, M., Tun, Y.K., Manzoor, A., Hong, C.S.: A crowdsourcing framework for on-device federated learning. IEEE Trans. Wireless Commun. **19**(5), 3241–3256 (2020)
16. Shapley, L.S.: Stochastic games. Proc. Natl. Acad. Sci. **39**(10), 1095–1100 (1953)
17. Štrumbelj, E., Kononenko, I.: Explaining prediction models and individual predictions with feature contributions. Knowl. Inf. Syst. **41**(3), 647–665 (2014)
18. Sundararajan, M., Najmi, A.: The many shapley values for model explanation. In: International Conference on Machine Learning, pp. 9269–9278. PMLR (2020)
19. Sundararajan, M., Taly, A., Yan, Q.: Axiomatic attribution for deep networks. In: International Conference on Machine Learning, pp. 3319–3328. PMLR (2017)
20. Wang, S., et al.: Adaptive federated learning in resource constrained edge computing systems. IEEE J. Sel. Areas Commun. **37**(6), 1205–1221 (2019)
21. Wang, X., Han, Y., Wang, C., Zhao, Q., Chen, X., Chen, M.: In-edge AI: intelligentizing mobile edge computing, caching and communication by federated learning. IEEE Network **33**(5), 156–165 (2019)
22. Yan, T., Procaccia, A.D.: If you like shapley then you'll love the core. In: Proceedings of the AAAI Conference on Artificial Intelligence, vol. 35, pp. 5751–5759 (2021)
23. Zeng, R., Zhang, S., Wang, J., Chu, X.: Fmore: an incentive scheme of multi-dimensional auction for federated learning in MEC. In: 2020 IEEE 40th International Conference on Distributed Computing Systems (ICDCS), pp. 278–288. IEEE (2020)

24. Zhang, J., Wu, Y., Pan, R.: Incentive mechanism for horizontal federated learning based on reputation and reverse auction. In: Proceedings of the Web Conference 2021, pp. 947–956 (2021)
25. Zhang, M., Wei, E., Berry, R.: Faithful edge federated learning: scalability and privacy. IEEE J. Sel. Areas Commun. **39**(12), 3790–3804 (2021)

MetaEM: Meta Embedding Mapping for Federated Cross-domain Recommendation to Cold-Start Users

Dongyi Zheng[1], Yeting Guo[1], Fang Liu[2(✉)], Nong Xiao[1], and Lu Gao[3]

[1] College of Computer, National University of Defense Technology, Changsha, China
[2] School of Design, HuNan University, Changsha, China
fangl@hnu.edu.cn
[3] School of History, Hubei University, Wuhan, China

Abstract. Cross-domain recommendation exploits the rich data from source domain to solve the cold-start problem of target domain. Considering the recommendation system contains some user private information, how to provide accurate suggestions for cold-start users on the basis of protecting privacy is an important issue. Federated recommendation systems keep user private data on mobile devices to protect user privacy. However, compared to federated single-domain recommendation, federated cross-domain recommendation needs to train more models, making resource-constrained mobile devices infeasible to run large-scale models. In view of this, we design a meta embedding mapping method for federated cross-domain recommendation called MetaEM. The training stage of MetaEM includes pretraining and mapping. The pretrain stage learns user and item embeddings of source domain and target domain respectively. Items embeddings are divided into common and private. The common embeddings are shared by all users, and we train a meta-network to generate private embeddings for each user. The mapping stage learns to transfer user embeddings from source domain to target domain. In order to alleviate the negative impact of users with low number of ratings on mapping model, we employ a task-oriented optimization method. We implement the MetaEM prototype on large real-world datasets and extensive experiments demonstrate that MetaEM achieves the best performance and is more compatible with complicated models compared to other state-of-the-art baselines.

Keywords: Meta learning · Cross-domain recommendation · Federated learning · Cold-start · Embedding mapping

1 Introduction

Recommender systems have played an important role in various online applications of the Internet, which help users discover interesting content from massive

Supported by organization nudt.

© ICST Institute for Computer Sciences, Social Informatics and Telecommunications Engineering 2022
Published by Springer Nature Switzerland AG 2022. All Rights Reserved
H. Gao et al. (Eds.): CollaborateCom 2022, LNICST 460, pp. 154–172, 2022.
https://doi.org/10.1007/978-3-031-24383-7_9

information. Since the newly registered users of the system have not yet generated interaction data, it is difficult for the recommendation system to provide accurate recommendations for them, which is called the cold-start problem.

Cross-domain recommendation (CDR) provides a solution to the cold-start problem by utilizing the rich data of the source domain to improve the recommendation accuracy of the target domain. For example, recommend books to users based on their movie ratings. At present, cross-domain recommendation models can be divided into mapping-based [13], shared entity representation [5], heterogeneous graph embedding [19] and multi-domain collaborative training [17]. Among them, the mapping-based is the most used method, and the representative models of this method include EMCDR [13], TMCDR [20], PTUPCDR [22] and so on. However, these models all belong to the centralized training method, and dedicated to training high-performance cross-domain models. There is a risk of user data leakage in centralized training process.

Federated learning is a distributed machine learning framework that can be applied in recommendation systems to solve privacy protection issues. It saves users' private data on mobile devices, and then builds and trains recommendation models between mobile devices and cloud server. Existing federated recommendation models include FCF [1], FedRec [14], FedRec++ [8], FedFast [15], MetaMF [10], etc. However, these methods focus on addressing the privacy protection issue in single-domain recommendation scenarios. There is a lack of relevant research on privacy protection in cross-domain recommendation scenarios. Therefore, it is of great significance to study federated cross-domain recommendation, which can provide more accurate recommendation suggestions for cold-start users on the basis of protecting privacy. We mainly study federated cross-domain recommendation that belong to mapping-based.

We summarize the challenges faced by federated cross-domain recommendation as follows:

(1) Resource-constrained mobile devices. Compared with federated single-domain recommendation, map-based federated cross-domain recommendation requires federated training of three models: two pretrained models (including source and target domains) and a mapping model. Therefore, federated cross-domain recommendation requires more models to be trained on mobile devices than federated single-domain recommendation. Large-scale model training is difficult for resource-constrained mobile devices. In addition, since the mobile device needs to continuously download and upload the embedding and gradient information of the items in the pretrain stage, when the number of items is massive, the amount of data transmitted between mobile devices and cloud server increases sharply, which demands more RAM, and communication bandwidth on mobile phones. Therefore, it is not practical to allow resource-constrained mobile devices to participate in training. However, in the real world, most devices are resource constrained.

(2) Optimization Strategy. Existing cross-domain models such as [13,18] adopt a distance-oriented approach to optimize the mapping model, taking the Euclidean distance between the transformed embedding (prediction) and the target embedding (ground truth) as the optimization objective. However,

low-quality embeddings of users with fewer ratings can add negative effects to the mapping model. And each training sample consists of the user's target embedding and transformation embedding, and the number of total training samples depends on the number of training users, so the total number of samples is limited.

In response to the challenge of resource-constrained mobile devices, our goal is to design a light federated cross-domain recommendation model, which can significantly reduce the amount of data transferred between mobile devices and cloud servers, alleviating the communication and storage load of mobile devices. Facing the challenge of optimization strategy, we can use the transformed embedding for the prediction task. Our main contributions are summarized as follows:

- We design a meta embedding mapping method for federated cross-domain recommendation, MetaEM. It utilizes a meta-learner to generate small-scale private item embedding matrix for each user, thereby reducing the amount of data transferred between mobile devices and cloud servers.
- To stably learn the mapping model, we use a task-oriented optimization strategy to remove the side effects of low-quality user embeddings.
- We conduct extensive experiments to demonstrate the effectiveness and compatibility of MetaEM for cold-start users. It demonstrate that MetaEM achieves the best performance and is more compatible with complicated models compared to other state-of-the-art baselines.

2   Related Work

In this section, we discuss the existing related works, mainly including the application of federated learning in single-domain recommendation scenario and cross-domain recommendation models.

There are many applications of federated learning in single-domain recommendation scenarios. FedFast [15] puts forward an accelerated strategy of federated learning for recommendation. Because the traditional federated learning algorithm converges slowly for recommendation, it will continue to occupy the equipment resources of the client during model training. FedFast not only protects users' privacy and improves convergence speed, but also maintains fine recommendation performance. On the basis of user clustering, FedFast proposed two algorithms, user sampling and gradient aggregation, which can converge with fewer rounds. MetaMF [10] considers that traditional federated learning assumes that the server model is the same size as the client model, but not all users have high-quality mobile phones, so the client can't perform large-scale neural network training like the central server. Therefore, considering the resource limitations of clients, this paper proposes a federated recommendation algorithm based on meta-learning, aiming at learning a small personalized model for each client, so as to achieve accurate recommendation service. FedRec and FedRec++ [8,9] add randomly sampled items and simulated ratings to users, which makes the server unable to accurately identify users' preferences for items, thus improving the protection of users' privacy. These methods are the latest applications of federated learning in single-domain recommendation scenarios. When traditional federated learning schemes adapt to single-domain recommendation, it will face various problems, such as slow convergence speed, large model size of client and privacy leakage from gradient. In the cross-domain recommendation scenario, these problems will be more serious.

The goal of cross-domain recommendation is to enrich the knowledge of target domain with the data of source domain. Tong et al. proposed a single-target cross-domain recommendation algorithm based on domain mapping (EMCDR) [13] and [7]. The recommendation goal of EMCDR is for users or items with little information in the target domain. For example, for users or items newly added to the system, their latent factors can not be found in the target domain, but the users are active in the source domain and have accurate latent factors in the source domain. So EMCDR map the latent factors in the source domain to the target domain through the mapping function, and then complete the recommendation. CMF [16] was proposed to realize cross-domain knowledge integration by connecting multiple rating matrices and sharing user latent factor across domains. Yong et al. proposed TMCDR [21], which divided cross-domain recommendation into Transfer stage, Meta stage and prediction stage. The Transfer stage is similar to the stage of learning user and item latent factors in EMCDR, then the trained model is used as a pretraining model. The Meta stage draws on the idea of meta-learning, extracts some user data from the user set in the cross domain as tasks, and repeatedly extracts several tasks to form a batch for training. In the prediction stage, the cold start user can be recommended by using the trained meta-network to output the latent factor in the target domain. Yong et al. also proposes a novel framework PTUPCDR [22]. It uses a meta-learner to model a personalized preference bridge with user traits extracted from the user's interaction history. Then use the personalized bridge to complete the mapping of the source domain embeddings to the target domain. All these existing CDR methods adopt a centralized architecture and are dedicated to training high-performance cross-domain recommendation models, ignoring that the data collection stage is also included in the real recommendation scenario. Therefore, user privacy is at risk of being leaked [11,12].

Unlike federated single-domain recommendation, which is dedicated to enhancing privacy protection, cross-domain recommendation faces more complex challenges while solving privacy protection, such as more consumption of mobile resources, and we devote to study an light and compatible federated learning paradigm for cross-domain recommendation scenarios. Compared with centralized cross-domain recommendation dedicated to training high-performance cross-domain models, we hope to improve the privacy protection of cross-domain recommendation by studying the federated cross-domain recommendation procedure and get competitive recommendation performance, while enabling real-world resource-constrained mobile devices to train stably.

3   MODEL

3.1   Overview

In cross-domain recommendation, there are a source domain and a target domain. The source domain has user set $\mathcal{U}^s$, item set $\mathcal{V}^s$, and rich rating matrix R^s. The target domain has user set $\mathcal{U}^t$, item set $\mathcal{V}^t$, and sparse rating matrix R^t, and cold-start user set $\mathcal{U}^c$, where the cold-start users have ratings in source domain and no ratings in target domain. We define the overlapping users $\mathcal{U}^o = \mathcal{U}^s \cap \mathcal{U}^t$, where $\mathcal{U}^c \in \mathcal{U}^o$, and $\mathcal{V}^s$ and $\mathcal{V}^t$ are non-overlapping. Important notations are shown in Table 1.

Table 1. Important notations

Symbol	Definition
$*^s$ and $*^t$	The notations of source domain and target domain
k_c	Dimension of shared item embedding
k_p	Dimension of private item embedding
m, n	Number of users and items
D_i	Local data for u_i
$\mathcal{U}^o$	Overlapping user sets for source and target domains
$\mathcal{U}^c$	Cold-start user set of target domain
$\mathcal{U}^{train}$	Train users in overlapping users
$V^c \in \mathbb{R}^{n \times k_c}$	Common item embedding matrix
$V^p \in \mathbb{R}^{k_c \times k_p}$	Private item embedding matrix
U^*, V^*	User and item embedding matrix
$V_{u_i}^*$	Private item embedding matrix for user i
$Server\_pt_{paras}$	Server-side parameters in pretrain stage
$Server\_mp_{paras}$	Server-side parameters in mapping stage
$Device_{paras}$	Device-side parameters
u_i, v_j	Embedding of user i and item j
$R \in \mathbb{R}^{m \times n}$	User-item rating matrix
$r_{ij} \in R$	The rating of user u_i on item v_j
$\hat{r}_{ij}$	The predicted rating of user u_i on item v_j
g_ϕ	Meta-network
f_θ	Mapping-network

Our goal is to accurately recommend items for $\mathcal{U}^c$. Our approach is to model the relationship between the embeddings of $\mathcal{U}^o$ in the source and target domains, and then use the trained model to transfer the embeddings of $\mathcal{U}^c$ from the source domain to the target domain and finally complete the recommendation.

3.2   Build MetaEM

Before introducing the design of each module of MetaEM in detail, we first introduce how to use MetaEM to build a federated recommendation system between distributed mobile devices and cloud servers. The overview of MetaEM is shown in Fig. 1.

In aspect of module deployment, MetaEM is divided into MF module, meta-network module, mapping module and prediction module. In particular, we deploy the meta-network module, mapping module and MF module on the server side. The prediction module is deployed on mobile devices.

In the view of training stage. The modules and processes included in each stage are as follows:

(1) Pretrain stage. Both the source domain and the target domain need pre-train stage. The pretrain stage includes the MF module, the Meta module and the Prediction module. Server-side trainable parameters include: user embedding matrix, meta network, and MLP_{user}, called $Server\_pt_{paras}$. The trainable parameters on the mobile device side is MLP_{item}, called $Device_{paras}$. Taking the source domain as an example, the pretrain process of the target domain is similar to that of the source domain. In the training procedure, the server first initializes $Server\_pt_{paras}$, and then each mobile device downloads the latest output of $V^c, V_{u_i^p}$ and MLP_{user}, then the mobile device uses its local ratings data to calculate the gradients of $Server\_pt_{paras}$ and update $Device_{paras}$, then the server aggregates the gradients from all devices to update $Server\_pt_{paras}$ to complete a round of training. Servers and mobile devices continue to train until the loss stabilizes. When the pre-training phase is completed, the parameters of both the MF module, Meta module, MLP_{user} and MLP_{item} are fixed.

(2) Mapping stage. The Mapping stage is performed in the target domain. MLP_{user} firstly takes the train user's embedding in the source domain as input, and then the mapping network accepts the output of MLP_{user} as input, and outputs the predicted user's embedding in the target domain. The predicted embedding is used for rating prediction in the Prediction module. When the mapping phase is completed, the mapping network parameters are fixed. So far, all trainable parameters of MetaEM are trained.

(3) Cold-start stage. The cold-start stage generates accurate predicted ratings for cold-start users of the target domain. The scoring generation process is similar to the mapping stage. The cold-start user's embedding in the source domain is used as input, and the transformed embedding is generated through MLP_{user} and Mapping network. Then each mobile device downloads the predicted embedding and uses the local its Prediction module generates predicted ratings.

MetaEM can protect user privacy by saving user private data locally on the device. Typically, the strength of privacy protection depends on the content of the user gradient. MetaEM achieves a trade-off between privacy protection and recommendation performance. It deploys the module with the most model parameters on the server side, while the mobile device side only needs to deploy the rating prediction module with the least amount of parameters.

In the following sections, we introduce the implementation detail and technical process of each stage module of MetaEM.

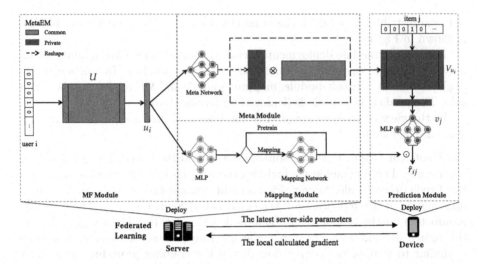

Fig. 1. An overview of MetaEM. It consists of four modules. The MF module generates user embeddings and common item embeddings, the Meta module generates private item embeddings for each user, the Mapping module transforms user embeddings from the source domain to the target domain, and the Prediction module is used to predict rating. The MF and Meta modules are deployed on the server (source and target) side, specifically, the Mapping module is deployed on the target server side, and the Prediction module is deployed on the mobile device side.

3.3 Pretrain Stage

Both the source and target domains need to obtain user and item embeddings information in the pretrain stage. The pretrain stage involves the MF, Meta and prediction modules, and the three modules cooperate to complete the entire pretrain process. The following subsections describe the design of each module in detail.

Matrix Factorization. The traditional matrix factorization algorithm decomposes the user rating matrix R into a user embedding matrix and an item embedding matrix, as shown in Eq. 1. R represents the rating matrix of $m \times n$, k is the dimension of the embedding, U represents the user embedding matrix of $k \times m$, where u_i represents the embedding of the user i. V represents the item embedding matrix of $k \times n$, where v_j represents the embedding of the item j. However, when the number of items is large, the scale of the item embedding matrix V will be very large. In the federated environment, the mobile devices need to continuously download the V and upload the gradient of the V, resulting in a serious communication load on the mobile device.

$$L = \min_{U,V} \left(\sum_i \sum_j \|I_{ij} \cdot \left(R_{ij} - u_i^T v_j\right)\|_F^2 \right) \tag{1}$$

To solve this problem, we propose to decompose the item embedding matrix into the product of the private item embedding matrix V^p and the common item embedding matrix V^c. The V^p is generated by a meta-network for each user. When V^c and V^p are transmitted to the mobile device, the amount of parameters is greatly reduced, thereby alleviating the communication load of the mobile device during the training process, as shown in Eq. 2, where $V_{u_i}^p$ denotes the private item embedding matrix of user i, V^c represents the common item embedding matrix shared by all users. Compared to directly generating V, which needs $O(k_s \times n)$ parameters, the MetaEM needs $O(k_s \times k_p + k_p \times n)$ parameters which $k_p < k_s$ and obviously reduces the item related parameters.

$$V_{u_i} = V^s \otimes V_{u_i}^p \tag{2}$$

Meta Recommemder Module. The meta-network takes the embedding of user i in source domain as input, and the outputs $V_{u_i}^p$. The definition of the meta-network is shown in Eq. 3, where $g(\cdot)$ is the meta-network, its parameter is ϕ, the input is the embedding of the user u_i, and the output dimension is $k_p \times k_s$ vector w_{u_i}, which is then reshaped into matrix $V_i^p \in \mathbb{R}^{k_c \times k_p}$.

$$w_{u_i} = g(u_i; \phi) \tag{3}$$

We define the meta-network as a multi-layer perceptron (MLP), where l represents the number of layers of the MLP, W_l and b_l are the weights and biases of the l layer, respectively.

$$h_1 = ReLU(W_1 u_i + b_1),$$

$$\dots$$

$$h_l = ReLU(W_l h_{l-1} + b_l),$$

$$h_{l+1} = ReLU(W_{l+1} h_l + b_{l+1}) \tag{4}$$

Prediction Module. We generate the prediction model for each user, and define the prediction model as MLP_{user} and MLP_{item}, which are used to represent the nonlinear relationship between user embeddings and item embeddings, respectively. So we need to generate weights and biases for each layer. For the number of layers l, the weights and biases for this layer are $W_l^u \in \mathbb{R}^{f_{out} \times f_{in}}$ and $b_l^u \in \mathbb{R}^{f_{out}}$, where f_{in} represents the number of input layer parameters, f_{out} represents the number of output layer parameters. The outputs of MLP_{user} and MLP_{item} are calculated by Eqs. 5 and 6, respectively, and where l represents the number of layers, W_l and b_l are the weights and biases, u_i represents the embedding of user i, $\hat{u}_i$ represents the output of MLP_{user}, $V_{u_i,j}$ represents the embedding of item j, as shown in Eq. 2, and $\hat{v}_j$ represents the output of MLP_{item}.

$$h_1 = ReLU(W_1 u_i + b_1),$$

$$\dots$$

$$h_l = ReLU(W_l h_{l-1} + b_l),$$

$$\hat{U}_i = ReLU(W_{l+1} h_l + b_{l+1}) \tag{5}$$

$$h_1 = ReLU(W_1 V_{u_{i,j}} + b_1),$$

$$\ldots$$

$$h_l = ReLU(W_l h_{l-1} + b_l),$$

$$\hat{v}_j = ReLU(W_{l+1} h_l + b_{l+1})$$

(6)

Then, we use the dot product of $\hat{U}_i$ and $\hat{V}_{u_{i,j}}$ as the predicted score for user u_i to item v_j, as shown in Eq. 7.

$$\hat{r}_{ij} = \hat{u}_i \odot \hat{v}_j$$

(7)

Loss. In order to learn the pretrain stage of MetaEM, we formulate the RP task as a regression problem and the loss function is defined as:

$$L_{rp} = \frac{1}{D_{train}} \sum_{r_{i,j} \in D_{train}} (r_{i,j} - \hat{r}_{i,j})^2$$

(8)

To avoid overfitting, we add the $L2$ regularization term:

$$L_{reg} = \frac{1}{2} \|\Theta\|_2^2,$$

(9)

where Θ represents all the trainable parameters in the pretrain stage, including the user embeddings and item embeddings, the parameters of the meta network and the parameters of the prediction model.

The final loss L is a linear combination of L_{rp} and L_{reg}:

$$L = L_{rp} + \lambda L_{reg},$$

(10)

where λ is the weight of L_{reg}. The whole procedure of pretrain stage can be efficiently trained using back propagation with federated learning on distributed mobile devices. The whole procedure of pretrain stage is shown in Algorithm 1.

3.4 Mapping Stage

The mapping stage is carried out in the target domain. After the pretrain of the source and target domains, the embedding sets of users and items can be obtained { $U^s, V^{cs}, g_\phi^s, U^t, V^{ct}, g_\phi^t$}, contains the overlapped user and all item embeddings and meta-learners for the source and target domains. We use a MLP to capture the nonlinear relationship between source domain embeddings and target domain embeddings. In particular, we capture the relations between user embeddings transformed by MLP_{user}, as this can be conveniently used directly for recommendation tasks. The source domain server needs to share the embeddings of $\mathcal{U}^{train}$ to the target domain. The parameters of the mapping model are described as $Server\_mp_{paras} = \theta$. The mapping model is defined as follows:

$$\hat{u}_i^t = f_i(MLP_{user}(u_i^s); \theta)$$

(11)

Algorithm 1. Pretrain stage

Input: The user set $\mathcal{U}$, for user i, his local data D_i stored in his device; † means the code is executed in the server.

Output: $Server\_pt_{paras}$, $Device_{paras}$.

1: Initialize U, V^c, ϕ, MLP_{user} randomly in the server; Initialize MLP_{item} randomly in user i' device.
2: **while** not convergent **do**
3:    Sample a batch user S from $\mathcal{U}$.
4:    **for** user i in S **do**
5:       Calculate V^p based on g_ϕ;
6:       Download V^p, V^c from server; †
7:       Calculate the gradient of $Server\_pt_{paras}$ based on D_i; †
8:       Upload the gradient of $Server\_pt_{paras}$ to the server; †
9:       Update $Device_{paras}$ based on D_{u_i}; †
10:   **end for**
11:   Accumulate the gradient of $Server\_pt_{paras}$ gathered from S.
12:   Update $Server\_pt_{paras}$ based on the accumulated gradient.
13: **end while**
14: **for** user i in $\mathcal{U}^o$ **do**
15:   Calculate V^p based on g_ϕ;
16:   Deploy latest V^c, V^p in his device; †
17: **end for**

where the input to the mapping model is the output of MLP_{user}, $\hat{u}_i^t$ represents the transformed result of the embedding u_i^s.

To train the mapping model, we can optimize the distance between the input and output embeddings:

$$L = \sum_{user \in \mathcal{U}^{train}} \|\hat{u}_i^t - MLP_{user}(u_i^t)\|^2, \qquad (12)$$

This optimization strategy is called distance-oriented, making $\hat{u}_i^t$ as close as possible to u_i^t.

However, since some users of the target domain have very few ratings, their embeddings may be unreasonable and inaccurate. Learning towards this inaccurate embeddings will adds negative impact to the mapping. Therefore, we adopt a task-oriented optimization strategy to directly use the final predicted rating as the optimization objective. The task-oriented loss function is defined as follows:

$$\hat{r}_{i,j} = \hat{u}_i^t \odot MLP_{item}(V_{u_i,j}) \qquad (13)$$

$$L = \sum_{user \in D_{train}} (r_{i,j} - \hat{r}_{i,j})^2 + \lambda \frac{1}{2}\|\Theta\|_2^2 \qquad (14)$$

where θ represents the parameters of the mapping model, λ represents the weight of the regularization term.

Compared with distance-oriented optimization, task-oriented can eliminate the influence of unreasonable user embedding, and have more training samples. The number of samples in the distance-oriented optimization is $|m|$, the number of samples in the task-oriented optimization is $|m \times n|$. The whole framework of cross-domain stage can be efficiently trained using back propagation with federated learning on distributed mobile devices. The whole procedure of mapping stage is shown in Algorithm 2.

Algorithm 2. Mapping stage

Input: The user set $\mathcal{U}^{train}$; For user i, his local data D_i^t and V^{ct}, V^p are stored in his device; † means the code is executed in the source App; ‡ means the code is executed in the target App.

Output: $Server\_mp_{paras}$

1: Initialize $Server\_mp_{paras}$ randomly in the target server.
2: **while** not convergent **do**
3:     Sample a batch user S from $\mathcal{U}^o$.
4:     **for** user i in S **do**
5:         Calculate the gradient of $Server\_mp_{paras}$ based D_i^t and Prediction module; ‡
6:         Upload the gradient of $Server\_mp_{paras}$ to the target server; ‡
7:     **end for**
8:     Accumulate the gradients of $Server\_mp_{paras}$ gathered from S.
9:     Update $Server\_mp_{paras}$ based on the accumulated gradients.
10: **end while**

3.5   Cold-Start Stage

Since cold-start users do not have accurate embeddings in the target domain, we cannot recommend items of interest for them accurately. However, these users have rich ratings in the source domain, and the behavior of the same user in the source domain and the target domain is related. Based on this assumption, we can generate reasonable embedding for each cold-start user in the target domain, thus recommending items for them based on locally deployed Prediction module. Given the trained mapping model f_θ and embedding u_i^s, we can get the embedding of user in the target domain as shown in Eq. 11. Then, we can use the trained RP model to recommend items of interest to cold-start users, as shown in Eq. 14.

4   Experiments

We define three cross-domain tasks using the real-world Amazon review dataset and conduct sufficient experiments to answer the following questions:

- **Q1:** How does MetaEM perform in cold-start users comparing to the baseline cross-domain models?
- **Q2:** What is the contribution of meta-learner for the performance improvement?
- **Q3:** How does MetaEM perform in more practical scenarios of real-world recommendation?

4.1 Datasets

Following the existing methods [20,22], we adopted the large Amazon review dataset[1] for experiments. Specially, we use the Amazon-5scores dataset where the rating from 1 to 5.

Following [20,22], we choose three popular categories in total: Movie, Music and Book. We define three CDR tasks as Task 1: Movie → Music, Task 2: Book → Movie, and Task 3: Book → Music. The detailed statistics of the three datasets are shown in Table 2. In each CDR task, the number of ratings in the source domain is much larger than that in the target domain. There are many existing works that use only a small subset of the Amazon dataset, we use the entire dataset for experiments.

Table 2. Statistics about Amazon Dataset

CDR tasks	Domain		Item		User			Rating	
	Source	Target	Source	Target	Overlap	Source	Target	Source	Target
Task1	Movie	Music	5,0052	6,4443	1,8031	12,3960	7,6258	169,7533	109,7592
Task2	Book	Movie	36,7982	5,0052	3,7388	60,3668	12,3960	889,8041	169,7533
Task3	Book	Music	36,7982	6,4443	1,6738	60,3668	7,5258	889,8041	109,7592

4.2 Implementation Details

We use the Pytorch to implement our MetaEM and baselines. For each method, we use Adam optimizer and the initial learning rate are tuned within 0.0001, 0.001, 0.01, and set the regularization weight to 0.0001. Following [13,22], for all methods, We randomly select a fraction of overlapping users in the target domain and as test users, the other overlapping users are train users. We set the proportions of test users β as 20%, 50%, 80%. For all models, we set the batch size as 256. For all baselines, We set the dimension of user embeddings and item embeddings as 32. In addition, for each method, we report the mean results over ten random runs.

For MetaEM, we set the dimension of pravite item embeddings as 8 and common item embeddings as 32. The meta-network, mapping model and RP

---

[1] http://jmcauley.ucsd.edu/data/amazon.

model are defined as a three-layer network with hidden units 128. We use the *ReLU* function as the activation function. During training, we initialize all user embeddings and common item embeddings randomly with a normal distribution.

In our experiments, We implement CMF based on released code of the author[2]. We implement EMCDR based on released code of the author[3]. We implement PTUPCDR based on released code of the author[4]. If this paper is accepted, we will publish the codes of DCDCSR, SSCDR and MetaEM at github.

4.3 Baselines

Therefore, MetaEM belongs to the mapping-based method, so for fairness, we mainly choose the following methods as the baselines for comparison.

- TGT: TGT indicates that the target domain only uses its own data to complete MF training, which belongs to single-domain recommendation.
- CMF [16]: CMF achieves knowledge integration across multiple domains by connecting user rating matrices from multiple domains and sharing overlapped user embeddings across domains.
- DCDCSR [18]: This model continues the idea of EMCDR, but the learned mapping function is the mapping function from the target domain to the standard domain: the standard domain is a embedding space that fuses the source domain and the target domain together.
- SSCDR [6]: This model transforms the entire model into a semi-supervised learning process by designing an unsupervised loss function: it can utilize the rich non-overlapping entity data in the field, making the learned mapping function more robust and improving the recommendation performance.
- EMCDR [13]: EMCDR use MLP to capture the nonlinear mapping function between source domain and target domain, and propose only the users with sufficient data should be used to learn the mapping model, thus guaranteeing its effectiveness.
- PTUPCDR [22]. PTUPCDR uses a meta-learner to model a personalized preference bridge with user traits extracted from the user's interaction history in the source domain as input. Then use the personalized bridge to complete the mapping of the source domain embeddings to the target domain. This method is one the state-of-art method for cross-domain recommendation.

4.4 Evaluate Metrics

We adopt the recommendation scenario of explicit feedback of predicted ratings. We choose Root Mean Square Error (RMSE) and Evaluation Absolute Error

---

[2] https://github.com/VincentLiu3/CMF.
[3] https://github.com/masonmsh/EMCDR_PyTorch.
[4] https://github.com/easezyc/WSDM2022-PTUPCDR.

(MAE) as our evaluation metrics, as follows:

$$MAE = \frac{1}{m} \sum_{i=1}^{m} |(y_i - \hat{y}_i)|$$

$$RMSE = \sqrt{\frac{1}{m} \sum_{i=1}^{m} (y_i - \hat{y}_i)^2}$$

(15)

4.5 Experimental Results and Analysis

Cold-Start Experiments (Q1). This section presents the experimental results and analyzes the performance of MetaEM in cold-start scenario in details. We evaluate the effectiveness of MetaEM and the existing methods [6,13,16,18,22] on three cold-start scenarios under different values of β. The experiments are shown in Table 3 and the best result is marked with *. From the experimental results, we have the following findings:

(1) TGT is a single-domain recommendation model that only uses data from its own domain for training. Since cold-start users do not have enough ratings, their embedding quality is unsatisfactory. The recommended performance of TGT is unsatisfying. Compared with TGT, other cross-domain recommendation models use the rich data of the source domain to enrich the information of the target domain, so the cold-start users of the target domain can have better recommendation results. Therefore, the ability of single-domain recommendation to solve the cold-start problem is limited, and cross-domain recommendation performs better than single-domain recommendation in cold-start scenarios.

(2) CMF achieves knowledge integration across multiple domains by connecting user rating matrixcs from multiple domains and sharing overlapped user embeddings across domains. But it ignores that the embedding space between domains is different, and there is the problem of domain shift. So the recommendation result of CMF is better than that of single domain recommendation. On the contrary, the mapping-based models transform the embedding from source domain to the target domain, that can alleviates the influence of domain shift. Therefore, the way of cross-domain recommendation is very important for the recommendation results.

(3) EMCDR trains a mapping model that maps source-domain embeddings to target-domain, making full use of source-domain information to improve target-domain recommendation performance. So EMCDR outperform TGT and CMF. But EMCDR trains a common mapping model for all overlapping users, ignoring personalization among users. PTUPCDR trains a personalized mapping model for each overlapping user, and achieves better recommendation results than EMCDR. Therefore, we need to consider the differences between users when recommending.

(4) We find that MetaEM outperforms the best baseline model(PTUPCDR) in most scenarios, demonstrating the effectiveness of MetaEM on the cold-start problem. Unlike PTUPCDR, which trains a private mapping model for each user, MetaEM trains private item embeddings for each user. The private item matrix can represent the personalization of user interests. Consistent with PTUPCDR, MetaEM transfers the user embeddings from the source domain to the target domain. The difference is that in the cold-start phase, each cold-start user in the target domain uses the transferred embeddings to generate his private item matrix, getting better personalized recommendation results than PTUPCDR. In general, MetaEM belongs to personalization of interests, while PTUPCDR belongs to personalization of embedding mapping. Therefore, private item embeddings can perform better than private mapping models on the cold start problem.

Table 3. Experiment results (MAE & RMSE) for CDR tasks (the best result is marked with *)

	β	Metric	TGT	CMF	DCDCSR	SSCDR	EMCDR	PTUPCDR	MetaEM
Task1	20%	MAE	4.4765	1.5305	1.4869	1.3217	1.2364	1.1365	0.8138*
		RMSE	5.1374	2.0214	1.9052	1.6754	1.5574	1.1974	1.1226*
	50%	MAE	4.4886	1.6698	1.8023	1.3799	1.3201	1.2698	0.8394*
		RMSE	5.1985	2.2065	2.3341	1.7421	1.6568	1.6284	1.1359*
	80%	MAE	4.5095	2.4155	2.7021	1.5001	1.5009	1.4012	0.9373*
		RMSE	5.1845	3.0856	3.3069	1.9202	1.8765	1.8322	1.2051*
Task2	20%	MAE	4.1801	1.3622	1.4032	1.2399	1.1211	0.9972	0.8948*
		RMSE	4.7533	1.7898	1.7465	1.6549	1.4201	1.3319	1.1918*
	50%	MAE	4.2212	1.5765	1.6687	1.2136	1.1987	1.0874	0.9507*
		RMSE	4.8012	2.0598	2.0679	1.5618	1.5031	1.4232	1.2028*
	80%	MAE	4.2015	2.1487	2.3556	1.3088	1.3064	1.2012	1.1215*
		RMSE	4.8256	2.6508	2.7684	1.6979	1.6854	1.6031	1.4252*
Task3	20%	MAE	4.4812	1.8919	1.8319	1.5482	1.3602	1.2397	0.9897*
		RMSE	5.1564	2.3987	2.2916	1.9269	1.7015	1.6089	1.4116*
	50%	MAE	4.5179	2.1387	2.1862	1.4697	1.4697	1.3649	1.2299*
		RMSE	5.1849	2.7348	2.6597	1.8379	1.8006	1.7349	1.7335*
	80%	MAE	4.5316	3.0132	3.1467	1.6418	1.7095	1.5882	1.4468*
		RMSE	5.2465	3.7016	3.5947	2.1487	2.0948	2.0732	1.9648*

Explanation of the Performance Improvement (Q2). In this section, we conduct extensive experiments and analyze the contribution of private item embeddings, thereby explaining the improvement brought by MetaEM, and answer Q2.

We performed a visualization of target embeddings and transformed embeddings. We analyze the distribution of target embeddings and transformation embeddings in the embedding space. We further explore why MetaEM performs better than PTUPCDR from the embedding distribution, then demonstrate the capability of meta-network to generate private item embedding matrix for each user.

We use t-SNE [4] to visualize user embeddings learned by MetaEM and PTUPCDR on Task1 with $\beta = 0.2$. Figure 2(a) and 2(b) denote the embeddings of training and test users by PTUPCDR. Figure 2(c) and 2(d) denote the embeddings of trianing and test users by MetaEM. To be fair, we set the training and testing users for the MetaEM and PTUPCDR user visualizations to be the same. We selected 256 users from training users and test users for visualization, respectively. The red points represent the target embeddings (ground trouth) taken from target domain, while the green points denote the transformed embeddings.

Ideally, the t-SNE distribution of the transformed embeddings should be close to the target embeddings. From Fig. 2(a) and 2(b), We can see that there is a certain shift in the distributions of target embeddings and transformation embeddings. This shows that the recommendation results of PTUPCDR are not ideal. The main reason is that PTUPCDR multiplies the transformed embedding and item embedding to get the predicted score. This way is essentially a non-personalized matrix factorization. Therefore, PTUPCDR only realizes personalized transformation, but does not realize personalized recommendation.

As shown in Fig. 2(c) and 2(d), we can find that the distribution of transformed embeddings by MetaEM can better fit the target embeddings distribution, demonstrating the capacity of the meta-network in MetaEM. The main reason is that the meta-network generates private item embeddings for each user, and the private item embeddings can represent the user's personalized preferences for items. After the cold-start user obtains the transformed embedding, the meta-network takes the transformed embedding as input, and generates the user's private item embeddings, so as to obtain the personalized preferences of cold-start users in the target domain. Therefore, we can recommend personalized items for cold-start users of the target domain, which could be the fundamental reason why MetaEM could achieve better overall performance.

Generalization Experiments Q(3). In this section, we perform extensive experiments to verify the compatibility of MetaEM on more complicated models.

Mapping-based cross-domain models are devoted to improving the quality of mapping models, and they mostly use MF to extract user and item embeddings. However, MF does not perform well for large-scale real-world recommendation. Therefore, we investigate the compatibility of MetaEM on two complicated models: GMF [2] and DNN [3]. For comparison, we follow [22], applying GMF and DNN on EMCDR and PTUPCDR. Unlike MF, which uses the vector inner product as the prediction, GMF uses the dot product of the user latent vector and the item latent vector as the output. DNN is a two-tower model. For GMF, the mapping function directly transforms the user embeddings of source domain. For DNN, the mapping function transforms the output of the user tower. We conduct generalization experiments on Task 1 with $\beta = 20\%$.

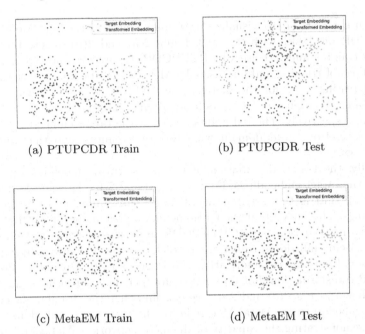

Fig. 2. The t-SNE visualization of MetaEM and PTUPCDR. We set the scenario as Task 1 and $\beta = 0.2$.

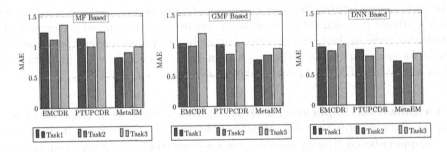

Fig. 3. Generalization experiments: using three base models MF, GMF, DNN for EMCDR, PTUPCDR and MetaEM, respectively. We set the scenario as Task 1 and $\beta = 0.2$

The generalization experiment results are shown in Fig. 3. We have several important observations: (1) The mapping-based cross-domain recommendation method is compatible with different embedding extraction models. EMCDR, PTUPCDR and MetaEM all significantly improve the recommendation performance on the target domain on GMF and DNN. Since DNN can extract more accurate embeddings than GMF, the improvement on DNN is higher than that of GMF, indicating that the quality of embedding can determine the recommendation performance of cross-domain models. (2) MetaEM has satisfying performance on different embedding models, which shows that MetaEM has good compatibility with complicated models in large-scale real-word recommendation. Furthermore, the recommendation performance of MetaEM can constantly better than EMCDR and PTUPCDR when using the same embedding model.

5 Conclusion

The existing cross-domain recommendation models lack the protection of user privacy, and in the federated learning environment, federated cross-domain recommendation will bring communication load to mobile devices. To address the challenge of limited mobile device resources in federated cross-domain recommendation, we propose a light federated cross-domain recommendation model MetaEM based on embedding mapping. MetaEM is divided into pretrain stage, mapping stage and cold-start stage. Each stage follows the federated learning paradigm. In particular, we deploy a meta-learner on the server. It generates a private small-scale item embedding matrix for each user, thus reducing the communication load on mobile devices. To learn the mapping model stably, we employ a task-oriented optimization method. Experimental results on real-world datasets show that MetaEM has satisfying recommendation performance while well protecting user privacy data. In addition, MetmEM has well compatibility in different embedding models. MetaEM can play an important role in cross-domain recommendation c with limited mobile resources and a large number of items.

Acknowledgement. This work is supported by National Natural Science Foundation of China (62172155, 62072465).

References

1. Ammad-Ud-Din, M., et al.: Federated collaborative filtering for privacy-preserving personalized recommendation system. arXiv preprint arXiv:1901.09888 (2019)
2. Böhm, J., Niell, A., Tregoning, P., Schuh, H.: Global mapping function (GMF): a new empirical mapping function based on numerical weather model data. Geophys. Res. Lett. **33**(7) (2006)
3. Covington, P., Adams, J., Sargin, E.: Deep neural networks for youtube recommendations. In: Proceedings of the 10th ACM Conference on Recommender Systems, pp. 191–198 (2016)
4. Donahue, J., et al.: DeCAF: a deep convolutional activation feature for generic visual recognition. In: International Conference on Machine Learning, pp. 647–655. PMLR (2014)
5. Hazrati, N., Shams, B., Haratizadeh, S.: Entity representation for pairwise collaborative ranking using restricted Boltzmann machine. Expert Syst. Appl. **116**, 161–171 (2019)
6. Kang, S., Hwang, J., Lee, D., Yu, H.: Semi-supervised learning for cross-domain recommendation to cold-start users. In: Proceedings of the 28th ACM International Conference on Information and Knowledge Management, pp. 1563–1572 (2019)
7. Kazama, M., Varga, I.: Cross domain recommendation using vector space transfer learning. In: RecSys Posters. Citeseer (2016)

8. Liang, F., Pan, W., Ming, Z.: FedRec++: lossless federated recommendation with explicit feedback. In: Proceedings of the AAAI Conference on Artificial Intelligence, vol. 35, pp. 4224–4231 (2021)

9. Lin, G., Liang, F., Pan, W., Ming, Z.: FedRec: federated recommendation with explicit feedback. IEEE Intell. Syst. **36**(5), 21–30 (2020)

10. Lin, Y., et al.: Meta matrix factorization for federated rating predictions. In: Proceedings of the 43rd International ACM SIGIR Conference on Research and Development in Information Retrieval, pp. 981–990 (2020)

11. Liu, J., Liu, X., Yang, Y., Wang, S., Zhou, S.: Hierarchical multiple kernel clustering. In: Thirty-Fifth AAAI Conference on Artificial Intelligence, AAAI, pp. 2–9 (2021)

12. Liu, X., et al.: One pass late fusion multi-view clustering. In: International Conference on Machine Learning, pp. 6850–6859. PMLR (2021)

13. Man, T., Shen, H., Jin, X., Cheng, X.: Cross-domain recommendation: an embedding and mapping approach. In: IJCAI, vol. 17, pp. 2464–2470 (2017)

14. Mashhadi, M.B., Shlezinger, N., Eldar, Y.C., Gunduz, D.: FedRec: federated learning of universal receivers over fading channels (2020)

15. Muhammad, K., et al.: FedFast: going beyond average for faster training of federated recommender systems. In: Proceedings of the 26th ACM SIGKDD International Conference on Knowledge Discovery & Data Mining, pp. 1234–1242 (2020)

16. Singh, A.P., Gordon, G.J.: Relational learning via collective matrix factorization. In: Proceedings of the 14th ACM SIGKDD International Conference on Knowledge Discovery and Data Mining, pp. 650–658 (2008)

17. Zhang, Y., Cao, B., Yeung, D.Y.: Multi-domain collaborative filtering. arXiv preprint arXiv:1203.3535 (2012)

18. Zhu, F., Wang, Y., Chen, C., Liu, G., Orgun, M., Wu, J.: A deep framework for cross-domain and cross-system recommendations. arXiv preprint arXiv:2009.06215 (2020)

19. Zhu, F., Wang, Y., Chen, C., Liu, G., Zheng, X.: A graphical and attentional framework for dual-target cross-domain recommendation. In: IJCAI, pp. 3001–3008 (2020)

20. Zhu, Y., et al.: Transfer-meta framework for cross-domain recommendation to cold-start users. In: Proceedings of the 44th International ACM SIGIR Conference on Research and Development in Information Retrieval, pp. 1813–1817 (2021)

21. Zhu, Y., et al.: Transfer-meta framework for cross-domain recommendation to cold-start users, pp. 1813–1817. Association for Computing Machinery, New York (2021). https://doi.org/10.1145/3404835.3463010

22. Zhu, Y., et al.: Personalized transfer of user preferences for cross-domain recommendation. In: Proceedings of the Fifteenth ACM International Conference on Web Search and Data Mining, pp. 1507–1515 (2022)

A Reliable Service Function Chain Orchestration Method Based on Federated Reinforcement Learning

Zhiwen Xiao$^{(\boxtimes)}$ ⓘ, Tao Tao, Zhuo Chen, Meng Yang, Jing Shang, Zhihui Wu, and Zhiwei Guo

China Mobile Information Technology Center, Beijing 100033, China
xiaozhiwen@chinamobile.com
http://it.10086.cn

Abstract. The novel cloud-edge collaborative computing architecture can provide more efficient and intelligent services close to users. Reliable service function chain orchestration among datacenters is critical to ensuring computing efficiency. In this study, a service orchestration model is proposed to improve the reliability while reducing cost. The solution is a federated reinforcement learning framework that shares decision-making experiences to obtain reliable and effective service orchestration results between different datacenter environments. The simulation results demonstrate that the proposed orchestration method reaches convergence faster and has a significant performance in terms of improving service reliability.

Keywords: Service function chain · Cloud-edge collaborative computing · Federated reinforcement learning · Reliability

1 Introduction

With the rapid development of Internet of Things and its corresponding online applications, analyzing large volumes of geographically distributed data is a critical issue for data analysts and real-time application decision-making. To tackle this issue, the computing mode has gradually changed from cloud-centric to cloud-edge collaboration to cater to real-time data processing requirements. Cloud service providers deploy multiple edge datacenters in multiple locations [1]. The key to provide stable computing services is that the service function chain formed by geo-distributed datacenters is reliable. Subsequently, network function virtualization (NFV) is proposed to virtualize the large-scale data tasks as VNF instances that can run on geo-distributed datacenters to provide users with quick access to their services [2].

Meanwhile, the orchestration based on NFV brings additional reliability problems [3,4]. Because it is necessary to introduce more complex functions on the basis of traditional physical nodes to support node virtualization. However,

H. Gao et al. (Eds.): CollaborateCom 2022, LNICST 460, pp. 173–189, 2022.
https://doi.org/10.1007/978-3-031-24383-7_10

due to the objective existence of software defects and other factors, virtual nodes built on reliable physical nodes may themselves be faulty. Existing research usually solves the reliability problem through a backup strategy [5] and network protection strategy [3], but it will bring additional and redundant equipment overhead. Considering reliability at the beginning of service deployment is a better solution. Therefore, service orchestration not only needs to consider the minimization of the orchestration overhead but also the reliability of the service. This paper establishes the orchestration model to jointly optimize the cost and service reliability.

To solve optimization and obtain service function chain orchestration decision, the reinforcement learning method is widely used [6–8]. Because of its dynamic decision-making adaptability, it can contribute to the reliability of the service function chain. However, the reinforcement learning model requires intensive interaction with network environment to learn an effective strategy. The reinforcement learning model in a single datacenter is trained based on the local data to learn local experience. The independent model only maintains good performance in the specific service and network environment, and cannot adapt to the environment of multiple datacenters. For geo-distribution datacenters in different regions, their user groups and user services may slightly overlap. At the same time, due to different services, there are also differences in the feature spaces of the datasets between the two datacenters [10,11]. Besides, the business data of different datacenters may be under the jurisdiction of different companies, and it is difficult to collect all business data to train the overall model. Therefore, service orchestration across datacenters cannot be limited to local data only. The non-interoperable datacenters are hard to share decision-making experiences leads to the reinforcement learning model must collect new training samples and retrain the neural network so that the model can converge when building a service chain in a new datacenter [9]. This process leads to slow convergence and poor model performance of the reinforcement learning, making it difficult to ensure the effect of service orchestration for geo-distributed datacenters.

It therefore remains necessary to address the aforementioned challenges to improve the convergence efficiency and stability of reinforcement learning model for reliable service orchestration in geo-distributed datacenters. Federated learning [12] provides a framework for collaborative orchestration for datacenters to solve the problem of non-sharing of experience between independent models. Federated learning aggregates the orchestration experience of multiple data centers, and delivers the aggregated model to each data center. By integrating the training parameters of reinforcement learning in each datacenter environment, optimal service orchestration decisions can be obtained.

The main contribution of this paper is as follows: We propose a service function chain orchestration method to jointly optimize cost and the service reliability for geo-distributed datacenters in the cloud-edge collaborative computing architecture. First, for the reliability assurance of service function chain orchestration in multiple datacenters, we model service function chain orchestration problem with both cost function and reliability assessment of service function chain. Then, for cross-regional multi-datacenter scenarios, we introduce a federated reinforcement learning framework to obtain the orchestration decision. This method uses the reinforcement learning model as the training basis and then obtains the federated reinforcement model by fusing the training parameters in different datacenters. The model implemented in the training and new datacenter environments can achieve convergence faster and obtain the optimal decision with better service reliability while reducing cost.

The remainder of this paper is organized as follows: Sect. 2 provides an overview of related work into the service function chain orchestration. Section 3 outlines the federated reinforcement learning model for computing datacenters orchestration. Section 4 describes the simulation experiments and analyzes the performance of the proposed model. In the final section, we provide conclusions and recommendations for further research.

2 Related Work

In terms of service function chain orchestration, existing studies use different methods to solve this problem. Dieye et al. [13] modelled service function chain orchestration as an integer linear programming problem and proposed a cost-effective active VNF placement and linking algorithm. The algorithm can find the optimal number of VNFs and their positions to minimise costs while satisfying QoS. Sang et al. [14] constructed an integer linear programming model to solve the VNF dynamic placement problem. Yang et al. [15] used a path-based integer linear programming model to minimise network energy consumption when solving service orchestration problems. Kar et al. [16] designed a dynamic energy-saving model with M/M/c queuing network and minimum capacity strategy, improving machine utilisation and avoiding frequent changes in machine state. For the placement of service function chains, the authors defined an energy cost optimisation problem constrained by capacity and proposed a heuristic dynamic VNF chain placement solution. Varasteh et al. [17] proposed a fast heuristic framework that can effectively solve the power-aware and delay-constrained VNF placement and routing problems. Troia et al. [6] studied the application of reinforcement learning to perform dynamic SFC quotas in NFV-SDN-enabled metro core optical networks. The authors constructed a reinforcement learning system that optimises SFC quotas in multi-layer networks. Quan et al. [18] applied deep reinforcement learning (DRL) to solve the placement problem of virtual network function-forwarding graphs and developed a simulation platform based on the Mininet and containers to demonstrate the advantages of DRL over existing methods. Pei et al. [19] proposed a VNF placement algorithm (DDQN-VNFPA) based on a double deep Q-network using deep reinforcement learning technology. DDQN obtains the best solution from a considerable solution space, and DDQN-VNFPA places or releases VNF instances (VNFIs) according to threshold-based policies. This algorithm can improve overall network performance.

All researches above, which face single-agent service orchestration schemes, propose various optimization goals. However, when the environment changes and training data is limited, performing high-quality resource orchestration decisions is difficult. Multi-agent service orchestration schemes have also been widely discussed. Shah et al. [7] pointed out that the service function chain orchestration problem under the constraints of IoT systems can be expressed as a Markov decision process (MDP). A multi-agent deep reinforcement learning algorithm can solve the MDP problem, where each agent serves a service function chain. They proposed two Q-networks in the specific implementation. One Q-network solves the service function chain placement problem. It generates virtual agent interactions with the environment to receive accumulated rewards and uses the learned experience to update the policy. The other updates the Q-value by tracking long-term policy change weight. Liu et al. [8] developed a multi-agent reinforcement learning framework that uses an independent learner-based multi-agent Q-learning (IL-based MA-Q) algorithm to solve distributed computing offloading problems in Edge Computing. However, none of these methods considers data security and interfaces protection issues between multiple edge networks.

Federated learning provides a reasonable framework for non-interoperable data in multi-agent collaborative computing. Huang et al. [10] proposed an extensible orchestration method based on federated reinforcement learning, which introduces federated learning into global model training and deep reinforcement learning into local model training to achieve an extensible services function chain. This method works as follows: First, this method divides the entire network into regions and assigns an agent in each region to train a local model of service function chain orchestration. Then, the cloud specifies an initial pre-trained model and sends it to each edge datacenter. Afterwards, each agent trains its local model and reports it to the cloud for global model aggregation through federated learning. Finally, it places the VNF into the network according to the learned policy. However, these federated learning training environments are different regions of the same network. This work is hard to apply in different datacenter environments or a new edge environment under the cloud-edge collaboration mode.

3   Proposed Method

In this section, the design proposal for the service function chain orchestration model is presented. We also describe our federated reinforcement learning framework to show the principle of the reliable computing service orchestration method.

3.1   Service Function Chain Orchestration Model

In order to construct the orchestration of service function chains, we model an orchestration problem. The following definitions are given to describe the orchestration problem of service function chains.

Definition 1. *The physical network $G_p = (V_p, E_p)$ is composed of a set of physical nodes V_p and a set of physical links E_P, with physical nodes $v \in V_p$ and physical links $e \in E_p$. A physical node represents a physical server carrying virtual functions, and a physical link is an actual link between physical nodes.*

Definition 2. *The virtual network $G_v = (V_v, E_v)$ comprises a virtual node set V_v and virtual link set E_v, with virtual node $f \in V_v$ and virtual link $z \in E_v$. The virtual node represents a VNF on the service function chain, and the virtual link represents the logical concatenation relationship between the VNFs.*

Definition 3. *For service $s \in S$, there is resource mapping $g_s = (g_s^V, g_s^E)$. Where S represents the service set, g_s^V represents the mapping $V_v \to V_p$ of virtual node set V_v to physical node set V_p, g_s^E represents the mapping $E_v \to E_p$ of virtual link set E_v to physical link set E_p.*

Definition 4. *$a_{f \to v}$ represents the act of placing virtual node f to physical node v, $a_{f \to v} \in g_s^V$. Similarly, $a_{z \to e}$ represents the act of placing virtual link z to physical link e, $a_{z \to e} \in g_s^E$.*

Definition 5. *$\lambda : \{\lambda_v^f, \lambda_e^z\}$ represents the VNF placement decision. λ_v^f means to execute a decision of $a_{f \to v}$. λ_e^z means to execute a decision of $a_{z \to e}$ The value range of λ is $\{0, 1\}$, 1 means to place on a physical node or link, and 0 means not to place. For $\forall \lambda \in \Pi^s$, Π^s represents a set of policies that map all virtual links on service s to physical links.*

Under the above definition, the service function chain orchestration problem can be expressed as follows: the service in the virtual network needs to find an optimal placement strategy to realize the one-to-one mapping of virtual resources to physical resources. The optimization goal is improving reliability and reducing operating costs. We define the calculation methods of cost and reliability as follows, and give a formalized optimization problem.

$$Cost = \sum_x \sum_f \lambda_v^f \cdot k_x + \sum_z \sum_{x,y} \lambda_e^z \cdot k_z \tag{1}$$

where k_x represents the cost of the unit resource on the node x, and k_z represents the cost of the unit resource on the link z.

The reliability of the service defined as r_s:

$$r_s = \prod_e r_e \cdot \prod_v r_v \tag{2}$$

where r_e represents the reliability of the physical link e and r_v represents the reliability of the physical node v. The reliability assessment process of the above physical links and nodes (r_e and r_v) can refer to [20].

Based on the above analysis, service function chain orchestration problem can be formulated as:

$$\max_\lambda \frac{\beta r_s}{Cost}$$
$$s.t. \sum_z \lambda_e^z \le C_E(t)$$
$$\sum_f \lambda_v^f \le C_V(t) \tag{3}$$
$$\sum_{v \in V_p} a_{f \to v} = 1$$
$$\sum_{e \in E_p} a_{z \to e} = 1$$

where β is an adjustment coefficient which controls the weight of the reliability and cost. The first constraint $\sum_z \lambda_e^z \leq C_E(t)$ is the resource constraint on links, $C_E(t)$ represents the total resources of physical link e at time t. The second constraint $\sum_f \lambda_v^f \leq C_V(t)$ is the resource constraint on nodes, $C_V(t)$ represents the total resources of the physical node v at time t. The third and fourth are constraints on decision variables. In order to simplify the analysis of the orchestration problem, this paper does not consider the backup of resources. At this time, $\sum_{v \in V_p} a_{f \to v} = 1$ means a virtual node can only be mapped to one physical node; meanwhile, $\sum_{e \in E_p} a_{z \to e} = 1$ means a virtual link can only be mapped to one physical link.

After modelling this problem, we build the federated reinforcement learning solution with the optimization goal of improving reliability and reducing operating costs in the next two sections.

3.2 Reinforcement Learning Model in Single Datacenter

The service function chain orchestration process can be split into the sequential placement of VNFs, accompanied by the connection of links. The impact of each VNF placement on the overall service function chain is related to the VNF placed previously. The reinforcement learning model can obtain the optimal policy by calculating the reward of each action, which is suitable for solving the step-by-step orchestration problem of the service function chain.

In order to solve the service function orchestration problem using the reinforcement learning model, several essential parts of the reinforcement learning model need to be defined and analyzed: state, action, reward and target. The target of service orchestration in this study is to improve service reliability. When designing the reward function, the reliability and cost factors of the service need to be considered.

State: $S_t = \{C(t), F_{new}, F_{old}\}$ represents the state at time t, where $C(t)$ represents the occupation of physical resources at time t, F_{new} represents the VNF node to be placed, and F_{old} represents the previously placed VNF node.

Action: $A_t = \{\lambda_t\}$ represents the action at time t, where λ_t represents the placement decision at time t, and λ is defined in Definition 5.

Reward Function: Since the optimization objectives of orchestration are to improve the reliability of services and reduce costs, the reward function is defined by reliability and cost-benefit under resource-constrained. Then, the reward function R is presented by Eq. 4:

$$R = \begin{cases} \beta \cdot \frac{r_z \times 100}{Cost}, & if \sum_z \lambda_e^z \leq C_E(t) \ or \ \sum_f \lambda_v^f \leq C_V(t) \\ -1, & otherwise \end{cases} \tag{4}$$

The objective of reinforcement learning is to find the optimal policy $\pi^*(A_t|O_t)$, which can obtain the maximum the reward from the initial state

O_t, as shown in Eq. 5:

$$\max_{\pi} E[\sum_{t=0}^{H} \gamma^t R(S_t, A_t, S_{t+1})|\pi] \tag{5}$$

In this work, we introduce Q-learning as the basis learner. Because Q-learning is a model-free reinforcement learning method that learns how to find the optimal action selection policy through interaction with the environment. An optimal policy can be found by updating the Q-table, which is the mapping table between the state-action and the estimated future reward. The update process of Q-table $Q(s_t, a_t)$ is presented by Eq. 6:

$$Q(s_t, a_t) \leftarrow Q(s_t, a_t) + \alpha(r_{t+1} + \gamma Q(s_{t+1}, a') - Q(s_t, a_t)) \tag{6}$$

where $a \in \{0, 1\}$ is the learning factor, $\gamma \in \{0, 1\}$ is the discount factor and a' represents the behavior under strategy π. Then the currently selected action is presented by Eq. 7:

$$\pi(s_{t+1}) = \arg \max_{a'} Q(s_{t+1}, a') \tag{7}$$

In order to ensure the generalization function of Q-learning and avoid falling into the local optimum of the result, we generally use the ϵ-greedy method for action selection. The mechanism selects an optional action uniformly and randomly with a small probability ϵ of exploring and selects the current best action according to the above formula with a probability of $1 - \epsilon$.

The reinforcement learning model can obtain the optimal orchestration strategy after training. The limitation of this method is that it relies on a large amount of training experience, and the orchestration scheme cannot learn quickly in a new environment. Therefore, we introduce the federated learning model to realize the sharing of training experience between different datacenter environments.

3.3   Federated Reinforcement Learning Model in Multiple Datacenters

Service function chain orchestration decisions are learned from the interaction of the environment and the agent through reinforcement learning. In the cross-datacenter service orchestration scenario in this paper, a single datacenter has insufficient experience in orchestrating different types of services in different network environments, and needs to rely on the business processing experience of multiple datacenters. However, the business data of different datacenters may be under the jurisdiction of different companies, and it is difficult to collect training. Therefore, it is necessary to use the secure fusion of federated learning to achieve experience sharing and improve the reinforcement learning model proposed in the previous section. This section will introduce the generation, transfer, and correction process of federated reinforcement learning models.

After obtaining the reinforcement learning models of different datacenter environments, a federated reinforcement model is trained through the federated learning framework. The federated learning framework used in this work is shown in Fig. 1. Each participant obtains its reinforcement learning model after local training. Model parameters are stored in a private Q-table, which is a map of state-action and reward in reinforcement learning. Q-table information in different training environments is encrypted and transmitted by homomorphic encryption. After the encrypted results are sent to the aggregation server, model parameters are decrypted and securely aggregated as a federated Q-table. In each iteration, the aggregation server sends the generated federated learning model back to each training environment for updating. With the fusion of local and federal model parameters, multiple datacenters can share decision-making experiences. In addition to sharing models in the training environment, our method can also serve as a basis for model training in the new environment and participating in subsequent training.

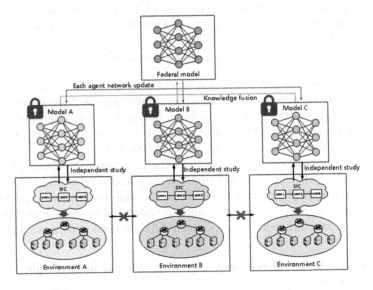

Fig. 1. The proposed federated learning framework.

In the generation process of the federated learning model, the placement action in the current state depends on the confidence of different datacenters. For example, in a certain state, the Q-table trained in the environment of datacenter A evaluates the Q-value of the current action as (5, 4, 4, 5, 6, 5, 5, 5, 5), and the Q-value in the environment of datacenter B is (3, 1, 10, 2, 2, 1, 1, 2, 10, 1). Then, it can be considered that datacenter B has higher confidence because of the more significant variance. However, the comparison by variance ignores the influence of extreme values. In contrast, information entropy is more suitable for measuring the uncertainty of information. In this work, we therefore use information entropy to define confidence.

For the main-body j, the confidence value under state x is defined as:

$$c_{xj} = -\frac{reward_{ij}}{\sum_{i=1}^{m} reward_{ij}} \cdot ln(\frac{reward_{ij}}{\sum_{i=1}^{m} reward_{ij}}) \tag{8}$$

where n is the number of the main-body, m is the action dimension (the number of nodes can be selected), $reward$ represents the return value. The confidence level w_{xj} is defined as shown in Eq. 9:

$$w_{xj} = \frac{(1 - c_{xj})}{\sum_{j=1}^{n} (1 - c_{xj})} \tag{9}$$

Assuming that there are k states in the reinforcement learning environment, and the Q-table is a $k \times m$ dimensional matrix, the federated model generation formula is shown in Eq. 10:

$$Q_{fl} = \sum_{j=1}^{n} Q_j \cdot \begin{pmatrix} w_{11}, w_{12}, \ldots, w_{1m} \\ \vdots \\ w_{k1}, w_{k2}, \ldots, w_{km} \end{pmatrix}^{T} \tag{10}$$

where Q_j is the main-body j participating in the training Q-table.

After the federated learning model is generated, the aggregation server will send the model to the training subjects in different environments to ensure the adaptability of the federated learning model.

The training subjects use Eq. 11 to update the local model so that the local model can learn more features.

$$Q_{new} = \frac{\alpha \cdot Q_{old} + Q_{fl}}{\alpha + 1} \tag{11}$$

where Q_{old} represents the original Q-table, Q_{new} represents the newly obtained Q-table, a represents the weight of the original Q-table. The federated model is sent to the original training environment and new environments to fuse models. Continue the training of reinforcement learning until the model converges. The iteration termination condition is defined as the difference between each new and the original Q-table is less than a pre-set threshold. The calculation by Euclidean distance is shown as:

$$\|Q_{old} - Q_{new}\| = \sqrt{(Q_{old} - Q_{new})(Q_{old} - Q_{new})^{T}} \leq \delta \tag{12}$$

In order to prevent leakage of the training data in different environments the federated learning framework needs to encrypt the Q table of the trained reinforcement learning. This process can ensure the safety and reliability of the transmission process as well as the privacy of the training data.

During the parameter transfer process of the federated learning model, we adopt homomorphic encryption to ensure the security of the model. Homomorphic encryption is a classic encryption algorithm. Homomorphic refers to a map from an algebraic structure to a similar algebraic structure, which can keep all relevant structures unchanged. Since the result obtained by decrypting the homomorphic encrypted ciphertext after specific operations is consistent with the result obtained by decrypting the ciphertext and then performing specific operations, it can effectively ensure the confidentiality of data operations in the federated model fusion stage, so it is very suitable for federated learning scenarios. Compared with the method of secure multi-party computing, the data interaction using homomorphic encryption is less. Therefore, the communication overhead is less, and the efficiency of model fusion can be improved in federated learning scenarios that require multi-party participation.

The process of model transmission using homomorphic encryption is as follows: First, the aggregation server generates a homomorphic encryption public-private key pair, and distributes the public key to each participant of federated learning. Second, each participant transmits the calculation result to the aggregation server in the form of homomorphic ciphertext. The aggregation server performs summary calculations and decrypts the results based on private key and ciphertext. Finally, the aggregation server send the decrypted results to all the participants, and the participants update their model parameters according to the results. So far, the process of aggregation and distribution of a model based on homomorphic encryption has been completed. This process is repeated periodically to guarantee the performance of federated learning model. By using a secure federated fusion algorithm with homomorphic encryption technology in the model transmission and model fusion stages, participants of different datacenters are prevented from private information leakage at any stage of model training.

In order to ensure the adaptability of the federated learning model in the new environment, it is necessary to migrate and correct the obtained federated learning model to reduce the number of training times required to obtain the orchestration model in the new environment. Figure 2 shows the basic process of federated learning model migration and correction. First, the reinforcement learning models obtained in different training environments are fused to generate a federated model. Secondly, it is necessary to transfer the federated model to the original training environment and the new environment. The model in the training environment is fused with the federated model. The model fusion method is shown in Eq. (11) in the new environment, the federated model is used as the pre-trained model. Continue the training of reinforcement learning until the model converges. In practical applications, the above training and fusion steps are usually repeated several times.

4   Simulation Analysis

In this section, we describe the design of the experiments and present the analysis of empirical results.

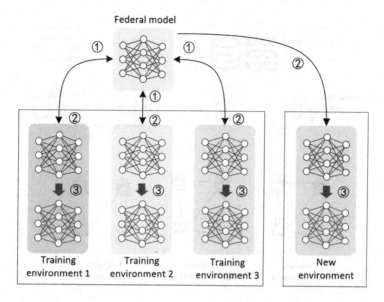

Fig. 2. Model migration and calibration process.

4.1 Design of Simulation Experiment

In order to verify the service orchestration effect of the federated reinforcement learning model proposed in this paper, it is necessary to design an appropriate simulation environment and orchestration tasks. We took a video analysis scenario as an example for simulation analysis. There are four VNFs in the video surveillance service that are placed and linked in the simulated network to provide users with video surveillance services, namely Motion Analyzer, Video Processor, Policy Decision and Mobile Proxy.

Three different training environments are designed in simulation, corresponding to different datacenters. Two are training environments with previous orchestration experience, and one is a new environment without orchestration experience. The simulation framework is shown in Fig. 3. The training processes of the three environments are independent of each other, and only after the federated reinforcement model is generated will the model information be exchanged.

The training processes of the three environments are independent of each other, and model information can only be exchanged after the federated reinforcement model has been generated. We sets 20 nodes to deploy the service function chain in each environment. The reliability and VNF load are different in each node. The cost of placing VNF is proportional to the spatial distance between nodes. The service function chain is to be arranged by four VNF serial compositions.

We train the reinforcement learning models in two environments independently to simulate the process of obtaining experience in the early stage. After models converge, training environments have orchestration experiences. The

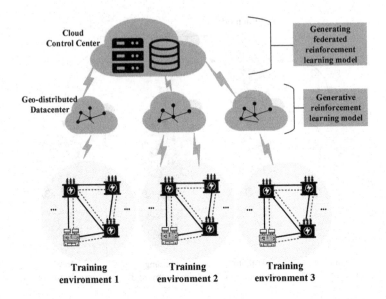

Fig. 3. Simulation framework.

training models are federated through the framework of federated learning. Then the generated federated model is sent to two training environments and a new environment for model fusion. We compare the proposed model with commonly used methods in terms of service reliability, resource overhead and efficiency, respectively. The VNF in the simulation is set up as a medium OpenStack VM with 2 vCPUs, 40 GB disk and 4 GB memory.

4.2 Empirical Results

We design three parts of simulation experiment for the service function chain orchestration method proposed in this paper. First, we analyze the convergence of the proposed federated reinforcement learning. Second, we verify the effectiveness of the proposed federated reinforcement learning framework in service function chain orchestration. Third, we verify the performance of the proposed service function chain orchestration method in jointly optimizing cost and reliability. The following is a detailed analysis of the experimental results.

Figure 4 shows the convergence of algorithm under different values of learning rate. Learning rate is one of the important hyperparameters in neural networks that affects the performance of federated reinforcement learning. As shown in Fig. 4, the model achieves the best performance when the learning rate is set as 0.01. When learning rate is set smaller as 0.001, The model converges at the local optimal solution and cannot reach a better reward. When the learning rate is set too large as 0.1, the model will skip some of the learning process since the step size of the neural network exploration will be larger. At this time, the effect of the model is in an oscillating state, and the convergence performance is not good. Therefore, in subsequent experiments we set the learning rate to 0.01.

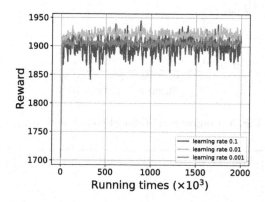

Fig. 4. Convergence performance of the model.

Figure 5 shows the training process of models in the new environment. The retrained Q-learning model converges after 800,000 iterations, and our method converges after 10,000 iterations. In this work, by comparing rewards of models during different iterations, we can prove that the convergence rate of reinforcement learning will be accelerated under the federated framework due to the experience of pre-training. In addition, the retrained Q-learning is trained based on random initialization parameters and local data. Therefore, at the beginning of the experiment, a low reward is obtained due to lack of experience in orchestration. And subsequent training is used to gradually obtain better orchestration decisions. While the federated reinforcement learning uses a model aggregated based on the orchestration experience of multiple datacenters. It has a certain orchestration experience at the beginning of the experiment, so better orchestration decisions can be obtained in early stage of training. As the training progresses, the optimal decision is gradually obtained.

To verify the effectiveness of the proposed federated learning framework in this work. We compare it with the independently retrained reinforcement learning model in the new and training environments. The simulation results of reliability and cost are shown in Fig. 6 and Fig. 7.

Figure 6 shows the comparison of the learning effects of our method (federated reinforcement learning model) and the retrained Q-learning model in the training environment. Regarding service reliability, our method can achieve high reliability and maintain stability at the beginning of training, while the retrained

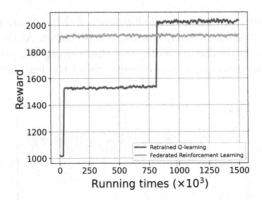

Fig. 5. Comparison of model convergence rates.

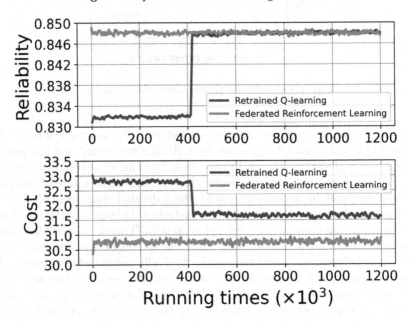

Fig. 6. Comparison of federated learning and reinforcement learning in training environment.

Q-learning model needs about 400,000 trainings to achieve high-reliability values. Regarding resource overhead, our method can consume lower costs, while the retrained Q-learning model still cannot reach the level that the federated model can achieve in a limited number of trainings. The reason is that our method integrates the training parameters of multiple environments, which can avoid a single environment training falling into local optimum. Generally speaking, the federated learning framework can achieve higher service reliability and consume fewer resources for training and decision-making in a training environment.

Figure 7 shows the comparison of the learning effects of our method and the retrained Q-learning model in the new environment. The emulation results show that our method can quickly reach a convergence state regarding training service reliability. Besides, the service reliability is maintained at a high value throughout the training process. In terms of resource overhead of the service function chain, our method can achieve rapid convergence and consume lower costs. The reason is that our method contains training experience obtained in other training environments, which achieve faster convergence when completing similar tasks. In general, our method for training and decision-making in the new environment can achieve higher service reliability and consume fewer costs.

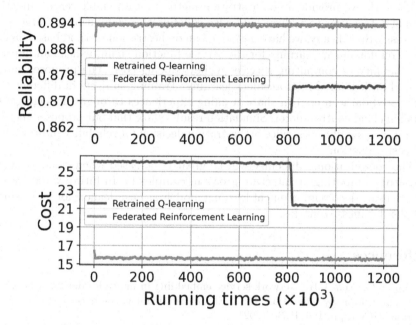

Fig. 7. Comparison of federated learning and reinforcement learning in the new environment.

To verify the performance of our proposed orchestration method, we select two greedy algorithms to compare the reliability and costs of service orchestration: the reliability-first greedy algorithm and the cost-first greedy algorithm. Table 1 shows experimental metrics in each case, which were statistically analyzed using average values over the 10 experiments. The best values of metrics in different cases are highlighted in bold.

Our proposed orchestration method based on federated reinforcement learning has significant reliability. In comparison with the reliability-first greedy algorithm, our method performs the best service reliability at a lower cost. Cost-first greedy algorithm leads to the lowest cost, and the overhead of our method is slightly higher. We can observe that the performance of our proposed method is better than other two methods, or it is close to the best value of metrics.

Table 1. Comparison of algorithm effects.

	Federated reinforcement learning model	Reliability-first greedy algorithm	Cost-first greedy algorithm
Service reliability	**0.993**	0.991	0.982
Cost	7.038	11.759	**7.000**

5   Conclusion

In this work, we provide an orchestration method for a reliable service function chain of datacenters to realize cloud-edge collaborative computing for large-scale data tasks. Specifically, we have developed an orchestration method based on federated reinforcement learning for the service function chain, which can improve the reliability of computing services while reducing cost. The proposed model is based on federated reinforcement learning. Training subjects in different geo-distributed datacenters can share training experiences through the aggregation model in cloud control center. Simulation results show that our proposed method can obtain a significant service orchestration decision for reliability improvement and cost reduction.

The computational difficulty will be greatly increased when cloud-edge collaborative computing architecture grows in complexity. In future work, we will explore using deep reinforcement learning models as basis leaners for increasingly complex business scenarios.

References

1. Tai, Y.C., Yen, L.H.: Network service embedding in multiple edge systems: profit maximization by federation. In: IEEE International Conference on Communications (ICC), pp. 1–6. IEEE (2021)
2. Jia, Y., Wu, C., Li, Z., et al.: Online scaling of NFV service chains across geo-distributed datacenters. IEEE/ACM Trans. Netw. **26**(2), 699–710 (2018). https://doi.org/10.1109/tnet.2018.2800400
3. Qing, H., Weifei, Z., Julong, L.: Virtual network protection strategy to ensure the reliability of SFC in NFV. In: Proceedings of the 6th International Conference on Information Engineering, pp. 1–5. ACM, New York (2017)
4. Wang, S., Zhou, A., Yang, M., et al.: Service composition in cyber-physical-social systems. IEEE Trans. Emerg. Topics Comput. **8**(1), 82–91 (2020). https://doi.org/10.1109/TETC.2017.2675479
5. Qu, L., Assi, C., Khabbaz, M.J., et al.: Reliability-aware service function chaining with function decomposition and multipath routing. IEEE Trans. Netw. Serv. Manag. **17**(2), 835–848 (2020)
6. Troia, S., Alvizu, R., Maier, G.: Reinforcement learning for service function chain reconfiguration in NFV-SDN metro-core optical networks. IEEE Access **7**, 167944–167957 (2019). https://doi.org/10.1109/ACCESS.2019.2953498

7. Shah, H.A., Zhao, L.: Multiagent deep-reinforcement-learning-based virtual resource allocation through network function virtualization in internet of things. IEEE Internet Things J. **8**(5), 3066–3074 (2020). https://doi.org/10.1109/JIOT.2020.3023111

8. Liu, X., Yu, J., Feng, Z., et al.: Multi-agent reinforcement learning for resource allocation in IoT networks with edge computing. China Commun. **17**(9), 220–236 (2020). https://doi.org/10.23919/JCC.2020.09.017

9. Chen, H.M., Chen, S.Y., Wang, S.K., et al.: Designing a reinforcement learning approach for the NFV orchestration system with energy saving optimization. In 2022 8th International Conference on Applied System Innovation (ICASI), pp. 98–10. IEEE (2022)

10. Huang, H., Zeng, C., Zhao, Y., et al.: Scalable orchestration of service function chains in NFV-enabled networks: a federated reinforcement learning approach. IEEE J. Sel. Areas Commun. **39**(8), 2558–2571 (2021). https://doi.org/10.1109/JSAC.2021.3087227

11. Zhang, P., Wang, C., Jiang, C., et al.: Deep reinforcement learning assisted federated learning algorithm for data management of IIoT. IEEE Trans. Industr. Inform. **17**(12), 8475–8484 (2021). https://doi.org/10.1109/TII.2021.3064351

12. Nguyen, D.C., Ding, M., Pathirana, P.N., et al.: Federated learning for internet of things: a comprehensive survey. IEEE Commun. Surv. Tutor. **23**(3), 1622–1658 (2021). https://doi.org/10.1109/JIOT.2022.3170449

13. Dieye, M., Ahvar, S., Sahoo, J., et al.: CPVNF: cost-efficient proactive VNF placement and chaining for value-added services in content delivery networks. IEEE Trans. Netw. Service Manag. **15**(2), 774–786 (2018). https://doi.org/10.1109/TNSM.2018.2815986

14. Sang, I.K., Kim, H.S.: A VNF placement method based on VNF characteristics. In: International Conference on Information Networking, Jeju Island, pp. 864–869. IEEE (2021)

15. Yang, Z., Chen, B., Dai, M., et al.: VNF placement for service chaining in IP over WDM networks. In: Asia Communications and Photonics Conference, Hangzhou, pp. 1–3. IEEE (2018)

16. Kar, B., Wu, E.H.K., Lin, Y.D., et al.: Energy cost optimization in dynamic placement of virtualized network function chains. IEEE Trans. Netw. Service Manag. **15**(1), 372–386 (2018). https://doi.org/10.1109/TNSM.2017.2782370

17. Varasteh, A., Madiwalar, B., Bemten, A.V., et al.: Holu: power-aware and delay-constrained VNF placement and chaining. IEEE Trans. Netw. Service Manag. **18**(2), 1524–1539 (2021). https://doi.org/10.1109/TNSM.2021.3055693

18. Quang, P., Hadjadj-Aoul, Y., Outtagarts, A.: On using deep reinforcement learning for VNF forwarding graphs placement. In: 11th International Conference on Network of the Future, Bordeaux, pp. 126–128. IEEE (2020)

19. Pei, J., Hong, P., Pan, M., et al.: Optimal VNF placement via deep reinforcement learning in SDN/NFV-enabled networks. IEEE J. Sel. Areas Commun. **38**(2), 263–278 (2020). https://doi.org/10.1109/JSAC.2019.2959181

20. Rui, L., Chen, X., Gao, Z., et al.: Petri net-based reliability assessment and migration optimization strategy of SFC. IEEE Trans. Netw. Service Manag. **18**(1), 167–181 (2020). https://doi.org/10.1109/tnsm.2020.3045705

Edge Computing and Collaborative Working

A Context-Aware Approach to Scheduling of Multi-Data-Source Tasks in Mobile Edge Computing

Jifeng Chen and Yang Yang[✉]

College of Computer and Information Science College of Software, Southwest University, Chongqing, People's Republic of China
chenjifeng@email.swu.edu.cn, yycia@swu.edu.cn

Abstract. The multi-data-source tasks are prevalent in the Mobile Edge Computing environment due to the distributed data storage of continuous data streams sent by various mobile devices. Many existing studies on context-aware task scheduling in MEC mainly aim to reduce energy consumption and improve performance by computation offloading among the MEC nodes. However, task context implies not only the locations of data sources but also the receivers of the result of task execution. Therefore, in this paper, we build a context-aware model for the multi-data-source tasks to analyze the objectives of task execution and data management in MEC and propose a related approach to scheduling the multi-data-source tasks. In the proposed approach, the task and environment contexts are used to determine the data sources involved, generate the task execution strategy, and resolve the target receivers. We discuss the task scheduling scheme in detail, including its architecture, metadata and data management, context-aware scheduling algorithm, and task offloading. We evaluate the feasibility and effectiveness of the proposed approach on a dataset of taxi trajectories in a city. The results illustrate that the proposed approach can effectively schedule the context-aware multi-data-source tasks in a MEC environment.

Keywords: Multi-data-source task · Context-aware scheduling · Mobile edge computing

1 Introduction

Internet of Everything is ascendant with the rapid development of mobile networks and 5G technology. Numerous sensors carried by various mobile devices, such as mobile phones, portable computers, and vehicles, send massive data via mobile internet. There are two inevitable severe challenges if all the data are sent and stored in a CDC (Cloud Data Center). First, it will put high force on network bandwidth and network stability due to the continuous data stream to the cloud data center via mobile internet. Second, the CDC will face a vast computing load when processing massive data, and then the performance of data processes is hard to be guaranteed [3,10].

© ICST Institute for Computer Sciences, Social Informatics and Telecommunications Engineering 2022
Published by Springer Nature Switzerland AG 2022. All Rights Reserved
H. Gao et al. (Eds.): CollaborateCom 2022, LNICST 460, pp. 193–212, 2022.
https://doi.org/10.1007/978-3-031-24383-7_11

To address the above issues, MEC (Mobile Edge Computing) arose at the right moment as a supplement to cloud computing and has a pivotal place in the 5G ecosystem. In the MEC paradigm, numerous edge servers are deployed at the edge of the mobile network [1]. On the one hand, they are placed with base stations side by side to serve for network access of mobile devices. On the other hand, since they store and process data close to the data source, they can effectively reduce the networking overhead, lower the demand for the stability of network access, and improve data processing performance by sharing the workload of centralized processing in the cloud.

In MEC scenarios, data generated and sent by mobile devices will be stored in multiple edge servers because the mobile devices will switch the connections to different base stations as they move. To reduce the load on bandwidth, edge servers usually don't transparent forward the data to the CDC in real-time. Instead, edge servers will periodically send the statistical data or the compressed data of the raw data to the CDC according to the business requirements. Consequently, the real-time tasks need to be executed on edge servers to obtain the correct results on the latest data. For example, when a vehicle is turning at a cross, the edge servers should send warnings to other vehicles to avoid traffic collision based on the velocity, direction, and driving track of the vehicles, especially for the vehicles beyond the sights of their drivers. This task is a typical multi-data-source one in MEC. It accesses the data stored in multiple distributed edge servers, locally processes them, and sends the results to targets connected with multiple base stations according to the task context. This kind of task is considerable prevalent in practice.

There has been many studies on task scheduling in MEC. For example, the various studies on task offloading focused on the number of users and computing nodes and the optimization objectives [2,7]. However, most of the studies haven't specialized on the multi-data-source tasks. Such a task should be accomplished through the cooperation of multiple edge servers and CDC in which the data are stored.

Therefore, we propose a context-aware approach to scheduling the multi-data-source tasks in MEC. The proposed approach uses the task context and the real-time load of edge servers to determine the data sources involved and generate the task execution strategy. The result of data processing will be sent to a specific range of edge servers determined by task context and then forwarded to the necessary mobile devices.

The contributions of this paper can be summarized as follows.

- We propose a context-aware model for the multi-data-source tasks to analyze the objectives of task execution and data management in MEC.
- We propose a context-aware approach to scheduling the multi-data-source tasks based on the task contexts and the real-time status of edge servers. If necessary, the computation will be offloaded among edge servers.

2 Related Works

Many distributed data storage services have been proposed for MEC in recent years. For example, Garg et al. [8] offered an edge time-series data storage service named TorqueDB based on ElfStore, which executes distributed queries on time-series data in edge-local storage. Zhou et al. [16] proposed a collaborative edge-edge data storage service called DECS, which can offload storage or computation among the MEC nodes and proactively replicate or migrate data by predicting data's popularity. Wang et al. [15] proposed an enhanced version of DECS to reduce the data access latency in the cold start and workload burst situations. Oyekanlu et al. [12] discussed that the real-time results of data processing could be obtained by deploying the computing on edge because such a way can filter most of the useless data, reduce resource consumption, and protect data privacy. In summary, the mainstream data storages are cloud-edge collaborative ones in which the data are distributed in multiple nodes, including the cloud data center, and migrated among the nodes. Hence, the multi-data-source task scheduling is of great research significance because the ubiquitous real-time tasks must be multi-data-source.

Concerning task scheduling in MEC, many types of research focus on optimizing energy consumption, execution performance, or resource utilization. For example, Saleem et al. [13] put forward a method to minimize the latency by D2D-enabled partial computation offloading. Huang et al. [9] studied on the energy-efficient offloading decision-making in vehicular networks. Bi et al. [4] proposed energy-optimized partial computation offloading with genetic simulated-annealing-based particle swarm optimization. Chen et al. [5] proposed a deep-reinforcement-learning-based context-aware online offloading strategy to reduce the overhead caused by user mobility. In general, these studies focused on generalized task scheduling, which aims to reduce energy consumption and improve performance by computation offloading among the MEC nodes. However, before assigning tasks to MEC nodes, we need to decide which MEC nodes will process their locally stored data. Moreover, we need to decide which target users will receive the result of data processing. Both the two decisions are made in the task contexts.

As for multi-data-source tasks, we also can find some related studies. For example, Chen et al. [6] proposed a non-cooperative game-theoretic offloading framework for multi-data-source task accomplishment. However, the MEC nodes either process data locally or fully offload computation to other nodes in this framework. There is no partial offloading allowed, which is a rather rigid restriction. Many studies on the application of MEC also involve distributed data processing. For example, Sonmez et al. [14] offered a machine-learning-based workload orchestrator for vehicular edge computing. Mehrabi et al. [11] put forward multi-tier cloudvr to Leverage edge computing for remote render of virtual reality. Existing studies on multi-data-source task scheduling have proposed some scenario-specific approaches. However, the more generic approach still needs to be developed for more scenarios.

3   System Model and Problem Formulation

3.1   A Scenario of Multi-Data-Source Task

The early warning of safe vehicle traveling is a typical context-aware multi-data-source task in MEC. In Fig. 1, all the vehicles send their status data to the connected base stations. After receiving the raw data, base stations store them on the local edge servers and send their digest as the metadata to CDC. The edge servers periodically compress and send the raw data to CDC at a relatively low frequency to reduce the bandwidth overhead. Hence, the real-time data are always held in edge servers. When performing real-time analysis, CDC assigns subtasks to base stations by the context of the analysis task. The base stations send the processing results back to CDC, and then the latter reduces all the results to determine what early warnings will be sent to which vehicles.

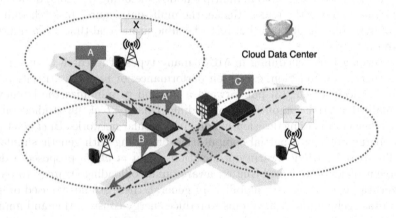

Fig. 1. A scenario of multiple data sources (Color figure online)

Car A, represented by the red flat cuboid, is traveling on the road in the direction of the red arrow. It enters the coverage area of base station Y after traveling through the coverage area of base station X. Then, car A will turn right at the cross while A and car C (represented by the blue flat cuboid and in the coverage area of base station Z) can't observe each other due to the high building at the corner. However, C must be early warned that it should take some risk avoidance measures because there is a possibility of collision with A. Meanwhile, car B(represented by the green flat cuboid) will not receive any warnings though B and C are almost the same far away from A and both B and A are in the coverage area of Y because the distance between A and B will not be shortened since B's traveling direction will not conflict with A.

Each base station with the collocated several edge servers forms a MEC node for data collecting, storing, and processing. The CDC continuously sends data analysis tasks to MEC nodes in the above scenario. The status of A, including the speed, traveling direction, current location, destination, and the geographical positions of other cars, will be used to determine the target cars of the early warnings. Consequently, the early warnings depend on the context-aware data from multiple sources, including the status data of A in a short period held in X and Y and the locations of cars in the coverage areas of geographically adjacent MEC nodes, such as Z.

It is inevitable for some MEC nodes to be incapable of completing the assigned data analysis tasks due to their overhigh real-time load. Accordingly, they have to offload part or all of the computation to directly connected MEC nodes to ensure the tasks will be accomplished. In addition to involving multiple data sources, the scheduling of such tasks should also take the collaboration among MEC nodes into account.

It is noticeable that even if the geographically adjacent MEC nodes are interconnected, a coordinator is still necessary to coordinate the collaboration among them because the peer-to-peer pattern is inefficient for the real-time multi-data-source tasks. Consequently, the reasonable way is to reduce the results returned by data processing MEC nodes in CDC, which will send the warnings to the target MEC nodes by their geographical locations.

Besides the early warning of the safe vehicle traveling, there are many other similar scenarios of the context-aware multi-data-source tasks in the real world, such as autonomous driving and mobile service recommendation. For this reason, it is well worth designing approaches to scheduling such tasks in MEC.

3.2   System Model

Suppose the application platform is composed of a remote cloud data center and N MEC nodes like X, Y, and Z shown in Fig. 1. The MEC nodes are represented as $E = \{e_i\}, i \in [0, n]$, where n is the number of MEC nodes and e_0 represents CDC. Each MEC node connects to CDC and its adjacent nodes. Thus, it is feasible for the computation to be effectively offloaded among the MEC nodes to achieve the global load balance.

In MEC, numerous data will be uploaded by mobile users and distributedly stored in the MEC nodes connected to them along the trajectories of users. When a user establishes a connection to a MEC node and closes the connection for switching to another MEC node, the MEC node will send a real-time message to CDC, and the latter will store the message as a piece of metadata. The message is represented as a quadruple $m = (e_{id}, u_{id}, a, t)$, where e_{id} is the MEC node ID, u_{id} is the user ID, a is the action of establishing or closing the connection, and t is the timestamp.

The MEC nodes will periodically compress and upload the raw user data to CDC, but this process is transparent to users. That is, users do not need to know the exact location of data storage. Once they connect to a MEC node, they can access all the data authorized to them.

CDC will maintain the metadata to locate the storage location of the users' data in the specified time slot. Each piece of the metadata is represented as $h = (u_{id}, e_{id}, t_e, t_l)$, where u_{id} is the user ID, t_e and t_l are the start and end timestamps of the time slot, e_{id} is the ID of the MEC node where stores the user's data generated in the time slot from t_e to t_l. When the MEC node uploads the stored data to CDC, the metadata will be updated to reflect the real-time change in the storage location. Moreover, CDC will merge the metadata by the contiguity of time slots to reduce the size of metadata. The initial values of t_e and t_l are the timestamps when the user enters and leaves the coverage area of e_{id}, but their final values are e_0, which represents CDC because the data are finally uploaded to it. Note that the storage location obtained by querying metadata is at the granularity of the MEC node or CDC. As for the specific storage mechanism, it depends on the implementation of the application platform, for example, using a time-series database to store the raw data.

3.3 Task Model

Each multi-data-source task, such as the prediction of traveling direction and speed of the cars in the safe vehicle traveling, is represented as $s = (u_{id}, f, \hat{t}_e, \hat{t}_l)$, where u_{id} is the user ID, f is the business function like prediction of traveling direction, $\hat{t}_e$ and $\hat{t}_l$ indicate the start and end timestamps of the time slot required by f.

When scheduling the task s, CDC will query the metadata to determine a set of MEC nodes $M = \{e_i\}$, $M \subset E$ which hold the data in the time slot from $\hat{t}_e$ to $\hat{t}_l$. Then, CDC assigns f to all the nodes in M, receives their return results, and reduces the results to obtain the final result. If s is a single-data-source task, its associated M contains only a single element.

The business function f will predict the mobile features of u_{id}, including the location, speed, and direction of u_{id}. CDC will send the warnings to some target users based on the prediction, just like car C receives the warning message about car A in Fig. 1. CDC determines the set of target users according to the geographical location and the mobile features of the users.

Therefore, context awareness of multi-data-source task scheduling has two aspects: on the one hand, the set of MEC nodes to which the task is assigned is determined by the context of the task. Thus, the data will be processed close to where they are generated and stored to save the network overhead and improve the processing performance. On the other hand, CDC will send the reduced result to a set of MEC nodes according to the task context. Then, the MEC nodes forward the result to the specified users.

3.4 Problem Formulation

In MEC, when CDC performs multi-data-source task scheduling, its target is the set of tasks $S = \{s_j\}, j \in [0, k]$ where k is the number of the tasks. The context-aware task scheduling has the following aspects:

Locating Data Sources and Assigning Tasks. For each s_j, suppose D_j is the data of u_{id}^j in time slot from $\hat{t}_e^j$ to $\hat{t}_l^j$. CDC will select the appropriate MEC nodes to form M_j by querying the metadata. Assuming $d_{e_i}^j$ is the data stored in the MEC node e_i, where $e_i \in M_j$. D_j and $d_{e_i}^j$ will satisfy the following condition:

$$D_j \subset \bigcup_{e_i \in M_j} d_{e_i}^j \tag{1}$$

That is, the data stored in all e_i of M_j chosen by CDC covers the required data D_j of s_j.

Reducing and Forwarding Result. Each s_j in S will return the result of f to CDC which includes the function-specific result, such as the evaluation of environment or the available services, and the prediction of the mobile features of u_{id}^j denoted as $r_j = (u_{id}^j, l_j, v_j, d_j)$, where l_j, v_j, and d_j respectively represent the location, speed, and direction of u_{id}^j at the next moment.

Suppose $U = \{u_{id}^j\}, j \in [1, k]$ contains all the users involved in S, CDC will create the set U' which contains all the users who are geographically away from some user in U less than a given threshold of y. For all the users in $\hat{U} = U \cup U'$, CDC will create a set of user pairs $P = \{p_i\}$, where $p_i = < u_f^i, u_s^i >$ for any pair of users between which the distance is less than the dangerous threshold y_h. For each pair, u_f^i and u_s^i will receive the warnings sent by CDC, and the warnings will contain the predicted mobile features of the other party and the function-specific result of f.

Offloading Computation. When some MEC nodes are overloaded, they can partially offload the tasks to other low-load or high-performance edge nodes. Considering the overhead and delay of data transmission caused by the computation offloading, we specify that a MEC node should only offload the computation to its directly connected MEC nodes. We require just the regional load balancing but not the global load balancing of all MEC nodes.

For each M_j of s_j in S, there is a set M_j' containing all the MEC nodes directly connect to any e_i^j in M_j. Suppose $\hat{M}_j = M_j \cup M_j'$ and L_{e_i} is the load of e_i, $e_i \in \hat{M}_j$, the optimization objective of the offloading decision is formulated as:

$$min(\sum_{e_i \in \hat{M}_j} (L_{e_i} - \overline{L})^2) \tag{2}$$

where $\overline{L}$ is the average load of all the edge nodes. Namely, our objective is to minimize the fluctuation of workloads of all the MEC nodes in $\hat{M}_j$.

4   Task Scheduling Scheme

Figure 2 is the overall architecture of the proposed scheduling scheme for multi-data-source tasks, which includes three functional modules: data management, metadata management, and context-aware task scheduling. We will discuss the specific design of the functional modules in the following subsections.

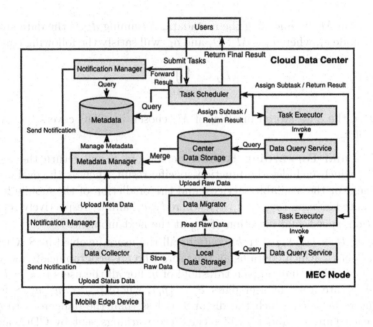

Fig. 2. The overall architecture of task scheduling scheme

4.1   Metadata Management

As mentioned in Sect. 3.2, the Data Collector of the MEC node will collect the data sent by MEDs(Mobile Edge Devices) and send two messages of $m = (e_{id}, u_{id}, a, t)$ to the Metadata Manager of CDC when u_{id} connects and disconnects with e_{id}. If a in m denotes connecting, Metadata Manager will create a new record in the metadata as $h = (u_{id}, e_{id}, t_e, t_l)$, where t_e is t in m and t_l is NULL indicating u_{id} hasn't disconnected to e_{id}. If a in m denotes disconnecting, Metadata Manager will search the records in metadata which matches u_{id} and e_{id} in m and whose t_l is NULL, then update t_l with t in m.

For example. In Fig. 3, when A enters the coverage area of X, X will send a message $m_1 = (X, A, Enter, t_1)$ to Metadata Manager. The latter will create a new record $h_1 = (A, X, t_1, NULL)$ in metadata. When A leaves X and enters the coverage area of Y, X and Y will respectively send the message $m_2 = (X, A, Leave, t_2)$ and $m_3 = (Y, A, Enter, t_2)$ to Metadata Manager, and the latter will update $h_1 = (A, X, t_1, t_2)$ and create a new record $h_2 = (A, Y, t_2, NULL)$.

When MEC nodes upload local data to the Central Data Storage of CDC, Metadata Manager will merge some records to reduce metadata size. The data uploaded by Data Migrator are divided into blocks by users. Each block contains all the data of a specific user and with a message $h = (u_{id}, e_{id}, t_e, t_l)$ in the same format as metadata. Metadata Manager will search the record exactly matching u_{id}, t_e, and t_l and update its e_{id} with e_0, indicating that these data have been migrated to CDC. Next, Metadata Manager will filter out all the records related

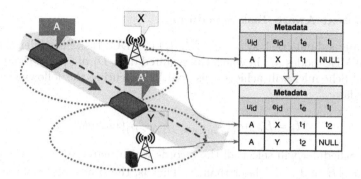

Fig. 3. An example of metadata management

to u_{id} whose e_{id} fields are e_0 and merge the records whose the time slots denoted by t_e and t_l are adjacent. For example, suppose A left the coverage area of Y at t_3, and both X and Y have uploaded A's data to CDC. Metadata Manager will merge the two records in Fig. 3 into one record as $h_1 = (A, e_0, t_1, t_3)$.

Besides the metadata of the dynamic data sent by MEDs, the static data of MEC nodes are also maintained by the Metadata Manager, including the geographical locations and the coverage area of the MEC nodes, and the connections among the MEC nodes. These data will be used in context-aware task scheduling.

4.2 Data Management

The Data Collector of the MEC node will collect the data sent by MEDs and store them in the local data storage. The Data Migrator will divide the local data into blocks by users and periodically migrate them from the local data storage of the MEC node to the central data storage of CDC. The application platform will store the migrated data in its specific database management system. The Metadata Manager will maintain the metadata of data locations in the way given in Sect. 4.1 when data are collected or migrated.

Every piece of data sent by MEDs to MEC node is denoted as $\mathbf{c} = <c_p, c_m>$, including the data specific to the application platform c_p and the mobile features c_m. c_m is denoted as (u_{id}, l, v, d) in the way given in Sect. 3.4 to represent the location, speed, and direction of u_{id}.

The local data storage of MEC nodes and the central data storage of CDC will build the 2d spatial index on users' locations l in c_m to support the search of users by the geographical distance. The positioning system of MEDs can obtain users' locations in the form of $< longitude, latitude >$. Many Database Management Systems support indexing on spatial data. For example, MySQL supports an R-tree structure index on spatial data.

4.3   Context-Aware Task Scheduling

When a user submits task $s_j = (u_{id}^j, f, \hat{t}_e^j, \hat{t}_l^j)$ to CDC, Task Scheduler will locate the set of MEC nodes M_j in which the required data D_j of s_j are stored at first. The Task Scheduler will achieve this goal by executing the following query in the metadata:

$$M_j = \Pi_{e_{id}}(\sigma_{u_{id}=u_{id}^j \wedge (t_l > \hat{t}_e^j \vee t_e < \hat{t}_l^j)}(metadata)) \tag{3}$$

Task Scheduler will select all the records which match u_{id}^j and whose t_e are earlier than $\hat{t}_l^j$ and t_l are later than $\hat{t}_e^j$. That is, the time slots of these records are fully or partly in the time period from $\hat{t}_e^j$ to $\hat{t}_l^j$. All the e_{id} projected from these records forms M_j.

For each e_i in M_j, $d_{e_i}^j$ is the subset of its stored data which is related to s_j. According to Eq. 3, the union of $d_{e_i}^j$ must cover D_j and therefore satisfy the constraint of Eq. 1.

Task Scheduler will obtain M_j' which contains all the MEC nodes directly connect to any e_i in M_j by querying the connections among MEC nodes in metadata and make decision on the policy of task execution for $\hat{M}_j = M_j \cup M_j'$. Then, Task Scheduler will send s_j along with the computation offloading decision to the MEC nodes of M_j to execute the task. We will discuss the specific algorithm of computation offloading in Subsect. 4.4.

Every MEC node and CDC has a Task Executor and a Data Query Service. The former executes the tasks sent by Task Scheduler and offloads computation to other nodes if necessary. The latter extracts required data from local data storage for the task execution. Since the function f of s_j operates on a distributed dataset, it should be a MapReduce job. Consequently, the Task Executor will execute $f.map()$ on the local dataset, and if necessary, it will offload partial computation to its directly connected nodes and execute $f.reduce()$ on the results they returned. Then, the Task Executor will send the final local result to Task Scheduler.

The special MEC node e_h in M_j is the one to which u_{id}^j is currently connected. The metadata record of this node is $(u_{id}^j, e_{id}, t, NULL)$. This node will send the locally-stored location l of u_{id}^j to the MEC nodes to which it directly connects. e_h and its adjacent nodes will find all the users who are geographically away from u_{id}^j less than a given threshold of y by searching in the local 2d spatial indexes. e_h will collect the found users in the set U_j'.

The Task Scheduler will obtain a set of the MEC nodes M_j^a in which each MEC node is geographically less than the threshold y away from and not directly connected to e_h. All the u_{id} currently connected with any nodes in M_j^a and geographically less than the threshold y away from e_h are added into U_j'. We calculate the distance between u_{id} and e_h instead of the one between u_{id} and u_{id}^j because the nodes in M_j^a can't obtain the location of u_{id}^j from e_h as they are not interconnected. That's why we set a larger threshold y at first to obtain potential targets and then use a smaller threshold y_h to filter out the final targets. Finally, the MEC nodes will send U'_j and their mobile features in the set $C_m^{U'_j}$, then send the two sets to Task Scheduler.

After all the Task Executors of the MEC nodes in M_j return the results to the Task Scheduler, the Task Scheduler will execute $f.reduce()$ on the results. For all the tasks in S, the Task Scheduler will generate the union U' of all the sets of U'_j, and further generate $\hat{U}$ of the union of U and U'. The Task Scheduler will iterate the users in $\hat{U}$ to find all the user pairs $p_i =< u_f^i, u_s^i >$ in each of which the distance between the two users is less than the dangerous threshold y_h in the next moment according to their locations, speeds, and traveling direction in $C_m^{U'_j}$. Finally, for each pair p_i, the Task Scheduler will search the MEC nodes where u_f^i and u_s^i are currently connecting in the metadata and send them the prediction of the mobile features of u_f^i and u_s^i. These MEC nodes will forward the predictions to u_f^i and u_s^i.

When determining whether the distance between two users u_F and u_S at the next moment will be less than the dangerous distance y_h, the task scheduler will use the following way to calculate the location $hatl$ of every individual user at the next moment:

$$\hat{l} =< v * \sin \alpha * \Delta t + l.longitude, v * \cos \alpha * \Delta t + l.latitude > \tag{4}$$

In Eq. 4, α is the angle between the traveling direction d and the positive axis of X in the plane coordinate system. The user's speed v is orthogonally decomposed into horizontal and vertical components, which are used to calculate the horizontal and vertical displacements in Δt from the current time to the next moment. The future location $\hat{l}$ is obtained by adding the displacements to the current location l.

When calculating the distance $\hat{y}$ between u_f and u_s at the next moment, the Task Scheduler can delegate the calculation to the navigation application if it is available. Otherwise, the Task Scheduler will calculate the Euclidean distance between the users. If the distance between the pair of users is enlarged and exceeds the threshold y_h, they will not receive the warnings about each other even though they are connecting to the same MEC nodes. On the contrary, if the distance is less than y_h, both the users will receive the warnings even though they are connecting to different MEC nodes.

The complete context-aware task scheduling process is shown in Algorithm 1, which invokes Algorithm 2 to find the geographically adjacent users of e_h and Algorithm 3 to send warnings to the target users.

4.4   Computation Offloading

When s_j is assigned to the MEC nodes in M_j, the sizes of the data related to s_j in all nodes are different. Moreover, the nodes have different workloads and are potentially heterogeneous with each other in computing powers. Thus, it is inevitable that some nodes perhaps can not accomplish the assigned subtask of s_j on demand. Consequently, these nodes need to offload full or partial computation

---

Algorithm 1: Context-aware Task Scheduling

Input: Task set $S = \{s_j\}_{j=1}^k$, The set of MEC nodes $E = \{e_i\}_{i=0}^n$, Metadata
　　　　 $metadata$
Output: NULL

1　**Function** TaskScheduling(S, E, $metadata$):
2　　　$U, U' \leftarrow \{\}$;
3　　　**foreach** $s_j = (u_{id}^j, f, \hat{t}_e^j, \hat{t}_{lj})$ in S **do**
4　　　　　$U \leftarrow U \cup \{u_{id}^j\}$;
5　　　　　$M_j \leftarrow \Pi_{e_{id}}(\sigma_{u_{id}=u_{id}^j \wedge (t_l > \hat{t}_e^j \vee t_e < \hat{t}_l^j)}(metadata))$;
6　　　　　$M_j', result \leftarrow \{\}$;
7　　　　　**foreach** e_i in M_j **do**
8　　　　　　| $M_j' \leftarrow M_j' \cup \{metadata.getDirectNeighbors(e_i)\}$;
9　　　　　**end**
10　　　　$\hat{M}_j \leftarrow M_j \cup M_j'$;
11　　　　TaskDispatch(s_j, $\hat{M}_j$);
12　　　　**foreach** e_i in $\hat{M}_j$ **do**
13　　　　　　$result_i \leftarrow f.map(d_{e_i}^j)$;
14　　　　　　**if** $e_i == e_h$ **then**
15　　　　　　　| $U_j' \leftarrow \text{FindAdjacentUsers}(e_h)$;
16　　　　　　　$result_i.add(C_m^{U_j'})$;
17　　　　　　**end**
18　　　　　　$result.add(result_i)$;
19　　　　**end**
20　　　　$U' \leftarrow U' \cup U_j'$;
21　　　　$f.reduce(result)$;
22　　　**end**
23　　　$\hat{U} \leftarrow U \cup U'$;
24　　　SendWarnings($\hat{U}$)
25　**End Function**

---

to other nodes. That's why the Task Scheduler builds $\hat{M}_j$ containing the nodes of M_j and their directly connected MEC nodes. Due to the time cost and network overhead caused by computation offloading, $\hat{M}_j$ doesn't include the indirectly connected MEC nodes.

Each MEC node e_i will send the heartbeat to CDC periodically to report its current workload L_{e_i}. Considering the heterogeneity among the nodes, we use $L_{e_i} = d_{e_i}/f_{e_i}$ to denote the workload of e_i, where f_{e_i} is the CPU frequency of e_i. We just consider the CPU frequency but not other factors, such as the memory size, bandwidth, or disk capacity, because the data processing tasks are most affected by CPU frequency, and the reasonable simplified model can reduce the computational complexity.

Task Scheduler will assign the subtasks of s_j to each MEC node e_i in M_j. If the current workload of e_i is L_{e_i}, and the extra workload brought by s_j is $\Delta L_{e_i} = d_{e_i}^j/f_{e_i}$, then the workload of e_i after it accepts the assigned subtask is

---

Algorithm 2: Finding Ajacent Users

Input: The MEC node e_h, The user u_{id}, Metadata *metadata*

Output: U'_j

1 **Function** FindAdjacentUsers(e_h,u_{id}, *metadata*):

2     $U'_j \leftarrow \{\}$;

3     $M^a_j \leftarrow metadata.getAjacentNeighbors(e_h)$;

4   **foreach** u^j_{id} in $e_h.getUsers()$ **do**

5   **if** $distance(u^j_{id},u_{id}) < y$ **then**

6           $U'_j \leftarrow U'_j \cup \{u^j_{id}\}$;

7   **end**

8   **end**

9   **foreach** e_i in M^a_j **do**

10   **foreach** u^j_{id} in $e_i.getUsers()$ **do**

11   **if** $distance(u^j_{id},e_h) < y$ **then**

12              $U'_j \leftarrow U'_j \cup \{u^j_{id}\}$

13   **end**

14   **end**

15   **end**

16   **return** U'_j

17 **End Function**

$L'_{e_i} = L_{e_i} + \Delta L_{e_i}$. If L_{e_i}' is not higher than the threshold L, e_i is not overloaded and it will locally process $d^j_{e_i}$. Otherwise, the Task Scheduler will choose a node directly connected to e_i in $\hat{M}_j$ to fully or partially offload computation.

We apply a simple algorithm when determining offloading targets due to the computational complexity. For each node e_i whose L'_{e_i} is greater than L, the Task Scheduler will sort the set of its directly connected MEC nodes M_i and iterate the nodes. At first, it finds the node e^0_i with the lowest workload. The $L'_{e_i} - L$ part of e_i's workload will be offloaded to e^0_i if the offloading doesn't incur the overloading of the latter. Otherwise, the part $L - L_{e^0_i}$ of e_i's workload will be offloaded to e^0_i. Then, the Task Scheduler checks the node e^1_i with the second-lowest workload in turn. The iteration proceeds until all the $L'_{e_i} - L$ part of e_i's workload is offloaded or all the nodes are iterated. The latter case means all the nodes in M_i will be overloaded, and the total computing power is not enough to accomplish the task in time. Consequently, e_i has to process the rest data by itself locally. Once the offloading decision is made, all the workloads of the nodes will be updated. Since each node only offloads the computation to its directly connected neighbors, the network overhead can be ignored in a 5G network. The nodes in M_i will send their processing results back to e_i, and the latter will perform $f.reduce$ on them before sending the final result to Task Scheduler. The complete task dispatching and computation offloading process are shown in Algorithm 4.

Algorithm 3: Sending warnings

Input: The user set $\hat{U}$
Output: NULL

1 **Function** SendWarnings(e_h,u_{id}, *metadata*):
2   **foreach** $< u_f^i, u_s^i >$ in $\hat{U}$ **do**
3       $\hat{y} \leftarrow distanceAtNextMoment(u_f^i, u_s^i)$;
4   **if** $\hat{y} < y_h$ **then**
5   sendWarnings($C_m^{u_f^i}, C_m^{u_s^i}, e_{u_f^i}, e_{u_s^i}$);
6   **end**
7   **end**
8 **End Function**

---

5 Evaluation

5.1 Simulation Setup

We use 2 servers with 32 cores and 128GB RAM to simulate 12 MEC nodes, each simulated with a service container and a MongoDB container. The components in MEC nodes shown in Fig. 2 are running in the service container while the data are stored in the MongoDB container. We also use a PC with 8 cores and 16 GB RAM to simulate the CDC in which we deploy the components of CDC and a MongoDB instance. Additionally, a script is deployed in the PC to simulate the vehicles sending data to the MEC nodes.

We download a data set of taxi trajectories in the city from Kaggle[1] for evaluation. This dataset contains a whole year (from 01/07/2013 to 30/06/2014) of the trajectories for all the 442 taxis running in the city of Porto in Portugal. We extracted a subset of the dataset containing all the taxi trajectories in four hours from 15:30 to 19:30 on July 1st, 2013. Considering that most multi-data-source tasks are real-time tasks, we interpolate data points in the original dataset to reduce the time interval between two successive data from 15 s to 1 s. Since the original has no speed of any taxi, we calculate the taxi speed by dividing distance by time to insert them into the dataset.

The preprocessed dataset is divided into a grid with 12 cells by the latitude and longitude of the taxi, as shown in Fig. 4. The blue dots are the taxi locations, and the solid black lines are the borders of the grid cells. We suppose a MEC node is deployed in each cell to collect the status data of all the taxis in the cell.

5.2 Analysis of Data Storage and Management

We simulate the taxis sending their status data to the MEC nodes. The Fig. 5 and Fig. 6 respectively show the data counts and the data sizes of CDC and MEC nodes at 24 time points with 10 min interval from 15:30 to 19:30 on July

---

[1] The dataset is available at https://www.kaggle.com/crailtap/taxi-trajectory.

Algorithm 4: Task Dispatching

Input: The task s_j, The set of MEC nodes $\hat{M}_j$
Output: NULL

1 **Function** TaskDispatch(s_j, $\hat{M}_j$):
2   **foreach** e_i *in* M_j **do**
3       $\Delta L_{e_i} = d_{e_i}^j / f_{e_i}$;
4       $L'_{e_i} = L_{e_i} + \Delta L_{e_i}$
5   **if** $L'_{e_i} > L$ **then**
6          $M_i \leftarrow metadata.getAjacentNeighbors(e_i)$;
7   **foreach** e_i^k *in* M_i **do**
8   **if** $(L_{e_i^k} + (L'_{e_i} - L)) < L$ **then**
9                $offloadComputation(e_i, e_i^k, L'_{e_i} - L)$;
10                $L'_{e_i} \leftarrow L$;
11                $L_{e_i}^k \leftarrow L_{e_i}^k + (L'_{e_i} - L)$;
12   break;
13   **else**
14                $offloadComputation(e_i, e_i^k, L - L_{e_i}^k)$;
15                $L'_{e_i} \leftarrow L'_{e_i} - (L - L_{e_i}^k)$;
16                $L_{e_i}^k \leftarrow L$;
17   **end**
18   **end**
19   **end**
20   **end**
21 **End Function**

1st, 2013. The Y coordinate values in Fig. 5 are the data count, while the Y coordinate values in Fig. 6 are the number of bytes of the MongoDB blocks storing the data, and each bar in both figures is stacked by the values of CDC and MEC nodes. We set the MEC nodes to migrate their data to CDC every 25 min after the first hour.

We have the following insights about the data storage:

The total data count keeps increasing over time, and the data are migrated from MEC nodes to CDC. At the beginning of the simulation, CDC has no data, and MEC nodes begin collecting data from taxis. Later, CDC has more and more data due to the data migration from MEC nodes. Once a MEC node migrates some data to CDC, its data count will reduce. So the storage loads of all MEC nodes fluctuate in a small range.

The total data size will be reduced after merging migrated data and metadata in CDC. Since MongoDB stores data in blocks, even a single document will occupy a whole block in which some space is wasted. If the data are divided into many slices, much space will be wasted in blocks. Consequently, when CDC merges the data migrated from MEC nodes, the wasted space will be reduced due to the contiguous storage.

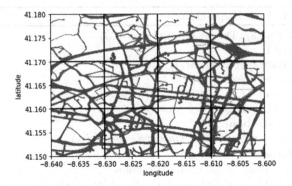

Fig. 4. The extracted dataset and its partitions

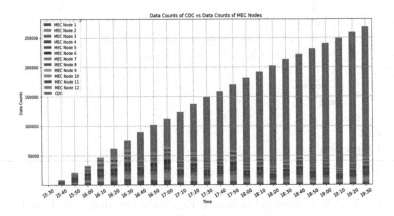

Fig. 5. Data counts of CDC and MEC nodes

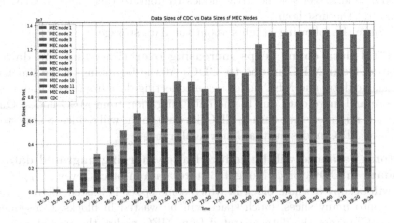

Fig. 6. Data sizes of CDC and MEC nodes

5.3 Validation of Context-Aware Task Scheduling

We use the application of early warning of safe vehicle traveling to illustrate the effectiveness and feasibility of the proposed approach to context-aware task scheduling. We choose the taxi with id 20000649 as the test target, whose location was $< -8.6253012, 41.1645144 >$ at 15:42:00 on July 1st, 2013.

The Task Scheduler assigns subtasks to the MEC node to which taxi 20000649 is connecting and its adjacent MEC nodes. All the MEC nodes return the nearby taxis by initial filtering, and CDC reduces the results and selects all the taxis less than 1 KM away from the target taxi. The final filtering results are shown in Fig. 7. The red dot is taxi 20000649, and the other dots are the taxis after initial filtering, among which the blue dots are the taxis less than 1 KM away from taxi 20000649, while the green dots are the taxis beyond the range of 1KM. All the taxis are in the coverage areas of 4 different MEC nodes represented by the grid. The final set of filtered taxis is [20000499, 20000472, 20000546, 20000007, 20000077].

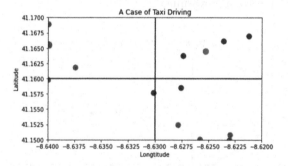

Fig. 7. A case of taxi driving

Then, Task Scheduler receives the trajectories of the filtered taxis from the MEC nodes and reduces them to obtain the complete trajectories. The first subfigure of Fig. 8 shows the trajectories of the 5 filtered taxis denoted as blue dots in Fig. 7. Each trajectory is plotted in a different color, and the black dot is the beginning end of the trajectory. The second subfigure of Fig. 8 shows the data distribution of the taxis. We can find that the trajectories of 2 taxis are respectively reduced with the results from 2 MEC nodes.

Finally, Task Scheduler calculates the distances between the target taxi and the filtered taxis every second in the next 30 s based on the predicted future trajectories and finds the destinations of the warnings. Figure 9 shows the trajectories of the target taxi and the potential destination taxis of the warnings. The blue and orange curves are the current and predicted future trajectories of the taxis, respectively. The green curve is the predicted future of the target taxi 20000649, and its beginning end is denoted by the black dot. According to

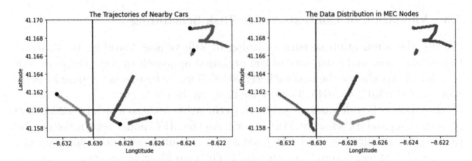

Fig. 8. Trajectories of the sample taxis

the calculated distances, only one taxi, 20000007, will be less than the dangerous threshold of 100 m away from taxi 20000649. Taxi 20000007 will be 89 m away from taxi 20000649 at 15:42:08. So taxi 20000649 and 20000007 receive the warning about each other, while other taxis, 20000499, 20000472, 20000546, and 20000077, won't receive any warnings.

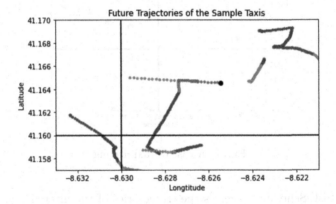

Fig. 9. Future trajectories of the sample taxis

This case demonstrates the two aspects of the proposed context-aware multi-data-source task scheduling. On the one hand, 4 MEC nodes are chosen to execute the early warning task by the task context, and CDC reduces the results of multiple MEC nodes to obtain the complete trajectories. On the other hand, the warnings are sent to the specified taxis according to the task context.

5.4   Discussion on Computation Offloading

In our simulation, all the service instances and MongoDB instances of the 12 MEC nodes are deployed in containers on 2 servers. Hence, all the MEC nodes are interconnected with each other. The data size of the extracted dataset is only

14 MiB, and we simulate they are collected by 12 MEC nodes and migrated to CDC periodically. Thus, the amount of data locally stored in each MEC node is not larger than 1 MiB, and the workload of each MEC node is always relatively low during the simulation. So no computation offloading is necessary for the simulation. However, if the dataset is large enough and a large number of tasks need to be executed, the computation offloading would happen. In our approach, if the computation is fully or partially offloaded from a MEC node to its directly connected nodes, the latter will send the task results back to the former to locally reduce the results before sending them to CDC. Consequently, it is reasonable to believe that computation offloading works in the proposed approach.

6   Conclusion

This paper analyzes the typical scenario of multi-data-source tasks in MEC and proposes a context-aware approach to scheduling this type of task. In the proposed approach, the task and environment contexts are used to locate the data sources involved, generate the task execution strategy, and resolve the target receivers of the task result. We offer the design of the task scheduling scheme, including its architecture, metadata and data management, context-aware scheduling algorithm, and task offloading. The feasibility and effectiveness of the proposed approach are evaluated on a dataset of taxi trajectories in a city.

In future, we should apply the proposed approach to more practical applications to verify its generalization in future work. Meanwhile, we should improve the performance of the proposed approach by optimizing the offloading algorithm and reducing the computational complexity of the algorithms.

References

1. Abbas, N., Zhang, Y., Taherkordi, A., Skeie, T.: Mobile edge computing: a survey. IEEE Internet Things J. **5**(1), 450–465 (2017)
2. Al-Ansi, A., Al-Ansi, A.M., Muthanna, A., Elgendy, I.A., Koucheryavy, A.: Survey on intelligence edge computing in 6G: characteristics, challenges, potential use cases, and market drivers. Future Internet **13**(5), 118 (2021)
3. de Assuncao, M.D., da Silva Veith, A., Buyya, R.: Distributed data stream processing and edge computing: a survey on resource elasticity and future directions. J. Netw. Comput. Appl. **103**, 1–17 (2018)
4. Bi, J., Yuan, H., Duanmu, S., Zhou, M., Abusorrah, A.: Energy-optimized partial computation offloading in mobile-edge computing with genetic simulated-annealing-based particle swarm optimization. IEEE Internet Things J. **8**(5), 3774–3785 (2020)
5. Chen, S., Chen, H., Ruan, J., Wang, Z.: Context-aware online offloading strategy with mobility prediction for mobile edge computing. In: 2021 International Conference on Computer Communications and Networks (ICCCN), pp. 1–9. IEEE (2021)

6. Chen, S., Sun, S., Chen, H., Ruan, J., Wang, Z.: A game theoretic approach to task offloading for multi-data-source tasks in mobile edge computing. In: 2021 IEEE International Conference on Parallel & Distributed Processing with Applications, Big Data & Cloud Computing, Sustainable Computing & Communications, Social Computing & Networking (ISPA/BDCloud/SocialCom/SustainCom), pp. 776–784. IEEE (2021)

7. Cong, P., Zhou, J., Li, L., Cao, K., Wei, T., Li, K.: A survey of hierarchical energy optimization for mobile edge computing: a perspective from end devices to the cloud. ACM Comput. Surv. (CSUR) 53(2), 1–44 (2020)

8. Garg, D., Shirolkar, P., Shukla, A., Simmhan, Y.: *TorqueDB*: distributed querying of time-series data from edge-local storage. In: Malawski, M., Rzadca, K. (eds.) Euro-Par 2020. LNCS, vol. 12247, pp. 281–295. Springer, Cham (2020). https://doi.org/10.1007/978-3-030-57675-2_18

9. Huang, X., Xu, K., Lai, C., Chen, Q., Zhang, J.: Energy-efficient offloading decision-making for mobile edge computing in vehicular networks. EURASIP J. Wirel. Commun. Netw. 2020(1), 1–16 (2020). https://doi.org/10.1186/s13638-020-1652-5

10. Khan, W.Z., Ahmed, E., Hakak, S., Yaqoob, I., Ahmed, A.: Edge computing: a survey. Futur. Gener. Comput. Syst. 97, 219–235 (2019)

11. Mehrabi, A., Siekkinen, M., Kämäräinen, T., ylä-Jääski, A.: Multi-tier CloudVR: leveraging edge computing in remote rendered virtual reality. ACM Trans. Multimedia Comput. Commun. Appl. (TOMM) 17(2), 1–24 (2021)

12. Oyekanlu, E.: Predictive edge computing for time series of industrial IoT and large scale critical infrastructure based on open-source software analytic of big data. In: 2017 IEEE International Conference on Big Data (Big Data), pp. 1663–1669. IEEE (2017)

13. Saleem, U., Liu, Y., Jangsher, S., Tao, X., Li, Y.: Latency minimization for D2D-enabled partial computation offloading in mobile edge computing. IEEE Trans. Veh. Technol. 69(4), 4472–4486 (2020)

14. Sonmez, C., Tunca, C., Ozgovde, A., Ersoy, C.: Machine learning-based workload orchestrator for vehicular edge computing. IEEE Trans. Intell. Transp. Syst. 22(4), 2239–2251 (2020)

15. Wang, J., Chen, H., Zhou, F., Sun, M., Huang, Z., Zhang, Z.: A-DECS: enhanced collaborative edge-edge data storage service for edge computing with adaptive prediction. Comput. Netw. 193, 108087 (2021)

16. Zhou, F., Chen, H.: DECS: collaborative edge-edge data storage service for edge computing. In: Gao, H., Wang, X., Iqbal, M., Yin, Y., Yin, J., Gu, N. (eds.) CollaborateCom 2020. LNICST, vol. 349, pp. 373–391. Springer, Cham (2021). https://doi.org/10.1007/978-3-030-67537-0_23

Secure and Private Coding for Edge Computing Against Cooperative Attack with Low Communication Cost and Computational Load

Xiaotian Zou, Jin Wang$^{(\boxtimes)}$, Can Liu, Lingzhi Li, Fei Gu, and Guojing Li

Department of Computer Science and Technology, Soochow University,
Suzhou, China
{20204227064,20214027012,20204227039}@stu.suda.edu.cn,
{wjin1985,lilingzhi,gufei}@suda.edu.cn

Abstract. Edge computing is an efficient computing paradigm, which can utilize computing devices at the edge of network to provide real-time proximity service. Since edge devices lack centralized management, they are more vulnerable to being attacked. Therefore, the issues of data security and user privacy in edge computing are particularly important. A large number of existing literature focus on the data security and user privacy with independent attackers. However, cooperative attacks, in which multiple attackers can collaborate to obtain the data content and user privacy, have not been fully investigated. In particular, we take the matrix-vector multiplication which is a basic component of most machine learning algorithms as the basic task. Therefore, in this paper, we focus on the *Secure and Privacy Matrix-vector Multiplication* (SPMM) issue for edge computing against cooperative attack and design a general coded computation scheme to achieve lowest system resource consumption, *i.e.* communication cost and computational load. Specifically, we propose two coding schemes: *Secure and Private Coding with lower communication Cost* (SPCC) and *Secure and Private Coding with lower computational Load* (SPCL). We also conduct solid theoretical analyses and extensive experiments to demonstrate that both two proposed coding schemes can achieve lower communication cost and computational load than existing work. Finally, we perform extensive analyses to the superiority of the proposed schemes.

This work is supported in part by National Natural Science Foundation of China (62072321, 61972272), Six Talent Peak Project of Jiangsu Province (XYDXX-084), China Postdoctoral Science Foundation (2020M671597), Jiangsu Postdoctoral Research Foundation (2020Z100), Suzhou Planning Project of Science and Technology (SNG2020073, SS202023, SYG202024), Tang Scholar of Soochow University, Collaborative Innovation Center of Novel Software Technology and Industrialization, and Soochow University Interdisciplinary Research Project for Young Scholars in the Humanities.
Responding author: Jin Wang, wjin1985@suda.edu.cn

H. Gao et al. (Eds.): CollaborateCom 2022, LNICST 460, pp. 213–232, 2022.
https://doi.org/10.1007/978-3-031-24383-7_12

Keywords: Edge computing · Security · Privacy · Communication cost · Computational load

1 Introduction

With the rapid arrival of the 5G era, it is unrealistic to transmit massive data to the cloud for real-time processing due to the bandwidth limitation between the cloud and the edge network [1]. Since edge devices are closer to the user, edge computing can provide efficient and real-time computing to the user [1–4]. Nowadays, with the development of artificial intelligence, edge computing has been used in extensive fields, such as *virtual reality* (VR) [2], smart city [3], autonomous vehicle [4], *etc.*, paving the way for the application of artificial intelligence [2–5].

Despite the enormous potential of edge computing, there are still many challenges [1,5–23]. The first major issue is the straggler problem [6–9]. Due to the differences in network environment and devices, edge devices return computation results at different speeds. Therefore, the user needs to wait for slower edge devices, namely stragglers, to complete the computation, which is the straggler problem. This greatly affects the calculation latency. In addition, since edge devices are at the edge of the network, they are more vulnerable to being attacked [10–23]. This seriously threatens the security of data. Therefore, the original data must be encoded before being allocated to edge devices [10–16]. Finally, due to the trustlessness of edge devices, they are more likely to leak the privacy of user when they participate in computing [17–23]. Matrix-vector multiplication, as one of the key modules of machine learning, image processing and deep learning, is the starting point to study the above problems [6–23].

To solve the above problems, researchers proposed many *coded distributed computing* (CDC) schemes in different scenarios [6–23]. In CDC, the user first divides the original data into blocks and encodes them, *i.e.* linearly combines

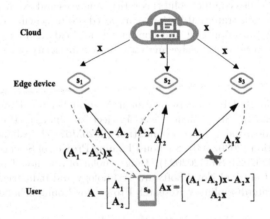

Fig. 1. Traditional distributed computing.

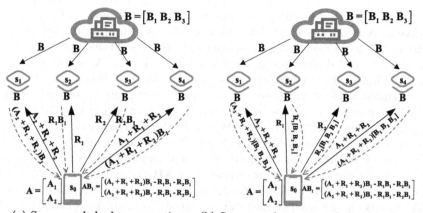

(a) Secure coded edge computing.   (b) Secure and private coded edge computing.

Fig. 2. An example of coded edge computing.

blocks. Then, the user allocates the coded blocks to edge devices. After receiving the coded blocks, edge devices calculate and return the computation results, *i.e.* intermediate results, to the user. Finally, once the user receives sufficient intermediate results, the user can decode and obtain the final result.

Through redundant calculation of data, the recovery threshold which is the number of intermediate results required to decode the final result can be reduced [6–9]. This greatly alleviates the straggler problem. As shown in Fig. 1, when the edge devices s_1 and s_2 return the results, the user can decode the final results without waiting for slower edge device s_3. However, the above research on CDC do not consider security issues. To solve the data security problems, an increasing number of researchers begin to investigate *secure coded distributed computing* (SCDC) [10–16] to satisfy *information-theoretic security* (ITS) [24], *i.e.* edge devices cannot obtain a linear combination of the original blocks. As shown in Fig. 2(a), the user protects data security by adding random blocks to the original blocks in the coding phase. Moreover, the scheme in Fig. 2(a) can protect the data security in the case of cooperative attack by any two devices. However, edge devices are curious about whichever piece of data in public data the user operates because the user typically has a variety of computing needs. This seriously undermines the privacy of user. Consequently, a large number of researchers are dedicated to studying *private coded distributed computing* (PCDC), *i.e.* edge devices have no way of knowing which piece of public data the user wants to calculate [17–23].

Next, we give an example in Fig. 2(a) (b) to show the coded edge computing system that we study. In this example, the goal of the user is to compute $\mathbf{AB}_1$. The system we considered consists of a user device s_0, a cloud and 4 edge devices s_1, s_2, s_3, s_4, where any two edge devices can cooperate to attack. Data $\mathbf{A}$ is stored on s_0 and $\mathbf{B} = [\mathbf{B}_1 \ \mathbf{B}_2 \ \mathbf{B}_3]$ as a small public data is stored on the cloud. The cloud sends data $\mathbf{B} = [\mathbf{B}_1 \ \mathbf{B}_2 \ \mathbf{B}_3]$ to edge devices before the calculation starts. Then, the cloud no longer communicates with edge devices. Firstly, the user divides $\mathbf{A}$ into 2 blocks by row which are $\mathbf{A}_1$, $\mathbf{A}_2$. In order to protect the security of $\mathbf{A}$, the user generates 2 random blocks $\mathbf{R}_1$, $\mathbf{R}_2$ of the same size as $\mathbf{A}_1$. Then, in secure coded edge computing, the user encodes $\mathbf{A}_1$, $\mathbf{A}_2$ with them and allocates coded blocks to edge devices as shown in Fig. 2(a). When edge devices receive a coded block of $\mathbf{A}$, the edge devices perform the calculation and return the results (intermediate results) to the user. When the 4 edge devices all return intermediate results, the final result $\mathbf{AB}_1$ can be decoded as shown in Fig. 2(a). Since the user encodes each block of $\mathbf{A}$ with two random blocks, the original information of $\mathbf{A}$ cannot be obtained when any two edge devices cooperate. However, since the user device wants to calculate $\mathbf{AB}_1$, edge devices only operate $\mathbf{B}_1$ with the coded blocks of $\mathbf{A}$. Thus, edge devices can know $\mathbf{B}_1$ is different from $\mathbf{B}_2$, $\mathbf{B}_3$ and $\mathbf{B}_1$ is the content that the user needs to calculate. Therefore, the scheme in Fig. 2(a) leaks the privacy of the user. As shown in Fig. 2(b), similar to Fig. 2(a), this scheme can protect the security of $\mathbf{A}$ when any two devices cooperate to attack. Since operations on $\mathbf{B}_1$, $\mathbf{B}_2$, $\mathbf{B}_3$ are consistent, edge devices have no way of knowing which column of $\mathbf{B}$ we want to calculate. In addition, in the case of cooperative attack by any two devices, edge devices cannot know computing goal of the user. Therefore, the scheme protects the security of $\mathbf{A}$ and privacy of user. In this paper, we proposed two secure and private coding schemes which can achieve lower communication cost and computational load than existing work when there are stragglers in the system. The contributions of this paper are as follows:

- We give the system model, attack model, privacy condition and security condition and define SPMM problem.
- We propose SPCC for the SPMM problem. In SPCC, although the communication cost of intermediate results returned by edge devices to the user is large, the communication cost of the user sending coded blocks to edge devices is improved. In addition, SPCC has lower communication cost than the existing work.
- In order to obtain a lower computational load, we further design SPCL for the SPMM problem and give the proof of security and privacy. SPCL has lower computational load than SPCC.
- Finally, we conduct extensive simulation experiments under different parameter settings, which demonstrate that SPCC can achieve lower communication cost and SPCL can achieve lower computational load compared with the existing work.

The rest of the paper is organized as follows. The related work is investigated in Sect. 2. In Sect. 3, we introduce a detailed description of the system model and define the SPMM problem. In Sect. 4, we propose SPCC and SPCL for SPMM. Besides, we perform a theoretical analysis of the two schemes that we proposed. In Sect. 5, we conduct extensive experiments to demonstrate the superiority of SPCC and SPCL. Finally, we conclude the paper in Sect. 6.

2 Related Work

Recently, a large number of researchers begin to study CDC because CDC can provide efficient computing and mitigate the impact of stragglers [6–9]. In [6], Li et al. proposed distributed fog computing coding scheme which can make full use of the devices scattered around the user for calculation. Lee et al. [7] proposed *maximum-distance-separable* (MDS) codes which can mitigate the impact of stragglers to speed up distributed machine learning. In [9], Dutta et al. proposed MatDot codes which reduce the recovery threshold of the system by sacrificing communication. Moreover, in [8], Soto et al. proposed a coding scheme that minimize the recovery threshold for batch matrix multiplication. However, none of the above schemes considers the security of the system.

Since edge devices are at the edge of the network, they are more vulnerable to being attacked. A growing number of researchers are committed to solving the problem of data security [10–14]. In [10], Yang et al. proposed secure polynomial coding scheme which can be applied not only to matrix-vector multiplication but also to image convolution. Besides, Bitar et al. [11] designed *Staircase Codes* and analysed the latency of *Staircase Codes* is always less than the latency of secret sharing. In [12], Bitar et al. proposed a solution based on *Staircase Codes* to minimize latency for SCDC. In [15], Cao et al. proposed secure coded edge computing schemes for the heterogeneous edge computing systems which can acquire the minimal total cost. Moreover, for the collusion of edge devices, a variety of secure schemes have been proposed. In [13], Chang et al. proposed a secure polynomial coding scheme to achieve the maximized ratio of effective blocks to total blocks for collusion attacks. In [14], Doliveira et al. proposed GASP codes to minimize the recovery threshold for distributed matrix multiplication with protecting both matrix security. In [16], Zhu et al. proposed a secure scheme in the case of collusion and minimize the total cost of the distributed matrix multiplication. However, the above schemes does not consider the privacy of the user.

For protecting the privacy, Kim et al. [17] proposed a privacy coding scheme by setting up special evaluation points to reduces the stragglers effect. In addition, Kim et al. [18] proposed a secure privacy coding scheme based on [17] to ensure security of data and privacy of the user. In [19], Chang et al. studied the correlation between upload and download for secure and private distributed matrix multiplication. In [20], Qian et al. employ entangled polynomial coding, which lowers the total computing cost and the recovery threshold for secure and private distributed matrix multiplication. Moreover, in order to deal with privacy issues in case of devices collusion, Vaidya et al. [21] firstly proposed a secure and privacy scheme for distributing computing in the case of collusion of edge devices. In this scheme, the privacy of the user is protected by sending random blocks, which greatly increases communication cost. Jia et al. [22] proposed X-secure and T-private coding scheme against the cooperative attacks through multiple rounds of calculation. Kim et al. [23] proposed a coding scheme to protect the privacy of two databases for collusion issues in a distributing computing system. However, in the above schemes, only [21, 22] considered the secure and private coded scheme against colluding devices, but there is no focus on the overhead of the system. Although the above studies have proposed methods for security and privacy issues in the case of collusion of edge devices, we believe that their schemes can be better optimized to achieve lower communication cost and computational load. In this paper, we focus on security and privacy issues and propose effective solutions to further reduce the communication cost and computational load.

3   Problem Modeling

In this section, firstly, we present a full description of the system model. Next, we propose our attack model, as well as security and privacy conditions. Finally, the SPMM problem is formally defined.

3.1   System Model

In this paper, we investigate an edge computing system that includes a user device, a cloud, and a large number of edge devices. Since edge devices are at the edge of the network, they lack centralized and unified management. Therefore, they are more vulnerable to being attacked. We assume any L ($L \geq 1$) edge devices can collude. Without losing generality, we focus on the matrix-vector multiplication, which is an important module for machine learning, image processing and federation learning [7–9,13–17]. In particular, data $\mathbf{A}$ ($\mathbf{A} \in \mathbb{F}_q^{t \times p}$ and $\mathbb{F}_q$ is a finite field) is the user data. Data $\mathbf{B}$ ($\mathbf{B} \in \mathbb{F}_q^{p \times n}$) is public data which is stored in the cloud. The goal of the user is to compute the multiplication of $\mathbf{A}$ and a column vector of $\mathbf{B}$, i.e. $\mathbf{AB}_d$ ($1 \leq d \leq n$), in the case of ensuring data security and privacy of user. Before computing, the cloud will send data $\mathbf{B}$ to edge devices[1]. After that, the cloud will not communicate with edge devices.

Firstly, the user divides $\mathbf{A}$ into m blocks according to rows[2] ($m \leq t$) to obtain $\mathbf{A} = \begin{bmatrix} \mathbf{A}_1^\top, \mathbf{A}_2^\top, \cdots, \mathbf{A}_m^\top \end{bmatrix}^\top$ where $\mathbf{A}_i \in \mathbb{F}_q^{\frac{t}{m} \times p}$ ($1 \leq i \leq m$). Then, to ensure the security of $\mathbf{A}$ and optimize the system sufficiently, the user generates L random blocks $\mathbf{R} = [\mathbf{R}_1, \mathbf{R}_2, \cdots, \mathbf{R}_L]$, where $\mathbf{R}_i \in \mathbb{F}_q^{\frac{t}{m} \times p}$ ($1 \leq i \leq L$). Next, the user encodes $\mathbf{A}$ with $\mathbf{R}$ by function $f(x)$, where $f(x)$ can be shown as follows:

$$f(x) = \sum_{i=1}^{m} \mathbf{A}_i x^{\alpha_i} + \sum_{j=1}^{L} \mathbf{R}_j x^{\alpha_{m+j}}. \tag{1}$$

The value of α_i ($\forall i \in \{1, \cdots, m+L\}$) will be shown in Sect. 4. The user selects T ($T \geq 1$) non-zero values $\{x_1, \cdots, x_T\}$ to obtain the coded matrix $\widetilde{\mathbf{A}} = \begin{bmatrix} \widetilde{\mathbf{A}}_1^\top, \widetilde{\mathbf{A}}_2^\top, \cdots, \widetilde{\mathbf{A}}_T^\top \end{bmatrix}^\top$, where $\widetilde{\mathbf{A}}_i = f(x_i)$, $\forall i \in \{1, \cdots, T\}$.

At this point, we define the recovery threshold:

---

[1] Since the data $\mathbf{B}$ can be stored on the edge device, $t >> n > 1$.
[2] When $\frac{s}{m}$ is not an integer, we add $\mathbf{0}$ vector to the row of matrix $\mathbf{A}$ to make $\frac{s}{m}$ an integer.

Definition 1 *(Recovery threshold).* *The recovery threshold N is the minimal number of intermediate results returned by the edge devices can be used to decode the final result $\boldsymbol{AB}_d$.*

To ensure that user can get $\mathbf{AB}_d$, we give the decodability condition as follows:

Definition 2 *(Decodability Condition).* *The user can obtain $\boldsymbol{AB}_d$ iff $T \geq N$ and the exponent of $\boldsymbol{A}_i\boldsymbol{B}_d$ in each intermediate result is unique $\forall i \in \{1, \cdots, m\}$.*

3.2   Attack Model, Secure Condition and Privacy Condition

In this paper, we assume that edge devices are passive attackers or controlled by passive attackers [10–24]. The security model that we consider is based on ITS [10–16,24]. Specially, we need to make sure that any L edge devices collusion can not obtain the linear combination of $\mathbf{A}_1, \cdots, \mathbf{A}_m$. Moreover, similarly, the privacy model that we consider any edge device can not obtain the relevant information of d [17–23].

Let $I(\varrho; \sigma)$ denote the mutual information between ϱ and σ. In addition, $\widetilde{\mathbf{A}}_{s_L}$ represents the set of coded blocks of $\mathbf{A}$ on any L edge devices. At this point, we define security [10–16,24] and privacy conditions [17–23].

Definition 3 *(Security Condition).* *The solution of SPMM satisfies the security condition iff*

$$I(\boldsymbol{A}; \widetilde{\boldsymbol{A}}_{s_L}) = 0. \tag{2}$$

Definition 4 *(Privacy Condition).* *The solution of SPMM satisfies the privacy condition iff any L colluding edge devices cannot obtain relevant information about d.*

3.3   Communication Cost and Computational Load

To measure communication and computation metrics, we define the communication cost and computational load [21] as follows:

Definition 5 *(Communication Cost).* *The communication cost is the number of elements that sent by the user to edge devices and returned by edge devices to the user.*

Definition 6 *(Computational Load).* *The computational load is defined as the number of multiplication operation on each edge device participating in the calculation.*

4   Secure and Private Coded Computation Schemes

In this section, we propose SPCC for SPMM. Next, we proof the security and privacy of SPCC and make theoretical analysis. Then, to get lower computational load, we propose SPCL and analyze its performance. Finally, we give an example for SPCC and SPCL, respectively.

4.1 Secure and Private Coding Scheme with Low Communication Cost (SPCC)

In this section, we first propose SPCC for SPMM. Next, we proof the security, privacy and decodability conditions of SPCC. Finally, we analyze communication cost and computational load of SPCC.

For the given m, L, the α_i is shown as follows:

$$\alpha_i = i - 1, \forall 1 \leq i \leq m + L. \tag{3}$$

In this scheme, the computation process can be shown as follows:

- Firstly, the user encodes data $\mathbf{A}$ according to Eq. (1) and Eq. (3). Then, the user allocates $\widetilde{\mathbf{A}}_i$ $(1 \leq i \leq T)$ to the i-th edge device.
- When the i-th edge device receives the coded block $\widetilde{\mathbf{A}}_i$, the edge device performs the calculation $\widetilde{\mathbf{A}}_i \mathbf{B}_1, \cdots, \widetilde{\mathbf{A}}_i \mathbf{B}_n$ and returns all results to the user.
- Once the user receives intermediate results from N_{SPCC} edge devices (N_{SPCC} is the recovery threshold of SPCC and $N_{SPCC} \leq T$), the user can decode the final results $\mathbf{AB}_d$ by using polynomial interpolation [10].

Theorem 1. *The SPCC is secure in the case of collusion of any L edge devices, i.e. the security condition Eq. (2) is satisfied.*

Proof. According to [10] and Eq. (3), it is clear that all α_i $(1 \leq i \leq m + L)$ are different. Therefore, the security condition Eq. (2) is satisfied.

Theorem 2. *The SPCC is private in the case of collusion of any L edge devices, i.e. the privacy condition is satisfied.*

Proof. Since the i-th edge device receives the coded block $\widetilde{\mathbf{A}}_i$, the edge device performs the calculation $\widetilde{\mathbf{A}}_i \mathbf{B}_1, \cdots, \widetilde{\mathbf{A}}_i \mathbf{B}_n$, this is equivalent to i-th edge device receiving the coding sequence Θ $(\Theta \in \mathbb{F}_q^{n \times 1})$ and the elements in Θ are all 1. When any L devices collude, the coding sequence that edge devices can obtain is still Θ. At this time, according to [17–23] the privacy condition is equivalent to

$$I(d; \Theta, \widetilde{\mathbf{A}}_{s_L}, \mathbf{B}) = 0. \tag{4}$$

Therefore, we need to prove Eq. (4). According to the chain rule, the privacy condition is given as follows:

$$\begin{aligned} I(d; \Theta, \widetilde{\mathbf{A}}_{s_L}, \mathbf{B}) &= I(d; \Theta) + I(d; \widetilde{\mathbf{A}}_{s_L}, \mathbf{B}|\Theta) \\ &= I(d; \Theta) + I(d; \widetilde{\mathbf{A}}_{s_L}|\Theta) + I(d; \mathbf{B}|\widetilde{\mathbf{A}}_{s_L}, \Theta). \end{aligned} \tag{5}$$

Firstly, since all elements of Θ are the same, the uncertainty of d cannot be reduced when any L edge devices conspire to obtain Θ. Hence, $I(d; \Theta) = 0$. Secondly, since each element in $\widetilde{\mathbf{A}}_{s_L}$ is generated according to Eq. (1) and Eq. (3). In SPCC, Eq. (1) is a deterministic function and d is independent of Θ, we can get $I(d; \widetilde{\mathbf{A}}_{s_L}|\Theta) = 0$. Thirdly, since the user does not know the content of the data $\mathbf{B}$ and d is independent of $\mathbf{B}$, we can get $I(d; \mathbf{B}|\widetilde{\mathbf{A}}_{s_L}, \Theta) = 0$. To sum up the above, we can get $I(d; \Theta, \widetilde{\mathbf{A}}_{s_L}, \mathbf{B}) = 0$, *i.e.* the privacy condition is satisfied.

Theorem 3. *The SPCC satisfies the decodability condition iff* $T \geq m + L$.

Proof. Since the polynomial of Eq. (1) in SPCC has degree $m + L - 1$, we can decode the final results when $m + L$ edge devices return intermediate results. Therefore, the recovery threshold of SPCC is $N_{SPCC} = m + L$. On one hand, if $T \geq m + L$, we can get $T \geq N_{SPCC}$. According to Eq. (1) and Eq. (3), we can know that the exponent of $\mathbf{A}_i \mathbf{B}_d$ in each intermediate result is unique $\forall i \in \{1, \cdots, m\}$. Therefore, the decodability condition is satisfied. On the other hand, if SPCC satisfies the decodability condition, the number of blocks generated after encoding $\mathbf{A}$ is greater than N_{SPCC}, *i.e.* $T \geq N_{SPCC} = m + L$. To sum up, the SPCC satisfies the decodability condition iff $T \geq m + L$.

Next, we give the analysis of communication cost and computational load of SPCC.

For communication cost of SPCC, firstly, the user sends T coded blocks of $\mathbf{A}$ to the edge devices in total and the dimension of each block is $\frac{t}{m} \times p$. The communication cost of sending is $\frac{tpT}{m}$. Secondly, in order to protect the privacy of data $\mathbf{B}$, each edge device returns n calculation results, *i.e.* $\widetilde{\mathbf{A}}_i \mathbf{B}_1, \cdots, \widetilde{\mathbf{A}}_i \mathbf{B}_n$, and the dimension of them is $\frac{t}{m} \times 1$. In addition, when edge devices return $m + L$ intermediate results, we can decode the final results. The communication cost of intermediate results returned by edge devices is $\frac{n(m+L)t}{m}$. Therefore, the communication cost of SPCC is $(Tp + n(m + L))\frac{t}{m}$.

For computational load of SPCC, in order to protect the privacy of data $\mathbf{B}$, each edge device needs to perform n matrix-vector multiplication. The size of the matrix is $\frac{t}{m} \times p$ and the size of the vector is $p \times 1$. Therefore, the computational load is $\frac{npt}{m}$.

4.2 Secure and Private Coding Scheme with Low Computational Load (SPCL)

However, in SPCC, since edge devices need to perform n matrix-vector multiplication, SPCC obtains a high computational load. Therefore, in this section, we propose the SPCL. Similarly, we prove the security, privacy and decodability conditions of SPCL. Finally, we analyze the communication cost and computational load of SPCL.

In SPCL, to satisfy the privacy condition, the user needs to send the coding sequences $\mathbf{Q}$ to edge devices [17–23]. Firstly, the user lets θ be the d-th column of $n \times n$ identity matrix and generates L random vectors $\mathbf{Z} = [\mathbf{Z}_1, \cdots, \mathbf{Z}_L]$, where $\mathbf{Z}_i \in \mathbb{F}_q^{n \times 1}$, $i \in \{1, \cdots, L\}$. Then, the user selects T non-zero value $\{x_1, \cdots, x_T\}$ to get $\mathbf{Q} = [\mathbf{Q}_1, \cdots, \mathbf{Q}_T]$, where $\mathbf{Q}_i = \mathbf{Q}_{(x_i)}$ and the general expression $\mathbf{Q}_{(x)}$ of $\mathbf{Q}_{(x_i)}$ is shown in Eq. (6).

For the given m, L, we redesign the $\mathbf{Q}_{(x)}$ based on [23] and give α_i are shown as follows:

$$\mathbf{Q}_{(x)} = \frac{\theta}{x} + \mathbf{Z}_1 + x\mathbf{Z}_2 + \cdots + x^{L-1}\mathbf{Z}_L, \tag{6}$$

Table 1. The exponents of x in $f(x)g(x)$ when using SPCL.

	$\theta : -1$	$\mathbf{Z}_1 : 0$	$\cdots$	$\mathbf{Z}_L : L - 1$
$\mathbf{A}_1 : 0$	-1	0	$\ldots$	$L - 1$
$\mathbf{A}_2 : L + 1$	L	$L + 1$	$\cdots$	$2L$
$\cdots$	$\cdots$	$\cdots$	$\cdots$	$\cdots$
$\mathbf{A}_m : (m-1)(L+1)$	$(m-1)(L+1)-1$	$(m-1)(L+1)$	$\cdots$	$(m-1)(L+1)+L-1$
$\mathbf{R}_1 : mL-L+m$	$(m-1)(L+1)$	$(m-1)(L+1)+1$	$\cdots$	$(m-1)(L+1)+L$
$\mathbf{R}_2 : mL-L+m+1$	$(m-1)(L+1)+1$	$(m-1)(L+1)+2$	$\cdots$	$(m-1)(L+1)+L+1$
$\cdots$	$\cdots$	$\cdots$	$\cdots$	$\cdots$
$\mathbf{R}_L : mL+m-1$	$(m-1)(L+1)+L-1$	$(m-1)(L+1)+L$	$\cdots$	$(m-1)(L+1)+2L-1$

$$\alpha_i = \begin{cases} (i - 1)(L + 1), & \forall 1 \leq i \leq m; \\ mL - L + i - m, & \forall m + 1 \leq i \leq m + L. \end{cases} \tag{7}$$

In this scheme, in order to prevent edge devices from getting relevant information of d in the case of collusion of any L edge devices, we add L random vectors to each coding sequence of $\mathbf{Q}$ in the process of coding. Therefore, one coding sequence is composed of $L + 1$ vectors and only θ is valid. As shown in Table 1, in order to guarantee the decodability condition of the scheme, the values from rows $\mathbf{A}_1$ to $\mathbf{A}_m$ of the θ column are unique. The exponential interval of the first m term in $f(x)$ is $m + L$. In addition, for the rows from $\mathbf{R}_1$ to $\mathbf{R}_L$, we need to overlap these items as much as possible. Therefore, the value of α_i ($m + 1 \leq i \leq m + L$) is different from α_j ($1 \leq j \leq m$). By setting Eq. (6) and Eq. (7), we make the interference terms overlap as much as possible and decrease the degree of the highest term of the polynomial.

The computation process are as follows:

– Firstly, the user encodes data $\mathbf{A}$ according to Eq. (1) and Eq. (7) to obtain $\widetilde{\mathbf{A}} = \left[\widetilde{\mathbf{A}}_1^\top, \widetilde{\mathbf{A}}_2^\top, \cdots, \widetilde{\mathbf{A}}_T^\top\right]^\top$. Besides, the user also generates $\mathbf{Q} = [\mathbf{Q}_1, \cdots, \mathbf{Q}_T]$, where $\mathbf{Q}_i = \mathbf{Q}_{(x_i)}$ according to Eq. (6). Then, $\widetilde{\mathbf{A}}_i^\top$ and $\mathbf{Q}_i$ are sent to the i-th edge device.
– Then, when the edge device receives the coded block $\widetilde{\mathbf{A}}_i$ and coding sequence $\mathbf{Q}_i$, the i-th edge device firstly performs the calculation $g(x_i)$ where the general expression $g(x)$ of $g(x_i)$ is shown as below:

$$g(x) = \mathbf{B}\mathbf{Q}_{(x)}. \tag{8}$$

After i-th edge devices obtaining $g(x_i)$, the edge device performs the computation $f(x_i)g(x_i)$ and returns the intermediate result.
– Finally, once the user receives N_{SPCL} intermediate results (N_{SPCL} is the recovery threshold of SPCL and $N_{SPCL} \leq T$), the user can obtain the final result $\mathbf{AB}_d$ by using polynomial interpolation [10]. The general expression of the intermediate result $f(x_i)g(x_i)$ can be shown in Eq. (9).

$$f(x)g(x) = (\sum_{i=1}^{m} \mathbf{A}_i x^{\alpha_i} + \sum_{j=1}^{L} \mathbf{R}_j x^{\alpha_{m+j}})\mathbf{B}\mathbf{Q}_{(x)}$$

$$= \sum_{i=1}^{m} \mathbf{A}_i x^{\alpha_i} \mathbf{B}\mathbf{Q}_{(x)} + \sum_{j=1}^{L} \mathbf{R}_j x^{\alpha_{m+j}} \mathbf{B}\mathbf{Q}_{(x)}. \tag{9}$$

Similar to the proof of Theorem 1, we can get the SPCL meets the security condition.

Theorem 4. *The SPCL is private in the case of collusion of any L edge devices, i.e. the privacy condition is satisfied.*

Proof. We let $\mathbf{Q}_{s_L}$ be the set of coding sequences on any L edge devices. When we use SPCL, according to [17–23] the privacy condition is equivalent to

$$I(d; \mathbf{Q}_{s_L}, \widetilde{\mathbf{A}}_{s_L}, \mathbf{B}) = 0. \tag{10}$$

Therefore, we need to prove Eq. (10). According to the chain rule, the privacy condition is given as follows:

$$I(d; \mathbf{Q}_{s_L}, \widetilde{\mathbf{A}}_{s_L}, \mathbf{B}) = I(d; \mathbf{Q}_{s_L}) + I(d; \widetilde{\mathbf{A}}_{s_L}, \mathbf{B}|\mathbf{Q}_{s_L})$$

$$= I(d; \mathbf{Q}_{s_L}) + I(d; \widetilde{\mathbf{A}}_{s_L}|\mathbf{Q}_{s_L}) + I(d; \mathbf{B}|\widetilde{\mathbf{A}}_{s_L}, \mathbf{Q}_{s_L}). \tag{11}$$

Firstly, since each element in $\mathbf{Q}_{s_L}$ is by encoding θ with L random vector according to Eq. (6) by the user, any L colluding edge devices can not obtain relevant information of θ, i.e. $I(\theta; \mathbf{Q}_{s_L}) = 0$. In addition, since θ contains the information of d, we can know that any L edge devices cannot acquire information of d, i.e. $I(d; \mathbf{Q}_{s_L}) = 0$. Secondly, since each element in $\widetilde{\mathbf{A}}_{s_L}$ is generated according to Eq. (1) and Eq. (7) and both are certain function, the d is independent of $\widetilde{\mathbf{A}}_{s_L}$. Hence, $I(d; \widetilde{\mathbf{A}}_{s_L}|\mathbf{Q}_{s_L}) = 0$. Thirdly, similar to the proof of Theorem 2, we can get $I(d; \mathbf{B}|\widetilde{\mathbf{A}}_{s_L}, \mathbf{Q}_{s_L}) = 0$. To sum up the above, we can get $I(d; \mathbf{Q}_{s_L}, \widetilde{\mathbf{A}}_{s_L}, \mathbf{B}) = 0$, i.e. the privacy condition is satisfied.

Theorem 5. *The SPCL satisfies the decodability condition iff $T \geq (m-1)(L+1) + 2L + 1$.*

Proof. According to Eq. (6) and Eq. (7), we can obtain the exponents of x in $f(x)g(x)$ in Table 1. As shown in Table 1, we can get the recovery threshold of SPCL is $N_{SPCL} = (m-1)(L+1) + 2L + 1$. On one hand, if $T \geq (m-1)(L+1) + 2L + 1$, we can get $T \geq N_{SPCL}$. In addition, by designing $\mathbf{Q}_{(x)}$ and α_i, we can make that the values from rows $\mathbf{A}_1$ to $\mathbf{A}_m$ of the θ column in Table 1 are unique. Further, we can get the exponents of $\mathbf{A}_i \mathbf{B}_d$ in each intermediate result is unique $\forall i \in \{1, \cdots, m\}$. Therefore, the decodability condition is satisfied. On the other hand, if SPCC satisfies the decodability condition, the number of blocks generated after encoding $\mathbf{A}$ is greater than N_{SPCL}, i.e. $T \geq N_{SPCL} = (m-1)(L+1) + 2L + 1$. To sum up, the SPCL satisfies the decodability condition iff $T \geq (m-1)(L+1) + 2L + 1$.

Next, we give the analysis of communication cost and computational load of SPCL.

For communication cost of SPCL, firstly, the user sends T coded blocks of $\mathbf{A}$ and coding sequence $\mathbf{Q}_x$ to edge devices in total. The dimension of each coded blocks of $\mathbf{A}$ is $\frac{t}{m} \times p$ and the dimension of each coding sequence $\mathbf{Q}_x$ is $n \times 1$. Therefore, the communication of data sent by the user to the edge devices is $nT + \frac{tpT}{m}$. Moreover, the dimension of an intermediate result is $\frac{t}{m} \times 1$, and the recovery threshold of SPCL is $(m-1)(L+1) + 2L + 1$. Therefore, the communication cost of intermediate results sent by edge devices to the user is $((m-1)(L+1) + 2L + 1)\frac{t}{m}$. Therefore, the communication cost of the system SPCL is $T(\frac{tp}{m} + n) + ((m-1)(L+1) + 2L + 1)\frac{t}{m}$.

For computational load of SPCL, firstly, in order to protect the privacy of data $\mathbf{B}$, the user needs to send one coding sequence to each edge device. Then, the i-th edge device performs one matrix-vector multiplication. The size of the matrix is $p \times n$ and the size of the vector is $n \times 1$. After that, each device can obtain a vector and the dimension of it is $p \times 1$. The computational load of this process is np. Then, the i-th edge device perform $f(x_i)g(x_i)$. The computational load of the process is $\frac{tp}{m}$. Therefore, the computational load of SPCL is $\frac{tp}{m} + np$.

4.3   Example of SPCC and SPCL

In this section, we give two examples of the two schemes proposed in this paper. In the following example, we assume $t = 6$, $m = 3$, $p = 2$, $n = 3$ $L = 2$. The goal of the user is computing $\mathbf{AB}_1$ satisfying security, privacy and decodability conditions. For clarity, we assume $T = N$. The detailed example of SPCC can be shown as follows:

Example of SPCC

- **Coding** Firstly, the user divides $\mathbf{A}$ by rows to obtain $\mathbf{A} = \left[\mathbf{A}_1^\top, \mathbf{A}_2^\top, \mathbf{A}_3^\top\right]^\top$. Then, the cloud sends $\mathbf{B} = [\mathbf{B}_1, \mathbf{B}_2, \mathbf{B}_3]$ to edge devices before computing. Next, the cloud will not communicate with edge devices. The user randomly generates 2 blocks $\mathbf{R}_1, \mathbf{R}_2$ where $\mathbf{R}_1, \mathbf{R}_2 \in \mathbb{F}_q^{2 \times p}$. Moreover, the user selects 5 values $x_1, \cdots, x_5$ for encoding $\mathbf{A}$ according to Eq. (12) to obtain 5 coded blocks $\widetilde{\mathbf{A}}_1, \cdots, \widetilde{\mathbf{A}}_5$ where $\widetilde{\mathbf{A}}_i = f(x_i)$, $\forall i \in \{1, \cdots, 5\}$. Finally, the user sends $\widetilde{\mathbf{A}}_1, \cdots, \widetilde{\mathbf{A}}_5$ to 5 edge devices respectively.

$$f(x) = \mathbf{A}_1 x^0 + \mathbf{A}_2 x^1 + \mathbf{A}_3 x^2 + \mathbf{R}_1 x^3 + \mathbf{R}_2 x^4. \tag{12}$$

- **Computing** After the i-th edge device receives $\widetilde{\mathbf{A}}_i$, edge devices perform calculation $\widetilde{\mathbf{A}}_i \mathbf{B}_1, \cdots, \widetilde{\mathbf{A}}_i \mathbf{B}_n$. Finally, the i-th edge device return $\widetilde{\mathbf{A}}_i \mathbf{B}_1, \cdots, \widetilde{\mathbf{A}}_i \mathbf{B}_n$ to the user.
- **Decoding** The user receives $\widetilde{\mathbf{A}}_i \mathbf{B}_1, \cdots, \widetilde{\mathbf{A}}_i \mathbf{B}_n$, $\forall i \in \{1, \cdots, 5\}$. The user only uses $\widetilde{\mathbf{A}}_i \mathbf{B}_1$, $\forall i \in \{1, \cdots, 5\}$, where $\widetilde{\mathbf{A}}_i \mathbf{B}_1$ can be shown as follows:

$$\widetilde{\mathbf{A}}_i \mathbf{B}_1 = \mathbf{A}_1 \mathbf{B}_1 + \mathbf{A}_2 \mathbf{B}_1 x_i + \mathbf{A}_3 \mathbf{B}_1 x_i^2$$
$$+ \mathbf{R}_1 \mathbf{B}_1 x_i^3 + \mathbf{R}_2 \mathbf{B}_1 x_i^4.$$

The recovery threshold, communication cost, and computational load are 5, 25, and 12 respectively.

Example of SPCL

- **Coding** In the coding stage, the user select 11 values $\{x_1, \cdots, x_{11}\}$ to encode **A** and generate coding sequence **Q** according to Eq. (13) where $\theta = [1\ 0\ 0]^\top$.

$$f(x) = \mathbf{A}_1 x^0 + \mathbf{A}_2 x^3 + \mathbf{A}_3 x^6 + \mathbf{R}_1 x^9 + \mathbf{R}_2 x^{12},$$

$$\mathbf{Q}_{(x)} = \frac{\theta}{x} + \mathbf{Z}_1 + x\mathbf{Z}_2. \tag{13}$$

- **Computing** After coding phase, the user sends coded block $\widetilde{\mathbf{A}}_i$ and coding sequence $\mathbf{Q}_{(x_i)}$ to the i-th edge devices for computation. When the i-th edge device receives the coding sequence $\mathbf{Q}_{(x_i)}$, they encode **B** according to $g(x)$ in Eq. (14). Finally, the i-th edge device computes $f(x_i)g(x_i)$ and returns the result.

$$g(x) = [\mathbf{B}_1\ \mathbf{B}_2\ \mathbf{B}_3]\mathbf{Q}_{(x)}. \tag{14}$$

- **Decoding** Once the user receives 11 intermediate results, the user can decode the result $\mathbf{AB}_d$. The intermediate result $f(x)g(x)$ can be shown in Eq. (15). In Eq. (15), J_i is the interference term, $\forall i \in \{1, \cdots, 8\}$.

$$\begin{aligned}f(x)g(x) = {} & \mathbf{A}_1\mathbf{B}_1 x^{-1} + \mathbf{A}_2\mathbf{B}_1 x^2 + \mathbf{A}_3\mathbf{B}_1 x^5 \\ & + J_1 x^0 + J_2 x^1 + J_3 x^3 + J_4 x^4 + J_5 x^6 + J_6 x^7 + J_7 x^8 + J_8 x^9\end{aligned} \tag{15}$$

The recovery threshold, communication cost, and computational load are 11, 66, and 10 respectively.

5 Experiments

In this section, we compare the proposed schemes SPCC and SPCL with the existing schemes SPC [21] and XSTP [22] in the case that one round calculation can obtain the final result. We conduct extensive experiments to demonstrate that both the two proposed coding schemes can achieve lower communication cost and computational load than existing work.

5.1 Parameter Settings

To ensure that each scheme can be decoded in the simulation experiment, we do not limit the number of edge devices but we must ensure $T \geq N$ for each scheme. Specifically, we consider the changes of the following six parameters to compare the performances of the two baseline schemes: (1) t, the number of rows in **A**, (2) m, the number of blocks divided by **A**, (3) p, the number of columns in **A**, (4) n, the number of columns in **B**, (5) L, the number of collusive edge devices (6) $\beta = \frac{N}{T}$, the percentage of edge devices that return the intermediate results on time. Besides, we set $t = 2000$, $m = 200$, $p = 100$, $n = 20$, $L = 15$ and $\beta = 0.8$ as the default parameters. For the convenience of observation, we will use the natural logarithm of the y-axis in the experiment.

5.2   Experimental Results of Communication Cost

As shown in Fig. 3(a), the communication cost of SPCC, SPCL, SPC, and XSTP rise as t increases. This is because the row numbers in $\mathbf{A}$ increase but the block numbers divided by $\mathbf{A}$ remain the same. This means an increase in the row numbers in each coded block of $\mathbf{A}$. In addition, since the threshold does not change with the change of t, the user's communication cost to the edge device and the edge device's communication cost to the user both rise. Therefore, the communication cost of all schemes rise. In all cases, the proposed SPCC can achieve the least amount of communication cost.

In Fig. 3(b), as m increases, the communication cost of SPCL remains essentially unchanged. However, the communication cost of SPCC and SPC decrease, and the communication cost of XSTP increases. This is because the number of blocks divided by $\mathbf{A}$ increases, and the row numbers of $\mathbf{A}$ does not change. This means the row numbers of coded blocks in $\mathbf{A}$ decreases. Besides, the recovery thresholds of SPCC, SPCL, SPC, and XSTP all increase. However, in SPCL, the communication cost gained from the decrease in the row numbers per coded block is generated by increasing m. This compensates for the communication cost created by the increased recovery threshold. For SPCC and SPC, when m is set a small value, the row numbers of the coded blocks are large, which means the row numbers of intermediate results are large. With the increase of m, the communication cost decreases, which means that the influence of threshold on communication cost is less than that of block size. For XSTP, although the row numbers of coded blocks of $\mathbf{A}$ decreases, the user needs to send m coded blocks of $\mathbf{A}$ to each device, and the threshold increases, the communication cost of XSTP increases. In all cases, the proposed SPCC can achieve the least amount of communication cost.

In Fig. 3(c), with the increase of p, the communication cost of SPCC, SPCL, SPC, and XSTP all increase. Besides, the communication cost between SPCC and SPC is significantly different. This is due to the fact that the column numbers of per coded block in $\mathbf{A}$ increase as p increases. This means that the number of elements in each block of $\mathbf{A}$ increases. In addition, since the threshold does not change with the change of p, the user's communication cost to the edge device and the edge device's communication cost to the user increase. Therefore, the communication cost of all schemes rise. In all cases, the proposed SPCC can achieve the least amount of communication cost.

In Fig. 3(d), with the increase of n, the communication cost of SPCC and SPC increase. However, SPCL and XSTP are basically unchanged. Besides, when $n < 22$, the communication cost of SPCL is greater than SPC. With the increase of n, the communication cost of SPCL is lower than SPC. This is because each edge device needs to return n results in SPCC. For SPC, the user needs to send n coded blocks to each edge device. As n increases, the communication cost will increase significantly. For SPCL and XSTP, since the thresholds of the two schemes do not change, and the intermediate results and coding sequences account for only a small part of the communication cost of the two schemes, so the communication cost will not change significantly. When n is set to a small

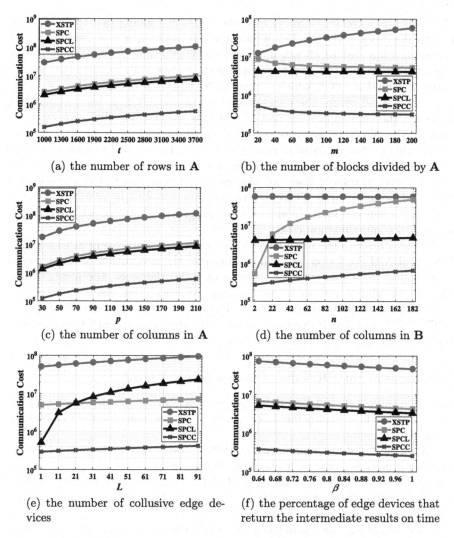

(a) the number of rows in **A**

(b) the number of blocks divided by **A**

(c) the number of columns in **A**

(d) the number of columns in **B**

(e) the number of collusive edge devices

(f) the percentage of edge devices that return the intermediate results on time

Fig. 3. The communication cost when changing different parameters: t, m, p, n, L and β.

value, in SPC, the block numbers sent by the user to each edge device are small. However, at this time, due to the large recovery threshold of SPCL scheme, the communication cost brought by coding sequences and coded blocks is large. When n is set to a large value, since each edge device needs to send n coded blocks to each edge device in SPC, the communication cost of SPC is larger than SPCL. In all cases, the proposed SPCC can achieve the least amount of communication cost.

In Fig. 3(e), with the increase of L, the communication cost of SPCL, SPCC, SPC, and XSTP increase. This is due to the fact that the recovery thresholds of all schemes increase. Consequently, the number of blocks that the user sends to edge devices and the number of intermediate results increase. This means the communication cost of all schemes increase. Furthermore, the communication cost of SPCL changes the greatest. because the increase of L leads to the increase of the threshold of SPCL, which is much larger than that of other schemes. When L is set a small value, the communication cost of SPCL is lower than SPC. However, the communication cost of SPCL is larger than SPC when $L > 21$ because the SPCL recovery threshold is small when L is small and the user sends only one coded blocks to each edge device. Therefore, the communication cost of SPCL is lower than SPC. However, when L is set a large value, the SPC recovery threshold does not change considerably. In SPCL, the recovery threshold becomes large. Therefore, the communication cost of SPCL is larger than SPC when L is large. In all cases, the proposed SPCC can achieve the least amount of communication cost.

In Fig. 3(f), with the increase of β, the communication cost of SPCC, SPCL, SPC, and XSTP all decrease. This is because the proportion of stragglers in edge devices decreases with the increase of β. Furthermore, the percentage of edge devices allocated to tasks and returning results on time rises, while the cost of incorrect communication falls. Therefore, the communication cost of SPCC, SPCL, SPC, and XSTP decrease. In all cases, the proposed SPCC can achieve the least amount of communication cost.

5.3   Experimental Results of Computational Load

Since the computational load only change with t, m, p, and n, we consider the changes of the four parameters to compare the performances of the two baseline schemes.

In all the following experiments, in SPCC, since each edge device needs to perform n matrix-vector multiplication, the size of the matrix is $\frac{t}{m} \times p$ and the size of the vector is $p \times 1$. Similarly, in SPC, each edge device needs to perform n matrix-vector multiplication of size $\frac{t}{m} \times p$ and $p \times 1$. Therefore, the computational load of them is the same.

As shown in Fig. 4(a), with the increase of t, the computational load of SPCC, SPCL, SPC, and XSTP all increase. This is because the row numbers in **A** increase. It means an increase in the row numbers in each coded block of **A** and each edge device needs to more row operations. However, for SPCL and XSTP, the change in computational load is not obvious. For SPCL, this is because although the rows of each coded block become large, the computational load of $g(x)$ is larger than $f(x)g(x)$. For XSTP, this is because the computational load of coding sequence accounts for a large part of the computational load. In all cases, the proposed SPCL can achieve the least amount of computational load.

As shown in Fig. 4(b), with the increase of m, the computational load of SPCC, SPCL, and SPC all decrease. However, the computational load of XSTP increase. Besides, when m is set a enough large value, the computational load of SPCL is close to SPC and SPCC. This is because the block numbers divided by **A** increase and the row numbers of **A** do not change. This means the row numbers

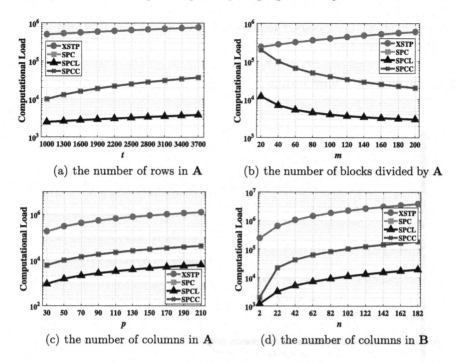

Fig. 4. The computational load when changing different parameters: t, m, p and n.

in coded blocks of **A** decrease. In SPCC and SPC, the computational load of them decrease considerably because of performing n matrix-vector multiplication of size $\frac{t}{m} \times p$ and $p \times 1$. For SPCL, only the computational load of $f(x)g(x)$ decreases, and the computational load of $g(x)$ remains unchanged. For XSTP, each device needs to calculate the sum of m coded blocks multiplied by the coding sequence. In all cases, the proposed SPCL can achieve the least amount of computational load.

In Fig. 4(c), with the increase of p, the computational load of SPCC, SPCL, SPC, and XSTP all increase. This is due to the fact that the column numbers in per coded block of **A** increases as p increases. This means that the number of elements in each block of **A** increases. In SPCC and SPC, the computational load of them decrease considerably because of performing n matrix-vector multiplication of size $\frac{t}{m} \times p$ and $p \times 1$. For SPCL and XSTP, except that the coded block of **A** leads to an increase in the amount of computational load, the coding sequence also leads to an increase in the amount of computational load. In all cases, the proposed SPCL can achieve the least amount of computational load.

In Fig. 4(d), with the increase of n, the computational load of SPCC, SPCL, SPC, and XSTP all increase. This is because each edge device performs n matrix-vector multiplication in SPCC and SPC. In addition, for SPCL and XSTP, the size of coding sequences becomes large. Therefore, the computational load of all schemes increase. In all cases, the proposed SPCL can achieve the least amount of computational load.

5.4   Intuitive Understanding

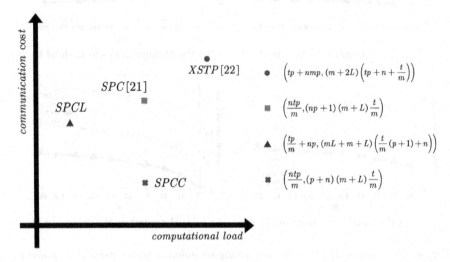

Fig. 5. Relationship between computational load volume and communication cost in all schemes

Finally, in order to give an intuitive understanding, Fig. 5 is given which is related with computational load and communication cost. For the convenience of comparison, we do not consider the straggler problem, $i.e.$ $T = N$ in all schemes. The advantages of the two schemes we proposed are shown in the Fig. 5.

6   Conclusion

In this paper, we study the SPMM issue for edge computing against cooperative attack and design a general coded computation scheme to achieve lowest system resource consumptions, $i.e.$ communication cost and computational load. Specially, we propose two coding schemes, $i.e.$ SPCC and SPCL, to protect the security of data and the privacy of the user. In addition, we give the communication cost and computational load under the two schemes and discover that it is lower than existing work. Specifically, SPCC has more advantages in communication cost, while SPCL has more advantages in computational load. Therefore, they can be flexibly chosen for different scenarios. However, in this paper, we do not consider multi-round calculation and more complex attack models such as active attack. In our future work, we will consider designing the coding scheme to adapt to more complex attack models.

References

1. Asim, M., Wang, Y., Wang, K., Huang, P.Q.: A review on computational intelligence techniques in cloud and edge computing. IEEE Trans. Emerg. Top. Comput. Intell. **4**(6), 742–763 (2020)
2. Wang, L., Jiao, L., He, T., Li, J., Mühlhäuser, M.: Service entity placement for social virtual reality applications in edge computing. In: Proceedings of INFOCOM Conference on Computer Communications, pp. 468–476 (2018)
3. Lv, Z., Chen, D., Lou, R., Wang, Q.: Intelligent edge computing based on machine learning for smart city. Futur. Gener. Comput. Syst. **115**, 90–99 (2021)
4. Liu, S., Liu, L., Tang, J., Yu, B., Wang, Y., Shi, W.: Edge computing for autonomous driving: opportunities and challenges. Proc. IEEE **107**(8), 1697–1716 (2019)
5. Zhou, Z., Chen, X., Li, E., Zeng, L., Luo, K., Zhang, J.: Edge intelligence: paving the last mile of artificial intelligence with edge computing. Proc. IEEE **107**, 1738–1762 (2019)
6. Li, S., Maddah-Ali, A.M., Avestimehr, S.A.: Coding for distributed fog computing. IEEE Commun. Mag. **55**(4), 34–40 (2017)
7. Lee, K., Lam, M., Pedarsani, R., Papailiopoulos, D., Ramchandran, K.: Speeding up distributed machine learning using codes. IEEE Trans. Inf. Theory **64**(3), 1514–1529 (2017)
8. Soto, P., Li, J.: Straggler-free coding for concurrent matrix multiplications. In: Proceedings of International Symposium on Information Theory (ISIT), pp. 233–238 (2020)
9. Dutta, S., Fahim, M., Haddadpour, F., Jeong, H., Cadambe, R.V., Grover, P.: On the optimal recovery threshold of coded matrix multiplication. IEEE Trans. Inf. Theory **66**, 278–301 (2020)
10. Yang, H., Lee, J.: Secure distributed computing with straggling servers using polynomial codes. IEEE Trans. Inf. Forensics Secur. **14**, 141–150 (2019)
11. Bitar, R., Parag, P., Rouayheb, S.E.: Minimizing latency for secure distributed computing. In: Proceedings of International Symposium on Information Theory (ISIT), pp. 2900–2904 (2017)
12. Bitar, R., Parag, P., Rouayheb, S.E.: Minimizing latency for secure coded computing using secret sharing via staircase codes. IEEE Trans. Commun. **68**(8), 4609–4619 (2020)
13. Chang, W., Tandon, R.: On the capacity of secure distributed matrix multiplication. In: Proceedings of Global Communications Conference (GLOBECOM), pp. 1–6 (2019)
14. D'Oliveira, G.L.R., Rouayheb, E.S., Karpuk, D.: GASP codes for secure distributed matrix multiplication. IEEE Trans. Inf. Theory **66**(7), 4038–4050 (2020)
15. Wang, J., Cao, C., Wang, J., Lu, K., Jukan, A., Zhao, W.: Optimal task allocation and coding design for secure edge computing with heterogeneous edge devices. IEEE Trans. Cloud Comput. (2021)
16. Zhu, L., Wang, J., Shi, L., Zhou, J., Lu, K., Wang, J.: Secure coded matrix multiplication against cooperative attack in edge computing. In: Proceedings of International Conference on Trust, Security and Privacy in Computing and Communications (TrustCom), pp. 547–556 (2020)
17. Kim, M., Yang, H., Lee, J.: Private coded computation for machine learning. arXiv:1807.01170 (2018)

18. Kim, M., Lee, J.: Private secure coded computation. IEEE Commun. Lett. 1918–1921 (2019)
19. Chang, W.T., Tandon, R.: On the upload versus download cost for secure and private matrix multiplication. In: IEEE Information Theory Workshop (ITW), pp. 469–473 (2019)
20. Yu, Q., Avestimehr, S.A.: Coded computing for resilient, secure, and privacy-preserving distributed matrix multiplication. IEEE Trans. Commun. **69**, 59–72 (2021)
21. Vaidya, K., Rajan, S.B.: Distributed computation-privacy, straggler mitigation, and security against colluding workers. In: Proceedings of Global Communications Conference (GLOBECOM), pp. 1–6 (2020)
22. Jia, Z., Jafar, S.A.: X-secure T-private information retrieval from MDS coded storage with byzantine and unresponsive servers. IEEE Trans. Inf. Theory **66**, 7427–7438 (2020)
23. Kim, M., Yang, H., Lee, J.: Fully private coded matrix multiplication from colluding workers. IEEE Commun. Lett. **25**, 730–733 (2021)
24. Cai, N., Chan, T.: Theory of secure network coding. Proc. IEEE **99**(3), 421–437 (2011)

Availability-Constrained Application Deployment in Hybrid Cloud-Edge Collaborative Environment

Wei Xu[1,2], Bing Tang[1,2(✉)], Feiyan Guo[1,2], and Xiaoyuan Zhang[1,2]

[1] School of Computer Science and Engineering, Hunan University of Science and Technology, Xiangtan 411201, China
[2] Hunan Key Laboratory for Service Computing and Novel Software Technology, Hunan University of Science and Technology, Xiangtan 411201, China
btang@hnust.edu.cn

Abstract. Cloud computing offers strong availability and lower cost, while edge computing has lower delay. Deployment of applications by placing microservices in containers in a cloud-edge collaborative environment is adopted by more and more enterprise application providers. For users, they care more about application response time and application availability. For application providers, they also need to save deployment costs to the maximum extent. Therefore, the application deployment in hybrid cloud-edge collaborative environment is a multi-objective optimization problem. In this paper, a genetic algorithm named DP-GA based on improved NSGA-II has been proposed to solve the multi-objective NP-hard problem. We balance the two objectives of minimizing deployment cost and average response time under availability constraints. Using the real dataset of Shanghai Telecom, the experimental results show that the proposed DP-GA is superior to the existing methods, reducing average response time by about 35% and saving deployment cost by about 15%.

Keywords: Composite application · Microservice deployment · Availability · Genetic algorithm · Cloud-edge collaboration

1 Introduction

With the advent of the era of the Internet of Everything and the advent of the 5G era, the data generated by network edge devices are growing rapidly. At this time, the centralized processing in the cloud computing center will not be able to efficiently process the data generated by edge devices. With the wide application of edge computing, some problems are constantly exposed, such as more expensive deployment costs and poor availability. Therefore, this paper discusses deploying applications in the cloud-edge collaboration environment, taking advantage of the two computing modes, cloud computing and edge computing.

The application deployed in this paper is based on the microservice architecture. In recent years, the microservice architecture has received extensive

© ICST Institute for Computer Sciences, Social Informatics and Telecommunications Engineering 2022
Published by Springer Nature Switzerland AG 2022. All Rights Reserved
H. Gao et al. (Eds.): CollaborateCom 2022, LNICST 460, pp. 233–248, 2022.
https://doi.org/10.1007/978-3-031-24383-7_13

attentions. Through combining microservices to build composite applications, it brings strong scalability and flexibility, which has become the deployment method widely chosen by many application providers. In this paper, we encapsulate microservices through containers, and then deploy the containers in virtual machines (VM) which are hosted by physical machines (PM). Both edge data center and cloud data center can deploy microservices.

Based on traditional cloud computing, due to its large response delay, it is urgent to shorten the application response time, especially for applications that require timely response. At the same time, edge computing has relatively poor availability and high deployment costs. Therefore, we combine the needs of both application providers and users, and we mainly focus on the following issues:

(1) The availability of edge data centers closer to the city center is worse due to electromagnetic interference in the city center and higher frequency of user access. At the same time, compared with edge computing, cloud computing often has higher availability due to centralized management.

(2) Because edge data center is often located in the urban area, its management cost is relatively high, and cloud data center is often far away from the urban area, centralized management cost is usually relatively low.

(3) If the microservice is deployed in an edge data center that is closer to the city center, the closer it is to the user, the shorter the response time will be, and the farther it is from the user center, the higher the response time. In addition, the response time of the cloud computing center is often the farthest from the user and has the highest application response time [3,11].

(4) When deploying microservices, we should consider whether the deployed microservices encapsulated in containers exceed the maximum resource capacity of virtual machines.

In response to the above problems, under the conditions of availability and resource constraints, we study minimizing deployment cost and minimizing application response time based on the microservice architecture. It is an NP-hard problem. We propose a new algorithm named DP-GA based on the genetic algorithm to realize the optimal application deployment in the hybrid cloud-edge collaborative environment.

The main contributions of this paper are summarized as follows:

– First, we define the optimal application deployment problem in the cloud-edge collaborative environment as a constrained multi-objective optimization problem. The goal is to deploy composite applications under resource constraints and availability constraints, so as to minimize the response time and deployment cost.

– Secondly, we propose a new method based on genetic algorithm to solve the multi-objective application deployment problem for composite applications, which is characterized by a specially designed population initialization method to obtain a better initial population to achieve better experimental results.

– Finally, to evaluate the proposed method, we obtain multiple Shanghai edge data centers and Western China Cloud Computing Center through clustering algorithm using the real Shanghai Telecom dataset to construct a cloud-edge collaborative environment. We compared our method with several existing algorithms by changing the number of microservices, and the availability constraint coefficient. The experimental results show that our method outperforms the existing methods.

The remainder of this paper is organized as follows. Section 2 discusses the related work on microservice allocation in container-based edge clouds and existing microservice deployment in cloud-edge environments. Section 3 defines the problem model. Section 4 introduces the improved algorithm DP-GA. Section 5 describes the experimental results and analysis. Section 6 summarizes the whole paper and discusses future work.

2   Related Work

This section presents related work on container-based microservice allocation and existing microservice deployment in cloud-edge environments. The main challenges that need to be addressed in our problem are also highlighted.

In recent years, cloud computing is emerging as a hosting model for delivering business applications. How to deploy application services with the best quality of service becomes a key issue [10,13]. Several research efforts have investigated the service deployment problem. For example, Wen et al. studied application deployment on federated clouds to minimize deployment costs while meeting the security and reliability requirements of deployment [13]. Shi et al. minimized the product of deployment cost and response time of business applications through an algorithm based on genetic algorithm [12], and there are also some multi-objective studies such as network transmission time [4,6,8,9], load balancing or energy consumption [1,4–6,8,9], availability [1,6] and other similar requirements [8]. However, most of these studies consider the problem of microservice allocation in cloud environments. With the continuous development of the Internet era and the arrival of the 5G era, Internet mobile devices and smart wear are becoming more and more popular, and in some situation, cloud computing can not satisfy the requirements of rapid application response without the assistance of the edge computing. Focusing on cloud computing alone will not suffice. The research in this paper is based on the deployment of microservices in the cloud-edge collaborative environment.

The research on container-based microservice deployment of composite applications considers a wide range of goals. Most of the works apply multi-objective optimization algorithms such as Ant Colony Algorithm (ACO) [6], NSGA-II [2], Particle Swarm Optimization (PSO) [5] to solve the problem. However, since these works are conventional multi-objective algorithms, in order to achieve better results and deal with more complex multi-layer (microservice-container-VM-PM) deployment problems, we intend to develop a new multi-objective algorithm to solve microservice multi-instance deployment problem of multiply composite applications in container-based cloud-edge collaborative environment.

3   Problem Description

3.1   Resource Model

In this paper, we study the deployment of composite application in the cloud-edge collaborative environment. The problem is that a set of composite applications $CA = \{ca_1, ca_2, ..., ca_i, ..., ca_s\}$, where ca_i represents the i-th composite application, s represents the number of composite applications, and each application consists of a set of microservices $MS = \{ms_1, ms_2, ..., ms_l, ..., ms_o\}$, where ms_l represents the l-th microservice, and o represents the number of microservices. Here, we assume that each microservice has two instances, and each instance is mapped to the container $C = \{c_{11}, c_{12}, c_{21}, c_{22}, ..., c_{l1}, c_{l2}, ..., c_{o1}, c_{o2}\}$, where c_{l1}, c_{l2} means that the two instances of the l-th microservice are mapped to the corresponding two containers, and c_{lj} is used to represent a specific container, where $j \in \{1, 2\}$. The memory capacity of each container is $\alpha(c_{lj})$.

There is a set of virtual machine types $\Psi = \{\psi_1, \psi_2, ..., \psi_q, ..., \psi_t\}$ used to allocate containers, where ψ_q represents the q-th virtual machine type, and t represents the total number of virtual machine types. For the type of virtual machine selected by the cloud-edge data center to host the container, we use $VM = \{vm_1, vm_2, ..., vm_p, ..., vm_x, vm_{x+1}\}$ to represent, where vm_p denotes the type of virtual machine selected when the p-th edge data center allocates the container, x represents the total number of edge data centers, and vm_{x+1} represents when the virtual machine type selected when the cloud data center needs to host containers. The capacity of each virtual machine is represented by $\delta(vm_p)$. The cost corresponding to each virtual machine is represented by $VMF = \{vmf_1, vmf_2, ..., vmf_p, ..., vmf_x, vmf_{x+1}\}$, where vmf_p represents the cost of the p-th virtual machine.

We define $DC = \{dc_1, dc_2, ..., dc_p, ..., dc_x, dc_{x+1}\}$ to represent the cloud-edge data center location set, where dc_p represents the location of the p-th edge data center, x represents the total number of edge data centers, dc_{x+1} represents the specified cloud data center location, and the corresponding capacity of PM in this data center is represented by $\Lambda(dc_p)$. Depending on the location of the data center, the availability is different. The availability of the cloud computing center is determined by the SLA provided by the VM, and the edge data center determines its availability by a given PM. For the convenience of calculation, the failure rate of a set of edge data centers and cloud computing centers can be defined as $F = \{f_1, f_2, ..., f_p, ..., f_x, f_{x+1}\}$, where f_p represents the failure rate of the PM of the p-th edge data center, and f_{x+1} represents the failure rate of VMs in the cloud data center. The set of user center locations is represented by $UC = \{uc_1, uc_2, ..., uc_k, ..., uc_r\}$, where uc_k represents the k-th user center in the city, and r represents the total number of user centers.

3.2   Time Model

The total amount of work of the i-th composite application ca_i is determined as: $tw_i = \sum_{k=1}^{r} r_{ik}$, where r_{ik} represents the request rate of the k-th user center of the application ca_i. Each service instance is modeled as a $M/M/1$ queue, since a service can be shared by multiple applications, service aggregation workloads can be accessed through

$$wl = \sum_{i=1}^{s} tw_i \quad s.t. \quad ms_l \in ca_i \tag{1}$$

For a VM instance with a processing capacity of ϕ, according to Little's law [7], the average request time for a service ms_l is

$$st_l = \frac{1}{\phi - wl} \tag{2}$$

Average latency between user center and the i-th application is

$$ua_i = \frac{\sum_{k=1}^{r} r_{ik}(Bt_{ik} + Et_{ik})}{tw_i} \tag{3}$$

where Bt_{ik} represents the delay from the k-th user center to the i-th application's starting service, Et_{ik} represents the network delay from the i-th application's ending service to the k-th user center.

We assume that mst_{ab} represents the network latency between the service mst_a and its successor service mst_b, and ua_i, mst_{ab} are usually determined by several immutable factors in the communication network. So, ART_i is calculated by $ART_i = ua_i + MS(ca_i)$, where $MS(ca_i)$ refers to the response time of the ca_i in the workflow. We define two functions EST (Earliest Start Time) and FT (Finish Time) for each service to calculate the application makespan. The computing process begins with the starting service, and the MS is the finish time of the ending service.

$$
\begin{aligned}
EST(start_i) &= 0 \\
FT(ms_l) &= EST(ms_l) + st_l \\
EST(ms_l) &= \max_{ms_a \in Pre(ms_l)} \{FT(ms_a) + mst_{al}\} \\
MS(ca_i) &= FT(end_i)
\end{aligned}
\tag{4}
$$

So, the average response time TRT is expressed by:

$$TRT = \frac{\sum_{i=1}^{s} tw_i ART_i}{\sum_{i=1}^{s} tw_i} \tag{5}$$

3.3   Cost Model

We define a binary variable D_{lj}^{p} to represent the location of the cloud-edge data center where the container is deployed.

$$D_{lj}^{p} = \begin{cases} 1 & \text{if } c_{lj} \text{ is placed on } dc_p \\ 0 & \text{otherwise} \end{cases} \tag{6}$$

We define the cost of deploying the microservice ms_l as

$$ msf_l = \sum_{j=1}^{2} \sum_{p=1}^{x+1} vmf_p D_{lj}^p \tag{7} $$

So, the total cost of composite application deployment is calculated through

$$ Cost = \sum_{l=1}^{o} msf_l \tag{8} $$

3.4   Availability Constraints

The microservice ms_l obtains the failure rate of the corresponding container where it is deployed:

$$ Dep(f_p) = \begin{cases} f_p & \text{if } (\sum_{j=1}^{2} \sum_{p}^{x+1} D_{lj}^p) > 0 \\ 1 & \text{else} \end{cases} \tag{9} $$

Then, the availability of the corresponding microservice ms_l can be defined as

$$ Msa_l = 1 - \prod_{p=1}^{x+1} Dep(f_p) \tag{10} $$

The availability of application ca_i can be defined as

$$ A_i = \prod_{l=1}^{o} Msa_l \quad s.t. \quad ms_l \in ca_i \tag{11} $$

The average availability for a set of composite applications is

$$ Availability = \frac{\sum_{i=1}^{s} A_i}{s} \geq a \tag{12} $$

where a is the minimum availability specified by the application provider, and we use feasible solutions under availability constraints to satisfy the availability constraints as reference solutions:

$$ a = A_{minimum} + k(A_{maximum} - A_{minimum}) \tag{13} $$

Among them, $A_{maximum}$ and $A_{minimum}$ are the highest availability and the lowest availability among various schemes deployed. k is the strictness coefficient that controls availability, and $k \in [0, 1]$. The larger the k, the more stringent the availability specified by the application provider.

3.5   Resource Constraints

It is required that the total resources of all containers allocated to each created virtual machine cannot exceed its capacity, and for each virtual machine type vm_p selected in the cloud-edge data center, it must satisfies

$$ \sum_{l=1}^{o} \sum_{j=1}^{2} \alpha(c_{lj}) D_{lj}^p \leq vm_p \tag{14} $$

At the same time, it also needs to satisfy that the total capacity of the virtual machines created by each PM does not exceed the corresponding PM's capacity. For the PM's capacity $\Lambda(dc_p)$ of each cloud-edge data center, it must satisfies

$$vm_p \leq \Lambda(dc_p) \tag{15}$$

3.6 Problem Definition

Here, a dual-objective optimization problem is defined to solve the optimal deployment under the conditions of minimizing cost and delay, subject to availability constraints and resource constraints, as shown in Eq. (16).

$$
\begin{aligned}
\min Cost &= \sum_{l=1}^{o} msf_l \\
\min TRT &= \frac{\sum_{i=1}^{s} tw_i ART_i}{\sum_{i=1}^{s} tw_i} \\
s.t. \quad Availability &= \frac{\sum_{i=1}^{s} A_i}{s} \geq a \\
&\sum_{l=1}^{o} \sum_{j=1}^{2} \alpha(c_{lj}) D_{lj}^{p} \leq vm_p \\
&vm_p \leq \Lambda(dc_p)
\end{aligned}
\tag{16}
$$

4 Algorithm Implementation

This section proposes a microservice deployment method based on cloud-edge collaboration. Firstly, the K-means clustering algorithm is used to cluster and group the edge server coordinates, and the edge servers in the same cluster are clustered to the same location, which can greatly reduce the search space. Then, an improved multi-objective genetic algorithm DP-GA based on NSGA-II is used to solve the microservice deployment to achieve a balance between dual objectives under constraints.

4.1 Chromosome Coding

We use chromosomes to encode service deployment solutions, and use an array of real integers to represent microservice placement strategies. Each chromosome represents a deployment strategy. Each code on each chromosome represents the location where each microservice is deployed, which carries the container where the microservice is located and its corresponding VM.

4.2 Fitness Function and Constraints

The fitness function is used to judge the pros and cons of individuals, each solution is represented by each individual, and all solutions constitute the overall population. The fitness function in this paper includes two categories: TRT and $Cost$. In addition to the fitness function, the constraints in this paper include two aspects. The first is the availability constraint. Any deployment scheme must meet the availability constraints. The closer to the city center, the higher the cost, the shorter the response time, and the worse of the availability. Secondly, resource constraints must be met. The virtual machine hosted by each physical machine must not exceed the capacity of the physical machine, and the resource of the container hosted by the virtual machine must not exceed the available resource of the virtual machine.

4.3   Population Initialization

The purpose of initialization is to create a set of different solutions. First, we heuristically assign the containers containing microservices to a set of VMs with random types (uniformly selected from the VM table) using First Fit (FF). Then, use FF to assign the VM to the PM. The use of FF guarantees an efficient solution as well as a unified VM/PM allocation problem.

In general, GAs randomly generate an initial population to ensure the diversity of the population. In order to improve the solution quality and convergence speed, this paper firstly uses the Differential Evolution Algorithm (DE) to determine a part of the population, and the rest of the population will be randomly initialized. The differential evolution algorithm is an efficient global optimization algorithm to prevent falling into a local optimum. By determining a part of the population first through the differential optimization algorithm, the quality of the evolutionary solution can be greatly improved.

4.4   Selection Operator

The improved genetic algorithm DP-GA selection operator in this paper adopts the elite reserved tournament selection operator (etour). Through the replacement sampling method, it is guaranteed that the optimal individual will be selected to participate in the tournament. This method can retain the optimal individual to the next generation of population until the matching pool is sufficient.

4.5   Crossover Operator

The crossover operator adopts the simulated binary crossover (recbx), which adopts the single-point crossover method. The selection of the crossover point is random, and the selection range of the crossover point is from 1 to the number of genes on each chromosome. Small damage can better maintain excellent individuals.

4.6   Mutation Operator

The mutation operator is to adopt two point swapping mutation (mutswap). After determining the deployment location of the microservice, we also determine the cost and response time of the microservice deployment. Since the composite application deployment problem in this paper is modeled as having to the acyclic graph (DAG) form, fully consider the dependence between services, the response time and deployment cost of different services are different when the containers are deployed in different locations. It does not destroy excellent individuals, reduces the probability of rapid convergence, and can continuously seek the optimal two goals through mutation.

4.7   Algorithm Description

Our proposed DP-GA algorithm, as shown in Algorithm 1, follows the standard framework of NSGA-II, a multi-objective genetic algorithm. The algorithm initializes the population through the differential evolution algorithm and the random generation combination method, and the solution is represented as a group of containers containing microservices corresponding to the location number of the VM where the VM is located. The pareto dominance relationship is obtained by fast non-dominated sorting, and then the priority between individuals is determined by calculating the crowding degree, so that the individuals in the quasi-pareto solution can be extended to the entire pareto domain, and evenly distributed to maintain the diversity of the population, the elite strategy is introduced, the sampling space is expanded, the parent population and the child population are merged to ensure that the excellent individuals can be retained, and then iteratively iterates through the crossover and two-point exchange mutation methods. This evolutionary process ends when a predetermined number of generations or a satisfactory fitness value level is reached.

Algorithm 1. Genetic algorithm DP-GA based on NSGA-II.

Input: A set of microservices
Output: The allocation of microservices
 1: Initialize a population P with individuals;
 2: **while** Termination Condition is not meet **do**
 3:     **for** each individual **do**
 4:         evaluate the fitness values;
 5:     **end for**
 6:     **while** children number is less than the population size **do**
 7:         apply binary elite tournament selection to select two parents;
 8:         apply simulated binary crossover over the selected parents;
 9:         apply two point swapping mutation on two children;
10:         add the children into a new population U;
11:     **end while**
12:     evaluate individuals from U;
13:     non-dominated sorting of $P \cup U$;
14:     calculate crowding distance of $P \cup U$;
15:     $P \leftarrow$ select population size of individuals from $P \cup U$;
16: **end while**
17: return the Pareto front of solutions;

---

5   Experimental Results and Analysis

In this paper, we study the deployment of applications in a cloud-edge collaboration environment based on availability and resource constraints, measuring and evaluating average response time and deployment costs. We compare our proposed algorithm with three other algorithms including differential evolution algorithm (DE), ant colony algorithm (ACO), and particle swarm optimization algorithm (PSO).

5.1   Dataset

The experiment is conducted using the real dataset of Shanghai Telecom, which contains the locations of around 3,000 base stations. We cluster the base stations through a K-means clustering algorithm to form 27 edge data centers. Together with the Western China Cloud Computing Center, we obtain a total of 28 cloud-edge data centers which are used as locations for microservice deployment. The center of the 16 districts in Shanghai is taken as the location of user centers. Here, it is assumed that the total number of visits in the whole Shanghai city is 100 times/second, according to the proportion of the population of each district, we calculated the visit frequency of each user center, as shown in Table 1.

Table 1. User center visit frequency.

User centers	User center visit frequency (times/s)
Huangpu District	2.7
Xuhui District	4.5
Changning District	2.8
Jingan District	3.9
Putuo District	4.9
Hongkou District	3
Yangpu District	5
Minhang District	10.7
Baoshan District	9
Jiading District	7.4
Pudong New Area	22.8
Jinshan District	3.3
Songjiang District	7.7
Qingpu District	5.1
Fengxian District	4.6
Chongming District	2.6

According to the location of each data center and the distance from the city center, the cost of each virtual machine type and the failure rate of the physical machine in each data center are determined. The closer to the city center, the higher the virtual machine rental cost. Due to the interference of various signals in the city center and the high frequency of user visits, the corresponding failure rate is also higher. Here, the Western China Cloud Computing Center has the

Table 2. Virtual machine price and failure rate.

Data center location	Virtual machine price ($/month)			Failure rate
	1Core 1G	2Core 2G	2Core 4G	
Huangpu District	12	23	45	0.047
Xuhui District	10.2	20.1	39.6	0.037
Changning District	11.5	22.7	43.9	0.043
Jingan District	10.6	20.8	40.2	0.039
Putuo District	7.9	15.8	30.9	0.02
Hongkou District	9.1	17.8	36.5	0.028
Yangpu District	9.7	19.2	37.7	0.032
Minhang District	8.7	17.2	33.9	0.025
Baoshan District	9.5	18.6	36.9	0.03
Jiading District	9.9	19.4	38.1	0.035
Pudong New Area	10.9	21.3	41.7	0.041
Jinshan District	7	13.8	26.5	0.01
Songjiang District	7.3	14.1	27.5	0.016
Qingpu District	8.3	16.2	32.1	0.022
Fengxian District	7.7	14.9	29.3	0.018
Chongming District	6.8	13.1	25.7	0.009
Western China Cloud Computing Center	5.4	10.2	19.6	0.0000001

lowest virtual machine rental cost, the lowest failure rate, and is the farthest from the city. Table 2 shows the price of different virtual machine types and the failure rate for the edge data centers in Shanghai and the Western China Cloud Computing Center.

5.2 Simulation Settings and Parameter Settings

Table 3. Parameter value for GA.

Key parameter	Value
Crossover probability	0.9
Mutation probability	0.1
The maximum number of iterations	100
Population proportion of differential evolution algorithm	20%
The number of populations	500
Time delay of each microservice processing request	[3 ms, 6 ms]

In our experiment, we simulate three application and 10 microservices as shown in Fig. 1. We assume that each microservice can be loaded and run with the virtual machine type of "1Core1G", which is the minimum environment to run a microservice.

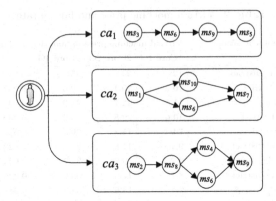

Fig. 1. Three applications with 10 microservices in our experiments.

Assuming that all requests are sent by user centers in Shanghai, and the total number of requests is fixed. According to the population proportion of each user center, the number of requests sent by each user center is calculated. Experiment environment are described as follows: the operating system is Windows 11; CPU is Intel Core i7-8700 with 3.2 GHz; the memory is 16 GB. The programming language is Python, and NSGA-II is implemented using Python Geatpy package. The values of the parameters for genetic algorithm we set are shown in Table 3.

5.3   Results and Analysis

Comparison of TRT and Cost Under Different Numbers of Microservices. We take the application ca_1 as an example, and change the number of deployed microservices. The minimum number of microservices is 3, the maximum number is 7, and the step size is 1. Each microservice is deployed in different cloud-edge data centers, and the availability constraint is fixed at 92%. DP-GA is compared with PSO, ACO and DE, in terms of the average response time and deployment cost.

First of all, the comparison results of average response time are shown in Fig. 2. It can be seen from this figure that no matter how many microservices there are, the TRT obtained by DP-GA is the smallest and it is about 35% better than other algorithms which shows that DP-GA is optimal. At the same time, it shows that when the number of microservices reaches 7, the TRT is greatly increased. The increase is due to the fact that when there are 7 microservices and the constraint is 92%, the cloud computing center participates in the deployment of microservices to increase the availability and reduce the failure rate.

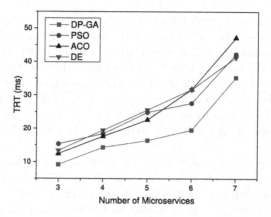

Fig. 2. Comparison of average response time with different numbers of microservices.

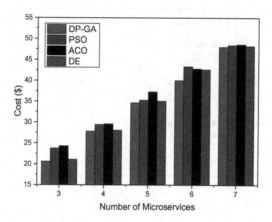

Fig. 3. Comparison of deployment cost with different numbers of microservices.

Next, we compare the effects of four algorithms in deployment cost. The results are shown in Fig. 3. From the information in the figure, it can be seen that DP-GA can always get the least cost among the four algorithms and save about 15% in deployment costs.

Comparison of TRT and Cost Under Different Availability Control Coefficient. We also take the application ca_1 as an example, deploy four microservices, and each microservice has two instances. The availability of the application can be greatly improved through multiple instances. Here, we control the availability in different degrees. Under the same conditions, the deployment schemes obtained by the four algorithms are compared to verify the effectiveness of DP-GA. In order to maximize the application availability, the instances of each microservice are also deployed in different cloud-edge data centers. For each user center in each deployment scheme, the shortest path with the least time-consuming is selected when the user center requesting applications.

First, we compare average response time, and the experimental results are shown in Fig. 4. We can conclude from this figure that as the availability constraint continues to increase, the location where we deploy microservices will be farther and farther away from the densely populated city center, and the TRT at this time will continue to increase. The TRT is always the smallest in the deployment scheme given by DP-GA, and when k is 0.5, the TRT is reduced by about 30%.

Next, we compare the deployment cost of the four algorithms under different availability control coefficient, as shown in Fig. 5. Comparison results in the figure shows that with the continuous improvement of availability constraints, the deployment location is getting farther and farther away from the city center,

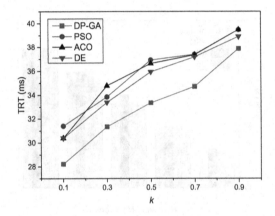

Fig. 4. Comparing average response time with different availability control coefficient.

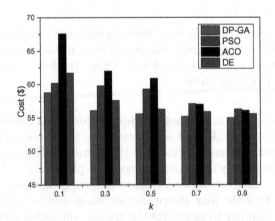

Fig. 5. Comparing deployment cost with different availability control coefficient.

and the cost at this time is constantly decreasing, when k is 0.5, the deployment cost is saved by about 10%. It can be seen that DP-GA is better than other algorithms.

6   Conclusion

In this paper, we studied the problem of optimal application deployment in cloud-edge environments considering availability constraints. To address this problem, we propose a novel genetic algorithm-based method to solve a multi-objective optimization problem with two objectives, that is to minimize the average response time and deployment cost. This method can allocate appropriate virtual machines to microservices, and deploy microservices in appropriate cloud-edge centers to achieve the goal. Based on the real dataset of Shanghai Telecom, we have confirmed through a large number of experimental results that the proposed multi-objective optimization algorithm DP-GA is superior to PSO, ACO and DE.

However, the proposed model and method have certain limitations, and for future work we will adjust and extend our method to adapt to more complex problems. For example, we will further comprehensively consider issues such as privacy, fault tolerance and reliability in the cloud-edge environment to cope with more dynamic environments and more complex user needs.

Acknowledgement. This work is supported by Natural Science Foundation of Hunan Province (No. 2021JJ30278).

References

1. Guerrero, C., Lera, I., Juiz, C.: Genetic algorithm for multi-objective optimization of container allocation in cloud architecture. J. Grid Comput. **16**(1), 113–135 (2018)
2. Guerrero, C., Lera, I., Juiz, C.: Resource optimization of container orchestration: a case study in multi-cloud microservices-based applications. J. Supercomput. **74**(7), 2956–2983 (2018). https://doi.org/10.1007/s11227-018-2345-2
3. Heilig, L., Buyya, R., Voß, S.: Location-aware brokering for consumers in multi-cloud computing environments. J. Netw. Comput. Appl. **95**, 79–93 (2017)
4. Hu, Y., De Laat, C., Zhao, Z.: Multi-objective container deployment on heterogeneous clusters. In: 2019 19th IEEE/ACM International Symposium on Cluster, Cloud and Grid Computing (CCGRID), pp. 592–599. IEEE (2019)
5. Li, L., Chen, J., Yan, W.: A particle swarm optimization-based container scheduling algorithm of docker platform. In: Proceedings of the 4th International Conference on Communication and Information Processing, pp. 12–17 (2018)
6. Lin, M., Xi, J., Bai, W., Wu, J.: Ant colony algorithm for multi-objective optimization of container-based microservice scheduling in cloud. IEEE Access **7**, 83088–83100 (2019)
7. Little, J.D., Graves, S.C.: Little's law. In: Chhajed, D., Lowe, T.J. (eds.) Building Intuition, pp. 81–100. Springer, Boston (2008). https://doi.org/10.1007/978-0-387-73699-0_5

8. Liu, B., Li, P., Lin, W., Shu, N., Li, Y., Chang, V.: A new container scheduling algorithm based on multi-objective optimization. Soft. Comput. **22**(23), 7741–7752 (2018). https://doi.org/10.1007/s00500-018-3403-7

9. Lv, L., et al.: Communication-aware container placement and reassignment in large-scale internet data centers. IEEE J. Sel. Areas Commun. **37**(3), 540–555 (2019)

10. Mao, Z., Yang, J., Shang, Y., Liu, C., Chen, J.: A game theory of cloud service deployment. In: 2013 IEEE Ninth World Congress on Services, pp. 436–443. IEEE (2013)

11. Shi, T., Ma, H., Chen, G.: A genetic-based approach to location-aware cloud service brokering in multi-cloud environment. In: 2019 IEEE International Conference on Services Computing (SCC), pp. 146–153. IEEE (2019)

12. Shi, T., Ma, H., Chen, G.: A seeding-based GA for location-aware workflow deployment in multi-cloud environment. In: 2019 IEEE Congress on Evolutionary Computation (CEC), pp. 3364–3371. IEEE (2019)

13. Wen, Z., Cała, J., Watson, P., Romanovsky, A.: Cost effective, reliable and secure workflow deployment over federated clouds. IEEE Trans. Serv. Comput. **10**(6), 929–941 (2016)

EBA: An Adaptive Large Neighborhood Search-Based Approach for Edge Bandwidth Allocation

Qinghong Hu[1,2], Qinglan Peng[3], Jiaxing Shang[1,2(✉)], Yong Li[1,2],
and Junjie He[4]

[1] College of Computer Science, Chongqing University, Chongqing, China
qinghonghu@yeah.net, {shangjx,yongli}@cqu.edu.cn
[2] Key Laboratory of Dependable Service Computing in Cyber Physical Society,
Ministry of Education, Chongqing, China
[3] School of Artificial Intelligence, Henan University, Zhengzhou, China
qinglan.peng@hotmail.com
[4] Information and Data Center, Guizhou Minzu University, Guiyang, China
18212727047@163.com

Abstract. As a promising computing paradigm, edge computing aims at delivering high-response and low-latency computing, storage, and bandwidth resources to end-users at the edge of the network. However, those edge-based novel applications (e.g., live broadcast, edge cloud game, real-time AR/VR rendering, etc.) are usually bandwidth-consuming, which has made a considerable contribution to the operating costs of edge application providers. Meanwhile, the bandwidth pricing modes of edge infrastructure providers are also complicated. Therefore, how to allocate the bandwidth demands of edge users to suitable edge servers to minimize the monetary cost of edge application providers becomes an important issue. In this paper, we consider the widely adopted 95th-percentile bandwidth billing mode and Quality-of-Service constrained edge bandwidth allocation problem, and propose a neighborhood search-based approach, shorts for EBA. It firstly employs a network flow-based heuristic to find a feasible initial solution quickly. Then, an adaptive large neighborhood search-based method is utilized to perform iterative optimization, which contains hill climbing and simulated annealing mechanisms. Therefore, the proposed EBA approach can expand the searching space, accelerate the optimization convergence speed, and avoid falling into local optimal. Experiments based on a real-world edge bandwidth consumption dataset illustrate the effectiveness of the proposed approach.

Keywords: Edge computing · Edge bandwidth allocation · 95th-percentile billing

© ICST Institute for Computer Sciences, Social Informatics and Telecommunications Engineering 2022
Published by Springer Nature Switzerland AG 2022. All Rights Reserved
H. Gao et al. (Eds.): CollaborateCom 2022, LNICST 460, pp. 249–268, 2022.
https://doi.org/10.1007/978-3-031-24383-7_14

1 Introduction

With the rapid development of advanced communication technologies and novel Internet of Things (IoT) technologies, nowadays we are surrounded by various kinds of smart mobile devices, which continuously generate a large amount of data day and night, thus creating the demand for processing local data using local computing resources [22]. To this end, the multi-access edge computing (MEC) paradigm emerged and has been widely used to support those computing-intensive, latency-sensitive, and privacy-preserving applications. The key idea of MEC is to sink the computing, storage, and bandwidth resources to the edge of the network, i.e., closer to the end-users [14,19]. Benefitting from edge computing-offloading technologies, the MEC paradigm has successfully supported the realization and prosperity of various novel applications, such as extreme-low-latency live broadcasting, online video game rendering, and immersion metaverse.

However, different from the traditional cloud computing paradigm with infinite resources, edge computing is usually constrained by limited resources [9] and high prices, especially for bandwidth resources. According to Gartner's prediction [2], by 2025 bandwidth cost will be the primary driver for new edge computing deployments, especially for those heavy content delivery applications (e.g., live streaming, cloud games, etc.). For these edge application providers, bandwidth accounts for a significant portion of their operating costs. Therefore, for edge application providers, it is of great practical significance to study how to properly allocate the bandwidth demands of edge users to appropriate edge servers while fulfilling the Quality-of-Service (QoS) constraint to reduce the cost.

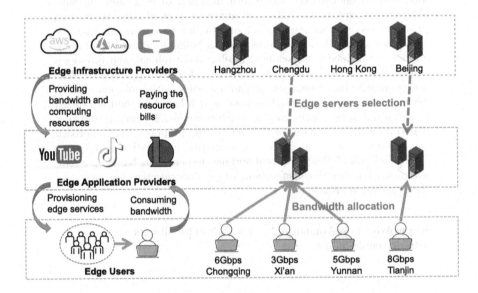

Fig. 1. Edge bandwidth allocation problem.

As shown in Fig. 1, where edge user refers to a group of end-users located in a certain area (e.g., all Tiktok users in Singapore), and its bandwidth demands are the aggregation of all individual end-users in that group at a certain time point. Note that, different user groups could have different bandwidth demands, which fluctuate over time. Edge application providers need to employ suitable edge servers, and properly schedule edge users' bandwidth demands to minimize their operating costs to improve their competitiveness. In this study, we consider the 95th-percentile billing mode, widely adopted by edge cloud infrastructure providers to provision bandwidth resources in real-world application scenarios [4, 15, 21]. As shown in Fig. 2, the billing period of the 95th-percentile billing mode is usually a month. Bandwidth providers sample the real-time bandwidth usage every 5 min (i.e., 8640 checkpoints for a month), discard the top 5% checkpoints, and choose the rest highest value as the actual billing bandwidth amount. The 95th-percentile billing is also called burstable billing. In this mode, since the top 5% of bandwidth usage is ignored, a great deal of cost could be saved if the bandwidth demands are properly allocated, and this is the edge bandwidth allocation problem.

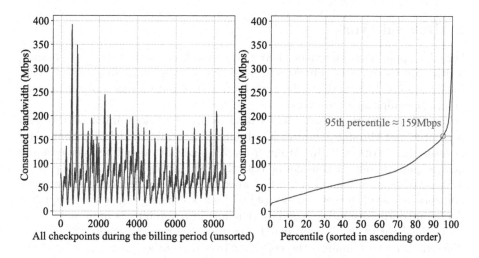

Fig. 2. The 95th-percentile billing mode.

The challenge of this problem also comes from the 95th-percentile billing mode, which has been proved to be an NP-hard problem [11]. Although many previous studies have been carried out, the existing methods rarely consider the network latency constraint in the edge bandwidth allocation problem. To fill this gap, in this paper we propose an adaptive large neighborhood search-based approach named EBA to solve the edge bandwidth allocation problem. Our approach mainly consists of two phrases. In the first phase, to quickly generate a good enough and feasible initial solution, we introduce intuitive sorting strategies which take full advantage of the top 5% non-billing checkpoints, and gradually increase the billing volume of the servers using the previously allocated information. In the second phase, to achieve load consolidation, we propose an iterative continuous optimization method which combines hill climbing and simulated annealing mechanisms based on adaptive large neighborhood search. In order to efficiently verify the feasibility of the neighborhood of the current solution, we design OptDinic suitable for this optimization based on the Dinic algorithm.

In sum, the main contributions of this paper are as follows:

1) Different from the traditional works of considering on-demand bandwidth billing [5] or static quota bandwidth billing, we consider 95th-percentile billing, which is more complicated and closer to the reality.
2) In our system model, we take the geographical distribution of edge users and edge servers, the various communication distances, and the resulting latency as QoS constraints.
3) Our EBA approach can expand the searching space, accelerate the optimization convergence speed, and avoid falling into local optimal.
4) We conducted a series of experiments based on a real-world edge application bandwidth demand tracking dataset to demonstrate the effectiveness of the proposed approach.

2   Related Work

For edge application providers, their goal is to minimize the total cost of bandwidth paid to the edge infrastructure providers while maintaining the QoS to the edge users. Extensive studies have been carried out on this problem of great practical significance till now.

For Delay-Tolerant Bulk (DTB) data, a lot of works minimized the 95th percentile cost through job-level scheduling, specifically by delaying some data to future time slots [8,10,13]. Wang et al. [23] made a trade-off between cost and delayed performance by considering both the cost charged by ISP and the penalty for delayed service. Wang et al. [24] studied how to selectively delay some traffic demands to save Internet access costs without sacrificing much service quality. An offline optimal solution based on dynamic programming is proposed.

Goldenberg et al. [7] considered how to allocate users' traffic demands to different ISPs to minimize the cost based on percentile billing without delay. For this purpose, they designed a series of intelligent routing algorithms. Adler et al. [3] provided an optimal offline algorithm that routes traffic to minimize the total bandwidth cost incurred in ISPs with AVG and MAX contracts. Peng et al. [16,25] took the long-term edge user allocation rate and edge server leasing cost as scheduling targets and proposed a decentralized collaborative and fuzzy-control-based approach to yielding real-time user-edge-server allocation schedules. Khare et al. [12] proposed NetReq to assign users' requests to reduce servers' billing volume. To solve the 95th percentile billing problem, Zhan et al. [27] proposed a mixed-integer linear programming (MILP) problem. Singh et al. [20] transformed percentile cost into K-max problem and developed an efficient online TE framework, CASCARA. Yang et al. [26] expressed the problem of network bandwidth allocation as an integer programming model.

However, methods such as [8,10,13,23,24] do not apply to real-time scenarios such as live streaming, because it is unrealistic to delay sending users' data. In addition, [3,7,12,20,26,27] do not take into account the importance of network latency in bandwidth allocation, which is closely related to geographical distribution. For example, to ensure the real-time and QoS, it is not practical to allocate the demands of an edge user in Guangxi to an edge server in Beijing, which has a high network latency.

3   System Model and Problem Formulation

In this section, we first present the system model of the proposed edge bandwidth allocation problem, and then give its corresponding problem formulation. Table 1 has listed the notations frequently used in this study.

Table 1. List of notations

Notation	Description
t_k	k-th time slot in T, also known as checkpoint
T	Set of checkpoints, also known as the billing period
s_i	i-th edge server in S
S	Set of edge servers
m	The number of edge servers
b_i	The bandwidth capacity of s_i
B	The bandwidth capacity of all edge servers
u_j	j-th edge user in U
U	Set of edge users
n	The number of edge users
y_j^k	Bandwidth demands of the u_j at t_k
Y	Bandwidth demands of all edge users in the billing period T
l_{ij}	Network latency between s_i and u_j
L	Network latency matrix between all edge servers and all edge users
τ	The upper limit of network latency the edge servers must meet
x_{ij}^k	The amount of bandwidth allocated by s_i to u_j at t_k
X	Bandwidth allocation matrix during the billing period
w_i^k	Total bandwidth allocated by s_i to all edge users at t_k
W_i	All allocation records of s_i during the billing period
$O_{95}(A)$	The $\lceil 95\% \times |A| \rceil$-th value in A_{sorted}, where A_{sorted} is A sorted in non-decreasing order, and $|A|$ is the number of elements in A
q_i	The billing volume of s_i
p	The unit price of bandwidth provided by edge servers (i.e., USD per Mbps)
C	Total cost during the billing period
Θ	The initial temperature of simulated annealing
Γ	Number of the outer loop of simulated annealing
Φ	Number of the inner loop of simulated annealing
α	Temperature attenuation coefficient of simulated annealing
λ	Frequency of simulated annealing in neighborhood search

3.1 System Model

In the 95th-percentile billing mode, for every employed edge server, the billing period T is usually a month, and the bandwidth usages are sampled every 5 min as shown in Fig. 2. Thus the billing period T can be split into 8640 time slots. Suppose that there are m edge servers available for edge application providers to rent. We use $S = \{s_1, s_2, \cdots, s_m\}$ to denote the set of edge servers, b_i is the maximum bandwidth that the i-th server can provide at each time slot. Since the edge servers in S could be geographically distributed in different locations, they may present different communication latency for the same edge user.

We use $U = \{u_1, u_2, \cdots, u_n\}$ to represent the set of edge users, where u_j is the j-th edge user which refers to a group of end-users located in a certain area. And we use l_{ij} to denote the network latency between edge server s_i and edge user u_j. At time slot t_k, we use y_j^k to denote the bandwidth demands of edge user u_j. To guarantee the QoS, edge user u_j can only connect to edge servers whose communication latency to u_j is less than τ. We use x_{ij}^k to denote the amount of bandwidth allocated by s_i to u_j at t_k. Thus, the total bandwidth allocated by s_i at t_k can be calculated as:

$$w_i^k = \sum_{j=1}^{n} x_{ij}^k \tag{1}$$

In this way, the consumed bandwidth trace can be represented as $W_i = \left\{ w_i^1, w_i^2, \cdots, w_i^{|T|} \right\}$. Thus, the billing volume of s_i can be given as:

$$q_i = O_{95}(W_i) \tag{2}$$

Therefore, the total cost of an edge application provider renting edge servers to meet the needs of edge users can be calculated as:

$$C = \sum_{i=1}^{m} q_i \times p \tag{3}$$

3.2 Problem Formulation

Based on the above formulation, the proposed edge bandwidth allocation problem can be formulated as follow:

$$Min : C \tag{4}$$

$$s.t : \sum_{i=1}^{m} x_{ij}^k = y_j^k \tag{5}$$

$$\sum_{j=1}^{n} x_{ij}^k \leq b_i \tag{6}$$

$$l_{ij} < \tau, \quad \forall x_{ij}^k > 0 \tag{7}$$

$$x_{ij}^k \in \mathbb{N}, \quad i \in [1, m], \quad j \in [1, n], \quad k \in [1, |T|]$$

As shown in Eq. (4), the target of this problem is to minimize the total bandwidth overhead of edge application providers. Equation (5) indicates that every edge user's bandwidth demands need to be met, and Eq. (6) is the bandwidth capacity constraint for every edge server. Meanwhile, Eq. (7) is the constraint that implies the available candidate serves for every edge user.

For the 95th-percentile billing optimization problem, Jalaparti et al. [11] have proved it is NP-hard. Similarly, for the problem we formulated above, if we relax the 95th-percentile billing mode to the 100th-percentile billing mode (i.e., billing amount is equal to the highest bandwidth usage), the problem discussed above reduces into an integer linear programming, which is well-known to be an NP-hard one. Thus the proposed edge bandwidth allocation problem is also an NP-hard one.

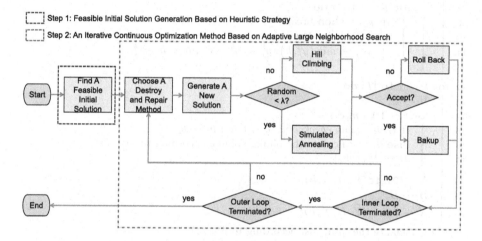

Fig. 3. The process of the proposed EBA approach.

4   Proposed EBA Approch

To address the aforementioned problem, we propose an adaptive large neighborhood search (ALNS) based approach, shorts for EBA. ALNS [18] is a kind of heuristic search method. It brings the adaptive operators (destroy and repair) selection feature to traditional local search, and thus expands the searching space and accelerates the optimization convergence speed. Figure 3 illustrates the process of the proposed EBA approach. It firstly employs a heuristic strategy to find a feasible initial solution quickly. Then, an ALNS-based method, which contains a Hill Climbing (HC) and Simulated Annealing (SA) mechanisms, is utilized to perform iterative optimization.

Algorithm 1: Feasible Initial Solution Generation (FISG)

Input : Billing period T; Edge servers S; Edge users U; Bandwidth capacity B; Bandwidth demands Y; Network latency matrix L; Network latency constraint τ; Unit price of bandwidth p;

Output: Bandwidth allocation matrix X; Total cost C;

1 $\widehat{Y} \leftarrow Y$; $f \leftarrow |T| - \lceil |T| \times 0.95 \rceil$;
2 sort edge servers in ascending order of connectivity;
3 **for** $i \leftarrow 1$ **to** m **do**
4 $\quad$ sort checkpoints in descending order by the sum of remaining bandwidth demands;
5 $\quad$ **for** $k \leftarrow 1$ **to** f **do**
6 $\quad\quad$ $h \leftarrow b_i$;
7 $\quad\quad$ sort edge users in ascending order of connectivity;
8 $\quad\quad$ **for** $j \leftarrow 1$ **to** n **do**
9 $\quad\quad\quad$ **if** $h = 0$ **then** break;
10 $\quad\quad\quad$ **else if** $l_{ij} < \tau$ **then**
11 $\quad\quad\quad\quad$ $x_{ij}^k \leftarrow \min\left(y_j^k, h\right)$; $y_j^k \leftarrow y_j^k - x_{ij}^k$; $h \leftarrow h - x_{ij}^k$;

12 **for** $k \leftarrow 1$ **to** $|T|$ **do**
13 $\quad$ $H \leftarrow \varnothing$;
14 $\quad$ **for** $i \leftarrow 1$ **to** m **do**
15 $\quad\quad$ **if** t_k *is a peak checkpoint of* s_i **then** $h_i \leftarrow b_i$;
16 $\quad\quad$ **else** $h_i \leftarrow$ calculate the billing volume according to Eq. (2);
17 $\quad\quad$ $H \leftarrow H \cup \{h_i\}$;
18 $\quad$ $\widehat{X} \leftarrow \texttt{Dinic}(\widehat{Y}, H, X, k)$;
19 $\quad$ $H \leftarrow B$;
20 $\quad$ $X \leftarrow \texttt{Dinic}(\widehat{Y}, H, \widehat{X}, k)$;

21 $C \leftarrow$ calculate the total cost according to Eq. (3);
22 **return** X, C;

4.1 Feasible Initial Solution Generation

For the first phase of the EBA approach, we develop a network flow-based feasible initial solution generation method, shorts for FISG. As shown in Algorithm 1, FISG has two main steps: 1) Allocating as much bandwidth as possible to each edge server at peak checkpoints. Here we have three sorting strategies: ascending order for edge servers and edge users according to connectivity while descending order for checkpoints according to the sum of remaining demands. These ideas are intuitive, because less connected servers or users are more difficult to meet the conditions later on and peak checkpoints are better suited for high demands (as shown in lines 2–11); 2) For the remaining user demands at each checkpoint, we preset the bandwidth capacity of each server and try to solve it by Dinic, an efficient network flow algorithm to find the max flow in a graph [6]. If Dinic fails to find a feasible max flow, FISG will increase the bandwidth capacity of servers to the upper limit before trying again (if successful, this step has no impact, as shown in lines 12–20). The time complexity of the algorithm is $O\left(|T|\, nm\,(n+m)^2\right)$.

4.2 ALNS-Based Iterative Continuous Optimization

Obviously, the initial solution obtained by FISG satisfies all constraints defined in Eqs. (5–7). However, its total cost can be further improved by performing load consolidation. Therefore, in the second phase of the proposed EBA approach, we develop an ALNS-based method to carry out the iterative continuous optimization. To avoid falling into local optimum, the proposed method also includes a SA mechanism to explore more feasible solutions.

Algorithm 2: ALNS-based Iterative Continuous Optimization (ICO)

Input : Initial solution X; Initial total cost C; Initial temperature Θ; Number of the outer loop Γ; Number of the inner loop Φ; Temperature attenuation coefficient α; Simulated annealing frequency λ;

Output: Bandwidth allocation matrix X; Total cost C;

1   $\bar{X}, \bar{C} \leftarrow X, C$; // current best solution
2   $\widehat{X}, \widehat{C} \leftarrow X, C$; // backup solution
3   $\rho^- \leftarrow (1, \cdots, 1)$; $\rho^+ \leftarrow (1, \cdots, 1)$;
4   **for** $e \leftarrow 1$ **to** Γ **do**
5   **for** $g \leftarrow 1$ **to** Φ **do**
6   select destroy method $\mathtt{d}() \in \Omega^-$ and repair method $\mathtt{r}() \in \Omega^+$ using ρ^- and ρ^+;
7         $s_i \leftarrow \mathtt{d}()$; $O \leftarrow \mathtt{r}()$; $\delta \leftarrow \mathtt{random}(0,1)$; $\psi \leftarrow$ false;
8   **if** $\delta \geq \lambda$ **then**
9   **if** $\mathtt{HCO}(\Theta, X, C, \widehat{X}, \widehat{C}, s_i, O) = true$ **then** $\psi \leftarrow$ true ;
10   **else**
11   **if** $\mathtt{SAO}(\Theta, X, C, \widehat{X}, \widehat{C}, s_i, O) = true$ **then** $\psi \leftarrow$ true ;
12   **if** $\psi = true$ **then** $\widehat{X}, \widehat{C} \leftarrow X, C$;
13   **else** $X, C \leftarrow \widehat{X}, \widehat{C}$;
14   **if** $C < \bar{C}$ **then** $\bar{X}, \bar{C} \leftarrow X, C$;
15   update ρ^-, ρ^+ according to Eq. (9);
16      $\Theta \leftarrow \Theta \times \alpha$;
17 **return** $\bar{X}, \bar{C}$;

As shown in Algorithm 2, the detailed steps of ICO are shown below:

1) Copy the initial solution to the current best solution and backup solution (for the rollback operation). And then initialize the weights of all destroy and repair methods to 1 (as shown in lines 1–3).

2) After initialization, ICO searches Φ times under the current SA-related temperature Θ. For each inner loop, ICO selects a destroy method and a repair method in a roulette manner. We use λ to determine the proportion of two neighborhood search mechanisms (e.g., HC and SA). Whichever mechanism is chosen, if it performs successfully (i.e., leads to cost reduction), ICO will update the backup solution. If it fails to optimize cost, ICO will roll back from the backup solution. The best solution is constantly updated if a solution with a lower total cost than the current best solution is found. The weights of the destroy and repair methods are dynamically adjusted based on their performance in the search process (as shown in lines 5–15).

3) After a cooling down event occurs (i.e., the inner loop of ICO is finished), ICO goes to step 2) and continues until the termination condition is reached (as shown in lines 4 and 16).

Destroy and repair operators are the key components of ALNS. Here we have designed three ways to destroy and repair the allocation solutions to explore further improvement. Specially, the destroy operators in ICO are to select which server to reduce its cost, i.e., the billing volume. The details of the three destroy methods employed by ICO are as follows:

1. Select a server randomly.
2. Select a server that has recently successfully updated the current solution.
3. Select a server with the highest billing volume.

After the destroy method has selected a server s_i, we need to reallocate the bandwidth allocated to s_i at some checkpoints to other servers. We can modify the order of building the edges in the Dinic algorithm to determine which servers take on first. The details of the three employed repair methods are as follows:

1. The priority of the servers is sorted randomly.
2. The priority of the servers is sorted by connectivity.
3. The priority of the servers is the order in which data files are read.

For each destroy and repair method, we maintain a count η and a score Ψ, which are initialized to 0. For each selected method, η is increased by 1, and the amount of Ψ increased is based on the following rules [17]:

$$\Psi = \Psi + \max \begin{cases} \omega_1 & \text{if } C < \bar{C} \\ \omega_2 & \text{if } C < \hat{C} \\ \omega_3 & \text{if the new solution is accept} \\ \omega_4 & \text{if the new solution is rejected} \end{cases} \tag{8}$$

Given a weight attenuation coefficient $\sigma \in [0, 1]$, the weight of each method can be updated as follows:

$$\rho = \begin{cases} \sigma \times \rho & \text{if } \eta = 0 \\ \sigma \times \rho + (1 - \sigma) \times \dfrac{\Psi}{\eta} & \text{if } \eta > 0 \end{cases} \tag{9}$$

Algorithm 3: Hill Climbing-based Optimization (HCO)

Input : Current temperature Θ; Current solution X; Current total cost C; Backup solution $\widehat{X}$; Backup total cost $\widehat{C}$; Selected server s_i; Servers' priority list O;

Output: Whether the optimization is successful

1 $step \leftarrow \texttt{random}(1, \Theta)$; $f \leftarrow 0$; $G \leftarrow \varnothing$;
2 $q_i \leftarrow$ calculate the billing volume according to Eq. (2);
3 **for** $k \leftarrow 1$ **to** $|T|$ **do**
4   **if** $\sum_{j=1}^{n} x_{ij}^k = q_i$ **then**
5          $G \leftarrow G \cup \{t_k\}$;
6   **if** t_k is not a peak checkpoint of s_i **then** $f \leftarrow f + 1$;

7 **while** $step > 0$ **do**
8      $cnt \leftarrow 0$;
9   **foreach** $t_k \in G$ **do**
10   **if** $\sum_{j=1}^{n} x_{ij}^k \geq step$ **then**
11             $H \leftarrow \varnothing$;
12   **for** $e \leftarrow 1$ **to** m **do**
13   **if** t_k is a peak checkpoint of s_e **then** $h_e \leftarrow b_e$;
14   **else** $h_e \leftarrow$ calculate the billing volume according to Eq. (2);
15                 $H \leftarrow H \cup \{h_e\}$;

16   **if** $\texttt{OptDinic}(H, X, s_i, O, step, k)$ **then**
17                 $cnt \leftarrow cnt + 1$;
18   **if** $cnt = f$ **then**
19   **return** true;

20     $X, C \leftarrow \widehat{X}, \widehat{C}$; $step \leftarrow \frac{step}{2}$;

21 **return** false;

Given a specific edge server s_i, the HCO aims to reduce the billing volume by at least 1Mbps without increasing other edge servers' costs. As shown in Algorithm 3, the HCO includes two main steps: 1) Find all checkpoints of s_i such that the load at that checkpoint is equal to the billing volume, and calculate the number of checkpoints that need to be lowered (as shown in lines 1–6). 2) Try to reduce the billing volume by $step$. If it fails, halve the current *step* before trying again. The OptDinic proposed by us is used to verify whether it is feasible (as shown in lines 7–20). The time complexity of the HCO is $O\left(|T| \, nm \, (n+m)^2 \log \Theta\right)$.

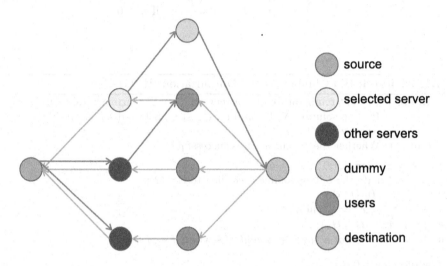

Fig. 4. Residual network of OptDinic. (Color figure online)

To verify the feasibility of the current solution, OptDinic is proposed based on the original Dinic algorithm [6]. As shown in Fig. 4, there are six kinds of nodes and two kinds of edges. The green edges represent the bandwidth that has been allocated, i.e., the current solution at one checkpoint. In contrast, the red edges denote the unallocated bandwidth. To reduce the actual load of the selected server by *step* at the checkpoint, we add the dummy node and let its bandwidth demands equal to *step*. It is worth noting that there is no unallocated bandwidth from the source to the selected server, while the dummy node is only connected to the selected server but not other servers. Therefore, when the bandwidth traffic from the source to the destination increases by *step*, it must be that the selected server allocates the *step* size bandwidth to the dummy node, and other servers increase the *step* size altogether to meet the users' demands. As for which server tries to increase its load first, we can control the order of edge building through the servers' priority.

Given a specific edge server s_i, the SAO aims to select a peak checkpoint to reduce its load at that checkpoint to below the billing volume. As shown in Algorithm 4, the SAO involves two main steps: 1) Try to reduce the load by *step* at a peak checkpoint without increasing the others' cost. If the current checkpoint t_k is the peak checkpoint of a server, its bandwidth capacity is defaulted to the upper limit. Otherwise, it will be set to the billing volume. Here we also use OptDinic to verify the feasibility of the optimized solution (as shown in lines 2–9). 2)Increase the bandwidth capacity of servers to the

---

Algorithm 4: Simulated Annealing-based Optimization (SAO)

Input   : the same as HCO
Output: Whether the optimization is successful

1 **foreach** $t_k \in$ *peak checkpoints of* s_i **do**
2 | $q_i \leftarrow$ calculate the billing volume according to Eq. (2);
3 | $step \leftarrow \sum_{j=1}^{n} x_{ij}^k - \max(q_i - 1, 0); H \leftarrow \varnothing$;
4 | **for** $e \leftarrow 1$ **to** m **do**
5 | | **if** t_k *is a peak checkpoint of* s_e **then** $h_e \leftarrow b_e$;
6 | | **else** $h_e \leftarrow$ calculate the billing volume according to Eq. (2);
7 | | $H \leftarrow H \cup \{h_e\}$;
8 | **if** $\mathtt{OptDinic}(H, X, s_i, O, step, k)$ **then**
9 | | **return** true
10 | $H \leftarrow B; \delta \leftarrow \mathtt{random}(0, 1)$;
11 | **if** $\mathtt{OptDinic}(H, X, s_i, O, step, k)$ *and* $\delta < \exp\left(\frac{\widehat{C} - C}{\Theta}\right)$ **then**
12 | | **return** true
13 | **else** $X, C \leftarrow \widehat{X}, \widehat{C}$;
14 **return** false;

---

upper limit before trying again. If the total cost rises, accept it with a certain probability. If it fails, roll back from the backup solution and try the next peak checkpoint (as shown in lines 10–13). The time complexity of the SAO is $O\left(|T| nm (n + m)^2\right)$. Therefore, the total time complexity of proposed EBA approach is $O\left(\Gamma\Phi |T| nm (n + m)^2 \log\Theta\right)$.

5   Experiments and Analysis

In this section, we conducted a series of experiments based on a real-world edge bandwidth load dataset to verify the effectiveness of the proposed approach.

5.1   Experiment Settings

For a real-world short video and live streaming application, we have tracked the bandwidth demands within a monthly billing period. Here edge user refers to a group of end-users located in a certain area (i.e., end-users in the same province), and its bandwidth demands are the aggregation of all individual end-users in that group at a certain time point. Figure 5 shows the overall bandwidth demands of edge users. It can be seen that the demands present a noticeable periodical change, the period is one month, and the highest whole network bandwidth demand is about 4 Tbps. In our experiment, we consider 110 edge servers distributed among different provinces in China, in which the bandwidth capacity of edge servers follows the normal distribution with 512 Gbps bandwidth expectation, and the network latency between edge servers and edge users is set to be

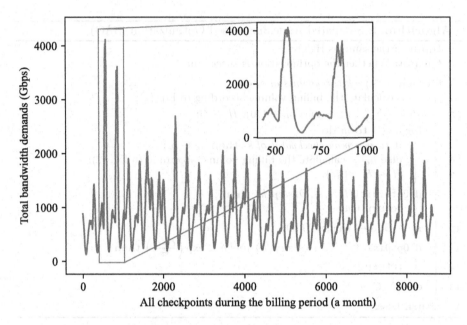

Fig. 5. Bandwidth demands during the billing period.

uniformly distributed from 140 ms to 540 ms. The bandwidth price is obtained from the latest Aliyun ECS price table [1].

Some hyperparameter settings during the experiment are shown in Table 2.

Table 2. Parameter setting

Hyperparameter	Value
Θ	8192
Γ	400
Φ	50
α	0.95
λ	0.25
ω_1	100
ω_2	10
ω_3	1
ω_4	0

We compare EBA against the following baseline algorithms:

- Load Balance (LB): For each edge user at every checkpoint during the billing period, the LB heuristic randomly selects d feasible edge servers. Note that, those servers with remaining bandwidth capacity at peak checkpoints will be preferentially selected. And then, edge users' bandwidth demands are allocated to the selected server with the lowest load.
- Round robin (RR): For each edge user at every checkpoint during the billing period, the target server is rotated by a polling strategy. If the selected server does not have enough capacity, the remaining demands will be allocated to other servers in the same way of polling.
- Equal Split (ES): For each edge user at every checkpoint during the billing period, the servers are sorted in ascending order in terms of capacity. And in this order, the amount of bandwidth allocated to the current server is less than the remaining capacity and the average remaining demands.
- FISG: Our proposed network flow-based approach described in Sect. 4.1.
- EBA-ALNS: Our proposed EBA approach without the ALNS module. Specifically, the destroy and repair method always choose the random strategy.
- EBA-SA: Our proposed EBA approach without the SA mechanism.

5.2 Performance Comparison

Results Under Different Demands Constraints: In Fig. 6, we evaluate the performance of the proposed EBA approach and its peers in terms of bandwidth monetary costs. It can be seen that LB, ES, and RR algorithms achieve the top 3 highest cost. The FISG algorithm we proposed obviously outperforms them, whose cost is only 19.82% of the RR algorithm with the scaling of demands on average, and 22.27% of the RR algorithm with the scaling of edge users on average. We also learn from the Fig. 6 that compared with the FISG, the proposed EBA approach is capable of reducing by 37.45% and 35.31% of the total cost on average. Besides, in most cases of Fig. 6(b), the total cost shows a rising trend regardless of whether the ALNS or SA are removed. In addition, with the increase in demands and the number of edge users, the total cost tends to rise in all cases.

Analysis: Because the LB algorithm randomly selects servers each time, the billing volume of each server is relatively high. The cost of the ES algorithm is higher than that of the RR algorithm because the former tends to employ more servers to fulfill each user's demands. While our FISG algorithm takes into account three intuitive sorting strategies in the first phase and gradually updates the billing volume of the servers in the second phase. In this way, each server is fully utilized in both peak and non-peak time slots. Compared with the native local search method, the ALNS-based approach can expand the neighborhood

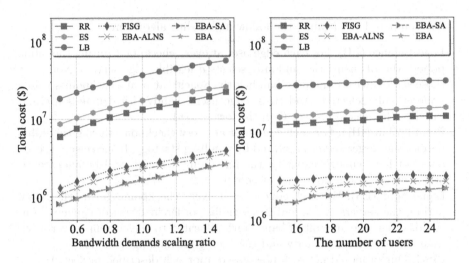

Fig. 6. (a) Comparison of the total cost under different bandwidth demands. (b) Comparison of the total cost under different numbers of users.

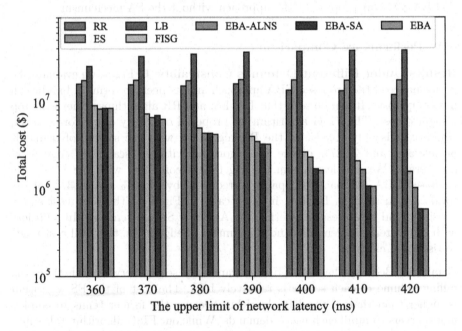

Fig. 7. Comparison of the total cost under different latency constraints.

search range, and SA can jump out of the local optimum. That is why the proposed EBA outperforms other baselines in all experimental cases.

Results Under Different Latency Constraints: In Fig. 7, we compare the total cost under different latency constraints. It can be seen that LB, ES, and

RR are still the three algorithms with the highest total cost. Moreover, our EBA achieves the lowest cost. In addition, with the relaxation of the latency constraint, our proposed FISG algorithm and EBA algorithm show a gradual increasing advantage over other baselines. When the latency constraint is set to 360 ms, the total cost of the FISG algorithm is 56.78% of the RR algorithm, and the EBA reduces by 7.15% compared to FISG. However, when the latency constraint is set to 420 ms, the total cost of FISG is 13.18% of RR, and the EBA reduces by 63.02% compared to FISG.

Analysis: Our FISG algorithm is improving because the number of servers available increases when the latency constraint is relaxed. Besides, the importance of taking full advantage of 95th-percentile billing becomes apparent and helps a lot. When the number of available servers increases, it also means that more neighborhood solutions meet the conditions for ALNS-based approaches, which result in a high success rate of optimization and thus improve the quality of yield solutions. Therefore, the total cost of the EBA approach drops more than other baselines with the increase in latency constraints.

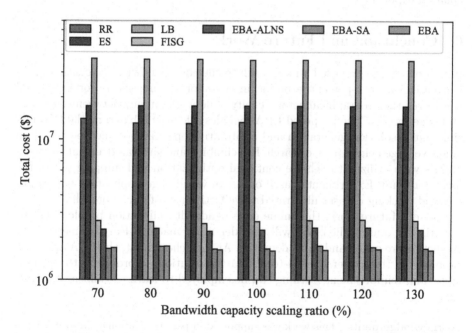

Fig. 8. Comparison of the total cost under different bandwidth capacities.

Results Under Different Capacity Constraints: Figure 8 compares the total cost under different bandwidth capacities. The top four algorithms with the highest total cost are LB, ES, RR, and FISG. The total cost of EBA-ALNS decreased by 12.16% based on the FISG algorithm on average, while EBA-SA decreased by 35.11% on average. EBA achieves the lowest cost, and the total cost is reduced by 36.57% on average compared to the FISG algorithm.

Analysis: Due to the large search space resulting from the complex 95th-percentile optimization problem, it is difficult for a single search strategy to find an appropriate descent route. In addition, the SA mechanism has a certain probability of accepting worse solutions during the search. Thus it is capable of jumping out of the local optimum. However, restricted by a single destroy and repair operator, SA fails to improve the quality of the solution further. In contrast, the ALNS-based approach expands the optimization range by introducing multiple operators and an adaptive switching mechanism.

The above experimental results also show that our proposed FISG can obtain high-quality initial solutions. No matter how to scale users' bandwidth demands, the number of users, latency constraints, or servers' bandwidth capacity, the proposed EBA approach always achieves considerable optimization based on the initial solution. We also verified the effectiveness of ALNS and SA. Since the hill climbing mechanism does not lead to a cost increase, it is not included in the ablation experiment.

6   Conclusion and Future Work

In this paper, we proposed an approach to the edge bandwidth allocation problem based on 95th-percentile billing in edge computing, shorts for EBA, and considered the geographical heterogeneity of network latency between edge users and edge servers. The proposed EBA includes a heuristic-based method for feasible initial solution generation and an iterative optimization method based on adaptive large neighborhood search. Hill climbing and simulated annealing mechanisms were utilized to achieve continual optimization and jumping out of the local optimum. Experiments based on a real-world edge application bandwidth demand tracking dataset illustrated the effectiveness of our approach.

For our future work, the online edge bandwidth allocation problem will be investigated and studied. We will consider using machine learning methods to predict future edge bandwidth demands. At each checkpoint, the EBA approach proposed in this paper is used to obtain the solution according to the current state, and reinforcement learning can be employed to learn the allocation strategy.

Acknowledgements. This work was supported in part by: National Natural Science Foundation of China (Nos. 61966008, U2033213), Sichuan and Chongqing Joint Key R&D Project (No. 2021YFQ0058).

References

1. Aliyun ECS pricing-calculator. https://www.aliyun.com/pricing-calculator?#/commodity/vm. Accessed 12 June 2022

2. Predicts 2022: The distributed enterprise drives computing to the edge. https://www.gartner.com/en/documents/4007176. Accessed 12 June 2022

3. Adler, M., Sitaraman, R.K., Venkataramani, H.: Algorithms for optimizing the bandwidth cost of content delivery. Comput. Netw. **55**(18), 4007–4020 (2011)

4. Dimitropoulos, X., Hurley, P., Kind, A., Stoecklin, M.P.: On the 95-percentile billing method. In: Moon, S.B., Teixeira, R., Uhlig, S. (eds.) PAM 2009. LNCS, vol. 5448, pp. 207–216. Springer, Heidelberg (2009). https://doi.org/10.1007/978-3-642-00975-4_21

5. Ding, J.W., Deng, D.J., Wu, T.Y., Chen, H.H.: Quality-aware bandwidth allocation for scalable on-demand streaming in wireless networks. IEEE J. Sel. Areas Commun. **28**(3), 366–376 (2010)

6. Dinic, E.: Algorithm for solution of a problem of maximum flow in a network with power estimation. Soviet Math. Doll. **11**(5), 1277–1280 (1970). English translation by RF. Rinehart (1970)

7. Goldenberg, D.K., Qiuy, L., Xie, H., Yang, Y.R., Zhang, Y.: Optimizing cost and performance for multihoming. ACM SIGCOMM Comput. Commun. Rev. **34**(4), 79–92 (2004)

8. Golubchik, L., Khuller, S., Mukherjee, K., Yao, Y.: To send or not to send: reducing the cost of data transmission. In: 2013 Proceedings IEEE INFOCOM, pp. 2472–2478. IEEE (2013)

9. Hong, C.H., Varghese, B.: Resource management in fog/edge computing: a survey on architectures, infrastructure, and algorithms. ACM Comput. Surv. (CSUR) **52**(5), 1–37 (2019)

10. Jain, S., Fall, K., Patra, R.: Routing in a delay tolerant network. In: Proceedings of the 2004 Conference on Applications, Technologies, Architectures, and Protocols for Computer Communications, pp. 145–158 (2004)

11. Jalaparti, V., Bliznets, I., Kandula, S., Lucier, B., Menache, I.: Dynamic pricing and traffic engineering for timely inter-datacenter transfers. In: Proceedings of the 2016 ACM SIGCOMM Conference, pp. 73–86 (2016)

12. Khare, V., Zhang, B.: CDN request routing to reduce network access cost. In: 37th Annual IEEE Conference on Local Computer Networks, pp. 610–617. IEEE (2012)

13. Laoutaris, N., Smaragdakis, G., Stanojevic, R., Rodriguez, P., Sundaram, R.: Delay-tolerant bulk data transfers on the internet. IEEE/ACM Trans. Netw. **21**(6), 1852–1865 (2013)

14. Liyanage, M., Porambage, P., Ding, A.Y., Kalla, A.: Driving forces for multi-access edge computing (MEC) IoT integration in 5G. ICT Express **7**(2), 127–137 (2021)

15. Mukerjee, M.K., Naylor, D., Jiang, J., Han, D., Seshan, S., Zhang, H.: Practical, real-time centralized control for CDN-based live video delivery. In: Proceedings of the 2015 ACM Conference on Special Interest Group on Data Communication, pp. 311–324 (2015)

16. Peng, Q., et al.: A decentralized collaborative approach to online edge user allocation in edge computing environments. In: 2020 IEEE International Conference on Web Services (ICWS), pp. 294–301. IEEE (2020)

17. Pisinger, D., Ropke, S.: Large neighborhood search. In: Gendreau, M., Potvin, J.Y. (eds.) Handbook of Metaheuristics, pp. 399–419. Springer, Boston (2010). https://doi.org/10.1007/978-1-4419-1665-5_13

18. Ropke, S., Pisinger, D.: An adaptive large neighborhood search heuristic for the pickup and delivery problem with time windows. Transp. Sci. **40**(4), 455–472 (2006)

19. Satyanarayanan, M.: The emergence of edge computing. Computer **50**(1), 30–39 (2017)

20. Singh, R., Agarwal, S., Calder, M., Bahl, P.: Cost-effective cloud edge traffic engineering with cascara. In: 18th USENIX Symposium on Networked Systems Design and Implementation (NSDI 2021), pp. 201–216 (2021)
21. Stanojevic, R., Laoutaris, N., Rodriguez, P.: On economic heavy hitters: shapley value analysis of 95th-percentile pricing. In: Proceedings of the 10th ACM SIGCOMM Conference on Internet Measurement, pp. 75–80 (2010)
22. Tseng, C.W., Tseng, F.H., Yang, Y.T., Liu, C.C., Chou, L.D.: Task scheduling for edge computing with agile VNFs on-demand service model toward 5G and beyond. Wirel. Commun. Mob. Comput. **2018** (2018)
23. Wang, J.: Traffic regulation under the percentile-based pricing policy. In: Proceedings of the 1st International Conference on Scalable Information Systems, pp. 4-es (2006)
24. Wang, J., Chen, J., Yang, M., Zheng, S.: Traffic regulation with single-and dual-homed ISPS under a percentile-based pricing policy. J. Comb. Optim. **17**(3), 247–273 (2009)
25. Wu, C., et al.: Online user allocation in mobile edge computing environments: a decentralized reactive approach. J. Syst. Architect. **113**, 101904 (2021)
26. Yang, C., You, J., Yuan, X., Zhao, P.: Network bandwidth allocation problem for cloud computing. arXiv preprint arXiv:2203.06725 (2022)
27. Zhan, Y., Ghamkhari, M., Akhavan-Hejazi, H., Xu, D., Mohsenian-Rad, H.: Optimal response to burstable billing under demand uncertainty. arXiv preprint arXiv:1603.05752 (2016)

System Completion Time Minimization with Edge Server Onboard Unmanned Vehicle

Wen Peng[1], Hongyue Wu[1], Shizhan Chen[1(✉)], Lei Dong[1], Zhuofeng Zhao[2], and Zhiyong Feng[1]

[1] College of Intelligence and Computing, Tianjin University, Tianjin, China
{peng_wen,hongyue.wu,shizhan,2118218002,zyfeng}@tju.edu.cn
[2] Beijing Key Laboratory On Integration and Analysis of Large-Scale Stream Data, North China University of Technology, Beijing, China
edzhao@ncut.edu.cn

Abstract. With the advantages of flexibility and powerful computing resources, edge servers mounted on unmanned vehicles (V-edge) have attracted significant interest in mobile edge computing (MEC). In this paper, we design an offloading scheme for vehicle-mounted edge rescue systems with the consideration of road limitations. In these systems, edge servers can receive data and process them while on the move. The objective is to minimize the completion time of tasks within the system under both time-varying communication and computation resource constraints. The formulated problem is decomposed into two subproblems, i.e., task completion time minimization within communities and V-edge travel time minimization between communities. For task completion time minimization, we propose an SQP-based iterative algorithm, which can generate feasible stopping points by using quadratic programming. V-edge travel time minimization problem can be converted to a TSP problem and thus can be solved by some existing methods. Finally, experiments are conducted to verify the usability of the proposed approach.

Keywords: Edge computing · Computation offloading · Mobility server · Unmanned vehicle

1 Introduction

In recent years, natural disasters such as hurricanes and wildfires are part of our daily life which have significant devastating effects, including but not limited to network failures [2]. Hence, numerous emergency management officials will undertake rescue operations, with rescuers carrying rescue devices for exploration, identification, and detection, which will generate intensive computation.

However, due to the limitations of computing power, storage capacity and battery capacity, the intelligent devices cannot meet the needs of these various computationally intensive applications. Therefore, how to solve these computationally intensive tasks quickly is a huge challenge. Cloud computing is

© ICST Institute for Computer Sciences, Social Informatics and Telecommunications Engineering 2022
Published by Springer Nature Switzerland AG 2022. All Rights Reserved
H. Gao et al. (Eds.): CollaborateCom 2022, LNICST 460, pp. 269–289, 2022.
https://doi.org/10.1007/978-3-031-24383-7_15

a worthy solution to consider. However, service requests cannot be responded promptly due to the long transmission latency. To address this challenge, a novel paradigm, Edge Computing (EC), has been proposed. Compute-intensive tasks can be offloaded to edge servers with shorter latency compared to offloading to the cloud, which can also free up the device's resources earlier.

Traditional EC-based base stations (BSs) are powerful enough to handle many complex service requests in most cases with low latency and high QoS requirements of users. However, edge servers are prone to failures due to adverse weathers, earthquake disasters, etc. [11], which will make it impossible to respond to users' requests until they are repaired. Especially, the rescue equipment cannot rely on infrastructure of BSs for communication in the case of server failure after disaster. There are many literature has raised the issue of failure recovery and user migration, such as [4,11]. But these proposed approaches either require waiting for failure recovery or cannot migrate all service demands. On the other hand, a more flexible MEC mechanism is quite necessary in rural environments and military exercises, due to high deployment costs resulting in limited BSs and APs infrastructure.

Thus, an mobile on-demand offload services are needed to ease their burden. UAVs and unmanned vehicles are integrated with EC to provide computing power and storage resource capacity. Therefore, EC can be classified into two types according to the state of edge servers: static edge servers connected to BSs and mobile edge servers mounted on vehicles or unmanned aerial vehicles (UAVs) [10].

Compared to static edge servers, mobile edge servers are more flexible and can be applied to a richer set of scenarios. In many studies of mobile edge servers, UAVs have shown their capabilities [5,8,14], but their battery endurance, computational power, and storage resources are worse compared to mobile edge servers mounted on vehicles (V-edge [10]). There is no doubt that V-edge is a better choice with a large volume of data and few road obstacles.

Accordingly, we designed a vehicle-mounted edge server rescue system to provide computational offload services. Considering the importance of each task, we need to complete all tasks in the shortest possible time. However, V-edge travels around each device to provide the service is relatively wasteful of resources. To this end, we divide the requesting devices in close proximity together according to their geographical location to form a requesting community, so that V-edge can handle the tasks of the devices in that community at the same time. Moreover, when the data size of task is large, V-edge cannot finish processing the tasks while it is moving, so that it needs to stop at a point to continue processing. However, differences in stopping positions can make a gap in the distance between the V-edge and devices, affecting the transmission time and subsequently the time to complete tasks. In order to complete all tasks as quickly as possible, we need to choose the best point to stop for V-edge. Then, complete all community tasks one by one. The main contributions of the paper are summarized as follows:

- We propose a vehicle-mounted edge server rescue system for emergency rescue, with the goal of minimizing the system completion time.
- We jointly optimize the communication and computation of the mobile and divide the original minimization problem into community task completion time minimization subproblem and V-edge travel time minimization problem between communities. For the first subproblem, quadratic programming and positive definite Hessian approximation techniques are used to formulate and solve the feasible solution by iteration. Therefore, an iterative approach based on the sequential quadratic programming (SQP) algorithm is proposed to address the complexity of joint optimization.
- The effectiveness of the algorithm is evaluated with extensive simulation results. Numerical results show that the algorithm is effective in ensuring that the system completion time is minimized.

The rest of the paper is organized as follows. Section 2 presents the related work. Section 3 demonstrates the system model. Section 4 formulates the optimization problem into a TSP problem. Section 5 shows the methods to solve the optimization problem. The simulation results are described in Sect. 6, followed immediately by the conclusion in Sect. 7.

2 Related Work

In recent years, computation offloading has become an integral part of service computing and has been a popular research topic.

We hereby review the studies of computation offloading from two aspects in the following: (1) offloading to a server at a fixed location and (2) offloading to mobile devices with some computing power or edge servers.

2.1 Static Edge Computation Offloading

Many studies have investigated the offloading strategies of EC systems in static scenarios. In general, these works are made for various optimization targets [17,18,21], such as latency minimization, energy consumption minimization, and resource allocation. For instance, In [18], the authors investigated the collaboration between cloud and edge server to minimize request's latency. In [22], the authors jointly considered computational offloading and resource management to minimize network-wide weighted energy consumption. Considering the mobility of users, zhao et al. [21] proposed a mobility-aware cross-edge computation offloading framework to reduce the latency.

The above works can meet the tasks in general scenarios, but in rural areas or areas outside the range of servers, these fixed-location servers are out of reach and cannot provide service support, making it difficult for users' requests to be fulfilled. In particular, during the disaster scenarios, servers are prone to failure which will prevent it from processing user requests.

2.2 Mobile Edge Computation Offloading

Existing work has proposed that users can offload their tasks to neighboring devices or to a mobile edge server mounted on unmanned aerial vehicles (UAVs) or vehicles. For instance, In [3], chen et al. proposed a task offloading scheme merely relying on vehicle-to-vehicle (V2V) communication which can fully exploring the idle resources of vehicles and complete tasks quickly. In [14], ning et al. designed a 5G-enabled UAV-to-community offloading system and jointly considered trajectory designing and task scheduling, with the objective of maximizing the system throughput. Liu et al. [10] designed a novel vehicle-mounted edge mechanism, and jointly optimize path planning and resource allocation to maximize the returned data with deadline constrains.

In the literature, we can find that servers mounted on UAVs or unmanned vehicles can be applicable to many scenarios and make up for the shortcomings of traditional base stations. Therefore, we optimize the system in terms of the completion time of the minimized system.

3 System Model

3.1 System Model

Fig. 1 shows a real emergency rescue scenario, where many rescuers carry intelligent devices (SD in Fig. 1) for detection, identification, collection, and classification which will generate a large number of computational tasks. Each device can communicate with the server individually. Suppose that there are K devices performing rescue tasks, indexed by $\mathcal{K}=\{1, 2, ..., K\}$. Let $p_i = (x_i, y_i)$ denote the location of device i. Affected by the disaster, large communication facilities such as base stations may experience power outages or failures. Therefore, devices cannot offload computation-intensive tasks through edge computing base stations, etc., and need V-edge to provide various services. Thus, a V-edge assisted offloading system is designed. By optimizing the location in community and path of V-edge, computational support can be provided to the devices in the shortest possible time. For simplicity, a quasi-static network scenario [10] is considered in which the locations of devices do not change during the system time period T. We assume that the devices always perform their tasks in system time T, i.e., the number of devices is constant. Therefore, we investigate the computational offloading problem between V-edge and smart devices with the aim of minimizing the time to complete all tasks(system completion time), including the time to complete tasks within the community and the time for V-edge to reach the community.

Additionally, we assume that V-edge is full-duplex communication, which means that task uploading and result downloading can be executed simultaneously and V-edge can interact with multiple devices at the same time by using processor sharing [19]. For convenience, we assume that V-edge needs to receive all the task data before it can process the task.

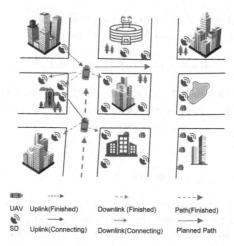

| UAV | Uplink(Finished) | Downlink (Finished) | Path(Finished) |
| SD | Uplink(Connecting) | Downlink(Connecting) | Planned Path |

Fig. 1. Simulation result for the network.

3.2 Computing Task Offloading Model

With the objective of minimizing the system completion time, we designed a V-edge-based task offloading model. The task generated by the device i can be given by a 4-tuple $A_i(I_i, f_i, O_i, p_i)$, where I_i is the input data size (in bit), f_i denotes the CPU frequency of device (in CPU cycles per bit), O_i denotes the data size of computing result (in bits), which is depended on tasks and is smaller than I_i, p_i is the location of device i. At the beginning, V-edge can only receive demands information instead of demands data from rescue devices relying on a bootstrapping program [15]. Only within the communication range can V-edge start computation task offloading.

In V-edge, we assume that the computational resources are sufficient and by using processor sharing, V-edge can provide parallel computation for multiple computational tasks. Its maximum CPU frequency is designed as F (in CPU cycles per second).

Here are the steps for V-edge offloading process. (i) V-edge received corresponding profile of tasks A_i according to the bootstrapping program. (ii) devices upload their tasks to V-edge within the community via the uplink. (iii) V-edge processes the tasks. (iv) devices obtain the results via the downlink. (v) V-edge travels to the next community.

3.3 Communication Model

To offload the computation tasks for V-edge execution, corresponding input bits of the task need to be delivered to V-edge via uplink. Similarly, computation results need to be delivered by V-edge via downlink. We assume the wireless channels between devices and V-edge are i.i.d line-of-sight (LOS) channel [1].

Given device i located at $p_i = (x_i, y_i)$ as well as V-edge located at (x_0, y_0), the distance between device i and V-edge can be given by

$$d_{i,0} = [(x_i - x_0)^2 + (y_i - y_0)^2]^{\frac{1}{2}} \tag{1}$$

Therefore, the path loss between device i and V-edge when V-edge is moving at time t $(L_{m,i}(t))$ or when V-edge stays in a certain position $(L_{p,i})$ can be expressed as

$$L_{m,i}(t) = \eta\mu^2((l_i - vt)^2 + h_i^2), \tag{2}$$
$$L_{p,i} = \eta\mu^2((L_i + x - l_i)^2 + h_i^2) \tag{3}$$

where we denote the attenuation factors by η, and the correlation coefficient by μ which is equal to $\frac{4\pi g}{c}$, and the maximum speed of V-edge by v. Let L_i denote the distance between the position where device i can connect to V-edge with the position where all the devices within the community can connect to V-edge, as shown in the red segment in Fig. 2. And let x indicate the location of V-edge where V-edge can connect to all tasks at the same time. Let l_i the communication radius of device i on the road (as shown in Fig. 2), and h_i the vertical distance from device i to the road segment (as shown in Fig. 2).

When V-edge is moving, the transmission rates of uplink $(R_{m,i}^u(t))$ and downlink $(R_{m,i}^d(t))$ between device i and V-edge at time t can be formulated by

$$\begin{cases} R_{m,i}^u(t) = B\log_2(1 + \dfrac{p_{TX}}{L_{m,i}(t)\sigma^2 B}) \\ R_{m,i}^d(t) = B\log_2(1 + \dfrac{p_{RX}}{L_{m,i}(t)\sigma^2 B}) \end{cases} \tag{4}$$

where B represent the uplink and downlink bandwidth between device i and V-edge, and $p_{TX}(W), p_{RX}(W)$ is the transmission power and the receiving power, and σ^2 is the white Gaussian noise variance [7].

When V-edge stays in a certain position, the transmission rates of uplink $(R_{p,i}^u)$ and downlink $(R_{p,i}^d)$ between device i and V-edge can be formulated by

$$\begin{cases} R_{p,i}^u = B\log_2(1 + \dfrac{p_{TX}}{L_{p,i}\sigma^2 B}) \\ R_{p,i}^d = B\log_2(1 + \dfrac{p_{RX}}{L_{p,i}\sigma^2 B}) \end{cases} \tag{5}$$

3.4 Computational Model

Within the same community, the transmission time and computation time of each task are different due to the distinctions in data volume and their geographical locations. In order to complete all tasks better and faster, we optimally allocate the computational resources of V-edge. Let T^u, T^p, T^d denote The upload, computation, and download latency respectively. Since V-edge can

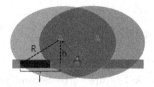

Fig. 2. Example of h,l,h of each device in a community

perform data transmission while moving, the communication distance between devices and V-edge will change over time, so do the communication rate, which affects uplink communication time and downlink communication time. When V-edge is moving, the uplink and downlink communication time $(T_m^u(i), T_m^d(i))$ can be calculated by

$$I_{m,i} = \int_0^{T_{m,i}^u} R_{m,i}^u(t)dt, \quad \forall i \in K \tag{6}$$

$$O_{m,i} = \int_0^{T_{m,i}^d} R_{m,i}^d(t)dt, \quad \forall i \in K \tag{7}$$

When V-edge interacts with devices at a point, the uplink and downlink communication time $(T_{p,i}^u, T_{p,i}^d)$ can be calculated by

$$T_{p,i}^u = \frac{I_i^r}{R_{p,i}^u}, \quad \forall i \in K \tag{8}$$

$$T_{m,i}^d = \frac{O_i^r}{R_{p,i}^d}, \quad \forall i \in K \tag{9}$$

where I_i^r and O_i^r are the residual input data or output data.

For task of device i, the processing time can be given by:

$$T_i^p = \frac{f_i I_i}{F_i}, \quad \forall i \in K \tag{10}$$

where F_i is the computational resources allocated to the task by V-edge.

3.5   Mobile Model

We assume that V-edge is driving on a straight road cleared in advance, regardless of turning. V-edge can only drive on roads. There is no doubt that the optimal location for V-edge is within the road to perform its task within the community. Within each community, the V-edge moves to the optimal position at the maximum speed v until the V-edge drives out of the communication range of the device just to return the result of the task. After driving away from the community, the V-edge moves at the maximum speed, expecting to reach the next community faster.

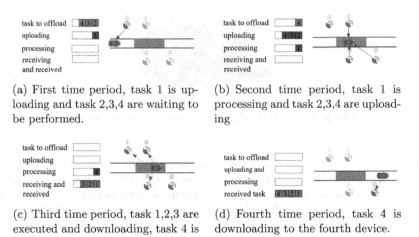

(a) First time period, task 1 is uploading and task 2,3,4 are waiting to be performed.

(b) Second time period, task 1 is processing and task 2,3,4 are uploading

(c) Third time period, task 1,2,3 are executed and downloading, task 4 is processing.

(d) Fourth time period, task 4 is downloading to the fourth device.

Fig. 3. An example of computing task offloading. V-edge finishes four tasks from four devices during different time period.

4   Problem Formulation

In this section, we analyzed the V-edge assisted offloading and formulated the problem of minimizing the system completion time.

4.1   Problem Overview

The V-edge assisted offloading process is given by an example illustrated in Fig. 3 where four subfigures display the offloading process in one community. In the Fig. 3(a), task 1 is uploading to the V-edge for execution because V-edge reaches its communication range, and the other devices wait for V-edge to enter their communication range. In the Fig. 3(b), V-edge moves to the optimal stopping position in the common communication segment (the red area in Fig. 2), and V-edge is processing the task 1 and receiving the data from task 2, task 3 and task 4 via uplink respectively. In the third subfigure, Fig. 3(c), V-edge just finished transmitting result to device 1, and is transmitting result to device 2 and device 3 via downlink respectively. At the same time, V-edge is processing the task 4. In the Fig. 3(d), task 4 is accomplished and the result is transmitted to device 4 via downlink.

With the objective of minimizing system completion time on the premise of completing all tasks, we need to optimize community completion time and travelling time of V-edge. To minimizing the community completion time, we need to divide the devices into different communities, then find the common communication road segment, and find an optimal stopping position for V-edge, which makes V-edge complete all tasks in the shortest time. Finally, the shortest path for V-edge to travel between communities is optimized.

4.2   Constraint Analysis

V-edge receives input data from the device via uplink and returns the result via downlink respectively. We assume that the V-edge moves into the community to perform the task, which may contain two parts, one that is performed on the move and one that is performed when it stops. Meanwhile, the input data may be transferred in two parts and the output results are the same. Thus, we can obtain the following equation constraints:

$$I_i = \int_0^{T_{m,i}^u} R_{m,i}^u(t)dt + R_{p,i}^u T_{p,i}^u, \forall i \in K \tag{11}$$

$$O_i = \int_0^{T_{m,i}^d} R_{m,i}^d(t)dt + R_{p,i}^d T_{p,i}^d, \forall i \in K \tag{12}$$

where both the uplink and downlink transmission rates vary with time because of changes of communication distance.

4.3   Problem Formulation

With the objective of minimizing the system completion time, intuitively, the time to complete tasks of each community and the travel time to access all communities need to be minimized. In one community, we optimized the community task completion time by optimizing the stopping points of the V-edge. Specifically, in order to ensure that each task is executed, V-edge needs to wait until all tasks are executed away from the community communication range.

To formulate the objective function, we designed some variables:

Let the binary variable α_i indicate whether the device i can complete result downloading during time τ which indicates the time that V-edge is away from the communication range of device i from the docking point, i.e.,

$$\alpha_i = \begin{cases} 1, \text{device } i \text{ can download result during } \tau \\ 0, \text{otherwise.} \end{cases} \tag{13}$$

Let the binary variable β_i represent whether V-edge can receiving the uploading data of device i before stopping if needed, i.e.,

$$\beta_i = \begin{cases} 1, \text{V-edge can receive the uploading data before} \\ \quad \text{stopping,} \\ 0, \text{otherwise.} \end{cases} \tag{14}$$

Let $\gamma_{i,1}$ denote whether the V-edge has completed task processing and device i has finished downloading the result during time τ, i.e.,

$$\gamma_{i,1} = \begin{cases} 1, \text{V-edge can complete processing and device } i \\ \quad \text{can receive the downloading data during } \tau, \\ 0, \text{otherwise.} \end{cases} \tag{15}$$

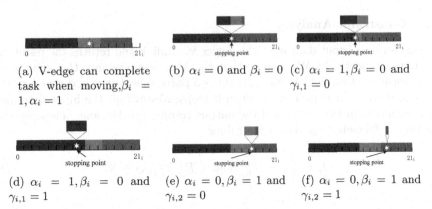

Fig. 4. Illustration of the uploading (blue), computing (green), downloading (orange) process in difference cases that $\alpha_i, \beta_i, \gamma_{i,1}, \gamma_{i,2}$ take different values. (Color figure online)

Let the binary variable $\gamma_{i,2}$ denote whether device i can complete the task uploading and V-edge can complete task processing when the V-edge moves to the stopping point, i.e.,

$$\gamma_{i,2} = \begin{cases} 1, \text{device } i \text{ can complete task uploading and V-edge} \\ \quad \text{can complete task processing before stopping,} \\ 0, \text{otherwise.} \end{cases} \quad (16)$$

Due to the difference in the size of tasks and and geographical differences, some tasks can be completed when the V-edge is moving (as shown in Fig. 4(a)), while others require the V-edge to stop at the stopping point to process the task. Figure 4(b) shows that device i cannot upload all the data to V-edge while V-edge is heading to the stopping point, and device i cannot download all the result of task from V-edge during time period τ, which means that V-edge needs to receive the uploading data, calculate the result and deliver part of the result to the device at the stopping point. Figure 4(c) shows that device i cannot uploading all the data to V-edge while V-edge is moving to the stopping point, and device i can download all the result of task during time period τ. Figure 4(d) shows that device i cannot uploading all the data to V-edge while V-edge is moving to the stopping point, and V-edge can calculate the task and device i can download all the result during τ. Figure 4(e) shows that device i can uploading all the data to V-edge while V-edge is moving to the stopping point, V-edge need to stop at the stopping point to calculate residual data and deliver part of result to device i. Figure 4(f) indicates that V-edge can complete the reception and calculation of the uploaded data while driving to the stopping point but still need to stop at the stopping point to deliver partial results to the device i, but V-edge needs to stop waiting for device i to download part of the results.

Therefore, the upload latency of task i can be classified to four cases, as shown in Fig. 4, which can be represented by:

$$T_i^u = \begin{cases} \text{solved by}: I_i = \int_0^{T_i^u} R_{m,i}^u(t)dt, & \text{if } \beta_i = 1 \\ \frac{L_i+x}{v} + \frac{I_i - \int_0^{\frac{L_i+x}{v}} R_{m,i}^u(t)dt}{R_{p,i}^u}, & \text{if } \beta_i = 0, \alpha_i = 1, \gamma_{i,1} = 0 \\ \frac{2l_i - v(T_i^d + T_i^p)}{v} + \frac{I_i - \int_0^{\frac{2l_i - v(T_i^d + T_i^p)}{v}} R_{m,i}^u(t)dt}{R_{p,i}^u}, & \text{if } \beta_i = 0, \alpha_i = 1, \gamma_{i,1} = 1 \\ \frac{L_i+x}{v} + \frac{I_i - \int_0^{\frac{L_i+x}{v}} R_{m,i}^u(t)dt}{R_{p,i}^u}, & \text{if } \beta_i = 0, \alpha_i = 0 \end{cases} \quad (17)$$

where T_i^d is the download latency of task i and T_i^p is the computation latency of task i.

Meanwhile, the download latency of task i can be classified to four cases, as shown in Fig. 4, which can be represented by:

$$T_i^d = \begin{cases} \text{solved by}: O_i = \int_0^{T_i^d} R_{m,i}^d(t)dt, & \text{if } \alpha_i = 1 \\ \frac{2l_i - L_i - x}{v} + \frac{O_i - \int_0^{\frac{2l_i - L_i - x}{v}} R_{m,i}^d(t)dt}{R_{p,i}^d}, & \text{if } \alpha_i = 0, \beta_i = 1, \gamma_{i,2} = 0 \\ \frac{2l_i - v(T_i^u + T_i^p)}{v} + \frac{O_i - \int_0^{\frac{2l_i - v(T_i^u + T_i^p)}{v}} R_{m,i}^d(t)dt}{R_{p,i}^d}, & \text{if } \alpha_i = 0, \beta_i = 1, \gamma_{i,2} = 1 \\ \frac{2l_i - L_i - x}{v} + \frac{O_i - \int_0^{\frac{2l_i - L_i - x}{v}} R_{m,i}^d(t)dt}{R_{p,i}^d}, & \text{if } \alpha_i = 0, \beta_i = 0 \end{cases} \quad (18)$$

Let binary variable ϕ_i represent whether the V-edge can complete the device task of device i while moving, i.e.,

$$\phi_i = \begin{cases} 1, T_i^u + T_i^p + T_i^d \geq 2l_i/v, \\ 0, \text{otherwise.} \end{cases} \quad (19)$$

Thus, the stopping time for V-edge to complete the task of device i can be given by

$$Q_i(x) = \phi_i(T_i^u + T_i^p + T_i^d - 2l_i/v) \quad (20)$$

Therefore, the stopping time minimization for V-edge to perform tasks in the jth community is formulated:

$$S(x) = \max_i \quad Q_i(x), \quad i = 1, 2, ..., n_j$$
$$\text{s.t} \quad x \geq 0$$
$$x \leq x_{max} \quad (21)$$
$$\text{Constraints } (11), (12)$$

where x_{max} is the upper limit of x in the community and n_j is demands number in community j.

Minimizing the stopping time of the V-edge within community j can be formulated as **P1**

$$\mathbf{P1} : \zeta_j = \min_{x} \max_{i} Q_i(x), i = 1, 2, ..., n_j$$
$$\text{s.t} \quad x \geq 0 \tag{22}$$
$$x \leq x_{max}$$
$$\text{Constraints} (11), (12)$$

In the community, the community completion time consists of two parts, the V-edge stopping time and the V-edge travel time in the community. The community task completion time minimization in community j can be formulated as **P2**

$$\mathbf{P2} : T = \zeta_j + \Gamma_j/v$$
$$\text{s.t} \quad x \geq 0 \tag{23}$$
$$x \leq x_{max}$$
$$\text{Constraints} (11), (12)$$

where Γ_j is the length of communication road segment in the community.

After obtaining the task completion times for all communities, the problem is transformed into a TSP problem which can be solved by many measures, such as [12]. And We design a graph G = (S, E), where S is the community set, and E is a set of undirected edges, which means the travelling time from communities to communities.

We associate with each edge a non-negative cost T_{ij} to denote the time cost between community i and community j. Similarly, each vertex (community) is associated with a non-negative cost T_i to denote the time cost within the community i. Let binary variable e_{ij} represent whether the V-edge is travelled T_{ij}, where $e_{ij} = 1$ indicates V-edge travelled from Community i to Community j; otherwise $e_{ij} = 0$. Similarly, let binary variable b_i represent whether the V-edge has completed the tasks in community i, where $b_i = 1$ indicates V-edge has completed the tasks, otherwise $b_i = 0$. Therefore, the problem can be formulated as follows based on the analyzed constraints:

$$\mathbf{P} : \min \sum_{i,j \in S} e_{ij} T_{ij} + b_i * T_i$$

Due to the maneuverability of the V-edge, the major challenge in solving the problem P is the nonlinear transmission under Eqs. (6), (7) as well as constraints (11), (12). At the same time, the Minimax problem is a typical non-fine optimization problem, i.e., a non-smooth optimization problem. It is a challenging to obtain the optimal solution by the algorithms with polynomial time complexity.

5   Proposed Optimization Method

In this section, we propose a Community Partition and an algorithm for jointly optimizing communication, computation and mobility to solve V-edge Location

Optimization subproblem, which reduces the optimization objective to a simple TSP problem (**P**) which can be solved by ant colony optimization algorithm [12].

5.1 Community Partition

Many existing works have investigated clustering methods, such as semi-dynamic user-specific clustering [9]. Most of the approaches are based on a random common center point where users within the community are close enough to the center point. However, due to road constraints, the V-edge can only be driven on roads, so that the communication center must be in the communication road segment. We model the community division problem as a coverage problem.

Algorithm 1. Community Partition Algorithm

Input: devices set K, crossroads set P
1: Initialization:$Q \leftarrow \emptyset, P \leftarrow \{p_1, ..., p_n\}$, $p_i = [(x_a, y_a), (x_b, y_b)]$, each device communication path Λ
2: divide all devices to the proper road $\{\Psi\}$, mark $\|\Psi\| = n$, and build road device sets $\mathbb{K}$
3: **for** each $p_i \in \Psi$ **do**
4:   **for** $k_{p_i} \subset \mathbb{K}$ **do**
5:     Calculate boundary device set $k_b \subseteq k_{p_i}$
6:     Set new sets $q_j \leftarrow k_b$ and communication path Π_{q_j}, and $\|q\| \leq \|k_b\|$
7:     **for** each $k \in k_{p_i} \backslash k_b$ **do**
8:       **if** device k communication path $\Pi_{q_j} \cap \Lambda_k \neq \emptyset$ **then**
9:         $q_j \leftarrow k$
10:        $\Pi_{q_j} \leftarrow \Pi_{q_j} \cap \Lambda_k$
11:      **else**
12:        set new set q $\leftarrow$ k, and $\Pi_q \leftarrow \Lambda_k$
13:      **end if**
14:    **end for**
15:    $Q \leftarrow Q \cup q$
16:   **end for**
17: **end for**
18: **return** Q, Π

As shown in Algorithm 1, we first divide the devices into different roads according to the road constraint, Specifically, for isolated devices, i.e., there are no other devices within the communication range, they are directly classified as the one with the closest road. For other devices, they are jointly divided according to the number of neighboring devices and the road distance (Line 2). Then calculate the boundary devices for each divided road and give them a higher priority to create communities, mainly to prevent omissions (Line 5–6). Obviously, the number of communities is less than the number of devices (Line 6). For other devices, they are divided according to the distance from the existing community and the length of the effective communication road segment (Line8-10), and the devices that exceed the communication range are reclassified into a new community (Line 12). Finally, merge into communities collection (Line 15).

5.2 V-edge Location Optimization Method

In this subsection, we consider the global optimization of sub problem **P1**. In order to minimize the task completion time within the community, we need to determine an optimal stopping location for V-edge to process all task requests within the community simultaneously.

Since function $S(x)$ (21) is generally non-integrable, it is necessary to transform the function $S(x)$ into a smooth function, so we introduce an auxiliary variable t to transform the min-max problem **P1** (22) into a minimization problem **P3**. For simplicity, we rearranged the inequality constraints associated with the independent variables in **P1**. Specifically, let $g(x)$ denote the inequality constraint function.

$$\textbf{P3} : \min_{x} \quad t$$
$$s.t \quad Q_i(x) - t \leq 0, i = 1, 2, ..., n_j$$
$$g_1(x) = -x \leq 0 \quad\quad\quad\quad (24)$$
$$g_2(x) = x - x_{max} \leq 0$$

where n_j is the number of demands in community j.

Based on the theory of successive convex approximations and SQP algorithm, we proposed a novel task completion time minimization strategy that jointly optimizes computation and communication and considers server mobility (jointCCM). Firstly, we present a convex programming subproblem at each iteration point to approximate the original model, and then find the feasible directions to search for locally optimal solutions within the neighborhood of each iteration point.

For **P3**, let x_k denote the feasible point of the kth iteration, obtained from the previous iteration k-1. We can yield the next feasible point by:

$$x_{k+1} = x_k + \theta_k d_k \quad\quad\quad\quad (25)$$

where θ_k is the step length parameter that is determined by an appropriate line search procedure so that a sufficient decrease in a merit function is obtained, and d_k represents the feasible search direction within a certain neighborhood of x_k. Initially, x_1 is an initial feasible point in a deterministic scope, and in order to obtain the optimal solution, we keep finding the search direction and appropriate step size for the next step and iterate. To solve this problem, we will present the algorithm design of jointCCM in detail.

A. Convex Approximation Transformation. The Lagrangian function associated with Problem is described by

$$L(x, \lambda, \rho) = \sum_{i \in I} \lambda_i Q_i(x) + \sum_{j \in J} \rho_j g_j(x). \quad\quad\quad\quad (26)$$

where the variables λ and ρ are the non-negative Lagrange multiplier vector, and $I = \{1, 2, ..., n_j\}$, $J = \{1, 2\}$.

Based on (26) and SQP algorithm, given the current iteration point x_k and the Lagrange multipliers vector λ, ρ, we can develop a convex quadratic programming(QP) subproblem **P4** to obtain a search direction for x_{k+1} as follows:

$$\mathbf{P4}: \min_{(d,t) \in R^{n+1}} \quad t_k + \frac{1}{2} d_k^T W_k d_k$$
$$s.t \quad Q_i(x_k) + \nabla Q_i(x_k)^T d_k - S(x_k) \leq t, i \in I, \tag{27}$$
$$g_j(x_k) + \nabla g_j(x_k)^T d_k \leq \eta_k t, j \in J$$

where η_k is the non-negative auxiliary variable, the matrix W_k is a positive definite approximation of the Hessian matrix of the Lagrangian function which will be covered in detail in the next section.

The above problem(**P4**) can be solved by any QP algorithm such as active-set method [6].

In summary, based on the quadratic programming subproblem, i.e., **P4**, we can obtain the iterative search direction for Eq. (25).

B. Positive-Definite Hessian Approximation. At each iteration, subproblem **P4** requires a positive definite Hessian approximation, we adopt Powell's modification of Broyden-Fletcher-Goldfarb-Shanno formula (BFGS) [16] to perform the calculation:

$$W_{k+1} = W_k + \frac{p_k p_k^T}{p_k^T B_k} - \frac{W_k B_k B_k^T W_k^T}{B_k^T W_k B_k} \tag{28}$$

where $B_k = x_{k+1} - x_k$, and p_k is the linear combination of $W_k B_k$ and y_k, as follows:

$$p_k = \epsilon_k y_k + (1 - \epsilon_k) W_k B_k, \epsilon \in [0, 1] \tag{29}$$

where $y_k = \nabla_x L(x_{k+1}, \lambda_k, \rho_k) - \nabla_x L(x_k, \lambda_k, \rho_k)$, and ϵ is designed to keep that the positive definitions of Hessian approximation, and is can be expressed as follows:

$$\epsilon_k = \begin{cases} 1, & \text{if } B_k^T y_k \geq 0.2 B_k^T W_k B_k \\ \dfrac{0.8 B_k^T W_k B_k}{B_k^T W_k B_k - y_k^T B_k}, & \text{if } B_k^T y_k < 0.2 B_k^T W_k B_k. \end{cases} \tag{30}$$

where the factor 0.2 was chosen empirically. Initially, the Hessian approximation is set up as a unit matrix.

Under appropriate conditions, theoretical analysis shows that the algorithm can converge globally [20].

We describe the V-edge position optimization algorithm in detail. First, we obtain the community data by Algorithm 1 (Line 1). For each community, we allocate the computation resources of V-edge for devices (Line 4), then we generate the stopping time function $Q_i(x)$ (Line 5). Initialize the position of V-edge

---

Algorithm 2. JointCCM Algorithm Based On Sequential Quadratic Programming

---

Input: community sets Q
Output: the time for serve each community T
 1: Initialize Q $\leftarrow$ Algorithm 1, $T \leftarrow 0$, $j \leftarrow 0$,
 2: **for** $q \in Q$ **do**
 3:     $x_0 \in \mathbb{R}$, $H_0 \leftarrow$ E, $k \leftarrow 0$
 4:     allocate F to each user in the community
 5:     set the function $Q_i(x)$ according to Equation (20)
 6:     solve QP subproblem: compute (d_k, t_k) by the quadratic programming problem
         (27) at x_k with corresponding KKT multiplier vectors λ_k, ρ_k. If $d_k = 0$, then
         $T_j = t_k + \Gamma_j/v$, j $\leftarrow$ j+1; continue next community.
 7:     update $x_{k+1} = x_k + \alpha_k d_k$, H_{k+1}
 8:     k $\leftarrow$ k+1. Go back to Step 5.
 9: **end for**
10: **return** T

---

x_0 (Line 3), simplify the original problem to a quadratic programming problem (18) at iteration point x_k, then solve the programming problem to get the direction d_k and the function value, if $d_k = 0$, then stop and set value for T_j (Line 6), then get the next iteration point x_{k+1} (Line 7). Correct Hessian matrix H according to BFGS and continue to the next iteration until the optimal solution is found (Line 7–8).

After obtain all the time of completing community demands, we can transform the problem into a classical TSP problem. For simplicity, we can use existing algorithms to solve the problem, which is to optimize a path to minimize the V-edge travel time. For example, ant colony optimization algorithm, dynamic programming algorithm, branch and bound method, etc.

6   Simulation Results

In this section, extensive simulation experiments are performed to verify the effectiveness of our solution and compare it with the optimal solution, and analyze the performance under different parameters.

6.1   Evaluation Setup

We simulated a 1000*1000 m^2 non-functional square area with a random distribution of users. For convenience, the initial location of V-edge is in the center of the area. The simulation uses the communication model in [7]. The basic parameters of the simulation are summarized in Table 1. We randomly generated the computational task size of the device and conducted several experiments to eliminate the effect of randomness. To observe the effect of task size on the experiment, we divided the data size into three levels: (0, 100) MB, (100, 500) MB

Table 1. Simulation parameters

Definition	Parameters	Values
Bandwidth	W	40 MHz
Attenuation factors	η	1
White Gaussian noise power	σ^2	$5 * 10^{-15}$
Max velocity of V-edge	v_{max}	20 m/s
Transmitting power	P_{TX}	1.8 W
Receiving power	P_{RX}	2 W
Computation intensity	f	unif(200, 1000) cycles/bit
V-edge CPU frequency	F	5 GHz
The carrier frequency	g	2.4 GHz
The speed of light	c	$3 * 10^8$ m/s

and (500, 1000) MB. All algorithms in this paper are performed on a computer with Intel Core i7-10700 2.90 GHz CPU and 16G RAM.

In this evaluation, we will consider a key performance metric, namely the system completion time.

Inspired by [10,14], our proposed algorithm is compared with the following six methods:

– Optimal Static (OS): V-edge provides services for uploading, computing and downloading operations after stopping at the optimal point.
– Shortest Path (SPS): The stopping location of V-edge is determined based on the shortest sum of distances from devices in the community to a point.
– Random (Random): V-edge randomly selects a point from the community's common communication segment to serve.
– Sine Cosine Algorithm (SCA): It is a novel population-based optimization algorithm which will create multiple initial random candidate solutions and requires them to fluctuate outwards or towards the best solution using a mathematical model based on sine and cosine functions [13].
– Shortest Distance Point for each device (SDP): V-edge travels to the closest point to each device to provide service and does not consider mobility communication.
– Shortest Distance Point with Communication for each device (SDPC): V-edge travels to the closest point to each device to provide service and considers communication during the movement.

In next section, the algorithm is analyzed for different system parameters using the benchmark algorithm described above. We performed 40 independent evaluation experiments in this section.

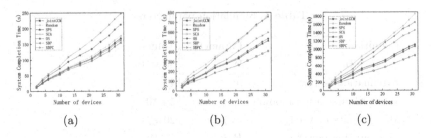

Fig. 5. System completion time under different numbers of devices. (a) $I_k \sim$ unif(1, 100) MB. (b) $I_k \sim$ unif(100, 500) MB. (c) $I_k \sim$ unif(500, 1000) MB.

6.2 Numerical Results

The system completion time of seven algorithms under different number of devices is plotted in Fig. 5. We can observe that system completion time increases when K grows. It is because more service demands need to be satisfied with growing number of devices.

System completion time under proposed jointCCM algorithm, as shown in Figs. 5(a), 5(b), and 5(c), is the lowest, compared to other algorithms. Simultaneously, we can notice that the system performance is more superior under jointCCM algorithm as the task size grows. In Fig. 5(a), the jointCCM algorithm performs 14%, 9%, 37%, 5% and 60% better than the compared Random, SPS, OS, SDP and SDPC methods respectively when number of devices is thirty-one. And in Fig. 5(b), these ratios vary to 91%, 25%, 31%, 86% and 47% respectively. And in Fig. 5(c), these ratios vary to 117%, 30%, 25%, 93% and 71% respectively. From the ratios in these three plots, we can notice that the ratios of Random and SPS increase when task size grows. This is because the stopping point of jointCCM algorithm is closer to devices so that the communication latency is shorter, compared to Random and SPS. The communication latency gap is greater when the task size increases. However, the ratios of OS algorithm in three plot decrease when task size grows, this is because a smaller portion of tasks are completed when V-edge is moving with the same time. Similarly, it can be found that as the amount of tasks increases, the jointCCM algorithm is more effective compared to SDP and SDPC. It also shows the importance of optimizing the stopping point of V-edge. In summary, jointCCM algorithm outperforms the compared methods in terms of system completion time. The algorithm performs better when the task size increases.

To investigate the effect of V-edge's computational resources, Fig. 6 shows the system completion time at different CPU frequencies. We set the maximum CPU frequency to 20 GHz in Fig. 6. As we can see, the system completion time decreases with the increase of computational resources. This is because when the CPU frequency increases, more computational resources are allocated to each task, thus reducing the computing latency. And, we can observe that the effect of computational resources on the system completion time is limited, i.e., the increasing trend becomes much slower when the CPU frequency exceeds

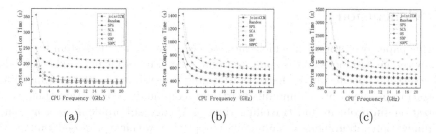

Fig. 6. System completion time under different numbers of CPU frequency. (a) $I_k \sim$ unif(1, 100) MB. (b) $I_k \sim$ unif(100, 500) MB. (c) $I_k \sim$ unif(500, 1000) MB.

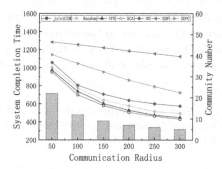

Fig. 7. System completion time and community number under different communication radius.

10 GHz. Therefore, system performance at CPU frequencies below 10 GHz is mainly affected by the lack of computational resources, which leads to an increase in task completion time. Meanwhile, it can be found that the task size has less impact on the decreasing trend from Figs. 6(a), 6(b), and 6(c) when the CPU frequency exceeds 10 GHz, and has some impact on the decreasing trend when the CPU frequency is small.

In Fig. 7, we considered the effect of the communication radius of devices on the system completion time. We set the number of devices at 30 and compared seven algorithms. The left axis of the graph is the system completion time, which is represented using a line graph, and the right axis is the number of communities, which is represented using a bar graph. We can observe that when the communication radius increases, the number of communities decreases. Meanwhile, due to the reduction of the number of communities, V-edge can complete more task demands within a community at the same time and reduce its traveling time to other communities.

In summary, it can be observed that the jointCCM algorithm based on SQP algorithm can achieve the best results. Although the SCA algorithm can also achieve this result, its convergence time is longer than that of jointCCM. In a computational offloading environment, it is preferred to choose the algorithm with faster execution time.

7   Conclusion

In this paper, we propose a vehicle-mounted edge server rescue system for emergency rescue and focus on the computational offloading problem based on mobile edge servers. Specifically, we have transforming the system completion time minimization problem into community partition, community completion time minimization subproblem and travelling time of V-edge subproblem. To solve the minimization subproblem of community completion, we have proposed jointCCM method based SQP algorithm. Numerical results have showed that the algorithm performs well.

Due to the limited coverage area of V-edge, we will consider the cooperation between V-edge and UAVs. The V-edge can carry multiple UAVs, and the V-edge can provide service to the devices on the planned path and provide energy to the UAVs, while the UAVs provide service to the devices further away or act as relays to deliver requests. The above issues will be investigated in our future work.

Acknowledgement. This work is supported by the National Natural Science Key Foundation of China grant No. 62032016 and No. 61832014, and the National Natural Science Foundation of China grant No. 62102281.

References

1. Al-Hourani, A., Kandeepan, S., Lardner, S.: Optimal lap altitude for maximum coverage. IEEE Wirel. Commun. Let. **3**(6), 569–572 (2014)
2. Ashraf, M.W., Idrus, S.M., Iqbal, F., Butt, R.A., Faheem, M.: Disaster-resilient optical network survivability: a comprehensive survey. In: Photonics, vol. 5, p. 35. Multidisciplinary Digital Publishing Institute (2018)
3. Chen, C., et al.: Delay-optimized v2v-based computation offloading in urban vehicular edge computing and networks. IEEE Access **8**, 18863–18873 (2020)
4. Du, W., He, Q., Ji, Y., Cai, C., Zhao, X.: Optimal user migration upon server failures in edge computing environment. In: 2021 IEEE International Conference on Web Services (ICWS), pp. 272–281. IEEE (2021)
5. Faraci, G., Grasso, C., Schembra, G.: Fog in the clouds: UAVs to provide edge computing to IoT devices. ACM Trans. Internet Technol. (TOIT) **20**(3), 1–26 (2020)
6. Gill, P.E., Murray, W., Saunders, M.A., Wright, M.H.: Procedures for optimization problems with a mixture of bounds and general linear constraints. ACM Trans. Math. Softw. (TOMS) **10**(3), 282–298 (1984)
7. Hou, X., Ren, Z., Wang, J., Zheng, S., Zhang, H.: Latency and reliability oriented collaborative optimization for multi-UAV aided mobile edge computing system. In: IEEE INFOCOM 2020-IEEE Conference on Computer Communications Workshops (INFOCOM WKSHPS), pp. 150–156. IEEE (2020)
8. Jeong, S., Simeone, O., Kang, J.: Mobile edge computing via a UAV-mounted cloudlet: optimization of bit allocation and path planning. IEEE Trans. Veh. Technol. **67**(3), 2049–2063 (2017)

9. Liu, D., Han, S., Yang, C., Zhang, Q.: Semi-dynamic user-specific clustering for downlink cloud radio access network. IEEE Trans. Veh. Technol. **65**(4), 2063–2077 (2015)

10. Liu, Y., Li, Y., Niu, Y., Jin, D.: Joint optimization of path planning and resource allocation in mobile edge computing. IEEE Trans. Mob. Comput. **19**(9), 2129–2144 (2019)

11. Lu, W., Shen, Y., Wang, T., Zhang, M., Jagadish, H.V., Du, X.: Fast failure recovery in vertex-centric distributed graph processing systems. IEEE Trans. Knowl. Data Eng. **31**(4), 733–746 (2018)

12. Meng, L., Lin, Y., Qing, S., Wenjing, F.: Research on generalized traveling salesman problem based on modified ant colony optimization. In: 2019 Chinese Control And Decision Conference (CCDC), pp. 4570–4574. IEEE (2019)

13. Mirjalili, S.: SCA: a sine cosine algorithm for solving optimization problems. Knowl. Based Syst. **96**, 120–133 (2016)

14. Ning, Z., et al.: 5g-enabled UAV-to-community offloading: Joint trajectory design and task scheduling. IEEE J. Sel. Areas Commun. **39**, 3306–3320 (2021)

15. Niu, Y., Liu, Y., Li, Y., Chen, X., Zhong, Z., Han, Z.: Device-to-device communications enabled energy efficient multicast scheduling in mmwave small cells. IEEE Trans. Commun. **66**(3), 1093–1109 (2017)

16. Powell, M.J.: The convergence of variable metric methods for nonlinearly constrained optimization calculations. In: Nonlinear Programming, vol. 3, pp. 27–63. Elsevier (1978)

17. Ren, J., Yu, G., Cai, Y., He, Y.: Latency optimization for resource allocation in mobile-edge computation offloading. IEEE Trans. Wirel. Commun. **17**(8), 5506–5519 (2018)

18. Ren, J., Yu, G., He, Y., Li, G.Y.: Collaborative cloud and edge computing for latency minimization. IEEE Trans. Veh. Technol. **68**(5), 5031–5044 (2019)

19. Sun, Y., Zhou, S., Xu, J.: EMM: energy-aware mobility management for mobile edge computing in ultra dense networks. IEEE J. Sel. Areas Commun. **35**(11), 2637–2646 (2017)

20. Wang, L., Luo, Z.: A simple SQP algorithm for constrained finite minimax problems. Sci. World J. **2014**, 159754 (2014)

21. Zhao, H., Deng, S., Zhang, C., Du, W., He, Q., Yin, J.: A mobility-aware cross-edge computation offloading framework for partitionable applications. In: 2019 IEEE International Conference on Web Services (ICWS), pp. 193–200. IEEE (2019)

22. Zhou, T., Qin, D., Nie, X., Li, X., Li, C.: Energy-efficient computation offloading and resource management in ultradense heterogeneous networks. IEEE Trans. Veh. Technol. **70**, 13101–13114 (2021)

An Approach to the Synchronization of Dynamic Complex Network Combining Degree Distribution and Eigenvector Criteria

Rong Xie[✉], Yuchen Wang, and Mengting Jiang

School of Computer Science, Wuhan University,
Wuhan 430072, People's Republic of China
{xierong,wyc2722}@whu.edu.cn

Abstract. Synchronization is an important behavior of a dynamic complex network. Traditional methods, like changing network structure, enhancing coupling capability and utilizing external control strategies, etc., cannot achieve complete network synchronization. As it is easier for the small-world networks to achieve topology synchronization than regular networks and random networks, from the viewpoint of the topology of complex networks, we propose the method of Degree Distribution Connection (DDC) for balancing the degree distribution of nodes in a network. And further, we propose the method of Enhanced Synchronization Small-World (ESSW) for constructing the network combining degree distribution and eigenvector criteria, deleting connecting edge by preferentially selecting the node with a larger degree and reconnecting the edge according to the eigenvector criterion. The experimental results show that our solution is effective that can solve the network synchronization problem well by improving network topology.

Keywords: Dynamic complex network · Synchronization · Degree distribution · Eigenvector criterion · Degree Distribution Connection (DDC) · Enhanced Synchronization Small-World (ESSW)

1 Introduction

A dynamic complex network is usually a network of basic units formed by a series of nodes and their interconnecting edges. The phenomenon that the behaviors of different nodes gradually tend to be the same or similar over time is called synchronization, which is a significant characteristic of behavior of dynamic network. As synchronization behavior and its regular patterns can explain how complex systems work together, the study of network synchronization has always been an important research direction in the field of complex networks, which has a wide range of applications, including industrial robots' cooperation in factory, unmanned aerial vehicles (UAVs) formation, epidemic spread suppression, etc.

H. Gao et al. (Eds.): CollaborateCom 2022, LNICST 460, pp. 290–308, 2022.
https://doi.org/10.1007/978-3-031-24383-7_16

Many traditional methods were proposed to improve the capability of synchronization, including enhancing coupling capability [1–3], changing network structure [12,18,20–23], etc. In addition, when a network itself could not reach its state of synchronization, some external control strategies [4–11] were also applied to promote network to synchronization state. Since it was not easy to change the coupling mode and the dynamic properties, also it was mostly uncontrollable to dominate the results of external control, these methods could not fundamentally achieve complete synchronization.

Watts and Strogatz [12] pioneerely proposed their significant discovery of small-world and established a WS small-world network model. Their results proved that small-world network had both large clustering coefficient and small average path length, which had great advantages for many applications related to collaboration. Based on their work, many researchers had devoted themselves to studying the synchronization problem of complex networks with the properties of small-world; and found that the small-worlds could significantly improve the synchronization capability of dynamic networks [13], which were generally believed that the topology of small-world was easier to achieve synchronization than regular network and random network.

Analyzing the internal causes for the dynamic network synchronization, we think that, from the perspective of basic components of complex networks and their interactions, subtle changes in network topology will have a greater impact on the synchronization of complex networks, and it is required for us to consider both local dynamics of nodes and global interactions among topologies. Therefore, we propose an approach to small-world network synchronization that combines degree distribution and eigenvector criteria. Nodes are no longer selected randomly for reconnection, but selected that can keep degree distribution of network as uniform as possible. At the same time, reconnection edges are handled by the eigenvector criteria. This method can improve synchronization capability of the small-world network.

The rest of the paper is organized as follows. Section 2 discusses related work. Section 3 presents the overview framework of our method. Our methods of DDC and ESSW are proposed in Sect. 4 and Sect. 5, respectively. Section 6 gives experiment results. Conclusions are finally presented in Sect. 7.

2   Related Work

Focusing on solving the network synchronization problem, many researchers have carried out a lot of work from different aspects such as node degree distribution, adding edges and network topology, etc.

Node Degree Distribution. Nishikawa et al. [14] proposed that large variance of node degree distribution would inhibit network synchronization, even if average path length of network was long, a uniform node degree distribution could still make network better synchronization. But, Hong et al. [15] pointed out that a short average path length could improve synchronization, and if network degree distribution showed an uneven state, it would also enhance synchronization capability. Lv and Li [16] once designed a PA algorithm for the construction of small-world network through a selective reconnection strategy. Their method randomly selected node connections according to a weight proportional to node degree, however, synchronization was slightly lower than WS small-world. Their results showed that the uneven degree distribution could inhibit network synchronization.

Adding Edges. Hagberg and Schult [17] selected those edges that had the greatest impact on synchronization based on eigenvector of Laplacian matrix of network, and achieved network synchronization by deleting the selected edges. The method could effectively maintain the number of edges in network, but the effect of synchronization was not as good as those methods of adding edges. Dai and Wang [18] presented that clustering coefficient and average path length could not determine network synchronization independently. Based on eigenvector criterion, they proposed small-world network algorithm SOSW-I and SOSW-II with the improved strategy of adding edge and reconnecting edge, respectively, which made good effects of synchronization. Wang et al. [19] improved synchronization by adding new edges to nodes with smaller degree in the nearest neighbors, but the method required to change some characteristic parameters of network, which would have a certain impact on process of synchronization evolution. Zeng et al. [20] proposed a method of residual edge-betweenness gradient (REBG) to select edge according to the betweenness of edge to improve synchronization, but the method might be hindered under some certain conditions, causing the network to not be fully synchronized.

Network Topology. Many researchers tried to solve the network synchronization problem by changing network topology [12,18,20–23]. Classical WS model suggested to modify the network topology by rewiring certain amount of the existing links based on a certain probability [12]. Dai and Wang made their experiments on SOSW-I and SOSW-II, which showed that different networks with similar topological characteristics could have different synchronization capabilities [18]. Through the comparison of small-world algorithms, Allan presented that synchronization could be achieved if it was promoted by manipulating topology appropriately [21]. Some other related methods were also proposed. Based on Zeng et al.'s work [20], Hou et al. [22] further divided candidate nodes into four different categories, improved network structure using a maximum forward matching strategy, and improved the overall network with local topological features. Wen et al. [23] studied the network synchronization problem with directed switching topology, and proposed a Lyapunov function to analyze synchronization. Reviewing these methods, it was necessary to find a solution by exploring the internal causes for the improvements of synchronization capability of network.

3   Overview Framework

3.1   Network Synchronization Problem

Suppose a continuous-time coupled dynamic network with N nodes is $G(V, E)$, where V is a set of nodes and E is a set of edges connecting nodes. The state equation of node i in G is represented by

$$\dot{x}_i = f(x_i) + c\sum_{j=1}^{N} a_{ij}x_j, \quad i = 1, 2, \ldots, N \tag{1}$$

where x_i is the state variable of node i, f is the function of state transition, c is constant of coupling strength of network, $c > 0$.

The network topology is represented by a negative Laplace matrix, called coupling matrix, which is defined as $A = (a_{ij}) \in R^{N \times N}$. If there exists an edge between node i and node j, then it corresponds to the value of element a_{ij} in A. Set the weight of edge be m, $m > 0$. Since coupling matrix is undirected, which is a symmetric matrix, then $a_{ji} = a_{ij}$. If there is no edge between node i and node j, then element a_{ij} in A is 0. Similarly, $a_{ji} = 0$. The diagonal element of a negative Laplacian matrix is the inverse of the sum of elements in each row, and its value is less than 0, i.e. $a_{ii} = -\sum\limits_{j=1, j\neq i}^{N} a_{ij}$, $i = 1, 2, \ldots, N$. When $t \to \infty$, if the dynamic network defined by Eq. (1) satisfies Eq. (2), then it reaches a fully synchronized state, that is,

$$x_1(t) = x_2(t) = \ldots = x_N(t) = s(t) \tag{2}$$

where $x_i(t)$ represents the state of node i in network at time t, and $s(t)$ represents the synchronization state of dynamic network (1), that is, a solution that satisfies the network conditions.

Definition 1 (Network Synchronization Problem, NSP): Let the size of nodes of dynamic network be N, $x_i(t)$ is the state variable of node i in network at time t, $s(t)$ is a solution where the isolated node satisfies the coupling condition. If there is $t > 0$, that the state of the nodes of the entire network are roughly consistent, approaching a certain same state, then the network is called to achieve identity synchronization, satisfying

$$\lim_{t \to \infty} \|x_i(t) - s(t)\|_2 \to 0, \quad i = 1, 2, \ldots, N \tag{3}$$

where $\|x_i(t) - s(t)\|_2$ is the 2-norm of $x_i(t) - s(t)$.

A is a symmetric irreducible matrix, and A of dynamic network (1) is a negative Laplace matrix. Since the minimum eigenvalue of Laplacian matrix is 0, the sum of each row of A is equal to 0, and the maximum eigenvalue is 0, other eigenvalues are negative. So, the N eigenvalues of A satisfy

$$0 = \lambda_1 > \lambda_2 \geqslant \lambda_3 \geqslant \ldots \geqslant \lambda_N \tag{4}$$

It can be seen that the second eigenvalue λ_2 is a negative number. The smaller the value of λ_2, the larger its absolute value $|\lambda_2|$.

When dynamic network (1) satisfies Eq. (5), then its state reaches asymptotic stability [24].

$$c \geqslant \left|\frac{r}{\lambda_2}\right| \tag{5}$$

where r is a constant determined by dynamic equation of node. Therefore, c is actually determined by λ_2. For dynamic network (1), if A is constant, then network can achieve synchronization with a small coupling strength c, and synchronization capability of network is strong. Inequality (4) shows that synchronization capability of dynamic network can be measured by λ_2 of its coupling matrix. The smaller the value of λ_2 is, the stronger the synchronization capability is.

3.2 Our Method

The goal of the paper is to propose an improved small-world network based on the combination of degree distribution and eigenvector criterion to improve the capability of network synchronization.

After analyzing the influence of node degree distribution on network synchronization, we can see, uneven degree distribution of nodes will inhibit network synchronization to a certain extent. So, we propose a method of degree distribution based on connection (DDC). Define and calculate the variance of network degree distribution. According to the value of variance, the node with smaller degree is preferentially selected, and degree distribution of nodes in network is kept as uniform as possible. On this basis, combined with the eigenvector criterion, we further propose the method of modeling Enhanced Synchronization Small-World (ESSW) network. Select nodes to delete edges according to the probability proportional to the value of weight of node. When reconnecting edges, select two nodes according to the eigenvector criterion to connect edges selectively. We can further analyze how to improve network synchronization capability by changing small-world network topology, so as to find a way to solve the network synchronization problem.

4   Network Connection Based on Degree Distribution

4.1   Degree Distribution

Degree distribution of node in network is an important characteristic parameter used to describe network topology, and its distribution can be judged by the degree distribution variance.

Definition 2 (Degree distribution variance): Suppose the total number of network nodes is N, and d_i is degree of node i. The variance of degree distribution σ satisfies

$$\sigma^2 = \frac{\sum\limits_{1}^{N} d_i^2 - \dfrac{(\sum\limits_{1}^{N} d_i)^2}{N}}{N} \tag{6}$$

Hong et al. [15] presented that making node degree distribution of network uneven could improve network synchronization capability. Lv and Li [16] presented a different opinion. They proposed a PA algorithm for the construction of small-world. And their experiments showed that the gradual increase in the variance of degree distribution was not the main reason for enhancing synchronization capability of small-world network.

When the reconnection probability P is small, with reconnection of edges, the average path length of small-world network will decrease rapidly. So, synchronization capability of network is mainly determined by the change of average path length. However, when the change rate of average path length of small-world network is almost 0, if the variance of degree distribution of the current network is greater than a certain threshold, synchronization capability of network will be then inhibited. Therefore, we think, the uneven node degree distribution of small-world network will inhibit the improvement of synchronization capability of network to some extent.

4.2 The Method of DDC

The reconnection edge of WS small-world was not prioritized, but connected completely randomly. In the paper, we design a network connection method based on degree distribution. In the reconnection, the node with a smaller degree is preferentially selected for connection, and the node degree distribution of network is kept as uniform as possible.

Give preference to those nodes that can make the node degree distribution more uniform, which can reduce the uneven distribution of degrees during the reconnection process. The weight is set for node by the probability inversely proportional to the network node degree, and then the reconnection strategy is set according to the probability proportional to the node weight. Nodes with a larger degree are not easy to participate in edge connection, so the degree of node generally does not increase; Nodes with a smaller degree have a greater probability of connecting new edges, and the degree will increase. Thus, the node degree distribution will tend to be average.

The weight W_i of a node i $(i = 1, 2, \ldots, N)$ in network is represented by

$$W_i = \begin{cases} \left(\dfrac{1}{d_i} \right)^x , d_i \neq 0 \\ \qquad 1 \quad , \text{othervise} \end{cases} \tag{7}$$

where x is weight coefficient of the adjusted node. The larger x is, the easier it is for those nodes with smaller degrees to be selected. d_i is degree of node i. When degree is 0, then weight $W_i = 1$.

4.3 The Algorithm of DDC

Let the total number of network nodes be N, the initial number of neighbors is k (must be an even number), reconnection probability is P, and weight coefficient is x. The steps of the implementation of DDC algorithm are described as follows.

Step 1: According to k, each node in network is connected to the $k/2$ nearest neighbor nodes, and the initial network G is obtained.

Step 2: Traverse the edge set E of G, and generate a random number p for each edge in E. If $p > P$, then skip this edge and continue to traverse the next edge in the set; otherwise, perform a selective reconnection operation.

Step 3: Calculate the degree distribution of node of network. Calculate the inverse of the degree of each node, i.e., $1/d_i$. If the degree is 0, then set its reciprocal to 1.

Step 4: Calculate the x-th power of the reciprocal of the degree of each node, that is $(1/d_i)^x$, to obtain the weight value of the node.

Step 5: Select the node to connect an edge according to the probability proportional to the value of node weight.

Step 6: Update the current network and check whether all edges in E have been traversed. If not, then continue to traverse the next edge and return to **Step 2**; otherwise, the algorithm ends.

5   Enhanced Synchronization Small-World

On the basis of Sect. 4, further combining the eigenvector criterion, we propose our modeling ESSW method, which has stronger capability of synchronization, but not losing the small-world characteristics.

5.1   Eigenvector Criterion

It can be known from inequality (4) that, in order to improve the capability of network synchronization, the second eigenvalue λ_2 of the coupling matrix A of the network should be made as small as possible. Suppose that n edges with weight m are added to the current network. If the newly added edges can minimize λ_2 of A, then the added edges are the optimal solution for network synchronization.

The coupling matrix of the network after adding an edge is defined as $A(m) = A + m\Delta A$, where $\Delta A = (\Delta a_{ij})_{N \times N}$, representing the change of A after adding edges to the network. If an edge is added between node i and node j, and the weight is m, then $\Delta a_{ij} = \Delta a_{ji} = m$; otherwise $\Delta a_{ij} = \Delta a_{ji} = 0$. Diagonal element is $\Delta a_{ii} = -\sum\limits_{j=1, j \neq i}^{N} \Delta a_{ij}$, $i = 1, 2, ..., N$. After adding edges, the eigenvalues of $A(m)$ are denoted as $0 = \lambda_1(m) > \lambda_2(m) \geq \lambda_3(m) \geq ... \geq \lambda_N(m)$. Since a new edge is added to the original network, the value of λ_2 always decreases, i.e., $\lambda_2(m) < \lambda_2 < 0$. In order to improve the capability of network synchronization, it is necessary to change the network topology by adding edges to satisfy $min(\lambda_2(m))$.

Give the corresponding unit eigenvector $\xi(m)$ for $\lambda_2(m)$ of $A(m)$. It can be obtained $A(m)\xi(m) = \lambda_2(m)\xi(m)$ from the matrix definition, and after transformation, it can be obtained as

$$\lambda_2(m) = \xi(m)^T (A + m\Delta A)\xi(m) \tag{8}$$

Taking the partial derivative with respect to m on both sides of Eqs. (8), (9) is obtained.

$$\frac{\partial \lambda_2(m)}{\partial m} = \xi(m)^T \Delta A \xi(m) + 2\lambda_2(m)\xi(m)^T \frac{\partial \xi(m)}{\partial m} \qquad (9)$$

Due to $\xi(m)^T \xi(m) = 1$, Eq. (9) can be simplified as

$$\frac{\partial \lambda_2(m)}{\partial m} = \xi(m)^T \Delta A \xi(m) \qquad (10)$$

In the formula, if m is small enough, then the size of λ_2 has nothing to do with the weight m of the edge. Therefore, the problem can turn into how to add a new edge to the original network to get a new coupling matrix $A(m)$, which minimizes $\lambda_2(m)$.

It is known from Eq. (10) that making the value of the left side of the equation smaller $\lambda_2(m)$ is equivalent to how to construct ΔA, so that the value of the right side of the equation $\xi^T \Delta A \xi$ is the smallest. Since the result is independent of the size of m, here $\xi \triangleq [\xi_1, \xi_2, ..., \xi_N]$ is the unit feature vector corresponding to λ_2 of A of the initial network.

For the convenience of calculation, we only add one edge to the original network each time. After the new coupling matrix is obtained, it is used as the new network coupling matrix, and then the calculation is performed, and the subsequent edge is added. The eigenvector criterion for adding edge is defined as shown in Eq. (11).

$$\min \xi^T \Delta A \xi = \min_{i,j \in E} \{-(\xi_i - \xi_j)^2\} \qquad (11)$$

where E is the set of edges of network. In order to minimize the value of the right side of the equation, two nodes i and j should be selected so as to minimize $-(\xi_i - \xi_j)^2$, that is, to maximize $|\xi_i - \xi_j|$. Therefore, in the process of network construction, we can refer to the nodes obtained by the eigenvector criterion and connect them, the value of $\lambda_2(m)$ can be then minimized, and the capability of network synchronization can be improved to the greatest extent.

5.2   The Method of ESSW

For the classical WS small-world network, the reconnection edges are random, that is, the connection nodes are not selected, but reconnected randomly, which depends on the reconnection probability P. Although random reconnection can improve the capability of network synchronization, it is not the optimal. In order to solve the problem of complex network synchronization, we propose an ESSW small-world network modeling method that combines degree distribution and eigenvector criteria. When constructing a small-world network, reconnect edges selectively, so that network can be more synchronized than those networks by random reconnection edges.

Give scale of the given network N, number of neighbors k, and reconnection probability P. Calculate the maximum number of iterations T of the algorithm according to Formula (12), where T is also the number of reconnected edges in ESSW.

$$T = \frac{P \times N \times k}{2} \tag{12}$$

When reconnecting edges, the selection is made according to the eigenvector criterion. For the network G_t of the t-th iteration, find λ_2 corresponding to A and the corresponding unit eigenvector ξ, where $\xi \triangleq [\xi_1, \xi_2, ..., \xi_N]^T$. If the corresponding element $a_{ij} = 0$ in A, it means that there is no connection between nodes i and j. Then, the distance gap between the components ξ_i and ξ_j of ξ corresponding to i and j is calculated.

Traverse the nodes in network, and add an edge between i and j for the node pair (i, j) with the largest distance gap, satisfying

$$\max gap = \max_{i,j \in E} |\xi_i - \xi_j| \tag{13}$$

where E is the set of edges of network.

The network obtained by our method can make it converge the fastest, get the optimal solution, and have stronger synchronization capability.

5.3   The Algorithm of ESSW

Let the total number of nodes in network be N, the number of neighbors be k (must be an even number), the maximum number of iterations be T, and reconnection probability is P. The steps of the implementation of ESSW are described as follows.

Step 1: According to k, each node in network is connected to the $k/2$ nearest neighbor nodes, and the initial network G is obtained.

Step 2: According to P and the number of edges e of the initial network, the number T of iterations of the algorithm is calculated.

Step 3: In the $(t+1)$-th iteration, the network obtained in the t-th iteration is taken as the network G_t of this iteration.

Step 4: Find the node degree distribution of the current network G_t, and select a node according to the probability proportional to the node degree, and delete the edge connected to it.

Step 5: Obtain A of network G_t' after deleting edge, calculate the λ_2 of A, and obtain the unit feature vector ξ corresponding to λ_2.

Step 6: According to the reconnection policy of ESSW, add a new edge between node i and node j.

Step 7: Update the network and check whether the algorithm has reached the maximum number of iterations T. If it is not reached, then return to **Step 3**, and take the network G_{t+1} obtained by the $(t + 1)$-th iteration as a new network, and continue to perform the reconnection operation; otherwise, the algorithm ends.

6   Experiments

6.1   Evaluation Indexes

Parameters, such as average path length of network, clustering coefficient, network betweenness, maximum node degree, and network diameter, determine the basic characteristics of topology of complex network. They are reflected in the network topology, which makes network have topological properties different from other networks, and promotes or inhibits certain dynamic behaviors of network.

Definition 3 (Average Path Length): It is defined as the minimum number of edges through which two pairs of nodes are related to each other in network, denoted by L. It can be calculated by Formula (14).

$$L = \frac{\sum\limits_{i,j} d(v_i, v_j)}{N(N-1)} \tag{14}$$

where N is the total number of nodes in network. When $v_i = v_j$ or no path between v_i and v_j, then $d(v_i, v_j) = 0$.

Definition 4 (Clustering Coefficient): It is defined as the ratio of the actual number of connections between nodes to the total number of connections, denoted as C_i, which is expressed as the degree of association between node i and its neighbor nodes. It can be calculated by Formula (15).

$$C_i = \frac{2n_i}{k_i(k_i - 1)} \tag{15}$$

where k_i represents the degree of node i, and n_i represents the actual number of connections between node i and all adjacent nodes.

Definition 5 (Network Betweenness): The betweenness of node k in network satisfies Formula (16).

$$BC_k = \frac{\sum\limits_{i \neq j} \frac{n_k(i,j)}{n(i,j)}}{(N-1)(N-2)} \tag{16}$$

where $n(i,j)$ is the number of shortest paths between node i and node j. $n_k(i,j)$ is the number of shortest paths between node i and node j through node k. The larger the node betweenness is, the more important the node plays in interacting with other nodes.

Definition 6 (maximum node degree): It is defined as the maximum value of degree distribution of node in network, denoted as d_{max}, which can be calculated by Formula (17). To a certain extent, it reflects the unevenness of degree distribution of network.

$$d_{\max} = \max_{v_i \in Nodes} d_i \tag{17}$$

where $Nodes$ is a collection of nodes in network. d_i is degree of node i as defined in the **Definition** 2.

Definition 7 (Network diameter): It is defined as the maximum distance between any two node pairs in network, denoted as D, which has an important impact on the stability of the entire network. It can be calculated by Formula (18).

$$D = \max_{v_i, v_j \in Nodes} l(v_i, v_j) \qquad (18)$$

where $l(v_i, v_j)$ represents the distance between node i and node j.

6.2   The Experiments of DDC

Figure 1 shows the results of the effects of number of network nodes N, number of neighbors k and weight coefficient x on the synchronization of small-world network based on degree distribution.

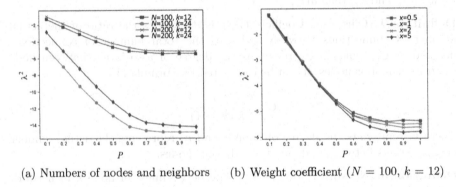

(a) Numbers of nodes and neighbors   (b) Weight coefficient ($N = 100$, $k = 12$)

Fig. 1. The influence of various parameters on the synchronization of small-world network based on degree distribution

Figure 1(a) represents the effects of N and k on the capability of network synchronization. From the figure, each curve presents a trend of monotonically decreasing, indicating that, under different parameter combinations, as P increases, λ_2 becomes smaller, and synchronization capability of small-world network is gradually improved. For the same N, the larger the k is, the stronger the network synchronization is. For the same k, the smaller N is, the stronger the network synchronization is.

Figure 1(b) represents the effect of x on the capability of network synchronization. As can be seen from the figure, with the increase of P, the synchronization capability gradually improves. When $P > 0.4$, different x has different effects on the synchronization. The larger x is, the faster the value of λ_2 decreases, indicating that the synchronization is stronger.

Table 1. Comparison of the λ_2 of different weight coefficients in small-world network based on degree distribution

P	x			
	0.5	1	2	5
0.1	−1.242	−1.237	−1.259	−1.319
0.2	−2.223	−2.183	−2.205	−2.165
0.3	−3.122	−3.090	−3.166	−3.154
0.4	−3.884	−3.958	−3.946	−4.030
0.5	−4.590	−4.604	−4.719	−4.770
0.6	−5.042	−5.201	−5.305	−5.355
0.7	−5.297	−5.364	−5.480	−5.628
0.8	−5.394	−5.469	−5.570	−5.815
0.9	−5.377	−5.522	−5.644	−5.823
1	−5.360	−5.571	−5.662	−5.807

The values corresponding to Fig. 1(b) are shown in Table 1.

As can be seen from Table 1, when $P = 0.2$, the value of λ_2 for $x = 5$ is larger than that for $x = 0.5$, $x = 1$, and $x = 2$, representing that although the increase of x can effectively improve the synchronization capability of small-world network, when P is small, too much pursuit of the uniformity of degree distribution may reduce the chance of adding edges that can greatly improve synchronization in random reconnection. Therefore, in practical application, it is necessary to set x reasonably according to the requirements.

Set $N = 100$ and $k = 12$, Fig. 2 compares the variance of degree distribution and network synchronization as the reconnection probability increases between WS [12] and our DDC method.

As can be seen from Fig. 2(a), when $P > 0.5$, the difference between the variances of degree distributions of node of the two networks gradually widens. This is because the larger P is, the larger the proportion of reconnected edges in network is, and DDC preferentially selects nodes with smaller degree for reconnection each time. Also, as can be seen from Fig. 2(b), when $P < 0.5$, the values of λ_2 of the two networks is not significantly different. It is because there is little difference in the variance of the degree distribution of node, so the impact on the capability of network synchronization is small. When $P > 0.5$, the capability of synchronization of DDC is stronger than that of WS small-world network.

It can be seen from Fig. 3, when N and k are constant, the larger P is, the stronger the synchronization capability of small-world network is. When N and P are constant, the larger the k is, the stronger the synchronization capability of small-world network is; At the same time, when k and P are constant, the smaller N is, the stronger the synchronization capability of small-world network is. Therefore, N and k not only determine the strength of network synchronization, but also determine the strength of the network synchronization obtained at the end of the algorithm iteration. It shows that topology plays an important role in determining the synchronization of ESSW.

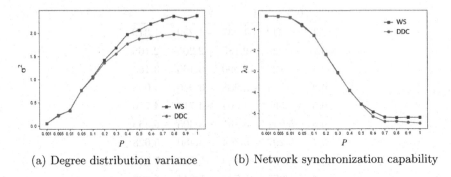

(a) Degree distribution variance   (b) Network synchronization capability

Fig. 2. Parameters comparison of WS and DDC based on degree distribution ($N = 100$, $k = 12$)

6.3   The Experiments of ESSW

Figure 3 shows the results of the influence of different parameter combinations of number of network nodes N and number of neighbors k on the ESSW algorithm.

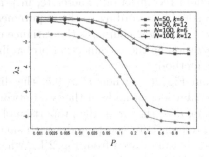

Fig. 3. Parameter analysis of ESSW

In order to demonstrate the improvement of synchronization capability of ESSW, in the following, we compare ESSW with WS [12] as well as some improved small-world networks related to synchronization, such as SOSW-II [18] and PA [16]. Given $N = 100$ and $k = 12$. All connections are assumed to be symmetrical with the same coupling strength. The comparison results of synchronization capabilities of the four algorithms are shown in Fig. 4, and the values are shown in Table 2.

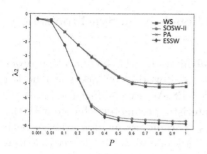
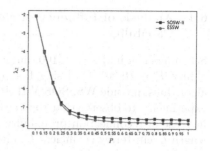

Fig. 4. Comparison of capability of network synchronization of algorithms

Fig. 5. Comparison of synchronization capabilities of SOSW-II and ESSW

As can be seen from Fig. 4 and Table 2, when $P = 0.8$, the difference of λ_2 between ESSW and SOSW-II is the largest, the former is 0.205 smaller than the latter, and ESSW has stronger synchronization capability. Compared with WS and PA, the λ_2 of ESSW has the largest difference at $P = 0.4$ and $P = 0.3$, the difference is 3.505 and 3.572, respectively, representing that the capability of synchronization of ESSW is stronger than WS and PA.

Table 2. Comparison of λ_2 of different algorithms

P	WS	SOSW-II	PA	ESSW
0.001	−0.356	−0.356	−0.356	−0.356
0.01	−0.426	−0.555	−0.413	−0.554
0.1	−1.284	−2.228	−1.309	−2.229
0.2	−2.225	−4.583	−2.219	−4.629
0.3	−3.097	−6.475	−3.017	−6.589
0.4	−3.854	−7.187	−3.789	−7.359
0.5	−4.532	−7.41	−4.448	−7.581
0.6	−4.973	−7.497	−4.866	−7.677
0.7	−5.166	−7.549	−4.930	−7.745
0.8	−5.206	−7.569	−4.976	−7.774
0.9	−5.200	−7.630	−5.002	−7.805
1	−5.159	−7.638	−4.879	−7.828

For SOSW-II algorithm, it also adopted the eigenvector criterion as the reconnection strategy. We compare it with our ESSW, and the result is shown in Fig. 5. When ESSW deletes edge, it selects nodes based on the node degree distribution, because it adjusts the subtle changes of topology, we can see, ESSW can always have better synchronization capability than that of SOSW-II with the increase of P.

6.4   Analysis of Influence of Network Topology on Synchronization Capability

Set number of nodes $N = 100$, number of neighbors $k = 12$, reconnection probability $P \in (0.001, 1)$. Using four different small-world network construction algorithms, include WS, SOSW-II, PA and our ESSW, we conduct the following experiments to observe that the basic characteristic parameters change with the increase of reconnection probability P. These parameters include average path length L, clustering coefficient C, maximum betweenness B^{max}, degree distribution variance σ^2, maximum degree d^{max} and diameter D, which can represent the characteristics of small-world network. The experimental results are shown in Fig. 6.

From Fig. 6(a), all L decreases monotonically as P increases. Therefore, the reduction of L may improve synchronization to a certain extent. On the other hand, the L of SOSW-II and ESSW almost coincide, but their synchronization capability is quite different, showing that L cannot determine synchronization alone. From Fig. 6(b), as P increases, all C decreases monotonically, so C may affect synchronization. However, referring to Fig. 6(a), when L and C are similar, synchronization performance is still quite different. From Fig. 6(c), when $P > 0.01$, all B^{max} gradually decreased with increasing P. The B^{max} of ESSW and SOSW-II are very similar, however, comparing with Figs. 4 and 5, when $P > 0.1$, B^{max} of ESSW and SOSW-II are almost the same, but their synchronization ability is quite different. Hence, synchronization cannot be judged by B^{max} only. From Figs. 6(d) and 6(e), σ^2 of WS and PA shows a monotonically increasing trend with the increase of P, d^{max} also increases gradually, indicating that node degree distribution is becoming more and more uneven. From Fig. 6(f), all D decreases monotonically with the increase of P. When $P = 0.1$, D of different networks is almost the same, However, it can be seen from Fig. 4 that synchronization capability varies greatly, which means that synchronization cannot be judged simply based on D.

According to these results, we can conclude that the difference of topology structure will lead to the change of network synchronization capability. But this change is not absolute but the result of a combination of multiple parameters.

1) Each network parameters cannot independently determine network synchronization. Some characteristics are similar but may also represent completely different synchronization capability.
2) Maximum betweenness cannot be used as the only criterion for judging synchronization capability.
3) If the node degree distribution is too uneven, the inhibition effect is more obvious on network synchronization. Only a small average path length and a uniform network degree distribution can make small-world network more synchronous.

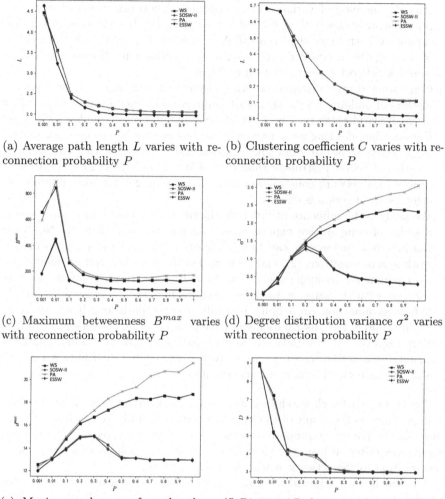

(a) Average path length L varies with reconnection probability P

(b) Clustering coefficient C varies with reconnection probability P

(c) Maximum betweenness B^{max} varies with reconnection probability P

(d) Degree distribution variance σ^2 varies with reconnection probability P

(e) Maximum degree of node dmax changes with reconnection probability P

(f) Diameter D changes with reconnection probability P

Fig. 6. Analysis of influence of network topology on synchronization capability

7   Conclusions

Our main work is summarized as follows.

1) By analyzing the influence of degree distribution on network synchronization, we define the variance of degree distribution of network, and propose the method of degree distribution connection. This method does not select nodes randomly, but those nodes with smaller degree according to the calculation weight to set the reconnection strategy. The experimental results show

that the increase of variance of the optimized network degree distribution is significantly slower than that of WS small-world, but the synchronization capability is stronger than that of WS, which it is proved that the method of making the network degree distribution uniform is effective for solving complex network synchronization problem.

2) Combining degree distribution with eigenvector criterion, we propose the method of building ESSW network to improve the synchronization capability of small-world network. The method preferentially selects nodes with larger degrees when deleting network edges, and reconnect edges to network according to eigenvector criterion. The experimental results show that the synchronization of ESSW is stronger than that of WS, SOSW-II and PA. Which it is proved that network construction method combining degree distribution and eigenvector criterion is effective.

3) We analyze the influence of different algorithms on synchronization through a series of comparative experiments. The results show that, (1) No single characteristic parameter can independently determine the strength of network synchronization; (2) The network betweenness has certain limitations as a parameter to judge synchronization. In some cases, network synchronization with the same network betweenness may still be quite different; (3) When reconnection probability is small, average path length will decrease rapidly, and degree distribution will have little effect on network synchronization. However, when variation of average path length decreases and gradually maintains a certain constant, excessively large degree distribution variance will inhibit network synchronization ability.

To sum up, network synchronization may change due to the slight topology change, which is the result of the joint interaction of multiple topological properties. In the paper, we propose a method of combining degree distribution and eigenvector criterion from the viewpoint of network topology, which provides a new solution to the network synchronization problem.

Our further work includes: 1) In real systems, nodes in network may often interfered by environment, causing failure sometimes, which will affect synchronization capability of network. So, we shall improve our algorithms to enhance synchronization robustness, so that complex network can adapt to changes of environment. 2) The methods proposed in the paper are modeled from the mathematical description. We shall improve our algorithms to fit the real applications.

Acknowledgement. This work was partially supported by National Key Research and Development Program of China under grant no. 2018YFB1003800).

References

1. Plotnikov, S.A., Lehnert, J., Fradkov, A.L., et al.: Control of synchronization in delay-coupled neural networks of heterogeneous nodes. Int. J. Bifurc. Chaos **23**, 435–455 (2015)

2. Yu, W., DeLellis, P., Chen, G., et al.: Distributed adaptive control of synchronization in complex networks. IEEE Trans. Autom. Control **57**(8), 2153–2158 (2012)
3. Wang, L., Zhao, L., Shi, H., et al.: Realizing generalized outer synchronization of complex dynamical networks with stochastically adaptive coupling. Math. Comput. Simul. **187**, 379–390 (2021)
4. Coelho, L.S., Bernert, D.L.A.: PID control design for chaotic synchronization using a tribes optimization approach. Chaos, Solitons Fractals **42**(1), 634–640 (2009)
5. Guan, Z.H., Liu, Z.W., Feng, G., et al.: Synchronization of complex dynamical networks with time-varying delays via impulsive distributed control. IEEE Trans. Circuits Syst. I Regul. Pap. **57**(8), 2182–2195 (2010)
6. Yang, X., Cao, J., Lu, J.: Stochastic synchronization of complex networks with nonidentical nodes via hybrid adaptive and impulsive control. IEEE Trans. Circuits Syst. **59**(2), 371–384 (2011)
7. Yang, X., Cao, J., Qiu, J.: Pth moment exponential stochastic synchronization of coupled memristor-based neural networks with mixed delays via delayed impulsive control. Neural Netw. **65**, 80–91 (2015)
8. Li, H., Liao, X., Chen, G., et al.: Event-triggered asynchronous intermittent communication strategy for synchronization in complex dynamical networks. Neural Netw. **66**, 1–10 (2015)
9. He, D., Xu, L.: Ultimate boundedness of nonautonomous dynamical complex networks under impulsive control. IEEE Trans. Circuits Syst. **62**(10), 997–1001 (2015)
10. Chandrasekar, A., Rakkiyappan, R.: Impulsive controller design for exponential synchronization of delayed stochastic memristor-based recurrent neural networks. Neurocomputing **173**, 1348–1355 (2016)
11. Li, J.: Prescribed performance synchronization of complex dynamical networks with event-based communication protocols. Inf. Sci. **564**, 254–272 (2021)
12. Watts, D.J., Strogatz, S.H.: Collective dynamics of "small-world" networks. Nature **393**(6684), 440–442 (1998)
13. Hu, T., Liu, C., Wang, Z.: Design and analysis of UHF tag antenna structure. In: China-Japan Joint Microwave Conference, pp. 1–4. IEEE, Hangzhou, China (2011)
14. Nishikawa, T., Motter, A.E., Lai, Y.C., et al.: Heterogeneity in oscillator networks: are smaller worlds easier to synchronize? Phys. Rev. Lett. **91**(1), 014101 (2003)
15. Hong, H., Kim, B.J., Choi, M.Y., et al.: Factors that predict better synchronizability on complex networks. Phys. Rev. E **69**(6), 067105 (2004)
16. Lv, Y., Li, Y.: Study on synchronizability of SWN with preferential attachment. J. App. Electron. Techn. **46**(2), 73–76 (2020). (In Chinese)
17. Hagberg, A., Schult, D.A.: Rewiring networks for synchronization, Chaos: an interdisciplinary. J. Nonlinear Sci. **18**(3), 037105 (2008)
18. Dai, K., Wang, X.: Optimizing the capability of network synchronization based on eigenvector criterion. In: 4th National Academic Forum of Network Science, pp. 262–272. CCAST, Qingdao, China (2009). (In Chinese)
19. Wang, S.J., Wu, Z.X., Dong, H.R., et al.: Enhancing the synchronizability of scale-free networks by adding edges. Int. J. Mod. Phys. C **21**(1), 67–77 (2010)
20. Zeng, A., Son, S.W., Yeung, C.H., et al.: Enhancing synchronization by directionality in complex networks. Phys. Rev. E **83**(4), 045101 (2011)
21. Sanchez, A.G., Castillo, C.P., Gonzalez, E.G., et al.: Determining efficiency of small-world algorithms: a comparative approach. Math. Comput. Simul. **187**, 687–699 (2021)
22. Hou, L., Lao, S., Small, M., et al.: Enhancing complex network controllability by minimum link direction reversal. Phys. Lett. A. **379**(20, 21), 1321–1325 (2015)

23. Wen, G., Yu, W., Hu, G., et al.: Pinning synchronization of directed networks with switching topologies: a multiple Lyapunov functions approach. IEEE Trans. Neural Netw. Learn. Syst. **26**(12), 3239–3250 (2015)
24. Zhou, C., Kurths, J.: Dynamical weights and enhanced synchronization in adaptive complex networks. Phys. Rev. Lett. **96**(16), 164102 (2006)

An Energy-Saving Strategy for 5G Base Stations in Vehicular Edge Computing

Fei Zhao[1,3], Lei Shi[1,3(✉)], Yi Shi[2], Shuangliang Zhao[1,3], and Zengwei Lv[1,3]

[1] The School of Computer Science and Information Engineering, Hefei University of Technology, Hefei 230009, China
[2] Department of ECE, The Virginia Tech, Blacksburg, VA 24061, USA
[3] The Engineering Research Center of Safety Critical Industrial Measurement and Control Technology, Ministry of Education, Hefei 230009, China
`shilei@hfut.edu.cn`

Abstract. With the rapid development of the Internet of Vehicles (IoV), various types of compute-intensive vehicle applications are emerging and present significant challenges to resource-constrained vehicles. Emerging vehicular edge computing (VEC) can alleviate this situation by offloading computational tasks from vehicles to base stations (BSs) with edge servers at the roadside. And the excellent transmission performance of 5G provides more reliable support for VEC. However, due to the drawbacks of small coverage area and high energy cost of 5G BSs, long-term usage will result in huge costly resource investment. In this paper, we design a new 4G–5G hybrid task offloading framework for the VEC scenario. We consider switching some of the 5G BSs to sleep state during low traffic and low data consumption conditions, while letting the 4G BS process the tasks generated in these areas. We first build the mathematical model and find that it cannot be solved directly. Then we design the algorithm for the offline case and the online case, respectively. Simulation results show that our scheme significantly reduces the energy cost while ensuring high task success rate.

Keywords: 5G · Energy saving · Vehicular edge computing · Task offloading · Internet of vehicles

1 Introduction

In recent years, the rapid development of vehicle technology and wireless communication has enabled the modern vehicles to be more intelligent. Many new vehicle applications are emerging, such as autonomous driving, real-time video analytics and on-board infotainment services [1,2]. These applications all require intensive real-time computation. However, due to limited computing resources,

The work is supported by the major science and technology projects in Anhui Province, Grant No. 202003a05020009 and innovation foundation of the city of Bengbu, Grant No. JZ2022YDZJ0019.

H. Gao et al. (Eds.): CollaborateCom 2022, LNICST 460, pp. 309–325, 2022.
https://doi.org/10.1007/978-3-031-24383-7_17

vehicle local computing units are often unable to satisfy the computing demands of such applications. To overcome the limitation, vehicular edge computing (VEC) is an emerging and promising paradigm that provides fast computing services for vehicle users [3–5]. Specifically, through vehicle-to-infrastructure (V2I) communications, resource-constrained vehicle users are allowed to offload their latency-sensitive, compute-intensive tasks to 5G BSs configured with edge servers for processing [6–8]. In addition, compared to the conventional cloud computing, VEC can provide lower communication latency due to the proximity of edge servers to vehicles [9,10]. Consequently, vehicle users can receive better quality of service (QoS) [11].

However, in order to support the high density of vehicle users in cities, transportation systems need dense deployment of 5G BSs at the roadside. For now, 5G BSs have the disadvantages of high energy consumption and small coverage area [12], long-term usage will result in huge costly resource investment. In addition, the large amount of energy consumption will also accelerate global warming and deteriorate the environment. Therefore, how to reduce the energy consumption in VEC deserves investigation.

Previous studies have made some contributions to reducing the energy cost of VEC [13,14]. In these works, they focus on the energy consumed during task offloading and computation. In fact, more energy is wasted during low-traffic periods [15]. It is not necessary to keep 5G BSs active all the time. We can save energy by switching 5G BSs to sleep status during low-traffic periods. However, switching 5G BSs to sleep status raises a new problem. Unlike 5G BSs in cells, 5G BSs in VEC are arranged along roads and each segment of the road is served by only one 5G BS. When a 5G BS switches to sleep state in low-traffic periods, vehicles within its coverage will not be able to offload tasks. This makes it very demanding for 5G BSs to sleep without affecting vehicle users.

Motivated by the aforementioned discussion, we aim to give a new and more suitable solution. In this paper, we further investigate the problem of minimizing the energy consumption of 5G BSs in VEC. The contributions of this paper are summarized as follows.

– We propose a new hybrid 4G-5G offloading framework for VEC scenarios, where 5G BSs can be switched to sleep status during low-traffic periods, while tasks are offloaded to 4G BS while satisfying latency constraints.
– We developed a mathematical model in terms of both energy consumption and latency, and our work is among the few efforts to consider BS switching cost in the formulation of the problem.
– We design the heuristic algorithm for the offline case and the online case, respectively. Through experimental simulations, it is confirmed that our scheme significantly reduce the energy cost of 5G BSs while ensuring a high task success rate.

The rest of this paper is organized as follows. In Sect. 2, the related works are introduced. In Sect. 3, the system model is presented, including the 5G BS energy consumption model and the task delay model. In Sect. 4, our offline and online algorithms are described. Detailed simulation results and conclusions of the paper are given in Sects. 5 and 6, respectively.

2   Related Works

There has been a lot of studies on energy cost optimization for vehicle edge computing, mainly focused on two aspects, one is the optimization of energy consumption for vehicles, and the other is the optimization of energy consumption for infrastructure such as base stations.

First, we briefly introduce the research on vehicle energy consumption optimization. Authors in [16] propose a multi-device and multi-server task Joint Task Offloading Game (JTOG) algorithm in order to minimize the energy consumption for all vehicular terminal devices generating tasks. Authors in [17] jointly optimize the offloading proportion and uplink/computation/downlink bit allocation of multiple vehicles, for the purpose of minimizing the total energy consumption of the vehicles under the delay constraint. Authors in [13,14] jointly optimize the latency and cost by considering both offloading decisions, communication and computational resource allocation.

Next, we introduce the research on energy consumption optimization of 5G BSs. Authors in [18] save infrastructure costs by using coherent beamforming techniques to reduce the density of 5G BS placement at the roadside. They designed a heuristic algorithm for the Iterative Coherent Beamforming Node Design (ICBND) algorithm to obtain the approximate optimal solution. And they significantly reduce the cost of communication network infrastructure. Authors in [19] propose a sleep model for base stations in cellular networks and investigates the benefits of turning off a portion of base stations during low traffic. In the article, the authors propose a simple analytical model that determines the optimal base station shutdown time based on daily traffic patterns. However, in that paper the authors consider only one switchover for the base station, and the effect of this switchover on reducing the energy consumption and operating costs of the base station is relatively small. Authors in [20] reduce the power consumption of BSs by having unloaded BSs alternate between on and off in a cyclical manner. Authors in [21] propose an efficient algorithm to minimize the energy consumption by jointing the cell association and on-off scheme. Authors in [22] optimize the task latency while allowing the candidate BSs to randomly switch states between sleep and work to save energy consumption. Authors in [23] minimize energy consumption by forcing idle BSs to sleep or dynamically adjusting the signal range of BSs through a software-defined network, considering connectivity, communication, and power perspectives, respectively. Authors in [24] consider the scenario where multiple mobile users share multiple heterogeneous edge servers and propose an approximation algorithm to minimize the energy consumption of the MEC system. Authors in [25] consider optimizing the quality of user experience under a long-term energy budget constraint.

However, the above studies mainly focus on the base station switching approach for cellular network environments, and they do not consider the switching costs incurred when the base station switches states. In light of the existing works, we propose a new hybrid 4G–5G offloading framework for VEC scenarios. In this offloading framework, the 5G BSs can dynamically adjust its state, and vehicles can dynamically select the offloading method according to the state

of the 5G BS. Meanwhile, we design the heuristic algorithm for the offline case
and the online case, respectively. Through experimental simulations, it is confirmed that our scheme significantly reduce the energy cost of 5G BSs while
ensuring a high task success rate.

3   System Model

We first describe the system model (see Fig. 1). Suppose a straight road with a
long distance is covered by one 4G BS and several 5G BSs. Suppose the 5G BSs
hava a quicker data transmission speed, a bigger energy consuming and a smaller
cover area comparing with the 4G BS. Suppose the whole road is divided into
many segments, each segment is covered by one 5G BS and the whole road can
be covered by the 4G BS. Suppose these base stations are connected by wired
links, so the communication time among them can be ignored. Suppose each
BS is equipped with an edge server with the same computing capability, which
means these BSs can do communicating jobs and computing jobs simultaneously.
Suppose during the whole scheduling time vehicles will pass through the road,
and when they pass through it, they may have tasks needed to be transmitted
for handling. However, since the 5G BS energy consuming is high, we want to
design an algorithm for "turn on/off " these 5G BSs appropriately, so that we
can save energy while not influence vehicles work.

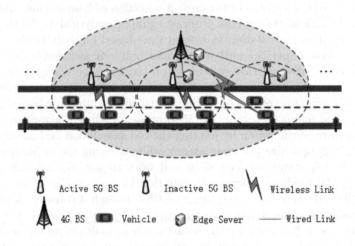

Fig. 1. 4G-5G hybrid task offloading framework in VEC.

3.1   Energy Model

We first discuss the energy model. Suppose the whole scheduling time T can
be divided into h time slots τ equally and we normalize $\tau = 1$. Denote $t(t \in T, 1 \leq t \leq h)$ as a time slot. Denote $s_i(s_i \in N, 1 \leq i \leq n)$ as a 5G BS. Denote
$l_j(l_j \in L, 1 \leq j \leq m)$ as a task. We divide the total energy consumption of 5G

BSs into three parts, including static energy consumption(energy consumption of power transmission and cooling, etc.), load-related dynamic energy consumption and state-switching energy consumption [26]. Denote E^{total} as the total energy consumed by all 5G BSs in time period T. Therefore E^{total} can be expressed as

$$E^{total} = E^s + E^d + E^{switch},$$ (1)

where E^s and E^d are the static energy and dynamic energy consumed by all 5G BSs in the time period T, respectively. E^{switch} is the state-switching energy consumed by all 5G BSs in the time period T. In the following, we will give the specific formula for each component.

For the first item E^s, we use a binary variable $\alpha_i(t)$ to indicate the state of s_i at time slot t, then we have

$$\alpha_i(t) = \begin{cases} 1 : s_i \text{ is active at time slot } t; \\ 0 : \text{otherwise}. \end{cases}$$ (2)

Thus E^s can be expressed as

$$E^s = \sum_{t=1}^{h} \sum_{i=1}^{n} (\alpha_i(t) \cdot E^a + (1 - \alpha_i(t)) \cdot E^{ua}),$$ (3)

where E^a and E^{ua} are the static energy that a 5G BS needs to consume when it is active and inactive in a time slot, respectively.

For the second item E^d, suppose that there are m tasks needed to be offloaded and processed in time period T, and all tasks are equivalent. We describe these tasks with three attributes. One, the task data size, and we denote it as D. Two, the computing resource required for accomplishing the task which is quantified by the number of CPU cycles, and we denote it as W. Three, the maximum tolerable delay for tasks, and we denote it as T^{max}.

There are two possibilities for offloading tasks. First, the task is transmitted to the 4G BS. Second, the task is transmitted to the 5G BS. For each task, it can only be transmitted to one base station, and we use μ_j to indicate the offloading result for task l_j, then we have

$$\mu_j = \begin{cases} 1 : l_j \text{ is transmitted to the 4G BS}; \\ 0 : l_j \text{ is transmitted to one 5G BS}. \end{cases}$$ (4)

Then E^d can be expressed as

$$E^d = \sum_{j=1}^{m} (1 - \mu_j) \cdot \zeta \cdot D,$$ (5)

where ζ is the dynamic energy consumed by a 5G BS to process a unit of task data.

For the third item E^{switch}, we use x_i^{on} and x_i^{off} to represent the number of times that s_i is turn on and off in time T respectively. We have

$$x_i^{on} = \sum_{t=1}^{h} max\{(\alpha_i(t) - \alpha_i(t-1)), 0\},$$ (6)

$$x_i^{off} = \sum_{t=1}^{h} max\{(\alpha_i(t-1) - \alpha_i(t)), 0\}. \tag{7}$$

Then E^{switch} can be expressed as

$$E^{switch} = \sum_{i=1}^{n} (x_i^{on} \cdot E^{on} + x_i^{off} \cdot E^{off}), \tag{8}$$

where E^{on} and E^{off} are the energy cost of turning on and off a 5G BS once, respectively.

3.2   Delay Model

In this subsection we continue to discuss the delay model. Suppose tasks generated at any time slot can be completed before the next time slot. The total task delay includes the transmission delay, the waiting delay and the calculation delay. Then for task l_j, we have

$$T_j^{total} = T_j^{trans} + T_j^{w} + T_j^{comp}, \tag{9}$$

where T_j^{trans}, T_j^{w} and T_j^{comp} correspond to the transmission delay, the waiting delay and the calculation delay for l_j respectively. In the following, we will give the specific formula for each component.

For the first item T_j^{trans}, suppose tasks received by the same BS in the same time slot have the same transmission rate after the communication resources are allocated. Then when l_j is transmitted to the 4G BS, we can get the data transmission rate as

$$r_j^{4G} = \frac{R^{4G}}{k^{4G}(t_j)}, \tag{10}$$

where R^{4G} is the maximum transmission rate between a vehicle and the 4G BS, t_j is the time slot when l_j is generated, and $k^{4G}(t_j)$ is the number of tasks transmitted to the 4G BS at time slot t_j.

We can similarly get the data transmission rate between the corresponding vehicle and the 5G BS s_i as

$$r_{i,j}^{5G} = \frac{R^{5G}}{k_i^{5G}(t_j)}, \tag{11}$$

where R^{5G} is the maximum transmission rate between a vehicle and the 5G BS, $k_i^{5G}(t_j)$ is the number of tasks transmitted to s_i at time slot t_j. We use $\beta_{i,j}(t)$ to indicate whether the vehicle generating l_j is within the coverage of s_i at time slot t, then we have

$$\beta_{i,j}(t) = \begin{cases} 1 : \text{the vehicle generating } l_j \text{ is within } s_i\text{'s coverage at time slot } t; \\ 0 : \text{otherwise.} \end{cases} \tag{12}$$

Therefore, the transmission rate of l_j can be expressed as

$$r_j = \begin{cases} r_j^{4G} : \text{if } \mu_j = 1; \\ r_{i,j}^{5G} : \text{if } \mu_j = 0, \beta_{i,j}(t_j) = 1, \alpha_i(t_j) = 1. \end{cases} \tag{13}$$

Then, we have:

$$T_j^{trans} = \frac{D}{r_j}. \tag{14}$$

For the second item T_j^w, we assume that edge servers use non-preemptive CPU allocation and allocate computing resources to one task at a time until the task is completed. We use $\gamma_{j'}(l_j)$ to indicate whether $l_{j'}$ is the previous task in the task queue of l_j, then we have

$$\gamma_{j'}(l_j) = \begin{cases} 1 : l_{j'} \text{ is the previous task in the task queue of } l_j; \\ 0 : \text{otherwise.} \end{cases} \tag{15}$$

So T_j^w can be expressed as

$$T_j^w = \max\{\sum_{j'=1}^{m} \gamma_{j'}(l_j) \cdot ((t_{j'} + T_{j'}^{trans} + T_{j'}^w + \frac{W}{f}) - (t_j + T_j^{trans})), 0\}, \tag{16}$$

where f is the computing capability of an edge server.

For the third item T_j^{comp}, it can be expressed as

$$T_j^{comp} = \frac{W}{f}. \tag{17}$$

Based on the above discussion, we can get the total delay of l_j. We have

$$T_j^{total} \leq T^{max}. \tag{18}$$

Then our problem can be formulated as

$$\begin{aligned} \min\ & \frac{E^{total}}{T} \\ \text{s.t.}\ & (1), (3), (5) - (11), (13), (14), (16) - (18) \\ & \alpha_i(t) \in \{0, 1\}, \forall i \in [1, n], \forall t \in [1, h] \\ & \mu_j \in \{0, 1\}, \forall j \in [1, m]. \end{aligned} \tag{19}$$

In (19), $\alpha_i(t)$ and μ_j are binary variables. T, h, m, and other symbols are all constants or determinable values. However, these binary variables almost appear in all items with different forms. In real scenarios, we may only know the tasks that have been generated or being generated. So the values of $\alpha_i(t)$ and μ_j are difficult to be solved directly. We will try to get an approximate optimal solution in the next section.

4   Algorithms

In Sect. 3, we give the original problem model and show it is difficult to be solved directly. In this section, we will try to find a feasible solution for the problem. First, we design an offline algorithm. In the offline algorithm, we suppose that we know the total number of tasks and the time slot in which any task is generated.

Then we design an online algorithm. In the online algorithm, we only know tasks that have been or are being generated, while tasks that will be generated are not known. This means that we need to dynamically change the state of the 5G BSs and the way for transmitted tasks based on the situation of past and current time slots. In the following, we first discuss the offline algorithm in sub Sect. 4.1. Then we discuss the online algorithm in sub Sect. 4.2.

4.1 Offline Strategy

For the offline strategy, we assume that we know the corresponding location and time slot when any task is generated. Based on this information, we will first determine cases on where tasks transmitted to the 4G BS cannot satisfy the delay constraint. Then, we further determine cases on where 5G BSs should be in sleep. Then main idea for the offline strategy can be summarized into four steps as the following.

Algorithm 1. Offline Algorithm

Input: L:The task set; t_j:The time slot when any task l_j is generated; $\beta_{i,j}(t_j)$:The location when any task l_j is generated;

Output: $\frac{E^{total}}{T}$

1: **for** 5G BS $s_i \in N$ **do**
2:    **for** Task $l_j \in L$ $(\beta_{i,j}(t_j) = 1)$**do**
3:        Calculate T_j^{total} according to formula (9) under the condition that l_j is transmitted to the 4G BS;
4:        **if**$(T_j^{total} \leq T^{max})$ **then**
5:            $\alpha_i(t_j) = 0$, $\mu_j = 1$;
6:        **else**
7:            $\alpha_i(t_j) = 1$, $\mu_j = 0$;
8:        **end if**
9:    **end for**
10:    Get all values of $\alpha_i(t)$ $(\forall t \in T)$, select all periods when $\alpha_i(t)$ is equal to 0 continuously and get the set $\mathbb{T}$;
11:    **for** $T_q^{ua} \in \mathbb{T}$ **do**
12:        **if**$(T_q^{ua} < T_{on} + T_{off} || (E^a - E^{ua}) \cdot T_q^{ua} \leq E^{on} + E^{off})$
13:            $\alpha_i(t) = 1(t \in T_q^{ua})$;
14:            Remove T_q^{ua} from $\mathbb{T}$;
15:        **end if**
16:    **end for**
17: **end for**
18: Calculate the final optimization total energy efficiency $\frac{E^{total}}{T}$;

Step one, we first randomly select a 5G BS s_i and pick out all tasks generated within its coverage. When no task is generated within the coverage of s_i in a time slot, the state of s_i in this time slot is tentatively set as inactive. For a task generated within range of s_i, we try to transmit it to the 4G BS and calculate its total delay. If the total delay can satisfy the delay constraint, the state of s_i in this time slot is tentatively set as inactive too. Otherwise, let s_i be active at this time slot and let generated tasks at this time slot transmit to s_i.

Step two, after obtaining the state of s_i at each time slot by step one, we can find time slots which are adjacent and have the same state. Denote $T_q^{ua}(T_q^{ua} \in \mathbb{T}, q = 1, ...)$ as a time period consisting of a series of adjacent time slots in which the state of s_i is inactive.

Step three, judge if s_i can be switched into the sleep state in time period T_q^{ua}. We notice that if two conditions are satisfied then s_i can be switched into the sleep state. First, $T_q^{ua} \geqslant T_{on} + T_{off}$, where T^{on} and T^{off} are the time required to turn on and off a 5G BS once, respectively. Second, $(E^a - E^{ua}) \cdot T_q^{ua} > E^{on} + E^{off}$. When both conditions T_q^{ua} are satisfied, it is reasonable and can reduce energy consumption for s_i to switch to sleep state at time period T_q^{ua}. Judge the rest of the time period in $\mathbb{T}$ like this.

Step four, repeat the above operation for all other 5G BSs.

Based on these discussions, we can get the offline algorithm as shown in Algorithm 1.

4.2   Online Strategy

For the online strategy, we only know tasks that have been generated and are being generated. We should make strategies based on this information in real time. In this subsection, we will first discuss the case where we need to increase the active 5G BSs, and then we will discuss the case where we need to decrease the active 5G BSs. After that, we will give the steps of the online algorithm.

First, we determine the situation where we need to increase an active 5G BS. Denote $k(t)$ as the total number of tasks generated at time slot t. Denote k^{max} as the maximum number of tasks that can be transmitted to the 4G BS at the same time slot while satisfying the time delay constraint. Then we have $\frac{k^{max} \cdot D}{R^{4G}} + \frac{k^{max} \cdot W}{f} \leq T^{max}$. When both sides of the formula are equal, we can get $k^{max} = \lfloor \frac{T^{max} \cdot R^{4G} \cdot f}{D \cdot f + R^{4G} \cdot W} \rfloor$. Denote $s(t)$ as the number of 5G BSs in sleep state at time slot t. Denote $a(t)$ as the number of 5G BSs in active state at time slot t. Suppose that vehicles are evenly distributed on the road, i.e., tasks are generated with equal probability in the coverage area of each 5G BS. Based on this, we can use $\frac{s(t)}{n} \cdot k(t)$ to approximate the number of tasks transmitted to the 4G BS at time slot t. We notice that if $\frac{s(t)}{n} \cdot k(t) > k^{max}$, the number of currently active 5G BSs is not enough to match the number of tasks. Therefore, when $s(t) > 0$ and $k(t) > \frac{n}{s(t)} \cdot k^{max}$, we turn on a 5G BS in a sleeping state.

Second, we determine the situation where we need to decrease an active 5G BS. We notice that two conditions need to be met. First, similar to the last paragraph, $a(t) > 0$ and $k(t) < \frac{n}{n-a(t)+1} \cdot k^{max}$. Because we need to ensure that after an active 5G BS is turned off, all tasks generated at the current time slot still meet the delay constraint. Second, the first condition has been maintained for a period of time, which is at least the shortest time that a 5G BS is worth sleeping. In this case it is reasonable to assume that the decrease in the number of tasks is not episodic. From the offline algorithm we can obtain the minimum time that a 5G BS is worth sleeping is $\frac{E^{on}+E^{off}}{E^a-E^{ua}}$. When both of these conditions hold, we turn off an active 5G BS.

So the main idea for the online strategy can be summarized into three steps as the following.

Step one, we first initialize all 5G BSs to be in sleep state.

Step two, for time slot $t = 1$, tasks generated within the range of an active 5G BS are transmitted to the corresponding 5G BS, and tasks generated within the range of an inactive 5G BS are transmitted to the 4G BS. Determines whether the number of 5G BSs currently active matches the number of current generated tasks. If the status of the current time slot meets the condition of increase an active 5G BS, then turn on a 5G BS in a sleeping state. If the status of the current time slot meets the condition of decrease an active 5G BS, then turn off an active 5G BS. Otherwise, all 5G BSs remain in their current state.

Step three, repeat the above judgment operation until $t = h$.

Based on these discussions, we can get the online algorithm as shown in Algorithm 2.

Algorithm 2. Online Algorithm

1: **Initialization**;
2: Initialize all 5G BSs to sleep state;
3: **End Initialization**;
4: **for** Time slot $t \in [1, h]$ **do**
5:    **for** $s_i \in N$ **do**
6:      **if**$(\alpha_i(t) = 0)$ **then**
7:        $\mu_j = 1(\beta_{i,j}(t_j) = 1, t_j = t)$;
8:      **else**
9:        $\mu_j = 0(\beta_{i,j}(t_j) = 1, t_j = t)$;
10:     **end if**
11:   **end for**
12:   **if**$(s(t) > 0$ && $k(t) > \frac{n}{s(t)} \cdot k^{max})$**then**
13:      Turn on a 5G BS;
14:   **else if**$(a(t) > 0$ && all values from $k(t - \frac{E^{on}+E^{off}}{E^a-E^{ua}})$ to $k(t)$ are less than $\frac{n}{n-a(t)+1} \cdot k^{max})$ **then**
15:      Turn off a 5G BS;
16:   **else**
17:      all 5G BSs remain in their current state;
18:   **end if**
19: **end for**
20: Calculate the final optimization total energy efficiency $\frac{E^{total}}{T}$;

---

5   Simulation

In this section, we conduct simulations and present representative numerical results to evaluate the performance of the proposed online algorithm. We first describe the simulation setup and then discuss the simulation results.

5.1   Simulation Setup

In the simulation, we consider a one-way road with a length of 800 m. A 4G BS is deployed in the middle of the roadside, and its coverage radius is 400 m. Since the coverage of 5G BS is generally 200–300 m, we set the number of 5G BSs to 3, that is, n = 3. We set the length of a time slot $\tau = 1$ s. The detailed parameters setting about tasks and base stations is shown in Table 1.

Table 1. PARAMETER SETTINGS

Description	Value
Computing capability of edge server(f)	300 M CPU/s
Maximum transmission rate between vehicle and 4G BS/5G BS(R^{4G}, R^{5G})	10 Mbit/s, 80 Mbit/s
Static energy consumed by an active/inactive 5G BS in one time slot(E^a, E^{ua})	3 kJ, 0.5 kJ
Switching time of 5G BS(T^{on}, T^{off})	5 s, 5 s
Switching energy of 5G BS(E^{on}, E^{off})	40 kJ, 40 kJ
Data size of task (D)	{0.2 ∼ 1Mbit}
Computation size of task (W)	10M CPU cycles
Maximum delay of task (T^{max})	1 s
Efficiency of dynamic energy consumption of 5G BS (ζ)	0.1 kJ/Mbit
Number of tasks(m)	441000 ∼ 882000

5.2   Simulation Results

We consider the following schemes as benchmarks to evaluate our proposed algorithms.

- **Always-Active:** where all 5G BSs are always in active state.
- **Always-Sleep:** where all 5G BSs are always in sleeping state.
- **Random-Switch:** where all 5G BSs are turned on and off randomly.
- **Greedy-Algorithm:** When reducing an active 5G BS, only the first condition corresponding to the online algorithm needs to be satisfied, and other parts are the same as the online algorithm.

We first evaluate the performance of the proposed online algorithm in terms of task success rate. In our experiments, we set T=86400 s , which means that the scheduling time in our simulation is a whole day consisting of 86400 time slots. We use a traffic flow dataset from a freeway near Heathrow Airport in the UK as reference, and generate tasks in proportion to the number of vehicles in the corresponding time period. The task succeeds when the total delay of the task is less than or equal to the maximum tolerable delay, otherwise the task fails. Figure 2 shows the relationship between the task success rate and the number of tasks when we set $D = 0.8M$, $W = 10M$ CPU cycles. It can be seen that task success rate of all schemes decrease with the increasing of the number of tasks except the Always-Active scheme and the offline algorithm. Because an increase in the total number of tasks equates to faster task generation. This will increase the burden on the base station, strain communication and computing resources, and ultimately increase the possibility that the total task delay exceeds the maximum tolerable delay. In contrast, except for the Always-Active scheme and the offline algorithm, the effectiveness of our online algorithm is better than other algorithms.

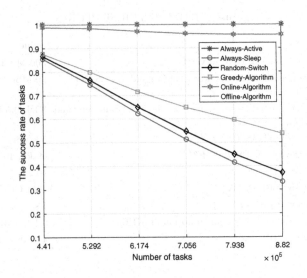

Fig. 2. The success rate of tasks under different number of tasks.

Then, we evaluate the performance of the proposed online algorithm in reducing energy cost. Figure 3 shows the relationship between the average energy cost of 5G BSs and the number of tasks when we set $D = 0.8M$, $W = 10M$ CPU cycles. It can be seen that the average energy cost of 5G BSs of all schemes increase with the increasing of the number of tasks except the Random-Switch scheme and the Always-Sleep scheme. In the Random-Switch scheme, since all 5G BSs are switched randomly under any cases, the energy consumption does not change much. However, due to the frequent switching of states of 5G BSs under this scheme, a large amount of switching energy consumption will be generated, resulting in the highest energy cost compared with other schemes. In the Always-Sleep scheme, since all 5G BSs are in a sleep state under any cases and do not process any tasks, the energy consumption remains unchanged, and only the static energy in the inactive state is consumed. Although this scheme consumes the lowest energy cost, it can be seen from Fig. 2 that the success rate of the tasks under the Always-Sleep scheme is very low. Therefore, this scheme is not effective. In the Greedy-Algorithm, the switching of 5G BSs is greatly affected by the occasional fluctuation of traffic flow, which results in many very short sleep periods that are not worthy of sleep for 5G BSs. This increases the energy cost and also affects the offloading of tasks, resulting in a lower task success rate. In contrast, it can be seen that the energy saving effect of our online algorithm is very close to the offline algorithm. In the case of the same task success rate, the energy saving effect is slightly weaker than that of the offline algorithm, but significantly better than other schemes except the Always-Sleep scheme.

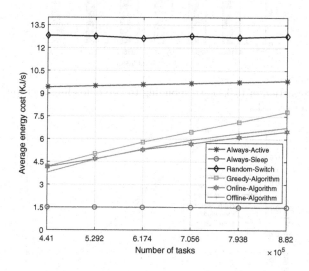

Fig. 3. The average energy cost of 5G BSs under different number of tasks.

To provide a more straightforward understanding, we present in Fig. 4 the proportion of tasks corresponding to the two offloading decisions of the online algorithm in Figs. 2 and 3. It can be seen that the proportion of tasks transmitted to the 5G BSs increases with the total number of tasks. Because this can ensure a higher task success rate.

Figure 5 shows the relationship between task success rate and task data size when we set $m = 705600$, $W = 10M$ CPU cycles. It can be seen that task success rate of all schemes decrease with the increasing of the task data size except the Always-Active scheme and the offline algorithm. Because a larger data size requires more communication resources, this increases the probability of task failure. It can be seen that the advantages of our online algorithm are still obvious.

Figure 6 shows the relationship between the average energy cost of 5G BSs and task data size when we set $m = 705600$, $W = 10M$ CPU cycles. It can

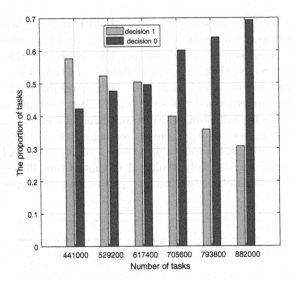

Fig. 4. The proportion of tasks corresponding to two offloading decisions under different total number of tasks.

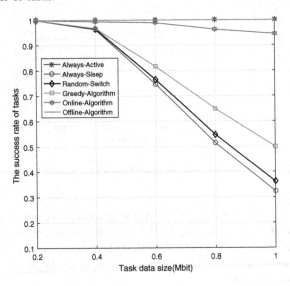

Fig. 5. The success rate of tasks under different task data size.

be seen that the average energy cost of 5G BSs of all schemes increase with the increasing of the task data size except the Always-Active scheme and the Random-Switch scheme. Although the energy-saving performance of our online algorithm is slightly inferior to that of the Greedy-Algorithm when the task data size is small, it is more stable and effective in guaranteeing a high task success rate.

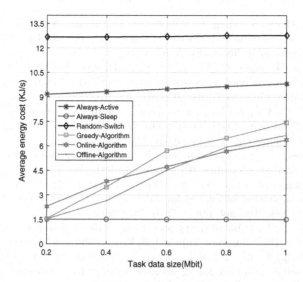

Fig. 6. The average energy cost of 5G BSs under different task data size.

Based on the above analysis, it can be concluded that our online algorithm can significantly reduce the energy cost while ensuring a high task success rate.

6 Conclusion

In this paper, we have investigated the problem of minimizing the energy cost of 5G BSs in VEC, and we propose a new hybrid 4G-5G task offloading framework which combines the respective advantages of 4G BS and 5G BS. Specifically, we first establish a mathematical model which cannot be solved directly. Then we propose offline algorithms that can be iteratively tuned to achieve 100% success of the task. Considering the real-time requirements of realistic scenarios, we also proposed corresponding online algorithm. Finally, we use a real-world traffic flow dataset to implement the simulation. Simulation experiments demonstrate that our scheme significantly reduces the energy cost while ensuring high task success rate.

In the future, we will consider offloading for different types of tasks. Of course, we should also consider cases where tasks are allowed to be partially offloaded.

References

1. Peng, H., Shen, X.: Deep reinforcement learning based resource management for multi-access edge computing in vehicular networks. IEEE Trans. Netw. Sci. Eng. **7**(4), 2416–2428 (2020)
2. Gao, J., Li, M., Zhao, L., Shen, X.: Contention intensity based distributed coordination for v2v safety message broadcast. IEEE Trans. Veh. Technol. **67**(12), 12288–12301 (2018)

3. Zhang, N., Zhang, S., Yang, P., Alhussein, O., Zhuang, W., Shen, X.S.: Software defined space-air-ground integrated vehicular networks: challenges and solutions. IEEE Commun. Mag. **55**(7), 101–109 (2017)

4. Liu, J., Wan, J., Zeng, B., Wang, Q., Song, H., Qiu, M.: A scalable and quick-response software defined vehicular network assisted by mobile edge computing. IEEE Commun. Mag. **55**(7), 94–100 (2017)

5. Shi, T., Li, Y., Cai, Z.: To process a large number of concurrent top-k queries towards IoT data on an edge server. The 42nd IEEE International Conference on Distributed Computing Systems (ICDCS 2022) (2022)

6. Cai, Z., Zheng, X., Yu, J.: A differential-private framework for urban traffic flows estimation via taxi companies. IEEE Trans. Industr. Inf. **15**(12), 6492–6499 (2019)

7. Ke, H., Wang, J., Deng, L., Ge, Y., Wang, H.: Deep reinforcement learning-based adaptive computation offloading for MEC in heterogeneous vehicular networks. IEEE Trans. Veh. Technol. **69**(7), 7916–7929 (2020)

8. Cai, Z., Shi, T.: Distributed query processing in the edge-assisted IoT data monitoring system. IEEE Internet Things J. **8**(16), 12679–12693 (2021)

9. Xu, X., Zhang, X., Liu, X., Jiang, J., Qi, L., Bhuiyan, M.Z.A.: Adaptive computation offloading with edge for 5g-envisioned internet of connected vehicles. IEEE Trans. Intell. Transp. Syst. **22**(8), 5213–5222 (2021)

10. Gu, X., Zhang, G., Cao, Y.: Cooperative mobile edge computing-cloud computing in internet of vehicle: architecture and energy-efficient workload allocation. Trans. Emerg. Telecommun. Technol. **32**(8), e4095 (2021)

11. Wheeb, A.H.: Performance analysis of VOIP in wireless networks. Int. J. Comput. Netw. Wirel. Commun. (IJCNWC) **7**(4), 1–5 (2017)

12. Cheng, X., Chen, C., Zhang, W., Yang, Y.: 5g-enabled cooperative intelligent vehicular (5genciv) framework: when Benz meets Marconi. IEEE Intell. Syst. **32**(3), 53–59 (2017)

13. Luo, Q., Li, C., Luan, T., Shi, W.: Minimizing the delay and cost of computation offloading for vehicular edge computing. IEEE Trans. Serv. Comput. **15**, 2897–2909 (2021)

14. Luo, Q., Li, C., Luan, T.H., Shi, W., Wu, W.: Self-learning based computation offloading for internet of vehicles: model and algorithm. IEEE Trans. Wirel. Commun. **20**(9), 5913–5925 (2021)

15. Auer, G.: How much energy is needed to run a wireless network? IEEE Wirel. Commun. **18**(5), 40–49 (2011)

16. Zhang, X., Debroy, S.: Energy efficient task offloading for compute-intensive mobile edge applications. In: ICC 2020–2020 IEEE International Conference on Communications (ICC), pp. 1–6 (2020)

17. Jang, Y., Na, J., Jeong, S., Kang, J.: Energy-efficient task offloading for vehicular edge computing: Joint optimization of offloading and bit allocation. In: 2020 IEEE 91st Vehicular Technology Conference (VTC2020-Spring), pp. 1–5 (2020)

18. Wu, L., Xu, J., Shi, L., Bi, X., Shi, Y.: Jointly optimizing throughput and cost of IoV based on coherent beamforming and successive interference cancellation technology. In: The 16th International Conference on Wireless Algorithms, Systems, and Applications(WASA), Nanjing, China, 25–27 June, pp. 235–243 (2021)

19. Ciullo, D., Marsan, M.A., Chiaraviglio, L., Meo, M.: Jointly optimizing throughput and cost of iov based on coherent beamforming and successive interference cancellation technology. In: 2012 Fourth International Conference on Communications and Electronics (ICCE), pp. 245–250 (2012)

20. Wen, C., Zheng, J.: An RSU on/off scheduling mechanism for energy efficiency in sparse vehicular networks. In: 2015 International Conference on Wireless Communications Signal Processing (WCSP), pp. 1–5 (2015)
21. Chavarria-Reyes, E., Akyildiz, I.F., Fadel, E.: Energy consumption analysis and minimization in multi-layer heterogeneous wireless systems. IEEE Trans. Mob. Comput. **14**(12), 2474–2487 (2015)
22. Sun, Y., Zhou, S., Xu, J.: EMM: energy-aware mobility management for mobile edge computing in ultra dense networks. IEEE J. Sel. Areas Commun. **35**(11), 2637–2646 (2017)
23. Zhao, Q., Gerla, M.: Energy efficiency enhancement in 5g mobile wireless networks. In: 2019 IEEE 20th International Symposium on "A World of Wireless, Mobile and Multimedia Networks" (WoWMoM), pp. 1–3 (2019)
24. Zhu, T., Shi, T., Li, J., Cai, Z., Zhou, X.: Task scheduling in deadline-aware mobile edge computing systems. IEEE Internet Things J. **6**(3), 4854–4866 (2019)
25. Jiang, H., Dai, X., Xiao, Z., Iyengar, A.K.: Joint task offloading and resource allocation for energy-constrained mobile edge computing. IEEE Trans. Mob. Comput. 1 (2022)
26. Elsherif, F., Chong, E.K.P., Kim, J.H.: Energy-efficient base station control framework for 5g cellular networks based on Markov decision process. IEEE Trans. Veh. Technol. **68**(9), 9267–9279 (2019)

An Efficient Scheduling Strategy for Containers Based on Kubernetes

Xurong Zhang[1], Xiaofeng Wang[1,2(✉)], Yuan Liu[1], and Zhaohong Deng[1]

[1] School of Artificial Intelligence and Computer Science, Jiangnan University, Wuxi, China
wangxf@jiangnan.edu.cn
[2] Peng Cheng Laboratory, Shenzhen, China

Abstract. Container clouds are an important supporting technology for collaborative edge computing, and Kubernetes has become the de facto standard for container orchestration. To solve the problem that the scheduling mechanism of Kubernetes has a single scheduling resource index and is unable to adapt the refined resource scheduling requirements in collaborative edge computing, this paper proposes an efficient multicriteria container online scheduling strategy based on Kubernetes, named E-KCSS. To improve the resource utilization of the cluster, the proposed E-KCSS strategy takes into account the global view of edge nodes and containers. An adaptive weight mechanism based on real-time utilization is proposed to solve the problem that preset Kubernetes weighting coefficients do not meet the individual resource requirements of applications. The experimental results show that compared with the scheduling mechanism of Kubernetes, the deployment efficiency of E-KCSS is improved by 35.22%, the upper limit of container application deployment is increased by 29.82%, and the cluster resource imbalance is reduced by 6.87%, which can make the multi-dimensional resource utilization of the cluster more balanced.

Keywords: Collaborative edge computing · Kubernetes · Container online scheduling strategy · Adaptive weight mechanism · Resource utilization

1 Introduction

With the large growth of intelligent terminal data traffic, edge computing can significantly improve computing performance by enabling cloud computing services to be deployed at the edge of the network to alleviate the great pressure of data [1]. Edge computing can decompose large-scale services into smaller and easier to manage parts, which enables real-time processing and analysis of data at the source of data generation. It is considered an effective distributed computing architecture [2].

However, with the emerging applications of computation-intensive and delay-sensitive [3] requirements, the limited computing power of edge nodes has been greatly challenged. Collaborative edge computing uses different edge nodes to collaborate by sharing computing resources and data, which provides a low time delay and highly reliable computing services [4]. In the collaborative edge computing scenario, computing

H. Gao et al. (Eds.): CollaborateCom 2022, LNICST 460, pp. 326–342, 2022.
https://doi.org/10.1007/978-3-031-24383-7_18

tasks are scheduled to edge nodes to fully use the advantages of edge nodes in computing and storage and reduce the network burden of cloud data centres.

In recent years, relevant research has further explored the fusion of containers and collaborative edge computing [5–8]. Most studies sink the container to the edge node and use its features of second-level deployment, easy portability and elastic scaling [7] to perform task computing. The fusion of containers and collaborative edge computing considers the collaboration among edge nodes to achieve mobile container scheduling. The lightweight nature of containers enables the cluster to quickly deploy application instances when needed, which provides technical support for scheduling the computing power of edge nodes by flexibly adjusting the number of service applications [8].

Before the public release of Kubernetes, it was difficult to jointly develop complex collaborative computing systems due to hardware differences between computing infrastructures [8]. However, since Kubernetes provides a declarative interface for upwards services, it can use software virtualization to abstract resources and provide unified objects to the outside world [9], which perfectly fits with the collaborative edge computing scenario.

The Kubernetes resource scheduler plays a decisive role in cluster and resource utilization and is the core of the container cloud. However, it faces the problems of a single scheduling mechanism and fixed resource scheduling weight and it cannot ensure that the computing power of edge nodes will be available on demand. Therefore, it is necessary to explore a new container scheduling mechanism for collaborative edge computing according to the container characteristics, system state and optimization objectives.

To overcome the shortcomings of Kubernetes scheduling in collaborative edge computing scenarios, an efficient scheduling strategy for containers based on Kubernetes, named E-KCSS, is presented. The novelty of E-KCSS lies in the introduction of a multicriteria scheduling strategy and an adaptive weight mechanism for resources. This strategy is considered at the node and container levels to achieve the load balancing of the cluster.

In summary, our main contributions are as follows:

1. A multicriteria container scheduling strategy for Kubernetes for collaborative edge computing is proposed, which selects nodes with a good compromise among multiple criteria for each container.
2. An adaptive weight algorithm is proposed, which can automatically model and solve the container resource weight set according to the dynamically obtained multidimensional resource utilization of edge nodes.
3. Based on the global node load balancing of the cluster as the objective function, the scheduling of a set of containers submitted online is optimized considering the multi-dimensional resource idleness and resource imbalance of the nodes.

The remainder of this article is organized as follows. In Sect. 2, some related works are introduced. Section 3 describes the proposed E-KCSS architecture and key technologies of E-KCSS in detail. Section 4 presents the exhaustive experiments and analysis to validate the E-KCSS method. Finally, Sect. 5 summarizes the full text and describes future research.

2 Related Work

The resource scheduling module in the container cloud platform plays a decisive role in the cluster performance [9]. There have been considerable studies on scheduling strategies for container technology, which mainly focus on collaborative computing, improving system resource utilization, achieving system load balancing, and predicting models based on machine learning.

Reference [4] proposes a dynamic offloading strategy based on a probabilistic evolutionary game-theoretic model. The mechanism comprehensively considers computing power and task requirements, establishes a resource consumption model and a time computing model, and uses a greedy algorithm to determine the optimal scheduling node of the container in the mobile edge computing scenario. Reference [10] proposes a cloud container-based collaboration framework that performs dynamic resource provisioning according to different workloads in collaborative computing scenarios, which outperforms virtual machine-based systems in terms of completion time and throughput.

The authors of [11] perform network prioritization of containers by introducing a quality of service mechanism to provide priority delivery services for containers. It can effectively determine the scheduling and allocation of bandwidth-sensitive containers and reduce operating costs. In [12], the authors analyse the correlation between absolute and relative CPU utilization under different workload scenarios and select the most appropriate performance metric for automatic scaling control while ensuring service quality constraints. This method can reduce the energy consumption of the cloud infrastructure platform and maximize the CPU utilization. Reference [13] proposes an I/O scheduling strategy at the cluster and node levels for the contention of I/O shared resources by containers. The disk usage is collected in real time at the cluster level, and the container priority is set at the node level, to achieve node-level throttling and cluster-level load balancing. References [11–13] are optimized based on single-resource scheduling, which plays an optimization role when the container focuses on such resources.

Reference [14] investigates and introduces a scheduling mechanism based on the resource utilization rate for index weight self-learning, which calculates the resource weight set of containers through dynamic perception of the real-time resource utilization rate, and improves the resource utilization in the container cloud environment. Reference [15] proposes a container scheduling method based on the multi-dimensional resource idle rate to achieve OpenShift cluster load balancing. It mathematically models the factors that affect scheduling, automatically solves the dynamic weights of multi-dimensional resources required by the container, and ensures the efficient use of node resources. References [14, 15] aim to improve the utilization of system resources, and they simulate the container cloud environment on the ContainerCloudSim [16] simulator to verify the scheduling strategy.

With the development of artificial intelligence, some predictive algorithms based on machine learning have emerged in the field of container scheduling. The authors of [17] consider the threshold distance of container replicas, use a genetic algorithm to address the problems of container scheduling and automatic scalability of containers, optimize the uniform distribution of microservices, enhance system resource allocation, and reduce network overhead. Reference [18] proposes a microservice container scheduling strategy based on a multi-objective ant colony optimization algorithm from the four dimensions of node computing resource utilization, storage resource utilization, number of microservice requests and failure rate and improves the cluster service reliability and resource utilization. Reference [19] proposes a forecasting model based on time series, which collects the historical resource usage of nodes, and predicts future resource usage through the forecasting model. However, scheduling strategies based on heuristic algorithms and machine learning predictive algorithms must learn a large number of data sets in advance, which will increase the difficulty of practical application. Based on these studies, there is less research on container scheduling in container clouds. The traditional scheduling method cannot fully consider the characteristics of containers, which often leads to low resource utilization and load imbalance in container clouds. More research should consider both.

3   E-KCSS Scheduling Strategy

In this section, we propose a new Kubernetes multicriteria container scheduling strategy, E-KCSS, to optimize the container scheduling performance in edge collaboration scenarios. This strategy considers the differences in multi-dimensional resource utilization on edge nodes and individual requirements of containers and combines the adaptive weight mechanism to perform load balancing of cluster resources.

3.1   E-KCSS Architecture

In Kubernetes, the node is the carrier to execute tasks, and the pod is the smallest unit of scheduling. The scheduler plays an important role in linking the preceding and the following. It is responsible for receiving requests to create pods, and it notifies the service process to manage the life cycle of the pod.

As shown in Fig. 1, the E-KCSS architecture is divided into two independent control loops: the Informer Path and Scheduling Path. The Informer Path starts a series of informers, monitors the changes to the multi-dimensional resources in the database, and adds the pods to be scheduled to the scheduling priority queue. The main logic of the Scheduling Path is to constantly pull pods out of the scheduling priority queue. First, the Predicates strategy is called to obtain a list of all nodes that meet pod requirements. Then, taking the responsible balance of the cluster as the objective function, the nodes are prioritized through the Priorities strategy, and the optimal node is selected. In addition, the scheduling part of E-KCSS is responsible for updating the scheduler cache and caching as much cluster information as possible to fundamentally improve the execution efficiency of the Predicates strategy and Priorities strategy.

The Scheduling mechanism is the key point of the Scheduling Path. It mainly introduces multicriteria indicators, combines the adaptive weight mechanism for resources, and takes the load balance of the cluster nodes as the objective function to select the optimal node for a pod. First, Sect. 3.2 introduces the Kubernetes multicriteria metrics. Then, Sect. 3.3 introduces the adaptive weight mechanism. Finally, Sect. 3.4 takes the global node load balancing of the cluster as the objective function to optimize the container scheduling performance.

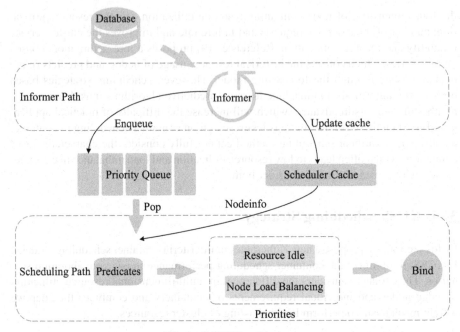

Fig. 1. E-KCSS architecture

3.2 Multicriteria Indicators

The scheduling algorithm of Kubernetes only considers the CPU and memory, and does not consider the needs of pod applications for other resources. Reference [14] adds two evaluation indicators, bandwidth and disk utilization, to the scheduler to avoid deploying containers to nodes that cannot adapt to edge computing scenarios. However, this strategy deploys many pods to a certain node. Therefore, E-KCSS additionally considers the number of pods deployed. Pods are added to the E-KCSS consideration to more evenly deploy containers to different nodes of the cluster.

Because edge nodes are limited by the deployment environment, network edge storage, computing, bandwidth and other resources are very scarce. According to the characteristics of the container, E-KCSS introduces multicriteria indicators, which additionally take the bandwidth, disk utilization, and number of deployed pods as the basis for scoring, to avoid deploying pod applications to nodes in which bandwidth, disk, and pod resources are saturated. Another aspect of E-KCSS considering bandwidth is to pull container images from container repositories faster. The transmission speed of the image directly affects the normal operation of the pod application and startup speed of the business. E-KCSS considers the disk factor to more reasonably schedule disk-intensive containers.

E-KCSS integrates a monitoring component to monitor resource changes on each node, collects the usage and total amount of resources in each dimension on each node, and calculates the idle utilization of various resources on the node. Assume that the number of filtered Kubernetes working nodes to satisfy the pod's requirement is K; this is expressed as $M = (m_1, m_2, \cdots, m_k)$. The nodes in the cluster consider resources in N dimensions. In E-KCSS, there are five types of resources: CPU, memory, bandwidth, disk utilization, and number of pods, so $N = 5$. The total resources of the nodes in the cluster are expressed as $R = \left(r_1^n, r_2^n, \cdots, r_k^n\right), \forall n \in N$, where r_k^n is the total number of n th-dimension resources owned by node k. The resource usage of the node is expressed as $U = \left(u_1^n, u_2^n, \cdots, u_k^n\right), \forall n \in N$, where u_k^n is the usage of the n th-dimension resource owned by node k. Therefore, the idle rate of the n th-dimension resource on node k $Free_k^n$ is expressed as

$$Free_k^n = \left(1 - \frac{u_k^n}{r_k^n}\right), \forall n \in N \tag{1}$$

3.3 Adaptive Weight Mechanism

When Kubernetes deploys pod applications, because the importance of pods to multidimensional resource requirements often varies, a scheduling policy using a fixed weight coefficient cannot satisfy the individual requirements of pod applications. Reference [15] adopts the fuzzy analytic hierarchy process to automatically model and solve the multi-dimensional resource weight parameters of container applications. Although the utilization of resources and cluster performance improve, this is more related to weight prediction at the subjective level. Based on the above research, E-KCSS obtains the dynamic weight coefficient triggered by dynamic events. E-KCSS automatically generates multi-dimensional resource weights according to the specific resource requirements of pod applications and combines the weights with the idle resource rates of the cluster nodes to calculate the scores of candidate nodes. This idea considers the actual situation of edge nodes and actual needs of pod applications, and their combination is applied to E-KCSS.

E-KCSS calculates the dynamic weight of a pod according to the proportion of the resources of the pod to the CPU, memory, bandwidth, disk, and pod number in the corresponding total resources of the cluster. The total amounts of various resources on the node are collected through the monitoring module, and the total resource R_n on each node is calculated.

$$R_n = \left(r_1^n, r_2^n, \cdots, r_k^n\right), \forall n \in N \tag{2}$$

where R_n is the n th-dimensional resource set of each node in the Kubernetes cluster and r_k^n is the total amount of n th-dimensional resources owned by node k. Therefore, the total resource S_n of the n th dimension of the cluster is expressed as

$$S_n = \sum_{i=1}^{k} r_i^n \tag{3}$$

The mathematical model is built according to the resource requirements of the pod, and the pod application container records the set of resource requirements as $P = (p_1, p_2, \cdots, p_n)$. Therefore, the proportion w_n of the resource demand of the n th-dimension of the pod with respect to the total global resources can be obtained by combining formula (3) to obtain

$$w_n = \frac{P_n}{S_n} = \frac{P_n}{\sum_{i=1}^{k} r_i^n}, \forall n \in N \tag{4}$$

Therefore, the set of resources required by the pod application in the overall resource weight of the cluster is set to $Weight = (w_1, w_2, \cdots, w_n)$. Thus, deploying the pod application consumes w_1 CPU resources, w_2 memory resources, w_3 bandwidth resources, w_4 disk resources, and w_5 pod quantity resources in the cluster.

Finally, the weight set is normalized. Define the weight coefficients $\beta_i, \forall i \in [1, 5]$, which represent the weights of the CPU, memory, bandwidth, disk, and pod number after normalization, respectively; $\beta_1 + \beta_2 + \beta_3 + \beta_4 + \beta_5 = 1$, where β_i is expressed as

$$\beta_i = \frac{w_i}{\sum_{j=1}^{N} w_j}, \forall i \in N \tag{5}$$

The adaptive weight algorithm is shown in Algorithm 1. The input of Algorithm 1 is all candidate node information (nodeInfo), pod application information (PodInfo) and dimension resource name sets (resourceSet). The output is the weight vector (weightVector) of the pod, which is used to save the dynamic weight coefficient.

Algorithm 1. Adaptive Weight Algorithm

Input: *nodeInfo, PodInfo, resourceSet*;

Output: *weightVector*;

1. *weightVector, PodVector, nodeVector, Sum* ← {};
2. **for** *Pod* in *PodInfo* **do:**
3.   *PodVector* ← Get the resource demand the of pod from *PodInfo*;
4. **end for**
5. **for** *node* in *nodeInfo* **do:**
6.   *nodeVector* ← Get the total resources of the node from *nodeInfo*;
7.   *Sum* += *nodeVector*;
8. **end for**
9. *weight* ← According to *Sum* and *PodVector*, calculate the proportion of resources required by pod to the overall global resources, and judge the tendency of the pod;
10. *weightVector* ← Normalize *weight*;
11. **return** *weightVector*

3.4 Load Balancing Strategy

The load balancing strategy of E-KCSS is jointly determined by the node resource idle module and multi-dimensional resource balancing module. The node resource idle module implies that a higher idle resource rate of the candidate node corresponds to a higher score; the multi-dimensional resource balance module implies that a more balanced resource utilization of the candidate node corresponds to a higher score. The final score of the candidate node is determined by the weighted sum of the two scores.

E-KCSS calculates the n th-dimension resource idleness on node K as $Free_k^n$ based on formula (1). According to formula (5), the pod resource weight set $W = (\beta_1, \beta_2, \cdots, \beta_n)$ is obtained. Therefore, the idle resource score S_k of the pod deployed on node k is expressed as

$$S_k = \sum_{i=1}^{n} Free_k^n \times \beta_i \tag{6}$$

Therefore, scoring set S of the idle resource degree of the cluster nodes is

$$S = (S_1, S_2, \cdots, S_j), \forall j \in K \tag{7}$$

E-KCSS obtains the multi-dimensional resource utilization set on the candidate node k according to formula (1), which is denoted as $U_k = (u_k^1, u_k^2, \cdots, u_k^n), \forall n \in N$. Therefore, the average resource utilization U_{avg} on candidate node k is expressed as

$$U_k^{avg} = \sum_{i=1}^{N} u_k^i \tag{8}$$

In probability theory, variance is often used to measure the degree of deviation between a random variable and the mean; it describes the distribution range of variable values. A larger variance corresponds to a larger data fluctuation, more unbalanced resources of the cluster, and a lower node score. Therefore, the multi-dimensional resource balance score B_k on node k is expressed as

$$B_k = \sqrt{\frac{1}{n} \sum_{i=1}^{N} (u_k^i - u_k^{avg})^2} \tag{9}$$

To obtain B_k, after amplification, score set B of the multi-dimensional resource balance degree of the cluster nodes is expressed as

$$B = (B_1, B_2, \cdots, B_j), \forall j < K \tag{10}$$

Therefore, according to formula (7) and formula (10), the comprehensive score of candidate node k is expressed as $f_k = S_k + B_k$. Therefore, the comprehensive score set F of cluster candidate nodes is expressed as

$$F = (f_1, f_2, \cdots, f_j), \forall j < K \tag{11}$$

4 Experimental Evaluation

In this section, we verify the analysis of E-KCSS through the following experiments: 1) comparison of cluster resource imbalance, 2) comparison of deployment efficiency, and 3) comparison of resource utilization.

Table 1. Kubernetes node information.

Node number	CPU/core	Memory/GB	Disk/GB	Bandwidth/Mbps
Master1	4	8	200	1000
Node1	8	8	1000	1000
Node2	8	12	1000	1000
Node3	16	24	1000	1000
Node4	16	32	1700	1000
Node5	12	64	1100	1000

4.1 Experimental Environment

To verify the validity and feasibility of the proposed E-KCSS, a Kubernetes cluster was built, including one master node and five worker nodes. The total resource information of each node is shown in Table 1.

Simultaneously, T pod applications for scheduling are constructed, and their resource requirements simulate four different resource-intensive applications in terms of the CPU, memory, bandwidth and disk in the cloud computing platform. The resource specifications are shown in Table 2.

Table 2. Pod application resource specifications.

Number	CPU/MHz	Memory/MB	Disk/GB	Bandwidth/Mbps	Pod
1	400	230	8	20	1
2	100	700	2	10	1
3	150	100	20	20	1
4	75	175	7	10	1
...	...	...	...	...	...
T	200	100	5	80	1

The normalized multi-dimensional resource weights of the T pods in Table 2 are solved according to the adaptive weight mechanism, and the corresponding multi-dimensional weight parameters are shown in Table 3.

Table 3. Pod multi-dimensional resource weight parameters.

Number	CPU/MHz	Memory/MB	Disk/GB	Bandwidth/Mbps	Pod
1	0.517	0.128	0.124	0.154	0.077
2	0.181	0.552	0.045	0.111	0.111
3	0.245	0.070	0.392	0.196	0.097
4	0.209	0.209	0.206	0.209	0.167
...	...	...	...	...	...
T	0.238	0.051	0.071	0.569	0.071

4.2 Performance Indicators

There are three main performance indicators.
1) Cluster resource imbalance
    For nodes, the standard deviation of multi-dimensional resource utilization can reflect the resource balance of nodes. We calculate the average utilization rate U_k^{avg} of each resource dimension for node k according to formula (1), which is expressed as

$$U_k^{avg} = \frac{1}{N}\sum_{i=1}^{N}(1 - Free_k^i) \tag{12}$$

Therefore, the standard deviation of the node k resource utilization SD_k is expressed as

$$SD_k = \sqrt{\sum_{i=1}^{N}(1 - Free_k^i - U_k^{avg})^2} \tag{13}$$

Define the cluster resource imbalance degree $IBD = \frac{1}{K}\sum_{i=1}^{K}SD_i$. A smaller value corresponds to less cluster resource imbalance, more balanced overall resource utilization, and a higher load balance.

2) Deployment efficiency
    The pod deployment time is the time from when the control node issues the deployment command until the pod becomes available. A shorter pod deployment time corresponds to a higher deployment efficiency.
3) Resource utilization of each dimension
    The resource utilization of each dimension on the cluster node measures whether the resources of the node are overloaded. A smaller probability of node resource tilt corresponds to better scheduling performance.

4.3 Comparison of Cluster Resource Imbalance

In the experiment, the Kubernetes scheduler and scheduler based on the E-KCSS mechanism were used to maximally deploy pod applications. To fully use cluster resources as much as possible, the application with pod number 4 in Table 2 was selected for scheduling. The experiment deployed as many pod applications as possible in order, where each round lasted 60 s, and recorded the CPU, memory, bandwidth, and disk utilization of each node and the proportion of the number of deployed pods to the total number of pods on the node. The imbalance degree of cluster resources was calculated according to formula (12) and formula (13), and the experimental results are shown in Fig. 2.

After E-KCSS scheduling, the cluster resource imbalance degree is better than that of the Kubernetes scheduling strategy on the whole, with an average reduction of 6.87%. The Kubernetes scheduler node failed in the 173rd round; the pod application could not be deployed on the node, and 285 pods were deployed in total. The E-KCSS scheduler counted 253 rounds of information and deployed a total of 370 pods, which is 29.82% greater than the number scheduled by the Kubernetes scheduler. E-KCSS maximized the use of multi-dimensional cluster resources, which greatly improved the utilization of resources. The reason is that E-KCSS considers the weights of the four resources and the number of node pod deployments at the pod and node levels, which effectively reduces the possibility that one node in a cluster is exhausted and other resources are too often unused. E-KCSS also takes the load balance of the cluster nodes as the objective function, which combines the idle rate of multi-dimensional resources and the resource imbalance between nodes. As a result, the imbalance of cluster resources is reduced to satisfy the deployment requirements of more pod applications.

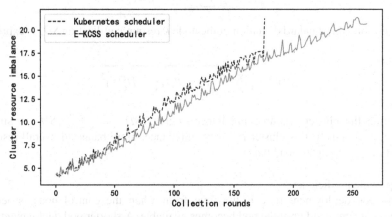

Fig. 2. Comparison of cluster resource imbalance

4.4 Comparison of Deployment Efficiency

In the experiment, the Kubernetes scheduler and E-KCSS scheduler were used to deploy pod applications, and the total time required to deploy 20 pods, deployment time of each pod, and network load rate before deploying each pod were compared. The method to determine the total time consumption of pod deployment in the experiment took the deployment request time of the first pod as the start time; the remaining pods were deployed at intervals of 10 s, and the time at which all pods became available was considered the completion time.

The experimental results are shown in Fig. 3. Figure 3(a) shows the total time taken from the creation command delivery to the pod successful creation for each pod. Figure 3(b) shows the network load rate before the node creates the pod. From the experimental result calculations, the Kubernetes scheduler takes 521 s to deploy 20 pods and 157.7 s to deploy one pod on average. E-KCSS takes 345 s to deploy 20 pods, and it takes 102.15 s to deploy one pod on average, a decrease of 0.35 times in deployment time. Figure 3(b) shows that the network load rate of the node selected by E-KCSS before creating the pod is lower than that of the node selected by the Kubernetes scheduler. In contrast to the Kubernetes scheduling policy, the improved E-KCSS takes the network load rate of the nodes as a reference factor for scheduling during the scheduling process, and preferentially selects nodes with a low network load rate for scheduling. Therefore, the efficiency of the container image distribution will be improved and reduce the speed of pod deployment. In summary, E-KCSS determines the network bandwidth utilization of nodes; it has higher deployment efficiency than the Kubernetes scheduler and can rapidly deploy containers.

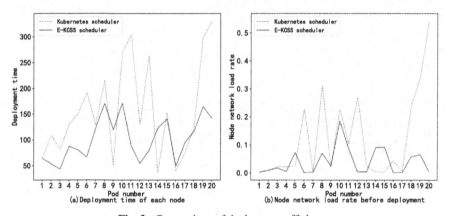

Fig. 3. Comparison of deployment efficiency

4.5 Comparison of Resource Utilization

In the experiment, the Kubernetes scheduler and scheduler based on E-KCSS were used to deploy CPU-intensive pod applications, memory-intensive pod applications and disk-intensive pod applications, corresponding to the applications with pod numbers 1, 2 and 3, respectively, in Table 2. The experiment deployed 100 pod applications in order, and compared the CPU utilization, memory utilization, disk utilization and pod distribution of each work node after deployment. The experimental results of deploying CPU-intensive pod applications are shown in Fig. 4. The experimental results of deploying memory-intensive pod applications are shown in Fig. 5. The experimental results of deploying disk-intensive pod applications are shown in Fig. 6.

As seen from Fig. 4(d), compared with the Kubernetes scheduler, the pod distribution of E-KCSS after deploying CPU-intensive applications is 12, 13, 26, 29, and 20, and many pods are deployed on node4. Table 1 shows that node4 has the most CPU resources, so E-KCSS solves the multi-dimensional resource weight parameters of the specific pod application according to the resource demand characteristics of pod applications and node resource utilization, enlarges the proportion of the CPU resource weight, and prioritizes the deployment of nodes with more CPU resources. Simultaneously, as shown in Fig. 4(a), the Kubernetes scheduler deploys a large number of pods on node5, which makes the CPU utilization of node5 reaching 96.40%, while the E-KCSS more evenly deploys pods on all cluster nodes. The CPU utilization of node5 decreases by 27.50%, and the CPU utilization of the other nodes increases by 6.15% on average to avoid resource utilization overload.

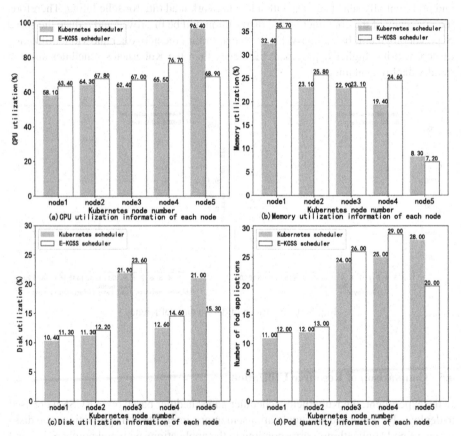

Fig. 4. CPU intensive pod application resource utilization

As Fig. 5 shows, compared with the Kubernetes scheduler, E-KCSS is more balanced in deploying memory-intensive applications. As shown in Fig. 5(d), the pod distribution of E-KCSS after deploying memory-intensive applications is 7, 11, 21, 22, and 39. Because node1 and node2 have relatively tight memory resources, while node5 has the most memory resources, combined with the adaptive weight mechanism, E-KCSS deploys many pods on node5 to alleviate the memory pressure on the other working nodes. As shown in Fig. 5(b), the memory utilization of node5 increased by 15.50%, and the memory utilization of the other nodes decreased by 8.53%.

As Fig. 6 shows, the deployment of disk-intensive pod applications using E-KCSS-based schedulers is more balanced than that using Kubernetes schedulers. According to Table 1, node4 has the most disk resources, followed by node5. Simultaneously, as shown in Fig. 6(c), the Kubernetes scheduler deploys a large number of pods on node3, which makes the Disk utilization of node3 reaching 61.40%, while the E-KCSS more evenly deploys pods on all cluster nodes. According to Fig. 6(d), the pod distribution of E-KCSS after deploying disk-intensive applications is 13, 15, 19, 30, and 23. Many disk-intensive pod applications are deployed on node4 and node5. In summary, E-KCSS makes the disk utilization of cluster nodes more balanced.

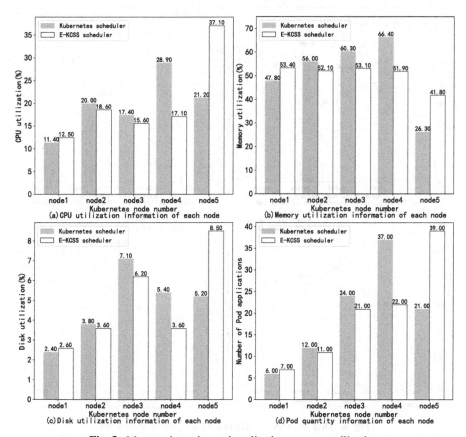

Fig. 5. Memory intensive pod application resource utilization

The Kubernetes scheduler considers only the resource utilization of nodes, while E-KCSS considers the pod application requirements and multi-dimensional resource utilization of nodes. E-KCSS automatically adjusts the multi-dimensional resource weight and gives higher weight to the high-performance resource nodes to deploy more pods to these nodes. In addition, E-KCSS also uses the load balancing strategy to take into account the resource requirements of the pod and the actual surplus of the node. Using this strategy, the pod can be deployed on cluster nodes more evenly.

As the number of Pods increases, the Kubernetes scheduler does not consider factors such as disk resources and the number of pod deployments. Once a work node in the cluster is overloaded with resources, it will cause the waste of other resources, and the scheduler will be unable to schedule pod applications to the node. However, E-KCSS uses the adaptive weight algorithm to obtain the dynamic weight coefficient triggered by the dynamic event, and combines the resource idle rate of node to obtain the optimal solution. To sum up, compared with the Kubernetes scheduler, E-KCSS makes the node resource utilization more balanced.

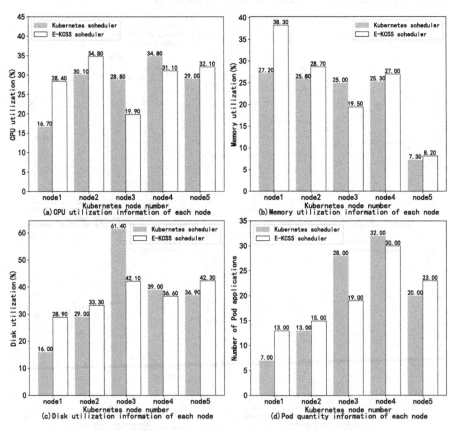

Fig. 6. Disk intensive pod application resource utilization

5 Conclusion

Container clouds are an important supporting technology for collaborative edge computing. The resources of edge nodes are relatively scarce, and the difference between edge applications and traditional applications brings new requirements for the scheduling mechanism of container clouds. Based on research on the Kubernetes scheduling policy, this paper proposes a Kubernetes container scheduling policy for collaborative edge computing to address the shortcomings of its single-criteria scheduling mechanism. This strategy comprehensively considers the CPU, memory, bandwidth, disk, and number of pods, automatically calculates multi-dimensional resource weights according to the application's resource requirements, and schedules pod applications based on the node resource load balance. Finally, experiments are designed to verify the performance of the E-KCSS scheduling method proposed in this paper and scheduling method of Kubernetes. Compared with the Kubernetes scheduling strategy, the deployment efficiency of E-KCSS increases by 35.22%, the upper limit of deployment increases by 29.82%, and the cluster resource imbalance decreases by 6.87%. The experiments show that the new scheduling method can effectively improve multi-dimensional resource utilization and cluster load balancing. In the future, more factors, such as node affinity and anti-affinity, internal load interference and data localization of pod applications, will be considered to make the cluster resource scheduling more balanced and efficient and satisfy the real-time needs of multiple tenants.

Acknowledgements. This research was funded by the National Natural Science Foundation of China (grant nos. 62172191 and 61972182), the National Key R&D Program of China (grant no. 2016YFB0800803), and the Peng Cheng Laboratory Project (grant no. PCL2021A02).

References s

1. Ren, J., Yu, J., He, Y.: Collaborative cloud and edge computing for latency minimization. IEEE Trans. Veh. Technol. **68**(5), 5031–5044 (2019)
2. Chiang, M., Zhang, T.: Fog and IoT: an overview of research opportunities. IEEE Internet Things J. **3**(6), 854–864 (2016)
3. Yang, L., Cao, J., Cheng, H.: Multi-user computation partitioning for latency sensitive mobile cloud applications. IEEE Trans. Comput. **64**(8), 2253–2266 (2014)
4. Lei, Y., Zheng, W., Ma, Y., Xia, Y., Xia, Q.: A novel probabilistic-performance-aware and evolutionary game-theoretic approach to task offloading in the hybrid cloud-edge environment. In: Gao, H., Wang, X., Iqbal, M., Yin, Y., Yin, J., Ning, G. (eds.) Collaborative Computing: Networking, Applications and Worksharing. LNICSSITE, vol. 349, pp. 255–270. Springer, Cham (2021). https://doi.org/10.1007/978-3-030-67537-0_16
5. Xiao, X., Li, Y., Xia, Y., Ma, Y., Jiang, C., Zhong, X.: Location-aware edge service migration for mobile user reallocation in crowded scenes. In: Gao, H., Wang, X., Iqbal, M., Yin, Y., Yin, J., Ning, G. (eds.) Collaborative Computing: Networking, Applications and Worksharing. LNICSSITE, vol. 349, pp. 441–457. Springer, Cham (2021). https://doi.org/10.1007/978-3-030-67537-0_27
6. Gao, H., Huang, W., Zou, Q., Yang, X.: A dynamic planning framework for QOS-based mobile service composition under cloud-edge hybrid environments. In: Wang, X., Gao, H., Iqbal,

M., Min, G. (eds.) Collaborative Computing: Networking, Applications and Worksharing. LNICSSITE, vol. 292, pp. 58–70. Springer, Cham (2019). https://doi.org/10.1007/978-3-030-30146-0_5

7. Zhang, J., Li, Y., Zhou, L., Ren, Z., Wan, J., Wang, Y.: Priority-Based optimization of I/O isolation for hybrid deployed services. In: Wang, X., Gao, H., Iqbal, M., Min, G. (eds.) Collaborative Computing: Networking, Applications and Worksharing. LNICSSITE, vol. 292, pp. 28–44. Springer, Cham (2019). https://doi.org/10.1007/978-3-030-30146-0_3

8. Xu, Y., Chen, L.: An adaptive mechanism for dynamically collaborative computing power and task scheduling in edge environment. IEEE Internet Things J. 1(1), 232–245 (2021)

9. Li, J.: Design and implementation of machine learning cloud platform based on Kubernetes. Master thesis, Nanjing University of Posts and Telecommunications (2021)

10. Suresh, S., Manjunatha, R.: CCCORE: cloud container for collaborative research. Int. J. Elect. Comput. Eng. 8(3), 1659–1670 (2018)

11. Dusia, A., Yang, Y., Taufer, M.: Network quality of service in docker containers. In: 2015 IEEE International Conference on Cluster Computing, pp. 527–528. IEEE (2015)

12. Casalicchio, E.: A study on performance measures for auto-scaling CPU-intensive container-ized applications. Clust. Comput. 22(3), 995–1006 (2019). https://doi.org/10.1007/s10586-018-02890-1

13. McDaniel, S., Herbein, S., Taufer, M.: A two-tiered approach to I/O quality of service in docker containers. In: 2015 IEEE International Conference on Cluster Computing, pp. 490–491. IEEE (2015)

14. Kong, D., Yao, X.: Kubernetes resource scheduling strategy for 5G edge computing. Comput. Eng. 47(2), 32–38 (2021)

15. Gong, K., Wu, Y., Chen, K.: Container cloud multi-dimensional resource utilization balanced scheduling. App. Res. Comput. 37(4), 1102–1106 (2018)

16. Piraghaj, S., Dastjerdi, A., Calheiros, R.: ContainerCloudSim: an environment for modeling and simulation of containers in cloud data centers. Softw. Pract. Exp. 47(4), 505–521 (2017)

17. Guerrero, C., Lera, I., Juiz, C.: Genetic algorithm for multi-objective optimization of container allocation in cloud architecture. J. Gird Comput. 16(1), 113–135 (2018)

18. Lin, M., Xi, J., Bai, W.: Ant colony algorithm for multi-objective optimization of container-based microservice scheduling in cloud. IEEE Access. 7, 83088–83100 (2019)

19. Yang, M., Rao, R., Xin, Z.: CRUPA: a container resource utilization prediction for auto-scale based on time series analysis. In: 2016 International Conference on Progress in Informatics and Computing, pp. 468–472. IEEE (2016)

NOMA-Based Task Offloading and Allocation in Vehicular Edge Computing Networks

Shuangliang Zhao[1,3], Lei Shi[1,3(✉)], Yi Shi[2], Fei Zhao[1,3], and Yuqi Fan[1,3]

[1] School of Computer Science and Information Engineering,
Hefei University of Technology, Hefei 230009, China
`shilei@hfut.edu.cn`
[2] Department of ECE, Virginia Tech, Blacksburg, VA 24061, USA
[3] Engineering Research Center of Safety Critical Industrial Measurement
and Control Technology, Ministry of Education, Hefei 230009, China

Abstract. Vehicular Edge Computing (VEC) is envisioned as a promising approach to process explosive vehicle tasks. In the VEC system, vehicles can choose to upload tasks to nearby edge nodes for processing. This approach requires an efficient communication method, and Non-Orthogonal Multiple Access (NOMA) can improve channel spectrum efficiency and capacity. However, in the VEC system, the channel condition is complex due to the fast mobility of vehicles, and the arrival time of each task is stochastic. These characteristics greatly affect the latency of tasks. In this paper, we adopt a NOMA-based task offloading and allocation scheme to improve the VEC system. To cope with complex channel conditions, we use NOMA to upload tasks in batches. We first establish the mathematical model, and divide the offloading and allocation of tasks into two processes: transmission and computation. Then we determine appropriate edge nodes for transmission and computation according to the position and speed of vehicles. We define the optimization objective as maximizing the number of tasks completed, and find that it is an integer nonlinear problem. Since there are more integer variables, this optimization problem is difficult to solve directly. Through further analysis, we design Asymptotic Inference Greedy Strategy (AIGS) algorithm based on heuristics. Simulation results demonstrate that our algorithm has great advantages.

Keywords: VEC · NOMA · Task offloading · Task allocation · Collaborative processing

The work is supported by the major science and technology projects in Anhui Province, NO. 202003a05020009 and the innovation foundation of the city of Bengbu, Grant No. JZ2022YDZJ0019.

H. Gao et al. (Eds.): CollaborateCom 2022, LNICST 460, pp. 343–359, 2022.
https://doi.org/10.1007/978-3-031-24383-7_19

1   Introduction

With the rapid development of the Internet of Things (IoT), a large number of intelligent devices and other smart IoT devices are flooding into wireless networks [1]. Various smart applications have been flourishing, such as smart city, smart manufacturing, automatic driving [2,3], etc. Moreover, The Internet of Vehicles (IoV) has received a lot of attention in recent years, and the rapid development of IoV has also brought some challenges that need to be solved. Most vehicular applications are usually latency critical, and solving this problem requires strong processing capability. In addition, because of the extreme scarcity of wireless resources, large amounts of IoV device need to allocate wireless resources more efficiently [2,5]. Edge Computing (EC) has been regarded as a promising technology to reduce latency [4], and VEC is the application of EC in IoV [25]. Meanwhile, the development of NOMA can effectively utilize wireless resources and improve communication quality [6–8]. The combination of these two technologies has greatly contributed to solving the challenges in IoV [9–11].

In EC, Edge Nodes (ENs) can efficiently allocate communication and computing resources to users [12,14]. Compared to traditional cloud server, ENs are closer to users, so they can give feedback to requests in time [15]. Moreover, NOMA can effectively improve the channel utilization [13]. Therefore, the application of NOMA-assisted ENs has gradually become a mainstream scheme [16–20]. In addition, this scheme can achieve secure power allocation and reduce processing latency in industrial applications [21,22]. And using Unmanned Aerial Vehicle (UAV) to join this scheme can also achieve great results, but this approach also brings additional power consumption and scheduling problems [23,24].

In VEC, vehicles have a higher speed of movement and the requirements for communication are more demanding [26]. NOMA can increase the task of simultaneous transmission and improve the service quality of the system [27]. However, adopting NOMA technology in VEC also presents some challenges. First, since the speed of vehicle is fast, it is very critical to determine a suitable edge node in transmission process. Second, NOMA has a threshold requirement for Signal to Interference plus Noise Ratio (SINR) [14], and determining the order of task transmission has an important role in transmission process. Third, after uploading the task, the vehicle may leave the current edge node, so it is very important to select the appropriate edge node to process the task for the improvement of system performance, etc. These considerations motivate the study of this article and the main contributions of our work are summarized as follows,

1) For the high-speed mobility of the vehicle, we select the appropriate edge node to upload the task according to the location and speed of the vehicle. In this way, we can ensure that the task can be successfully uploaded to the edge node. After the task is uploaded, we determine the appropriate edge node to compute the task according to the location of the vehicle and the load of the edge nodes.
2) In order to increase the number of tasks transmitted simultaneously, we use NOMA to transmit tasks in the transmission process. Moreover, we transmit tasks in batches according to the position of the vehicle and the size of the task, In this way, the communication quality of NOMA can be improved.

3) For the optimization problem, we design the Asymptotic Inference Greedy Strategy (AIGS) algorithm to deal with situations in real roads. We execute many simulation experiments by simulating real-time road conditions, and the results show that our algorithm has great advantages.

The remainder of this article is organized as follows. Related works are presented in Sect. 2. Our system model and problem formulation are described in Sect. 3. Section 4 introduces our algorithm. The simulation and experiments are provided in Sect. 5. Finally, this paper is concluded in Sect. 6.

2   Related Work

With the rapid development of IoV, the study on VEC has become one of the hot study topics in recent years. Some scholars have done a lot of researches on VEC from the following aspects.

The allocation of communication resources and computing resources in VEC is very important. Wang et al. proposed a multilayer data flow processing system to integrally utilize the computing capacity throughout the whole work, and efficient data processing can be achieved in this way [28]. Liu et al. explored a vehicle edge computing network architecture to maximize the long-term utility of the vehicle edge computing network [29]. Some other scholars also used Deep Reinforcement Learning (DRL) to solve the problems in VEC. Li et al. developed a collaborative edge computing framework to reduce the computing service latency and improve service reliability for vehicular networks, and the offloading and computing problem were formulated as a Markov decision process [30]. Ke et al. designed a task computation offloading model in a heterogeneous vehicular network, and they proposed an adaptive computation offloading method based on DRL to obtain the tradeoff between the cost of energy consumption and the cost of data transmission delay [31]. Load balancing is one of the focuses of VEC. Zhang et al. introduced Fiber-Wireless (FiWi) technology to enhance Vehicular Edge Computing Networks (VECNs), and they proposed a Software-Defined Networking (SDN) based load-balancing task offloading scheme in FiWi enhanced VECNs [32]. Dai et al. proposed integrating load balancing with offloading and studied resource allocation for a multiuser multiserver VEC system. They formulated the joint load balancing and offloading problem as a mixed integer nonlinear programming problem to maximize system utility [33].

The combination of NOMA and VEC has become a new hot research topic. Qian et al. investigated NOMA assisted vehicular edge computing via underlay spectrum sharing. They optimized the vehicular computing-users partial offloading and the allocation of the communication and computing resources to minimize the delay [27]. Zhu et al. constructed a decentralized DRL framework to formulate the power allocation optimization problem due to uncertain multi-input multi-out NOMA channel and stochastic tasks. They adopted the deep deterministic policy gradient algorithm to learn the optimal power allocation scheme based on the decentralized DRL framework [25]. Qian et al. formulated a joint optimization of the computation resource allocations and radio resource allocations for NOMA transmission, with the objective of minimizing a system wise cost [34].

The above [25–34] have done a great deal of work on vehicle networks from various aspects, and our focus is mainly on the aspect of NOMA-assisted VEC. Although some scholars have conducted research on computational offloading of NOMA-assisted VEC, few scholars have paid attention to the transmission waiting time in the NOMA-transmission process and the selection of edge nodes in the process of vehicle movement, etc. In this paper, we mainly study the transmission batch problem of NOMA and the selection of edge nodes.

3   System Model and Problem Formulation

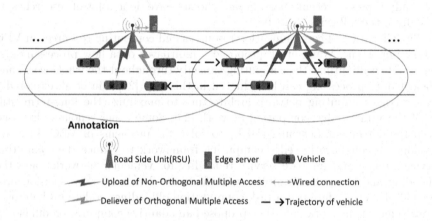

Fig. 1. Network model

Consider the number of equidistant Road Side Units (RSUs) deployed along a straight road, as shown in Fig. 1. Suppose these RSUs are equipped with edge servers, which means they can be used for transmitting and computing simultaneously. In the following we refer to RSUs as edge nodes. Consider vehicles passing the road are generating tasks needed to be handled by these edge nodes, we use the NOMA communication technique for uploading tasks, and NOMA can eliminate the collision between signals from different vehicles. Assume that each task can only choose one edge node for transmission. For one edge node, it may have many tasks to be handled at a time, so it may send some tasks to other nodes for computing. Additionally, we divide the whole schedule time T into multiple identical time slots $t(t \in \mathcal{T})$, where $\mathcal{T}$ is the set of time slots, and we normalize the length of these time slots. Due to the small length of these time slots, each vehicle generates at most one task in each time slot, and tasks generated in the same time slot can be approximately generated at the same time. Because of the fast mobility of vehicles, the number of vehicles on the road in different time slots will be various, and we define $\mathcal{M}_t$ as the set of vehicles in time slot t.

Define $\mathcal{N}$ as the set of edge nodes. Define $f_{m,t}$ as the task generated by vehicle m at time slot t. The total processing time required for task $f_{m,t}$ can be expressed as follows,

$$T_{m,t}^{Total} = \sum_{x \in \mathcal{N}} \alpha_{m,x,t} \left(T_{m,x,t}^{wait} + T_{m,x,t}^{up} \right) + \sum_{y \in \mathcal{N}} \gamma_{m,y,t} \left(T_{m,y,t}^{que} + T_{m,y,t}^{com} \right), \quad (1)$$

where $T_{m,x,t}^{wait}$ is the waiting time for task $f_{m,t}$ to be uploaded to edge node x, and $T_{m,x,t}^{up}$ is the uploading time for task $f_{m,t}$ to be uploaded to edge node x, and $T_{m,y,t}^{que}$ is the waiting time for task $f_{m,t}$ to be computed on edge node y, and $T_{m,y,t}^{com}$ is the computation time for task $f_{m,t}$ to be computed on edge node y. $\alpha_{m,x,t}$ and $\gamma_{m,y,t}$ are $\{0, 1\}$ variables,

$$\alpha_{m,x,t} = \begin{cases} 1, & \text{if task } f_{m,t} \text{ is transmitted to edge node } x; \\ 0, & \text{otherwise.} \end{cases}$$

$$\gamma_{m,y,t} = \begin{cases} 1, & \text{if task } f_{m,t} \text{ is computed at edge node } y; \\ 0, & \text{otherwise.} \end{cases}$$

Since the data returned by the task is relatively small, we ignore the task return time.

Next, we will introduce the transmission process model and the computation process model respectively.

3.1   Transmission Model

Since we use the NOMA technique, several tasks may be received by one edge node simultaneously. However, the possibility of simultaneous reception is restricted by SINR. So in the transmission model, we combine tasks which can be transmitted together into a batch, and let tasks which cannot be transmitted together join different batches. Then some batches may wait for other batches finishing transmission. As an example shown in Fig. 2. We can see that the second batch is combined with four tasks, and it should wait for the transmitted completion of the first batch. Therefore, we define a $\{0, 1\}$ variable $\theta_{m,n,t}^{j}$ to indicate whether the task $f_{m,t}$ starts to upload in the j-th batch.

$$\theta_{m,n,t}^{j} = \begin{cases} 1, & \text{if } \alpha_{m,n,t} = 1 \text{ and task } f_{m,t} \text{ is uploaded in the } j\text{-th batch}; \\ 0, & \text{otherwise.} \end{cases}$$

So if task $f_{m,t}$ is uploaded in the j-th batch, $T_{m,n,t}^{wait}$ can be expressed as follows,

$$T_{m,n,t}^{wait} = \max_{\forall j | \theta_{m,n,t}^{j} = 1} \left\{ t_n^{j-1} - t, 0 \right\}, \quad (2)$$

where t_n^{j-1} is the time slot for all tasks in the $(j-1)$-th batch to complete the transmission, and it can be expressed as the following formula,

$$t_n^{j-1} = \max_{\forall f_{x,y}|x \in \mathcal{M}_y, y \in \mathcal{T}} \theta_{x,n,y}^{j-1} \left(y + T_{x,n,y}^{wait} + T_{x,n,y}^{up}\right). \tag{3}$$

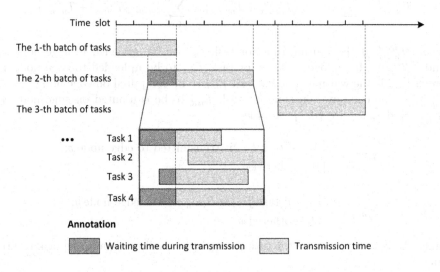

Fig. 2. An example of transmission process

For the convenience of consideration, we approximate the channel gain of vehicle m during the entire transmission process to a constant value, and SINR during the transmission can be expressed as follows,

$$SINR_{m,n,t} = \frac{\theta_{m,n,t}^j p g_{m,n,t}}{N_0 + \sum_{\theta_{x,n,y}^j p g_{x,n,y} < \theta_{m,n,t}^j p g_{m,n,t}} \theta_{x,n,y}^j p g_{x,n,y}} \geq \theta_{m,n,t}^j \beta, \tag{4}$$

where p is the transmission power of the vehicle, and we suppose all vehicles have the same transmission power. In addition, N_0 is Gaussian white noise, and β is the custom threshold that SINR needs to meet. Moreover, $g_{m,n,t}$ is the channel gain of task $f_{m,t}$, and it can be expressed as follows,

$$g_{m,n,t} = |d_n - d_{m,t}|^{-\lambda}, \tag{5}$$

where $d_{m,t}$ is the position where vehicle m generates task $f_{m,t}$, and d_n is the position of edge node n, and λ is the path loss coefficient [19].

Therefore, The transmission rate $R_{m,n,t}$ of the task $f_{m,t}$ transmitted to the edge node n can be expressed as follows,

$$R_{m,n,t} = W \log_2 \left(1 + SINR_{m,n,t}\right), \tag{6}$$

where W is the uplink bandwidth. According to the above content, we can get the transmission time $T_{m,n,t}^{up}$ of the task $f_{m,t}$,

$$T_{m,n,t}^{up} = \frac{D_{m,t}}{R_{m,n,t}} + T^{RSU}, \tag{7}$$

where $D_{m,t}$ is the amount of data that needs to be transmitted for task $f_{m,t}$, and T^{RSU} is the transmission time between edge nodes. Moreover, since edge nodes are connected by wire, the transmission time between them is quick enough to be ignored. Therefore, we do not consider the T^{RSU} in our system model.

3.2 Computation Model

After the task is transmitted to the edge node n, we will select the appropriate edge node to compute according to the task situation in each edge node and the location of the vehicle. Moreover, we consider edge nodes to compute only one task at a time, so there is a queue waiting time in the computation process. The time slot for task $f_{m,t}$ to reach edge node n can be expressed as follows,

$$a_{m,n,t} = t + T_{m,n,t}^{wait} + T_{m,n,t}^{up}. \tag{8}$$

For tasks arriving at the same time in the time slot $a_{m,n,t}$, they are represented by the set $\mathcal{F}(a_{m,n,t})$. We define a $\{0,1\}$ variable $\rho_{m,n,t}^{j}$, and it indicates whether the task $f_{m,t}$ is computed as the j-th task,

$$\rho_{m,n,t}^{j} = \begin{cases} 1, & \text{if } \gamma_{m,n,t} = 1 \text{ and task } f_{m,t} \text{ is computed as the } j\text{-th task;} \\ 0, & \text{otherwise.} \end{cases}$$

Therefore, if the task $f_{m,t}$ is computed as the j-th task, $T_{m,n,t}^{que}$ is the time required for the $(j-1)$-th task to complete the remaining computation portion at the time slot t. Therefore, the waiting time of the task during the computation process can be expressed as follows,

$$T_{m,n,t}^{que} = \max_{\forall j | \rho_{m,n,t}^{j}=1} \left\{ a_n^{j-1} - a_{m,n,t}, 0 \right\}, \tag{9}$$

where a_n^{j-1} is the time slot for the $(j-1)$-th task to complete the computation, and it can be expressed as the following formula,

$$a_n^{j-1} = \sum_{i=1}^{a_{m,n,t}} \sum_{f_{x,y} \in \mathcal{F}(i)} \rho_{x,n,y}^{j-1} \left(a_{x,n,y} + T_{x,n,y}^{que} + T_{x,n,y}^{com} \right). \tag{10}$$

Finally, the computing time $T_{m,n,t}^{com}$ of task $f_{m,t}$ at edge node n can be obtained as follows,

$$T_{m,n,t}^{com} = \frac{Q_{m,t}}{C}, \tag{11}$$

where $Q_{m,t}$ is the number of CPU cycles required to complete the computation of task $f_{m,t}$, and C is the computing capability of the edge node, and each edge node has the same computing capability.

3.3   Problem Formulation

After a task completes the computation, we need to determine whether the current task is successfully executed. Therefore, we define a $\{0,1\}$ variable $\mu_{m,t}$, and it indicates whether the task $f_{m,t}$ can be completed within the delay constraint.

$$\mu_{m,t} = \begin{cases} 1, & \text{if, } T_{m,t}^{Total} \leq T_{m,t}^{max}; \\ 0, & \text{otherwise.} \end{cases} \tag{12}$$

In addition, $T_{m,t}^{max}$ is maximum delay constraint of task $f_{m,t}$.

The main objective of this paper is to maximize the number of tasks completed by all vehicles in time period T through allocation decisions. And we have the optimization problem as follows,

$$\max \sum_{t \in \mathcal{T}} \sum_{m \in \mathcal{M}_t} \mu_{m,t}, \tag{13}$$

s.t.

$$(1)(2)(3)(4)(5)(6)(7)(8)(9)(10)(11)(12). \tag{13a}$$

$$\sum_{n \in \mathcal{N}} \alpha_{m,n,t} = 1, \sum_{n \in \mathcal{N}} \gamma_{m,n,t} = 1. \quad \forall m, t \tag{13b}$$

$$\sum_{j} \theta_{m,n,t}^{j} = 1. \quad \forall m, n, t \tag{13c}$$

$$\sum_{t \in \mathcal{T}} \sum_{m \in \mathcal{M}_t} \sum_{j} \rho_{m,n,t}^{j} = 1. \quad \forall n \tag{13d}$$

(13a) indicates the architecture of the entire model. (13b) indicates that each task can only select one edge node in transmission or computation process. (13c) indicates that each task can only select one batch to start uploading. (13d) indicates that each task can only select one order to start computing.

4   Problem Analysis and Algorithm

In this section, we first analyze the optimization problem. In our system model, $\alpha_{m,n,t}$ and $\theta_{m,n,t}^{j}$ are optimization variables in the transmission process, and $\gamma_{m,n,t}$ and $\rho_{m,n,t}^{j}$ are optimization variables in the computation process. According to formula $(1), (2), (3)$, it can be known that $\alpha_{m,n,t}$ and $\theta_{m,n,t}^{j}$ are multiplied. Moreover, $\alpha_{m,n,t}$ and $\theta_{m,n,t}^{j}$ are $\{0,1\}$ variables. The relationship between $\gamma_{m,n,t}$ and $\rho_{m,n,t}^{j}$ is similar to $\alpha_{m,n,t}$ and $\theta_{m,n,t}^{j}$. Therefore, this is an integer nonlinear optimization problem. This problem is difficult to solve directly, and we consider solving for these variables by heuristics.

Through further analysis, it can be found that the interaction between transmission process and computation process is small, so we choose to solve the optimization variables in these two processes separately. As shown in Algorithm 1, we

---

Algorithm 1. Asymptotic Inference Greedy Strategy(AIGS) algorithm

---

Input: $\mathcal{T}$: The set of time slots; $\mathcal{N}$: The set of edge nodes; $\mathcal{M}_t$: The set of vehicle at time slot t; $\mathcal{F}_t$: The set of tasks waiting for transmission in slot t; $\mathcal{F}(t)$: The set of tasks waiting for computation in slot t.

Output: $\alpha_{m,n,t}$, $\theta^j_{m,n,t}$, $\gamma_{m,n,t}$, $\rho^j_{m,n,t}$.

1: **for** $t \in \mathcal{T}$ **do**
2:     When task $f_{m,t}$ is generated in time slot t, $f_{m,t} \to \mathcal{F}_t$.
3:     For any task $f_{x,y}$, if $f_{x,y}$ is being uploaded, release $f_{x,y}$ from $\mathcal{F}_t$. If $f_{x,y}$ has completed transmission, $f_{x,y} \to \mathcal{F}(t)$. If $f_{x,y}$ is being computed, release $f_{x,y}$ from $\mathcal{F}(t)$.
4:     **for** $f_{m,t} \in \mathcal{F}_t$ **do**
5:         In transmission process, get $\alpha_{m,n,t}$ and $\theta^j_{m,n,t}$ according to TPUD algorithm.
6:     **end for**
7:     **for** $f_{m,t} \in \mathcal{F}(t)$ **do**
8:         In compute process, get $\gamma_{m,n,t}$ and $\rho^j_{m,n,t}$ according to CPED algorithm.
9:     **end for**
10: **end for**

---

design the Asymptotic Inference Greedy Strategy (AIGS) algorithm to solve the optimization problem. We first determine $\alpha_{m,n,t}$ and $\theta^j_{m,n,t}$ in transmission process, and then we solve $\gamma_{m,n,t}$ and $\rho^j_{m,n,t}$ in computation process. In addition, the Transmission Process Upload Decision (TPUD) algorithm and Compute Process Execute Decision (CPED) algorithm will be described in detail in the following sections.

4.1 Problem Analysis in Transmission Process

In the transmission step, we design the TPUD algorithm to solve $\alpha_{m,n,t}$ and $\theta^j_{m,n,t}$. When vehicles generate tasks, edge nodes for uploading tasks should be determined first. We use the following steps for solving $\alpha_{m,n,t}$ and $\theta^j_{m,n,t}$. First, we get an initial method without considering the vehicle's speed. Then, we try to consider the influence of vehicle's speeds from the largest to the smallest. Finally, we try to adjust the initial method until we find an acceptable method.

Step 1: Initialize $\alpha_{m,n,t}$. First, we initialize $\alpha_{m,n,t}$ according to the initial position of the vehicle m. If $d^{min}_n < d_{m,t}$ and $d^{min}_{n+1} > d_{m,t}$, we have $\alpha_{m,n,t} = 1$. Otherwise, we have $\alpha_{m,n,t} = 0$. Moreover, d^{min}_n is the minimum coverage position of edge node n.

Step 2: Get $\theta^j_{m,n,t}$ **according to initial** $\alpha_{m,n,t}$. Second, we sort tasks according to channel gains from small to large, and use superposition coding to divide these tasks into different batches. Then all $\theta^j_{m,n,t}$ can be obtained.

Step 3: Adjust $\alpha_{m,n,t}$. Third, we narrow the adjustment range of $\alpha_{m,n,t}$, and let tasks only be uploaded to these edge nodes where vehicles can arrive within $T^{max}_{m,t}$. For task $f_{m,t}$ that fails to transmit due to v_m and $d_{m,t}$, we will upload the task to the next edge node and adjust $\alpha_{m,n,t}$.

Algorithm 2. Transmission Process Upload Decision(TPUD) algorithm

---

Input: $\mathcal{T}$: The set of time slots; $\mathcal{N}$: The set of edge nodes; $\mathcal{M}_t$: The set of vehicle at time slot t; W: Uplink bandwidth; S: Boolean variables used to judge decisions.
Output: $\alpha_{m,n,t}$, $\theta^j_{m,n,t}$.

1: **for** $n \in \mathcal{N}$ **do**
2:    Get the initial $\alpha_{m,n,t}$ according to $d_n^{min} < d_{m,t}$ and $d_{n+1}^{min} > d_{m,t}$.
3: **end for**
4: **while** $!S$ **do**
5:    $S = \text{TRUE}$.
6:    **for** $n \in \mathcal{N}$ **do**
7:       Update $\theta^j_{m,n,t}$ according to $SINR_{m,n,t}$.
8:       **if** $\left(\left(T^{wait}_{m,n,t} + T^{up}_{m,n,t} \right) > \frac{d_{n+1}^{min} - d_{m,t}}{v_m} \right)$ **then**
9:          Adjust $\alpha_{m,n,t}$ and $S = \text{FALSE}$.
10:       **end if**
11:    **end for**
12: **end while**

Step 4: Repeat Step 2 and Step 3. Finally, we will re-solve $\theta^j_{m,n,t}$ according to step 2 and step 3 until all tasks are uploaded successfully or $\alpha_{m,n,t}$ cannot adjust.

4.2 Problem Analysis in Computation Process

In the computation step, we design the CPED algorithm to solve $\gamma_{m,n,t}$ and $\rho^j_{m,n,t}$. After the task is uploaded to the edge node, the appropriate edge node should be selected for computing first. We use the following steps for solving $\gamma_{m,n,t}$ and $\rho^j_{m,n,t}$. First, we get an initial method without considering the cooperation of edge nodes, Then, we try to consider the influence of the cooperation of edge nodes. Finally, we try to adjust the initial method until we find an acceptable method.

Step 1: Initialize $\gamma_{m,n,t}$. First, we initialize $\gamma_{m,n,t}$ according to the $\alpha_{m,n,t}$. Specifically, the task is preferentially computed on the uploaded edge node. If $\alpha_{m,n,t} = 1$, we have $\gamma_{m,n,t} = 1$.

Step 2: Get $\rho^j_{m,n,t}$ **according to initial** $\gamma_{m,n,t}$. Second, we determine the computation order of each task according to the strategy of high response ratio. Specifically, by comparing $\frac{T^{que}_{m,n,t} + T^{com}_{m,n,t}}{T^{com}_{m,n,t}}$, the task with a highest response ratio will be computed first. Then all $\rho^j_{m,n,t}$ can be obtained.

Step 3: Adjust $\gamma_{m,n,t}$. Third, we narrow the adjustment range of $\gamma_{m,n,t}$, and let tasks only be computed on these edge nodes where vehicles can arrive within $T^{max}_{m,t}$. For task $f_{m,t}$ that fails to compute, if the vehicle m can leave the current edge node within $T^{max}_{m,t}$, we will put the task on the next edge node for computing and adjust $\alpha_{m,n,t}$.

Algorithm 3. Compute Process Execute Decision(CPED) algorithm

---

Input: $\mathcal{T}$: The set of time slots; $\mathcal{N}$: The set of edge nodes; $\mathcal{M}_t$: The set of vehicle at time slot t; S: Boolean variables used to judge decisions.

Output: $\gamma_{m,n,t}$, $\rho_{m,n,t}^j$.

1: **for** $n \in \mathcal{N}$ **do**
2:    Get the initial $\gamma_{m,n,t}$ according to $\alpha_{m,n,t}$.
3: **end for**
4: **while** !S **do**
5:    S = TRUE.
6:    **for** $n \in \mathcal{N}$ **do**
7:       Update $\rho_{m,n,t}^j$ according to $\frac{T_{m,n,t}^{que}+T_{m,n,t}^{com}}{T_{m,n,t}^{com}}$.
8:       **if** $\left(T_{m,n,t}^{Total} > T_{m,t}^{max}\right)$ and $\left(\left(d_{m,t} + v_m T_{m,t}^{max}\right) > d_{n+1}^{min}\right)$ **then**
9:          Adjust $\gamma_{m,n,t}$ and S = FALSE.
10:      **end if**
11:   **end for**
12: **end while**

Step 4: Repeat Step 2 and Step 3. Finally, we will re-solve $\rho_{m,n,t}^j$ according to step 2 and step 3 until all tasks are computed successfully or $\gamma_{m,n,t}$ cannot adjust.

5   Simulation and Experiment

In this section, we mainly introduce the related works of experiments and simulations. We assume that the simulation scene is two bidirectional intersection roads, and RSUs are deployed at roadside intervals of 200m, with each covering a radius of 250 m [30]. Moreover, there are 10 edge nodes serving in our simulation experiments, and these edge nodes communicate over wired connections. We assume that there are 100 vehicles on these roads, and when a vehicle on the road generates a task, it will request nearby edge nodes to assist with the task. And we use a random distribution method to initialize the positions of these vehicles on the two roads. After investigating some real road conditions and experimental data from other papers, we adopt the experimental data in Table 1 to conduct our simulation experiments.

First, we assume that the speed of vehicles is randomly distributed within the interval [40, 60] km/h, and the transmit power of the vehicle is 100 mW. Then, we assume that the threshold for SINR is 1, and the gaussian white noise is −100 dBm [29,34]. Finally, we assume that the size of each task is random, and the data size for task falls within the interval [5, 10]Mbits, and the number of required CPU cycles for task falls within the interval [1000, 3000]Megacycles, and the maximum delay constraint of task falls within the interval [1, 3]s [29,30]. Moreover, we mainly verify the performance of our algorithm by changing the number of tasks requested to be processed, communication bandwidth and edge node computing capability. We simulate the processing of tasks on the road in 30 time slots, and each time slot is 0.2 s long. Since the size of the task is

Table 1. Simulation parameters

Simulation parameters	Value
The transmission power of the vehicle	100 mW
Speed of vehicle	$[40, 60]$km/h
The custom threshold for SINR	1
Gaussian white noise	-100 dBm
Uplink bandwidth	$[5, 10]$MHz
The computing capability of the edge node	$[5, 10]$GHz
Maximum delay constraint of task	$[1, 3]$s
Data size for task	$[5, 10]$Mbits
The number of required CPU cycles for task	$[1000, 3000]$Megacycles

randomly generated, our experimental results are averaged from 50 groups of corresponding experiments.

In our simulation experiments, there are three comparison algorithms. The OMA-AIGS algorithm is obtained by modifying the AIGS algorithm, and the communication method is Orthogonal Multiple Access (OMA). By comparing these two algorithms, we can observe the superiority of NOMA. Moreover, the idea of Random algorithm is that the batches selected during transmission process and the order selected during computation process are random, and the strategy adopted by the FCFS algorithm is that the first come first service.

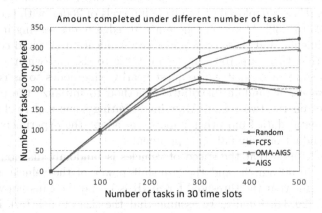

Fig. 3. Different number of tasks

In the first simulation experiment, we believe that the number of tasks requested to be processed has an important impact on algorithm performance. Therefore, we compare the performance of each algorithm under different number of tasks, and the number of tasks falls within the interval [100, 500]. Moreover, we assume that the uplink bandwidth is 7.5 MHz and the computing capability of the edge node is 7.5 GHz, and our measure of algorithm performance is the number of tasks completed. As shown in Fig. 3, we can know that when the number of tasks requested to be processed increases, the performance of AIGS algorithms is best. Through further observation, we can find that when the number of tasks is large, the performance of Random algorithm and FCFS algorithm begin to degrade, and our algorithm can still remain stable.

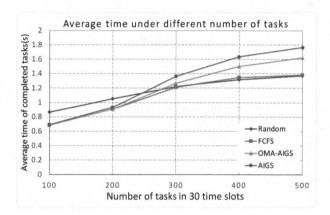

Fig. 4. Average time for complete tasks

In addition, we also compare the average processing time under different number of tasks for these algorithms. As can be seen from Fig. 4, when the number of tasks increases, although the average processing time of our algorithm is longer, the gap with other algorithms is not large, and we are able to accomplish more tasks in this situation. Through the above experimental results, we can know that our algorithm has better performance under different number of tasks.

In the second simulation experiment, we compare the effect of different bandwidth conditions on the performance of the algorithm. We assume that the uplink bandwidth falls within the interval [5, 10] MHz, and the computing capability of the edge node is 7.5 GHz, and the number of tasks is 300. The measure of algorithm performance is the number of tasks completed. As shown in Fig. 5, the number of tasks completed increases gradually for all algorithms as the bandwidth increases. But in general, our algorithm has better performance compared with other algorithms under different bandwidths. In addition, by comparing AIGS algorithm and OMA-AIGS algorithm, we can find that the NOMA method can effectively increase the number of tasks completed.

In the previous simulation experiment, we compare the impact of different bandwidth on the algorithm performance, so in this simulation experiment we compare the impact of different computing capabilities of edge nodes on the

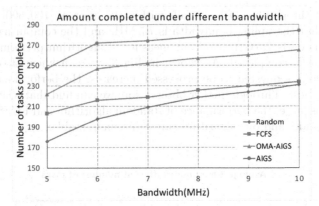

Fig. 5. Different bandwidth

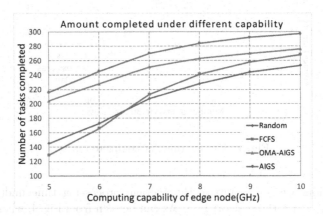

Fig. 6. Different computing capability

algorithm performance. In the final simulation experiment, we assume that computing capability of the edge node falls within the interval $[5, 10]$GHz, and the uplink bandwidth is 7.5 MHz, and the number of tasks is 300. As can be seen from Fig. 6, with the increase of computing power of edge nodes, the number of tasks completed by all algorithms increases gradually, and the overall performance of our algorithm has been the best. Moreover, compared with the impact of different bandwidths on algorithm performance, the impact of different computing power is more obvious.

6   Conclusion

In this paper, we have investigated the task offloading and allocation in IoV. We adopt NOMA-assisted VEC to solve this problem, and divide task processing into two processes. In the transmission process, the transmission method of

NOMA is determined to upload tasks, and according to the position and speed of vehicles, we select appropriate transmission batches for tasks to improve communication quality. In the computation process, the appropriate edge nodes are selected to compute the task according to the mobility of the vehicle. And we have designed AIGS algorithms based on heuristics to solve our problems. We have also presented abundant simulation results to demonstrate the algorithms, and simulation results have shown that our proposed method has effective performance. The main problem in the current research is that the connection between the transmission process and the computation process is ignored, which may not achieve the best results. Therefore, we will make further optimization on the basis of considering the connection between the two processes in future work, and the energy consumption will also be a factor to consider in our optimization problem.

References

1. Kiani, A., Ansari, N.: Edge computing aware NOMA for 5G networks. IEEE Internet Things J. **5**(2), 1299–1306 (2018)
2. Zhang, J., Letaief, K.B.: Mobile edge intelligence and computing for the internet of vehicles. Proc. IEEE **108**(2), 246–261 (2020)
3. Qian, L., Wu, Y., Jiang, F., Yu, N., Lu, W., Lin, B.: NOMA assisted multi-task multi-access mobile edge computing via deep reinforcement learning for industrial Internet of Things. IEEE Trans. Industr. Inf. **17**(8), 5688–5698 (2021)
4. Ding, Z., Fan, P., Poor, H.V.: Impact of non-orthogonal multiple access on the offloading of mobile edge computing. IEEE Trans. Commun. **67**(1), 375–390 (2019)
5. Mao, Y., You, C., Zhang, J., Huang, K., Letaief, K.B.: A survey on mobile edge computing: the communication perspective. IEEE Commun. Surv. Tutorials **19**(4), 2322–2358, Fourthquarter (2017)
6. Saito, Y., Kishiyama, Y., Benjebbour, A., Nakamura, T., Li, A., Higuchi, K.: Non-orthogonal multiple access (NOMA) for cellular future radio access. In: 2013 IEEE 77th Vehicular Technology Conference (VTC Spring), pp. 1–5 (2013)
7. Baghani, M., Parsaeefard, S., Derakhshani, M., Saad, W.: Dynamic non-orthogonal multiple access and orthogonal multiple access in 5G wireless networks. IEEE Trans. Commun. **67**(9), 6360–6373 (2019)
8. Saleem, U., Liu, Y., Jangsher, S., Tao, X., Li, Y.: Latency minimization for D2D-enabled partial computation offloading in mobile edge computing. IEEE Trans. Veh. Technol. **69**(4), 4472–4486 (2020)
9. Liu, Y., Peng, M., Shou, G., Chen, Y., Chen, S.: Toward edge intelligence: multiaccess edge computing for 5G and Internet of Things. IEEE Internet Things J. **7**(8), 6722–6747 (2020)
10. Cui, G., et al.: Demand response in NOMA-based mobile edge computing: a two-phase game-theoretical approach. IEEE Trans. Mobile Comput. (2021)
11. Qian, L., Wu, Y., Ouyang, J., Shi, Z., Lin, B., Jia, W.: Latency optimization for cellular assisted mobile edge computing via non-orthogonal multiple access. IEEE Trans. Veh. Technol. **69**(5), 5494–5507 (2020)
12. Zhang, L., et al.: Energy-efficient non-orthogonal multiple access for downlink communication in mobile edge computing systems. IEEE Trans. Mobile Comput. **21**(12), 4310–4322 (2022). https://doi.org/10.1109/TMC.2021.3083660

13. Hossain, M.A., Ansari, N.: Network slicing for NOMA-enabled edge computing. IEEE Trans. Cloud Comput. (2021)
14. Cui, G., et al.: OL-EUA: online user allocation for NOMA-based mobile edge computing. IEEE Trans. Mobile Comput. (2021)
15. Yang, Z., Liu, Y., Chen, Y., Al-Dhahir, N.: Cache-aided NOMA mobile edge computing: a reinforcement learning approach. IEEE Trans. Wireless Commun. **19**(10), 6899–6915 (2020)
16. Liu, Y.: Exploiting NOMA for cooperative edge computing. IEEE Wirel. Commun. **26**(5), 99–103 (2019)
17. Qian, L., Wu, W., Lu, W., Wu, Y., Lin, B., Quek, T.Q.S.: Secrecy-based energy-efficient mobile edge computing via cooperative non-orthogonal multiple access transmission. IEEE Trans. Commun. **69**(7), 4659–4677 (2021)
18. Tuong, V.D., Truong, T.P., Nguyen, T.-V., Noh, W., Cho, S.: Partial computation offloading in NOMA-assisted mobile-edge computing systems using deep reinforcement learning. IEEE Internet Things J. **8**(17), 13196–13208 (2021)
19. Yang, L., Guo, S., Yi, L., Wang, Q., Yang, Y.: NOSCM: a novel offloading strategy for NOMA-enabled hierarchical small cell mobile-edge computing. IEEE Internet Things J. **8**(10), 8107–8118 (2021)
20. Du, J., et al.: When Mobile-Edge Computing (MEC) meets nonorthogonal multiple access (NOMA) for the Internet of Things (IoT): system design and optimization. IEEE Internet Things J. **8**(10), 7849–7862 (2021)
21. Pei, X., Yu, H., Wang, X., Chen, Y., Wen, M., Wu, Y.-C.: NOMA-based pervasive edge computing: secure power allocation for IoV. IEEE Trans. Industr. Inf. **17**(7), 5021–5030 (2021)
22. Tuong, V.D., Noh, W., Cho, S.: Delay minimization for NOMA-enabled mobile edge computing in industrial Internet of Things. IEEE Trans. Industr. Inf. **18**(10), 7321–7331 (2022)
23. Feng, W., et al.: Hybrid beamforming design and resource allocation for UAV-aided wireless-powered mobile edge computing networks with NOMA. IEEE J. Sel. Areas Commun. **39**(11), 3271–3286 (2021)
24. Zhang, X., Zhang, J., Xiong, J., Zhou, L., Wei, J.: Energy-efficient multi-UAV-enabled multiaccess edge computing incorporating NOMA. IEEE Internet Things J. **7**(6), 5613–5627 (2020)
25. Zhu, H., Wu, Q., Wu, X.-J., Fan, Q., Fan, P., Wang, J.: Decentralized power allocation for MIMO-NOMA vehicular edge computing based on deep reinforcement learning. IEEE Internet Things J. **9**(14), 12770–12782 (2022)
26. Arthurs, P., Gillam, L., Krause, P., Wang, N., Halder, K., Mouzakitis, A.: A taxonomy and survey of edge cloud computing for intelligent transportation systems and connected vehicles. IEEE Trans. Intell. Transp. Syst. **23**(7), 6206–6221 (2022)
27. Qian, L., Wu, Y., Yu, N., Jiang, F., Zhou, H., Quek, T.Q.S.: Learning driven NOMA assisted vehicular edge computing via underlay spectrum sharing. IEEE Trans. Veh. Technol. **70**(1), 977–992 (2021)
28. Wang, P., Yao, C., Zheng, Z., Sun, G., Song, L.: Joint task assignment, transmission, and computing resource allocation in multilayer mobile edge computing systems. IEEE Internet Things J. **6**(2), 2872–2884 (2019)
29. Liu, Y., Yu, H., Xie, S., Zhang, Y.: Deep reinforcement learning for offloading and resource allocation in vehicle edge computing and networks. IEEE Trans. Veh. Technol. **68**(11), 11158–11168 (2019)
30. Li, M., Gao, J., Zhao, L., Shen, X.: Deep reinforcement learning for collaborative edge computing in vehicular networks. IEEE Trans. Cogn. Commun. Netw. **6**(4), 1122–1135 (2020)

31. Ke, H., Wang, J., Deng, L., Ge, Y., Wang, H.: Deep reinforcement learning-based adaptive computation offloading for MEC in heterogeneous vehicular networks. IEEE Trans. Veh. Technol. **69**(7), 7916–7929 (2020)
32. Zhang, J., Guo, H., Liu, J., Zhang, Y.: Task offloading in vehicular edge computing networks: a load-balancing solution. IEEE Trans. Veh. Technol. **69**(2), 2092–2104 (2020)
33. Dai, Y., Xu, D., Maharjan, S., Zhang, Y.: Joint load balancing and offloading in vehicular edge computing and networks. IEEE Internet Things J. **6**(3), 4377–4387 (2019)
34. Qian, L.P., Shi, B., Wu, Y., Sun, B., Tsang, D.H.K.: NOMA-enabled mobile edge computing for Internet of Things via joint communication and computation resource allocations. IEEE Internet Things J. **7**(1), 718–733 (2020)

A Collaborative Graph Convolutional Networks and Learning Styles Model for Courses Recommendation

Junyi Zhu[1], Liping Wang[1], Yanxiu Liu[1,2], Ping-Kuo Chen[3(✉)],
and Guodao Zhang[4(✉)]

[1] College of Computer Science and Technology, Zhejiang University of Technology,
Hangzhou 310023, China
[2] School of Data and Computer Science, Shandong Women's University, Jinan 250300, China
[3] Great Bar University, Dongguan 523000, China
a1104100@ms23.hinet.net
[4] School of Media and Design, Hangzhou Dianzi University, Hangzhou 310018, China
guodaozhang@zjut.edu.cn

Abstract. With the rise of Massive Open Online Courses (MOOCs) and the deepening of lifelong learning, there is a growing demand for learners to learn on online learning platforms. The vast amount of course resources provides learners with massive and easy access while posing challenges in terms of personalized and precise selection. Traditional recommendation models have room for improvement in performance and interpretability in massive open online course scenarios while under-utilizing the potential interaction signals in user-course interactions and ignoring the impact of the user's learning style as a learner. In order to solve the above problems, this paper proposes a collaborative graph convolutional networks and learning styles model for courses recommendation (CGCNLS). First, the course prediction rating is obtained by propagating the learner-course interaction information recursively through the graph convolutional networks; further, a course and learning styles matching scale is created to calculate the course learning styles similarity score; finally, the course prediction rating is combined with the course learning styles similarity score to make personalized course recommendations. The experimental results show that the model proposed in this paper can effectively recommend courses for learners and outperforms the baseline approach in terms of Precision, Recall, and NDCG performance metrics.

Keywords: Graph neural networks · Learning styles · Course recommendation · Collaborative models

This work was supported by the National Natural Science Foundation of China grant numbers 71872131 and Starting Research Fund of Great Bay University under grant YJKY220020 and Research Foundation of Hangzhou Dianzi University (KYS335622091; KYH333122029M).

H. Gao et al. (Eds.): CollaborateCom 2022, LNICST 460, pp. 360–377, 2022.
https://doi.org/10.1007/978-3-031-24383-7_20

1 Introduction

Nowadays, Massive Open Online Courses (MOOCs) are attracting the interest of many learners as an emerging educational model [1, 2]. With many different MOOC platforms in place, not only is the cost of learning reduced for learners, but they can also access quality courses from top universities around the world. Online education has greatly promoted the development of part-time learners. Still, those learners tend to be self-directed, lack guidance, and learn inefficiently, making personalized course recommendations particularly important for improving their learning efficiency. Therefore, scholars [3, 4] have devoted themselves to studying personalized learning resource systems, and customized learning resource recommendations include educational courses, learning paths, exercises, learning peers, etc.

In general, course recommendation methods are divided into course recommendation models based on traditional algorithms and course recommendation models based on deep learning techniques. Traditional course recommendation models use collaborative filtering (CF) techniques, which measure the similarity between users or courses to predict and recommend content that may interest users. In addition, with the development of deep learning techniques, deep networks are gradually being applied to educational resource recommendation. Many effective deep network recommendation models have been proposed to model user preferences in different ways. Deep learning techniques usually represent users and items as low-dimensional Embedding vectors [5–7] and iteratively optimize the parameters of the deep network and the Embedding vectors of users and items based on user behavior data or item information. Then, personalized recommendations are made by calculating the prediction rating of users and items or by feeding the embedding into the deep network to obtain the prediction rating of users for items to be recommended. Although the above methods are effective, the process of generating embedding vectors of users and courses lacks information to encode the key collaboration information, which is hidden in the interaction behavior of users and courses. This information can reveal the behavioral similarity between users/items. Specifically, CF approaches use only descriptive features (e.g., IDs and attributes) to construct embedding functions without considering the effects arising from user-course interactions. These interactions are used only to define the objective function for model training (e.g., inner product) without applying them to the process of generating embedding vectors.

With the development of online open courses and information technology, a large amount of data is easily accessible and stored, and with it comes the challenge of learners' privacy. Process behavior data mainly refers to human-computer interaction data, i.e., information about learners' course selection, learners' viewing of learning resources, etc., which can effectively protect personal privacy. Piao et al. [8] used processive data to construct Meta-Path-based graph convolutional networks for learning resource recommendation. Sheng et al. [9] used to process data to construct a heterogeneous information network-based model for online course recommendation and achieved good performance. It follows that learner modeling through processual behavioral data can effectively address individualized learner needs, i.e., recommending courses or learning resources that meet learners' needs.

In summary, this paper proposes a collaborative graph convolutional networks and learning styles course recommendation model to solve the above problem. The main work is as follows:

1. Construct an end-to-end graph convolutional network model to propagate learner-course interaction information in a recursive form, and apply higher-order interaction information to the embedding vector generation process to better compute the corresponding predicted course rating of learners.
2. To create a matching scale of course and learning styles based on pedagogical learning styles theory, and to obtain learners' corresponding course learning styles similarity score by cosine similarity calculation.
3. Collaborative prediction rating are obtained by graph convolutional network course prediction rating and course learning styles similarity score for personalized course recommendation. Multi-group experimental analysis in the real-world dataset shows that the course learning styles similarity score mechanism proposed in this paper can effectively improve the model performance, and the performance of the CGCNLS model is significantly better than that of the benchmark models.

The remainder of this paper is organized as follows. Section 2 reviews the latest relevant work. Section 3 describes the proposed approach in this paper. In Sect. 4, the experimental results and analysis are shown. In Sect. 5, a summary and outlook of this paper are presented.

2 Related Work

Learning style-based recommendation models have been a hot research topic in recent years [10–12]. For example, Hajri et al. [13] create learner learning style profiles based on learner profiles and dynamically provide learning resource recommendations to learners based on MOOC attributes. Sanjabi et al. [14] conducted a study on the personalization of e-learning environments based on the Kolb learning style model. Yan et al. [15] integrate learning style features into collaborative filtering algorithms for association rule mining. Sensuse et al. [16] surveyed personalization strategies based on Felder-Silverman learning styles and their impact on learning, finding insufficient theoretical research and a lack of user relevance studies in the literature. These methods have experimentally demonstrated the effectiveness of learning styles for the problem of learning resource recommendation. However, they are limited by the fact that they rely heavily on manual adjustment of parameters due to their traditional manual approach to students' learning styles and the selection of educational resources.

The rise of graph neural networks, especially the success of models such as graph convolutional network GCN [17], graph attention network GAT, and graph representation learning GraphSage [18], has led to the rapid development of graph neural network recommendation [19, 20]. For example, Xu et al. [21] proposed an algorithm combining knowledge graph and collaborative filtering (FKGCF), which utilizes not only the user's evaluation information of the course but also the semantic information of the course itself for course recommendation. Jibing Gong et al. [22] proposed a heterogeneous perspective of attention graph convolutional network for MOOC-oriented knowledge concept recommendation by an adaptive attention mechanism that incorporates contextual information from different meta-paths to capture students' different interests and make effective recommendations. Although these models have been successful, they ignore the user as a learner and suffer from poor performance in the course recommendation problem. Therefore, this paper proposes a collaborative graph convolutional network and learning style course recommendation model to solve the above problems.

3   The Proposed Model

Currently, recommendation algorithms based on graph convolutional networks usually use historical user interaction data without considering the influence of the learning styles possessed by the learners themselves. To address those problems, this paper proposes an algorithm called collaborative graph convolutional networks and learning styles course recommendation model (CGCNLS). The algorithm propagates learner-course interaction information in a recursive form, applies higher-order interaction information in the embedding vector generation process. And integrate the learning styles similarity of the recommended objects into the course prediction rating of the graph convolutional network, compensating for the shortcomings of existing recommendation algorithms that ignore the learning styles of the learners themselves. The algorithm model is shown in Fig. 1.

3.1   Problem Definition: Course Recommendation Models

The goal of the course recommendation algorithm is to predict the learners' rating for the untaken course:

$$\hat{y}_{u,c} = F(D_u, D_c) \tag{1}$$

To be specifically, using a prediction function F to estimate the likelihood that a user u will favor a course c, given the data D_u and D_c, to describe the user u and course c.

3.2   Course Learning Styles Similarity Score

Learning Styles Profile.   To clearly illustrate the course learning styles similarity score in this paper, we first introduce two definitions.

Definition 1 (learner profile): It is assumed that learner learning styles are represented by a real-valued vector LS_u from 0 to 1 in Eq. 1, where rea, tra, soc denote realistic, traditional, and social learning styles respectively. Equation 1 is as follows:

$$LS_u = (rea, tra, soc) \tag{2}$$

Examples of course-learning styles vectors are shown in Table 1, and these vectors were calculated using the information in Table 3 through the process shown in Fig. 2.

Definition 2 (course profile): Online courses cover many theoretical concepts. Different theoretical concepts belong to different areas of expertise, and different areas of

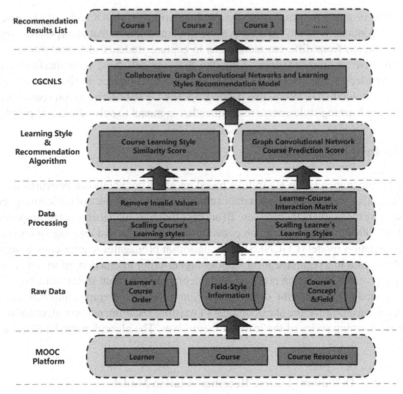

Fig. 1. CGCNLS model.

Table 1. Examples of learner learning styles vectors

Learner	rea	tra	soc
Learner 1	0.1029	0.7402	0.1569
Learner 2	0.8142	0.1858	0.0000
Learner 3	0.0000	0.2137	0.7863
...	...	...	...

expertise have their corresponding learning styles. Therefore, according to the correlation between course-concept-learning styles, the course profile can be represented by a learning styles vector, as in Eq. 2, which indicates the learning styles category that the course fits.

$$LS_c = (rea, tra, soc) \tag{3}$$

Examples of course-learning styles vectors are shown in Table 2, and these vectors were calculated using the information in Table 3 through the process shown in Fig. 2.

Table 2. Example of course learning styles vector

Course	rea	tra	soc
Course1	0.7532	0.1265	0.1203
Course2	0.2105	0.5789	0.2106
...	...	...	...

Calculating Learning Styles Vectors. Table 3 shows some examples of a field-learning styles matching measure based on an authentic questionnaire and guidance from educational professionals.

Table 3. Field-learning styles type matching metric representation example

Filed	Learning styles type
Computer Science and Technology	Realistic
Agronomy	Realistic
Mechanics	Traditional
Mathematics	Traditional
Psychology	Social
Pedagogy	Social
...	...

The learner learning styles vectors in Table 1 and the course learning styles vectors in Table 2 are calculated as shown in Fig. 2.

Calculating Learning Styles Similarity Score. Based on the learner learning styles vector and the course learning styles vector, the cosine similarity was used to calculate the learning styles similarity between the learner and the course, and obtain the course learning styles similarity score $Sim_{cls}(u, c)$, as shown in Eq. 3.

$$Sim_{cls}(u, c) = \frac{\sum_{i=1}^{n}\left(LS_{u_i} \times LS_{c_i}\right)}{\sqrt{\sum_{i=1}^{n}\left(LS_{u_i}\right)^2} \times \sqrt{\sum_{i=1}^{n}\left(LS_{c_i}\right)^2}} \tag{4}$$

where LS_{u_i} denotes the i-th value in the learner learning styles vector and LS_{c_i} denotes the i-th value in the course learning styles vector. The learning styles similarity score will be integrated into the subsequent collaborative prediction rating.

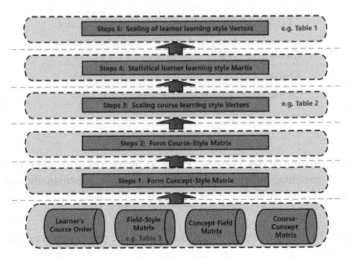

Fig. 2. Learning styles vector calculation process diagram

3.3 Graph Convolutional Network Course Prediction Rating

As with current recommendation models, we describe the learner u (course c) using the embedding vector $e_u \in \mathbb{R}^{dim} (e_c \in \mathbb{R}^{dim})$, where *dim* denotes the size of the embedding dimension. This process is seen as constructing a matrix of parameters as an embedding look-up table:

$$E = [\underbrace{e_{u_1}, \cdots, e_{u_N}}_{\text{learners embeddings}} , \underbrace{e_{c_1}, \cdots, e_{c_M}}_{\text{courses embeddings}}] \tag{5}$$

The main idea of graph convolutional networks is to propagate learner-course interaction information over a learner-course interaction graph, encoding higher-order interaction information into the embedding vector generation process. The graph convolutional network course prediction rating model consists of three main components: higher-order embedding propagation layer, embedding aggregation layer and prediction rating layer.

Higher-Order Embedding Propagation Layer.
As shown in Fig. 3, based on the above idea, we can encode the embedding information from learner u's connected course c as learner u's first-order embedding information for enhancing learner u's own embedding information by the following form. Definition as follows.

$$e_u^{(1)} = \sum_{c \in \mathcal{N}_u} \alpha_{uc} e_c \tag{6}$$

where $e_u^{(1)}$ denotes the first-order connectivity information for learner u, e_c denotes the initial embedding of course c, and α_{uc} denotes the decay coefficient for each propagation on edge (u, c). In this paper, we adopt the same idea as GCN[17] and set α_{uc} to $\frac{1}{\sqrt{|\mathcal{N}_u|}\sqrt{|\mathcal{N}_c|}}$, where $|\mathcal{N}_u|$ and $|\mathcal{N}_c|$ denote the number of first-hop neighbors of the learner u and the course c. α_{uc} not only takes on the function of equalizing how much the historical course c contributes to the preferences of the constituent learner u, but also in the process of embedding propagation different embedding information can be decayed as the path length changes.

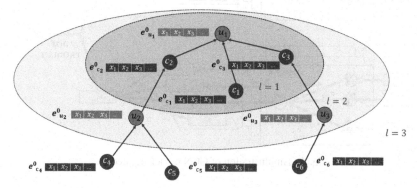

Fig. 3. An illustration of the learner-course interaction graph and the high-order interactive information

According to the form of propagation of first-order embedded information, the form of l-order embedded information for learner u in this method is as follows:

$$e_u^{(l)} = \sum_{c \in \mathcal{N}_u} \frac{1}{\sqrt{|\mathcal{N}_u|}\sqrt{|\mathcal{N}_c|}} e_c^{(l-1)} \tag{7}$$

Similarly, an expression for the l-order higher-order embedding information of course c can be obtained in the form:

$$e_c^{(l)} = \sum_{u \in \mathcal{N}_c} \frac{1}{\sqrt{|\mathcal{N}_c|}\sqrt{|\mathcal{N}_u|}} e_u^{(l-1)} \tag{8}$$

Embedding Aggregation Layer.
As shown in Fig. 4. After performing the embedding propagation of the L-layer, multiple higher-order information $\left\{e_u^{(0)}, \cdots, e_u^{(L)}\right\}$ of the learner node u was obtained, and the same for the course node. The outputs of the different layers emphasise the connectivity information of different orders. Therefore, an aggregation mechanism is used to aggregate the embedding information of each order into a single vector, as shown in Eqs. 8 and 9:

$$e_u^* = \sum_{l=0}^{L} p_l e_u^{(l)} \tag{9}$$

$$e_c^* = \sum_{l=0}^{K} p_l e_c^{(l)} \tag{10}$$

where p_l is $1/(L+1)$ to balance the effect of each layer of embedding propagation on the final embedding representation. The node embedding representation obtained

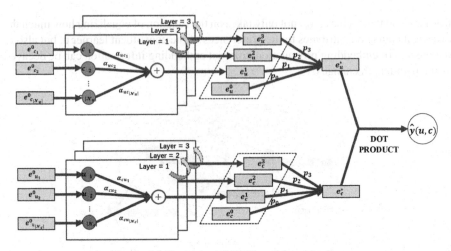

Fig. 4. An illustration of GCN model architecture

by aggregating the embedding information at each level in this way contains different semantic information in the graph structure, and the final embedding representation obtained will be more comprehensive.

Prediction Rating Layer. Finally, we perform inner product operations on the aggregated embedded representations of learner u and course c to predict the predicted rating of learner u for that course c:

$$\hat{y}(u, c) = e_u^{*\top} e_c^* \tag{11}$$

where $\hat{y}$ will be integrated into the subsequent collaborative prediction rating, which is used to generate the recommendation list.

Loss Functions and Trainers. The only parameter that needs to be trained in the whole graph collaborative filtering model is the embedding lookup table described earlier, i.e. the embedding representation of layer 0. To optimize the graph collaborative filtering model, the BPR loss function is chosen, which calculates the overall loss of the model by assuming that learners should have higher prediction values for learned courses than for unlearned courses.

$$L_{BPR} = -\sum_{(u,i,j)\in O} \ln \sigma \left(\hat{y}_{ui} - \hat{y}_{uj} \right) + \lambda \|\Theta\|^2 \tag{12}$$

where $O = \{(u, i, j) \mid (u, i) \in \mathcal{R}^+, (u, j) \in \mathcal{R}^-\}$ denotes the training set, where $\mathcal{R}^+$ denotes the set of courses that learners have learned. $\mathcal{R}^-$ is the set of courses that learners have not learned through a random negative σ is the sigmoid function; λ is used to control the L2 regularization strength, and Θ denotes the parameters of the model as a whole, i.e. the layer 0 embedding representation. We use the mini-batch Adam optimizer to optimize and update the model parameters.

3.4 Collaborative Prediction Rating

The prediction rating $\hat{y}_{CGCNLS}(u, c)$ of the CGCNLS model is a fusion of the graph convolutional network course prediction rating $\hat{y}(u, c)$ and the learning styles similarity score $Sim_{cls}(u, c)$.

For each learner u, after obtaining a list of predicted ratings of the course by learner u through the graph convolutional network recommendation algorithm $\{\hat{y}(u, c_1), \hat{y}(u, c_2), \ldots, \hat{y}(u, c_{|C|})\}$, the predicted ratings $\hat{y}(u, c)$ obtained from the graph convolutional network model are optimized by calculating the learning styles similarity between learner u and course c. The optimization equation is as follows.

$$\hat{y}_{CGCNLS}(u, c) = \hat{y}(u, c) + \varepsilon \times Sim_{cls}(u, c) \tag{13}$$

where ε is the predictive scoring collaborative weights. Based on the collaborative predicted rating, the Top-K courses of the collaborative predicted rating are selected as the final course recommendation results $R(u)\{c_1, c_2, \ldots, c_{Top-K}\}$.

4 Experiment Process

To evaluate the performance of our proposed collaborative graph convolutional network and learning style course recommendation model, we conducted experiments to answer the following research questions.

RQ1: How does our proposed CGCNLS course recommendation model perform compared to some existing baseline approaches?
RQ2: What is the impact of different co-weighting factors ε on the performance of the model?
RQ3: What is the performance of our proposed model when changing hyperparameters?

4.1 Experimental Environment and Data Set Processing

This paper conducted experiments on the real-world dataset MOOCCube [23] collected by XuetangX. In this paper, users with 10–20 course subscriptions were selected, and a total of 5738 users and 649 courses were used for the experiment. Detailed statistical information on these data is shown in Table 4. Each positive instance is paired with a randomly sampled negative instance during the training process. During testing, each historical course in the test set is considered a target course, and the corresponding course for the same user in the training set is considered a historical course. Finally, all courses of the user except the training set are rated, and the Top-K course recommendation list is obtained by sorting according to the predicted ratings.

Table 4. Statistical table of data sets

Dataset	#Courses	#Users	#Interactions
MOOCCube	649	5738	72148

To more accurately measure the performance of the algorithm, this paper uses five-fold cross-validation. That is, the experimental data are randomly grouped into 5 parts, one of which is used as the test set and the other 4 parts are used as the training set. A total of five tests were conducted and the average result of the five tests was used as the final evaluation result of the algorithm. All experiment results are obtained on a machine with Python 3.8, 3.80 GHz CPU, 12 GB of Video Memory and 32 GB of RAM。

4.2 Evaluation Metrics

Several metrics widely used in recommender system evaluation are used to measure the performance of our proposed model in different aspects, including the precision rate of Top-K items, the recall rate of Top-K items, and the normalized discounted cumulative return of Top-K items. In our experiments, we set the Top-K to 5, 10, 20, and 30.

Let R(u) represent the list of recommendations calculated by the model for the user based on the user's behavior on the training set, and T(u) represent the list of target courses for the user on the test set.

Precision@K is the calculation of how many courses in the predicted recommendation list are actually of interest to the user. The definition is as follows.

$$Precision = \frac{\sum_{u \in U} |R(u) \cap T(u)|}{\sum_{u \in U} |R(u)|} \tag{14}$$

Recall@K is a calculation of how many of the courses in a user's true favorite list are predicted by the recommendation algorithm. The definition is as follows.

$$Recall = \frac{\sum_{u \in U} |R(u) \cap T(u)|}{\sum_{u \in U} |T(u)|} \tag{15}$$

where R(u) represents the list of recommendations calculated by the model for the user based on the user's behavior on the training set, and T(u) represents the list of target courses for the user on the test set. Another ranking metric we use in our evaluation is the Normalized Discounted Cumulative Gain NDCG@K, which measures the performance of the retrieval system based on the hierarchical relevance of the retrieved entities and is a precision-based metric. The definition is as follows:

$$DCG_u@K = \sum_{k=1}^{K} \frac{2^{rel_u^i} - 1}{log_2(i+1)} \tag{16}$$

$$IDCG_u@K = \sum_{k=1}^{K} \frac{1}{log_2(i+1)} \tag{17}$$

$$NDCG@K = \frac{1}{|U|}\sum_{u=1}^{U} \frac{DCG_u@K}{IDCG_u@K} \qquad (18)$$

where $DCG_u@K$ indicates the discounted cumulative gain of the Top-K recommendation list for the user u, rel_u^i indicates the relevance (0 or 1) of the i-th recommendation result to user u, and $IDCG_u@K$ indicates the maximum discounted cumulative gain under ideal conditions.

4.3 Comparison with Baseline Method (RQ1)

To validate the performance of our proposed method CGCNLS, we will compare it with the following baseline approach.

GMF [24] decomposes the scoring matrix R into a user matrix U and an item matrix I. The product of U and I get closer to the true scoring matrix in a continuous iterative training.

NeuMF [24] combines GMF and MLP to operate on the embedding of target users and candidate courses to find the predicted ratings of users on candidate courses.

FISM [25] is an item-based collaborative filtering method for recommendations based on the average embedding of all historical courses of the user and the embedding of the target course.

NAIS [26] is also an item-based collaborative filtering method but distinguishes the weights of different historical courses through an attention mechanism.

NGCF [19] is the current baseline algorithm for recommendations based on graph neural networks.

Table 5 shows the experimental results of comparing our proposed model with some baseline methods on offline datasets. The experimental comparison shows that our proposed CGCNLS outperforms other baselines in all evaluation metrics, indicating the effectiveness of CGCNLS in MOOC course recommendations. Compared with the traditional neural network model, our graph convolutional network can better learn to model the complex interactions between learners and courses, thus improving accuracy, recall, and normalized discount cumulative gain. Compared with the graph neural network baseline model, our proposed collaborative learning style strategy is somewhat advanced and further enhances the overall interpretability of the model while ensuring its performance.

Table 5. Results obtained with different models on the MOOCCube dataset

Model	Precision@Top-K				Recall@Top-K				NDCG@Top-K			
	K = 5	K = 10	K = 20	K = 30	K = 5	K = 10	K = 20	K = 30	K = 5	K = 10	K = 20	K = 30
GMF	0.1221	0.0896	0.0640	0.0505	0.2372	0.3411	0.4862	0.5691	0.2119	0.2551	0.3048	0.3291
NueMF	0.1269	0.0898	0.0631	0.0499	0.2470	0.3446	0.4766	0.5653	0.2204	0.2542	0.3043	0.3285
FISM	0.1272	0.0878	0.0628	0.0496	0.2443	0.3335	0.4749	0.5599	0.2173	0.2504	0.3019	0.3249
NAIS	0.1324	0.9561	0.0647	0.0496	0.2554	0.3651	0.4903	0.5603	0.2254	0.2721	0.3119	0.3241
NGCF	0.1328	0.0955	0.0665	0.0525	0.2588	0.3668	0.5054	0.5952	0.2312	0.2757	0.3221	0.3476
CGCNLS (ours)	0.1470*	0.1055*	0.0711*	0.0550*	0.2856*	0.4029*	0.5375*	0.6254*	0.2526*	0.3012*	0.3465*	0.3711*

We use **bold** to mark the best performance and underline to indicate the best performance other than CGCNLS.

4.4   Experiments of Different Collaborative Weight Factor ε (RQ2)

The predictive scoring co-weight ε controls the proportion of learning style similarity score in the final collaborative predictive rating and is a key factor in the proposed algorithm. We vary the predictive scoring co-weights ε in the set of {0, 0.001, 0.005, 0.01, 0.02, 0.05} for the experiments. In addition, layer number l is set to 3, embedding dimension d is set to 64, and compared under different list lengths Top-K. The final experimental results are shown in Fig. 5. We can see that different weights ε settings affect the model differently. When the weight ε is less than 0.02, the evaluation indexes of the proposed algorithm are better than our proposed single graph convolutional network model. When the weight ε is 0.005, the accuracy and recall of the proposed method reach the best value. The results prove that The cooperative graph convolutional network and learning style approach can make our model more reliable and accurate.

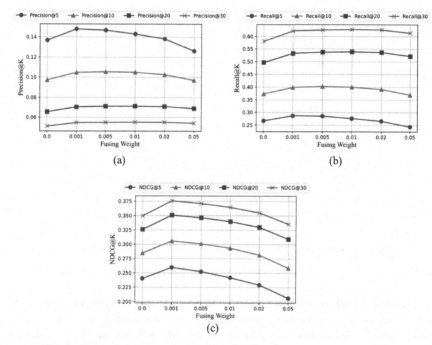

(a)   (b)

(c)

Fig. 5. Comparison of results for different prediction score fusion weights ε

4.5   Parameter Settings (RQ3)

Here, we investigate the sensitivity of different parameters and report the results of CGCNLS under each of them. As shown in Fig. 6 and Fig. 7.

Experiments of Different GCN Embedding Dimension d. When training a predictive scoring model for graph convolutional network, using different embedding dimension d produces different results. We vary the embedding dimension d in the set of {16,

32, 64}, in addition, the layer number l is set to 3, and the prediction scoring co-weight
ε is set to 0.0, and conduct experiments at different recommendation list lengths Top-K.
The final experimental results are shown in Fig. 6. We can see that the model has better
evaluation indexes when d is 64, the overall performance of the model is stable when
changing the embedding dimension, and the model performance gradually increases
with dimensionality.

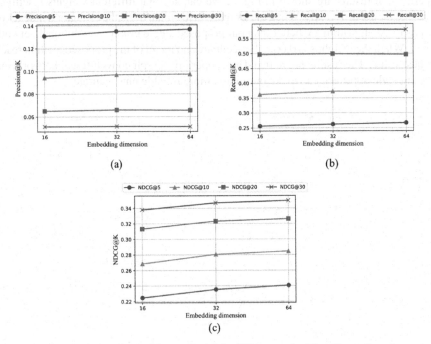

Fig. 6. Comparison of the results of the different embedding dimensions d

Experiments of Different GCN Layers *l.* Meanwhile, the higher-order information
contained in the final embedding representation of the learner (course) obtained for
different Graph convolutional network layers (GCNL) is different. We vary the layer
number l in the set of {1,2,3}. In addition, the embedding dimension d is set to 64,
the prediction scoring co-weight ε is set to 0.0, and the experiments are conducted at
different recommendation list lengths Top-K. The final experimental results are shown
in Fig. 7. We can see that different layers of the graph convolutional network have a
large impact on the model performance, and the model performs best when l = 3.

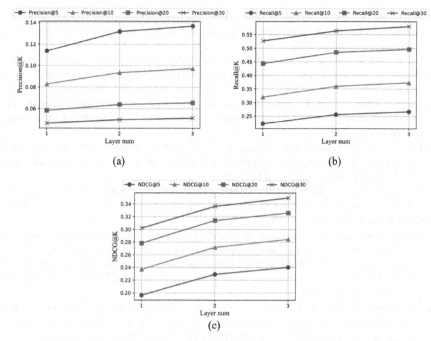

Fig. 7. Comparison of the results of the different number of GCN layers l

5 Conclusion

In this paper we propose a collaborative graph convolutional network and learning style course recommendation model (CGCNLS), which uses a graph convolutional network to learn embedding information that can effectively represent the relevance differences between learners and courses. We also introduce a collaborative weighted to synergize course prediction score and learning styles similarity score. The accuracy of the recommendations is improved while considering the learning styles of the learners. We conducted extensive comparative and ablation experiments on the public dataset, and the experimental results show that the performance of CGCNLS is advanced compared to the baseline methods.

References

1. Khanal, S.S., Prasad, P.W.C., Alsadoon, A., Maag, A.: A systematic review: machine learning based recommendation systems for e-learning. Educ. Inf. Technol. **25**(4), 2635–2664 (2019). https://doi.org/10.1007/s10639-019-10063-9
2. Guruge, D.B., Kadel, R., Halder, S.J.: The state of the art in methodologies of course recommender systems—a review of recent research. Data **6**(2), 18 (2021)
3. Khalid, A., Lundqvist, K., Yates, A.: A literature review of implemented recommendation techniques used in massive open online courses. Expert Syst. Appl. **187**, 115926 (2022)
4. Qiu, F., Zhu, L., Zhang, G., et al.: E-learning performance prediction: mining the feature space of effective learning behavior. Entropy **24**(5), 722 (2022)

5. Wu, L., He, X., Wang, X., et al.: A survey on accuracy-oriented neural recommendation: from collaborative filtering to information-rich recommendation. IEEE Transactions on Knowledge and Data Engineering (2022)
6. Wu, L., He, X., Wang, X., et al.: A survey on neural recommendation: from collaborative filtering to content and context enriched recommendation (2021). arXiv preprint arXiv:2104.13030
7. Gao, C., Wang, X., He, X., et al.: Graph neural networks for recommender system. In: Proceedings of the Fifteenth ACM International Conference on Web Search and Data Mining, pp. 1623–1625 (2022)
8. Piao, G.: Recommending knowledge concepts on MOOC platforms with meta-path-based representation learning. In: Proceedings of The 14th International Conference on Educational Data Mining (EDM21), pp. 487–494 (2021)
9. Sheng, D., Yuan, J., Xie, Q., et al.: ACMF: an attention collaborative extended matrix factorization based model for MOOC course service via a heterogeneous view. Futur. Gener. Comput. Syst. **126**, 211–224 (2022)
10. Truong, H.M.: Integrating learning styles and adaptive e-learning system: current developments, problems and opportunities. Comput. Hum. Behav. **55**, 1185–1193 (2016)
11. Gope, J., Jain, S.K.: A learning styles based recommender system prototype for edX courses. In: 2017 International Conference on Smart Technologies for Smart Nation (SmartTechCon), pp. 414–419. IEEE (2017)
12. Laksitowening, K.A., Yanuarifiani, A.P., Wibowo, Y.F.A.: Enhancing e-learning system to support learning style based personalization. In: 2016 2nd International Conference on Science in Information Technology (ICSITech), pp. 329–333. IEEE (2016)
13. Hajri, H., Bourda, Y., Popineau, F.: Personalized recommendation of open educational resources in MOOCs. In: McLaren, B.M., Reilly, R., Zvacek, S., Uhomoibhi, J. (eds.) CSEDU 2018. CCIS, vol. 1022, pp. 166–190. Springer, Cham (2019). https://doi.org/10.1007/978-3-030-21151-6_9
14. Sanjabi, T., Montazer, G.A.: Personalization of E-learning environment using the kolb's learning style model. In: 2020 6th International Conference on Web Research (ICWR), pp. 89–92. IEEE (2020)
15. Yan, L., Yin, C., Chen, H., Rong, W., Xiong, Z., David, B.: Learning resource recommendation in e-learning systems based on online learning style. In: Qiu, H., Zhang, C., Fei, Z., Qiu, M., Kung, S.-Y. (eds.) KSEM 2021. LNCS (LNAI), vol. 12817, pp. 373–385. Springer, Cham (2021). https://doi.org/10.1007/978-3-030-82153-1_31
16. Sensuse, D.I., Hasani, L.M., Bagustari, B.: Personalization strategies based on Felder-Silverman learning styles and its impact on learning: a literature review. In: 2020 3rd International Conference on Computer and Informatics Engineering (IC2IE), pp. 293–298. IEEE (2020)
17. Kipf, T.N., Welling, M.: Semi-supervised classification with graph convolutional networks (2016). arXiv preprint arXiv:1609.02907
18. Hamilton, W., Ying, Z., Leskovec, J.: Inductive representation learning on large graphs. In: Proceedings of the 31st International Conference on Neural Information Processing Systems, pp. 1025–1035 (2017)
19. Wang, X., He, X., Wang, M., et al.: Neural graph collaborative filtering. In: Proceedings of the 42nd International ACM SIGIR Conference on Research and Development in Information Retrieval, pp. 165–174 (2019)
20. Ying, R., He, R., Chen, K., et al.: Graph convolutional neural networks for web-scale recommender systems. In: Proceedings of the 24th ACM SIGKDD International Conference on Knowledge Discovery & Data Mining, pp. 974–983 (2018)

21. Xu, G., Jia, G., Shi, L., et al.: Personalized course recommendation system fusing with knowledge graph and collaborative filtering. Computational Intelligence and Neuroscience 2021 (2021)
22. Gong, J., Wang, S., Wang, J., et al.: Attentional graph convolutional networks for knowledge concept recommendation in MOOCs in a heterogeneous view. In: Proceedings of the 43rd International ACM SIGIR Conference on Research and Development in Information Retrieval, pp. 79–88 (2020)
23. Yu, J., Luo, G., Xiao, T., et al.: MOOCCube: a large-scale data repository for NLP applications in MOOCs. In: Proceedings of the 58th Annual Meeting of the Association for Computational Linguistics, pp. 3135–3142 (2020)
24. He, X., Liao, L., Zhang, H., et al.: Neural collaborative filtering. In: Proceedings of the 26th International Conference on World Wide Web, pp. 173–182 (2017)
25. Kabbur, S., Ning, X., Karypis, G.: Fism: factored item similarity models for top-n recommender systems. In: Proceedings of the 19th ACM SIGKDD international conference on Knowledge discovery and data mining, pp. 659–667 (2013)
26. He, X., He, Z., Song, J., et al.: Nais: neural attentive item similarity model for recommendation. IEEE Trans. Knowl. Data Eng. 30(12), 2354–2366 (2018)

Exploring the Impact of Structural Holes on the Value Creation in Service Ecosystems

Lu Zhang, Shizhan Chen, Xiao Xue, Hongyue Wu[✉], Guodong Fan,
Chao Wang, and Zhiyong Feng

Department of Intelligence and Computing, Tianjin University,
Tianjin 300350, China
{zlu_4435,shizhan,jzxuexiao,hongyue.wu,guodongfan,
taracw,zyfeng}@tju.edu.cn

Abstract. A service ecosystem (SE) is essentially a value creation system, and changes in the organizational structure of services affect the value change of SE. No research work has been found on the impact of structural holes (SH) on the value creation of SE. Existing works on the value creation of SE have been carried out from the perspective of service ecology, ignoring the consideration of individual services. Therefore, we firstly construct a SE value creation model. Secondly, we propose an analysis method to explore the impact of SH on SE value creation from the level of both individual service and SE. In addition, we construct a computational experiment for experimental comparison and analysis, which reveals how changes in SH affect the value creation of SE. The findings of this paper can be used to induce the evolution of SE and promote its value maximization.

Keywords: Service ecosystem · Structural holes · Value creation · Analysis method · Computational experiment

1 Introduction

The constant development of big data, the Internet of Things, and other technologies have brought in new prospects for traditional services. Service is gradually penetrating various industries, e.g., education, healthcare, and transportation. The number and variety of services available are increasing. Complex correlations are developed between different services in the process of long-term competition and collaboration, and a service ecosystem (SE) is gradually formed to satisfy diversified, dynamic, and individualized user demands.

SE is essentially a value creation system, and value is created by the process of service interaction between many participants (e.g., users, and service providers) [20]. The socio-economic participants in SE are users and service providers [14]. If the services provided by providers can satisfy the demands

© ICST Institute for Computer Sciences, Social Informatics and Telecommunications Engineering 2022
Published by Springer Nature Switzerland AG 2022. All Rights Reserved
H. Gao et al. (Eds.): CollaborateCom 2022, LNICST 460, pp. 378–395, 2022.
https://doi.org/10.1007/978-3-031-24383-7_21

proposed by users, the services will obtain value. In summary, around diverse user demands, different participants in SE integrate resources and create value based on the service network [4,19], which can achieve mutual integration and interconnection between value chains.

It is important to study the value creation of SE for the sustainable development of SE. The value creation of SE is the result of the joint action of many participants (e.g., users, services, and service providers), and the factors affecting the value creation of SE are also multi-level and multi-perspective. At present, there have been some studies on the factors influencing the value creation of SE. Maglio et al. [15] argue that a service system is a configuration of people, technologies, and other resources that interact with others. Thus, people, technologies, and resources influence value creation in a SE. Akaka et al. [2] argue that the embeddedness of social networks and the multiplicity of institutions within a SE influence the complexity of context, and that value (co-)creation interacts with and influences the environment at different levels. However, current research on the factors influencing value creation in SE is still coarse-grained, and there are many limitations in terms of the scope of the research objects and how each factor influences value creation in SE.

In SE, the competitive advantage of the service is mostly based on its quality and the complementary resources brought by cooperation with other services. Therefore, the value of services is closely related to the competitive and cooperative relationships among services, and changes in the organizational structure of services affect the value evolution of SE. Structural holes (SH) is an important characteristic that can reflect the organizational relationship between services. In 1992, Burt [3] first proposed the concept of SH, which is "SH refers to a non-repetitive relationship between two persons", i.e., SH is a non-redundant connection between two actors. From the perspective of the network, SH is a "cave"-like structure, where a node occupying the location of SH can connect two nodes or communities that are not directly connected. SH plays an important role in identifying the important nodes in complex networks [5,11] and controlling the public opinion dissemination in social networks [7,12].

In response to the current problems in the study of factors influencing the value creation of SE, we focus on exploring the impact of the SH on the value creation of SE and propose a value creation model of SE. Then, the impact analysis method is studied from two levels: individual service and SE. Finally, the paper constructs a computational experimental system for experimental validation. The main contributions of this paper are as follows:

1. A value creation model of SE is constructed, which helps us better understand the process of SE value creation.
2. We propose an impact analysis method, and research it from two levels of individual services and SE, which effectively extends the traditional research.
3. We design and construct a computational experiment system, which effectively reveals how the changes of SH affect the value creation of SE through experimental comparison and analysis.

The rest of the paper is organized as follows. Section 2 presents the value creation model of the SE. Section 3 proposes the methodology of this paper. Section 4 designs the computational experiment system and analyzes the experimental results. Section 5 introduces the related works, and Sect. 6 concludes the paper.

2   Value Creation Model of SE

In *Competitive Advantage*, Porter believed that value was the amount customers are willing to pay for what a company provides [17]. In this paper, value in a SE is the revenue generated during the complex and dynamic interaction between developers, providers, users, and many other actors, i.e., the revenue generated when developers provide services to users that satisfy their demands.

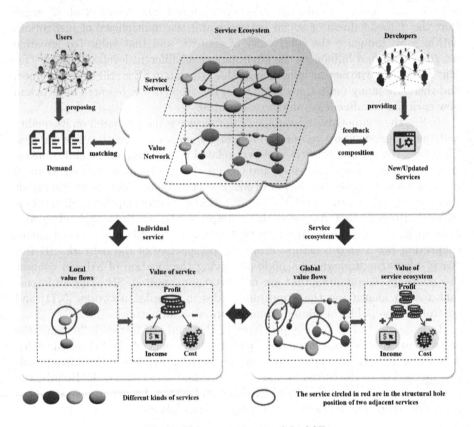

Fig. 1. Value creation model of SE.

The value creation process of the SE is shown in Fig. 1. In the figure, the circles represent service nodes, and the different colors of the circles represent the different types of service nodes. The size of the circle represents the capability and attributes of the service node, and the larger the size of the service node, the stronger the service capability. The services framed by the red circles occupy the position of the SH formed between neighboring nodes. Only some of the services occupying the SH positions are exemplified in the figure, and not all the services occupying the SH positions are labeled. The SE mainly includes three types of roles: users, developers, and services. To match the diverse and personalized demands of users, developers continuously improve or provide new services. At the same time, the competitive and collaborative relationships between services continue to evolve. In this dynamic process, value is also generated and flows, forming a value network. A value network is a topological mapping of a service network. The nodes in the value network are the service nodes, and the edges in the value network represent the value flow and transfer relationship between the service nodes.

In the dynamic process of value creation, the value of service nodes changes dynamically in real-time, but not every node can create value in real-time. Therefore, the edges of the value network are not the same as those in the service network, and they will change with the value flow. Changes in services (e.g., usage frequency decreases, service function changes) can affect the value creation of service nodes or even the whole SE.

We focus on the impact of SH on the value creation of the SE. The value creation of individual services is influenced by the organizational relationship between individual services and their neighbors. SE value is also subject to the constraints of its structure. Therefore, the influence of SH on SE value creation is researched at the levels of both individual services and SE.

3   Methodology

3.1   Research Questions

To explore the impact of SH on value creation in SE, we propose the following two research questions.

RQ1: How does the SH of an individual service affect its value creation?
RQ2: How does the SH of a SE affect its value creation?

3.2   Impact Analysis Method

To investigate the impact of SH on the value creation of SE, we propose an impact analysis method. It can be studied from two levels: the individual service level and the SE level. The method is shown in Fig. 2.

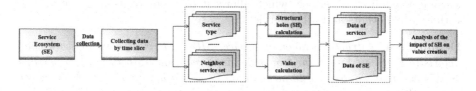

Fig. 2. Impact analysis method.

The impact analysis method is carried out in four main steps. Firstly, the rules and strategies of the computational experimental environment are designed to construct a simulated SE that matches the characteristics of the real SE. The construction method is described in the next section. Secondly, the data of SE at different times are collected separately according to the time slice. The data mainly includes the number of services in SE, the set of neighboring nodes, the value of each service node, etc. Thirdly, SH and values of service nodes and SE are calculated separately. The calculation method is described in the next subsection. Finally, the impact of SH on value creation in SE is analyzed and answered by comparing changes in SH and value at the individual service level and SE level through statistical and visual methods of data.

3.3   Concepts and Definitions

We provide a formal description of the service network and value network, and then define the relevant concepts and computational methods for individual services and SE, respectively.

Definition 1. *(Service network, SN). SN is a complex network structure consisting of competing and collaborative relationships between services. It can be represented by the two-tuple SN(S, R). $S = \{S_1, S_2, \cdots, S_n\}$ represents the service set, which is a representation of the individual vertices in SN. and $R = \{< S_i, S_j > | S_i, S_j \in S\}$ represents edge set (i.e., coupling relationship between services), which represents the edge in SN.*

Definition 2. *(Value network, VN). VN is a mapping of value flow relationships between SN, with services as its nodes and the value flows between services represent its edges. Therefore, VN can be represented by the two-tuple VN(S, E). $S = \{S_1, S_2, \cdots, S_n\}$ represents the vertex set of VN. $E = \{< S_i, S_j > | S_i, S_j \in S\}$ represents the edge set of VN.*

Definition 3. *(Service, s). The service is expressed as follows.*

$$s_i = <R, S_t, E_t, V_t, Y_t> \tag{1}$$

R is the stable capability property of individual service, which remains unchanged for a relatively long time; S_t is the dynamic capability property of individual service, which will change with time; E_t is the perception capability of individual service; V_t is the response capability of individual service; Y_t is the learning capability of service, which allows it to promote itself by interacting with external events and other services.

Definition 4. *(Structural holes of service, SHS): SH is a social network characteristic that can reflect the non-redundant relationship between two persons. In this paper, it will be used to measure the organizational structure between services. SHS is the degree of SH occupied by the individual service. The closeness of the network environment in which an individual node is located can reflect its SHS to a certain extent. The closer the relationship between the node and the neighbor nodes, the fewer SH positions the individual service may occupy, i.e., the lower SHS of the individual service. The metric of SHS is constructed for* *reference to the calculation of clustering coefficients [13], while the formulae are divided into three categories based on the number of neighboring nodes and the degree of closure of nodes: 1) If there are two or more neighboring nodes of the service node and the service node is not completely closed, SHS is calculated as shown in Formula 2. 2) If the service node is completely closed, SHS is calculated as shown in Formula 4. 3) When the service node is independent and has no mutual relationship with other nodes or exists only with one service node, its SHS takes the value of 0.1. 0.05 and 0.1 was set empirically, and we also verified it by other structural hole calculation methods.*

$$SHS_{s_i} = \frac{|Neb\,(s_i)|}{\alpha} \times \left(1 - \frac{2E_i}{|Neb\,(s_i)|\,(|\text{Neb}\,(s_i)| - 1)}\right) \tag{2}$$

Simplified as:

$$SHS_{s_i} = \frac{\text{Neb}\,(s_i)\,|\,(|\text{Neb}\,(s_i)| - 1) - 2E_i}{\alpha\,(|\text{Neb}\,(s_i)| - 1)} \tag{3}$$

$$SHS_{s_i} = \frac{|Neb\,(s_i)|}{\alpha} \times 0.05 \tag{4}$$

$Neb(s_i)$ represents the neighbor service set, E_i represents the number of interconnection edges between neighboring nodes of S_i. α is the adjustment parameter, and it exists to control the value of SHS of individual services between 0 and 1. The value of α depends on the number of services in the SN, and its value is different for different SN.

Definition 5. *(Value of service, VS): VS is the value created by the individual service over a while minus its cost of value creating. The value created by the individual service includes the value created by the service and the value created by the interaction between the service and its neighbor services. The cost of individual service includes both the cost of the service itself and the cost of the service spent on interacting with neighboring services. Therefore, the calculation formula of VS is as follows.*

$$VS_i = g_i - c_i \tag{5}$$

$$g_i = vsel_i + vcol_i \tag{6}$$

$$c_i = csel_i + \sum_{s_j \in Neb(s_i)} cs_{ij} \tag{7}$$

g_i is the value created by the individual service, c_i is the cost of the individual service, $vsel_i$ is the value created by the individual service itself, $vcol_i$ is the value created by the interaction between the service and the neighbor services, $csel_i$ is the cost of the individual service itself, cs_{ij} is the cost of maintaining the relationship between the service and its neighbors.

Definition 6. *(SH of SE, SHSE): SHSE is the mean value of SHS in SE, so the calculation formula for SHSE is as follows:*

$$SHSE = \frac{\sum_{i=1}^{N} SHS_{s_i}}{N} \qquad (8)$$

N is the number of services in SE.

Definition 7. *(Value of SE, VSE): We ignore some external factors that affect the operation of SE, and only consider the interaction between services. Therefore, VSE is the sum of VS in SE.*

$$VSE = \sum_{i=1}^{N} VS_i \qquad (9)$$

4   Experimental Design and Analysis

4.1   Construction of Computational Experiment

There are many inconveniences in using a real environment for experimental validation. On the one hand, the research content of this paper involves specific service values. Due to the security and confidentiality demands of data, real data are not available in this paper. On the other hand, the value creation of services in the real environment may be disturbed by various internal and external factors, e.g., QoS and the market environment. This prevents us from intuitively discovering the impact of SH on service value creation, and the economic and time costs are too large. Computational experiments are one of the mainstream methods to analyze complex systems. It can be used to simulate the evolution process of complex systems under different rules. Therefore, to verify the impact of SH on value creation in SE, we use computational experimental [16,21] to simulate the dynamic evolution of services and user demands in SE. At the same time, we achieve a comparative analysis through the design of different parameters and evolutionary strategies.

The operation and evolution of SE can be seen as the process of the service continuously satisfying the demand of users. Therefore, as shown in Fig. 3, the computational experiment system is designed from both the service-side and the demand-side, including two types of agents: service and demand. The computational experiment system operates and evolves according to both a natural evolution and controlled evolution, respectively. The difference between natural and controlled evolution is how newly joined service nodes in the SE select cooperative nodes. During natural evolution, the newly joined nodes freely choose the cooperating nodes. During controlled evolution, newly joined nodes choose to cooperate with nodes that have greater connectivity. We believe that these two types of collaboration are already representative of what is possible in most SEs. The properties and behavior rules of the service-side and demand-side agents are designed based on the characteristics of the services and user requirements in real SEs, e.g. the demise of services and the increase in demand. The computational experiments are designed to satisfy the characteristics of SE, e.g., complexity and autonomy.

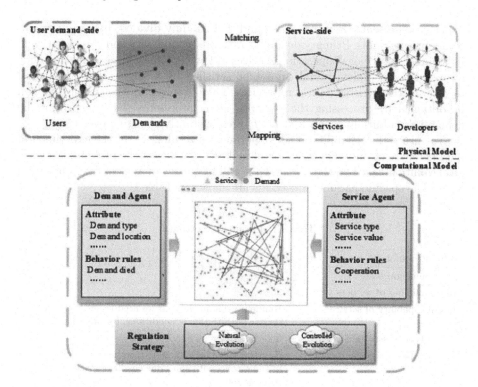

Fig. 3. Design of computational experiment system.

In the computational experiment system, the service-side agent represents the service node, which has the characteristics of autonomy and self-evolution. All agents can perceive the surrounding demands, and if they cannot satisfy the demands, they will seek cooperation from neighboring agents. The benefit distribution is carried out according to the capacity ratio of the service agent. The characteristics of the service agent are represented as shown in Formula 10.

$$SA = <Styp, Scap_t, Sval_t, Ssh_t> \tag{10}$$

$Styp$ represents the type of service, and different types of services have different functions. $Scap_t$ represents the capability of service. $Sval_t$ represents VS. Ssh_t represents SHS. In addition, $Scap_t$, $Sval_t$, Ssh_t are constantly changing with time.

In the computational experiment system, the demand-side agent represents user demands, and user demands are constantly changing. In the experiment, the complexity of demands is different. When the complexity of the demand is large, a single service cannot satisfy the demand. The cooperation of neighboring nodes needs to be sought for a win-win situation.

$$DA = <Dtyp, Dval_t, Dlif_t> \tag{11}$$

Dtyp represents the type of demand. It is mainly divided into primary and secondary demands. Primary demands are of low complexity and can be satisfied by a single service or cooperation services of low capability. Secondary demands are of higher complexity and cannot be satisfied by a single service and need to rely on the synergy between services. $Dval_t$ represents the profit that can be obtained by processing the demand. $Dlif_t$ represents the life cycle of the demand. In addition, $Dval_t$ and $Dlif_t$ are constantly changing over time.

To ensure the reliability of the experimental results, we set the experimental parameters regarding the operation of real SE, e.g., we set the probability of service evolution based on the update time and frequency of apps in the application store. The specific parameter settings are shown in Table 1.

Table 1. Parameter setting

System variable	Experiment setting
Environmental scale	$50 * 50$
Initial number of services	20
Initial capability of service	Random value in [1, 4]. If we need to set the initial service with the same conditions, its capability is 3
Initial type of service	6
Initial value of service	Random value in [130, 180]. If we need to set the initial service with the same conditions, its initial value is 150
Moving cost	$Y = k * x$ (x is the moving distance, $x > 0$), $k = 1.3$
Operation cost	Random value in [2, 6]
Cooperation cost	Random value in [3, 8]
Service evolution probability	Random value in [1.4%, 1.7%]
Service evolution capability	Random value in [0, 1]
Service types increase cycle	90 tick
Initial number of demands	200, and the ratio of the primary demand to the secondary demand is 4:6
Demand value	Primary demand: random value in [20, 70), Secondary demand: random value in [70, 110]
The growth trend of demand value	N(60,100)

4.2 Experimental Design

Scenario Design. We simulated four experimental scenarios to answer RQ1 and RQ2 using a computational experimental system with the configurations shown in Table 2.

To verify the impact of the SH of the individual service on value creation, we do two types of comparison experiments: 1) In Scenario 1 and Scenario 2, we compare the changes of SHS and VS of any two initial services at different ticks,

Table 2. Scenario design

Scenario	Environment configuration
Scenario 1	Natural evolution: All properties of the initial services are identical
Scenario 2	Controlled evolution: All properties of the initial services are identical
Scenario 3	Natural evolution: All properties of the initial service are set randomly
Scenario 4	Controlled evolution: All properties of the initial service are set randomly

respectively. 2) In Scenario 3 and Scenario 4, we compare the changes of SHS and average VS at different ticks, respectively.

To verify the impact of the SH of SE on value creation, we compare the changes of SHSE and VSE under Scenario 3 and Scenario 4 with different ticks, respectively.

Experimental Data. On the one hand, we obtain the data of all the initial services in Scenario1 and Scenario 2 from tick 1 to tick 320. On the other hand, based on the above scenarios and experimental design, we obtain two runs data of Scenario 3 and Scenario 4, and 4 different ticks are selected for each run: 80, 160, 240, and 320. The data for each scenario were obtained twice to reduce the effect of accidental factors. The specific data descriptions are shown in Table 3.

Table 3. Data description

Dataset	Descriptions
Data 1	This dataset contains the SH and VS of all initial nodes under all ticks during the Scenario 1 run
Data 2	This dataset contains the SH and VS of all initial nodes under all ticks during the Scenario 2 run
Data 3-1	This dataset contains the SH and VS of all nodes in
Data 3-2	the Scenario 3 run under 4 different ticks
Data 4-1	This dataset contains the SH and VS of all nodes in
Data 4-2	the Scenario 4 run under 4 different ticks

4.3   Analysis on Individual Services Level (RQ1)

The data of two initial service nodes are randomly selected from Data 1 and Data 2, respectively. Comparing the relationship between SHS and VS with the same initial conditions in the same scenario, the results are shown in Fig. 4. VS is much larger than SHS, and it is reduced in equal proportion to facilitate the comparison of the two indicators in the same graph. According to VS of different ticks and the graph display under different reduction ratios, the reduction ratio of VS is finally set to 500.

From Fig. 4, it can be seen that: 1) In both Scenario 1 and Scenario 2, the comparison between individual services yields that the larger the SHS, the higher its corresponding VS. 2) In different scenarios, for any service, when its SHS grows, the VS also grows. 3) In both Fig. 4(a) and Fig. 4(b), it can be found that the VS grows faster when the SHS is between 0.3 and 0.5. 4) In both Fig. 4(a) and Fig. 4(b), there is a phenomenon that the VS sometimes grows when the SHS does not change. This is because the VS is not influenced only by SH. The occasional growth may be influenced by the environment in which it is located, functional attributes, and other factors.

Compared with the behavior of individuals, the average behavior of similar nodes can more objectively reflect the characteristics of this class of nodes. So, we use the average value to represent the VS of a group of nodes with the same SHS. Based on Data3-1, Data 3-2, Data 4-1, and Data 4-2, we calculate the average VS corresponding to SHS at different ticks, and the obtained results of Data3-1 and Data3-2 show the same trend, as do Data4-1 and Data4-2, so only one set of results is shown in this paper (See Fig. 5). When SHS is equal to 0.1, SHS and its corresponding VS are represented by darker colored bars. When SHS is less than or greater than 0.1, SHS and its corresponding VS are represented by slightly lighter colored bars. Observing Fig. 5, we can see that: 1) When SHS is less than 0.1, VS gradually decreases as SHS increases. 2) When SHS is greater than 0.1, VS tends to increase and then decrease as SHS increases. 3) When SHS is greater than or equal to 0.7, VS increases abruptly as SHS increases. 4) When SHS is equal to 0.1, the VS increases compared to those nodes with SHS less than 0.1. This is because when the service node has many neighboring nodes but is completely closed, too much association with other services will increase the cost of relationship maintenance, and it will affect the efficiency of value creation.

Integrating the above experiments and the actual SE operation and evolution process, we can conclude as follows: 1) when the individual service is completely closed (i.e., the individual service does not occupy SH), the value created by it gradually decreases as the number of its neighboring nodes increases. 2) When the individual service occupies SH, it has a better advantage in creating value when its SHS is between 0.3 and 0.5. 3) When SHS is greater than or equal to 0.7 (i.e., the individual service has an absolute positional advantage), the individual service is also able to create value better. 4) A service node with only a single neighbor has a higher ability to create value than a service with many neighbor nodes but closed.

4.4   Analysis on SE Level (RQ2)

Based on Data3-1, Data 3-2, Data 4-1, and Data 4-2, we calculate SHSE and VSE for different ticks under different scenarios. Different SEs in our computational experiments have the same service growth trend, and they have the same number

Original Service_Data1

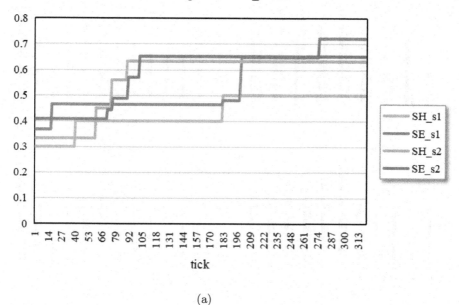

(a)

Original Service_Data2

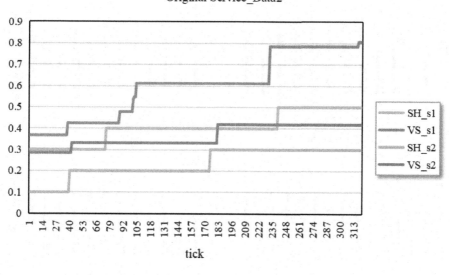

(b)

Fig. 4. The comparison of SHS and VS.

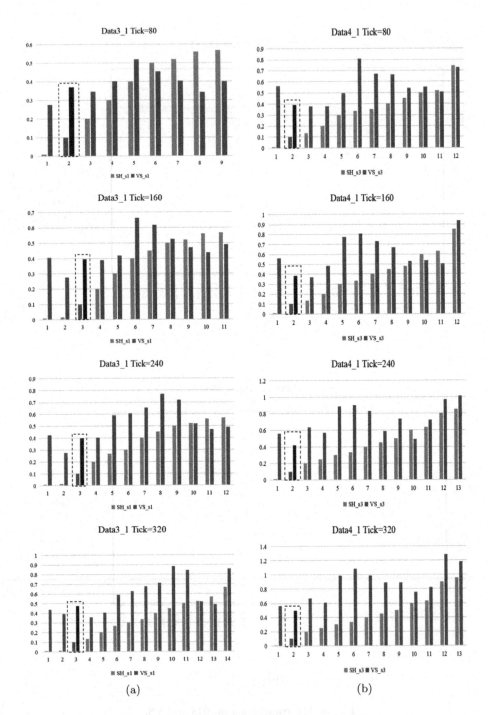

Fig. 5. The comparison of SHS and average VS.

of services under the same tick. The SHSE and VSE of the four datasets with different ticks were compared separately, and the results are shown in Fig. 6. VSE is also much larger than SHSE, so the reduction ratio of VSE is finally set to 20000.

From Fig. 6, it can be seen that: 1) The SHSE is consistently between 0.15 and 0.25 under five different ticks. It is not possible for all services in a SE to have a high SHS, so a low SHSE is a result of averaging the SHS. In real SEs, SHSE will not take high values either. 2) The comparison between SHSE and VSE under five different ticks all show the same phenomenon, i.e., the larger the SHSE, the greater its VSE.

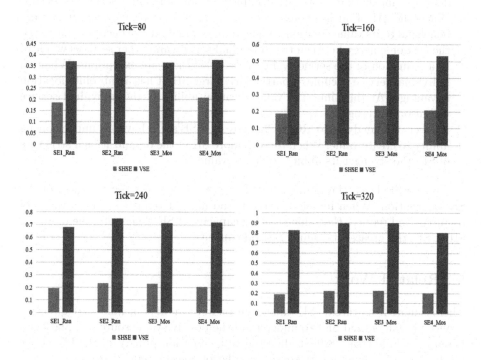

Fig. 6. The comparison of SHSE and VSE.

Therefore, we can get the conclusions as follows. Changes in the SH of a SE affect its ability to create value. The more SH exists in the organizational structure of a SE, the greater the ability of SE to create value.

4.5   Answers and Analysis to the Research Questions

Based on the process of value creation in SE and the above experimental analysis, it is possible to answer the 2 questions raised above.

1) Answer and analysis to RQ1. Changes in the SH of an individual service affect its ability to create value. When the individual service is completely closed, the value created by it decreases and then increases as its number of neighboring nodes increases. When the individual service occupies the SH, its value creation ability increases and then decreases with the enhancement of the SH. In addition, when the SH of the individual service has an absolute advantage, it is also able to create value better.

   From the level of individual services, the service that occupies the SH position has more competitive advantages compared with other services. Therefore, the value of services is higher when they have SH advantages. However, this does not mean that more SH occupied by an individual service is better. When the SH of an individual service is at an appropriate level, it is more beneficial to its value creation. When an individual service occupies many SH, the cost of synergy between the individual service and other services will lead to a reduction in the service value. Of course, there are exceptions. When an individual service occupies a particularly large SH, it has an absolute location advantage. At this time, the value creation ability of the individual service will also be strong.

2) Answer and analysis to RQ2. Changes in a SE's SH have an impact on its ability to create value. When there is more SH in the organizational structure of SE, the stronger its ability to create value.

   From a SE level, the number of SH in a SE represents the closeness of the SE aggregation. When its aggregation is too high, it tends to cause a waste of resources and reduces the value-creating capacity of SE. Therefore, the more the SH of SE, the greater its value creation capacity.

5   Related Work

There is more literature on SE value creation in terms of stakeholders (e.g., users, service providers) and SE. To understand the positive value sources of platform-based SE, Haile et al. [8,9] studied the value creation process of the IT service platform ecosystem and software service platform ecosystem, respectively. In the IT service platform ecosystem, application service users, service developers, and service platform providers are the main market players. In the software service platform ecosystem, the value creation process mainly involves three types of stakeholders: application users, service developers, and platform providers, and the parameters affecting value are divided into four categories: service type, QoS, cost, and user base. Zahid et al. [18] analyzed the interrelationships among stakeholders in the cybersecurity information sharing ecosystem and determined the value parameters. Their work better coordinates the value of stakeholders (i.e., utility and profit) and assists business managers in making decisions related to business strategies.

There is only small literature that considers how it affects the value creation of SE in terms of other factors. Akaka et al. [1] used structural modeling techniques to analyze the role of technology in service systems and how it interacts with human practices and institutions. They argued that technology is a resource that can act on other resources to create value and is a key resource for value co-creation, service innovation, and system re-engineering. Selam et al. [6] constructed a value creation model for an IT service platform, and analyzed the impact of the degree of openness (i.e., interoperability, portability, and availability) of cloud computing platforms on the value creation of IT service platforms.

There is also little literature on the analysis of SE impact factors from different levels. Haile et al. [10] used an economic perspective to study the value creation of providers and users at different levels of interoperability. Based on this, platform providers can not only understand how investments in interoperability and portability affect costs, but also design new strategies to optimize their investments.

In summary, the research on the influencing factors of SE value creation has made certain achievements, which provides a good reference for SE value co-creation research. However, there are two deficiencies in this research work at present. On the one hand, in terms of the research scope, most of the current studies have been conducted from the perspective of SE, ignoring the influence of individual behaviors and lacking consideration of how each factor affects the value creation of SE. On the other hand, in terms of research objects, most of the current studies promote value co-creation in SE by studying the value creation mechanism among different stakeholders. In this paper, we considered how to promote the value maximization of SE from the aspect of the organizational structure of services. There is no relevant literature that studies the impact of SH on value creation in SE.

6   Conclusion

In this paper, we studied the impact of SH on the value creation of SE, which promotes the maximization of SE value. By constructing a SE value creation model, we analyzed the dynamic process of SE value creation. Then, we proposed an impact analysis method and studied it from two levels: individual service and SE. Finally, we designed a computational experimental environment based on the Repast platform and concluded how the SH of individual service and SE affect their value creation through experimental comparison and analysis. The above conclusions obtained in this paper can guide the development and evolution of SE.

The experimental data in this paper were obtained from a simulated environment, but the simulated environment was designed based on the operation of real SEs, and the data obtained from the simulated environment were random and multi-sampled. Therefore, the research results in this paper are credible. In the future, we will consider more about how to induce and intervene in the value creation process of SE through the indicator of SH.

Acknowledgment. This work is supported by the National Natural Science Key Foundation of China grant No. 61832014 and No. 62032016, National Natural Science Foundation of China grant No. 62102281, and the Natural Science Foundation of Tianjin City grant No. 19JCQNJC00200.

References

1. Akaka, M.A., Vargo, S.L.: Technology as an operant resource in service (eco) systems. IseB **12**(3), 367–384 (2014)
2. Akaka, M.A., Vargo, S.L., Lusch, R.F.: The complexity of context: a service ecosystems approach for international marketing. J. Int. Mark. **21**(4), 1–20 (2013)
3. Burt, R.S.: Structural Holes: The Social Structure of Competition. Harvard University Press, Cambridge (1992)
4. Chen, S.Z., Feng, Z.Y., Wang, H.: Service relations and its application in services-oriented computing. Jisuanji Xuebao (Chin. J. Comput.) **33**(11), 2068–2083 (2010)
5. Feng, J., Shi, D., Luo, X.: An identification method for important nodes based on k-shell and structural hole. J. Complex Netw. **6**(3), 342–352 (2018)
6. Gebregiorgis, S.A., Altmann, J.: It service platforms: their value creation model and the impact of their level of openness on their adoption. Procedia Comput. Sci. **68**, 173–187 (2015)
7. Gong, C., et al.: Structural hole-based approach to control public opinion in a social network. Eng. Appl. Artif. Intell. **93**, 103690 (2020)
8. Haile, N., Altmann, J.: Value creation in IT service platforms through two-sided network effects. In: Vanmechelen, K., Altmann, J., Rana, O.F. (eds.) GECON 2012. LNCS, vol. 7714, pp. 139–153. Springer, Heidelberg (2012). https://doi.org/10.1007/978-3-642-35194-5_11
9. Haile, N., Altmann, J.: Value creation in software service platforms. Futur. Gener. Comput. Syst. **55**, 495–509 (2016)
10. Haile, N., Altmann, J.: Evaluating investments in portability and interoperability between software service platforms. Futur. Gener. Comput. Syst. **78**, 224–241 (2018)
11. Hu, P., Mei, T.: Ranking influential nodes in complex networks with structural holes. Physica A **490**, 624–631 (2018)
12. Huang, W., Wang, Q., Jie, C.: Tracing public opinion propagation and emotional evolution based on public emergencies in social networks. Int. J. Comput. Commun. Control **13**(1), 129–142 (2018)
13. Kartun-Giles, A.P., Bianconi, G.: Beyond the clustering coefficient: a topological analysis of node neighbourhoods in complex networks. Chaos, Solitons Fractals: X **1**, 100004 (2019)
14. Linghu, K.R., Jian, Z.Q., Lei, L.I.: Service ecosystem: origin, core viewpoints and theoretical framework. R&D Manage. **30**(05), 151–162 (2018)
15. Maglio, P.P., Vargo, S.L., Caswell, N., Spohrer, J.: The service system is the basic abstraction of service science. IseB **7**(4), 395–406 (2009)
16. Moiseev, S., Kalinina, N., Shevchenko, L., Poryadina, V.: Management models for complex socioeconomic systems. E3S Web Conf. **244**, 11002 (2021). EDP Sciences
17. Porter, M.E.: Competitive Advantage: Creating and Sustaining Superior Performance: with a New Introduction. FreePress, New York (1985)
18. Rashid, Z., Noor, U., Altmann, J.: Economic model for evaluating the value creation through information sharing within the cybersecurity information sharing ecosystem. Futur. Gener. Comput. Syst. **124**, 436–466 (2021)

19. Vargo, S.L., Lusch, R.F.: From repeat patronage to value co-creation in service ecosystems: a transcending conceptualization of relationship. J. Bus. Mark. Manag. **4**(4), 169–179 (2010)
20. Vargo, S.L., Lusch, R.F.: Institutions and axioms: an extension and update of service-dominant logic. J. Acad. Mark. Sci. **44**(1), 5–23 (2016)
21. Wang, F.Y.: Toward a paradigm shift in social computing: the ACP approach. IEEE Intell. Syst. **22**(5), 65–67 (2007)

Learning Dialogue Policy Efficiently Through Dyna Proximal Policy Optimization

Chenping Huang$^{(\boxtimes)}$ and Bin Cao

College of Computer Science and Technology, Zhejiang University of Technology, Hangzhou, China
{huangchenping,bincao}@zjut.edu.cn

Abstract. Many methods have been proposed to use reinforcement learning to train dialogue policy for task-oriented dialogue systems in recent years. However, the high cost of interacting with users has seriously hindered the development of this field. In order to reduce this interaction cost, the Deep Dyna-Q (DDQ) algorithm and several variants introduce a so-called *world model* to simulate the user's response and then use the generated simulated dialogue data to train the dialogue policy. Nevertheless, these methods suffer from two main issues. The first is limited training efficiency due to the Deep-Q Network used. The second is that low-quality simulation dialogue data generated by the world model may hurt the performance of the dialogue policy. To solve these drawbacks, we propose the Dyna Proximal Policy Optimization (DPPO) algorithm. DPPO combines the Proximal Policy Optimization (PPO) algorithm with the world model and uses a deactivation strategy to decide when to stop using the world model for subsequent training. We have conducted experiments on the task of movie ticket booking. Experiments show that our algorithm combines the advantages of DDQ and PPO, which significantly reduces the interaction cost required during training and has a higher task success rate.

Keywords: Dialogue policy · Reinforcement learning · World model deactivation · PPO

1 Introduction

Human-machine collaboration methods have been deployed in various scenarios. As a common way of Human-machine collaboration, dialogue systems have been used in E-commerce scenarios, where the dialogue system is used to answer simple questions from customers, while the human customer service is responsible for answering questions that are difficult for the dialogue system to handle. An important branch of dialogue systems is task-oriented dialogue systems, which is designed to help users complete specific tasks, such as booking movie tickets or hotels. This type of system is usually implemented in a pipeline manner [2], where

H. Gao et al. (Eds.): CollaborateCom 2022, LNICST 460, pp. 396–414, 2022.
https://doi.org/10.1007/978-3-031-24383-7_22

following four components are involved (as shown in the Fig. 1): (1) Natural Language Understanding (NLU) [4,24], which parses user utterance into intentions and entities; (2) Dialogue State Tracking (DST) [3,9], which manages the conversation history and outputs the current dialogue state; (3) Policy Learning (PL) [32,33], which learns how to choose the next action based on the current dialogue state; (4) Natural Language Generation (NLG) [16,28], which converts the system action into natural language as a response to the user. The work of this paper is to improve the PL component in the task-oriented dialogue system.

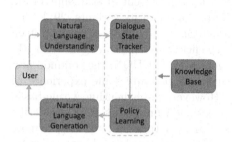

Fig. 1. Pipeline task-oriented dialogue system.

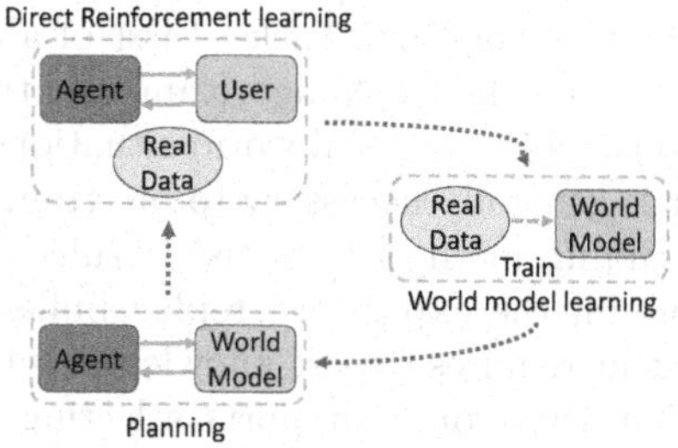

Fig. 2. The process of training the agent by combining a world model.

In recent years, Reinforcement Learning (RL) has been the primary method to optimize the dialogue policy [12,15,23,26,31], where the user and the dialogue system are regarded as the environment and the agent respectively. At the beginning of each conversation, the user performs the first action (makes an utterance) according to their goal, generating the initial state of the environment. After that, for each action (response) of the agent, the environment will give a reward and update the state of the environment. The agent optimizes the dialogue policy according to the reward value to maximize the expected value of the accumulated reward. When using RL to train an agent, it is necessary to let the agent interact with the environment many times. Due to the high labor cost, the cost of directly interacting with the user to train the agent is very high.

Researchers have proposed some methods to reduce the cost of training agents. The most common method is to adopt a user simulator that can simulate user behavior instead of the real user to train the agent, and then let the trained agent interact with the real user for further improvement [5,26,27,31]. However, due to the complexity of real conversations and biases in the design of user simulators, there always exists a discrepancy between real users and simulated users [21].

Another method is to reduce the number of user interactions required to optimize the dialogue policy. The most representative algorithm is Deep Dyna-Q (DDQ) [15], which combines the Dyna-Q framework [22] and the Deep-Q Network (DQN) [13]. After DDQ was proposed, some follow-up works [29,31] extended DDQ and proposed some variants of DDQ. The training process of DDQ is shown in Fig. 2, and it consists of three consecutive stages: (1) *direct reinforcement learning*, the agent interacts with the real user, and the agent is improved through RL; (2) *world model learning*, based on the real conversation data obtained in the previous stage, supervised learning is used to improve the world model to make it behave more like real user; (3) *indirect reinforcement learning*, or referred as *planning*, the agent interacts with the world model instead of the user, and improves the agent through RL. Because DDQ uses the world model to generate a large number of simulated dialogues to train the agent, it significantly reduces the number of interactions between the agent and the user required for training.

Although DDQ reduces the training cost to some extent, it still suffers from the following drawbacks. First of all, DDQ and most of its variants [29,31] are based on the DQN algorithm, and the characteristic of DQN does not lend itself to the following real-world situations: (1) To effectively train an agent with RL, it is generally necessary to pre-train the agent first. For DQN, the common pre-training method is to use a rule-based agent to generate some experience to pre-fill the experience replay buffer [15]. However, implementing a rule-based agent requires expert knowledge, which causes additional costs. (2) Considering that DQN only supports selecting one action at a turn and to contain more slots in the corresponding utterance, the size of the predefined action set for DQN could be very large. Specifically, for n slots, totally $2^n - 1$ actions could be predefined at most, and such a large action space leads to the exponential growth of computational requirements [30]. As shown in Fig. 3, three slots are involved and to support the system to recommend with different slots, the predefined action set for DQN contains all possible slot combinations, i.e., seven actions.

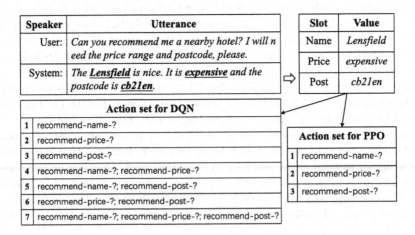

Fig. 3. An example for illustrating action set.

Furthermore, another limitation of DDQ occurs in planning, where the effectiveness of agent training largely depends on the quality of the simulated dialogue from the world model. Specifically, due to the complexity of user behavior, the simulated user experience inevitably has some deviations from the real user experience. Peng et al. [15] pointed out that in the early stage, training the agent with a large amount of low-quality simulated dialogue can improve the performance of the agent. However, in the later stage of training, low-quality simulated experience may hurt the agent's performance.

To address the above drawbacks of DDQ, we propose a new algorithm called Dyna Proximal Policy Optimization (DPPO). First, DPPO draws on the idea of integrating the world model, but the RL algorithm it uses is Proximal Policy Optimization (PPO) [19]. Compared with DQN, (1) PPO can directly use human-human dialogues to pre-train agents through imitation learning [6], without the need to use rule-based agents; (2) PPO supports multiple actions to be selected at a turn through thresholding the probability. So in the example shown in Fig. 3, the predefined action set for PPO only needs to contain three actions, thus avoiding the difficulty of training due to the large action set.

Second, DPPO uses a deactivation strategy to deal with the situation where simulated experience from the world model may harm the agent's performance. A similarity index is used to continuously monitor the similarity between the world model and the user during the training process. If the similarity is lower than a fixed threshold, we stop using the world model, and then the agent only learns by interacting with the user. Through this strategy, the agent can eliminate the harmful effects of simulated dialogue.

To summarize, our contributions are three-fold:

- To learn dialogue policy efficiently, we propose the DPPO algorithm, which can avoid the inherent shortcomings of DQN by integrating the PPO algorithm with a world model.
- We propose a world model deactivation strategy, which can stop the poorly performing world model in time to avoid the harmful influence of the world model on the agent's performance.
- We conduct extensive experiments on a movie-ticket booking dialogue dataset, and the results show that DPPO outperforms DDQ and its variant in terms of the task success rate.

The rest of this paper is organized as follows. Section 2 presents the preliminaries for dialogue system and reinforcement learning. Section 3 introduces our method in detail. Section 4 validates our method through a series of experiments. Section 5 summarizes related work in the field of dialogue systems. Section 6 concludes the content of the paper.

2   Preliminaries

2.1   Some Concepts of Pipeline System

In order to better understand the task-oriented dialogue system, it is necessary to understand some related concepts first.

- **slot**: In a task-oriented dialogue system, there is usually some task-related information. For example, the information involved in the task of booking movie tickets includes the movie ticket name, time, date, etc., while the information involved in the task of booking a hotel includes the hotel name, room number, and price range. Task-oriented dialogue systems usually use slots to store this information. These slots are usually designed in advance by domain experts.
- **knowledge base**: To accomplish user goals, task-oriented systems often require access to a task-related knowledge base. For example, the knowledge base may store information about all candidate movie theaters for a movie ticket booking task, including their names, cities, star ratings, movie titles and start times.
- **user goal**: When implementing a task-oriented dialogue system, it is usually assumed that the user has a goal to achieve, expressed as $G = (C, R)$ [17], where C is a set of constraints and R is a set of requests. Taking movie ticket booking as an example, the constraints specified by the user might be the name and date of the movie, while the requests could be the location of the movie theater and the start time of the movie. Figure 4 is an example of a user goal in a movie reservation scene. It specifies the user's requirements for booking tickets (movie name, number of tickets, movie start time), and the information the user wants to obtain (cinema name).
- **action**: For each user utterance, the natural language understanding model will parse out the corresponding user action, which is usually represented by the triple [intent, slot type, slot value]. For example, for the user's utterance "I want to watch the movie zootopia, can you book a ticket for me?", the user action extracted by the natural language understanding model may be [inform, movie name, zootopia]. System actions are also generally represented using such triples. For example, if the system wants to further ask the user for the movie's start time that the user wants to book, the system action may be [request, starttime, ?]. Then, the natural language generation model generates the utterance "What time would you like to see it?" based on [request, starttime, ?].
- **dialog state**: The dialog state tracking model maintains the current dialog state. When the research focus is on the dialogue policy learning model, in order to simplify the experiment, researchers often use a rule-based dialogue state tracker for dialogue state generation. The dialog state usually includes four parts: (1) the current user action; (2) the system action of the last turn; (3) the slots the user has informed or requested so far; (4) the knowledge base query result. Different system implementations may include some different additional information in the dialog state.

2.2 Reinforcement Learning

In reinforcement learning, two roles are shown in Fig. 5, namely the environment and the agent. The environment is the world in which the agent lives. At each

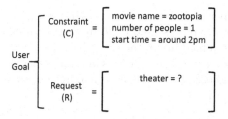

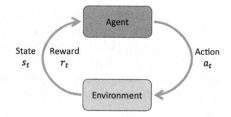

Fig. 4. An example of user goal.

Fig. 5. The agent-environment interaction in a Markov decision process.

time step t, the agent will observe the current state of the environment s_t and then make an action a_t. For a_t, the environment gives a reward r_t indicating whether a_t is good or bad. Moreover, based on a_t, the state of the environment changes, causing the agent to observe a new state s_{t+1} at the next time step. The interaction between the environment and the agent will form a sequence of states, actions, and rewards, which is called a trajectory:

$$\tau = (s_1, a_1, r_1, s_2, a_2, r_2, s_3, a_3, r_3, \cdots) \tag{1}$$

The finite-horizon undiscounted return is the sum of rewards obtained in a trajectory:

$$R(\tau) = \sum_{t=1}^{T} r_t \tag{2}$$

where T is the final time step. The goal of reinforcement learning is to optimize the policy so as to maximize the expected return:

$$J(\pi) = \underset{\tau \sim \pi}{E} [R(\tau)] \tag{3}$$

where π represents the agent's policy.

When training dialogue policies with reinforcement learning, the user can be seen as the environment, and the dialogue system can be seen as the agent. During the interaction between the user and the system, the dialogue state tracker will give the current dialog state s_t, and the dialogue policy in the system selects the action a_t based on s_t. Then, based on the user's new utterance, the dialogue state tracker gives a new dialogue state s_{t+1}. Moreover, the user needs to give a reward r in the form of a numerical value according to whether the system completes the user's goal. However, in the actual training process, generally, only at the end of each conversation can the user give a reward r according to whether the user goal is completed. In other turns, the reward may be fixed at -1, designed to drive the system to accomplish the user goal in a shorter interaction process.

The agent's policy π determines how the agent chooses actions in each state:

$$a_t \sim \pi(\cdot|s_t) \tag{4}$$

In deep reinforcement learning, a multi-layer perceptron can be used to represent the policy π. The input of the multi-layer perceptron is the state s, and the output is the probability of the agent performing the action a_t. For the multi-layer perceptron, its parameters are generally represented by θ. In task-oriented dialogue systems, the action space is determined in advance.

There is a class of methods called policy gradient algorithms in reinforcement learning. The basic idea of the policy gradient algorithms is to maximize $J(\pi_\theta)$ by using gradient ascent on θ, as shown in Eq. 5.

$$\theta_{k+1} = \theta_k + \alpha \nabla_\theta J(\pi_{\theta_k})$$
(5)

Since $J(\pi_\theta)$ is an expected value and cannot be calculated directly, it needs to be estimated by using some methods. The reinforcement learning method we use, PPO, belongs to the policy gradient method, which we describe in more detail in Sect. 3.2.

3   DPPO Implementation

We first describe the workflow of our proposed DPPO algorithm and then introduce its main components in detail.

3.1   The Workflow

As shown in Algorithm 1, the workflow of DPPO can be divided into the following four stages:

- **Direct reinforcement learning** (lines 3–9): The agent interacts with a user, collects real data, and uses the real data to optimize the dialogue policy.
- **World model training** (lines 11–12): The world model is trained via supervised learning based on the data collected in the direct reinforcement learning phase.
- **Planning** (lines 13–19): The world model plays the role of the user, and the agent interacts with the world model. The simulated experience from the world model is collected and used to optimize the dialogue policy.
- **World model deactivation** (lines 20–23): DPPO monitors the agent's performance interacting with different environments (user and world model) and sets the deactivation flag f_{stop} to true if necessary.

In the initial training phase, efficient training of the agent in the DPPO algorithm can be achieved by using the low-cost simulation dialogue from the world model. When the deactivation strategy is triggered and the flag f_{stop} is set to true, the DPPO algorithm will only perform direct reinforcement learning. Thus, the negative influence of the simulated experience from the world model can be avoided.

Algorithm 1. DPPO for Dialogue Policy Learning.

Parameter: b, N, K, α

1: $f_{stop} \leftarrow$ **false**
2: **for** $i = 1$ to N **do**
3:    # Direct Reinforcement Learning
4:    **repeat**
5:       agent interacts with user
6:       for per turn, save (s, a, r, t) to D^{ppo} and save (s, a, r, t, a^u) to $D^{worldmodel}$
7:    **until** $size(D^{ppo}) \geq b$
8:    optimize dialogue policy based on D^{ppo}, then clear D^{ppo}
9:    calculate success rate r^u based on these conversations
10:   **if not** f_{stop} **then**
11:      # Training World Model
12:      optimize world model based on $D^{worldmodel}$
13:      # Planning
14:      **repeat**
15:         agent interacts with world model
16:         for per turn, save (s, a, r, t) to D^{ppo}
17:      **until** $size(D^{ppo}) \geq (K - 1) * b$
18:      optimize dialogue policy based on D^{ppo}, then clear D^{ppo}
19:      calculate success rate r^w based on these conversations
20:      # Self-adaptive stopping
21:      **if** $\frac{r^w}{r^u} < \alpha$ **then**
22:         $f_{stop} \leftarrow$ **true**
23:      **end if**
24:   **end if**
25: **end for**

3.2   Direct Reinforcement Learning and Planning

The working mechanisms in direct reinforcement learning and planning phases are similar: the agent interacts with the environment, collects experience, and optimizes the dialogue policy. The main difference is the environment, i.e., the user and the world model. Therefore, when we discuss using PPO to optimize the dialogue policy below, we do not deliberately distinguish which environment the dialogue comes from.

The policy learning module contains two neural networks, namely the dialogue policy network π_θ and the value network V_ϕ, as shown in Fig. 6. The policy network π_θ indicates how the agent will act in the form of probability. For example, given a dialogue state s, $\pi_\theta(a_k|s) = 0.6$ means that the probability that the next action a_k taken by the agent is 0.6. The value network V_ϕ is used to estimate the value of the state s when the agent acts according to the policy network π_θ. When optimizing the policy network π_θ, the estimated value $v(s)$ calculated by V_ϕ needs to be used.

We treat task-completion dialogue as a Markov decision process which consists of a sequence of $<state, action, reward>$. Specifically, at each step, the agent observes the dialogue state s, then chooses an action a according to the

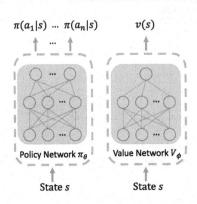

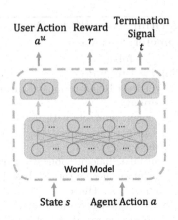

Fig. 6. Two networks in the Policy Learning module.

Fig. 7. The world model architecture.

policy π_θ. Afterward, the user or the world model responds with an action a^u and gives a reward r. The DST in the dialogue system updates the dialogue state s to s' according to a^u. From the perspective of the agent, a conversation of length T can be expressed as $\{(s_1, a_1, r_1), (s_2, a_2, r_2), \cdots, (s_T, a_T, r_T)\}$ where the triple $(s_t, a_t, r_t)(t \in [1, T])$ represents a turn of dialogue. These dialog data are all saved in a buffer D^{ppo}.

Given these data, we update the policy π_θ via

$$\theta = \arg\max_\theta \mathop{E}_{s,a \sim \pi_{\theta_{old}}} [\min(L_1, L_2)], \tag{6}$$

Here L_1 and L_2 are given by

$$L_1 = \frac{\pi_\theta(a|s)}{\pi_{\theta_{old}}(a|s)} \hat{A}^{\pi_{\theta_{old}}}(s, a) \tag{7}$$

$$L_2 = clip(\frac{\pi_\theta(a|s)}{\pi_{\theta_{old}}(a|s)}, 1 - \epsilon, 1 + \epsilon)\hat{A}^{\pi_{\theta_{old}}}(s, a) \tag{8}$$

where θ_{old} is the parameters of the policy network before the update, ϵ is a hyperparameter (usually $\epsilon \approx 0.2$), and $\hat{A}^{\pi_{\theta_{old}}}(s, a)$ is an estimator of the advantage function.

Let $r(\theta)$ denote the probability ratio $\frac{\pi_\theta(a|s)}{\pi_{\theta_{old}}(a|s)}$. L_1 and L_2 are very similar, except that the first term in L_2 is $clip(r(\theta), 1 - \epsilon, 1 + \epsilon)$ instead of $r(\theta)$. $clip(r(\theta), 1 - \epsilon, 1 + \epsilon)$ clip $r(\theta)$ into the range $[1 - \epsilon, 1 + \epsilon]$.

We use the general advantage estimation method [18] to calculate the estimator $\hat{A}_t^{\pi_{\theta_{old}}}(s, a)$ of the advantage function at timestep t:

$$\hat{A}_t^{\pi_{\theta_{old}}}(s, a) = \sum_{l=1}^{T-t} (\gamma\lambda)^{l-1} \delta_{t+l-1}^v \tag{9}$$

where

$$\delta_t^v = \begin{cases} -v(s_t), & t = T; \\ -v(s_t) + r_t + \gamma v(s_{t+1}) & t \in [1, T-1]. \end{cases} \tag{10}$$

in which $\gamma \in [0,1]$ and $\lambda \in [0,1]$ are hyperparameters.

For the value network V_ϕ, its loss is:

$$loss_v = (v(s_t) - v_t^{targ})^2 \tag{11}$$

where

$$v_t^{targ} = \begin{cases} r_t, & t = T; \\ r_t + \gamma v(s_{t+1}) & t \in [1, T-1]. \end{cases} \tag{12}$$

3.3   World Model Training

The world model we used is the same design as that of DDQ [15]. Specifically, it is implemented as a multi-task deep neural network (as shown in Fig. 7). In each dialogue turn, the world model takes the current dialogue state s and the last agent action a as input and outputs the predicted user action a^u, reward r, and termination signal t. Its calculation formula is as follows:

$$\begin{aligned} h &= tanh(W_h(s,a) + b_h) \\ a^u &= softmax(W_a h + b_a) \\ r &= W_r h + b_r \\ t &= sigmoid(W_t h + b_t) \end{aligned} \tag{13}$$

where (s, a) is the concatenation of s and a, and W and b are the trainable parameters of the world model.

In the direct reinforcement learning stage, the dialogue data (s, a, r, t, a^u) between the agent and the user will be saved in the buffer $D^{worldmodel}$. In the stage of world model training, we use the data in $D^{worldmodel}$ to train the world model so that it can predict user behavior. In the planning stage, the agent interacts with the world model and the simulated dialogue data is collected to optimize the policy network π_θ.

3.4   World Model Deactivation

Due to the complexity of user behavior, the world model may not simulate user behavior well. When using simulation data from the world model to train the agent, the inconsistency between the world model and the user's behavior will hurt the agent's performance. To address this issue, we propose the deactivation strategy in DPPO to stop training with the world model.

The world model deactivation strategy is designed based on the success rate which is the ratio of the number of successfully completed dialogues to the total number of dialogues. Specifically, we express the user goal as $G = (C, R)$ [17], where C is a set of constraint and R is a set of requests. Taking movie ticket booking as an example, the constraints specified by the user might be the name and date of the movie, while the requests could be the location of the movie theater and the start time of the movie. When the movie ticket is booked and the booked movie ticket meets the user's constraints, a dialogue is considered successful.

We use r^w to represent the success rate of the dialogue between the agent and the world model and r^u to denote the success rate of the dialogue between the agent and the user. From the agent's point of view, the inconsistency between the world model and the user can be reflected in the difference between r^w and r^u. Therefore, we use $\frac{r^w}{r^u}$ to represent the similarity between the world model and the user. Assuming that the world model can accurately predict the user's behavior, the expected value of $\frac{r^w}{r^u}$ is close to 1. However, due to the actual prediction deviation of the world model, $\frac{r^w}{r^u}$ will deviate from 1. Our deactivation strategy is that when $\frac{r^w}{r^u} < \alpha$, we set the flag f_{stop} to true to stop using the world model in subsequent training.

4   Experiments and Results

4.1   Dataset and User Simulator

For comparison with DDQ, we use the exact same dataset and user simulator as in paper [15].

Dataset. The original raw data in a movie-ticket booking scenario was collected via Amazon Mechanical Turk and then annotated based on a schema defined by domain experts. This annotation schema contains 11 intents and 16 slots. The dataset contains 280 conversations, and their average length is 11 turns.

User Simulator. Since the agent needs to interact with the user many times when training and the interaction cost of the real user is too high, we use a user simulator [10] to simulate the user's interaction with the agent in the experiment. For each agent's action, the user simulator will reply with a simulated user action. At the end of the dialogue, the user simulator will calculate a reward value based on whether the dialogue task is completed. At the end of the dialogue, if the task is completed successfully, the reward value is $2 * L$; if the task fails, the reward value is $-L$. L is the maximum length of the dialogue, set to 40 in the experiment. In order to encourage the agent to complete the task in a short conversation, the agent will receive a reward of -1 on each turn.

4.2   Baselines

In order to benchmark the performance of DPPO, we used several algorithms to train task-oriented dialogue agents:

- **DDQ**: The Deep Dyna-Q [15] algorithm, which uses DQN to optimize the agent and uses a continuously optimized world model to generate simulation data to expand the number of conversations.

- **D3Q**: The Discriminative Deep Dyna-Q [21] algorithm (a variant of DDQ), which trains a discriminator based on the idea of Generative Adversarial Network (GAN) to select a high-quality part from a large number of simulated data for training the agent.
- **PPO**: The Proximal Policy Optimization [19] algorithm, a policy-based RL algorithm using a clipping mechanism to ensure the stability of the training process.
- **DPPO**: Our Dyna Proximal Policy Optimization algorithm. The algorithm also uses the world model to expand the number of conversations. However, unlike DDQ, it uses PPO to optimize the agent and uses a deactivation strategy to control when to stop training with the world model.
- **DPPO w/o stop**: Except for not using the deactivation strategy, everything else is the same as DPPO.

For DDQ, the hidden layers of the Q-value network are two fully connected layers, and the hidden layer size is 80. The activation functions of the hidden layer are all tanh. Reward discount coefficient γ is 0.9. The ϵ-greedy strategy is used when selecting actions during training, where ϵ is 0.1. The agent's experience pool size for both user experience and simulation experience is 5000. The world model in DDQ uses two shared hidden layers and three hidden layers related to specific tasks. The parameter K in planning is set to 5. The size of these layers is 80.

For PPO and DPPO, the hidden layers of their policy and value networks are two fully connected layers with a size of 64 and an activation function of relu. According to the default parameter values of PPO in the code Baselines [1], the hyperparameter ϵ is set to 0.2, γ is set to 0.99, and λ is set to 0.95. In each stage of direct reinforcement learning, they need to collect 1024 turns of data. The configuration of the world model is the same as the configuration in DDQ. The parameter K in planning is also set to 5. In planning, the maximum length of a simulated dialogue is 40. Moreover, the experimental results reported in this paper are the average of five runs, and the random number seeds used in these five runs are all different.

4.3   Results

We conduct several experiments: (1) To find an appropriate value of α in the world model deactivation strategy, a parameter tuning experiment on α for DPPO is conducted; (2) To verify whether DPPO can achieve a higher task success rate, a comparative study among DPPO, DDQ and D3Q is performed; (3) To verify whether DPPO can use real conversation data more effectively, we compare DPPO with PPO; (4) To verify whether the world model deactivation strategy is useful, we perform an ablation study for DPPO.

---

[1] Openai baselines https://github.com/openai/baselines.

Tuning for α. Figure 8 shows the learning curves of several agents trained with DPPO when the parameter α takes different values, and Table 1 is the specific value at some time in Fig. 8. We propose DPPO not only to pursue a high final dialogue success rate, but also to hope that the algorithm can perform well when it can only interact with the environment a small number of times. In Fig. 8, each agent interacts with the environment the same number of times for each epoch in training. Around the 500th epoch, the performance of all agents tends to be stable, and we regard the performance of each agent at this moment as the final performance that the agent can achieve. At the 100th and 150th epochs, the number of interactions between the agent and the environment is still relatively small. We use the agent's performance at these moments to measure the algorithm's performance at low interaction times.

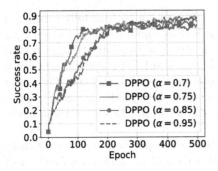

Fig. 8. Performance of DPPO with different α in the deactivation strategy.

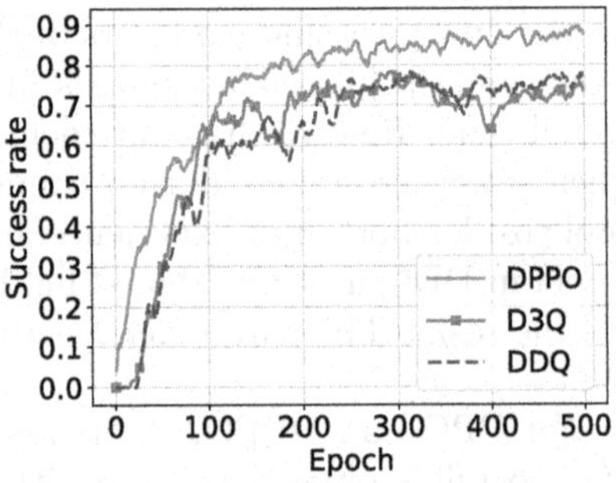

Fig. 9. DPPO vs. DDQs.

Table 1. The performance of DPPO when the parameter α in the world model deactivation strategy takes different values.

Agent (DPPO)	100th epochs			150th epochs			Final performance		
	Success	Reward	Turns	Success	Reward	Turns	Success	Reward	Turns
$\alpha = 0.70$	75.09%	40.46	21.28	76.81%	43.94	18.46	82.42%	52.28	15.24
$\alpha = 0.75$	64.16%	25.67	24.64	76.94%	42.56	21.53	86.93%	56.65	17.32
$\alpha = 0.85$	49.60%	8.01	25.04	64.53%	26.94	23.00	84.89%	54.6	16.55
$\alpha = 0.95$	43.76%	0.05	26.94	65.39%	28.43	22.08	87.51%	57.69	16.63

From Table 1, it can be found that at the 100th and 150th epoch, the dialogue success rates of DPPO ($\alpha = 0.7$) and DPPO ($\alpha = 0.75$) both reach 64% and 76%, while the dialogue success rates of DPPO ($\alpha = 0.85$) and DPPO ($\alpha = 0.95$)

are more than 10% lower. When considering final performance, the final dialogue success rate of DPPO ($\alpha = 0.75$) is 4% higher than that of DPPO ($\alpha = 0.7$). Therefore, we consider $\alpha = 0.75$ to be a suitable parameter, and in subsequent experiments, we set α for DPPO to be 0.75.

DPPO Vs. DDQs. Figure 9 and Table 2 show the results of the comparative experiment among DPPO, DDQ, and D3Q. D3Q is a variant of DDQ, so we refer to these two algorithms collectively as DDQs. The reinforcement learning methods they use to optimize dialogue policies are all DQN. In this comparative experiment, we mainly want to compare the final performance that DPPO and DDQs can achieve. It can be seen quantitatively from Table 2 that the task success rate of DPPO is more than 10% higher than that of DDQ and D3Q.

Table 2. Comparison between DPPO and DDQs.

Agent	Final performance		
	Success	Reward	Turns
DDQ	76.33%	42.41	20.37
D3Q	73.13%	41.23	15.06
DPPO	86.93%	56.65	17.32

Another thing worth noting in Fig. 9 is that at the beginning of training, both DDQ and D3Q have a task success rate of 0, while DPPO has a task success rate of approximately 0.05. This is because DPPO can facilitate imitation learning to pre-train the dialog policy using human-human dialogs, but DDQ and D3Q cannot.

DPPO vs. PPO. Figure 10 compares the learning curve of DPPO and PPO. Specifically, Fig. 10a shows the final performance of DPPO and PPO, while Fig. 10b highlights the performance they can achieve with relatively few interactions with the environment.

It can be found from Table 3 that although the final dialogue success rates of PPO and DPPO are very similar, the dialogue success rates of DPPO are about 30% and 28% higher than that of PPO at the 100th and 150th epochs, respectively. This is because, compared with PPO, DPPO uses the world model to generate a large amount of simulated data during the training process to assist the training of the agent, thereby speeding up the training speed of the agent. This feature of DPPO makes DPPO more suitable for use in real environments where interaction with the environment is expensive compared to PPO.

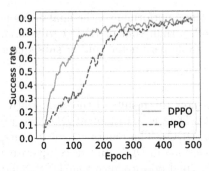
(a) Learning curve within 500 epochs.

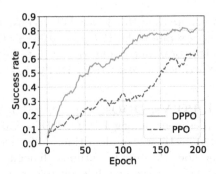
(b) Learning curve within 200 epochs.

Fig. 10. DPPO vs. PPO.

Table 3. Comparison between DPPO and PPO.

Agent	100th epochs			150th epochs			Final performance		
	Success	Reward	Turns	Success	Reward	Turns	Success	Reward	Turns
PPO	34.97%	−12.15	30.24	48.03%	5.89	25.47	86.31%	56.38	16.39
DPPO	64.16%	25.67	24.64	76.94%	42.56	21.53	86.93%	56.65	17.32

Unlike PPO discarding all real data immediately after optimizing the dialogue policy, DPPO will use these real data to train the world model, and in the subsequent epochs, the world model can continuously generate simulated data. In this way, DPPO indirectly extends the life cycle of each batch of real data. This explains why DPPO has higher data utilization than PPO.

Ablation Study. In order to verify the effect of the world model deactivation strategy, we compare DPPO with DPPO w/o stop, and the results are shown in Fig. 11. Although DPPO w/o stop can achieve better results in the early training stage than DPPO, the final dialogue success rate performance of DPPO w/o stop is about 3% lower than DPPO. Using DPPO w/o stop is not a bad option when interacting with the environment is very expensive. But if the final performance of the agent is more important than the training cost, using DPPO is better than DPPO w/o stop.

To further analyze why the final performance of DPPO w/o stop is lower than DPPO, we show in Fig. 12 the task success rate curves of DPPO w/o stop interacting with the user and world model respectively during the training process. During the initial period of training, the rising speeds of r^u and r^w are very similar; but after the 60th epoch, the gap between them gradually increases; in the later stage, there is always an apparent gap between r^u and r^w. The interval between r^u and r^w indicates the inconsistency between the user and world model. When the agent's performance is weak, the agent may not be aware of the inconsistency. However, when the agent's performance reaches a certain

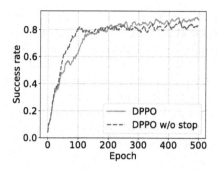 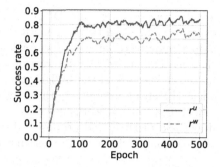

Fig. 11. DPPO vs. DPPO w/o stop.   **Fig. 12.** r^u and r^w for DPPO w/o stop.

level, the inconsistency will hinder the further improvement of the agent. The deactivation strategy used by DPPO continuously monitors the degree of inconsistency detected by the agent. When the degree reaches a specified threshold, DPPO will no longer use the simulation data generated by the world model for training.

5   Related Work

When using RL to train dialogue policy in a dialogue system, the high cost of interacting with users is a problem that must be carefully considered. Existing work focusing on this problem can be grouped into three types, and we discuss them as follows:

The first type is to build a user simulator to completely replace the user [1,7,8,20]. The most popular user simulator is built on hand-crafted rules with a stack-like agenda based on the user goal [10,17,34]. At present, most of the work that uses RL to learn dialogue policy uses this type of user simulator [5,26,31]. However, implementing an agenda-based user simulator requires much expert knowledge. Moreover, the agenda-based user simulator is tightly coupled with the corresponding dialogue scene, making it difficult to migrate to other scenes.

The second type of work is to treat both user and system as agents and train two agents directly from human-human dialogues [11,14,23,25]. Papangelis et al. [14] train the user and system agents end-to-end. In their work, these two agents can only communicate through natural language. Takanobu et al. [23] use the actor-critic framework to train user and system agents and conduct experiments on larger datasets. However, the environment in this type of work is dynamic, which makes it more difficult for training when compared with the static environment in DDQ or our method.

The third type is to design a training framework that reduces the number of interactions between the agent and the user during training instead of eliminating the user's participation like the previous two methods. An important representative of this method is DDQ [15], where a learnable world model is introduced to the dialogue policy training process. Afterward, some work [8,29,31] are devoted to improving DDQ. In order to control the quality of simulated experience, inspired by the generative adversarial network, Su et al. [21] trained a discriminator to filter out low-quality simulated data. Zhang et al. [31] assume that the number of user interactions available (budget) is fixed and small. To make the best use of the budget, they designed a scheduling method to control when the agent interacts with the user and when it interacts with the world model. Unlike these works, we replace DQN with PPO to overcome the inherent drawbacks of DDQ and propose a deactivation strategy to avoid the damage of the low-quality simulation experience to the agent's performance.

6   Conclusion

In this paper, we propose the Dyna Proximal Policy Optimization (DPPO) algorithm to learn dialogue policy efficiently. DPPO overcomes the drawbacks of existing methods of DDQ and its variants by (1) using Proximal Policy Optimization (PPO) to improve the training efficiency of the agent; (2) proposing a deactivation strategy to avoid the harmful effect from the low-quality simulated experience of the world model. The experimental results on the task of booking movie tickets confirm the effectiveness of our method. The idea behind the DPPO algorithm can also be extended to solve other reinforcement learning problems that are expensive to interact with the environment.

Acknowledgement. This work was supported by the Key Research Project of Zhejiang Province (2022C01145).

References

1. Asri, L.E., He, J., Suleman, K.: A sequence-to-sequence model for user simulation in spoken dialogue systems. arXiv preprint arXiv:1607.00070 (2016)
2. Chen, H., Liu, X., Yin, D., Tang, J.: A survey on dialogue systems: recent advances and new frontiers. ACM SIGKDD Explor. Newsl. **19**(2), 25–35 (2017)
3. Feng, Y., Wang, Y., Li, H.: A sequence-to-sequence approach to dialogue state tracking. In: Proceedings of the 59th Annual Meeting of the Association for Computational Linguistics and the 11th International Joint Conference on Natural Language Processing (Volume 1: Long Papers), pp. 1714–1725 (2021)
4. Firdaus, M., Golchha, H., Ekbal, A., Bhattacharyya, P.: A deep multi-task model for dialogue act classification, intent detection and slot filling. Cogn. Comput. **13**(3), 626–645 (2021)
5. Gordon-Hall, G., Gorinski, P., Cohen, S.B.: Learning dialog policies from weak demonstrations. In: Proceedings of the 58th Annual Meeting of the Association for Computational Linguistics, pp. 1394–1405 (2020)
6. Hussein, A., Gaber, M.M., Elyan, E., Jayne, C.: Imitation learning: a survey of learning methods. ACM Comput. Surv. (CSUR) **50**(2), 1–35 (2017)
7. Keizer, S., et al.: Parameter estimation for agenda-based user simulation. In: Proceedings of the SIGDIAL 2010 Conference, pp. 116–123 (2010)

8. Kreyssig, F., Casanueva, I., Budzianowski, P., Gasic, M.: Neural user simulation for corpus-based policy optimisation of spoken dialogue systems. In: Proceedings of the 19th Annual SIGdial Meeting on Discourse and Dialogue, pp. 60–69 (2018)

9. Lee, C.H., Cheng, H., Ostendorf, M.: Dialogue state tracking with a language model using schema-driven prompting. In: Proceedings of the 2021 Conference on Empirical Methods in Natural Language Processing, pp. 4937–4949 (2021)

10. Li, X., Lipton, Z.C., Dhingra, B., Li, L., Gao, J., Chen, Y.N.: A user simulator for task-completion dialogues. arXiv preprint arXiv:1612.05688 (2016)

11. Liu, B., Lane, I.: Iterative policy learning in end-to-end trainable task-oriented neural dialog models. In: 2017 IEEE Automatic Speech Recognition and Understanding Workshop (ASRU), pp. 482–489. IEEE (2017)

12. Lu, K., Zhang, S., Chen, X.: Goal-oriented dialogue policy learning from failures. In: Proceedings of the AAAI Conference on Artificial Intelligence, vol. 33, pp. 2596–2603 (2019)

13. Mnih, V., et al.: Human-level control through deep reinforcement learning. Nature **518**(7540), 529–533 (2015)

14. Papangelis, A., Wang, Y.C., Molino, P., Tur, G., Uber, A.: Collaborative multi-agent dialogue model training via reinforcement learning. In: 20th Annual Meeting of the Special Interest Group on Discourse and Dialogue, p. 92 (2019)

15. Peng, B., Li, X., Gao, J., Liu, J., Wong, K.F.: Deep Dyna-Q: integrating planning for task-completion dialogue policy learning. In: Proceedings of the 56th Annual Meeting of the Association for Computational Linguistics (Volume 1: Long Papers), pp. 2182–2192 (2018)

16. Peng, B., et al.: Few-shot natural language generation for task-oriented dialog. In: Findings of the Association for Computational Linguistics: EMNLP 2020, pp. 172–182 (2020)

17. Schatzmann, J., Thomson, B., Weilhammer, K., Ye, H., Young, S.: Agenda-based user simulation for bootstrapping a POMDP dialogue system. In: Human Language Technologies 2007: The Conference of the North American Chapter of the Association for Computational Linguistics; Companion Volume, Short Papers, pp. 149–152 (2007)

18. Schulman, J., Moritz, P., Levine, S., Jordan, M., Abbeel, P.: High-dimensional continuous control using generalized advantage estimation. arXiv e-prints arXiv:1506.02438, June 2015

19. Schulman, J., Wolski, F., Dhariwal, P., Radford, A., Klimov, O.: Proximal policy optimization algorithms. arXiv preprint arXiv:1707.06347 (2017)

20. Shi, W., Qian, K., Wang, X., Yu, Z.: How to build user simulators to train RL-based dialog systems. In: Proceedings of the 2019 Conference on Empirical Methods in Natural Language Processing and the 9th International Joint Conference on Natural Language Processing (EMNLP-IJCNLP), pp. 1990–2000 (2019)

21. Su, S.Y., Li, X., Gao, J., Liu, J., Chen, Y.N.: Discriminative deep Dyna-Q: robust planning for dialogue policy learning. In: Proceedings of the 2018 Conference on Empirical Methods in Natural Language Processing, pp. 3813–3823 (2018)

22. Sutton, R.S.: Integrated architectures for learning, planning, and reacting based on approximating dynamic programming. In: Machine Learning Proceedings 1990, pp. 216–224. Elsevier (1990)

23. Takanobu, R., Liang, R., Huang, M.: Multi-agent task-oriented dialog policy learning with role-aware reward decomposition. In: Proceedings of the 58th Annual Meeting of the Association for Computational Linguistics, pp. 625–638 (2020)

24. Teng, D., Qin, L., Che, W., Zhao, S., Liu, T.: Injecting word information with multi-level word adapter for Chinese spoken language understanding. In: ICASSP 2021–2021 IEEE International Conference on Acoustics, Speech and Signal Processing (ICASSP), pp. 8188–8192. IEEE (2021)
25. Tseng, B.H., Dai, Y., Kreyssig, F., Byrne, B.: Transferable dialogue systems and user simulators. In: Proceedings of the 59th Annual Meeting of the Association for Computational Linguistics and the 11th International Joint Conference on Natural Language Processing (Volume 1: Long Papers), pp. 152–166 (2021)
26. Wang, H., Peng, B., Wong, K.F.: Learning efficient dialogue policy from demonstrations through shaping. In: Proceedings of the 58th Annual Meeting of the Association for Computational Linguistics, pp. 6355–6365 (2020)
27. Wang, H., Wong, K.F.: A collaborative multi-agent reinforcement learning framework for dialog action decomposition. In: Proceedings of the 2021 Conference on Empirical Methods in Natural Language Processing, pp. 7882–7889 (2021)
28. Wen, T.H., Gasic, M., Mrksic, N., Su, P.H., Vandyke, D., Young, S.: Semantically conditioned lstm-based natural language generation for spoken dialogue systems. arXiv preprint arXiv:1508.01745 (2015)
29. Wu, Y., Li, X., Liu, J., Gao, J., Yang, Y.: Switch-based active deep Dyna-Q: efficient adaptive planning for task-completion dialogue policy learning. In: Proceedings of the AAAI Conference on Artificial Intelligence, vol. 33, pp. 7289–7296 (2019)
30. Zahavy, T., Haroush, M., Merlis, N., Mankowitz, D.J., Mannor, S.: Learn what not to learn: Action elimination with deep reinforcement learning. In: Bengio, S., Wallach, H., Larochelle, H., Grauman, K., Cesa-Bianchi, N., Garnett, R. (eds.) Advances in Neural Information Processing Systems, vol. 31. Curran Associates, Inc. (2018)
31. Zhang, Z., Li, X., Gao, J., Chen, E.: Budgeted policy learning for task-oriented dialogue systems. In: Proceedings of the 57th Annual Meeting of the Association for Computational Linguistics, pp. 3742–3751 (2019)
32. Zhao, Y., Wang, Z., Huang, Z.: Automatic curriculum learning with over repetition penalty for dialogue policy learning, vol. 35(16), pp. 14540–14548 (2021)
33. Zhao, Y., Wang, Z., Zhu, C., Wang, S.: Efficient dialogue complementary policy learning via deep Q-network policy and episodic memory policy. In: Proceedings of the 2021 Conference on Empirical Methods in Natural Language Processing, pp. 4311–4323 (2021)
34. Zhu, Q., et al.: ConvLab-2: an open-source toolkit for building, evaluating, and diagnosing dialogue systems. In: Proceedings of the 58th Annual Meeting of the Association for Computational Linguistics: System Demonstrations, pp. 142–149 (2020)

Self-gated FM: Revisiting the Weight of Feature Interactions for CTR Prediction

Zhongxue Li[1], Hao Wu[1(✉)], Xin Wang[2], Yiji Zhao[3], and Lei Zhang[4]

[1] School of Information Science and Engineering, Yunnan University,
Kunming, China
lzhxue@mail.ynu.edu.cn, haowu@ynu.edu.cn
[2] School of Computer Science, Wuhan University,Wuhan, China
[3] School of Computer Science, Beijing Jiaotong University, Beijing, China
[4] School of Electrical and Automation Engineering, Nanjing Normal University,
Nanjing, China

Abstract. With the successful application of factorization machine models in click-through rate prediction, the automatic selection of feature interactions has attracted extensive attention. As the most commonly-used strategies, automatic construction of limited high-order cross-feature and automatic learning of feature interaction weight have made great progress. However, most studies still face challenges of complex training and search process. Therefore, we propose a self-gating mechanism for automatic feature selection of factorization machine models and implement a portable self-gating layer. In the self-gating layer, the weight of feature interaction is revisited through the attention network with different attentive aspects, and then the gate status is dynamically determined according to the attention score to achieve the effect of automatic selection. Our method can be easily ported to FM and DeepFM. The experimental results on two real-world data sets show that our proposed methods are superior to many state-of-the-art methods.

Keywords: Factorization machines · Feature selection · Self-gating · Neural networks · Click-through rate prediction

1 Introduction

With the development of information overload, the problem is becoming more and more serious. Recommender systems came into being and developed into

Supported by the National Natural Science Foundation of China (61962061, 61562090), the Postgraduate Research and Innovation Foundation of Yunnan University (2021Y276), and partially supported by the Yunnan Provincial Foundation for Leaders of Disciplines in Science and Technology (202005AC160005), Yunnan High-Level Talent Training Support Plan: Young Top Talent Special Project (YNWR-QNBJ-2019-188).

© ICST Institute for Computer Sciences, Social Informatics and Telecommunications Engineering 2022
Published by Springer Nature Switzerland AG 2022. All Rights Reserved
H. Gao et al. (Eds.): CollaborateCom 2022, LNICST 460, pp. 415–432, 2022.
https://doi.org/10.1007/978-3-031-24383-7_23

a research hotspot. Click-through rate (CTR) prediction is a basic task of FM-based recommendation systems. The core issue of recommendation algorithms is effectively modeling feature interaction. For example, an 18-year-old female user tends to give feedback (e.g., click, purchase) to skirts. The interaction of gender and age can release a stronger signal to help predict the feedback probability. Making full use of feature interactions is essential for achieving potential benefits for recommender systems.

With the introduction of multiple contextual features into modeling user-item interaction, matrix decomposition methods become powerless regarding the generalization ability. Factorization Machines (FM) [20] can simulate most decomposition models through feature engineering, and thus can combine the universality of feature engineering with the advantages of the decomposition model to estimate the interaction between a wide range of features (e.g. categorical variables and continuous variables). In real life, not all features and feature interactions are equally helpful and predictive [5]. The introduction of noise features may increase the model complexity and damage the prediction performance. Therefore, it is necessary to distinguish useful feature interactions from useless ones to ensure the performance and efficiency of FM models.

Method such as DCN [25], xDeepFM [15], AutoInt [21], AutoCross [17], and FiBiNET [12] focuses on automatically constructing finite high-order cross features and learning the high-order interaction of input features. While these models can only search a small part of all interactive features. Another technical route is to automatically learn weight for feature interactions. Typical examples are AFM [26], FwFM [19], and IFM [9]. A significant disadvantage of such methods is that the noise features are involved in the prediction. The gating mechanism enables the gates to be closed for noise features and kept for the features that are favorable to the model. Based on this principle, AutoFIS [16] and GateNet [11] have been proposed and achieved state-of-the-art performance on feature selection in the FM models.

Although existing solutions have made great progress, they still face some challenges, e.g., the complex training method in AutoFIS, and the complex search process in AutoCross and AutoInt. A simple yet elegant manner is always worth exploring. Guided by these, this paper proposes self-gated factorization machines to address existing challenges. Different from existing solutions, our self-gating mechanism is based on the attention network where we revisit the role of feature interaction weight, and directly take these attention scores as signals to activate the gate status. By this, our method enables the gate status to be determined dynamically in a portable component and to learn the relative importance of the kept feature interaction simultaneously. Therefore, our method does not prescribe any additional search process. Also, our method concentrates on pooling the second-order cross-features which are the most commonly used instance of FMs, and thus is easily applied to most of the factorization machines.

Our contributions in this paper can be summarized as follows: (I)A novel self-gating method for automatic feature selection of cross-features is proposed based on the attention mechanism. Most importantly, the feature-field interaction scheme is proposed and explored to enhance the attention mechanism.

(II) Four variants of self-gating factorization machines (gFM, gFM+, gDeepFM, gDeepFM+) are proposed and demonstrate that our method is portable and easily migrated to the existing FM models to provide a thoroughly end-to-end solution. (III) We conduct extensive experiments on two large-scale datasets and show that migrating self-gating components significantly benefits the existing FM models. Also, our proposed self-gated FM models achieve competitive or superior results compared to the SOTA methods.

The following structure of this paper is organized as follows: Sect. 2 reviews the related work. Section 3 introduces the model of self-gating factorization machines and details the self-gating mechanism. Section 4 is the settings of the experiment. The analysis of experimental results and some influencing factors are carried out in Sect. 5. Section 6 shows the conclusion of this paper.

2 Related Work

2.1 Factorization Machines

Based on naive FM, there are many variants to enhance feature interaction. FFM [13] attributes features of the same properties to the same field and proposes an upgraded version of FM. FmFM [23] models the interactions of field pairs as a matrix. However, these FM models can not model high-order feature interaction until various neural components are employed to stack on naive FM to provide an effective solution for feature interaction to represent more complex learning tasks, such as NFM [8], DeepFM [7], and Wide & Deep [2]. FNN [27] is a forward neural network using FM to pre-train the embedding layer. However, FNN can capture only high-order feature interactions. FMs consider feature interactions among input features by using only polynomial expansion which fails to capture complex nonlinear patterns in data. Moreover, existing FMs do not provide interpretable predictions to users. SEFM [14] is thus proposed to overcome these two limitations by using non-parametric subspace feature mapping. In addition, many variants strengthen the FM model from different facets to solve specific problems.

2.2 Attention Mechanism

In the learning of neural network, more parameters mean stronger model expression ability. However, computing resources are limited, and we hope to use limited computing resources to process more important information. Inspired by human vision research, the attention mechanism is introduced to focus on more target-related information and ignore other irrelevant information, which has been widely used in research fields such as natural language processing and computer vision [1]. Thanks to the attention mechanism, the model focuses on learning input features that have a great impact on the results, so as to extract more critical and important information without bringing more overhead to the model's computation and storage. The self-attention mechanism [24] is that after the model receives the input information, it determines the currently important information according to the input information itself. AFM [26] proposes to apply an attention mechanism on feature interactions, thereby transforming the computation of interaction vectors from a simple summation to a selective weighted summation. DIN [28] adaptively adjusts the influence of historical information on the prediction of the current model by weighting the historical interest sequence features. Based on the multi-head self-attention mechanism, AutoInt [21] realizes the functions of explicitly constructing cross-features and mining the correlation between features.

2.3   Feature Selection for FMs

Despite the successful application of FM and its many deep learning variants, treating every feature interaction fairly may degrade the performance. Given this, the current feature selection focuses on *Embedded* methods where the selection algorithm is blended as part of the learning algorithm.

One kind of work focuses on automatically constructing finite high-order cross features and learning the high-order interaction of input features. DCN [25] is similar to DeepFM where CrossNet is used to capture explicit high-order cross-features and DNN is to capture implicit intersection features. Following DCN, xDeepFM [15] proposes compressing the interaction layer and AutoInt [21] introduces a new interaction layer based on multi-head self-attention mechanism. AutoCross [17] uses beam search to effectively generate cross features. FiBiNET [12] dynamically learns the feature importance via the Squeeze-Excitation network [10] and fine-grained feature interactions via bilinear function. In essence, these models are still the combination of deep network and FM, and only play the role of feature selection with the help of preset structure. The limitation of these models is that they can only search a small part of all interactive features. Another technical route is to automatically learn weight for feature interactions. AFM [26] learns the importance of each feature interaction through the neural attention network. FwFM [19] learns a weight for the field to which the feature belongs. Similarly, IFM [9] introduces Interaction-Aware Mechanism to learn flexible interactions on feature and field aspects.

The gating mechanism is introduced into the factorization machine models for automatic feature selection. The gates are closed for noise features, so that the model can only learn the features that are beneficial to the model [4]. AutoFIS [16] trains the factorization machine models with a gating mechanism in a phased approach. The first stage mainly removes noise features, and the second stage focuses on retraining beneficial features. GateNet [11] introduces embedding gates and hidden gates to explicitly select potential features and implicitly capture high-order interaction respectively.

3   Methodology

3.1   Self-gated Factorization Machines

Self-gated factorization machines (gFM) can be regarded as a minimum model with self-gating functionality. It contains the *Input* layer, *Embedding* layer, *Feature Interaction* layer, *Self-Gating* layer and *Prediction* layer. On this basis,

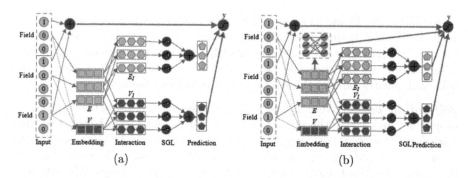

(a)   (b)

Fig. 1. The architecture of gFM+ and gDeepFM+.

we can demonstrate how to integrate the classical FM models with self-gating functionality (see Fig. 1).

Input Layer: Typical data preprocessing is to convert each data instance into a high-dimensional sparse vector through one-hot or k-hot encoding. The collection of all data instances is $X \in \mathbb{R}^{n \times m}$ where n is the total number of instances and m is the field number of each instance after coding. Each input instance is a sparse vector $x \in X$, and the **feature** value of i-th **field** of x is marked as x_i, i.e.: $x = [x_1, x_2, \ldots, x_m]$.

Embedding Layer: The function of embedding layer is to transform x into a $k \times m$ dense matrix. For each **feature** x_i, it will be projected into a k-dimensional dense vector e_i. The embedding matrix $E' = [e_1, e_2, \ldots, e_m]$ consists of m embedding vectors. Further, it is combined with x as $E = [e_1 x_1, e_2 x_2, \ldots, e_m x_m]$. In addition, to enable field-aware interaction, each **field** of the feature is also projected into a k-dimensional dense vector $v_i \in V$ where $i = 1 : m$.

Feature-Feature Interaction Layer: Feature interaction is a standard component in neural factorization machines [7,8,26]. Given m embedding vectors of features, it expands to $m(m-1)/2$ cross-feature vectors, where each cross-feature vector is the *Hadamard* product of two distinct vectors to encode their interaction. Formally, we have:

$$E_I = \{e_i x_i \odot e_j x_j | i = 1 : m - 1, j = i + 1 : m\}. \tag{1}$$

Feature-Field Interaction Layer: The importance of feature interaction is affected not only by itself but also by the field to which the feature belongs. For example, a male customer (a feature) may pay more attention to the price *field* than the brand *field* when selecting goods. The interaction between the male feature and the price field should be more important than that of the brand field, and vice versa. For this reason, we add a Feature-Field Interaction layer to model this effect. Formally, we have:

$$V_I = \{v_i \odot e_j x_j + e_i x_i \odot v_j | i = 1 : m - 1, j = i + 1 : m\}. \tag{2}$$

Similar to the Feature-Feature Interaction, each cross-feature is also modeled as the Hadamard product of two distinct vectors to encode their interaction. Considering that each feature is associated with a field and the bilateral symmetry of interaction, we integrate the two interactive operations of the feature to the field to implicitly capture the interaction of associated fields.

Self-gating Layer: We can use various subsequent neural network layers to project E_I and V_I to the prediction score. For example, NFM proposes using a *bilinear interaction pooling* with a fully connected layer; AFM proposes using an *attention-based pooling* and followed by a fully connected layer. However, these methods do not play the role of gating cross-features. Inspired by AutoFIS [16] and GateNet [11] which both attempt to use the gating mechanism for automatic feature selection, we design a novel self-gating layer based on the attention mechanism [18]. Let f_{SG} be a parameterized nonlinear function, it will compress E_I into a dense vector for further processing:

$$f_{SG}(E_I) = \sum_{i=1}^{m-1} \sum_{j=i+1}^{m} g_{ij}(e_i x_i \odot e_j x_j) \tag{3}$$

where g_{ij} indicates the gating status corresponding to the feature interaction of x_i and x_j, and will be learned from the data. In the same way, we can add another self-gating layer for the feature-field interactions as follows:

$$f_{SG}(V_I) = \sum_{i=1}^{m-1} \sum_{j=i+1}^{m} g_{ij}(v_i \odot e_j x_j + e_i x_i \odot v_j) \tag{4}$$

Prediction Layer: The output of the self-gating layer is a k-dimensional vector, which compresses all feature interactions in the embedding space after distinguishing their importance. And then, we use a fully connected layer to project it to the prediction score. At the same time, to preserve the general form of FMs, we give the overall formulation of our model as:

$$y_{gFM+} = w_0 + \sum_{i=1}^{m} w_i x_i + p_e^{\mathsf{T}} f_{SG}(E_I) + p_v^{\mathsf{T}} f_{SG}(V_I) \tag{5}$$

where $p_e, p_v \in \mathbb{R}^k$ denote the weights for the prediction layer.

Noted that our self-gated FM will degrade to a basic version without the feature-field interaction layer. The basic version follows the general form of factorization machines, so we marked the basic version as gFM, and named the full version as gFM+.

3.2   Self-gating Layer

Our self-gating mechanism focuses on pooling the second-order cross-features, which are the most effective and commonly used instances of FMs. The structural diagram of the self-gating layer is shown in Fig. 2.   The input of SGL is a set of

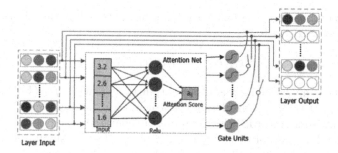

Fig. 2. The structure of the self-gating layer (SGL). The features that enter the SGL first acquire the attention score through the attention net, and then activate the gating status accordingly.

cross-feature vectors. To distinguish the contribution of different cross-features for a prediction task, an attention network [18] is used to assign different weights to each cross-feature automatically. The so-called attention is a mechanism that focuses on local information, such as a certain area of the visual field. The attention is often changed as the task changes. As for the implementation of the attention network, we use a multi-layer perceptron to parameterize the attention score (a.k.a weight of cross-feature) [26]. Given a set of cross-feature vectors (e.g. E_I), the weight α_{ij} for every vector is obtained as follows:

$$
\begin{aligned}
\alpha_{ij} &= \boldsymbol{q}^{\mathsf{T}}\mathbf{relu}(\boldsymbol{W}_e \boldsymbol{E}_I^{ij} + \boldsymbol{W}_v \boldsymbol{V}_I^{ij} + \boldsymbol{b}) \\
&= \boldsymbol{q}^{\mathsf{T}}\mathbf{relu}\left(\boldsymbol{W}_e(\boldsymbol{e}_i x_i \odot \boldsymbol{e}_j x_j) + \boldsymbol{W}_v(\boldsymbol{v}_i \odot \boldsymbol{e}_j x_j + \boldsymbol{e}_i x_i \odot \boldsymbol{v}_j) + \boldsymbol{b}\right)
\end{aligned}
\tag{6}
$$

where $\boldsymbol{q} \in \mathbb{R}^h$, $\boldsymbol{W}_e$, $\boldsymbol{W}_v \in \mathbb{R}^{h \times k}$, $\boldsymbol{b} \in \mathbb{R}^h$ are model parameters in the attention network and h denotes the hidden layer size of the attention network. For simplicity, we always let $h = k$. The activation function is *relu*.

According to the common practices [26], attention score α_{ij} are generally normalized with softmax function: $g_{ij} = \mathrm{softmax}(\alpha_{ij})$ and re-assigned to each cross-feature to achieve feature calibration:

$$
f_{Att}(\boldsymbol{E}_I^{ij}) = g_{ij}(\boldsymbol{e}_i x_i \odot \boldsymbol{e}_j x_j).
\tag{7}
$$

However, this treatment is under a defect. The softmax function in exponential form can enlarge the larger weight and suppress the smaller weight. In extreme cases, it will lead to one-hot activation where only one cross-feature is enabled. When the number of cross-features is counted in hundreds, many useful ones are killed by mistake. To avoid this drawback, it must learn a non-mutually-exclusive relationship, to ensure that more useful features are allowed to enter the subsequent propagation process [10]. For this, we revisit the role of feature interaction weights, and directly take these attention scores as signals to activate the gate status as $g_{ij} = \mathrm{sigmoid}(\alpha_{ij})$. By this, attention scores are projected to [0,1]. It can either let no flow or complete flow of information throughout the gates to play the role of excitation [10]. Here, gate status is only determined by the corresponding feature weight, so it can be called self-gating. Finally, we get the output of SGL with:

$$f_{SG}(\boldsymbol{E}_I^{ij}) = g_{ij}(\boldsymbol{e}_i x_i \odot \boldsymbol{e}_j x_j). \tag{8}$$

At the same time, we can get another output of SGL with: $f_{SG}(\boldsymbol{V}_I^{ij}) = g_{ij}(\boldsymbol{v}_i \odot \boldsymbol{e}_j x_j + \boldsymbol{e}_i x_i \odot \boldsymbol{v}_j)$ when considering the feature-field interactions.

Different from AutoFIS which requires a separated search stage to estimate g_{ij} and then its mask for deciding whether a cross-feature should be included in the model, our method enables g_{ij} to be determined dynamically in an attention network and to learn the relative importance of the kept feature interaction. Therefore, our methods do not prescribe an additional search process.

The gated recurrent neural network is to introduce a gating mechanism on the classical RNN to control the information transmission in the neural network [3,6]. The gating mechanism can be used to control which information in the memory unit needs to be left and which needs to be discarded. In this way, the gated recurrent neural network can learn the long-term dependence within a relatively long span, and will not lead to gradient explosion or gradient dispersion. Our self-gating layer is also inspired by the gating function in GRU, which also plays a role in controlling information transmission. The difference is that because our feature selection task focuses on suppressing unimportant information rather than learning long-term dependence, our gating layer is not a recurrent structure, and only one nonlinear activation is used to achieve the selection function.

3.3   Exploiting Self-gating Layer in Deep FM Models

SGL can be flexibly added to many existing FM models for feature selection to improve the model performance. For demonstrating this point, we select DeepFM which is a robust variant of deep factorization machines [29], to apply the Self-Gating mechanism. Table 1 summarizes the prediction rules and notations of four self-gated factorization machines: gFM, gFM+, gDeepFM, and gDeepFM+.

3.4   Objective Function and Optimization

Generally, CTR prediction is modeled as a classification task and uses the *binary cross entropy* loss function:

$$\mathcal{L}_{BCE} = -\frac{1}{n} \sum_{i=1}^{n} (y_i \log(\hat{y}_i) + (1 - y_i) \log(1 - \hat{y}_i)) \tag{9}$$

where n is the number of training instances, y_i and $\hat{y}_i$ indicates the real value and the prediction value respectively.

Over-fitting is a recurring problem in the process of optimizing machine learning models, particularly for the factorization machine models. If the neurons in the pairwise interaction layer are excessively adaptive and interdependent, which inevitably results in over-fitting when training these models. Two widely-used

Table 1. The prediction rules of the self-gated factorization machine models.

Model	Notations and prediction rule
gFM	$y = y_{LR} + y_{SG}$ $y_{SG} = \boldsymbol{p}_e^{\mathsf{T}} \sum\limits_{i=1}^{m-1} \sum\limits_{j=i+1}^{m} f_{SG}(\boldsymbol{E}_I^{ij})$ where $y_{LR} = w_0 + \sum\limits_{i=1}^{m} w_i x_i$, $\boldsymbol{p}_e \in \mathbb{R}^k$ is the weight vector of the prediction layer, y_{SG} performs feature selection only on the layer of feature-feature interaction.
gFM+	$y = y_{LR} + y'_{SG}$ $y'_{SG} = \boldsymbol{p}_e^{\mathsf{T}} \sum\limits_{i=1}^{m-1} \sum\limits_{j=i+1}^{m} f_{SG}(\boldsymbol{E}_I^{ij}) + \boldsymbol{p}_v^{\mathsf{T}} \sum\limits_{i=1}^{m-1} \sum\limits_{j=i+1}^{m} f_{SG}(\boldsymbol{V}_I^{ij})$ where $\boldsymbol{p}_e, \boldsymbol{p}_v \in \mathbb{R}^k$ is the weight vector of the prediction layer, y'_{SG} performs feature selection on both the layers of feature-feature interaction and feature-field interaction
gDeepFM	$y = y_{LR} + y_{SG} + y_{DNN}$ $y_{DNN} = \boldsymbol{p}^{\mathsf{T}} \sigma_L \left(\boldsymbol{W}_L \left(\ldots \sigma_1 \left(\boldsymbol{W}_1 (\boldsymbol{E}_{con}) + \boldsymbol{b}_1 \right) \ldots \right) + \boldsymbol{b}_L \right)$ $\boldsymbol{E}_{con} = \boldsymbol{e}_1 x_1 \oplus \boldsymbol{e}_2 x_2 \oplus \ldots \oplus \boldsymbol{e}_{m-1} x_{m-1} \oplus \boldsymbol{e}_m x_m$ where $\sigma_L, \boldsymbol{W}_L, \boldsymbol{b}_L$ are the activation function, weight matrix and bias vector of the L-th layer, and $\boldsymbol{p}$ is a weight vector, $\boldsymbol{E}_{con}$ is the concatenation of embedding vectors in $\boldsymbol{E}$, y_{SG} performs feature selection only on the layer of feature-feature interaction
gDeepFM+	$y = y_{LR} + y'_{SG} + y_{DNN}$ where y'_{SG} performs feature selection on both the layers of feature-feature interaction and feature-field interaction

methods to prevent over-fitting in deep learning are *dropout* and L_2 regularization. *Dropout* randomly disables a certain proportion (a.k.a $dr \in [0,1]$) of the feature detectors to prevent co-adaptation of neurons in each training batch. L_2 regularization imposes large penalties on sparse peaked values, and finally reduces the size of parameter values to reduce model complexity.

4 Experiment Settings

4.1 Datasets

To carry out the experimental evaluation, we use two large-scale datasets from different application fields. Statistics of datasets are summarized in Table 2. Criteo comes from the click logs of 45 million users within a week. There are 26 anonymous categorical features and 13 continuous features in the dataset [1]. Avazu is released in Kaggle's CTR prediction competition. It contains about 38.55M click records of ten days ordered by time [2]. We randomly divided each dataset in the same way: 80% of samples as the training set, 10% of samples as the validation set, and the rest as the test set.

4.2 Evaluation Methods

1. *FM* [20] is the naive factorization machine.

---

[1] https://www.kaggle.com/c/criteo-display-ad-challenge/.
[2] https://www.kaggle.com/c/avazu-ctr-prediction.

Table 2. Statistics of the datasets of Avazu and Criteo.

Dataset	#Instances	#Fields	#Features
Avazu	40,428,967	24	8.37M
Criteo	45,840,617	39	5.55M

2. *FFM* [13] is the field-aware FM.
3. *DeepFM* [7] combines an FM component to capture second-order interaction, and a deep component to simulate high-order interaction.
4. xDeepFM [15] introduces a compressed interaction layer to DeepFM and enables learning high-order feature interaction at the vector level.
5. *NFM* [8] stacks a MLP component over a bilinear interaction pooling layer.
6. *AFM* [26] distinguishes and learns the importance of feature interaction through an attention network.
7. *AutoFIS* [16] is recorded as AutoFM, AutoDeepFM, etc. The models are trained in a phased manner with a search stage and re-train stage.
8. *GateNet* [11] is recorded as GateFM(e), GateFM(h), etc. 'e' and 'h' represents the application embedding gates and hidden gates respectively.
9. *FiBiNet* learns feature importance via the squeeze-excitation network and fine-grained feature interactions via bilinear functions.
10. *Self-Gated FMs* are our proposed methods and marked with a prefix of 'g'.

4.3   Evaluation Criteria

For CTR prediction, two standard indicators AUC (area under ROC) and LogLoss (cross entry) are used. The improvement of AUC and logloss by 0.001 is significant in the performance of the model [2,21,23].

Table 3. The settings of FM models. k: embedding size, lr: learning rate, bs: batch size, λ: L_2 regularization, h: attention units, dr: dropout ratio, rd: reduction ratio, $cross$: cross-layer size, c and μ are parameters in gRDA optimizer.

Model	Avazu	Criteo
General	$k = 32$	$k = 64$
	$lr = 1e{-}3$	$lr = 1e{-}3$
	$bs = 4096$	$bs = 8192$
	$\lambda = 1e{-}6$	$\lambda = 1e{-}6$
	$h = 32$	$h = 64$
	$dr = 0.2$	$dr = 0.2$
	mlp $= (32,32)$	mlp $= (64,64)$
NFM	mlp $= (64,)$	mlp $= (64,)$
FFM	$k = 16$	$k = 16$
FiBiNet	$rd = 3$	$rd = 3$
xDeepFM	$cross = (16,16)$	$cross = (16,16)$
AutoFM	$c = 5e{-}3, \mu = 0.8$	$c = 5e{-}4, \mu = 0.8$
AutoDeepFM	$c = 5e{-}4, \mu = 0.8$	$c = 5e{-}4, \mu = 0.8$

4.4 Implementation Details

The gRDA optimizer is used in the AutoFIS model for the search stage. The parameters of other baseline models and our self-gated FMs are optimized by the Adam optimizer. An early-stopping strategy is taken to all models. All models are implemented with PyTorch and all experiments are conducted on a computer with Intel(R) Xeon(R) Bronze 3204 CPU @1.90 GHz, 128 GB memory, and NVIDIA Geforce RTX 3090.

For the evaluation methods, the hyper-parameter setting is carefully searched to follow the existing configuration disclosed in their papers. For model training, both L_2 regularization and *dropout* regularization are adopted for evaluation methods. For two datasets, the parameters of FM models are set as Table 3. For our models, we use the same hyper-parameters as the base models (i.e., FM and DeepFM accordingly) except for extra ones.

5 Experiment Analysis

The experimental results are analyzed for answering the following questions:

RQ 1: Can the self-gating mechanism work well when migrating to different FM models?

RQ 2: How do our methods perform as compared with other counterparts?

RQ 3: How do key parameters and mechanisms affect our methods?

RQ 4: How do our methods perform in terms of computational efficiency?

5.1 Migration to FM Models (RQ 1)

To answer RQ1, we apply the SGL to FM [20] and DeepFM [7] to automatically select cross-features and show the experimental results in Table 4. When comparing gFM with FM, we can find that gFM significantly improves AUC and reduces LogLoss on all datasets and gFM achieves slightly better performance than DeepFM. When comparing gDeepFM with DeepFM, we can still find that gDeepFM outperforms DeepFM on the Avazu and Criteo datasets. It can prove that the self-gating mechanism is effective for the selection of cross features.

When introducing the feature-field interactions, no significant gain is noted on gFM+, yet surprising benefits are observed on gDeepFM+. On the datasets of Avazu and Criteo, gDeepFM+ increases the AUC of gDeepFM by 0.0016 and 0.0005; at the same time, reduces the LogLoss of gDeeFM by 0.0009 and 0.0010. We speculate the main reason is that it is difficult for shallow FM to learn effective representations for features and fields when the underlying data is sparse (both for the Avazu and Criteo datasets), such as users with specific preferences or niche features with a narrow appeal [2]. In such cases, there should be not enough interactions between most field-feature pairs, but dense embeddings will lead to nonzero predictions for all field-features pairs, and thus can over-generalize and make less relevant predictions [2]. On the contrary, through multiple combinations of features, the deep component can explore the potential patterns in the data and even the correlation between rare features and the label. It indirectly has the potential to play the role of feature-field interaction patterns and improve the attention effect.

Table 4. Performance comparison of different FM models. The values in the first grade and the second grade are marked in **bold** and *italics*, respectively.

Dataset	Avazu		Criteo	
Model	AUC	LogLoss	AUC	LogLoss
AFM	0.7852	0.3778	0.8083	0.4435
NFM	0.7843	0.3776	0.8102	0.4416
FFM	0.7875	0.3769	0.8073	0.4447
FiBiNet	*0.7876*	0.3765	0.8090	0.4431
xDeepFM	0.7855	0.3787	0.8101	0.4417
AutoFM	0.7850	0.3789	0.8043	0.4478
GateFM(e)	0.7828	0.3792	0.8096	0.4421
AutoDeepFM	0.7861	0.3767	0.8087	0.4436
GateDeepFM(e)	*0.7876*	0.3766	0.8106	*0.4411*
GateDeepFM(h)	0.7848	0.3789	0.8078	0.4443
FM	0.7814	0.3793	0.8057	0.4462
gFM	0.7865	0.3761	0.8102	0.4418
gFM+	0.7865	0.3771	0.8094	0.4427
DeepFM	0.7865	0.3769	0.8085	0.4432
gDeepFM	*0.7876*	*0.3761*	*0.8111*	*0.4411*
gDeepFM+	**0.7892**	**0.3752**	**0.8116**	**0.4401**

Finally, we demonstrate the logloss changes on the validation set with each training epoch. According to Fig. 3, our proposed self-gating FM models converge faster than the naive FM and DeepFM. Since their logloss performance is much lower, it also implies that their generalization ability is better. This is also consistent with the above analysis.

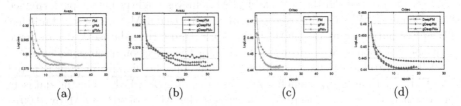

Fig. 3. Logloss on the validation set with each training epoch. (a–b) Avazu and (c–d) Criteo.

5.2   Performance Comparison (RQ 2)

To answer RQ2, our self-gated factorization machines is compared to seven baselines. The experimental results are also shown in Table 4. gDeepFM+ ranks in the 1st grade, and gDeepFM ranks in the 2nd grade on both datasets.

As above-mentioned that both AFM and NFM focus on pooling the second-order cross-features. gFM shares many components with them. gFM works much better on the Avazu dataset and shows comparable performance to NFM on the Criteo dataset. From the perspective of pooling, it is obvious that our strategy is superior to AFM and NFM. AutoFIS and GateNet are both based on gating mechanisms for the selection of cross-features. However, gFM is superior to AutoFM and GateFM(e) on all two datasets, and correspondingly gDeepFM outperforms AutoDeepFM and GateDeepFM(e) on the Avazu and Criteo datasets. Although GateNet is simpler and also competitive, it cannot be extended to model and exploit the effects of feature-field interactions. On the contrary, our mechanism is more scalable, which can result in more powerful models such as gDeepFM+. In AutoFIS, the search stage and retraining stage must be utilized to avoid co-adaptation of gating status and weight. This trims the parameter adjustment of AutoFIS in different scenarios more complex. Compared with AutoFIS, our models do not need phased training and use only one optimizer which makes the model easier to train and deploy in the context of real applications.

FFM shows its competitive edge as it also considers the effect of fields. However, FFM suffers from large-scale parameters and low efficiency. In contrast, our proposed gFM has advantages both in classification accuracy and computational efficiency (see Table 4). XDeepFM can be said to be a real "deep" factorization machine, but its complexity will be a major bottleneck and it needs to be carefully optimized to achieve a better prediction performance. Compared with SENETLayer used in FiBiNet, there are the following differences with our methods: (1) There is no squeeze stage and no pooling operations. (2) SENETLayer uses two full-connection layers to realize excitation, while SGL uses an attention network, which eliminates the operations of dimension reduction and promotion. (3) Instead of bilinear operation, the hadamard product is used for feature interactions in our method. (4) Most importantly, the feature-field interaction layer is proposed and explored to enhance the attention mechanism. DeepFM, xDeepFM, and FiBiNet are the most competitive variants of FM according to FuxiCTR which is an open benchmark for reproducible research and provides a rigorous comparison of different models for CTR prediction [29]. However, our proposed models especially for gDeepFM+ outperform them significantly.

5.3 Analysis of Influencing Factors (RQ 3)

Impact of Embedding Dimension: We keep the settings of L_2-regularization coefficient λ, dropout ratio, and learning rate unchanged, and observe the impact of embedding dimension (k) on self-gated factorization machines. As shown in Fig. 4, for the same dataset, the optimal embedding dimensions are different with various models. For gFM and gFM+, the optimal setting falls in $k \in [64, 128]$ on both datasets. When the value of k is larger than 64, it incurs overfitting and thus harms the generalization ability of the model. For gDeepFM and gDeepFM+, the optimal setting collapses in $k \in [32, 64]$. As the gDeepFM/gDeepFM+ is of the better generalization ability, increasing k empowers the prediction performance. Generally, the dimension determines the amount of information a

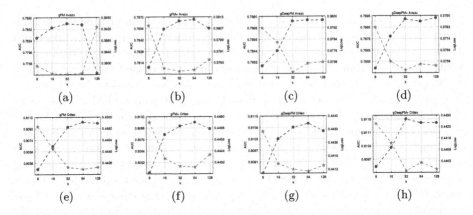

Fig. 4. The impact of embedding dimension (k) on self-gated factorization machines. (a–d) Avazu and (e–h) Criteo.

feature vector can carry. When the dimension is too small, the expression ability is insufficient, and when the dimension is too high, the cost of calculation and memory increases. Because embedding learning also has the risk of under-fitting or over-fitting, $k \in [32, 64]$ is appropriate for our proposed models.

Table 5. Performance comparison of different regularization strategies, where $k=32$, $bs=4096$ for Avazu and $bs=8192$ for Criteo, $lr=$1e-3.

Avazu						
Regularization	$dr=0$, $\lambda=0$		$dr=0.2$, $\lambda=$1e-6		$dr=0.2$, $\lambda=0$	
Metric	AUC	LogLoss	AUC	LogLoss	AUC	LogLoss
gFM	0.7841	0.3800	0.7865	0.3761	0.7861	0.3776
gFM+	0.7847	0.3789	0.7865	0.3771	0.7848	0.3787
gDeepFM	0.7866	0.3771	0.7875	0.3761	0.7864	0.3767
gDeepFM+	0.7883	0.3767	0.7892	0.3752	0.7876	0.3770
Criteo						
Regularization	$dr=0$, $\lambda=0$		$dr=0.2$, $\lambda=$1e-6		$dr=0.2$, $\lambda=0$	
Metric	AUC	LogLoss	AUC	LogLoss	AUC	LogLoss
gFM	0.8096	0.4423	0.8102	0.4418	0.8109	0.4412
gFM+	0.8102	0.4417	0.8094	0.4427	0.8105	0.4412
gDeepFM	0.8103	0.4417	0.8111	0.4411	0.8108	0.4411
gDeepFM+	0.8112	0.4407	0.8116	0.4401	0.8114	0.4402

Impact of Regularization Strategies: Both strategies of dropout and L_2 regularization can be used in avoiding the risk of the over-fitting problem. Additionally, two regularization strategies can play a complementary effect at the same time [22]. However, according to our experiments, the situation is not always as expected as shown in Table 5. Generally, the prediction performance of self-gated

FM models can be enhanced using dropout regularization. Compared with the case without regularization ($dr = 0$, $\lambda = 0$), enabling dropout ($dr = 0.2$ benefits the prediction accuracy on both the datasets of Avazu and Criteo, except the case of gDeepFM+ on the Avazu dataset. When enabling both L_2 and dropout regularizations ($dr = 0$ and $\lambda = 1e{-}6$), the situation becomes complicated. The performance gains can be seen in gFM, gDeepFM, and gDeepFM+ against the Avazu dataset, and gDeepFM+ against the Criteo dataset. However, it harms the prediction performance of gFM+ on the Avazu dataset, and that of gFM, gFM+, and gDeepFM on the Criteo dataset. The regularization strategies need to be carefully chosen.

Table 6. Model size of different FMs.

Models	Model size
FM	$n(1 + k)$
FFM	$n(1 + mk)$
AFM	$n(1 + k) + (hk + 2h + k)$
gFM	$n(1 + k) + (hk + 2h + k)$
gFM+	$n(1 + k) + 2(hk + h + k)$
DeepFM	$n(1 + k) + (mkh + Lh^2 + h)$
gDeepFM	$n(1 + k) + (hk + 2h + k) + (mkh + Lh^2 + h)$
gDeepFM+	$n(1 + k) + 2(hk + h + k) + (mkh + Lh^2 + h)$

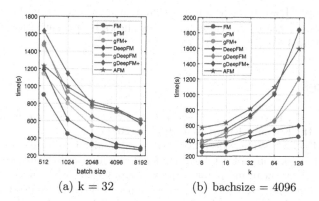

(a) k = 32   (b) bachsize = 4096

Fig. 5. The computational overheads with a) batch size and b) embedding dimension, against the Criteo cataset.

5.4   Computational Efficiency (RQ 4)

Regarding the model of FMs, space cost is mainly reflected in the total number of model parameters. Let n be the number of features, m be the number of fields, k be the embedding dimension, L be the total number of layers in MLP and h be the number of hidden units in each layer, the model size of selected FM models is shown in Table 6. Generally speaking, FM has the least space overhead and FFM has the greatest space overhead. AFM and gFM have the same space complexity. gFM+ introduces $hk+k$ parameters over gFM as it introduces a field-feature interaction layer. DeepFM/gDeepFM /gDeepFM+ add $mkh + Lh^2 + h$ parameters over FM/gFM/gFM+ since that the same MLP is used for modeling deep feature interactions.

Given the same training configuration, Fig. 5(a) and 5(b) show the comparison of the computational overhead of selected methods w.r.t the embedding dimension k and the batch size, respectively. The computational efficiency of various FM variants is linear with the batch size and the embedding dimension. Thanks to the acceleration of GPU, the overhead of our proposed methods is only 2–3 times higher than that of FM or DeepFM, especially compared with AFM. The latter uses the softmax function, which significantly introduces the overhead in the back-propagation process.

6   Conclusions

We have proposed a novel self-gating mechanism for automatic feature selection of cross-features in FM models. Different from previous research, we revisit the role of the attention score of feature interactions and directly take these attention scores as signals to activate the gate status. More importantly, our methods learn that attention score depends not only on the feature-feature interactions but also on the feature-field interactions. By porting the self-gating mechanism to FM and DeepFM, we further confirm that it works better together with neural components on feature selections, and thus shows its potential for migration to other models of FMs.

References

1. Brauwers, G., Frasincar, F.: A general survey on attention mechanisms in deep learning. IEEE Trans. Knowl. Data Eng. 1 (2021)
2. Cheng, H., et al.: Wide & deep learning for recommender systems. In: Proceedings of the 1st Workshop on Deep Learning for Recommender Systems, pp. 7–10 (2016)
3. Cho, K., et al.: Learning phrase representations using RNN encoder-decoder for statistical machine translation. In: Proceedings of the 2014 Conference on Empirical Methods in Natural Language Processing, EMNLP, pp. 1724–1734. ACL (2014)
4. Dauphin, Y.N., Fan, A., Auli, M., Grangier, D.: Language modeling with gated convolutional networks. In: Proceedings of the 34th International Conference on Machine Learning, ICML 2017, pp. 933–941. PMLR (2017)
5. Du, G., Zhou, L., Yang, Y., Lü, K., Wang, L.: Deep multiple auto-encoder-based multi-view clustering. Data Sci. Eng. 6(3), 323–338 (2021)
6. Greff, K., Srivastava, R.K., Koutník, J., Steunebrink, B.R., Schmidhuber, J.: LSTM: a search space odyssey. IEEE Trans. Neural Networks Learn. Syst. 28(10), 2222–2232 (2017)

7. Guo, H., Tang, R., Ye, Y., Li, Z., He, X.: DeepFM: a factorization-machine based neural network for CTR prediction. In: Proceedings of the Twenty-Sixth International Joint Conference on Artificial Intelligence, IJCAI 2017, pp. 1725–1731 (2017). ijcai.org

8. He, X., Chua, T.: Neural factorization machines for sparse predictive analytics. In: Proceedings of the 40th International ACM SIGIR Conference on Research and Development in Information Retrieval, pp. 355–364. ACM (2017)

9. Hong, F., Huang, D., Chen, G.: Interaction-aware factorization machines for recommender systems. In: The Thirty-Third AAAI Conference on Artificial Intelligence, AAAI 2019, pp. 3804–3811. AAAI Press (2019)

10. Hu, J., Shen, L., Albanie, S., Sun, G., Wu, E.: Squeeze-and-excitation networks. IEEE Trans. Pattern Anal. Mach. Intell. **42**(8), 2011–2023 (2020)

11. Huang, T., She, Q., Wang, Z., Zhang, J.: GateNet: gating-enhanced deep network for click-through rate prediction. CoRR abs/2007.03519 (2020)

12. Huang, T., Zhang, Z., Zhang, J.: FiBiNET: combining feature importance and bilinear feature interaction for click-through rate prediction. In: Proceedings of the 13th ACM Conference on Recommender Systems, 2019, pp. 169–177. ACM (2019)

13. Juan, Y., Zhuang, Y., Chin, W., Lin, C.: Field-aware factorization machines for CTR prediction. In: Proceedings of the 10th ACM Conference on Recommender Systems. pp. 43–50. ACM (2016)

14. Lan, L., Geng, Y.: Accurate and interpretable factorization machines. In: The Thirty-Third AAAI Conference on Artificial Intelligence, AAAI 2019, pp. 4139–4146. AAAI Press (2019)

15. Lian, J., Zhou, X., Zhang, F., Chen, Z., Xie, X., Sun, G.: xDeepFM: combining explicit and implicit feature interactions for recommender systems. In: Proceedings of the 24th ACM SIGKDD International Conference on Knowledge Discovery & Data Mining, KDD, pp. 1754–1763. ACM (2018)

16. Liu, B., et al.: AutoFIS: automatic feature interaction selection in factorization models for click-through rate prediction. In: Proceedings of the 26th ACM SIGKDD Conference on Knowledge Discovery and Data Mining, pp. 2636–2645. ACM (2020)

17. Luo, Y., et al.: AutoCross: automatic feature crossing for tabular data in real-world applications. In: Proceedings of the 25th ACM SIGKDD International Conference on Knowledge Discovery & Data Mining, KDD 2019, pp. 1936–1945. ACM (2019)

18. Luong, T., Pham, H., Manning, C.D.: Effective approaches to attention-based neural machine translation. In: Proceedings of the 2015 Conference on Empirical Methods in Natural Language Processing, EMNLP 2015, pp. 1412–1421. The Association for Computational Linguistics (2015)

19. Pan, J., et al.: Field-weighted factorization machines for click-through rate prediction in display advertising. In: Proceedings of the 2018 World Wide Web Conference on World Wide Web, WWW 2018, pp. 1349–1357. ACM (2018)

20. Rendle, S.: Factorization machines. In: ICDM 2010, The 10th IEEE International Conference on Data Mining, pp. 995–1000. IEEE Computer Society (2010)

21. Song, W., et al.: AutoInt: automatic feature interaction learning via self-attentive neural networks. In: Proceedings of the 28th ACM International Conference on Information and Knowledge Management, CIKM, pp. 1161–1170. ACM (2019)

22. Srivastava, N., Hinton, G.E., Krizhevsky, A., Sutskever, I., Salakhutdinov, R.: Dropout: a simple way to prevent neural networks from overfitting. J. Mach. Learn. Res. **15**(1), 1929–1958 (2014)

23. Sun, Y., Pan, J., Zhang, A., Flores, A.: FM^2: field-matrixed factorization machines for recommender systems. In: WWW 2021: The Web Conference 2021, pp. 2828–2837. ACM/IW3C2 (2021)

24. Vaswani, A., et al.: Attention is all you need. In: Advances in Neural Information Processing Systems, pp. 5998–6008 (2017)

25. Wang, R., Fu, B., Fu, G., Wang, M.: Deep & cross network for ad click predictions. In: Proceedings of the ADKDD 2017, pp. 12:1–12:7. ACM (2017)

26. Xiao, J., Ye, H., He, X., Zhang, H., Wu, F., Chua, T.: Attentional factorization machines: learning the weight of feature interactions via attention networks. In: Proceedings of the Twenty-Sixth International Joint Conference on Artificial Intelligence, IJCAI, pp. 3119–3125 (2017). ijcai.org

27. Zhang, W., Du, T., Wang, J.: Deep learning over multi-field categorical data. In: Ferro, N., et al. (eds.) ECIR 2016. LNCS, vol. 9626, pp. 45–57. Springer, Cham (2016). https://doi.org/10.1007/978-3-319-30671-1_4

28. Zhou, G., et al.: Deep interest network for click-through rate prediction. In: Proceedings of the 24th ACM SIGKDD International Conference on Knowledge Discovery & Data Mining, KDD, pp. 1059–1068. ACM (2018)

29. Zhu, J., Liu, J., Yang, S., Zhang, Q., He, X.: FuxiCTR: an open benchmark for click-through rate prediction. arXiv preprint arXiv:2009.05794 (2020)

Heterogeneous Graph Neural Network-Based Software Developer Recommendation

Zhixiong Ye[1], Zhiyong Feng[1], Jianmao Xiao[2(✉)], Yuqing Gao[3], Guodong Fan[1], Huwei Zhang[1], and Shizhan Chen[1]

[1] Tianjin University, Tianjin, China
{lailai_zxy,zyfeng,guodongfan,zhuwe,shizhan}@tju.edu.cn
[2] Jiangxi Normal University, Jiangxi, China
jm_xiao@jxnu.edu.cn
[3] Fujian Normal University, Fujian, China
lilyeatcandy@icloud.com

Abstract. In software maintenance, it is critical for project managers to assign software issues to the appropriate developers. However, finding suitable developers is challenging due to the general sparsity and the long-tail of developer-issue interactions. In this paper, we propose a novel **H**eterogeneous **G**raph Neural Network-based method for **D**eveloper **R**ecommendation (called HGDR), in which text information embedding and self-supervised learning (SSL) are incorporated. Specifically, to alleviate the sparsity of developer-issue interactions, we unify developer-issue interactions, developer-source code file interactions and issue-source code file relations into a heterogeneous graph, and we embed text descriptions to graph nodes as information supplements. In addition, to mitigate the long-tail influence, e.g., recommendation bias, the proficiency weight suppression link supplementation is proposed to complement the tail developers by adjusting proficiency weights. Finally, to fully utilize rich structural information of heterogeneous graph, we use the joint learning of metapath-guided heterogeneous graph neural network and SSL to learn the embedding representation. Extensive comparison experiments on three real-world datasets show that HGDR outperforms the state-of-the-art methods by 6.02% to 44.27% on recommended metric. The experimental results also demonstrate the efficacy of HGDR in the sparse and long-tail scenario. Our code is available at https://github.com/1qweasdzxc/HGDR.

Keywords: Developer recommendation · Heterogeneous graph neural network · Information supplement · Self-supervised learning

1 Introduction

In the process of software maintenance and evolution, issues will continue to emerge and accumulate [14]. On the open source platform, users can request

H. Gao et al. (Eds.): CollaborateCom 2022, LNICST 460, pp. 433–452, 2022.
https://doi.org/10.1007/978-3-031-24383-7_24

issues, such as new feature requests and bugs encountered. However, due to the limited familiarity of project managers in assigning issues to developers, or the way developers go to the platform to solve problems on their own, issues are not handled timely or even remain unresolved for a long time [4]. Therefore, how to automatically recommend suitable developers to answer issues in a timely and accurately manner is an important problem with practical needs [16,28].

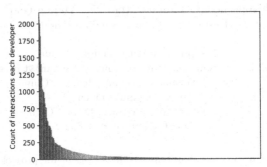

Fig. 1. Distribution of the number of issues solved by developers on the Tensorflow dataset

In recent years, to recommend suitable developers, a lot of efforts have been made in both research and practice. The matrix factorization (MF) [12] approach has been applied to recommend developers to solve issues [20,29,32], which is based on the hypothesis that developers have similar behavior [19,27]. Most of the current research methods focus only on developer-issue interactions and matching, while ignoring some useful information, such as the source code file as an intermediate bridge between the issue and the developer. This leads to low performance of recommendations. In addition, these approaches tend to recommend experienced developers. However, experienced developers are a minority, and it is difficult to solve the large number of issues raised by users timely. We argue that this is owning to two major limitations:

- **Scarcity of developer-issue interaction labels**: The solution to an issue usually involves only 1 to 3 developers, which leads to a sparse label of developer interactions. There may be other developers who are interested and capable of solving these problems, but these labels are difficult to collect.
- **Highly skewed data distribution**: Fig. 1 shows a long-tailed distribution of the number of issues solved by developers. The small number of experienced developers solve the majority of issues, which leads to a tendency to recommend experienced developers and a bias towards junior developers.

To solve the above problems, we find that the relationship between developers, issues, and the source code files can be well modeled by a heterogeneous graph. Recently, heterogeneous graph neural networks (HGNN) have been successful in various fields of processing heterogeneous information network (HIN) [17] data. The heterogeneous graph has a complex topology and rich relational information. Inspired by this, it can be applied to developer recommendation scenarios with sparse labels. Meanwhile, self-supervised learning (SSL) is used as a method to improve deep representation learning through unlabeled data and has been widely used in the fields of computer vision and natural language processing [1,3,6]. There have been some studies on network schema and meta-paths of heterogeneous graphs for SSL data augmentation [25]. However, there is few studies on the heterogeneous graphs of the long-tail distribution of the data, which do not take into account the feature distribution of recommended items. This makes it easy to recommend head items.

In this paper, we propose a novel **H**eterogeneous **G**raph Neural Network-based method for **D**eveloper **R**ecommendation (called HGDR), in which text information embedding and SSL are incorporated. Specifically, we unify developer-issue interaction, developer-source code interaction and issue-source code relations into a heterogeneous graph. Meanwhile, we embed text descriptions of developer commits and issues to graph nodes, which can well alleviate the sparsity of developer-issue interaction. To compensate for the recommendation bias caused by the long-tail, we propose a proficiency weight suppression label link supplementation to complement the tail developers who may have the ability to solve issues. In order to fully utilize rich structural information, we learn structural feature representations of developers and issues with the joint learning of HGNN and SSL. A novel data augmentation method based on SSL is proposed to better learn the latent relations of developer features. The main contributions of this work are as follows:

- To the best of my knowledge, HGDR is the first proposal to use heterogeneous graph neural networks to model the complex relationship between source code files, developers, and issues to recommend developers.
- We present a novel Heterogeneous Graph Neural Network-based model, HGDR. To address the sparsity and long tail of the developer-issue interactions, text information embedding and the proficiency weight suppression link supplementation are proposed, respectively. HGDR can also be used in many similar recommendation scenarios where label sparsity and long tails. In addition, we construct three real-world datasets for developer recommendation.
- Extensive experiments on three real-world datasets show that our HGDR outperforms existing state-of-the-art. The results demonstrate the effectiveness of HGDR in addressing the long-tail distributions and sparse labels of developer recommendation.

2 Preliminary

In this section, we define some basic concepts related to developer recommendation.

Definition 1 Developer Recommendation. In a software development platform, for an issue $i_i \in I$ recommends a set of suitable developers $\{d_1, d_2, ..., d_m\} \subseteq D$, where I represents the set of all issues, D represents the

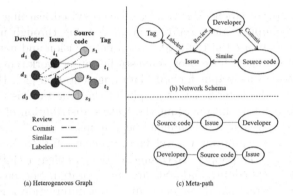

(a) Heterogeneous Graph   (c) Meta-path

Fig. 2. Heterogeneous information network structure and network model.

set of all developers, k represents the number of recommended developers. We construct HIN to model our developer recommendation task. A HIN is defined as $G = (V, E)$, where V and E denote the set of nodes and edges that have more than one node type or edge link type. For example, Fig. 2 (a) illustrates an example of a HIN including four node types: developer, source code file, issue, and tag, and four relationships between these nodes: review, commit, similar, and label. Here V includes the set of developer nodes D, the set of issue nodes I, the set of source code files nodes S and the set of issue label nodes T. Edge E is composed of relational edges between nodes, e.g., the developer-issue interaction edge (d, i) is $x_{di} = 1$.

Definition 2 Network Schema and Meta-path. A network schema is defined as $S_G = (O, R)$, which is the schema of a heterogeneous information network containing a directed graph of relationships R between all object types O. For example, Fig. 2 (b) shows the network schema, where developers are able to interact with issues by comments, with source code files through commits, and issues are related to the associated source code files. The meta-path P is defined as the path $O_1 O_2 ... O_{(l+1)}$, describing the complex relation $R = R_1 \circ R_2 ... \circ R_l$ between objects O_1 and $O_{(l+1)}$, and $\circ$ denotes the combinatorial operator of the relation. For example, Fig. 2 (c) shows two meta-paths in a network. SourceCode-Issue-Developer describes an issue that has been solved by the developer through comment replies, and submits some relevant source code files. Developer-SourceCode-Issue describes an issue that has been solved with some source code files. These source code files are also committed by some developers. Since meta-paths are combinations of multiple relations and contain complex semantics, they are considered as higher-order structures. The notations in this paper are shown in Table 1.

Table 1. Notations utilized in the paper.

Notations	Descriptions
I	$I = \{i_1, i_2, ..., i_n\}$ denotes a set of issues
D	$D = \{d_1, d_2, ..., d_m\}$ denotes a set of developers
S	$S = \{s_1, s_2, ..., s_p\}$ denotes a set of source code files
T	$T = \{t_1, t_2, ..., t_q\}$ denotes a set of tags
I-D-I	denotes issues solved by the same developer
D-I-D	denotes developers who have solved the same issue
I-T-I	denotes the same label issues
S-D-I	denotes developers who have solved this issue have also submitted some source code files
I-S-D	denotes some of the source code files submitted by the developer is related to some issue solving
D-S-I	denotes the issue is related to the source code files that has been modified by some developers' commits
S-I-D	denotes some issues solved by the developers are also related to some source code files

3   Approach

Figure 3 shows our model HGDR framework process for developer recommendation. First, we introduce data collection and heterogeneous graph construction. Second, We use text information embedding and link supplement methods to the heterogeneous graph. Third, joint learning based on meta-path and self-supervised is used to learn the embedding representation. Finally, with the embeddings of issues and developers, we predict the similarity score of developer-issue pair.

3.1   Data Collection and Heterogeneous Graph Construction

We collect the developer history commit records, issue related information and source code repository related information of open source projects from the popular open source platform Github. Then we preprocess the data to remove noisy data such as robot administrator data (some large projects set up robots to automatically submit simple actions), noisy source code file data (not in the set of source code files that have been submitted by developers), empty data, and duplicate data. To construct heterogeneous graph, we extract information about each issue's interaction with developer comments, the developer's commit records, the issue's tagging information, and the source code files associated with the issue solution. In particular, the source code files related to the issue solution are edge-linked using the issue description text after natural language processing preprocessing steps (including removing converting lowercase forms, removing punctuation, removing stop words, and stemming reduction lexical reduction word types). We use the NLTK [18] package to process the sentences, and the preprocessed words are compared with the words in the related source

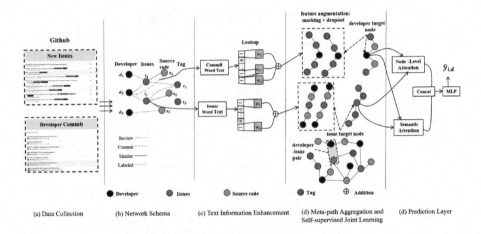

(a) Data Collection (b) Network Schema (c) Text Information Enhancement (d) Meta-path Aggregation and (d) Prediction Layer
                                                                           Self-supervised Joint Learning

Fig. 3. The overall framework of HGDR.

code files (identifiers in the code and words in the comments) calculate the cosine similarity. The definition is as follows:

$$Similarity = \frac{|IssueRequest \cap SourceCode|}{|SourceCode|}, \tag{1}$$

where $IssueRequest$ represents all words in the preprocessed issue request description, $SourceCode$ represents all words of the preprocessed source code in the source code file. Finally, a list of source code files is ranked by their similarity values to the issue, and we extract the relevant source code file which have the similarity value over a threshold (is set to 0.75 and the manual test issue correlates better with the source code file) to connect to the issue with similar edges. Using the data extracted above, we can construct a heterogeneous graph G. We describe the developer $e_d \in \mathbb{R}^N$, issue $e_i \in \mathbb{R}^N$, tag $e_t \in \mathbb{R}^N$, and source code file $e_s \in \mathbb{R}^N$ with embedding vectors, where the upper right N of $\mathbb{R}$ denotes the size of the vector dimension, and then construct an embedding matrix lookup table that can map the id to the embedding vector as follows,

$$E = [e_{i_1}, ..., e_{i_n}, e_{d_1}, ..., e_{d_m}, e_{t_1}, ..., e_{t_p}, e_{s_1}, ..., e_{s_q}]. \tag{2}$$

3.2   Text Information Enhancement and Link Supplement

In order to address the sparsity of newly arrived issue requests, we introduce text data to enhance the initial node embedding of heterogeneous graphs. First, we construct the corpus with the text description information committed by the developers and the text description information of the issue. It includes the text information of developer commit activity and issue content, respectively. Secondly, we extract the text information using Word2Vec [13] pre-training, and construct the dictionary $W = \{w_1, w_2, ..., w_{n-1}, w_n\}$ to get the word embedding.

Finally, we encode the text descriptive segment of the issue, and the text contains the sum of all word embeddings averaged as the initial embedding vector of the issue node. In particular, since the developer may have more than one history of submitting text descriptions, we also obtain the embedding of the text description segment after summing and averaging each word embedding. And we average these text description segments summations as the initial embedding vector of the developer node. In this way, when a newly arrived issue node has less information about other edges, we can also make good recommendation based on the embedding information constructed from the text descriptions. We apply the method equation as follows,

$$e_i = g(\{e_{w_1}, \ldots, e_{w_{n-1}}, e_{w_n}\}),$$
$$e_d = g(\{\{e_{w_1}, \ldots, e_{w_{n-1}}, e_{w_n}\}, \ldots, \{e_{w_1}, , e_{w_{n-1}}, e_{w_n}\}\}),$$

(3)

where e_{w_i} is the embedding of word w_i, e_i is the embedding of issue, e_d is the embedding of developer and the $g(\cdot)$ means the operation function applied to the words. In our experiments, we adopt the average function.

Since the developers' labels are in the long-tail distribution, this leads to a tendency to recommend experienced developers and a bias against developers with low proficiency. We propose a proficiency weight suppression link supplementation method for the proficiency bias of labels to mitigate the recommendation high proficiency tendency bias, which enables the recommendation to focus on finding the appropriate developer to solve the issue. The ranking indicator function DCG [9] is referenced to introduce an adaptive weighting mechanism that adaptively assigns weights based on the number of issues solved by the developer, while ensuring that the supplemented labels have solved similar issues before. Here the cosine similarity using the embedding information constructed from the text descriptions obtained above. We apply the method equation as follows,

$$S_{i,d} = w_d \cdot Rel_{d,i},$$
$$Rel_{d,i} = \sum_{i' \in I_d} Sim(i, i'),$$
$$w_d = 1 + weight/(1 + \log p_d),$$

(4)

where $Rel_{d,i}$ denotes the similarity of all issues solved by the developer's history with this issue, $Sim(,)$ denotes the cosine score similar to Eq. 1 and $S_{i,d}$ denotes the similarity score between the developer and this issue. The w_d denotes the weight assigned adaptively by the developer, where p_d denotes the number of issues solved by the developer. The *weight* is used as hyperparameters to control the degree of suppression. In order to weight the similarity between the developer and the issue in the supplemented link while appropriately reducing the proficiency bias, we present experiments to manually adjust the *weight* in Sect. 4.6.

3.3   Meta-path and Self-supervised Joint Learning

Supervised learning based on meta-paths as the main task of joint learning. Meta-path aggregation is the sequential semantics encoded by meta-paths that reveal different aspects of connected objects. For node information propagation, the information of all neighbors is step-by-step aggregated, which can save memory and computation time compared to classical graph neural networks (GNN), such as graph convolutional networks (GCN) [11] and graph attention networks (GAT) [21]. Since the goal of learning is developer and issue representation, it is intuitive to choose to end the meta-path with a developer or issue node, which ensures that the information aggregation on the meta-path is the end of the node we care about.

We extracted rich meta-path higher-order features and design eight meta-paths I-T-I, S-D-I, I-D-I, D-S-I, I-S-D, T-I-D, S-I-D, and D-I-D. The notations meanings are shown in Table 1. For example, D-S-I indicates that the source code files related to the issue and the solution has been submitted for modification by some developers. The impact of different meta-paths on our recommendation performance is studied in Sect. 5. The meta-path information aggregation is shown as follows,

$$X_{p,1} = \sigma(GNN_{p,1}(E, A_{p,1})), X_{p,2} = \sigma(GNN_{p,2}(X_{p,1}, A_{p,2})), \tag{5}$$

$$X_{p,k} = \sigma(GNN_{p,k}(X_{p,k-1}, A_{p,k})), \tag{6}$$

where E denotes the initial node embedding, $\sigma()$ is the activation function. $X_{p,k}$ is the node representation on meta-path p after the kth propagation. $A_{p,k}$ denotes the adjacency matrix of meta-path p at the step k. The $GNN_{p,k}$ denotes GNN layer of the meta-path p at the step k and propagation method is GAT, which aggregates neighboring nodes considering the importance of attention at the node level. By stacking multiple GNN layers, HGDR can be used not only to explicitly explore the multi-hop connectivity in a meta-path, but also to efficiently capture collaboration signals. SSL as an auxiliary task of joint learning in Fig. 4. We consider a developers d_i, given the same developer node i input, after augmented by transformation function f' and f'', i.e., masking nodes or edges with two perspectives. Finally, we use metapath-guided heterogeneous graph neural network g' and g'' encoding to get two perspectives of representation z_i' and z_i'', that is

$$z_i' \leftarrow g'(f'(e_i)), \ z_i'' \leftarrow g''(f''(e_i)). \tag{7}$$

Different from existing heterogeneous graphs with random masking mechanisms for edges or nodes. For example, a developer may loses the source code files submitted about the front-end sub-interface of the configuration software, but retains the source code file information of the configuration home page, which is not conducive to comparative learning to learn meaningful representation information. We could randomly divide the node neighbors into two mutually exclusive sets of neighbors for data augmentation. We call this method Random Dropout (RMD), and will use it as one of our baselines. We now introduce Similarity Meta-path Neighbor Masking (SMP) where we further explore

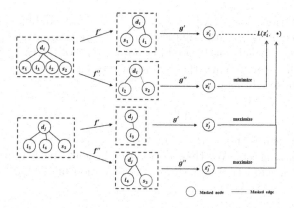

Fig. 4. Self-supervised learning framework illustration.

the feature correlations when creating masking patterns. Specifically, we can learn more meaningful comparative features by dividing the meta-path into two subsets of neighbors with large differences in similarity based on their embedded Euclidean Distance [2].

Similarity Meta-path Neighbor Masking. We randomly select the seed meta-paths Mp_{seed} for each batch developer, and use the pre-computed similarity. Here we split it into two equal number of mutually exclusive neighbor sets $N_d = \{Mp_{seed}, Mp_1, ...Mp_k\}$ by first order neighbor similarity. k is half the number of available neighbor nodes. We change the seed meta-paths for each batch so that the SSL task can learn various types of mask patterns.

After different data augmentation f' and f'', ensure that the model recognizes the representation of the same input node i. In other words, minimize the learning loss represented by the same nodes $z_i{'}$ and $z_i{''}$ and maximize the learning loss of different nodes $z_i{'}$ and $z_j{''}$ after data enhancement. We treat $(z_i{'}, z_i{''})$ as the positive pair and $(z_i{'}, z_j{''})$ as the negative pair for $i \neq j$. We define the SSL loss for a batch of developer $\{d_i\}$ as:

$$L_{ssl}\{d_i\} = -\frac{1}{n}\sum_{i \in D}^{n} \log \frac{exp(s(z_i{'}, z_i{''})/\tau)}{\sum_{j \in D}^{n} exp(s(z_i{'}, z_j{''})/\tau)}, \tag{8}$$

where $s(\cdot)$ measures the similarity of two embeddings, we still using the cosine similarity function. τ is a softmax hyperparameter. The above loss function $L_{ssl}\{d_i\}$ learns a robust embedding space, similar developers are close to each other after data augmentation, and random developers are pushed farther away. SSL can be performed for unlabeled scenarios.

3.4 Prediction Layer

After joint learning of the meta-path-aware subgraph, the semantic information revealed by all meta-paths is fused. Suppose that for a developer node d, its set of node representations $X_d = \{X_{p_1}^d, X_{p_2}^d, ..., X_{p_\lambda}^d\}$ is aggregated from λ meta-paths. The importance of meta-path semantics and node representation varies, and the contribution of each meta-path should be adjusted accordingly. Therefore, we use attention mechanism to learn the importance of each meta-path. We measure each meta-path weight as follows:

$$W_{mp}^d = \alpha^T \cdot X_d, \tag{9}$$

where W_{mp} measures the vector of meta-path importance and α is the matrix of learnable parameters. We then normalize the meta-path importance scores using the softmax function and obtain the attention factor for each meta-path as follows:

$$\beta_{mp_i}^d = \frac{exp(W_{mp_i}^d)}{\sum_{j=1}^{\lambda} exp(W_{mp_j}^d)}, \tag{10}$$

where $\beta_{mp_i}^d$ denotes the normalized attention factor of the meta-path mp_i on node d. Using the learned attention factors, we can fuse all meta-path aggregation node representations into the final meta-path-aware node representation z_d as follows:

$$z_d = \sum_{i=1}^{\lambda} \beta_{mp_i}^d X_{mp_i}^d, \tag{11}$$

z_i is obtained in the same way as z_d. We use a different pooling strategy which connects the embedding representation z_i of the target issue node with the embedding representation z_d aggregated representation of the developer node. i.e.,

$$z_g = concat(z_i, z_d). \tag{12}$$

Then, we use the 2-layer Multilayer Perceptron (MLP) to compute the matching scores of the issue-developer pairs. Let us denote by $\hat{y}_{i,d}$ the prediction function for the interaction score of issue i and developer d can be expressed as follows.

$$\hat{y}_{i,d} = w_2^T \sigma(w_1^T z_g + b_1) + b_2, \tag{13}$$

where w_1, w_2, b_1 and b_2 are trainable parameters of the MLP and σ is the nonlinear activation function.

3.5   Multi-task Training

In order to make the SSL representation contribute to improved learning of the supervised task, we utilize a multi-task training strategy in which the primary supervised task and the secondary SSL task are jointly optimized. Precisely, let $\{(i, d)\}$ be a batch of issue-developer pairs sampled from the training set, and let d be sampled from a batch of developer distribution D. The loss of joint learning is:

$$L = L_{main}(\{(i, d)\}) + \lambda_1 L_{ssl}(\{d\}) + \lambda_2 ||\theta||_2^2, \tag{14}$$

where L_{main} is the loss function of the main task HGNN recommendation. θ is the set of model parameters, λ_1 and λ_2 are the hyperparameters controlling the regularization strength of SSL and L_2, respectively.

Our main task uses pairwise Bayesian personalized ranking (BPR) loss [15], which is common for recommender systems. The BPR loss can be expressed as follows,

$$L_{main}(\{(i,d)\}) = \sum_{(i,d_+,d_-)\in B} -\log(\hat{y}(i,d_+) - \hat{y}(i,d_-)), \tag{15}$$

where $B = \{(i,d_+,i_-)|y_{(i,d_+)} \in Y_+, y_{(i,d_-)} \in Y_-\}$ is the training set, Y_+ is the observed issue-developer interaction (positive sample), while Y_- is the unobserved issue-developer interaction (negative sample).

4   Experiment Setup

Table 2. Statistics of three utilized real-world datasets.

Project	Commit	Total issue	Open issue	Developer	Source file	Time period
Tensorflow	123264	33683	2137	3046	24426	2015-11-12- 2021-01-16
Flutter	27032	63251	10649	957	6053	2015-04-30- 2022-01-06
Vscode	91053	125690	6427	1559	5593	2015-11-20- 2022-01-15

We provide empirical results to demonstrate the effectiveness of our proposed HGDR in real open source software projects. The experiments aim to answer the following research questions.

- **Q1:** Can our construction of a heterogeneous graph neural network model effectively improve the accuracy of recommendation developers compared to other baseline methods?
- **Q2:** Does the SSL, text information embedding module improve the model performance? Can it effectively address the recommendation bias caused by the long-tail distribution of developers, while alleviating the sparsity problem of labels?
- **Q3:** How does the meta-path relationship of the graph structure affect HGDR?
- **Q4:** How do the weight suppression parameters, SSL parameters data augmentation parameters and loss function parameters affect the model effect?

4.1   Datasets and Metrics

In this experiment, we collect 3 popular open source projects from GitHub based on the GitHub REST API[1], such as tensorflow, flutter, and vscode. The features

---

[1] https://docs.github.com/en/rest.

of each project are shown in Table 2. For Tensorflow projects, there are a total of 3046 active developers, 33683 total issues and 2137 open unsolved issues. Our datasets are targeted at open source projects with more issues, while there are a large number of issues in the open state not processed in a timely manner.

Metrics: To evaluate the performance of the recommended developers, we use the popular standard metrics Recall@K and Normalized Discounted Cumulative Gain (NDCG@K) to evaluate the recommended performance for each configuration of the experimental results. Recall@K measures the percentage of test datasets that have been included in the top-K ranking list, and NDCG @K complements recall by assigning higher scores to hits higher on the developer list.

4.2   Baselines and Hyper-parameters

To demonstrate the validity of our HGDR model, we compared it with the following five state-of-the-art methods in different aspects.

MFBPR [15]: This is a matrix decomposition method in the Bayesian personalized ranking pairwise learning framework, which is widely used in developer recommendations as an important baseline for our comparisons.

NeuMF [8]: Using neural networks to enhance matrix decomposition algorithms with nonlinearities, this is used to compare the advantages of our approach with the same addition of nonlinear neural networks.

NGCF [23]: This is a model of bipartite graphs, which uses graph neural networks to extract higher-order connectivity of recommendations. Only issues and developers are used here to construct the interaction bipartite graph, which is used to compare the advantages of our approach over the bipartite graph.

LightGCN [7]: This is a light bipartite graph state-of-the-art graph convolution model based on NGCF, that propagates linearly over the user-item interaction graph to learn user and item embeddings.

KGAT [22]: This is the advanced knowledge-based model for merging higher-order information by learning entity attention performing attentional embedding propagation over the knowledge graph, which compares our approach to knowledge graph approaches with the same kinds of relationships and nodes.

We train and test divide using Leave-One-Out Cross Validation [10], and set the number of negative sampling candidates to {10,20,50,99}. We use Adam optimizer and mini-batch of size 1024 or 2048 with embedding size 64. Learning rate is searched at {1e−5, 1e−4, 1e−3,1e−2}, L2 regularization term weight decay $\lambda2$ at {1e−7, 1e−6, 1e−5, 1e−4, 1e−3, 1e−2}. For MFBPR, NeuMF, NGCF, LightGCN and KGAT, we tested and reported the best performance for them. For other parameters, we follow the settings in their original papers. For the text embedding parameters, the parameter vector size is 64, the window is set to 8, and the number of training rounds is 8. For contrast learning, softmax temperature is set to {0.01,0.05,0.1,0.5,1}, λ = {0.1, 0.3, 1.0, 3.0}, dropout rate = {0.1, 0.2, ... , 0.9}. Finally, the best results are reported.

4.3 Effectiveness of HGDR Compared to Other Baseline Methods (to Q1)

HGDR is designed to automatically recommend the appropriate developers to solve issues, which helps to reduce the latency of issues and improve collaboration efficiency. Therefore, we need to know how it performs in terms of developer recommendation compared to existing developer recommendation methods. To answer this research question, we used our datasets in existing developer recommendation baselines as well as some classical recommendation baseline methods for the comparison. We try to use the method parameters as set in their original paper, and some common parameters are set the same as our method to ensure the fairness of the comparison. Table 3 shows the performance of HGDR against the baseline performance of the other five recommended methods.

We can observe that our model HGDR significantly outperforms all baselines in terms of Recall and NDCG metrics. Specifically, HGDR outperforms the

Table 3. Performance comparisons on three real-world datasets with six baselines.

Subject	Top k of Recall and NDCG	MFBPR	NeuMF	NGCF	LightGCN	KGAT	HGDR	%Impro
Tensorflow	5	0.5764	0.5731	0.5471	0.4939	0.6763	**0.8931**	32.06%
	10	0.6924	0.6844	0.6727	0.6256	0.8263	**0.9501**	14.98%
	20	0.7943	0.7805	0.781	0.7446	0.9105	**0.9879**	10.94%
	5	0.449	0.450	0.4196	0.3705	0.5030	**0.7257**	44.27%
	10	0.4866	0.4855	0.4603	0.4134	0.5516	**0.7504**	36.04%
	20	0.5125	0.5098	0.4878	0.4433	0.5780	**0.7581**	31.16%
Flutter	5	0.8288	0.8276	0.7194	0.8148	0.8843	**0.9495**	7.37%
	10	0.8729	0.8608	0.8066	0.8799	0.9143	**0.9799**	7.17%
	20	0.8438	0.858	0.8784	0.9248	0.9378	**0.9943**	6.02%
	5	0.7153	0.7225	0.5913	0.7054	0.7351	**0.8587**	16.81%
	10	0.7365	0.7434	0.6196	0.7266	0.7596	**0.8687**	14.36%
	20	0.7418	0.7503	0.6378	0.738	0.7631	**0.8724**	14.32%
Vscode	5	0.5292	0.5243	0.5087	0.5048	0.5321	**0.6058**	13.85%
	10	0.6587	0.645	0.6405	0.6327	0.7112	**0.8211**	15.45%
	20	0.7806	0.766	0.7674	0.7608	0.8572	**0.9591**	11.89%
	5	0.407	0.4068	0.3861	0.3835	0.4296	**0.4753**	10.64%
	10	0.4486	0.4459	0.4287	0.4248	0.5087	**0.6373**	25.28%
	20	0.4796	0.4765	0.4609	0.4573	0.5821	**0.6814**	17.06%

best baseline by 10.94%–44.27%, 6.02%–16.81%, and 10.64%–25.28% on Tensorflow, Flutter, and Vscode full datasets, respectively. The better performance of KGAT compared to the models (MFBPR, NeuMF, NGCF and LightGCN) using only developer-issue interaction information proves that multiple graph structure relationships are necessary.

Among all the methods of comparison, HGDR achieves the best performance in most cases for all these datasets. There are three main reasons for this: 1) HGDR models the complex relationships between source code, developer, and issue display encoded for developer and issue representation learning. From the developer perspective, unlike traditional matrix decomposition models (MFBPR, NeuMF) and the bipartite graph methods (NGCF and LightGCN), which simply use sparse developer-issue history interactions as developer representation. HGDR exploits to more precise information source code file code changes and the complex graph relationships between them, allowing more useful information to be extracted. 2) HGDR uses text information embedding supplement and encoded into the developer and issue representation learning, which helps to alleviate the interaction sparsity issue and improve the accuracy of recommendations(as will be demonstrated in Sect. 4.4)). 3) SSL of HGDR data augmentation that enables contrast learning to learn more meaningful contrast features for sparsity scenarios (as will be demonstrated in Sect. 4.4)).

4.4   Ablation Studies (to Q2)

By analyzing the maintenance process of open source projects on Github, we found that many developers have very few historical developer-issue interactions. In particular, the interaction sparsity problem is a real and common phenomenon for some newcomers developers. It usually degrades the performance of recommendations because the limited developer interactions make it difficult for previous methods to generate high-quality representations of developers and issues. Meanwhile, previous methods tend to recommend head developers with high proficiency. Here, we aim to evaluate the efficacy of different modules of HGDR in solving the interaction sparsity problem and improving the accuracy of tail developers.

To answer Q2, we evaluate the impact of SSL, text information embedding on model quality separately, we focus on using similarity meta-path neighbor masking (SMP) and random masking and dropout (RMD) as SSL data augmentation techniques and Word2vec text embedding as text data enhancement techniques.

HGDR without SSL as well as text information embedding module (NoSSLText-HGDR) can be considered as an ablation study to isolate text embedding (Text-HGDR) and SSL to observe the improvement effect separately. Finally, comparing our proposed contrast learning data augmentation method (SMP-HGDR) with the widely used baselines data augmentation method (RMD-HGDR).

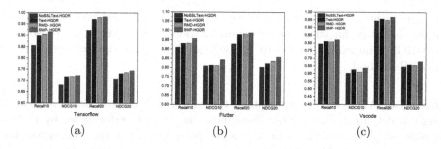

Fig. 5. Ablation study of key designs with different datasets.

As shown in Fig. 5, we observe that for the full dataset, SMP consistently performs best compared to no-SSL regularization techniques. On the Tensorflow dataset, the performance of SMP and the Text module is 6.62% and 5.36% higher respectively, relative to the pre-Ablation module. This helps to answer that RQ2, the proposed SSL framework, and text enhancement do improve the model performance of the recommender. By comparing SMP with RMD, it can be seen that SMP has better performance for SSL regularization.

Table 4. Experiment results trained on the sparse (30% down-sampled) datasets.

Model	30% Tensorflow		30% Flutter		30% Vscode	
	Recall@10	NDCG@10	Recall@10	NDCG@10	Recall@10	NDCG@10
MFBPR	0.4102	0.2548	0.7838	0.469	0.281	0.1659
NoTextSSL-HGDR	0.7810	0.6048	0.9183	0.8270	0.5581	0.2547
Text-HGDR	**0.9244**	**0.7145**	**0.9656**	**0.8374**	0.6802	0.4577
RMD-HGDR	0.7844	0.5855	0.9288	0.8100	0.6132	0.3179
SMP-HGDR	0.8745	0.6515	0.9488	0.8270	**0.6923**	**0.4894**

Table 5. Head and tail developer recommended performance results on the sparse datasets.

Model	30% Tensorflow				30% Flutter			
	Head		Tail		Head		Tail	
	Recall@10	NDCG@10	Recall@10	NDCG@10	Recall@10	NDCG@10	Recall@10	NDCG@10
MFBPR	0.6924	0.4866	0.479	0.3697	0.7838	0.469	0.5461	0.3659
NoTextSSL-HGDR	0.8831	0.5531	0.6135	0.3618	0.9234	0.8343	0.7107	0.5260
RMD-HGDR	0.9040	0.7032	0.6844	0.4855	0.9234	0.8343	0.7107	0.5260
HGDR	**0.9480**	**0.7491**	**0.8840**	**0.6787**	**0.9844**	**0.8999**	**0.8842**	**0.6468**

Label Sparsity Analysis. We study the effectiveness of HGDR in presence of sparse data to address Q2. We uniformly down-sampled 30% (too low can seriously affect the recommended performance) of training data and evaluate on the same (full) test dataset. The experimental results are shown in Table 4. Increasing data sparsity, HGDR provides a greater improvement. In addition, for some new incoming issues with very few labels, the text embedding information is better for such issue recommendations. For example, in Tensorflow, Text-HGDR improves Recall@10 125.35% on 30% sparse dataset compared to MFBPR method.

Head-Tail Analysis. To understand the gain from each module for mitigating long-tail developers, we further decompose the overall performance by looking at different developer slices by developer proficiency. For the Tensorflow test dataset, the header dataset contains examples where groundtruth developers are in the top 10% of the most frequent developers and the rest of the test developers are considered tails. Our hypothesis is that SSL usually helps to improve the performance of slices (e.g. tail developers) without much supervision. The results evaluated on the tail and head test sets are reported in Table 5. We observe that the proposed SSL approach improves the performance recommended by both head and tail developers, with greater gains for tail developers. For example, in Tensorflow, SMP improves Recall@10 by more than 51.5% on tail items and by 8.57% on heads.

4.5   Effects of Different Meta-paths (to Q3)

Unlike traditional models [20,30,31], which only focus on a single relationship between the interaction between developers and issues. HGDR extracts a rich set of meta-path higher-order feature relationships, which can effectively improve the recommendation performance. Here, we aim to evaluate the impact of integrating these meta-paths on recommendation results.

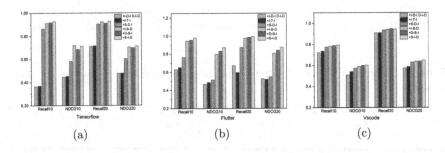

Fig. 6. Performances of HGDR with different meta-paths.

We choose to add meta-paths accordingly, and comparing the results as shown in Fig. 6. We have the following observations. First, the meta-paths I-D-I, D-I-D that only exploit the issue-developer synergy relationship have poor performance. For example, on the Tensorflow dataset, the Recall@10 and NDCG@10 for +I-D-I, D-I-D are 36.44%, 44.55%, respectively. Second, the improvement was not significant after adding the issue tagging relationship meta-path I-T-I. Until adding source code, developers, issue higher-order meta-path S-D-I relations, the recommendation performance has a large improvement. Here we consider only the collaborative relationship of developer-issue interaction, because the issue can only be solved by a small number of developers and then in a closed state, resulting in this collaborative relationship to disseminate limited information. We add source code information as a bridge between developers and the issue higher-order connection, so that the information disseminated between developers and the issue is richer and more accurate. Finally, adding I-S-D, D-S-I, and S-I-D meta-paths, the recommendation performance was also improved, proving that the higher-order graph structure relationship is helpful for recommendation effect improvement.

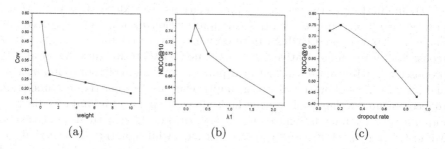

(a)   (b)   (c)

Fig. 7. Effect of different parameters on the model in the Tensorflow dataset.

4.6 Effects of Parameters (to Q4)

In order to analyze the impact of different weight suppression parameters on the model, we observe the change in the coverage of recommended developers to all developers. Coverage measures the ratio of distinct developers in all lists to all developers in an experiment instance. Cov value is calculated for each experiment instance as follows:

$$Cov = \frac{\sum_{u=1}^{m} distinct(pl(d))}{|L|}, \tag{16}$$

where $distinct(L)$ is the number of distinct developers in list L, $pl(d)$ is developers prediction list for each issue. We can see that the experimental results in Fig. 7 (a) show that when the weight is smaller, the coverage of recommended developers is higher, the more we suppress the developers with more interactions, and the recommended results are more diverse.

Figure 7 (b) summarizes the regularization strength evaluated on the Tensorflow dataset. We observe that as the regularization parameter increases, the model performance increases first and gets worse after a certain threshold. This is expected since the large SSL weights lead to a multitasking loss L dominating the loss function in Eq. (13). Figure 7 (c) shows the increase in model performance for different dropout rates as parameters, peaking at 0.2. It then deteriorates when we further increase the dropout rate. This observation is consistent with our expectation that when the dropout rate is too large, the input information becomes too small to learn a meaningful representation via SSL.

5 Related Work

5.1 Developer Recommendation

To find the appropriate developer, [20, 31] focus on developers-issues interactions and recommend developers based on matrix factorization (MF) [12, 30] or collaborative filtering (CF) [20, 31]. CF-based approaches typically suffer from severe sparsity and cold-start problems when the explicit interactions between developers and issues are sparse. For example, by analyzing the GitHub dataset, the data sparsity of the developer-issue explicit interaction matrix is as low as 0.1%, which greatly limits the effectiveness of recommendations. To address these limitations, previous work incorporates various side information into MF or CF. Recently, Sun et al. [20] proposed EDR_SI to recommend developers by exploring commit repositories using collaborative topic modeling (CTM) techniques. Xie et al. [30] proposed a SoftRec approach that incorporates developer collaboration relations and inter-task collaboration relations multi-relations into matrix decomposition to recommend developers. These methods alleviate sparsity and improve the performance of recommendation to some extent. Most of these methods are based on MF or CF traditional machine learning methods, while ignoring the fact that the relational information that may help improve recommendation performance, and cannot learn developer and issue representation due to sparsity and long-tail well.

5.2 Heterogeneous Graph Neural Networks

In recent years, graph neural networks (GNNs) have attracted considerable attention. Most of them have been proposed for homogeneous graphs [7, 23] and a detailed survey can be found in [26]. Recently, some researchers have focused on heterogeneous graphs. For example, HAN [24] uses hierarchical attention to describe node-level and semantic-level structures. PEAGNN [5] specifies meta-path node embeddings by means of features in a contrastive manner. The above methods greatly enrich the graph structure to represent the learning information, but there is no way to directly apply the methods for developer recommendation.

6 Conclusion

In this paper, we propose HGDR, a heterogeneous graph neural network-based method for developer recommendation. The text information embedding and the proficiency weight suppression link supplement are proposed to address the sparsity and long-tail of the developer-issue interactions. To the best of my knowledge, this is the first work to propose the use of HGNN to model source codes files, developers, and issues complexity relationships to recommend developers. Meanwhile, a generality SMP is used for SSL joint learning. Moreover, Extensive comparison experiments are conducted on three real-world datasets, which show that the performance outperforms state-of-the-art by a maximum of 44.27% in terms of NDCG. The experimental results also prove the efficacy of HGDR in sparse and long-tail scenario.

In the future, we plan to further explore the usefulness of HGDR for practical production. We hope to provide usable tools for some open source communities or commercial software companies, and further investigate some features related to developer recommendation.

Acknowledgement. This work is supported by the National Natural Science Key Foundation of China grant No. 61832014 and No. 62032016, the National Natural Science Foundation of China grant No. 62102281, the Natural Science Foundation of Tianjin City grant No. 19JCQNJC00200, and the Foundation of Jiangxi Educational Committee (GJJ210338).

References

1. Chen, T., Kornblith, S., Norouzi, M., Hinton, G.: A simple framework for contrastive learning of visual representations. In: International Conference on Machine Learning, pp. 1597–1607. PMLR (2020)
2. Danielsson, P.E.: Euclidean distance mapping. Comput. Graphics Image Process. **14**(3), 227–248 (1980)
3. Devlin, J., Chang, M.W., Lee, K., Toutanova, K.: BERT: pre-training of deep bidirectional transformers for language understanding. arXiv preprint arXiv:1810.04805 (2018)
4. Gousios, G., Zaidman, A., Storey, M.A., Van Deursen, A.: Work practices and challenges in pull-based development: the integrator's perspective. In: 2015 IEEE/ACM 37th IEEE International Conference on Software Engineering, vol. 1, pp. 358–368. IEEE (2015)
5. Han, Z., et al.: Metapath-and entity-aware graph neural network for recommendation. arXiv e-prints, arXiv-2010 (2020)
6. Hassani, K., Khasahmadi, A.H.: Contrastive multi-view representation learning on graphs. In: International Conference on Machine Learning, pp. 4116–4126. PMLR (2020)
7. He, X., Deng, K., Wang, X., Li, Y., Zhang, Y., Wang, M.: LightGCN: simplifying and powering graph convolution network for recommendation. In: Proceedings of the 43rd International ACM SIGIR Conference on Research and Development in Information Retrieval, pp. 639–648 (2020)
8. He, X., Liao, L., Zhang, H., Nie, L., Hu, X., Chua, T.S.: Neural collaborative filtering. In: Proceedings of the 26th International Conference on World Wide Web, pp. 173–182 (2017)
9. Järvelin, K., Kekäläinen, J.: Cumulated gain-based evaluation of IR techniques. ACM Trans. Inf. Syst. (TOIS) **20**(4), 422–446 (2002)
10. Kearns, M., Ron, D.: Algorithmic stability and sanity-check bounds for leave-one-out cross-validation. Neural Comput. **11**(6), 1427–1453 (1999)
11. Kipf, T.N., Welling, M.: Semi-supervised classification with graph convolutional networks. arXiv preprint arXiv:1609.02907 (2016)
12. Koren, Y., Bell, R., Volinsky, C.: Matrix factorization techniques for recommender systems. Computer **42**(8), 30–37 (2009)
13. Mikolov, T., Chen, K., Corrado, G., Dean, J.: Efficient estimation of word representations in vector space. arXiv preprint arXiv:1301.3781 (2013)
14. Rajlich, V.: Software evolution and maintenance. In: Future of Software Engineering Proceedings, pp. 133–144 (2014)

15. Rendle, S., Freudenthaler, C., Gantner, Z., Schmidt-Thieme, L.: BPR: Bayesian personalized ranking from implicit feedback. arXiv preprint arXiv:1205.2618 (2012)
16. Servant, F., Jones, J.A.: WhoseFault: automatic developer-to-fault assignment through fault localization. In: 2012 34th International Conference on Software Engineering (ICSE), pp. 36–46. IEEE (2012)
17. Shi, C., Li, Y., Zhang, J., Sun, Y., Philip, S.Y.: A survey of heterogeneous information network analysis. IEEE Trans. Knowl. Data Eng. **29**(1), 17–37 (2016)
18. Steven, B.: NLTK: the natural language toolkit in proceedings of the ACL 2004 on interactive poster and demonstration sessions. In: Association for Computational Linguistics, p. 31 (2004)
19. Sun, X., Yang, H., Leung, H., Li, B., Li, H.J., Liao, L.: Effectiveness of exploring historical commits for developer recommendation: an empirical study. Front. Comp. Sci. **12**(3), 528–544 (2018). https://doi.org/10.1007/s11704-016-6023-3
20. Sun, X., Yang, H., Xia, X., Li, B.: Enhancing developer recommendation with supplementary information via mining historical commits. J. Syst. Softw. **134**, 355–368 (2017)
21. Veličković, P., Cucurull, G., Casanova, A., Romero, A., Lio, P., Bengio, Y.: Graph attention networks. arXiv preprint arXiv:1710.10903 (2017)
22. Wang, X., He, X., Cao, Y., Liu, M., Chua, T.S.: KGAT: knowledge graph attention network for recommendation. In: Proceedings of the 25th ACM SIGKDD International Conference on Knowledge Discovery & Data Mining, pp. 950–958 (2019)
23. Wang, X., He, X., Wang, M., Feng, F., Chua, T.S.: Neural graph collaborative filtering. In: Proceedings of the 42nd International ACM SIGIR Conference on Research and Development in Information Retrieval, pp. 165–174 (2019)
24. Wang, X., et al.: Heterogeneous graph attention network. In: The World Wide Web Conference, pp. 2022–2032 (2019)
25. Wang, X., Liu, N., Han, H., Shi, C.: Self-supervised heterogeneous graph neural network with co-contrastive learning. arXiv preprint arXiv:2105.09111 (2021)
26. Wu, Z., Pan, S., Chen, F., Long, G., Zhang, C., Philip, S.Y.: A comprehensive survey on graph neural networks. IEEE Trans. Neural Netw. Learn. Syst. **32**(1), 4–24 (2020)
27. Xia, X., Lo, D., Wang, X., Yang, X.: Who should review this change?: Putting text and file location analyses together for more accurate recommendations. In: 2015 IEEE International Conference on Software Maintenance and Evolution (ICSME), pp. 261–270. IEEE (2015)
28. Xia, X., Lo, D., Wang, X., Zhou, B.: Dual analysis for recommending developers to resolve bugs. J. Softw. Evol. Process **27**(3), 195–220 (2015)
29. Xia, Z., Sun, H., Jiang, J., Wang, X., Liu, X.: A hybrid approach to code reviewer recommendation with collaborative filtering. In: 2017 6th International Workshop on Software Mining (SoftwareMining), pp. 24–31 (2017). https://doi.org/10.1109/SOFTWAREMINING.2017.8100850
30. Xie, X., Wang, B., Yang, X.: SoftRec: multi-relationship fused software developer recommendation. Appl. Sci. **10**(12), 4333 (2020)
31. Xin, X., He, X., Zhang, Y., Zhang, Y., Jose, J.: Relational collaborative filtering: modeling multiple item relations for recommendation. In: Proceedings of the 42nd International ACM SIGIR Conference on Research and Development in Information Retrieval, pp. 125–134 (2019)
32. Ye, L., Sun, H., Wang, X., Wang, J.: Personalized teammate recommendation for crowdsourced software developers. In: Proceedings of the 33rd ACM/IEEE International Conference on Automated Software Engineering, pp. 808–813 (2018)

Blockchain Applications

FAV-BFT: An Efficient File Authenticity Verification Protocol for Blockchain-Based File-Sharing System

Shuai Su[1,2(✉)], Chi Chen[1,2], and Xiaojie Zhu[3]

[1] State Key Laboratory of Information Security, Institute of Information Engineering, Chinese Academy of Science, Beijing 100093, China
[2] School of Cyber Security, University of Chinese Academy of Sciences, Beijing 100049, China
{sushuai,chenchi}@iie.ac.cn
[3] Abu Dhabi University, Abu Dhabi, UAE
xiaojie.zhu@adu.ac.ae

Abstract. Compared with traditional file-sharing system, the blockchain-based file-sharing system shows its superiority, such as electronic money incentive mechanism, decentralisation, information tamper resistance and so on. Benefiting from those properties, it has attracted tons of users to participate in blockchain-based file-sharing and eventually forms an indestructible electronic library. However, with such a huge amount of files, the problem of file authenticity verification is still not resolved. This paper attempts to address the challenge of file authenticity verification for blockchain-based file-sharing system, specifically, verifying that the file is really stored by the claimer and needed by the file-downloader before the file is downloaded. We propose an efficient file authenticity verification protocol, named File Authenticity Verification Byzantine Fault Tolerant (FAV-BFT). We first apply Verifiable Delay Function to bind the shared file, and then reconstruct it to a challenge-response interactive protocol for file-sharing, and finally embedded with Byzantine Fault Tolerant protocol. Due to the construction, with 2/3 of participants are honest, FAV-BFT can correctly prove how long a file has been stored and whether a file meets the requirement of the file downloader. Moreover, since all the file content is processed by hash function before transformation, FAV-BFT protects the shared-file from content disclosure during the verification process without trusted third parties.

Keywords: Blockchain · File-sharing · Authenticity verification · Efficient

1 Introduction

Peer-to-peer [1] systems allow users to share information in distributed environments because of their scalability and efficiency. Currently, the most popular P2P

H. Gao et al. (Eds.): CollaborateCom 2022, LNICST 460, pp. 455–474, 2022.
https://doi.org/10.1007/978-3-031-24383-7_25

file-sharing systems include BitTorrent, eDonkey, eMule [2], μTorrent, Napster, KaZaA [3] and so on. All these file-sharing systems requires file downloaders to search files through the central server or a *Distributed Hash Table* (DHT), and download shared-files from multiple file-sharers. The authenticity verification of the file (that is, before downloading the file, file-downloader can verify that the file is indeed the one that file-downloader needs) relies on the honesty of the central server or correctness of DHT. In practical, the central server or DHT may face various attacks, such as single point failure, information tampering, malicious nodes, and so on. Therefore, it is risky to simply rely on the trusted central server or DHT to verify the authenticity of the shared-files.

The development of Blockchain technology provides an inspiring solution to these problems. By applying blockchain technology to file-sharing system, the properties of blockchain, such as decentralization, data tamper proof and malicious peer tolerance, can solve the problems encountered by traditional file-sharing systems. Each node can use bounded resources to prove the existence of shared-files. Based on these file-existence proofs, file-sharers will obtain token rewards after sharing files. Therefore, they will form a competitive relationship in order to obtain tokens. At present, the research of file-sharing system based on blockchain is very popular. Many mature blockchain-based file-sharing mechanisms have been proposed and applied, such as BTFS [6], BlockIPFS [7], Filecoin [10], Siacoin [8], Storj [9], and so on. The goal of these systems is to use the reward mechanism to attract more users to participate in file-sharing, so as to form an indestructible electronic file-sharing library.

To maintain the quality of shared files, blockchain-based file-sharing system provides resource proof. Many consensus protocols are proposed to generate the proof, such as *Proof of Work* (PoW), *Proof of Stake* (PoS) [15], *Proof of Space* (PoSpace) [21], etc. However, these consensus protocols have their limitations. For example, PoW wastes a lot of electric power, PoS has the risk of being monopolized by oligarchs, PoSpace occupies large amount of space that is unrelated to the shared files. Moreover, these consensus protocols do not consider the file content. In such case, a user can claim a wrong file since the user only needs to show its existence instead of content. If the file content can be used as the evidence of resource proof, it can not only reduce resource consumption, but also verify the authenticity of the files. Therefore, in the blockchain based file-sharing community, the requirement of designing a practical solution that can not only prove the file existence with limited resource-consumption, but also prove the authenticity of the file.

For the proof of file existence, the existing solutions are inefficient, such as proof of sequential work [23,24], time-lock puzzle [27–29], and *Verifiable Delay Function* (VDF) [25]. Their solutions feature the time-consuming proof generation, not supported by parallel computing. In addition, for the file authenticity verification, all the previous work only considers the size of the stored file, such as PoSpace [21], *Proof of Space-Time* (PoST) [11,22]. They only support to prove the file size which is irrelevant to the file content. In order to solve above challenge, we observe that a feasible solution to this problem is to propose a mutual challenge mechanism between nodes. Fortunately, *Byzantine Fault-Tolerant* (BFT) protocol supporting state-machine replication, uses mutual challenge mechanism to tolerate malicious nodes. If above storage proof can be properly embedded into BFT, the problem of file authenticity verification for blockchain-based file-sharing system can be addressed. Particularly, the mutual challenge mechanism is responsible for matching the file content while the storage proof takes the responsibility of proving file existence.

In short, the contribution of this paper is summarised as follows.

1 VDF is adapted for file-sharing. It is bound together with the shared file content, and reconstructed to a challenge-response interactive protocol.
2 We proposes an efficient file authenticity verification protocol for blockchain-based file-sharing system, FAV-BFT. It novelly combines adapted VDF with *Reliable Broadcast* (RBC) algorithm of BFT to verify the authenticity of files. With more than two-thirds of participants are honest, this protocol can correctly verify the file authenticity. Meanwhile, the process of file authenticity verification does not disclose the content of shared files and does not rely on any trusted third party.
3 We evaluate the performance and security of FAV-BFT in theory and practice. The theoretical analysis results show that, compared with the protocol of Filecoin, the challenge-response protocol based on VDF has lower computation complexity in the prover and verifier proof phases. In addition, we also test the FAV-BFT, and the experimental result indicates that the FAV-BFT can indeed verify the authenticity of the file and the efficiency is higher than HoneyBadgerBFT [32].

The remainder of paper is organized as follows. Section 2 presents the related work. Subsequently, the specific construction of the FAV-BFT is described in Sect. 3. Section 4 analyzes the performance and security of FAV-BFT. In Sect. 5, the experiments and test results are given. Finally, Sect. 6 concludes this paper.

2 Related Work

At present, many researches on file authenticity verification for blockchain-based file-sharing system have emerged. Related work mainly includes two aspects, one is to directly combine distributed file-sharing system with existing mature blockchain mechanisms, and the other is to develop specific protocols oriented toward file-sharing scenarios.

For the first aspect, researches mainly focus on how to use the existing consensus protocol of blockchain to complete file storage and authenticity verification. For example, Sari, L. et al. and Khatal, S. et al. proposed FileTribe [4] and FileShare [5], both of them employs IPFS and Ethereum smart contract to govern, manage shared-files. *BitTorrent File System* (BTFS) [6] develops a file-sharing protocol utilizing the Tron Blockchain and the BitTorrent ecosystem. The consensus protocol of Tron is *Delegated-Proof-of-Stake* (DPoS) which is not associated with file content. Sia [8] combine cloud storage with the existing mature blockchain technology to develop blockchain-based cloud storage platform. Sia uses file contracts to restrict storage providers to store files for customers, and uses *Proof of Storage* (PoS) to verify whether files are stored continuously. These researches mainly study how to use the existing consensus protocol of blockchain to complete the storage proof of files. The consensus protocols are not associated with the file content. Users need to provide the proof of bounded resources while saving the shared files, which may cause a waste of resources-consumption.

For the second aspect, researches mainly focus on proposing specific protocols which can prove that files have been stored for a period of time. For example, Storj [9] uses *Proof of Retrievability* (PoR) [20] to promise that a verifier sends a file to a prover and later to request a proof that the prover really stored the file. However, it is difficult to ensure that files are stored continuously in Sia and Storj. Based on *InterPlanetary File System* (IPFS) [12], "Filecoin" [10] developed *Proof-of-SpaceTime* (PoST) and *Proof-of-Replication* (PoRep) [13] to prove that the prover stores the file for an elapsed time. However, the implementation of PoRep and PoST rely on cryptographic machinery (such as zk-SNARKs [14,16,17] and seal operation) requiring heavy computing resources. S. Dziembowski et al. proposed *Proof-of-Space* (PoSpace) [21] to replace *Proof of Work* (PoW), which prefer storage instead of computing resource to complete the qualification of mining. This consensus protocol is more energy-saving for the reason that storage consumes less cost than computing. However, PoSpace is not associated with file content, it cannot verify the authenticity of file. Benet et al. proposed *Proof-of-Replication* (PoRep) [13] which allows prover to prove that he/she is storing multiple redundant copies of a file, but it is hard to ensure that files are stored continuously. T. Moran et al. proposed *Proofs of Space-Time* (PoST) [11,22], which allow prover to convince to others that amount of "space-time" resource (storing data-space over a period of time) have been spend. PoST is also not associated with file content and cannot verify the authenticity of file. M. Mahmoody et al. and B. Cohen et al. proposed proofs of sequential work [23,24] that can prove to others that sequential computational work have been spent to solve a puzzle. D. Boneh el al proposed *Verifiable Delay Functions* (VDF) [25], which can prove that a period of time has been consumed. VDF algorithm requires a specified number of sequential steps to produce a unique output that can be efficiently and publicly verified. VDF algorithm can hardly be accelerated by parallel computing. K. Pietrzak et al. proposed a simple VDF [26] which make time-lock puzzle [27–29] to be publicly verifiable. B. Wesolowski el al proposed an efficient VDF [31], which has higher execution efficiency than previous VDF. The above VDF and proofs of sequential work can limit resource-consumption but not associated with file content, they cannot verify the authenticity of file. Shuai Su et al. proposed a efficient File-Sharing interactive verification protocol VoFSQ [35], it used storage-resources to prove that a particular file has indeed been stored for a period of time, but it is a protocol verified by both parties rather than multiple parties. The decentralization cannot be achieved.

In order to realize file authenticity verification, it is necessary to introduce a multi-party mutual verification mechanism.*Practical Byzantine Fault Tolerance* (PBFT) [18,19] uses mutual verification mechanism to tolerate malicious node.

PBFT has higher requirements for communication reliability, so it is weak practicability. HoneyBadgerBFT [32] is the first practical asynchronous BFT protocol, which guarantees liveness without making any timing assumptions. Dumbo [33] improves the consensus efficiency by implementing the *Asynchronous Binary Agreement* (ABA) algorithm through the election committee. Dumbo-MVBA [34] further improves the consensus efficiency by reducing the number of committees to a constant. The above BFT protocols are not associated with file content and cannot verify the authenticity of file. Table 1 shows details of these incentive mechanisms.

Table 1. Overview of the file authenticity verification protocols for Blockchain-based File-Sharing system

System, protocol	Description	Problems
FileTribe [4] FileShare Sia [5,8]	Combine Ethereum with file-sharing system	May cause a waste of resources
DPoS (in BTFS [6])	Prove that users own certain stake	Super nodes may appear
PoS, PoR (in Storj [9])	Prove that the file is stored	Hard to ensure that files are stored continuously
PoRep, PoST (in Filecoin [10])	Prove that files are continuously stored	Low efficiency and relies trusted third-party
PoSpace [21]	Prove that certain amount of space is occupied	Cannot verify the authenticity of file
PoRep [13]	Prove that the replication of file is stored	Hard to ensure that files are stored continuously
PoST [11,22]	Prove "space-time" have been spent	Cannot verify the authenticity of file
Proofs of sequential work [23,24]	Prove time-consuming sequential work has been done	Cannot verify the authenticity of file
VDF [25,31]	Prove time-consuming function is executed	Cannot verify the authenticity of file
VoFSQ [35]	Prove file has been stored for a period of time	Not decentralized
PBFT [18,19]	Can tolerate malicious node	Cannot verify the authenticity of file and weak practicability
HoneyBadgerBFT [32]	Asynchronous and high efficiency	Cannot verify the authenticity of file
Dumbo [33], Dumbo-MVBA [34]	Synchronous and high efficiency	Cannot verify the authenticity of file

In summary, there lack such protocol which can not only prove that the file is indeed stored for a period of time, but also prove that the file is really needed by the file-downloader on the premise of saving resource consumption. Therefore, this paper aim to design a protocol to solve these problems.

3   The Construction of FAV-BFT

This section mainly introduces the details of a consensus protocol, which is called *File-Authenticity Verification Byzantine Fault Tolerant* (FAV-BFT). FAV-BFT contains the following steps: 1. associating identity and file contents with VDF. 2. building a challenge-response protocol based on VDF. 3. verifying the file-consistence.

3.1   Associating Identity and File Contents with VDF

In order to verify the authenticity of the file, it is necessary to take file owner's identity and file content as the input of VDF [25]. There are three phases in this protocol: *Setup*, *Eval* and *Verify*. In *Setup* phase, initialization variables are generated. In *Eval* phase, the identity and file content are associated with the VDF process of generating proof. In *Verify* phase, the proof is verified. The improved VDF is a triple of algorithms as follows:

Protocol VDF associated with identity and file content

- $Setup(\lambda, t) \rightarrow \mathbf{pp} = (ek, pk)$. λ is a security parameter, t is difficulty, $\mathbf{pp}$ is a public parameter which contains an evaluation key ek and a verification key vk.
- $Eval(ek, x, id) \rightarrow (\pi)$. x stands for the file content or file hash value. id stands for the identity of file owner. *Eval* takes x as input and produces proof π. Algorithm *Eval* is time-consuming and difficult to be accelerated by parallel computing. Suppose that the fastest time of this step is t when using the fastest computing resources.
- $Verify(vk, x, id, \pi) \rightarrow \{Accept, Reject\}$. Algorithm *Verify* takes x, id, π as input and outputs *Accept* or *Reject*. *Verify* is much faster than *Eval*.

3.2   Building a Challenge-Response Protocol Based on VDF

The above mentioned VDF which can associate with identity and file contents is difficult to respond in real time when receiving the dynamic challenge. In order to achieve the purpose of real-time verification between nodes, it is necessary to build a challenge-response interactive protocol based on VDF. File-sharers verify each other through this protocol to check whether the same file has been preserved for a period time. The interactive protocol consists of three phases: initialization phase, proof phase, and verification phase. The two parties of the interactive protocol are prover P and verifier V. P can be viewed as a file-sharer who want to provide proof of file storage and authenticity, V acts as file-sharer who verify P. The process of VDF-based challenge-response protocol is shown in Fig. 1.

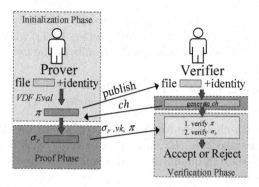

Fig. 1. A challenge-response protocol based on VDF.

Initialization Phase: P calculates the hash value of the verification key vk which generated in the VDF algorithm to generate identity ($id_P = hash(vk)$). Then P generates the VDF proof π according to the file-sharer's identity ($id_P \in \{0,1\}^*$) and file content f. The value of t can be adjusted dynamically which determines the difficulty of VDF. At the conclusion of this phase, P output proof ($\pi \in \{0,1\}^*$, respectively).

$$(\pi) \leftarrow \langle Eval_{init}(ek, id_P, t, f) \rangle \tag{1}$$

π will be used to generate the response within a certain time at the challenge-response phase, therefore, P should preserve π in the local storage. P broadcasts id_P and states that initialization phase has been completed.

In the initialization phase, P runs the VDF to generate the evidence-data. The VDF algorithm requires running given sequential steps and can hardly be accelerated by parallel computing. This progress is time consuming and has real-world cost.

Proof Phase: When V receives id_P from P, V sends a challenge $ch \in \{0,1\}^*$ to P. P should generate a response efficiently. P concatenates the value of id_P, f, π, ch and calculates its hash value. The calculation performed by P is as follows:

$$(\sigma_P) \leftarrow \langle hash(id_P||f||\pi||ch) \rangle \tag{2}$$

P sends (σ_P, vk, π) to V. Since P cannot obtain the challenge value ch in advance, she/he must run it after receiving the challenge value. If P does preserve the evidence-data, this process is efficient. Otherwise, P must rerun the initialization phase to generate the evidence-data. P will prefer continuous evidence-data preservation rather than dynamic evidence-data generation. As long as the evidence-data is preserved continuously, P can make the right response to V with a small computational cost. Preserving the evidence-data continuously should be cheaper than the cost of re-generating using computing resources.

Verification Phase: V owns the same file as the P. When V receive (σ_P, vk, π), V will recalculate the hash value according to the values of vk, f, π, ch and compare it with the value of σ_P received. Then V will verify the correctness of π. The V will output either accept or reject ($out_v \in \{0,1\}$, where 0 is interpreted as "reject" and 1 is "accept") based on the results of the two verifications.

$$(out_v) \leftarrow \left\langle \begin{array}{c} \sigma_P \overset{?}{=} (\sigma'_P) \leftarrow hash(hash(vk)||f||\pi||ch) \\ Verify\,(vk, f, hash(vk), \pi) \end{array} \right\rangle \tag{3}$$

This paper lists a challenge-response protocol based on Wesolowski's VDF [31]. All file-sharers who save the same file can verify with each other in order to compete for file-sharing qualification and win token reward. The description of this protocol is shown below:

Protocol A challenge-response protocol based on Wesolowski's VDF

Public Parameters: λ: security parameter, $N = p \cdot q$ with p and q two primes and N a λ-bits number, difficulty degree $\tau, t \in \mathbb{N}$.
Initialization Phase:(Performed by P)
Input: file content $m \in \{0,1\}^*$, identity $id \in \{0,1\}^*$.

1 $x \leftarrow H(m||id)$. (H stands for hash algorithm)
2 $y \leftarrow x$.
3 **for** (1 to τ)
  (a) $y \leftarrow y^2 \bmod N$.
4 $l \leftarrow H_{prime}(x + y)$.($H_{prime}(x)$ stands for the closest prime number larger or equal to $H(x)$)
5 $\pi = x^{\lfloor 2^\tau/l \rfloor} \bmod N$.
6 Publish the metadata of shared file, id, initialization outcome.

Proof Phase:(Performed by P)

Upon receiving a challenge ch from the V:

1 calculate $\sigma_P = H(id||m||\pi||ch)$
2 Send $\sigma_P, \tau, id, \pi, l, N$ to V.

Verification Phase:(Performed by V)
Generate a random challenge ch and send it to P. Wait to receive $\sigma_P, \tau, id, \pi, l, N$.

1 $\hat{x} \leftarrow H(m||id)$.
2 $r \leftarrow 2^\tau \bmod l$.
3 $\hat{y} \leftarrow \pi^l \cdot \hat{x}^r \bmod N$.
4 $\hat{l} \leftarrow H_{prime}(\hat{x} + \hat{y})$
5 $\hat{\sigma_P} = H(id||m||\pi||ch)$
6 if ($l == \hat{l}\&\&\hat{\sigma_P} == \sigma_P$)
  (a) return accept
7 else
  (a) return reject

3.3   Verifying the File-Consistence

This section formally introduces *Verification of File-Consistence* (VoFC) which can verify file authenticity on the premise that more than 2/3 nodes are honest.

In blockchain-based file-sharing scenario, multiple nodes will participate in file authenticity verification, which will form a network of N designated nodes (with distinct well-known identities (P_0 through P_{N-1})). The nodes utilize pre-served files to generate evidence-data. By using the evidence-data as input, their goal is to reach common agreement that these files have been preserved for a period of time and these files is really needed by the file-downloader on the premise that more than 2/3 nodes are honest. All the verification processes will not depend on the central server and do not disclose any privacy information about file content. This protocol particularly matches the deployment scenario of a "permissioned blockchain" where file-consistence verification can be submitted by arbitrary nodes, but the nodes responsible for carrying out the protocol are fixed.

VoFC combines VDF with *Reliable Broadcast* (RBC) algorithm of Honey-BadgerBFT [32], so that multiple nodes should to challenge with each other to complete file-consistence verification using storage resources. At the same time, VoFC also has the characteristics of high throughput, practical asynchronous and so on. There are multiple nodes in VoFC. The node initiating file authenticity verification can be viewed as a file-downloader, other nodes can be regarded as file-sharers participating in the verification. There are five phases in the VoFC, namely challenge, echo-challenge, val, echo, and ready. Each node needs to perform these phases.

1) Challenge phase

Before file authenticity verification, all nodes need to utilize VDF algorithm to generate evidence-data. This step consumes computing resources and a period of time. Nodes prefer to keep these evidence-data and wait for challenges. File-downloader generates random string ch and broadcasts m^{chal} message to the whole network.

$$(m^{chal}) \leftarrow \langle \langle \text{``challenge''}, id_d, ch \rangle , sign \rangle \tag{4}$$

where *"challenge"* is the request mark, id_d is the unique identity of file-downloader, *sign* is the digital signature of this request. When the node receives the ch value, it will execute the val and echo-challenge phase at the same time. Echo-challenge phase is to enable all nodes to challenge each other. The process of directly executing Val phase is shown in Fig. 2. The process of executing Val phase after echo-challenge phase is shown in Fig. 3.

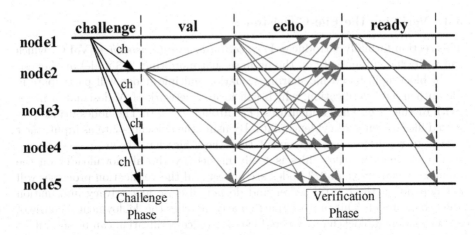

Fig. 2. The VoFC process of directly executing val phase.

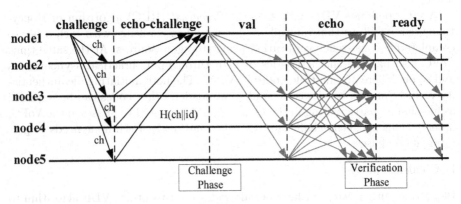

Fig. 3. The VoFC process of executing val phase after echo-challenge phase.

2) Echo-challenge phase

After receiving the message m^{chal} from file-downloader, the node verifies the digital signature. If the verification is passed, the node runs challenge phase of VDF to generate response m^{val} according to the challenge value ch, the implementation is described in val phase below. Then the node generates echo-challenge message $m^{echo-ch}$.

$$ech = hash\,(ch||id_d||id_f) \tag{5}$$

$$(m^{echo-ch}) \leftarrow \langle\langle\text{``}echo-chal\text{''}, id_s, ech\rangle, sign\rangle \tag{6}$$

where "$echo - chal$" is the mark of this phase, id_s is the unique identity of file-sharer. The node sends $m^{echo-ch}$ to other nodes.

3) Val phase

When receives m^{chal} or $m^{echo-ch}$, the node runs challenge phase of VDF to generate response m^{val}.

$$\sigma_P = hash\left(id_s||f||\pi||(ch\ or\ ech)\right) \tag{7}$$

$$(val) \leftarrow (\sigma_P||vk||\pi||id) \tag{8}$$

The node divides val into $N - f$ blocks (f is the maximum number of malicious nodes, less than $N/3$), and then uses erasure coding scheme to expend them to N blocks(that is, as long as $N - f$ blocks are received, the whole message can be recovered), and utilizes these nodes as leaf to build a Merkle tree. Denote h to represent the root node of this Merkle tree. The node sends m_j^{val} to node N_j, where b_j is the jth Merkle tree branch. Construct m_j^{val} and sent it to each node N_j. "ch" or "ech" indicates that this message is a response to the ch or ech.

$$(m_j^{val}) \leftarrow \langle\langle\text{``}val\text{''}, id_s, h, b_j, s_j, \langle\text{``}ch\text{''}\ or\ \text{``}ech\text{''}, ch\ or\ ech\rangle\rangle, sign\rangle \tag{9}$$

4) Echo phase

When receives m_j^{val}, the node needs to verifies the digital signature and check that b_j is a valid Merkle branch from leaf s_j to root h, otherwise discard. When all verification passes, the node constructs an m_j^{echo} message and sends it to other nodes.

$$(m_j^{echo}) \leftarrow \langle\langle\text{``}echo\text{''}, id_s, h, b_j, s_j, \langle\text{``}ch\text{''}\ or\ \text{``}ech\text{''}, ch\ or\ ech\rangle\rangle, sign\rangle \tag{10}$$

5) Ready phase

When receives m_j^{echo} message, the node verifies the corresponding Merkel path and signature value. If the verification passed, the node constructs m_j^{ready} message and sends it to other nodes.

$$(m_j^{ready}) \leftarrow \langle\langle\text{``}ready\text{''}, h, \langle\text{``}ch\text{''}\ or\ \text{``}ech\text{''}, ch\ or\ ech\rangle\rangle, sign\rangle \tag{11}$$

When node receives $N - f$ matching $ready(h)$ messages, he/she can use $N - f$ corresponding m^{val} messages to recover the original val message. Then, the node can perform the verification phase to verify the correctness of σ_P and π which contains val message. If the verification is passed, the corresponding Asynchronous Binary Byzantine Agreement (ABA) [32] (ABA is the next process to be executed after RBC algorithm in HoneyBadgerBFT) binary bit position will be set 1, otherwise it will be set 0.

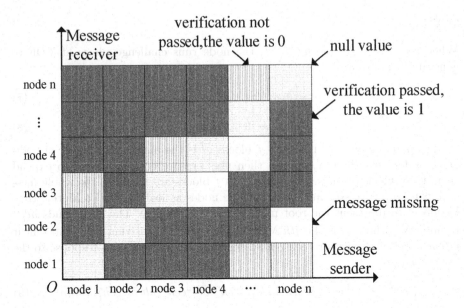

Fig. 4. ABA matrix.

After the above steps are completed, every node will receive the feedback to the corresponding challenge from other nodes, and generate a 0–1 matrix, as shown in Fig. 4. The x-axis is the message sender and the y-axis stands for the message receiver. When the verification is passed, the value is 1, otherwise the value is 0. Next, each node will execute ABA protocol, check whether the number of elements with 1 in each node matrix is greater than $2 * N/3$, if it is, set all element to 1. This step is the same as that in HoneyBadgerBFT.

Finally, every node will get a consistent matrix, showing that these nodes have preserved the same file and have afforded compute-time cost. If more than 2/3 nodes are honest, it can be sure that the shared file is exactly which file-downloader wants.

4   Evaluation of FAV-BFT

This section lists the theoretical performance analysis of the FAV-BFT, which include computing, time-consuming, storage and communication consumption. Then, we compare its differences with multiple BFT protocols, and finally analyzes its security.

4.1   Performance Evaluation

The performance evaluation includes memory M, time T, storage S, communication consumption.

Challenge-Response Protocol Based on VDF

Initialization Phase. In this phase, P have to run a computing and time consuming algorithm to generate the evidence-data. For Wesolowski's VDF, this algorithm is dominated by solving a puzzle, that is x^{2^τ}, which is conjectured to require τ sequential squarings. If $\phi(N) = (p-1)(q-1)$ is known, this algorithm can be accelerated, for the reason that:

$$y := x^{2^\tau} \ mod \ N = x^{2^\tau \ mod \ \phi(N)} \ mod \ N \tag{12}$$

It is very difficult to get $\phi(N)$ from N, so this algorithm needs to be calculated as follows:

$$x \rightarrow x^2 \rightarrow x^{2^2} \rightarrow x^{2^3} \rightarrow ... \rightarrow x^{2^\tau} \ mod \ N \tag{13}$$

There are many ways to accelerate modular multi-exponentiation algorithm [36,37]. On the premise of multithreading and s cores, the algorithm can be accelerated to at least $\frac{2\tau}{s \cdot log(\tau)}$. Computing the proof $\pi = x^{\lfloor 2^\tau/l \rfloor}$ requires a total of $O(\tau/log(\tau))$ group multiplications [30,31]. Let $t_{mul}(x^2)$ and $r_{mul}(x^2)$ denote running time and occupied memory of $\{x^2 : x \in [0,N]\}$. Using $t_{mod}(y \ mod \ N)$ and $r_{mod}(y \ mod \ N)$ to denote running time and occupied memory of $\{y \ mod \ N : y \in [0,(N-1)^2]\}$. Using $t_{hash}(z)$ and $r_{hash}(z)$ to denote running time and occupied memory of Hash algorithm $\{H(z) : z = lengthof(m||id) \in \{0,1\}^*\}$. So the results are as follows:

$$M_{init} := r_{mul}(x^2) + r_{mod}(y \ mod \ N) + r_{hash}(z) \tag{14}$$

$$T_{init} := (\frac{2\tau}{s \cdot log(\tau)} + O(\tau/log(\tau))) \cdot (t_{mul}(x^2) + t_{mod}(y \ mod \ N)) + t_{hash}(z) \tag{15}$$

$$S_{init} := sizeof(id||m||\pi||l) \tag{16}$$

It can be seen that the difficulty of generating the evidence-data is related to the value of τ. By dynamically adjusting τ, it can adjust the consumption of compute-time resource for generating the evidence-data. The consumption will cause real-world cost.

The setup phase of *Proof-of-Replication* (PoRep) in Filecoin uses file blocks as leaf nodes to generate a Merkel tree, the size of evidence-data is positively correlated with the file size. Wesolowski's VDF reduces the evidence-data to constant, therefore, it reduces storage resource consumption.

Proof Phase. P will generate a response σ_P when receiving a challenge ch. The calculation methods of computing and storage are as follows ($w = lengthof(id||m||\pi||ch)$):

$$M_{chal} := r_{hash}(w) \tag{17}$$

$$T_{chal} = t_{hash}(w) \tag{18}$$

$$S_{chal} := sizeof(\sigma_P||\tau||id||\pi||l||N) \tag{19}$$

Compared to the prove phase of *Proof-of-Replication* (PoRep) in Filecoin, this challenge phase does not use zk-SNARKS to hide the privacy information of file, but implement a less complex hash operation. Therefore, the efficiency of P proof phase is higher than PoRep.

Verification Phase. When receiving σ_P, τ, id, π, l, N, V begins to verify them. The consumption of computing and storage is as follows:

$$M_{ver} := r_{hash}(m||id) + r_{mul}(2^\tau) +$$
$$r_{mul}(\pi^l \cdot \hat{x}^r) + 2 \cdot r_{mod}(y \bmod l) \tag{20}$$
$$+ r_{hash}(\hat{x} + \hat{y}) + r_{hash}(id||m||\pi||ch)$$

$$T_{ver} := t_{hash}(m||id) + t_{mul}(2^\tau) +$$
$$t_{mul}(\pi^l \cdot \hat{x}^r) + 2 \cdot t_{mod}(y \bmod l) \tag{21}$$
$$+ t_{hash}(id||m||\pi||ch)$$

$$S_{ver} := S_{chal} \tag{22}$$

In this phase, the operations include multiplication, exponential operation, modular operation, etc. Comparing with the proof phase of *Proof-of-Replication* (PoRep) in Filecoin, verification phase does not use heavy cryptography mechanism zk-SNARKS. Therefore, the verification efficiency will be higher than that of PoRep.

Verification of File-Consistency. VoFC combines challenge and verification phases of VDF with the RBC algorithm of HoneyBadgerBFT. The total communication complexity of HoneyBadgerBFT is $O(N^2|v| + \lambda N^3 logN)$, where $|v|$ is the largest size of any node's input. VoFC increases challenge and echo-challenge phases compared with HoneyBadgerBFT, therefore, the communication complexity of FAV-BFT is $O(N^2|v| + \lambda N^3 logN + N^2 + N)$.

4.2   Comparison with Multiple BFT Protocol

At present, there are many popular BFT protocols, such as HoneyBadgerBFT [32], Dumbo [33], Dumbo-MVBA [34], etc. These popular BFT protocols all use RBC algorithm. FAV-BFT proposed in this paper only combines VDF with RBC protocol, while others remain unchanged. Compared with these BFT protocols, since the verification data of each stage of VoFC does not contain file privacy data, threshold encryption and randomly chosen sample can be removed. In theory, the efficiency of FAV-BFT proposed in this paper will be higher than these popular BFT protocols.

4.3   Security Analysis

The following contents introduce the security of challenge-response protocol based on VDF and VoFC respectively.

Challenge-Response Protocol Based on VDF. Challenge-response protocol based on VDF should satisfy the properties of completeness and soundness.

For completeness, it is required that for any honest P, the probability of passing the validation is close to 1.

Honest P uses the stored file to generate the evidence-data, and returns the response according to the V's challenge. When V receives the proof phase response corresponding to challenge ch, he/she will verify the correctness of the response. V holds the same file as P, so V can also calculate the value of $\hat{x}$ and r. Furthermore, V can verify the correctness of l. The completeness of this protocol is below:

Define k is the remainder of $2^\tau / l$:

$$k = 2^\tau \bmod l \tag{23}$$

Therefore:

$$\lfloor 2^\tau / l \rfloor = (2^\tau - k)/l \tag{24}$$

$$
\begin{aligned}
\pi^l \cdot x^r \bmod N &= x^{\lfloor 2^\tau / l \rfloor \cdot l} \cdot x^r \bmod N \\
&= x^{\lfloor 2^\tau / l \rfloor \cdot l} \cdot x^{2^\tau \bmod l} \bmod N \\
&= x^{(2^\tau - 2^\tau \bmod l)/l \cdot l} \cdot x^{2^\tau \bmod l} \bmod N \\
&= 2^{2^\tau} \bmod N
\end{aligned}
\tag{25}
$$

Therefore, for honest P, the possibility of passing the verification is 1.

For soundness, malicious file-sharers attempt to pass the verification without saving the file or affording the compute-time resources. If P does not save the file or pay the cost of compute-time, it will be difficult to generate the evidence-data, and thus cannot respond to the challenge of V. The probability of a malicious P passing the verification is close to 0.

Verification of File-Consistency. FAV-BFT combines challenge-response protocol base on VDF with RBC algorithm of BFT protocol. The communication and verification methods are consistent with RBC algorithm. Therefore, the security of FAV-BFT can be regulated to the security of these BFT protocols.

5   Experiment and Evaluation Result

This paper implements the FAV-BFT and tested its efficiency[1]. The experiment was performed on a machine with dual-core 12th Gen Intel(R) Core(TM) i7-12700F CPU @ 2.00 GHz, 8 GB RAM, Ubuntu 18.04 virtual machine, 20 GB

---

[1] The source code is open source on the website: https://github.com/buptis073114/FAV-BFT.

SATA hard disk. The challenge-response protocol based on VDF is implemented in C language and be compiled into so dynamic link library, in which GMP library is used for large number operation. RBC algorithm is implemented in Python language based on the open source code of HoneyBadgerBFT. The ctype library is used to call so shared libraries functions in Python3. Suppose that the shared file sizes are 1 MB, 5 MB, 50 MB, 100 MB, 500 MB, 700 MB and 1 GB respectively, the values of τ are 500, 5000, 10000, 50000, 100000, 300000, 500000 and 1000000 respectively. The size of N is 4096-bits.

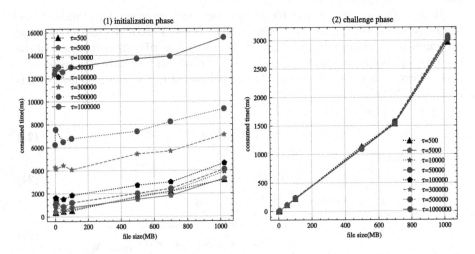

Fig. 5. Time consumed in initialization and challenge phases

Figure 5 (1) shows the consumed time of initialization phase with the different values of τ. As the shared-file size and the value of τ increase, the consumed time also increases. In this phase, the compute-time consumption can be adjusted by dynamically adjusting the value of τ. It is difficult to speed up this process by adding parallel computing. The size of evidence-data generated by this phase is 2231-bytes.

In proof phase, the experiment tested the efficiency for P to generate a response when receiving the challenge from V. The challenge is a 256-bit string randomly generated by P. The consumed time of P proof phase is shown in Fig. 5 (2). The consumed-time in this phase is positively correlated with file size and has little association with the value of τ. If the P does not hold the evidence-data, he/she must rerun the initialization phase, which will cause timeout and be rejected.

The experiment tests the efficiency of verification phase, which is shown in Fig. 6 (1). The consumed time in this phase is proportional to the file size. It can be shown that the consumed time mainly occurs in calculating the hash value of the file. We test the execution efficiency of VoFC and RBC algorithm, which is shown in Fig. 6 (2). The experimental results show that the efficiency of VoFC is higher than RBC under the premise that the input length is same.

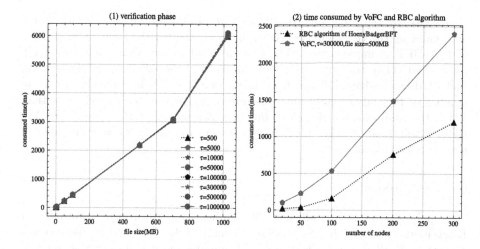

Fig. 6. Time consumed in verification phase, VoFC and RBC algorithm

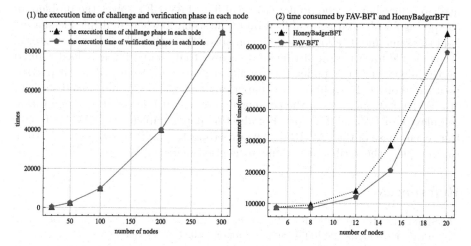

Fig. 7. Time consumed in verification phase, VoFC and RBC algorithm

In the above challenge and verification phases, verifying the hash value of the file takes most time. Therefore, the method of improving calculation efficiency is adopted by calculating the hash value of the file sampling instead of the hash value of the whole content of the file. The result shows that these two phases can be completed more efficiently.

The experiment also tests the efficiency of each node executing challenge and verification phases in VoFC, which is shown in Fig. 7 (1). The results show that each node will receive the challenge from all other nodes, and will verify all received responses. The execution number of challenge and verification phases is the square of node's number.

At last, by replacing the RBC algorithm of HoneyBadgerBFT with VoFC and removing the threshold encryption in HoneyBadgerBFT, the whole process of FAV-BFT is implemented. The experimental results show that FAV-BFT can indeed verify the authenticity of the file and the efficiency is higher than that of HoneyBadgerBFT which is shown in Fig. 7 (2). In addition, a certain number of bad participants are deliberately set in the experiment (less than 1/3 of the total number of nodes), but they can not affect the process of FAV-BFT, which demonstrates the characteristics of tolerating a certain number of malicious participants.

6   Conclusion

This paper proposes an efficient file authenticity verification protocol for Blockchain-based file-sharing system, namely *File Authenticity Verification Byzantine Fault Tolerant* (FAV-BFT). Compared with state-machine replication BFT protocol, FAV-BFT combines VDF with RBC algorithm to tolerate malicious file-sharers who do not save real files. FAV-BFT solves the problem of competing for file-sharing qualification in the scenario where multiple file-sharers hold the same file. It allows users to convince others that file-shares have stored the same file for a period of time and ensures that shared-file is indeed wanted by the file-downloader under the condition that more than 2/3 of all participants are honest. In addition, this paper analyzes the performance and security of FAV-BFT. Compared to the consensus protocol of Filecoin, the computation complexity of FAV-BFT is low. Finally, this paper implements FAV-BFT, and tests each phase of the FAV-BFT. The experimental results show that FAV-BFT can complete the verification of file authenticity efficiently.

References

1. Steinmetz, R., Wehrle, K.: Peer-to-Peer Systems and Applications, vol. 3485. Springer, Heidelberg (2005). https://doi.org/10.1007/11530657
2. Kulbak, Y., Bickson, D., et al.: The eMule protocol specification. eMule project (2005). http://sourceforge.net
3. Liang, J., Kumar, R., Ross, K.W.: Understanding kazaa
4. Sari, L., Sipos, M.: FileTribe: blockchain-based secure file sharing on IPFS. In: 25th European Wireless Conference, pp. 1–6 (2019)
5. Khatal, S., Rane, J., Patel, D., Patel, P., Busnel, Y.: FileShare: a blockchain and IPFS framework for secure file sharing and data provenance. In: Advances in Machine Learning and Computational Intelligence, pp. 825–833 (2021)
6. BTFS. https://www.bittorrent.com/token/bittorrent-file-system/
7. Nyaletey, E., Parizi, R.M., Zhang, Q., Choo, K.R.: BlockIPFS - blockchain-enabled interplanetary file system for forensic and trusted data traceability. In: 2019 IEEE International Conference on Blockchain (Blockchain), pp. 18–25 (2019)
8. Vorick, D., Champine, L.: Sia: simple decentralized storage. Nebulous Inc. (2014)
9. Storj Labs: Storj: a decentralized cloud storage network framework (2018)
10. Protocol Labs: Filecoin: a decentralized storage network (2017). https://filecoin.io/filecoin.pdf

11. Moran, T., Orlov, I.: Simple proofs of space-time and rational proofs of storage. In: Boldyreva, A., Micciancio, D. (eds.) CRYPTO 2019. LNCS, vol. 11692, pp. 381–409. Springer, Cham (2019). https://doi.org/10.1007/978-3-030-26948-7_14

12. Benet, J.: IPFS-content addressed, versioned, P2P file system. arXiv preprint arXiv:1407.3561 (2014)

13. Benet, J., Dalrymple, D., Greco, N.: Proof of replication, vol. 27, p. 20. Protocol Labs (2017)

14. Gennaro, R., Gentry, C., Parno, B., Raykova, M.: Quadratic span programs and succinct NIZKs without PCPs. In: Johansson, T., Nguyen, P.Q. (eds.) EUROCRYPT 2013. LNCS, vol. 7881, pp. 626–645. Springer, Heidelberg (2013). https://doi.org/10.1007/978-3-642-38348-9_37

15. King, S., Nadal, S.: PPCoin: peer-to-peer crypto-currency with proof-of-stake, 19 August 2012. Self-published paper

16. Bitansky, N., Chiesa, A., Ishai, Y., Paneth, O., Ostrovsky, R.: Succinct non-interactive arguments via linear interactive proofs. In: Sahai, A. (ed.) TCC 2013. LNCS, vol. 7785, pp. 315–333. Springer, Heidelberg (2013). https://doi.org/10.1007/978-3-642-36594-2_18

17. Ben-Sasson, E., Chiesa, A., Genkin, D., Tromer, E., Virza, M.: SNARKs for C: verifying program executions succinctly and in zero knowledge. In: Canetti, R., Garay, J.A. (eds.) CRYPTO 2013. LNCS, vol. 8043, pp. 90–108. Springer, Heidelberg (2013). https://doi.org/10.1007/978-3-642-40084-1_6

18. Castro, M., Liskov, B., et al.: Practical byzantine fault tolerance. In: OSDI 1999, vol. 99, pp. 173–186 (1999)

19. Schneider, F.B.: Implementing fault-tolerant services using the state machine approach: a tutorial. ACM Comput. Surv. (CSUR) 22(4), 299–319 (1990)

20. Juels, A., Kaliski Jr, B.S.: PORs: proofs of retrievability for large files. In: Proceedings of the 14th ACM Conference on Computer and Communications Security, pp. 584–597 (2007)

21. Dziembowski, S., Faust, S., Kolmogorov, V., Pietrzak, K.: Proofs of space. In: Gennaro, R., Robshaw, M. (eds.) CRYPTO 2015. LNCS, vol. 9216, pp. 585–605. Springer, Heidelberg (2015). https://doi.org/10.1007/978-3-662-48000-7_29

22. Moran, T., Orlov, I.: Rational proofs of space-time. Technical report. Cryptology ePrint Archive, vol. 35 (2016)

23. Mahmoody, M., Moran, T., Vadhan, S.: Publicly verifiable proofs of sequential work. In: Proceedings of the 4th Conference on Innovations in Theoretical Computer Science, pp. 373–388 (2013)

24. Cohen, B., Pietrzak, K.: Simple proofs of sequential work. In: Nielsen, J.B., Rijmen, V. (eds.) EUROCRYPT 2018. LNCS, vol. 10821, pp. 451–467. Springer, Cham (2018). https://doi.org/10.1007/978-3-319-78375-8_15

25. Boneh, D., Bonneau, J., Bünz, B., Fisch, B.: Verifiable delay functions. In: Shacham, H., Boldyreva, A. (eds.) CRYPTO 2018. LNCS, vol. 10991, pp. 757–788. Springer, Cham (2018). https://doi.org/10.1007/978-3-319-96884-1_25

26. Pietrzak, K.: Simple verifiable delay functions. In: 10th Innovations in Theoretical Computer Science Conference (ITCS 2019). Schloss Dagstuhl-Leibniz-Zentrum fuer Informatik (2018)

27. Rivest, R.L., Shamir, A., Wagner, D.A.: Time-lock puzzles and timed-release crypto (1996)

28. Mahmoody, M., Moran, T., Vadhan, S.: Time-lock puzzles in the random oracle model. In: Rogaway, P. (ed.) CRYPTO 2011. LNCS, vol. 6841, pp. 39–50. Springer, Heidelberg (2011). https://doi.org/10.1007/978-3-642-22792-9_3

29. Malavolta, G., Thyagarajan, S.A.K.: Homomorphic time-lock puzzles and applications. In: Boldyreva, A., Micciancio, D. (eds.) CRYPTO 2019. LNCS, vol. 11692, pp. 620–649. Springer, Cham (2019). https://doi.org/10.1007/978-3-030-26948-7_22

30. Boneh, D., Bünz, B., Fisch, B.: A survey of two verifiable delay functions. IACR Cryptology ePrint Archive 2018/712 (2018)

31. Wesolowski, B.: Efficient verifiable delay functions. In: Ishai, Y., Rijmen, V. (eds.) EUROCRYPT 2019. LNCS, vol. 11478, pp. 379–407. Springer, Cham (2019). https://doi.org/10.1007/978-3-030-17659-4_13

32. Miller, A., Xia, Y., Croman, K., Shi, E., Song, D.: The honey badger of BFT protocols. In: Proceedings of the 2016 ACM SIGSAC Conference on Computer and Communications Security, pp. 31–42 (2016)

33. Guo, B., Lu, Z., Tang, Q., Xu, J., Zhang, Z.: Dumbo: faster asynchronous BFT protocols. In: Proceedings of the 2020 ACM SIGSAC Conference on Computer and Communications Security, pp. 803–818 (2020)

34. Lu, Y., Lu, Z., Tang, Q., Wang, G.: Dumbo-MVBA: optimal multi-valued validated asynchronous byzantine agreement, revisited. In: Proceedings of the 39th Symposium on Principles of Distributed Computing, pp. 129–138 (2020)

35. Su, S., Yuan, F., Yuan, Y., Zeng, L., Chen, C.: VoFSQ: an efficient file-sharing interactive verification protocol. In: 2021 IEEE Symposium on Computers and Communications (ISCC), pp. 1–7 (2021)

36. Dimitrov, V., Jullien, G., Miller, W.: Complexity and fast algorithms for multiexponentiations. IEEE Trans. Comput. **49**, 141–147 (2000)

37. Chang, C., Lou, D.: Parallel computation of the multi-exponentiation for cryptosystems. Int. J. Comput. Math. **63**, 9–26 (1997)

Incentive Mechanism Design for Uncertain Tasks in Mobile Crowd Sensing Systems Utilizing Smart Contract in Blockchain

Xikun Jiang[1,4], Chenhao Ying[1,4], Xinchun Yu[2], Boris Düdder[3],
and Yuan Luo[1,4(✉)]

[1] Department of Computer Science and Engineering, Shanghai Jiao Tong University,
Shanghai, China
{xikunjiang,yingchh1565,yuanluo}@sjtu.edu.cn
[2] Tsinghua-Berkeley Shenzhen Institute, Tsinghua University, Beijing, China
yuxinchun@sz.tsinghua.edu.cn
[3] Department of Computer Science, University of Copenhagen,
Copenhagen, Denmark
boris.d@di.ku.dk
[4] Wuxi Blockchain Advanced Research Center, Beijing, China

Abstract. Mobile crowd sensing (MCS) systems recently have been regarded as a newly-emerged sensing paradigm, where the platform receives the requested tasks from requesters and outsources the collection of sensory data to participating workers. However, the centralized structure of the MCS system is vulnerable to a single point of failure, and there is a lack of trust between participants and the platform. Additionally, participating in MCS is often costly. So the paramount problem is how to solve these problems associated with centralized structures and incentivize more participation. Most existing works design the incentive mechanisms only considering static sensing tasks whose information is completely known a priori (*e.g.,* when and which task arrives). Due to the dynamic environment and severe resource constraints, the tasks are usually uncertain, *i.e.,* the information of tasks is incompletely known by the platform. Therefore, in this paper, we design an incentive mechanism, HERALD, for the uncertain tasks in MCS systems by using smart contracts. Specifically, the uncertain tasks are low sensitive to time (that is, tasks do not require real-time information) and arrive according to a probability distribution. HERALD utilizes the decentralized nature of the blockchain to eliminate the system's reliance on third parties and satisfies truthfulness, individual rationality, as well as low computational complexity and low social cost. The desirable properties of HERALD are validated through both theoretical analysis and extensive simulations.

Keywords: Incentive mechanism · Uncertain sensing tasks · Mobile crowd sensing · Smart contract

© ICST Institute for Computer Sciences, Social Informatics and Telecommunications Engineering 2022
Published by Springer Nature Switzerland AG 2022. All Rights Reserved
H. Gao et al. (Eds.): CollaborateCom 2022, LNICST 460, pp. 475–493, 2022.
https://doi.org/10.1007/978-3-031-24383-7_26

1   Introduction

The recent unprecedented development of mobile devices which are embedded with powerful processors and plentiful sensors (*e.g.,* GPS, microphone, camera) has impelled the rise of mobile crowd sensing, a newly emerged sensing paradigm that outsources the collection of sensory data to a crowd of workers who carry the mobile devices. Currently, numerous MCS systems have been devised and applied to a broad scope of applications [1–5], including smart transportation, traffic control, and so on.

However, in the process of data sharing, traditional MCS systems are generally proposed and implemented in a centralized manner under the control of the platform, are susceptible to a single point of failure, and need to rely on a trusted third party. Since it is not easy to solve the problems caused by a centralized structure, and it is difficult for participants to establish a trusting relationship with third parties, the establishment of such a platform is impractical. To solve this problem, we use the decentralized nature of the blockchain to eliminate the system's dependence on third parties. In fact, as a decentralized ledger, the blockchain is maintained by all participants in the network, effectively realizing the decentralization feature [6]. For more complex transactions in the blockchain, the smart contract is introduced, which was first implemented in the real world by Ethereum in 2014 [7]. The decentralized nature of blockchain prompted us to design an incentive mechanism using the smart contract.

A typical blockchain-based MCS system is shown in Fig. 1, all participants, including requesters and workers, must create their accounts and interact with the blockchain. Specifically, the requesters interact with the blockchain through the smart contract to publish their sensing tasks, and workers interact with the blockchain through the smart contract for the delivery of encrypted sensory data. Most applications of the MCS system depend on the sufficient participation of mobile workers such that the quality of service can be ensured. However, performing sensing tasks is usually costly for individual workers. For example, collecting the sensory data of requested tasks often consumes workers' battery power, storage resource, computing energy, and some additional costs for data transmission. Furthermore, it may also reveal workers' private information during collecting and exchanging data. It means a participant is not willing to provide the sensory data unless receiving a satisfying reward to compensate for the consumption. Therefore, it is necessary to design a proper incentive mechanism to attract more participation such that the corresponding applications of the MCS system can provide the sensing service with high quality.

Due to the paramount significance of incentives, many mechanisms [8–25] have been proposed in recent years to attract more participation. Thus far, some existing works considered the *offline* scenario [8,9], where the information of tasks and workers is known by the platform a priori, *e.g.,* when and which task or worker arrives. Furthermore, some works considered the *online* scenario [13], where the workers arrive dynamically in an online manner and the platform must collect the sensory data from the arrived workers without the information of future arriving workers. In particular, most of them are under the assumption

Fig. 1. A typical blockchain-based MCS system.

that the sensing tasks are static whose information is completely known by the platform a priori. However, due to the complicated practical environment, the sensing tasks are usually uncertain and their information is incompletely known by the platform *e.g.,* when and which task arrives. Therefore, it requires us to *use smart contracts to design a blockchain-based incentive mechanism in the MCS system under uncertain sensing tasks, which has nice properties* e.g., *truthfulness, individual rationality, and low social cost.*

Usually in the MCS system, for some tasks that do not require real-time performance, for example, when the requested task is to collect the number of bends on a road, the number of forks, or information about shops on both sides of the road, the platform can collect such task data in advance. It may incur heavy latency and lower efficiency if the platform collects the sensory data after the sensing tasks arrive. Therefore, the platform needs to collect the sensing tasks before the real tasks arrive such that the sensory data can be obtained once they arrive. Since the platform collects the tasks from the workers before the real tasks arrive, which causes it does not know any information about sensing tasks, *e.g.,* when and which tasks will arrive in the future. Therefore, we refer to this scenario as a *uncertain scenario.*

However, due to the uncertain nature of sensing tasks in the above practical scenario, it is difficult to design a proper incentive mechanism, which can guarantee the truthfulness and individual rationality which are two basic requirements in the design of an incentive mechanism, and meanwhile maintain the low computational complexity and low social cost. Therefore, to design a mechanism in the uncertain scenario, we assume that the tasks arrive in the future according to a probability distribution. Considering the above scenario with uncertain tasks, we propose an incentive mechanism based on blockchain and smart contracts, namely, HERALD[1], which utilizes the decentralized nature of blockchain to eliminate the system's dependence on third parties and satisfies the truthfulness and individual rationality, as well as the low computational complexity and social cost. In summary, the main contributions of this paper are as follows.

---

[1] The name HERALD is from incentive mec**H**anism for unc**ER**t**A**in tasks in mobi**L**e crow**D** sensing.

- *Mechanism:* Unlike the prior works, we propose a novel blockchain-based incentive mechanism, HERALD, using the smart contract. In particular, HERALD is designed for the uncertain scenario such that the smart contract can collect the sensory data before the real tasks arrive by assuming the tasks arrive in the future according to a probability distribution.
- *Properties of HERALD:* HERALD can stimulate the participation of workers and bears many desirable properties, including truthfulness, individual rationality, low computational complexity, and low social cost. Although some incentive mechanisms [8–11] have been proposed for the traditional MCS, they are simply designed to collect massive sensory data, which can not be applied in this work. Furthermore, we prove that its competitive ratio on expected social cost is $\mathcal{O}(\ln mn)$, where m and n are the numbers of workers and tasks published in advance.
- *Evaluations:* We further conduct extensive simulations to validate the desirable properties of HERALD. The simulation results show that compared with state-of-the-art approaches, HERALD has the lower expected social cost and expected total payment.

In the rest of this paper, we first present some existing works that are related to this work in Sect. 2 and introduce the preliminaries in Sect. 3. Then, the design details and theoretic analysis of HERALD are described in Sect. 4. In Sect. 5, we conduct extensive simulations to validate the desirable properties of HERALD. Finally, the conclusion of this paper is shown in Sect. 6.

2   Related Work

Due to the paramount significance of attracting more participation, various incentive mechanisms [8–25] for MCS systems have been developed recently. Apart from truthfulness and individual rationality, which are two critical properties in the incentive mechanism, these works also aim to guarantee the benefit of workers or platforms.

The authors in [8,9] designed the mechanisms to minimize the social cost. The proposed mechanisms in [10,11] maximized the platform's profit. The mechanisms designed in [12–18] minimized the platform's payment. Additionally, the authors in [19–21] devised the mechanisms that maximize social welfare. Apart from the above optimization objectives, there are also some works focusing on some other objectives. Hu *et al.* in [22] proposed a privacy-preserving incentive mechanism in dynamic spectrum sharing crowdsensing. Bhattacharjee *et al.* in [23] stimulated the workers to act honestly by investigating their data's quantity and quality. Han *et al.* in [24] considered the privacy-preserving in budget limited crowdsensing. Gong *et al.* in [25] proposed an incentive mechanism to stimulate workers to submit high-quality data.

Almost all existing works recruit workers to collect the corresponding sensory data under the static sensing tasks whose information is completely known by the platform a priori. However, due to the complicated practical environment and

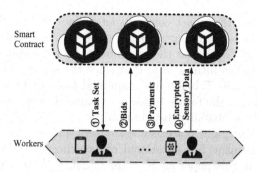

Fig. 2. Framework of HERALD where the tasks arrive according to a probability distribution. (The circled numbers represent the order of events).

severe resource constraints, the sensing tasks are usually uncertain, *i.e.,* their information is incompletely known by the platform. Therefore, different from the existing works, this paper is the first attempt to propose a novel incentive mechanism for the uncertain tasks in MCS systems by using smart contracts. Specifically, the uncertain tasks arrive according to a probability distribution and the platform does not know any information about these tasks.

3   Preliminaries

In this section, we introduce the system overview and design objectives.

3.1   System Overview

We consider a blockchain-based MCS system consisting of a smart contract and a set of participating workers which is denoted as $\mathcal{W} = \{1, 2, \ldots, m\}$. In HERALD, we assume that the smart contract has a set $\mathcal{T} = \{\tau_1, \ldots \tau_n\}$ of n sensing tasks known *a priori* and all requested tasks arriving in the future belong to $\mathcal{T}$. This assumption is rational since, in practice, the smart contract usually knows which tasks need to be completed. For example, in the service of a traffic monitor, the task set is the collection of forks on all roads in a region, with each task corresponding to the number of forks on each road. The task set in this service does not change over time and has no real-time requirements, and the data requests should be within the task set regardless of when they arrive. Similar service includes road curve monitor. The framework of HERALD is shown in Fig. 2, whose workflow is described as follows.

Incentive Mechanism for Uncertain Scenario: As shown in Fig. 2, the smart contract first publishes all sensing tasks in $\mathcal{T}$ to workers before the real requested tasks arrive (step ①). After receiving the task set $\mathcal{T}$, every worker i sends her preferred task set denoted as $\Gamma_i \subseteq \mathcal{T}$ to the smart contract, as well as a bid b_i, which is her bidding price for executing these tasks (step ②). Based on the received bids, the smart contract determines the set S of winners and the payment p_i to each winning worker i (step ③), and collects the winners' sensory data (step ④) such that the requested tasks are responded immediately when they arrive in the future. Note that since the smart contract collects the sensory data of tasks in T before the requested tasks arrive and do not know any information about the future tasks, we assume that all tasks in T arrive in the future following probability distribution.

Specifically, a loser does not execute any task and receives zero payment in the incentive mechanism. For notational convenience, we denote the payment profile of workers in this paper as $\overrightarrow{p} = (p_1, \ldots, p_m)$. When we denote the real cost of worker i as c_i in HERALD, her utility can be defined as

$$u_i = \begin{cases} p_i - c_i & \text{if worker } i \text{ wins} \\ 0 & \text{otherwise} \end{cases} \tag{1}$$

Without loss of generality, in this paper, we assume that the bid b_i of each worker i is bounded by $[b_{min}, b_{max}]$, where b_{min} is normalized to 1 and b_{max} is a constant. We further assume that for each worker i with a preferred task set Γ_i, there exist some workers j with preferred task sets Γ_j such that $\Gamma_i \subseteq \cup_j \Gamma_j$.

3.2   Blockchain and Smart Contract

The incentive mechanism proposed in this paper, HERALD, which is based on the blockchain with a smart contract, removes the centralized nature of a centralized MCS system to avoid single points of failure and resolve trust issues between participants. Specifically, each participant including requesters and workers needs to create their account and interact with the blockchain. The requesters and workers interact with the blockchain through the smart contract to complete their task publish and encrypted sensory data delivery, respectively.

Each worker registers at the registration authority (RA) and gets a certificate such that they can participate in the MCS. This step is described as follows.

Registration for the In-Chain Participants: RA generates a public-secret key pair for the certification and broadcasts. Then, each arrived worker with a unique ID creates a public-secret key pair for the signature and registers with RA. Furthermore, the worker gets a certificate from RA to bind the public key and her ID by utilizing the secret key. Similarly, each arrived requester with a unique ID creates a public-secret key pair for the signature and registers with RA. The requesters get a certificate from RA to bind the public key and their ID by utilizing the secret key.

The worker submits the encrypted data to the SC. The corresponding operations of workers are as follows.

Operation of Workers: After receiving the corresponding information, the worker encrypts the sensory data with the signature and address to obtain the ciphertext utilizing the public key of the requester. Then, the encrypted data is sent to Smart Contract and can be optionally saved on a decentralized storage system such as Swarm or IPFS. The truth of data is verified by an attestation service.

3.3   Design Objectives

In this paper, we aim to ensure that HERALD bears the following advantageous properties.

Due to workers' *selfish* and *strategic* nature, it is possible that any worker i may submit a bid b_i that differs from her real cost c_i for executing all of tasks in Γ_i. Therefore, one of our goals is to design a truthful incentive mechanism defined as follows.

Definition 1 (Truthfulness). *An incentive mechanism is truthful if for any worker $i \in \mathcal{W}$, her utility is maximized when bidding her real cost c_i.*

By Definition 1, we aim to ensure that workers bid truthfully to the smart contract. Apart from truthfulness, another desirable property that we aim to achieve is individual rationality defined as follows.

Definition 2 (Individual Rationality). *An incentive mechanism is individual rationality if, for any worker $i \in \mathcal{W}$, her utility u_i satisfies $u_i \geq 0$.*

Additionally, for HERALD, since the tasks in $\mathcal{T}$ arrive according to a probability distribution, we also aim to ensure it has a low expected social cost. To achieve this goal, we investigate its competitive ratio on expected social cost defined as follows.

Definition 3 (Competitive Ratio on Expected Social Cost). *When the tasks in sensing task set $\mathcal{T}$ arrive according to a probability distribution, for any set $\mathcal{A}$ of k tasks that possibly arrive simultaneously from $\mathcal{T}$, let $\mathcal{S}(\mathcal{A})$ be the set of winners selected by the mechanism such that $\mathcal{A} \subseteq \cup_{i \in \mathcal{S}(\mathcal{A})} \Gamma_i$ and $\Gamma_i \cap \mathcal{A} \neq \emptyset$ for $\forall i \in \mathcal{S}(\mathcal{A})$, $C(\mathcal{S}(\mathcal{A})) = \sum_{i \in \mathcal{S}(\mathcal{A})} c_i$ be the corresponding social cost, and $C_{\mathcal{OPT}}(\mathcal{A})$ be the minimum social cost of requested task set $\mathcal{A}$, respectively. The competitive ratio on expected social cost is defined as $\max_k \mathbb{E}_{\mathcal{A} \subseteq \mathcal{T}}[C(\mathcal{S}(\mathcal{A}))]/\mathbb{E}_{\mathcal{A} \subseteq \mathcal{T}}[C_{\mathcal{OPT}}(\mathcal{A})]$, where $\mathbb{E}_{\mathcal{A} \subseteq \mathcal{T}}[\cdot]$ is the expectation over all sets of possibly k arriving tasks in the future.*

Note that some tasks in task set $\mathcal{A}$ may be identical. Therefore, when we say $\mathcal{A} \subseteq \mathcal{T}$ in the investigation of competitive ratio, it means that every task in $\mathcal{A}$ is also in $\mathcal{T}$ since the tasks in $\mathcal{T}$ are distinct. Furthermore, the expectation $\mathbb{E}_{\mathcal{A} \subseteq \mathcal{T}}[\cdot]$ is caused by the variety of the set $\mathcal{A}$ of k requested tasks, and for convenience of notation, the subscript $\mathcal{A} \subseteq \mathcal{T}$ is omitted in the remainder of this paper, *i.e.,* this expectation is denoted as $\mathbb{E}[\cdot]$.

Finally, we aim for HERALD to be computational efficient which is defined as follows.

Definition 4. *An incentive mechanism is computationally efficient if it can be carried out in polynomial time.*

In short, our objectives are to ensure the proposed mechanisms are truthful and individual rationality, as well as have low social cost and low computational complexity.

4   Incentive Mechanism for Uncertain Scenario

In this section, we present an incentive mechanism for the uncertain scenario. It will be proved that our mechanism is individual rationality and truthfulness. Furthermore, we investigate its competitive ratios on expected social cost, which is shown in Theorem 3. Apart from the above properties, we also show its computational complexity in Proposition 1.

4.1   Design Rationale

When designing the incentive mechanism, we usually need to consider the number of tasks that arrive simultaneously since different numbers of tasks arrive simultaneously usually for different scenarios, and result in different mechanisms. In the offline scenario, all tasks arrive simultaneously such that the information of tasks is completely known by the smart contract a priori. However, in the uncertain scenario, due to the uncertain tasks, the number of tasks arriving simultaneously is also uncertain. The different numbers of the arrival of tasks follow a different probability distribution, which will be illustrated by the following simple example.

Example 1. In this example, the smart contract has a sensing task set $T = \{\tau_1, \tau_2, \tau_3\}$ with three tasks, each of which arrives in the future with probability $\frac{1}{3}$, *i.e.*, the arrival of tasks follows a uniform distribution. If only one task arrives simultaneously in the future, it may be τ_1, τ_2, or τ_3 with the same probability of $\frac{1}{3}$. While, if two tasks arrive simultaneously in the future, they maybe $\{\tau_1, \tau_1\}$, $\{\tau_2, \tau_2\}$ and $\{\tau_3, \tau_3\}$ with the same probability $\frac{1}{9}$, and may be $\{\tau_1, \tau_2\}$, $\{\tau_1, \tau_3\}$ and $\{\tau_2, \tau_3\}$ with the same probability $\frac{2}{9}$. Furthermore, if three tasks simultaneously arrive in the future, they maybe $\{\tau_1, \tau_2, \tau_3\}$ with probability $\frac{2}{9}$; $\{\tau_1, \tau_1, \tau_1\}$, $\{\tau_2, \tau_2, \tau_2\}$ and $\{\tau_3, \tau_3, \tau_3\}$ with the same probability $\frac{1}{27}$; and may be $\{\tau_1, \tau_2, \tau_2\}$, $\{\tau_1, \tau_3, \tau_3\}$, $\{\tau_1, \tau_1, \tau_2\}$, $\{\tau_1, \tau_1, \tau_3\}$, $\{\tau_2, \tau_2, \tau_3\}$, and $\{\tau_2, \tau_3, \tau_3\}$ with the same probability $\frac{1}{9}$.

As shown in the example, different from the existing works, where the number of tasks arriving simultaneously is fixed, in the uncertain scenario, due to the uncertainty of tasks, the number of tasks varies. Therefore, we propose the HERALD, which is an adaptive incentive mechanism based on the different numbers of tasks arriving simultaneously. In particular, we need to input an assumed number to the HERALD, which is the number of tasks arriving simultaneously. Then, according to the different input numbers, HERALD will output different results of winner selection and payment determination.

4.2   Design Details

To collect the sensory data of the uncertain tasks, we define a *selection threshold* (ST) $T \geq 0$ in HERALD. In particular, let $T = 64\mathbb{E}[C_{\mathcal{OPT}}(\mathcal{A})]$, where $\mathcal{A}$ is the set of k possibly simultaneously arriving tasks from the sensing task set T, and 64 is set for facilitating the proof mentioned later. HERALD works as follows.

Algorithm 1: HERALD in the Smart Contract

Input: The task set $\mathcal{T}$, worker set $\mathcal{W}$, workers' preferred task sets Γ_i, workers' bids b_i, the number k of tasks arriving simultaneously.

Output: The winner set $\mathcal{S}$, and payment $\overrightarrow{p}$;

1   $\mathcal{S} \leftarrow \emptyset$;

2   Smart contract calculates the selection threshold T;

    // Winner Selection Phase by Smart Contract:

3   **while** $\mathcal{T} \neq \emptyset$ **do**

4   **for** *each worker* $i \in \mathcal{W}$ **do**

5   Calculate the cost-effectiveness (CF) $\frac{b_i}{|\Gamma_i \cap \mathcal{T}|}$;

         // Type I Selection:

6   **if** $\exists i \in \mathcal{W},\ s.t\ \frac{b_i}{|\Gamma_i \cap \mathcal{T}|} \leq \frac{T}{|\mathcal{T}|}$ **then**

7   Choose a worker $i \in \mathcal{W}$ with the minimum value of CF denoted as $\frac{b_i}{|\Gamma_i \cap \mathcal{T}|}$ among the workers whose CFs are less than $\frac{T}{|\mathcal{T}|}$;

         // Type II Selection:

8   **else**

9   Choose a worker $i \in \mathcal{W}$, whose bid b_i is the least and preferred task set contains at least one uncovered task;

10         $\mathcal{S} \leftarrow \mathcal{S} \cup \{i\}$;

11         $\mathcal{T} \leftarrow \mathcal{T} \backslash \Gamma_i$;

    // Payment Determination Phase by Smart Contract:

12   **for** *each* $i \in \mathcal{S}$ **do**

13   Define a *copy set* $\mathcal{T}_i \leftarrow \Gamma_i$;

14   Build a *covering set* $\mathcal{W}_i = \{j | \forall j \in \mathcal{W} \backslash \{i\},\ \Gamma_j \cap \mathcal{T}_i \neq \emptyset\}$;

15   Define a *replaced set* $\mathcal{R}_i \leftarrow \emptyset$;

16   **while** $\mathcal{T}_i \neq \emptyset$ **do**

17   Choose a worker $j \in \mathcal{W}_i$ with the minimum CF denoted as $\frac{b_j}{|\Gamma_j \cap \mathcal{T}_i|}$;

18         $\mathcal{R}_i \leftarrow \mathcal{R}_i \cup \{j\}$;

19         $\mathcal{T}_i \leftarrow \mathcal{T}_i \backslash \Gamma_j$;

20      $p_i \leftarrow \max\{b_i, p_{\mathcal{R}_i}\}$ for $p_{\mathcal{R}_i} = \sum_{j \in \mathcal{R}_i} b_j$;

21   **Return** $\mathcal{S}$ and $\overrightarrow{p}$.

Winner Selection Phase: In each iteration, there exist two types of selections in HERALD, namely, *type I selection* and *type II selection*.

- *Type I Selection:* When there are some workers whose cost-effectiveness (CF) is less than or equal to $\frac{T}{|\mathcal{T}|}$, the smart contract selects a worker with the least CF as the winner. Note that, for worker i, if $\Gamma_i \cap \mathcal{T} = \emptyset$, then its CF $= +\infty$.
- *Type II Selection:* When the CFs of all workers are larger than $\frac{T}{|\mathcal{T}|}$, the smart contract selects a worker as the winner, whose bid is the least and preferred task set contains at least one uncovered task in $\mathcal{T}$.

It then adds the winner selected above to the winner set $\mathcal{S}$.

Payment Determination Phase: For each winner $i \in \mathcal{S}$, the smart contract defines a *copy set* $\mathcal{T}_i = \Gamma_i$ and builds a *covering set* $\mathcal{W}_i = \{j | \forall j \in \mathcal{W} \backslash \{i\}, \; \Gamma_j \cap \mathcal{T}_i \neq \emptyset\}$. It then derives a *replaced set* denoted as $\mathcal{R}_i$ consisting of workers in $\mathcal{W}_i$ with the least CFs in each iteration such that $\Gamma_i \subseteq \cup_{j \in \mathcal{R}_i} \Gamma_j$. The payment to winner i is $p_i = \max\{b_i, p_{\mathcal{R}_i}\}$, where $p_{\mathcal{R}_i} = \sum_{j \in \mathcal{R}_i} b_j$.

Example 2. In this example, the smart contract has a task set $\mathcal{T} = \{\tau_1, \tau_2, \tau_3, \tau_4, \tau_5\}$ with five tasks and there are seven workers with the preferred task sets $\Gamma_1 = \{\tau_1, \tau_2\}$, $\Gamma_2 = \{\tau_2, \tau_3\}$, $\Gamma_3 = \{\tau_3, \tau_1, \tau_4\}$, $\Gamma_4 = \{\tau_4, \tau_5\}$, $\Gamma_5 = \{\tau_4\}$, $\Gamma_6 = \{\tau_2, \tau_5\}$ and $\Gamma_7 = \{\tau_2, \tau_4, \tau_5\}$, as well as the costs $c_1 = 1.4$, $c_2 = 1.8$, $c_3 = 2.8$, $c_4 = 2.6$, $c_5 = 3.1$, $c_6 = 3.3$ and $c_7 = 3.6$. Since the mechanism HERALD is truthful which will be proved later, the workers' real costs are equal to their bids, i.e., $b_i = c_i$. We assume that the arrival of tasks follows a uniform distribution. When the input number of tasks arriving simultaneously is set to 1, *i.e.*, only one task arrives at each time, the task may be τ_1, τ_2, τ_3, τ_4, or τ_5 with the same probability $\frac{1}{5}$. Then, it can be obtained that the selection threshold $T = 125.44$. As shown in Algorithm 1, the smart contract will carry out the **winner selection phase**. For the first iteration, after calculating the cost-effectiveness of all workers, it can be seen that the condition in Line 6 of HERALD is satisfied. Therefore, the smart contract carries to `type I selection` and selects worker 1 as the winner. Then, the second iteration is carried out, where the condition in Line 6 of HERALD still holds. Thus, the `type I selection` is carried out, and worker 4 is selected as a winner. With the same iteration, it can be obtained that the final winner set selected by the HERALD is $\mathcal{S} = \{1, 2, 4\}$. Then, the smart contract carries out the **payment determination phase**. In particular, for worker 1 whose covering set is $\mathcal{W}_1 = \{2, 3, 6, 7\}$, it can be seen that the corresponding replace set is $\mathcal{R}_1 = \{2, 3\}$. Therefore, the smart contract to worker 1 is $p_1 = 1.8 + 2.8 = 4.6$. After the similar steps, it can be obtained that the payments to worker 2 and worker 4 are $p_2 = 1.4 + 2.8 = 4.2$ and $p_4 = 3.6$.

Furthermore, when the input number of tasks arriving simultaneously is set to 2, the tasks may be $\{\tau_1, \tau_1\}$, $\{\tau_2, \tau_2\}$, $\{\tau_3, \tau_3\}$, $\{\tau_4, \tau_4\}$, $\{\tau_5, \tau_5\}$ with the same probability $\frac{1}{25}$, and $\{\tau_1, \tau_2\}$, $\{\tau_1, \tau_3\}$, $\{\tau_1, \tau_4\}$, $\{\tau_1, \tau_5\}$, $\{\tau_2, \tau_3\}$, $\{\tau_2, \tau_4\}$, $\{\tau_2, \tau_5\}$, $\{\tau_3, \tau_4\}$, $\{\tau_3, \tau_5\}$, $\{\tau_4, \tau_5\}$ with the same probability $\frac{2}{25}$. The selection threshold is $T = 181.248$. Then, the smart contract can carry out the **winner selection phase** and **payment determination phase** of HERALD sequentially to obtain the winner set and the corresponding payments.

Remark 1. It can be seen that when we fix the input number as the total number of tasks n in the task set of the smart contract, HERALD has a probability of $\frac{A_n^n}{n^n}$ degraded to an offline incentive mechanism, which means that the HERALD can be applied to more scenarios compared with the existing offline incentive mechanisms.

4.3 Analysis

In this subsection, we will prove that HERALD satisfies the properties mentioned in Sect. 3.3.

Theorem 1 ([26]). *A mechanism is truthful if and only if*

1) *The selection rule is monotone: If worker i wins by bidding b_i, she also wins by bidding $b'_i \leq b_i$;*
2) *Each winner is paid the critical value: Worker i would not win if she bids higher than this value.*

Theorem 2. *HERALD is truthful.*

Proof. To prove the truthfulness of HERALD, we will show it satisfies the conditions mentioned in Theorem 1.

Monotone: For a worker i, once she wins by bidding b_i, we will show that she will also win by bidding $b'_i \leq b_i$ through the following two cases.

Case 1: In an iteration of the winner selection phase, when the CF of winning worker i satisfies $\frac{b_i}{|\Gamma_i \cap T|} \leq \frac{T}{|T|}$, it means that she has the minimum CF among all workers. Therefore, she will also win by bidding $b'_i \leq b_i$.

Case 2: In an iteration, when the CF of winning worker i satisfies $\frac{b_i}{|\Gamma_i \cap T|} > \frac{T}{|T|}$, it means that she has the minimum cost among workers and there is not any worker j with $\frac{b_j}{|\Gamma_j \cap T|} \leq \frac{T}{|T|}$. We then need to consider two subcases.

Subcase 2.1: When the bid $b'_i \leq b_i$ satisfies $\frac{b'_i}{|\Gamma_i \cap T|} > \frac{T}{|T|}$, it means that she will also win by bidding b'_i since b'_i is the minimum and there is not any worker j with $\frac{b_j}{|\Gamma_j \cap T|} \leq \frac{T}{|T|}$.

Subcase 2.2: When the bid $b'_i \leq b_i$ satisfies $\frac{b'_i}{|\Gamma_i \cap T|} \leq \frac{T}{|T|}$, it means that she will also win by bidding b'_i since she is the only worker with CF being less than or equal to T.

Critical Value: When a worker i wins, it can be seen that her payment is $p_i = \max\{b_i, p_{\mathcal{R}_i}\}$, where $p_{\mathcal{R}_i} = \sum_{j \in \mathcal{R}_i} b_j$. When worker i increases her bid b_i to $\tilde{b}_i$ such that $\tilde{b}_i \leq p_{\mathcal{R}_i}$, her payments are always the same. However, when $\tilde{b}_i > p_{\mathcal{R}_i}$, we need to consider the following two cases in each iteration of the winner selection phase.

Case 1: When CF of worker i satisfies $\frac{\tilde{b}_i}{|\Gamma_i \cap T|} \leq \frac{T}{|T|}$, we will prove that there is a worker k in $\mathcal{R}_i$ such that $\frac{b_k}{|\Gamma_k \cap T|} \leq \frac{\tilde{b}_i}{|\Gamma_i \cap T|}$. We have $\frac{\tilde{b}_i}{|\Gamma_i \cap T|} \geq \frac{\sum_{j \in \mathcal{R}_i} b_j}{\sum_{j \in \mathcal{R}_i} |\Gamma_j \cap T|}$. Then let worker k be the one with the minimum CF $\frac{b_k}{|\Gamma_k \cap T|}$ in $\mathcal{R}_i$, which means that $\frac{b_k}{|\Gamma_k \cap T|} \leq \frac{b_j}{|\Gamma_j \cap T|}$ for $\forall j \in \mathcal{R}_i$, i.e., $b_k |\Gamma_j \cap T| \leq b_j |\Gamma_k \cap T|$. Therefore, we have $b_k \sum_{j \in \mathcal{R}_i} |\Gamma_j \cap T| \leq |\Gamma_k \cap T| \sum_{j \in \mathcal{R}_i} b_j$, i.e., $\frac{b_k}{|\Gamma_k \cap T|} \leq \frac{\sum_{j \in \mathcal{R}_i} b_j}{\sum_{j \in \mathcal{R}_i} |\Gamma_j \cap T|}$. Since $\frac{b_k}{|\Gamma_k \cap T|} \leq \frac{\tilde{b}_i}{|\Gamma_i \cap T|}$, the smart contract will select worker k instead of worker i in this iteration.

Case 2: When CF of worker i satisfies $\frac{\tilde{b}_i}{|\Gamma_i \cap T|} > \frac{T}{|T|}$, we need to consider two subcases.

Subcase 2.1: Once there exist some workers $j \in \mathcal{R}_i$ such that $\frac{b_j}{|\Gamma_j \cap T|} \leq \frac{T}{|T|}$, the smart contract will select a worker k among them with the minimum CF instead of worker i.

Subcase 2.2: Once the CFs of all workers $j \in \mathcal{R}_i$ satisfies $\frac{b_j}{|\Gamma_j \cap T|} > \frac{T}{|T|}$, the smart contract will always find a worker k with the minimum bid b_k such that $b_k \leq p_{\mathcal{R}_i} \leq \tilde{b}_i$, which means that the smart contract will not select worker i.

Therefore, the conclusion holds.   □

Lemma 1. *HERALD is individual rationality.*

Proof. As proved in Theorem 2, each worker bids her real cost c_i. The individual rationality of HERALD is guaranteed by the fact that the payment to each winner i is $p_i = \max\{b_i, p_{\mathcal{R}_i}\} \geq b_i = c_i$.   □

Apart from truthfulness and individual rationality, it will be seen that HERALD has low computational complexity.

Proposition 1. *The computational complexity of the HERALD is $\mathcal{O}(m^2 + mn)$.*

Proof. To obtain the computational complexity of HERALD, we need to separately consider the winner selection phase and payment determination phase.

1) *Winner Selection Phase:* The main loop (Lines 4–11) of the winner selection phase terminates in the worst case after n iterations. In every iteration, it takes m times to carry out type I selection to find the worker with the minimum bidding price effectiveness (Lines 6–7), or type II selection to find the worker with the minimum bidding price (Lines 8–9). Therefore, the computational complexity of the winner selection phase is $\mathcal{O}(mn)$.

2) *Payment Determination Phase:* Similarly, the main loop (Lines 12–20) of the payment determination phase terminates at worst after m iterations. In each iteration, it takes m iterations to build a covering set (Line 14) and other n iterations to build a replaced set (Lines 16–19). Therefore, the computational complexity of the payment determination phase is $\mathcal{O}(m^2 + mn)$.

Combining the winner selection phase and payment determination phase, the computational complexity of HERALD is $\mathcal{O}(m^2 + mn)$.   □

In the following parts, we will show the competitive ratio on expected social cost achieved by HERALD when the tasks in T arrive following a uniform distribution. To derive the competitive ratio on the expected social cost of HERALD, we consider the costs of type I selection and type II selection separately.

Lemma 2. *When the arrivals of tasks in the task set T follow a uniform distribution, the competitive ratio on expected social cost achieved by HERALD through type I selection is $\mathcal{O}(\ln n)$.*

Proof. Let $\mathcal{S}_I = \{1, \ldots, h\}$ be the workers selected by HERALD through type I selection in this order. Moreover, let $\widetilde{T}_i$ denote the set of tasks whose sensory data is not collected just before worker i is selected. Since HERALD carries out type I selection, $c_i \leq |\Gamma_i \cap \mathcal{T}_i| \frac{64\mathbb{E}[C_{\mathcal{OPT}}(\mathcal{A})]}{|\widetilde{\mathcal{T}}_i|}$, where $\mathcal{A}$ is a subset of k tasks possibly arriving simultaneously from $\mathcal{T}$. Hence, the social cost of workers in $\mathcal{S}_I$ can be bounded by

$$\sum_{i \in \mathcal{S}_I} c_i \leq \sum_{i \in \mathcal{S}_I} \frac{64|\Gamma_i \cap \widetilde{\mathcal{T}}_i|\mathbb{E}[C_{\mathcal{OPT}}(\mathcal{A})]}{|\widetilde{\mathcal{T}}_i|} \leq 64\mathbb{E}[C_{\mathcal{OPT}}(\mathcal{A})] \sum_{t=1}^{m} \frac{1}{t}, \tag{2}$$

which is at most $64\mathbb{E}[C_{\mathcal{OPT}}(\mathcal{A})] \ln n$. Therefore, the conclusion holds due to the property of expectation. $\qquad\square$

It remains to bound the expected cost of workers selected by the type II selection. To show the expected social cost of workers selected by HERALD through type II selection, we need the following notations. Let $\mathcal{S}_{II} = \{1, \ldots, \ell\}$ be the workers selected by HERALD through type II selection in this order. Let $\widetilde{\mathcal{T}}_i$ be the set of tasks whose sensory data is not collected just before worker i is selected. Let $n_i = |\widetilde{\mathcal{T}}_i|$ and $k_i = n_i \frac{k}{n}$ be the number of tasks in $\widetilde{\mathcal{T}}_i$ and the expected number of requested tasks arriving from $\widetilde{\mathcal{T}}_i$, respectively. Denote by $\mathcal{A}_i$ the subset of $\mathcal{A}$ obtained by taking requested tasks only belonging to $\widetilde{\mathcal{T}}_i$. Furthermore, for any set of $\mathcal{A}$, let $\mathcal{S}^*(\mathcal{A})$ be the set of workers with the minimum social cost. Then, let $\mathcal{S}'(\mathcal{A}_i)$ be the subset of $\mathcal{S}^*(\mathcal{A})$ such that for each task $\tau_j \in \mathcal{A}_i$, the worker in $\mathcal{S}'(\mathcal{A}_i)$ has the preferred task set containing task τ_j and has the least cost among workers in $\mathcal{S}^*(\mathcal{A})$.

Lemma 3. *When the arrivals of tasks in the task set $\mathcal{T}$ follow a uniform distribution, the competitive ratio on expected social cost achieved by HERALD through type II selection is $\mathcal{O}(\ln mn)$.*

Proof. Recall that the set of workers selected by HERALD through type II selection is $\mathcal{S}_{II} = \{1, \ldots, \ell\}$. Set $k_{\ell+1} = 0$ and $c_0 = 0$ for notational convenience. Moreover, let j be $k_j \geq 8 \ln 2n$ but $k_{j+1} < 8 \ln 2n$. Hence, we see at most $8 \ln 2n$ tasks from $\widetilde{\mathcal{T}}_{j+1}$ in expectation. Since each of these tasks is carried out by a worker who does not cost more than the one carrying out it in $\mathcal{S}^*(\mathcal{A})$, the cost incurred by workers $j + 1, \ldots, \ell$ is bounded by $8 \ln 2n\mathbb{E}[C_{\mathcal{OPT}}(\mathcal{A})]$. Then, the expected cost incurred by using the remaining workers $1, \ldots, j$ satisfies

$$\sum_{i=1}^{j} c_i \Pr[\mathcal{A} \cap (\Gamma_i \cap \widetilde{\mathcal{T}}_i) \neq \emptyset]$$

$$\leq \sum_{i=1}^{j} c_i \mathbb{E}[|\mathcal{A} \cap (\Gamma_i \cap \widetilde{\mathcal{T}}_i)|] \overset{\widetilde{\mathcal{T}}_{i+1} \subseteq \widetilde{\mathcal{T}}_i \setminus \Gamma_i}{\leq} \sum_{i=1}^{j} c_i \mathbb{E}[|\mathcal{A} \cap (\widetilde{\mathcal{T}}_i \setminus \widetilde{\mathcal{T}}_{i+1})|]$$

$$\leq \sum_{i=1}^{j} c_i(k_i - k_{i+1}) \overset{c_0=0}{\leq} \sum_{i=1}^{j} k_i(c_i - c_{i-1}) \overset{(a)}{\leq} \sum_{i=1}^{j} 16\mathbb{E}[|\mathcal{S}'(\mathcal{A}_i)|] \ln m(c_i - c_{i-1}) \tag{3}$$

$$= 16 \ln m \left(c_j \mathbb{E}[|\mathcal{S}'(\mathcal{A}_{j+1})|] + \sum_{i=1}^{j} c_i \left(\mathbb{E}[|\mathcal{S}'(\mathcal{A}_i)|] - \mathbb{E}[|\mathcal{S}'(\mathcal{A}_{i+1})|] \right) \right)$$

$$\overset{(b)}{\leq} 16 \ln m \left(\mathbb{E}[C(\mathcal{S}'(\mathcal{A}_{j+1}))] + \sum_{i=1}^{j} \left(\mathbb{E}[C(\mathcal{S}'(\mathcal{A}_i))] - \mathbb{E}[C(\mathcal{S}'(\mathcal{A}_{i+1}))] \right) \right)$$

$$\leq 16 \ln m\mathbb{E}[C_{\mathcal{OPT}}(\mathcal{A})],$$

where inequalities (a) and (b) hold based on the Lemma 3.5 and Lemma 3.4 in the reference [27] respectively. As mentioned before, $\sum_{i=j+1}^{\ell} c_i \Pr[\mathcal{A} \cap (\Gamma_i \cap \tilde{\mathcal{T}}_i) \neq \emptyset] \leq 8 \ln 2n \mathbb{E}[C_{\mathcal{OPT}}(\mathcal{A})]$. Therefore, the expected cost incurred by workers $1, \ldots, \ell$ satisfies $\sum_{i=1}^{\ell} c_i \Pr[\mathcal{A} \cap (\Gamma_i \cap \tilde{\mathcal{T}}_i) \neq \emptyset] \leq [8 \ln 2n + 16 \ln m] \cdot \mathbb{E}[C_{\mathcal{OPT}}(\mathcal{A})]$. Then we have $\frac{\sum_{i=1}^{\ell} c_i \Pr[\mathcal{A} \cap (\Gamma_i \cap \tilde{\mathcal{T}}_i) \neq \emptyset]}{\mathbb{E}[C_{\mathcal{OPT}}(\mathcal{A})]} \leq \mathcal{O}(\ln mn)$, this proof is completed. □

Finally, by combining Lemma 2 and Lemma 3, we have the following theorem.

Theorem 3. *When the arrivals of tasks in the task set $\mathcal{T}$ follow a uniform distribution, the competitive ratio on expected social cost achieved by HERALD is $\mathcal{O}(\ln mn)$.*

According to Theorem 3, we can obtain the conclusion that HERALD achieves a low expected social cost, which means that it can be applied to many other scenarios with uncertain sensing tasks.

5   Performance Evaluation

In this section, we introduce the baseline methods, simulation settings, as well as simulation results of the performance evaluation of our proposed HERALD.

5.1   Baseline Methods

COst-effectiveNEss greedy auction (CONE): For the uncertain scenario, the smart contract only knows that the tasks in $\mathcal{T}$ arrive in the future with a probability distribution. Therefore, to collect sensory data for these tasks, the smart contract calculates the CF of each worker and selects worker i as a winner, whose CF $\frac{b_i}{|\Gamma_i \cap \mathcal{T}|}$ is the least among those of workers in each iteration. The smart contract then obtains the sensory data of worker i.

COSt greedY auction (COSY): For the uncertain scenario, to collect sensory data of these tasks, the smart contract compares the bids of workers and selects worker i as a winner, whose bid b_i is the minimum among those of workers and preferred task set Γ_i contains at least one uncovered task in each iteration. Then, the smart contract collects the sensory data of worker i.

The payment determination phases of both CONE and COSY are the same as HERALD. Clearly, CONE and COSY are truthful and individual rationality.

5.2   Simulation Settings

We show the evaluation parameters for different cases in Table 1, where c_i is the cost of worker i for executing her preferred task set Γ_i and $|\Gamma_i|$ is the number of tasks in the preferred task set. Furthermore, m, n are the numbers of workers in worker set $\mathcal{W}$ and sensing tasks in the task set $\mathcal{T}$, respectively. Additionally, k is the number of tasks possibly arriving simultaneously in the future in the

Table 1. Simulation Settings for HERALD.

Settings	Individual cost c_i	Number $\lvert\Gamma_i\rvert$ of preferred tasks	Number m of workers	Number n of sensing tasks	Number k of arriving tasks
I	$[5, 20]$	$[15, 20]$	$[70, 160]$	150	120
II	$[5, 20]$	$[15, 20]$	70	$[90, 180]$	$[60, 150]$
III	$[5, 10], [10, 15], [15, 20]$	$[20, 25]$	80	$[70, 160]$	$[50, 140]$
IV	$[15, 25]$	$[10, 15], [15, 20], [20, 25]$	$[60, 150]$	160	100

uncertain scenario. For the convenience of representation, k is briefly referred to as the number of arriving tasks.

In our evaluation, for HERALD, we show the influences of the numbers of workers and sensing tasks on the expected social cost and expected total payment. Specifically, to evaluate the impact of the quantity m of workers in worker set $\mathcal{W}$, we increase it from 70 to 160 by fixing the number n of sensing tasks and the number k of arriving tasks to 150 and 120, respectively, *i.e.*, setting I. Furthermore, to evaluate the impact of the quantity n of sensing tasks, we vary it from 90 to 180 and increase the number k of arriving tasks from 60 to 150 with the quantity m of workers fixed to 70, *i.e.*, setting II. Additionally, in setting I and setting II, the cost c_i of worker i and the number of tasks in her preferred task set Γ_i are sampled uniformly and independently at random in the intervals $[5, 20]$ and $[15, 20]$, respectively.

Nextly, we investigate the impacts of worker's costs on the expected social cost and expected total payment obtained by HERALD, respectively. In particular, to evaluate the impacts of worker's cost c_i, we select it in three distinct intervals, *i.e.*, $[5, 10]$, $[10, 15]$ and $[15, 20]$ in setting III, respectively, where the number $\lvert\Gamma_i\rvert$ of tasks in preferred task set is sampled in the interval $[20, 25]$. Furthermore, in setting III, the number m of workers is fixed to 80, while the number n of sensing tasks and the number k of arriving tasks vary from 70 to 160 and 50 to 140, respectively.

Finally, we evaluate the impacts of the number of workers' preferred tasks on the expected social cost and expected total payment derived by HERALD, respectively. Specifically, we select the number $\lvert\Gamma_i\rvert$ of tasks in each preferred task set in three distinct intervals, *i.e.*, $[10, 15]$, $[15, 20]$ and $[20, 25]$ in setting IV, respectively, where the cost c_i of each worker is sampled in the interval $[15, 25]$. Furthermore, in setting IV, the number n of sensing tasks and the number k of arriving tasks are fixed to 160 and 100, respectively, while the number m of workers varies from 60 to 160.

5.3   Simulation Results

In Fig. 3, we evaluate the impact of the number of workers. Specifically, Fig. 3(a) and Fig. 3(b) show the impact on the expected social cost and expected total payment derived by HERALD. It is shown that HERALD outperforms CONE and COSY. Interestingly, with the increasing number of workers, the expected social cost and expected total payment calculated by HERALD decrease. This is because with the increasing number of workers, for each task, the smart contract has more opportunities to collect sensory data from the worker whose cost is less.

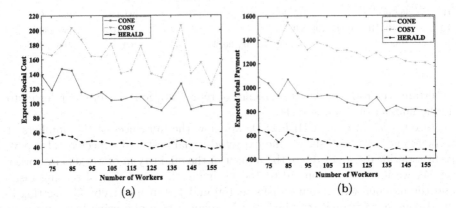

Fig. 3. (a) Expected social cost versus different numbers of workers for the uncertain scenario. (b) Expected total payment versus different numbers of workers for the uncertain scenario.

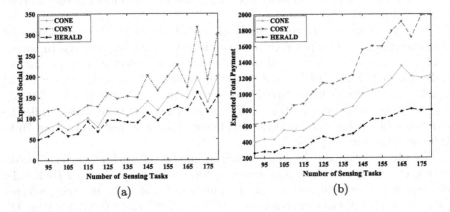

Fig. 4. (a) Expected social cost versus different numbers of sensing tasks for the uncertain scenario. (b) Expected total payment versus different numbers of sensing tasks for the uncertain scenario.

In Fig. 4, the impact of the number of tasks is also investigated. Specifically, Fig. 4(a) and Fig. 4(b) show the impact on the expected social cost and expected total payment derived by HERALD. Similarly, it can be seen that HERALD outperforms CONE and COSY. Additionally, with the increasing number of tasks, the expected social cost and expected total payment calculated by HERALD increase. This is because with the increasing number of tasks, the smart contract needs to collect sensory data from more workers.

In Fig. 5, we show the influence of the worker's cost. In particular, Fig. 5(a) and Fig. 5(b) plot the influence on the expected social cost and expected total payment obtained by HERALD. It can be seen that the higher worker's cost means the higher expected social cost and expected total payment in HERALD since the higher cost of the worker means that for the same tasks, the workers need more social cost and the smart contract needs more payment compared to the scenario with the lower cost of the worker.

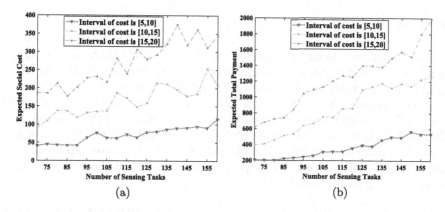

(a)   (b)

Fig. 5. (a) The impact of worker's cost on the expected social cost obtained by HERALD for uncertain scenario. (b) The impact of worker's cost on the expected total payment obtained by HERALD for uncertain scenario.

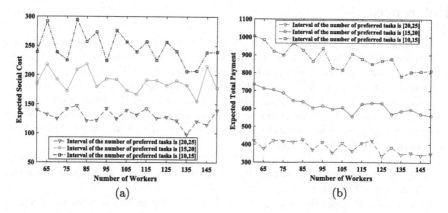

(a)   (b)

Fig. 6. (a) The impact of the number of worker's preferred tasks on the expected social cost obtained by HERALD for uncertain scenario. (b) The impact of the number of worker's preferred tasks on the expected total payment obtained by HERALD for uncertain scenario.

We finally investigate the influence of the number of workers' preferred tasks in Fig. 6. In particular, Fig. 6(a) and 6(b) give the impact on the expected social cost and expected total payment obtained by HERALD. It can be observed that the more preferred tasks of each worker decrease the expected social cost and expected total payment in HERALD. This is because compared to the scenario with the less preferred tasks of each worker, the smart contract needs fewer workers to execute the requested tasks due to the more preferred tasks of each worker, which results in the less expected social cost and expected total payment in HERALD.

6   Conclusion

In this paper, we design an incentive mechanism, HERALD, for the uncertain tasks in MCS systems by using smart contracts. Specifically, the uncertain tasks arrive according to a probability distribution such that the smart contract does not have any information on the tasks. HERALD utilizes the decentralized nature of the blockchain to eliminate the system's reliance on third parties. It is proved that HERALD satisfies truthfulness, individual rationality, low computational complexity, and achieves an $\ln mn$ competitive ratio on expected social cost. Finally, HERALD's desirable properties are validated through theoretical analysis and extensive simulations.

Acknowledgement. This work is supported by the grant PAPRICAS: Programming technology foundations for Accountability, Privacy-by-design & Robustness in Context-aware Systems. Independent Research Fund Denmark.

References

1. Ding, R., Yang, Z., Wei, Y., Jin, H., Wang, X.: Multi-agent reinforcement learning for urban crowd sensing with for-hire vehicles. In: Proceedings of IEEE International Conference on Computer Communications (INFOCOM) (2021)
2. Fan, G., et al.: Joint scheduling and incentive mechanism for spatio-temporal vehicular crowd sensing. IEEE Trans. Mob. Comput. **20**(4), 1449–1464 (2021)
3. Pan, M.S., Li, K.Y.: ezNavi: an easy-to-operate indoor navigation system based on pedestrian dead reckoning and crowdsourced user trajectories. IEEE Trans. Mob. Comput. **20**(2), 488–501 (2021)
4. Yu, S., Chen, X., Wang, S., Pu, L., Wu, D.: An edge computing-based photo crowdsourcing framework for real-time 3D reconstruction. IEEE Trans. Mob. Comput. **21**(2), 421–432 (2022)
5. Liu, Y., Yu, Z., Guo, B., Han, Q., Su, J., Liao, J.: CrowdOS: a ubiquitous operating system for crowdsourcing and mobile crowd sensing. IEEE Trans. Mob. Comput. **21**(3), 878–894 (2022)
6. Aitzhan, N.Z., Svetinovic, D.: Security and privacy in decentralized energy trading through multi-signatures, blockchain and anonymous messaging streams. IEEE Trans. Dependable Secure Comput. **15**(5), 840–852 (2018)
7. Buterin, V.: A next-generation smart contract and decentralized application platform. White paper, pp. 1–36 (2014)

8. Wang, Z., Li, J., Hu, J., Ren, J., Li, Z., Li, Y.: Towards privacy-preserving incentive for mobile crowdsensing under an untrusted platform. In: Proceedings of IEEE International Conference on Computer Communications (INFOCOM) (2019)

9. Zhou, R., Li, Z.P., Wu, C.: A truthful online mechanism for location-aware tasks in mobile crowd sensing. IEEE Trans. Mob. Comput. **17**(8), 1737–1749 (2018)

10. Cheung, M.H., Hou, F., Huang, J.: Delay-sensitive mobile crowdsensing: algorithm design and economics. IEEE Trans. Mob. Comput. **17**(12), 2761–2774 (2018)

11. Ma, Q., Gao, L., Liu, Y., Huang, J.: Incentivizing Wi-Fi network crowdsourcing: a contract theoretic approach. IEEE/ACM Trans. Netw. **26**(3), 1035–1048 (2018)

12. Wang, X., Wu, W., Qi, D.: Mobility-aware participant recruitment for vehicle-based mobile crowdsensing. IEEE Trans. Veh. Technol. **67**(5), 4415–4426 (2018)

13. Zhao, D., Ma, H., Liu, L.: Frugal online incentive mechanisms for mobile crowd sensing. IEEE Trans. Veh. Technol. **66**(4), 3319–3330 (2017)

14. Qu, Y., et al.: Posted pricing for chance constrained robust crowdsensing. IEEE Trans. Mob. Comput. **19**(1), 188–199 (2020)

15. Han, K., Huang, H., Luo, J.: Quality-aware pricing for mobile crowdsensing. IEEE/ACM Trans. Netw. **26**(4), 1728–1741 (2018)

16. Restuccia, F., Ferraro, P., Silvestri, S., Das, S.K., Re, G.L.: IncentMe: effective mechanism design to stimulate crowdsensing participants with uncertain mobility. IEEE Trans. Mob. Comput. **18**(7), 1571–1584 (2019)

17. Jin, W., Xiao, M., Li, M., Guo, L.: If you do not care about it, sell it: trading location privacy in mobile crowd sensing. In: Proceedings of IEEE International Conference on Computer Communications (INFOCOM) (2019)

18. Wang, L., Yu, Z., Han, Q., Guo, B., Xiong, H.: Multi-objective optimization based allocation of heterogeneous spatial crowdsourcing tasks. IEEE Trans. Mob. Comput. **17**(7), 1637–1650 (2018)

19. Zhang, X., Jiang, L., Wang, X.: Incentive mechanisms for mobile crowdsensing with heterogeneous sensing costs. IEEE Trans. Veh. Technol. **68**(4), 3992–4002 (2019)

20. Jin, H., Su, L., Chen, D., Guo, H., Nahrstedt, K., Xu, J.: Thanos: incentive mechanism with quality awareness for mobile crowd sensing. IEEE Trans. Mob. Comput. **18**(8), 1951–1964 (2019)

21. Karaliopoulos, M., Koutsopoulos, I., Spiliopoulos, L.: Optimal user choice engineering in mobile crowdsensing with bounded rational users. In: Proceedings of IEEE International Conference on Computer Communications (INFOCOM) (2019)

22. Hu, Y., Zhang, R.: Differentially-private incentive mechanism for crowdsourced radio environment map construction. In: Proceedings of IEEE International Conference on Computer Communications (INFOCOM) (2019)

23. Bhattacharjee, S., Ghosh, N., Shah, V.K., Das, S.K.: QnQ: quality and quantity based unified approach for secure and trustworthy mobile crowdsensing. IEEE Trans. Mob. Comput. **19**(1), 200–216 (2020)

24. Han, K., Liu, H., Tang, S., Xiao, M., Luo, J.: Differentially private mechanisms for budget limited mobile crowdsourcing. IEEE Trans. Mob. Comput. **18**(4), 934–946 (2019)

25. Gong, X., Shroff, N.B.: Truthful mobile crowdsensing for strategic users with private data quality. IEEE/ACM Trans. Netw. **27**(5), 1959–1972 (2019)

26. Singer, Y.: Budget feasible mechanisms. In: Proceedings of IEEE Symposium on Foundations of Computer Science (FOCS) (2010)

27. Grandoni, F., Gupta, A., Leonardi, S., Miettinen, P., Sankowski, P., Singh, M.: Set covering with our eyes closed. SIAM J. Comput. **42**(3), 808–830 (2013)

Research on the Update Method of CP-ABE Access Control Strategy Based on Smart Contract

Yu Hao, Bo Cui[✉], Ru Li, Tingting Song, and Wenhan Hou

College of Computer Science, Inner Mongolia Key Laboratory of Wireless Networking and Mobile Computing, Inner Mongolia University, Hohhot, China
{31909020,31809125,cshwh}@mail.imu.edu.cn, {cscb,
csliru}@imu.edu.cn

Abstract. The CP-ABE access control method based on blockchain realizes fine-grained access control of data and ensures the storage of ciphertext security. However, there are some problems in updating the access control policy. For example, the blockchain cannot be used as ample data storage. The ciphertext size increases with the number of attributes and the complexity of the access control policy, and the CP-ABE based on bilinear mapping is expensive to calculate. Therefore, this paper proposes dividing the ciphertext into data-related ciphertext and policy-related ciphertext, which are stored in blockchain and IPFS. It is worth noting that this paper uses the RSA-based CP-ABE encryption method, which can effectively reduce the computational cost of encryption and decryption and achieve a constant ciphertext size. In addition, we also systematically analyze and compare the advantages and costs generated by CP-ABE based on bilinear mapping and CP-ABE based on RSA. Through experimental analysis, security analysis, and formal analysis, compared with the existing access control policy update methods, the scheme proposed in this paper shows better performance when frequently updating the access control policy.

Keywords: Blockchain · CP-ABE · IPFS · Access Control · Policy update

1 Introduction

The ciphertext-policy attribute-based encryption (CP-ABE) [1] has attracted widespread attention as soon as it was proposed. The CP-ABE encryption method was initially used to store the ciphertext in a central server or cloud. However, there are some problems in traditional storage methods, such as single point of failure and trust crisis, which may cause the ciphertext to be lost and altered. Therefore, the combination of blockchain [2] and CP-ABE is used to achieve access control [3–8], which effectively solves the problems of traditional storage methods. But, blockchain is a tamper-proof distributed digital ledger. The old ciphertext cannot be deleted when an access control policy is

H. Gao et al. (Eds.): CollaborateCom 2022, LNICST 460, pp. 494–513, 2022.
https://doi.org/10.1007/978-3-031-24383-7_27

updated. The new ciphertext is continuously uploaded to the blockchain network, resulting in an increasing storage burden of blockchain. At the same time, as the ciphertext size increases, the update time also increases.

Researchers [9, 10] proposed reducing the time consumption and the size of the ciphertext when the access control policy is updated by decentralized storage of the ciphertext related to the data and the ciphertext related to the policy. But all data are stored in blockchain. Although the size of policy-related ciphertexts is reduced to reduce the consumption of update time, the storage burden of blockchain is not solved. Zhang et al. [11] suggested that data ciphertext should be stored in the cloud, and smart contract and CP-ABE should be combined to maintain an access control list. Although it can solve the burden of blockchain, the cloud is not trusted, and there will still be the threat of ciphertext tampering. Gao et al. [12] used the combination of InterPlanetary File System (IPFS) [13], which is tamper-proof, and blockchain to carry out the distributed storage of ciphertext. IPFS can effectively reduce the storage burden of the blockchain to realize the big data storage, make up for the defects of low storage efficiency and high cost of the blockchain, and avoid single points of failure and trust issues.

However, the CP-ABE encryption method is based on bilinear mapping in [12], and bilinear mapping is a complex calculation. Moreover, the time consumption of encryption and decryption and the ciphertext size is positively related to the number of attributes and complexity of the access control policy [14]. In other words, although scheme [12] relatively reduces the storage burden and update time consumption of blockchain, when the access control policy is frequently updated, the time consumed by encryption and decryption and the size of ciphertext generated will continue to increase with the increase of attributes and the complexity of the access control policy.

To further improve the performance of the access control policy updates, we propose to use the combination of IPFS and blockchain to reduce the burden of blockchain storage. Meanwhile, we use the RSA-based CP-ABE encryption method to avoid the time cost caused by bilinear mapping [15], effectively reducing the time consumption of encryption and decryption while achieving a constant ciphertext size. This method is more suitable for limited storage space, and where frequent access control policy updates are required. Besides, a Storage Smart Contract (SSC) and a Query Smart Contract (QSC) are designed to manage the new and old ciphertexts during the update process. Most importantly, we analyzed and compared CP-ABE based on bilinear mapping and CP-ABE based on RSA, and we conducted a safety analysis of the model and gave formal proof.

2   Related Work

CP-ABE can realize fine-grained access control, but traditional centralized ciphertext storage risks tampering and single point failure. Blockchain has a strong tamper-proof capability but lacks access control and privacy protection for the data. Literatures [3–8] proposed the integration of CP-ABE and blockchain technology to achieve secure data storage and fine-grained access control.

However, due to the limited storage capacity of blockchain, it is not suitable for ample data storage. To reduce the storage burden of blockchain, literature [16–21] proposed the on-chain and off-chain collaborative storage modes. In this mode, the big data generated by encryption is stored in the cloud or IPFS, and the data attributes, indexes, access rights, and other contents are stored on the blockchain. But none of the above researches considers the issue of access control policy update. Reference [22–24] studied the update of access control policy. Mounnan et al. [22] uploaded the ciphertext to the cloud, and entrusted the cloud to update the policy by updating the key. Ma et al. [23] proposed to entrust a trusted third party to update the access control policy through a ciphertext conversion algorithm. The ciphertext and the transform ciphertext are stored on the blockchain. Guo et al. [24] proposed dividing the cloud into storage and computing clouds. The storage cloud is used to store the ciphertext, and the computing cloud is used to convert the ciphertext to update the access control policy.

The three access policy update methods above need to update or convert all ciphertexts when updating, which is computationally expensive. Therefore, literature [9–12] proposed to store data-related ciphertexts and policy-related ciphertexts separately. Only the policy-related ciphertext can be updated to reduce the calculation cost when the policy is updated. Tian et al. [10] divided ciphertext encrypted by CP-ABE into data ciphertext and policy ciphertext, stored in the transaction block and policy block, respectively, and only the policy block needs to be updated when the policy is updated. In [9, 11, 12], data encrypted in other encryption modes is stored off-chain, and its decryption key is encrypted by CP-ABE and stored on the blockchain. When the policy is updated, only the ciphertext formed by the decryption key needs to be updated. The difference is the storage location of the data ciphertext in these three schemes. Yu et al. [9] used the chameleon hash to construct a redactable key chain and a standard data chain to store the ciphertext of the decryption key and the data ciphertext, respectively. Zhang et al. [11] recommended using cloud storage to store the data ciphertext and a smart contract to generate the corresponding access control list. Gao et al. [12] suggested using the distributed IPFS system to store the ciphertext of the data, and the smart contract realizes the management of the ciphertext and users.

However, the CP-ABE encryption methods used in the current research are all based on bilinear mapping, which will lead to expensive calculation costs. At the same time, as the number of attributes in an access control policy and the policy complexity increase, the ciphertext size and calculation time consumption also increase. For this reason, it is necessary to find a more efficient CP-ABE encryption method and control the size of ciphertext to improve the performance of the access control policy update.

3   Overview of Our Scheme

This section will introduce the access control policy update scheme combining on-chain and off-chain, as shown in Fig. 1. The proposed method combines IPFS and blockchain, and applies the RSA-based CP-ABE algorithm and smart contracts. There are five prominent roles in this method: Data Owner (DO), Data Requester (DR), blockchain, IPFS, and Certificate Authority (CA). In this paper, the default trusted CA is fully trusted, and its function description is shown in Table 1. The whole process of method is divided into nine processes:

Table 1. Function description of main roles

Name	Functional description
DO	Encrypt data, upload ciphertext and policy ciphertext, deploy smart contracts, update access control policies, maintain data information, query historical records
DR	Query data, decrypt policy ciphertext and data ciphertext
IPFS	Store data ciphertext
Blockchain	Store policy ciphertext, compile, store and execute smart contracts
CA	Generate system parameters and distribute public and private keys of RSA-based CP-ABE algorithm

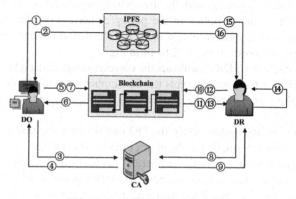

Fig. 1. Overall structure diagram.

- Upload data ciphertext: DO first encrypts the original data using symmetric encryption technology, then DO uploads the encrypted data ciphertext to IPFS. IPFS will calculate a hash value according to the content of the uploaded data ciphertext and return it to DO, where the hash value is used to find the uploaded data, corresponding to step 1 and step 2 in Fig. 1.
- Apply for public and private keys: CA first executes the initialization algorithm in the CP-ABE based on RSA and calculates the master public key (MPK) and the master secret key (MSK). When the DO request is received, the MPK used for encryption is sent to the DO, corresponding to steps 3 and 4 in Fig. 1.
- Upload policy ciphertext: DO designs an access control policy to limit DR access to the data. And then DO encrypts the hash value returned by IPFS, the decryption key of the data ciphertext, and the designed access control policy with MPK to form a policy ciphertext, and upload it to the blockchain to get the storage location of the transaction, corresponding to steps 5 and 6 in Fig. 1.
- Deploy smart contracts and upload data related information: DO first deploys SSC and QSC on the blockchain, then DO adds the relevant summary information of the data, the transaction location and the upload time of the policy ciphertext on the blockchain, as shown in step 7 in Fig. 1.

- Apply for a user private key: DR sends attributes to CA to apply for the user's private key. CA executes the key generation algorithm and sends the user private key corresponding to the user attribute to DR, as shown in step 8 and Step 9 in Fig. 1.
- Query policy ciphertext: DR retrieves whether the queried data exists by calling QSC. After receiving the query request, QSC calls SSC to query whether there is a record corresponding to the input information in the SSC. For example, to query if they have the same file name. If the record exists, the QSC returns the latest policy ciphertext storage location of the file to the DR according to the storage record of the SSC. Among them, only DO can choose to view the history of the policy ciphertext, corresponding to step 10 and step 11 in Fig. 1.
- Decrypt policy ciphertext: After receiving the storage location of the policy ciphertext returned by the QSC, the DR downloads the policy ciphertext from blockchain and decrypts the policy ciphertext with the user private key. Suppose the user's attributes satisfy the access control policy in the policy ciphertext. In that case, the policy ciphertext can be decrypted to obtain the IPFS's hash and the decryption key of the data ciphertext. as shown in steps 12 to 14 in Fig. 1.
- Decrypt data ciphertext: DR downloads the corresponding data ciphertext from IPFS through the IPFS's hash and decrypts the data ciphertext with the decryption key in the policy ciphertext to obtain the original data, corresponding to step 15 and step 16 in Fig. 1.
- Access control policy update: Only the DO can perform the update operation and update the relevant information of the policy ciphertext in the SSC. After DO decrypts the policy ciphertext, a new policy ciphertext is obtained by re-encryption. After it is re-uploaded to the blockchain, the new data information is published to the SSC. SSC first compares the data, if the data already exists, it will replace it and store the historical data in the historical information database. Otherwise, SSC will records the new information.

4   Implementation Details of Our Scheme

IN this section, the RSA-based CP-ABE algorithm used in this paper and other bilinear-mapping-based CP-ABE algorithms are firstly summarized and analyzed. Then, we will introduce the specific content of SSC and QSC.

4.1   Comparison of CP-ABE Based on RSA and CP-ABE Based on Bilinear Mapping

Different access structures are used to express the CP-ABE access policy based on the bilinear mapping. The most commonly used are tree, threshold, Linear Secret-Sharing Scheme (LSSS), and AND gates. The tree structure is the first proposed access structure. In the tree structure, the non-terminal nodes are composed of threshold gates, and the leaves are composed of attributes. LSSS is an improvement based on the tree structure, which is represented through a matrix. When forming the LSSS matrix, it makes the number of rows of the matrix equal the number of leaf nodes. In the access structure constructed by the threshold, the threshold t is set. (A, t) is used to encrypt the data so that the data requester can decrypt the ciphertext only if t attributes are met in attribute A. In the AND gate structure, a string composed of 0 and 1 is used to express whether the attribute exists. We assume that the access control policy attribute set and user's attributes set, where if and if, and the same is true. Then, $P \subseteq A$ only if for all, so we can say that the attribute set A satisfies the access policy P only if $P \subseteq A$.

The access tree and LSSS matrix methods are more flexible and convenient in the expression of access control policy. However, there are many non-attribute nodes in the access tree structure, and for a complex access control policy, the access tree structure will become more prominent. Therefore, more computational overhead is undoubtedly increased in encryption and decryption. Although the LSSS matrix effectively reduces the number of non-attribute nodes and tree structure, it does not fundamentally solve the computational overhead caused by non-attribute nodes. The threshold and AND gate methods are weaker and more straightforward in structure. Because it only involves the values of related attributes, it solves the problem of computational consumption of accessing non-attribute nodes in the tree and LSSS matrix. So, the threshold method and the AND gate method have certain advantages in terms of key length, ciphertext size, and encryption and decryption time consumption. Some scenarios with many attributes have a better practical application effect. Therefore, the algorithm used in this paper adopts the AND gate method to construct the access control policy.

LSK represents length of user secret key and LCT represents length of cipher-text. We use |G| and |Gt| to represent the prime order pairing (the group G is multiplicative group ZN, where N = pq), and use |Gc| and |Gtc| to represent the composite order pairing. Besides, the n represents the number of universal attributes, the nA represents the average number of values assigned to each attribute in attribute set A and the L represents length of plain-text M [15] in Table 1. In Table 2, we use p and e denote paring computation and exponentiation. Meanwhile, S denotes the size of an access formula, |I| denotes the number of attributes in user's decryption private key, m denotes the upper bound of attribute number in universal attributes U and s denotes the number of attributes in the chosen attribute set U [26].

This paper makes an overall summary analysis. Table 2 and Table 3 summarize the relevant data of some bilinear map-based CP-ABE under different access structures. Although they are all based on bilinear mapping, encryption and decryption time consumption are different in different access structures. For example, during encryption, BSW needs to perform two exponentiations on each leaf node, HLR needs to perform m+t+1 exponentiation, and SYGH needs to perform s + 3 exponentiations and a pairing computation. Although some CP-ABE schemes do not need pairing computation when encrypting, the key point is calculating $e(g,g)^{\alpha}$ during decryption, where α is a random parameter selected in the pairing calculation during the setup or the encryption phase. In the decryption stage, HLR and EMNOS need three pairing computations, MSC needs two pairing computations, AC needs six pairing computations, and so on. In addition, in the BSW, CN, LOSTB, and Waters schemes, the number of pairing computations depends on the number of attributes. Each attribute must be paired during the decryption process. But bilinear mapping is also an expensive calculation method, almost three times the time consumption of other calculations [32].

Table 2. CP-ABE encryption method ciphertext and attribute private key size

Scheme	Access structure	LSK	LCT
BSW [1]	Tree	$(2|A| + 1) |G|$	$(2|P| + 1) |G| + |Gt|$
HLR [25]	Threshold	$(n + |A|) |G|$	$2|G| + |Gt|$
SYGH [26]	Threshold	$(n + |A|) |G|$	$2|G| + |Gt|$
GZCMZ [27]	Threshold	$2n (n + |A|) |G|$	$2|G| + Gt$
EMNOS [28]	(n-n) Threshold	$2|G|$	$2|G| + |Gt|$
LOSTW [29]	LSSS	$(|A| + 1) |Gc|$	$(2|P| + 1) |Gc| + |Gtc|$
Waters [30]	LSSS	$(|A| + 1) |G|$	$(2|P| + 1) |G| + |Gt|$
LW [31]	LSSS	$(3 + |A|) |Gc|$	$(2|P| + 2) Gt + Gtc$
AC [32]	LSSS	$(3|A| + 6) |G|$	$(3|P| + 3) |G| + |Gt|$
MST [33]	LSSS	$(|A| + 2) |G|$	$(|P| + 1) |G| + |Gt|$
DJ [34]	AND gate	$(nA|A| + 2) |Gc|$	$2|Gc| + |Gtc|$
ZZCLL [45]	AND gate	$(n + 1) |G|$	$2|G| + |Gt|$
CN [36]	AND gates	$2(|A| + 1) |G|$	$(|P| + 1) |G| + |Gt|$
ZH [37]	AND gates	$(|A| + 1) |G|$	$2|G| + |Gt|$
GSWV [38]	AND gates	$2|G|$	$(n-P + 2) |G| + |Gt| + L$
YWGWDG [39]	AND gates	$(|A| + 2) |G|$	$2|G| + |Gt|$

Table 3. Encryption and decryption time of CP-ABE

Scheme	Encryption time	Decryption time	Scheme	Encryption time	Decryption time
BSW	$(2S + 2)e$	$(II)p$	EMNOS	$3e$	$2p + 3e$
HLR	$(m + t + 1)e$	$3p + O(t^2 + m)e$	Waters	$(2S + 2)e$	$(II)p$
SYGH	$p + (s + 3)e$	$2p + O(t^2 + s)e$	MST	$(m + 1)e$	$2p$
GZCMZ(CPA)	$3e$	$2p + 2Se$	DJ	$3e$	$2p$
GZCMZ(CCA)	$6e$	$6p + (2S + 2)e$	CN	$(n + 2)e$	$(n + 1)p$

The RSA-based CP-ABE encryption method eliminates the process of pairing calculation. Only exponentiation, multiplication, and hashing computation are involved in the encryption and decryption process. Therefore, the RSA-based CP-ABE used in our paper can effectively avoid the time consumption caused by complex paired calculation in the process of encryption and decryption. At the same time, the RSA-based CP-ABE achieves a constant ciphertext size, that this algorithm gets the attribute private key size is $2|G|$ and the ciphertext size generated is $3|G| + L$. Although there are methods to achieve constant ciphertext in the CP-ABE scheme based on bilinear mappings, such as HLR, SYGH, EMNOS, DJ, GZCMZ, and other schemes, as shown in Table 2. But these schemes consume more time for encryption and decryption. To sum up, RSA-based CP-ABE encryption has the advantages of minor time consumption and fixed ciphertext.

4.2 Sample Smart Contract Design

In order to implement the retrieval and management of the policy ciphertext after the access control policy is updated, two smart contracts with different functions are designed, which are SSC and QSC. SSC is responsible for recording data-related information, including data digest such as the file name, the position of transactions on the blockchain and upload time. When storing information in SSC, it is necessary to compare the uploaded data digest. SSC first calls the comparison function. Because the latest file update access control policy is more likely, this paper uses reverse order comparison can effectively save the time consumption of comparison. During the comparison, if there is a file with the same name as the newly uploaded file, the existing record will be stored in the historical information database. Then the new file position and the uploading time will be used to replace the original storage information of this file. If the same file name does not exist, a new record is added. It is important to note that DO can only call the SSC. QSC is responsible for the inquiry work. DR calls QSC to input the file name to be queried, and then QSC calls SSC to query whether the file name exists in SSC. If the file name exists, QSC returns the latest position of transactions on the blockchain corresponding to the file name. If not, it returns empty information. In addition, the DO has the right to call the SSC through the QSC to view the content in the historical information base.

Two data-related information structures, Massage and Record, are defined in SSC. Massage structure is used to store information related to the latest data, and Record structure is used to store historical data. Both structures contain three fields, namely Dataname, BCHash, and Time. Dataname is the summary information of the index data for the query. BCHash refers to the transaction position of the policy ciphertext in the blockchain. Time refers to the upload Time of the policy ciphertext to the blockchain. Meanwhile, two array variables, Mass and Historical, are defined for Massage and Record structures.

The Compare function is an internal function of the contract and can only be called by the SSC contract, as shown in Table 4. For the two input strings, first, compare whether the lengths of the strings are equal. If the lengths are not equal, return false directly. When the lengths are equal, compare the hash values of the strings. When the hash values of the two strings are the same, return true. Otherwise, return false.

The saveMassage function can only be executed by the contract creator, as shown in Table 5. That is, only the data owner DO can perform information management and update the policy ciphertext. To summarize the data uploaded by DO, the saveMassage function first calls the comparison function to perform a reverse order comparison to determine whether the information exists in the Message. If it does not exist, it means that the corresponding policy ciphertext is newly uploaded. The SSC contract records the new information (dataname, BChash, time) in the Massage for the freshly uploaded information. If the data exists, it means that the corresponding policy ciphertext has undergone an access control policy update operation. For the updated information, when the same summary information is found, the original record is stored in the Record, and then replace the original record with the new transaction location and upload time to complete an access control policy update.

Table 4. Compare function in the SSC

Input	Summary information about two data points (string a, string b)
Output	True or False
1.	if bytes(a).length != bytes(b).length then
2.	return false
3.	else
4.	return keccak256(a) == keccak256(b)
5.	end if

Table 5. SaveMassage function in the SSC.

Input	Data related information (dataname, BChash, time)
Output	success or fail
1.	If msg.sender is not owner then
2.	throw exception ("Do not have permission")
3.	end if
4.	for compare in reverse order
5.	if compare (Massage. Dataname, dataname) = true
6.	Historical.push(Record (Dataname, BCHash, Time))
7.	Mass.BCHash = BChash
8.	Mass.Time = time
9.	end
10.	else
11.	Mass.push(Massage (dataname, BChash, time))
12.	end if
13.	end for

The QueryMassage function is called by the QSC contract to query through the input data digest information, as shown in Table 6. This function does not perform authentication, and the query location is the data in the Massage. The function returns matching data-related information by comparing the input data digest with the digest information stored in the Message (BCHash, Time).

The QueryRecord function is called by the QSC contract to query the information in the Record, but the function needs to judge the caller's identity during execution. Only the contract creator can call this function through the QSC to query the data history, as shown in Table 7.

In QSC smart contract, the main function is to call the query function in the SSC to query according to the information input by the user and return the query result to the user through the QSC, as shown in Table 8. Anyone can call Research functions. First, the querier enters the information to be queried. The QSC automatically calls

Table 6. QueryMassage function in the SSC

Input	Data summary information (dataname)
Output	Transaction storage location (BCHash)and Upload time (Time)

1.   for compare in reverse order
2.   if compare (Mass. Dataname, dataname) = true then
3.   return (BCHash, Time)
4.   break
5.   end
6.   else
7.   throw exception ("No result is found")
8.   end if
9.   end for

Table 7. QueryRecord function in the SSC

Input	Data summary information (dataname)
Output	Transaction storage location (BCHash)and Upload time (Time)

1.   If msg.sender is not owner then
2.   throw exception ("Do not have permission")
3.   end if
4.   for compare in Record
5.   if compare (Historical. Dataname, dataname) = true then
6.   return (BCHash, Time)
7.   end
8.   throw exception ("No result is found")
9.   end if
10. end for

the QueryMassage function in the SSC to query the information in the Massage and returns the query result to the querier. At the same time, the inquirer can choose to query the history records. Querying the history begins by determining whether the caller is the originator of the contract. If not, an exception is thrown. Otherwise, all history is returned.

Table 8. Research function in the QSC

Input	Data summary information (dataname)
Output	Transaction storage location (BCHash)and Upload time (Time)

1.   function Research (dataname)
2.   Call the SSC QueryMassage function
3.   if Querying Historical Records
4.   Call the SSC QueryRecord function
5.   end if
6.   end

5 Security and Performance Analysis of the Proposed Scheme

5.1 Security Analysis

The CP-ABE algorithm used in this paper is proposed in the literature [15]. The author of the literature has fully proved the security of this algorithm, so we will not repeat the proof of its safety. In this section, we analyze the security of the proposed model in terms of privacy, security, and access control and provide formal proof.

Privacy Analysis. This paper uses symmetric encryption and CP-ABE encryption to protect privacy. The data is symmetrically encrypted and stored in IPFS, while its decryption key is encrypted and stored in blockchain by CP-ABE. To obtain the decryption key of the data, DR can decrypt the policy ciphertext encrypted by CP-ABE only when his attributes meet the access control policy. The decryption key is used to decrypt the data ciphertext on IPFS to obtain the original data. therefore, the privacy of the data is well guaranteed.

Security Analysis. IN this paper, we adopt a combination of IPFS and blockchain to ensure the security of data storage, publishing, and sharing. The original data is encrypted and stored on IPFS, and the IPFS'S hash of the data and decryption key are encrypted by CP-ABE and then released to the blockchain. Meanwhile, DR needs to query the data by invoking a smart contract to obtain relevant information for data sharing. Both IPFS and blockchain are distributed technologies. IPFS splits data and stores it in different nodes and computes hash from the data content, while blockchain stores data in a block and connects with the previous block for hash calculation. The features of IPFS and blockchain make data tamper-proof, ensuring data integrity and security while avoiding single points of failure.

Access Control Analysis. IN this paper, CP-ABE is used to achieve fine-grained data access control. It associates ciphertext with access control policy and the key with attributes to achieve access control with the granularity that can be refined to the attribute level. DO can make different access control policies according to the attributes of the DR to achieve fine-grained access control. Meanwhile, because DO completely determines the access control policy, DO has complete access control over the data.

Formal Analysis. WE divide the model into two layers. the top layer includes four alternative transitions: *Upload Data Ciphertext, Upload Policy Ciphertext, Data Information Operation* and *Decrypt Ciphertext*, which corresponds to the four bottom models respectively. The four places *DO, DR, IPFS*, and *BC* represent four main roles. the top-level model is shown in Fig. 2. It is worth noting that during the modeling process in this paper, the default DO has obtained the MPK required for encryption from the CA, and the DR has obtained the user's private key from the CA.

The Upload data ciphertext layer's content includes DO encrypt the original data, uploading the data ciphertext to IPFS, and receiving the hash value, as shown in Fig. 3. In the process of uploading data ciphertext, the original data can only be uploaded to IPFS after symmetric encryption, and IPFS can only return the hash value to DO after the data ciphertext is uploaded successfully. The Upload data ciphertext subpage first triggers the transition *symmetric encryption* to encrypt the data. The place *G1* is used to restrict only the original data to be encrypted to form the data ciphertext. After the data ciphertext is formed, the transitions *a1* and *b1* are fired. Then the transition *upload to IPFS* is fired, which satisfies the constraint that the data ciphertext can only be uploaded to IPFS after the data is encrypted. At this time, there is data ciphertext in IPFS. After the transition *c1* is fired, the transition *calculate the hash* and *Return Hash to DO* are fired successively to return the IPFS's hash value to DO, which satisfies the constraint that the hash value can be returned to DO only after the data ciphertext exists on IPFS.

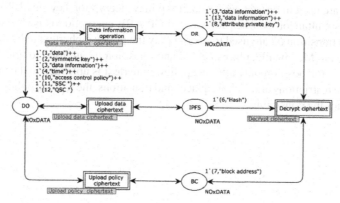

Fig. 2. The top layer of CPN model.

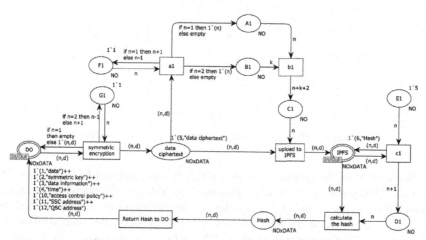

Fig. 3. The upload data ciphertext layer of CPN model.

The content of the Upload policy ciphertext layer includes DO uploading the policy ciphertext formed by RSA-based CP-ABE encryption to blockchain and obtaining the transaction position of the policy ciphertext in the blockchain, as shown in Fig. 4. Three constraints must be satisfied in this part. Firstly, RSA-based CP-ABE encryption can be performed only when the decryption key of the data ciphertext, the hash value returned by

IPFS, and the access control policy exist simultaneously. Secondly, it can be uploaded to the blockchain after encryption into the policy ciphertext. Finally, the transaction position can be returned only after the policy ciphertext is uploaded to the blockchain. When the DO receives the IPFS's hash in the Upload data ciphertext layer, the transition *blind1* is fired to bind the access control policy, decryption key, and IPFS's hash into a token. After the binding is completed, the transitions *CP-ABE encryption, upload to blockchain,* and *return block address to DO* are successively fired to complete the following operations, including RSA-based CP-ABE encryption, policy ciphertext upload to the blockchain, and return to the transaction location. Among them, places *A2, B2, G2,* and transitions *Blind1, C2* are used to restrict access control policy, decryption key, and IPFS's hash to be present simultaneously when RSA-based CP-ABE encryption is performed. Places *C2, D2* and transition *a2* are used to restrict only the policy ciphertext to be uploaded to the blockchain. Meanwhile, places *E2, F2* and transition *b2* are used to limit the return to the transaction position only after the policy ciphertext is uploaded to the blockchain. Through the restrictions of the above places and transitions, the Upload policy ciphertext layer satisfies the constraints.

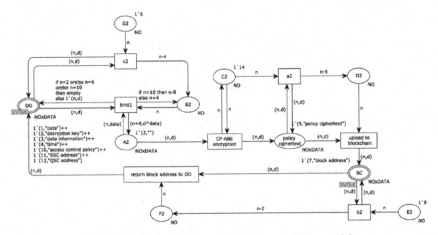

Fig. 4. The Upload policy ciphertext layer of CPN model.

The content of the data information operation layer includes DO deploying SSC and QSC, DO uploading data-related information to SSC, and DR querying information through QSC, as shown in Fig. 5. In this layer, four constraints need to be met: SSC and QSC can be deployed at any time, DR can call QSC to query after successful contract deployment, QSC returns query results to DR, and DR can always send query requests to QSC. Transition *Deploying the SSC* and *Deploying the QSC* can be fired at any time to deploy smart contracts. After that, the DR can trigger the transition *inquire* and *call SSC* to query the information, satisfying the first and second constraints. At this time, the transition *Release data information* is fired to upload the data-related information to the SSC. When the SSC is called by the QSC and receives the queried information, the transition *judge* can be fired for information matching. After the matching is successful, the transaction location and upload time are returned to the QSC through the trigger

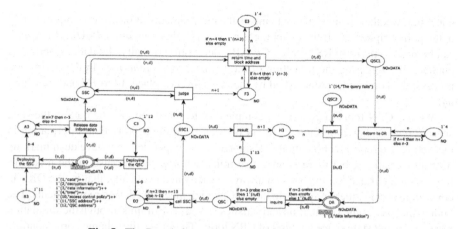

Fig. 5. The Data information operation layer of CPN model.

transition *return time and block address*, and then the transition *Return to DR* is fired to return the final query result to the DR. If the matching is unsuccessful, the transition *result* and *result1* will be fired successively and return the query failure information to the DR, thereby satisfying the third constraint condition. In addition, the transition *inquire* can always be fired to satisfy the fourth constraint. The places SSC and SSC1 represent the same contract, and QSC, QSC1 and QSC2 represent the same contract, represented by different places because they are in different states.

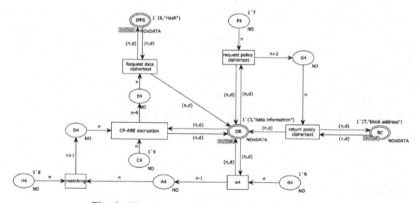

Fig. 6. The decrypt ciphertext layer of CPN model

The content of the Decrypt ciphertext layer includes DR downloading the data ciphertext from IPFS after DR decrypts the policy ciphertext, as shown in Fig. 6. In the process of decrypting the ciphertext, it is required to obtain the policy ciphertext first before the RSA-based CP-ABE decryption operation can be performed, and the data ciphertext can be downloaded only after the decryption is successful. The transition *request policy ciphertext* is fired first, and then the transition *return policy ciphertext* is fired to return the policy ciphertext from the blockchain. At this time, the transition *matching* is fired for matching, whether the user attribute meets the requirements of the access control policy in the policy ciphertext. If the matching is successful, the transition *CP-ABE decryption* can be fired to perform RSA-based CP-ABE decryption. Finally, the data ciphertext is obtained by triggering the transition of the *Request data ciphertext*. In the decryption process, the constraints are satisfied by the restriction of place *A4* to *H4* and transition *a4*.

We use CPN tools to generate a complete state space report. The data in the state space report is shown in Table 9. It can be seen from the activity data information in the state space report that the model designed in this paper does not have dead marking or dead transitions, but there is an active transition *inquire*. Because in the model of this paper, the transition *inquire* can always be activated cyclically, that is, the DR can continuously send query requests to the QSC, which meets the design requirements. The built model passes the verification and satisfies various constraints through the simulation verification and state space analysis of CPN tools. Therefore, the scheme corresponding to the model is correct and safe.

Table 9. Data in the state space

Variable	Value
State Space (Nodes)	619
State Space (Arcs)	2490
State Space (Secs)	0
State Space (Status)	Full
Scc Graph (Nodes)	619
Scc Graph (Arcs)	1706
Scc Graph (Secs)	0
Dead markings	None
Dead transition instances	None
Live transition instances	Data_information_operation'inquire 1

5.2 Performance Analysis

This section will test the associated time consumption of different CP-ABE encryption methods when updating the access control policy. The experimental environment requirements are shown in Table 10.

We first compare the performance of CP-ABE based on bilinear mapping and CP-ABE based on RSA. The test mainly aims at policy ciphertext generation. In our scheme, the data encrypted by CP-ABE is the IPFS's hash and the decryption key of the data ciphertext. Since the hash size of the IPFS address is fixed and the decryption key of the data ciphertext is also fixed once it is determined, we assume that the size of the data encrypted by CP-ABE is 128 bytes. We manually designed access control policies during

Table 10. Requirements of the experimental environment

Demand	Message
Processor	Intel(R) Core (TM) i5-3230M CPU @ 2.60 GHz
Operating system	64-bit Windows 7
Memory	4.00 GB
Programming language	Java with IPBC library
Blockchain	Ethereum

the test to ensure that the access control policies under different structures were the same. Simultaneously we set the number of attributes in the access control policy to 10–50 and the number of attributes in the private attribute key to 5–25. In the experiment, this paper compares the first proposed tree structure BSW scheme, the LW scheme under the LSSS structure, and the GZCMZ scheme under the threshold structure. GZCMZ is further upgraded to selected ciphertext attack (CCA) security under the proposed CP-ABE scheme of selective plaintext attack (CPA) security. Reference [14] makes a detailed comparison of the CP-ABE scheme under the AND gate structure, so this paper does not conduct a comparison test.

As shown in Fig. 7, the RSA-based CP-ABE scheme is significantly better than the other CP-ABE schemes based on bilinear mapping in terms of encryption and decryption time. Although the GZCMZ scheme also shows a better time advantage in the encryption stage, the time has increased rapidly in the decryption process. Because the GZCMZ does not need to perform pairing calculations during encryption, the encryption time consumption is relatively small during the encryption process. However, it is still necessary to perform pairing calculations on attributes in the decryption process. As the number of attributes increases, the calculation cost is increasing.

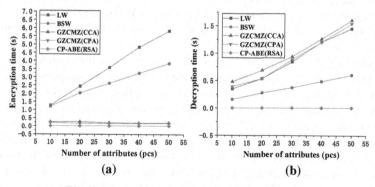

Fig. 7. Encryption time (a) and decryption time (b).

Moreover, the ciphertext size, policy ciphertext upload time, and total access control policy update time generated under different CP-ABE schemes are tested. The test results are shown in Fig. 8 and Fig. 9 (a). As shown in Fig. 8 (a), the ciphertext size of BSW and LW increases almost linearly with the number of attributes. Both the CP-ABE based on RSA and GZCMZ achieve a constant ciphertext size. Although the ciphertext size of the key generated by the CP-ABE based on RSA is larger than GZCMZ in terms of the ciphertext size, both ciphertexts do not exceed 1KB. However, from Fig. 7 (b), GZCMZ consumes about 480-1600ms more than the RSA-based CP-ABE in the decryption process. When the access control policy is updated, the update time consumption includes the sum of the decryption time, the re-encryption time, and the policy ciphertext upload time. As shown in Fig. 8 (b) and Fig. 9 (a), the RSA-based CP-ABE scheme offers higher update efficiency when updating the access control policy.

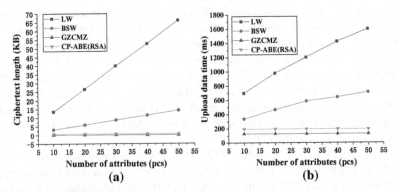

Fig. 8. Ciphertext length (a) and upload blockchain time (b).

We also conducted performance tests on SSC and QSC. In the process of querying and updating information, as shown in Fig. 9(b), the information stored first takes a higher time in querying and updating information. This is because the update and query operation designed in this paper use reverse order comparison when comparing data summaries. In this way, in the process of information update and query, the data stored later will be matched first, while the data stored first will be matched for more times, so it will consume more time.

According to the statistics in Fig. 9(b), in the process of information update, the time consumption is about 15–20 ms higher than the storage time consumption, because each information update is one step more than the information storage operation to put the historical records into the Record array. The information query time is about 350–400 ms higher than the storage time, because when querying, the SSC contract needs to be called through the QSC contract, and there will be a certain time cost in the process of calling the contract. For SSC, when the amount of stored data is less than 50, the storage and update times do not exceed 1200 ms. For QSC, the query time does not exceed 1550 ms. To sum up, the CP-ABE access control policy update method based on smart contract proposed in this paper shows better performance in time.

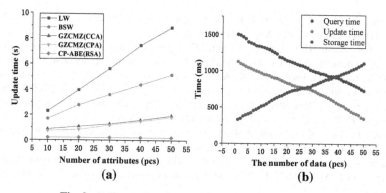

Fig. 9. Policy update time (a) and smart contract time(b).

6 Conclusion

In this paper, we propose an access control policy update scheme. In this paper, the RSA-based CP-ABE algorithm is used to improve the update efficiency of re-encryption. In addition, two smart contracts with different functions are designed to realize the storage management of old and new policy ciphertext and the retrieval of relevant information. Finally, the experiment results show that the proposed scheme has better strategy update efficiency in an environment with many attributes and frequent personnel changes. Our future work will focus on improving the functions of smart contracts of our scheme, which could implement the copyright control, keyword, and old policy ciphertext search functions.

Acknowledgment. This paper is supported by the National Natural Science Foundation of China (61962042) and Natural Science Foundation of Inner Mongolia (2018MS06028, 2022MS06020) and Science and Technology Program of Inner Mongolia Autonomous Region (2019GG376, 2020GG0188), and Open Topic of Inner Mongolia Discipline Inspection and Supervision Big Data Laboratory (IMDBD202008).

References

1. Bethencourt, J., Sahai, A., Waters, B.: Ciphertext-policy attribute-based encryption. In: 2007 IEEE symposium on security and privacy (SP'07), pp. 321–334. Berkeley, California (2007)
2. Nakamoto, S.: Bitcoin: A peer-to-peer electronic cash system. Consulted (2008)
3. Wen, Q., Gao, Y., Chen, Z., Wu, D.: A blockchain-based data sharing scheme in the supply chain by IIoT. In: 2019 IEEE International Conference on Industrial Cyber Physical Systems (ICPS), pp. 695–700. Taipei, China (2019)
4. Huang, D., Chung, C.J., Dong, Q., Luo J., Kang, M.: Building private blockchains over public blockchains (PoP) an attribute-based access control approach. In: Proceedings of the 34th ACM/SIGAPP Symposium on Applied Computing, pp. 355–363. Limassol, Cyprus (2019)
5. Yan, B., Yu, J., Wang, Y., Guo, Q., Chai B., Liu, S.: Blockchain-based service recommendation supporting data sharing. In: International Conference on Wireless Algorithms, Systems, and Applications, pp. 580–589. Qingdao, China (2020)

6. Huang, S., Chen, L.W., Fam, B.B.: Data security sharing method based on CP-ABE and blockchain. Comput. Syst. App. **28**(11), 79–86 (2019)

7. Qiu, Y.X., Zhang, H.X., Cao, Q., Zhang, J.C., Chen, X.S., Jin, H.J.: Blockchain data access control scheme based on CP-ABE algorithm. Chinese J. Netw. Inf. Secur. **6**(3), 88–98 (2020)

8. Qin, X., Huang, Y., Yang, Z., Li, X.: A blockchain-based access control scheme with multiple attribute authorities for secure cloud data sharing. J. Syst. Architect. **112**, 101854 (2021)

9. Yu, G., et al.: Enabling attribute revocation for fine-grained access control in blockchain-IoT systems. IEEE Trans. Eng. Manage. **67**(4), 1213–1230 (2020)

10. Tian, Y.L., Yang, K.D., Wang, Z., Feng, T.: Algorithm of blockchain data provenance based on ABE. J. Commun. **40**(11), 101–111 (2019)

11. Zhang, Y., He, D., Choo, K.K.R.: BaDS: blockchain-based architecture for data sharing with ABS and CP-ABE in IoT. In: Wireless Communications and Mobile Computing, pp. 1–9 (2018)

12. Gao, H., Ma, Z., Luo, S., Xu, Y., Wu, Z.: BSSPD: a blockchain-based security sharing scheme for personal data with fine-grained access control. In: Wireless Communications and Mobile Computing, pp. 1–20 (2021)

13. Benet, J.: IPFS - content addressed, versioned, P2P file system (DRAFT 3). arXiv preprint arXiv:1407.3561 (2014)

14. Odelu, V., Das, A.K., Khan, M.K., Choo, K.K.R., Jo, M.: Expressive CP-ABE scheme for mobile devices in IoT satisfying constant-size keys and ciphertexts. IEEE Access **5**, 3273–3283 (2017)

15. Khandla, D., Shahy, H., Bz, M.K., Pais, A.R., Raj, N.: Expressive CP-ABE scheme satisfying constant-size keys and ciphertexts. In: IACR Cryptol. ePrint Arch, p. 1257 (2019)

16. Jiang, S., Liu, J., Wang, L., Yoo, S.M.: Verifiable search meets blockchain: A privacy-preserving framework for outsourced encrypted data. In: ICC 2019–2019 IEEE International Conference on Communications (ICC), pp. 1–6. Tokio, Japan (2019)

17. Sun, S., Du, R., Chen, S.: A secure and computable blockchain-based data sharing scheme in IoT system. Information **12**(2), 47 (2021)

18. Li, X., Tan, M.: Electronic certificate sharing scheme with searchable attribute-based encryption on blockchain. J. Phys: Conf. Ser. **1757**(1), 012161 (2021)

19. Sun, J., Yao, X., Wang, S., Wu, Y.: Blockchain-based secure storage and access scheme for electronic medical records in IPFS. IEEE Access **8**, 59389–59401 (2020)

20. Pham, V.D., et al.: B-Box-a decentralized storage system using IPFS, attributed-based encryption, and blockchain. In: 2020 RIVF International Conference on Computing and Communication Technologies (RIVF), pp. 1–6. Ho Chi Minh City, Vietnam (2020)

21. Tan, H.B., et al.: Archival data protection and sharing method based on blockchain. J. Softw. **30**(9), 2620–2635 (2019)

22. Mounnan, O., Mouatasim, A.E., Manad, O., Outchakoucht, A., Es-samaali H., Boubchir, L.: A novel approach based on blockchain to enhance security with dynamic policy updating. In: 2020 7th International Conference on Internet of Things: Systems, Management and Security (IOTSMS), pp. 1-6. Paris, France (2020)

23. Ma, W., et al.: Attribute revocable data sharing scheme based on blockchain and CP-ABE. In: Proceedings of the 4th International Conference on Computer Science and Application Engineering, pp. 1–7. Sanya, China (2020)

24. Guo, R., Yang, G., Shi, H., Zhang, Y., Zheng, D.: O^3-R-CP-ABE: an efficient and revocable attribute-based encryption scheme in the cloud-assisted IoMT system. IEEE Internet of Things J. **8**(11), 8949–8963 (2021). https://doi.org/10.1109/JIOT.2021.3055541

25. Herranz, J., Laguillaumie, F., Ràfols, C.: Constant size ciphertexts in threshold attribute-based encryption. In: Nguyen, P.Q., Pointcheval, D. (eds.) Public Key Cryptography – PKC 2010. LNCS, vol. 6056, pp. 19–34. Springer, Heidelberg (2010). https://doi.org/10.1007/978-3-642-13013-7_2

26. Susilo, W., Yang, G., Guo, F., Huang, Q.: Constant-size ciphertexts in threshold attribute-based encryption without dummy attributes. Inf. Sci. **429**, 349–360 (2018). https://doi.org/10.1016/j.ins.2017.11.037

27. Ge, A., Zhang, R., Chen, C., Ma, C., Zhang, Z.: Threshold ciphertext policy attribute-based encryption with constant size ciphertexts. In: Susilo, W., Mu, Y., Seberry, J. (eds.) Information Security and Privacy. LNCS, vol. 7372, pp. 336–349. Springer, Heidelberg (2012). https://doi.org/10.1007/978-3-642-31448-3_25

28. Emura, K., Miyaji, A., Nomura, A., Omote, K., Soshi, M.: A ciphertext-policy attribute-based encryption scheme with constant ciphertext length. In: Bao, F., Li, H., Wang, G. (eds.) Information Security Practice and Experience. LNCS, vol. 5451, pp. 13–23. Springer, Heidelberg (2009). https://doi.org/10.1007/978-3-642-00843-6_2

29. Lewko, A., Okamoto, T., Sahai, A., Takashima, K., Waters, B.: Fully secure functional encryption: attribute-based encryption and (hierarchical) inner product encryption. In: Gilbert, H. (ed.) Advances in Cryptology – EUROCRYPT 2010. LNCS, vol. 6110, pp. 62–91. Springer, Heidelberg (2010). https://doi.org/10.1007/978-3-642-13190-5_4

30. Waters, B.: Ciphertext-policy attribute-based encryption: an expressive, efficient, and provably secure realization. In: Catalano, D., Fazio, N., Gennaro, R., Nicolosi, A. (eds.) Public Key Cryptography – PKC 2011. LNCS, vol. 6571, pp. 53–70. Springer, Heidelberg (2011). https://doi.org/10.1007/978-3-642-19379-8_4

31. Lewko, A., Waters, B.: New proof methods for attribute-based encryption: achieving full security through selective techniques. In: Safavi-Naini, R., Canetti, R. (eds.) Advances in Cryptology – CRYPTO 2012. LNCS, vol. 7417, pp. 180–198. Springer, Heidelberg (2012). https://doi.org/10.1007/978-3-642-32009-5_12

32. Agrawal, S., Chase, M.: FAME: fast attribute-based message encryption. In: Proceedings of the 2017 ACM SIGSAC Conference on Computer and Communications Security, pp.665–682. Dallas, TX, USA (2017)

33. Malluhi, Q.M., Shikfa, A., Trinh, V.C.: A ciphertext-policy attribute-based encryption scheme with optimized ciphertext size and fast decryption. In: Proceedings of the 2017 ACM on Asia Conference on Computer and Communications Security, pp. 230–240. United Arab Emirates, Dubai (2017)

34. Doshi, N., Jinwala, D.C.: Fully secure ciphertext policy attribute-based encryption with constant length ciphertext and faster decryption. Sec. Commun. Netwv **7**(11), 1988–2002 (2014)

35. Zhang, Y., Zheng, D., Chen, X., Li, J., Li, H.: Computationally efficient ciphertext-policy attribute-based encryption with constant-size ciphertexts. In: Chow, S.S.M., Liu, J.K., Hui, L.C.K., Yiu, S.M. (eds.) Provable Security. LNCS, vol. 8782, pp. 259–273. Springer, Cham (2014). https://doi.org/10.1007/978-3-319-12475-9_18

36. Cheung, L., Newport, C.: Provably secure ciphertext policy ABE. In: Proceedings of the 14th ACM Conference on Computer and Communications Security, CCS 2007, pp. 456–465. New York, NY, USA (2007)

37. Zhou, Z.B., Huang, D.J.: On efficient ciphertext-policy attribute based encryption and broadcast encryption: extended abstract. In: Proceedings of the 17th ACM Conference on Computer and Communications Security, CCS 2010, pp. 753–755. New York, NY, USA (2010)

38. Guo, F., Mu, Y., Susilo, W., Wong, D.S., Varadharajan, V.: CP-ABE with constant size keys for lightweight devices. IEEE Trans. Inf. Forensics Secur. **9**(5), 763–771 (2014)

39. ang, W., Wang, R., Guan, Z., Wu, L., Du, X.J., Guizani, M.: A lightweight attribute based encryption scheme with constant size ciphertext for Internet of Things. In: ICC 2020 IEEE International Conference on Communications (ICC), pp. 1–6. Dublin, Ireland (2020)

Effective Blockchain-Based Asynchronous Federated Learning for Edge-Computing

Zhipeng Gao, Huangqi Li$^{(\boxtimes)}$, Yijing Lin, Ze Chai, Yang Yang, and Lanlan Rui

State Key Laboratory of Networking and Switching Technology, Beijing University of Posts and Telecommunications, Beijing 100876, China
lhq320@bupt.edu.cn

Abstract. Since massive data are generated at the network's edge, the Internet of Things devices can exploit edge computing and federated learning to train artificial intelligence (AI) models while protecting data privacy. However, heterogeneous devices lead to low efficiency and single-point-of-failure. Moreover, malicious nodes may affect training accuracy. Therefore, we propose FedLyra, an effective blockchain-based asynchronous federated learning architecture, to improve the efficiency of aggregation and resist malicious nodes in a trusted and decentralized manner. We then propose a reputation mechanism that combines historical behaviors and the quality of local updates to resist disagreements and adversaries. With the help of the reputation mechanism, we propose a council-based decentralized aggregation mechanism to exclude malicious nodes. Experiments show that FedLyra can resist malicious nodes and ensure the accuracy of training results.

Keywords: Federated learning · Blockchain · Edge-computing · Asynchronous architecture · Decentralization

1 Introduction

The vast amount of data generated by edge devices can enhance various AI applications [5]. Edge devices can deliver computation-intensive AI tasks to edge servers without transferring large amounts of data to distant data centers [17,26]. However, data transferred from edge devices to edge servers involves privacy risks [26]. Federated learning is dedicated to solving the privacy problem in distributed learning. An edge computing-based federated learning system can learn a global statistical model with localized data on edge devices [13].

Every coin has two sides. First, federated learning suffers the single-point-of-failure due to the need for a central server. Second, there may be data inconsistency in the trustless environment. Third, heterogeneous devices make aggregation processes inefficient. Forth, attackers may disrupt the model aggregation process by hijacking devices or injecting malicious parameters.

The decentralization and asynchronous of federated learning can solve the above security problems. As a price, compared with the centralized counterpart,

H. Gao et al. (Eds.): CollaborateCom 2022, LNICST 460, pp. 514–532, 2022.
https://doi.org/10.1007/978-3-031-24383-7_28

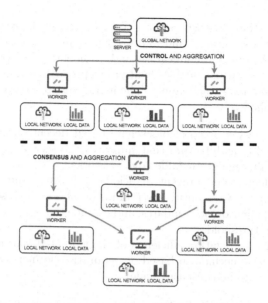

Fig. 1. Centralized vs. decentralized federated learning

decentralized asynchronous federated learning requires additional consideration. As shown in Fig. 1, centralized federated learning requires scheduling and aggregation through a central server. In contrast, in a decentralized network, all nodes are equal, and there is no authority responsible for control and storage. Therefore, the decentralized and asynchronous architecture needs to coordinate the nodes and ensure the consistency of global information such as global model, history, etc.

In recent years, blockchain has gradually become a promising solution for trusted decentralized systems with the characteristics of decentralization, tamper-proof, and transparency [1]. Many scholars have attempted to solve the aforementioned problems of federated learning by using blockchain to build consensus among untrusted workers, thus ensuring the consistency and reliability of the global model. However, there are several points often ignored. First, it is inefficient when reaching a consensus in a large-scale network [22]. Since each aggregation operation requires consensus in blockchain, adopting an inefficient consensus algorithm like Proof of Work (PoW) would severely reduce the aggregation efficiency. Second, limited resources for edge devices restrict the throughput of the blockchain. Furthermore, there may be huge delays caused by stragglers in the learning process [20]. Third, global synchronization can degrade the system's efficiency due to the unstable communication links [22]. Fourth, it is hard to find and exclude malicious nodes because traditional consensus cannot ensure the correctness of uploaded models, meaning that a poisoned model may be recorded in the blockchain since consensus will not verify the model itself.

In this paper, we propose FedLyra, an effective blockchain-based asynchronous federated learning framework to adapt to heterogeneous edge networks.

FedLyra restricts the consensus among a small group of particular nodes to reduce the consensus overhead and improve throughput. To reduce the latency caused by synchronous communication and stragglers, FedLyra adopts asynchronous aggregation, which enables FedLyra to process local updates uploaded by edge devices in a real-time manner. The main contributions of this paper are summarized as follows.

1. We propose FedLyra, a novel blockchain-based decentralized asynchronous federated learning architecture that improves the security and efficiency of federated learning under unstable edge networks.
2. In order to identify and prevent malicious nodes from interfering with the federated learning, we quantify the reputation of a node based on historical data and the quality of local updates, and exclude the malicious node through the reputation threshold.
3. To improve the aggregation efficiency of the federated learning, we design a council consensus mechanism based on reputation to increase the consensus speed by reducing the consensus scale.

This paper is organized as follows. Section 2 discusses the research related to blockchain and federated learning. Section 3 presents the core framework and mechanism proposed in this paper. Section 4 evaluates the performance of the system. Section 5 concludes the paper.

2   Related Work

Federated learning has attracted much attention from researchers since McMahan *et al.* proposed FedAvg, a federated learning method that learns a shared model between different devices through a synchronized weighted average method [18]. Li *et al.* [14] proposed FedProx, which limits the effect of non-i.i.d. data on the global model by introducing a proximal term. Reisizadeh and others proposed FedPAQ algorithm [19]. FedPAQ uses cycle averaging instead of global synchronous averaging. Xie *et al.* [24] proposed an asynchronous federated learning architecture FedAsync in which Worker and Updater work in parallel. Chen *et al.* [3] further improved on [24] by proposing FedSA, which accelerates training and improves communication efficiency by a two-stage training strategy and dynamical hyperparameters.

Since federated learning is privacy-preserving and can work between heterogeneous devices, some studies have attempted to combine federated learning with edge computing to enable distributed learning on edge heterogeneous networks. Wang *et al.* [21] combines deep reinforcement learning with federated learning to intelligently optimize communication and computing resources in the mobile edge computing. Jin *et al.* [7] explored approaches to adaptive adaptation of federated learning with limited resource budgets. Chen *et al.* [4] proposed an asynchronous federated learning method that can process continuous stream data on edge devices. Khan *et al.* [9] propose a Stackelberg-game-based incentive mechanism for federated learning. The above researches focus on optimizing the performance of federated learning or resource allocation in edge computing. They do not consider how to solve the trust between edge nodes.

As a decentralized immutable distributed digital ledger system [25], blockchain is suitable for processing distributed transactions in an untrusted environment. Kim et al. [10] proposed a blockchain-based distributed federated learning architecture BlockFL, in which each device will connect to a miner, who will verify the local updates uploaded by the device, and the miner who successfully mines a new valid block will aggregate the local updates and add the results to the blockchain. Li et al. [15] proposed a consensus approach based on a trusted small committee that can effectively avoid the influence of malicious nodes. Kang et al. [8] used reputation as a measure of device's reliability and trustworthiness and implemented a reputation-based reliable worker selection scheme, in addition to which they proposed an effective incentive mechanism that combines reputation with contract theory.

However, the above blockchain-based approaches implement in the synchronous scheme, which is unsuitable for edge environments with limited network bandwidth and low equipment reliability. Liu et al. [16] apply blockchain-based asynchronous federated learning methods to edge computing, but they lack consideration of practical conditions such as limited edge network resources and unstable devices. Feng et al. [6] proposed a blockchain-based asynchronous federated learning scheme, which is an improvement of [10] with an entropy-based node evaluation method for determining the weight of local update. These blockchain-based asynchronous federated learning methods attempt to improve efficiency by asynchronization. But, these methods adopt all devices to participate in consensus, which requires many resources for message synchronization. It may cause low throughput and significant delays due to the limited resource of edge devices and stragglers.

3 Core Technology of FedLyra

FedLyra employs a decentralized asynchronous federated learning mechanism based on council and reputation, which consists of asynchronous federated learning process, reputation quantification, and council consensus. This section first demonstrates the architecture of FedLyra, introduce the workflow, and then designs the three core mechanisms of FedLyra.

3.1 Architecture

In FedLyra, all devices in the edge network are treated as peer nodes and jointly maintain the blockchain ledger, as shown in Fig. 2. Nodes entitled to participate in learning are divided into common nodes and council nodes. Common nodes undertake local training and update uploading. Council nodes are a special type of common node that is additionally responsible for receiving updates from other nodes and performing aggregation. They will package aggregation results, upload updates, verification scores and reputation into blocks, then upload the blocks to

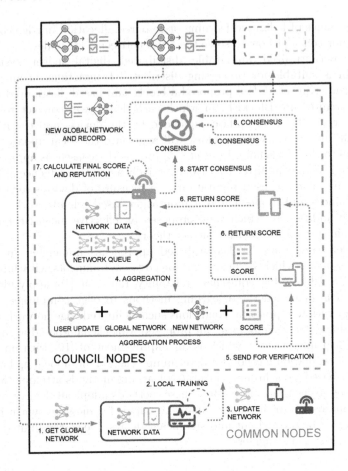

Fig. 2. Structure of FedLyra

blockchain after internal consensus among the council. It is worth noting that the council nodes are also common nodes, meaning that they still need to conduct model training and uploading. Each aggregation of FedLyra must be determined by consensus. By dividing the nodes, FedLyra limits the consensus process to a small council to reduce latency. Furthermore, since nodes outside the council do not have to perform aggregation, most nodes can concentrate on local training.

From a system-level perspective, FedLyra is divided into off-chain learning and on-chain verification. In the off-chain learning part, common nodes train the model based on local data, and council nodes aggregate the updates uploaded by common nodes. In the on-chain verification part, council nodes validate the global models and quantify model scores and node reputation. Blockchain stores the global model generated by each aggregation, local updates uploaded by nodes and other related records. Based on these records, we can quantitatively evaluate nodes' behaviors, assign roles to nodes and adjust the weight of node updates in

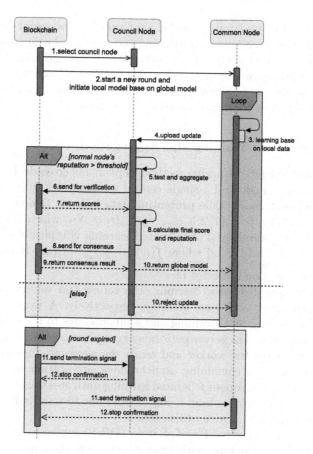

Fig. 3. Workflow of FedLyra in a round

aggregation. We can also penalize nodes with poor reputations, excluding them from the learning process.

3.2 Workflow

Figure 3 shows the workflow of FedLyra in a training round. Each common node first takes the latest global model from the local blockchain ledger and trains it according to the local dataset. After the training is completed, the common node broadcasts the local update to the council nodes and waits for them to complete the model aggregation. Once a council node receives the local update, it will test and aggregate the model, then broadcast the new model to other council nodes for scoring and validation. After the verification, this council node generates the final score of the common node's update based on the model scores quantified by others in council, then calculates the reputation of local update uploader based on the final score and the historical reputation. The new reputation and global model will be updated to blockchain through a successful consensus. The common node then continues local training and model uploading until the smart contract signal the end of the current round. Once a round ends, all nodes stop training, the learning process proceeds to the next round, and new council nodes will be determined. The learning process continues until a specified number of rounds are reached or the expected accuracy is met.

3.3   Asynchronous Training and Aggregation

The traditional federated learning method implements cross-device model training based on multi-node and a single central server, which fully leverages local data from different nodes while preventing data leakage. Denote the devices in the edge network by $D = \{1, 2, 3, \ldots, N_D\}$. $|D| = N_D$, which is the number of edge devices. The overall goal of federated learning is typically minimizing the objective function $\min_{w \in \mathbb{R}^{N_D}} f(w)$ where $f(w) := \frac{1}{n} \sum_n^{i=1} f_i(w)$. Here, $f_i(w)$ is the local objective function of device i.

In asynchronous federated learning, the server and worker perform asynchronous aggregation and local training, respectively. A worker continuously performs non-blocking local training and sends updates to the server once local training is completed. The server performs aggregation immediately after receiving the updates from the worker and sends the aggregated results to the corresponding worker. By combining asynchronous aggregation and non-blocking communication, asynchronous federated learning mitigates the influence of stragglers, prevents other devices from being blocked due to waiting for slow training devices, thus improving device utilization.

Inspired by the Delegated Proof of Stake (DPoS) consensus algorithm, we set up a council which cooperates with smart contracts to implement the scheduling and aggregation process in federated learning. The control function of the smart contract is shown in Algorithm 1. K is the number of council members. Upon the start of each round, the control function initializes the round termination flag in the contract, selects the council node by random or reputation sorting, and sends the node identity and the start signal to the corresponding node. It subsequently waits until $\frac{2}{3}$ of common nodes have completed the learning process and then reverses the round termination flag in the contract to alert all active nodes that the current round should be terminated.

The running process of common nodes is shown in Algorithm 2. In FedLyra, common nodes are only responsible for asynchronous training and local update upload meanwhile monitoring the round termination flag in the smart contract. Nodes can use the Adam algorithm for local training [11]. The global model used for node training can be obtained directly from the local blockchain records. When conducting an update upload, the node sends w_i, the local update, τ_i, the timestamp of the start of training, and d_i, the size of local dataset, to each council node.

Different from the common node, the council node needs to perform the duty of the common node (training and uploading) while aggregating model updates

---

Algorithm 1. Council selection and training control contract

Require: $round, K$
1: **for** $i = 0, 1, 2, ..., round - 1$ **do**
2:    Change termination flag in contract to False
3:    Randomly choose common node N_{common}
4:    **if** is the first time this function invoked and $i = 0$ **then**
5:        Randomly select K Nodes from N_{common} as $N_{council}$ with Verifiable Random Function
6:    **else**
7:        Sort N_{common} by reputation
8:        Select $N_{council}$ from top K in N_{common}
9:    **end if**
10:    Send identity and start signal to all node in N_{common}
11:    Wait until $2/3$ nodes in N_{common} have completed the learning process
12:    Change termination flag in contract to True
13: **end for**

Algorithm 2. Worker updating in FedLyra

Require: $epoch, \gamma$
1: Get latest w_{global} from blockchain with its timestamp t_{global}
2: $\tau_i \leftarrow t_{global}$
3: $w_i \leftarrow w_{global}$
4: $d_i \leftarrow$ size of dataset
5: **while** Termination flag in contract is False **do**
6:    **for** $i = 0, 1, 2, ..., epoch - 1$ **do**
7:        Update model using Adam algorithm with γ
8:    **end for**
9:    Broadcast (w_i, τ_i, d_i) to council
10:    Wait for aggregation
11: **end while**

---

from others, as well as evaluating and recording the updates. The aggregation process of council nodes is described in Algorithm 3. The receptor thread of the council node will store the data in the message queue if it receives the uploaded information from common nodes. Meanwhile, it will validate the aggregation result if it receives an aggregation massage from a council node, which will be described in the following section. The aggregator thread will take the model updates from the message queue in first-in-first-out (FIFO) order. If the uploader's reputation exceeds the threshold, the aggregator will test the model

---

Algorithm 3. Council aggregation in FedLyra

Require: t_{max}, ζ, a, b
Process: Council
 1: Initial *queue*
 2: Run Receptor thread and Aggregator thread in parallel
Thread: Receptor
 3: **while** Termination flag in contract is False **do**
 4:    **if** Receive (w_i, τ_i, d_i) from common node **then**
 5:       Push (w_i, τ_i, d_i) as msg_i into *queue*
 6:    **else if** Receive $(w_i, s_i^j, w'_{global})$ from other council node **then**
 7:       $s_i^k \leftarrow$ validates score of w_i by current node k
 8:       $s_{g'}^k \leftarrow$ validates score of w'_{global} by current node k
 9:       $s_g^k \leftarrow$ score of current global model w_{global}
10:       **if** $\left| s_i^j - s_i^k \right| < \varepsilon$ and $s_{g'}^k \geq s_g^k - \delta$ **then**
11:          Sign and return s_k^j to node j
12:       **end if**
13:    **end if**
14: **end while**
Thread: Aggregator
15: **while** Termination flag in contract is False **do**
16:    Get msg_i that has not been recorded in blockchain from *queue*
17:    Get (w_i, τ_i, d_i) from msg_i
18:    Get reputation r_i for node i from blockchain
19:    **if** $r_i \geq$ reputation threshold **then**
20:       Test w_i with local data and get correspond score s_i^j
21:       $w'_{global} \leftarrow$ Aggregate w_i according to equation (1)
22:       Send $(w_i, s_i^j, w'_{global})$ to other council node for verification
23:       Receive test score S_i from others and calculate r_i according to equation (5)
24:       Pack $(w'_{global}, msg_i, S_i, r_i)$ to start consensus
25:    **end if**
26: **end while**

---

using the local data, and record its test score. The score can be the average absolute error (MAE) or other indicators that can measure the quality of the model. Model aggregation is performed after the test according to the following equation:

$$w_{global} \leftarrow \alpha \times w_i + (1 - \alpha) \times w_{global} \qquad (1)$$

where α is the coefficient of aggregation, which is calculated according to the following formula:

$$\alpha \leftarrow \alpha_0 \times l\left(t - \tau\right) \times n\left(\frac{d_i}{d_{all}}\right) \times r_i \qquad (2)$$

where $l(t - \tau)$ is a function to measure the degree of staleness of the update. t is current time. τ is the generation time of the global model used by node i. $l(t - \tau)$ is represented by $l(t - \tau) = \begin{cases} \frac{1}{a(t - \tau - b) + 1}, & t - \tau < b \\ 1, & else \end{cases}$. r_i is the reputation value of the node i, which will be described in detail below. $n(\frac{d_i}{d_{all}})$ is a factor related to the amount of local data on node i. $n(\frac{d_i}{d_{all}})$ is represented by

$$n(\frac{d_i}{d_{all}}) = \beta \times arctan\left(\gamma \times \frac{d_i}{d_{all}}\right) \tag{3}$$

where d_i is the dataset size of node i, d_{all} is the dataset size of all nodes, and β and γ are scale factors.

After the aggregation of updates from node i, council node j packages the generated global model parameters w_g^j, node's local update w_i, test scores s_i^j, and original message of node i into a transaction and broadcasts it to others in council.

Other council nodes will extract local update and global model in the transaction and test them by local data respectively. Suppose that council node k receives a transaction from council node j and validates the aggregation result of common node i. Node k will check if the gap between the test score s_i^k for w_i and the score s_i^j in the transaction is within the specified range, i.e., $\left| s_i^j - s_i^k \right| < \varepsilon$, and if the test score of w_g^j is greater than or similar to the test score of the latest global model in the blockchain. If both conditions hold, the transaction passes the verification. Node k will return s_k^j to node j that proposed the transaction. Node j calculates the final test score and the reputation of node i based on the test scores of other council nodes. The detailed calculation for score and reputation is described in the next subsection.

3.4   Reputation of Node

All nodes have an initial reputation value at their first participation in the task. Suppose that in the subsequent learning process, when node k uploads a local update, the council node i processes this update. To prevent malicious nodes in council from deliberately providing wrong scores, node i sorts $S_k = \{s_k^j | j \in N_{council}\}$ in descending order, and exclude the top $1/6$ and bottom $1/6$ scores, then calculates the final test score s_k of this update for node k as follow

$$s_k = \frac{1}{|S_k|} \times \sum_{s' \in S_k} s' \tag{4}$$

The calculation of reputation is based on the final test score. Considering that a malicious node may increase its reputation, reputation must be iterative based on the historical reputation and current score

$$r_k = \zeta \times r_k + (1 - \zeta) \times (s_k / s_{compare})^2 \tag{5}$$

where ζ is the coefficient that balances the historical data and the current data. $s_k/s_{compare}$ is the normalized score. In the initial stage, the scores of local updates are low due to insufficient training. If the score is directly used as the base of the squared term, it will lead to a low reputation. In the later stage, the scores are high and need to be normalized to reflect the relative training quality. $s_{compare}$ is calculated as follows

$$s_{compare} = \begin{cases} s_{mid}, & |S| > 1/3 \cdot |N_{common}| \\ s_{compare} \text{ in last round,} & else \end{cases} \tag{6}$$

where $|N_{common}|$ is the number of common nodes. s_{mid} is the median score of S, $S = \{(j, s_j)|node\ j\ participated\ in\ learning\}$, which is a set of final score for all participating learning nodes in current round. S is maintained in the blockchain and updated through transaction as follow.

After the calculation of the reputation of node k, council node will update (k, s_k), the score of node k into S, generating a new score set S'. Then, it will package S', S_k, s_k together with other information mentioned above into a transaction and initiate a consensus in council. If consensus is successfully reached, the aggregation result will be permanently written to the blockchain.

3.5   Council Selection and Consensus

In FedLyra, only council members will participate in the aggregation and generation of the global model, while common nodes have no right to handle the local updates uploaded by other nodes. Meanwhile, common nodes are also excluded from the blockchain consensus, and only the council nodes will participate in the consensus. Since the council has the privilege to aggregate updates and write data to the blockchain by consensus, the council nodes must be selected cautiously. In principle, we want to grant these powers to good nodes, while malicious nodes are excluded from the council as much as possible. In FedLyra, the selection of council is mostly based on reputation, which is described in Lines 4 to 9 of Algorithm 1.

In the first round of the first learning task, the selection of council nodes is performed by random sampling due to the lack of historical data. With techniques such as Verifiable Random Function (VRF), FedLyra can complete council selection in a decentralized scenario. In the subsequent learning process, the selection of council nodes is performed based on node reputation generated in the last round. FedLyra sorts the reputation of nodes through smart contracts. At the beginning of the next round, nodes with the top K reputations are selected as the council nodes. It is worth noting that the reputations of nodes in the previous learning task can be applied to the next task. The council nodes in the first round of the next task can be selected by reputation ranking instead of random sampling.

After finishing model aggregation and reputation quantification and passing the council's validation, the council node that handles the uploaded update will pack the local update, update's score, the validated new global model, and node reputation into blocks and initiate consensus. Consensus is the final step of model aggregation, only global models that reach consensus can be released to others in the network for local training, so the efficiency of consensus has a significant impact on the system's throughput. Most blockchain-based federated learning architectures adopt the PoW consensus algorithm for consensus. Still, PoW suffers from low throughput rates, and consumes a lot of energy and computational resources, which is not suitable for energy-scarce edge devices. To further increase the throughput rate and reduce the energy consumption of edge devices, the consensus among council nodes adopts the Practical Byzantine Fault Tolerance (PBFT) algorithm [2]. PBFT has a high throughput in small-scale networks that can handle 100 transactions per second [22], more than ten times the PoW. PBFT can tolerate malicious nodes that account for less than $1/3$ of all nodes. Furthermore, PBFT does not require mining, which effectively reduces the energy consumption caused by consensus. In PBFT, each node takes turns to be the primary, and the primary will receive the request and launch a broadcast process to send the request to other nodes in the network. In FedLyra, the master node also needs to filter duplicate requests. A duplicate request is defined as an aggregation of the same local updates.

4   Evaluation Results

In this section, we evaluate the feasibility of FedLyra. We first analyze the training performance of FedLyra with different sizes of networks and different proportions of malicious nodes. Then, we analyze the impact of different reputation thresholds on the speed of detection and the risk of misclassification.

4.1   Experiment Setting

We conduct experiments on two benchmarks: Fashion-MNIST [23] and Cifar-10 [12]. We transform both into non-i.i.d. datasets, and each node will train based on its local dataset. We use Fashion-MNIST to construct evenly assigned dataset, meaning each node has the same number of local images. Fashion-MNIST contains a training set of 60,000 samples and a test set of 10,000 samples. We sort the training set by label, divide it into 200 slices, and distribute them equally to each node. In addition, we use Cifar-10 to construct unevenly assigned datasets. In experiments based on Cifar-10, we simulate 50 nodes and distribute the training set containing 50,000 images to these nodes unevenly. Figure 4 shows the size of the local dataset owned by each node. Nodes' training performance may have huge differences in experiments based on unevenly assigned datasets.

In the experiments, we adopt convolutional neural network (CNN) as the local training model[1,2]. The time limit for each round is 10 s. β and γ, the

---

[1] The CNN network trained on Cifar has 6 layer with the following structure: $3 \times 3 \times 64/128/256/512$ Convolutional $\rightarrow 2 \times 2$ MaxPool $\rightarrow 2048$ Fully connected $\rightarrow$ SoftMax.

[2] The CNN network trained on Fashion-MNIST has 5 layer with the following structure: $3 \times 3 \times 16/32/64$ Convolutional $\rightarrow 2 \times 2$ MaxPool $\rightarrow 576$ Fully connected $\rightarrow$ SoftMax.

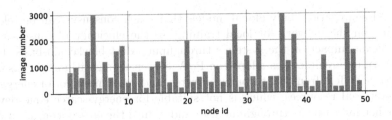

Fig. 4. Number of images owned by 50 nodes in experiment based on Cifar-10

weight of the dataset size in $n(\frac{d_i}{d_{all}})$, are fixed to 2 and 10, respectively. For the weight of historical reputation, $\zeta = 0.3$. Reputation threshold is 0.3 The initial weight of the aggregation α_0 is set to 0.9. The node learns 5 epochs locally before uploading the local update. The learning rate is set as 0.001.

In the experiment, we tested FedLyra's ability to resist malicious attacks by simulating malicious nodes. Malicious nodes will intentionally upload a neural network composed of random parameters. The parameters of the network are uniformly distributed random integers ranging from 0 to 10. These useless models may be involved in the aggregation, thereby disrupting the global model of the system.

4.2   Learning Performance of FedLyra

We first test the performance of FedLyra in scenarios where no malicious parties are involved. The FedAvg algorithm proposed by McMahan et al. [18] and the FedAsync algorithm proposed by Xie et al. [24] are adopted as the benchmark for synchronous federated learning and asynchronous federated learning, respectively. Figure 5 shows the performance of the three algorithms for the federated learning task base on unevenly assigned Cifar-10 in the absence of malicious nodes. The number of nodes is 50. As shown in Fig. 5, although the precision and loss of the three are not much different after the model approaches convergence, compared to the other two algorithms, FedLyra has a faster learning speed and the best learning effect. This is because FedLyra optimizes the weights of node updates in the aggregation process based on the size of local data. The weights of updates from nodes with more local data will be increased, and the quality of these updates tends to be better than updates from nodes with only a small amount of data. Figure 6 shows the accuracy and loss of the three algorithms for federated learning tasks on FashionMNIST with 100 goods nodes. We can conclude that FedLyra has a performance that is not inferior to the benchmark algorithm in a scenario with no malicious node interference.

We conduct experiments with malicious node participation based on an evenly assigned dataset, thereby better examining our proposed reputation mechanism by eliminating the influence of differences in the size of local data. Figure 7 shows the performance of each algorithm on FashionMNIST for federated learning tasks when 10% of the nodes are malicious nodes. The number of total nodes is 100. It is observed that FedAsync and FedAvg can hardly train an available model even

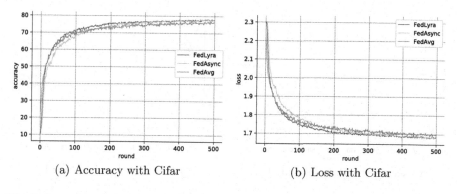

(a) Accuracy with Cifar   (b) Loss with Cifar

Fig. 5. Learning performance based on unevenly assigned dataset without malicious nodes

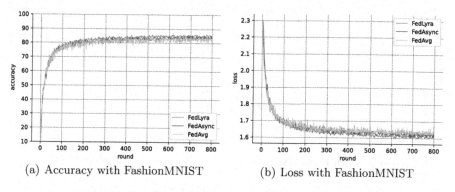

(a) Accuracy with FashionMNIST   (b) Loss with FashionMNIST

Fig. 6. Learning performance based on evenly assigned dataset without malicious nodes

if 90% of the nodes are good nodes. Compared to the two benchmark algorithms, FedLyra performs much better. After screening and excluding malicious nodes, FedLyra can perform federated learning based on the remaining common nodes, reaching accuracy rates of nearly 85% on FashionMNIST. In contrast, the accuracy rate of FedAsync and FedAvg cannot even reach 40%.

To verify the reliability of FedLyra in networks of different scales, we test FedLyra in networks with 25, 50, 75, and 100 nodes based on FashionMNIST. In these networks, 30% of the nodes are malicious. We distribute the dataset equally to each node. It can be seen from Fig. 8 that FedLyra can accomplish the learning task in networks of different sizes. As the number of nodes decreases, the learning performance improves, and the time affected by malicious nodes is relatively reduced. This phenomenon is due to 1) Compared with large-scale networks, small networks have fewer malicious nodes (a 100-node network contains 30 malicious nodes, compared to 25 nodes with only 7 malicious nodes) 2) In a small-scale network, the local data of a single node is larger, thus the quality of the trained model of the common node is higher, making the inefficient model uploaded by the malicious node more noticeable (in a 25-node network, each

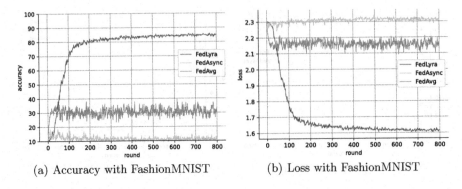

(a) Accuracy with FashionMNIST   (b) Loss with FashionMNIST

Fig. 7. Learning performance with 10% malicious nodes

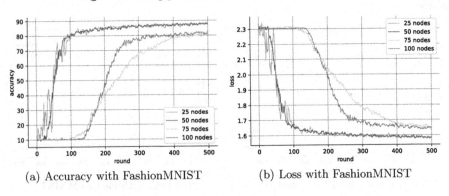

(a) Accuracy with FashionMNIST   (b) Loss with FashionMNIST

Fig. 8. Learning performance under different size networks

node has 1200 Pictures, and in a network of 100 nodes, each node has only 400 pictures).

In order to further analyze the influence of malicious nodes, we continue to conduct experiments on FashionMNIST to analyze the influence of different proportions (0% to 30%) of malicious nodes on model training. From Fig. 9, it can be seen that as the proportion of malicious nodes continues to rise, the number of rounds FedLyra needs to achieve the same accuracy continues to rise, meaning that more malicious nodes will lead to more time spent on eliminating them, which is also consistent with intuition. Meanwhile, after the model converges, the effect of learning with a smaller proportion of malicious nodes will be slightly better than the environment with more malicious nodes. However, the difference is not evident on the FashionMNIST dataset due to the relatively low difficulty of the FashionMNIST dataset. This influence will be more pronounced on more difficult datasets such as cifar100.

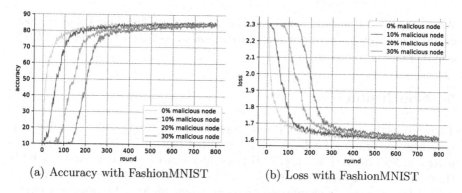

(a) Accuracy with FashionMNIST   (b) Loss with FashionMNIST

Fig. 9. Influence of different proportions of malicious nodes

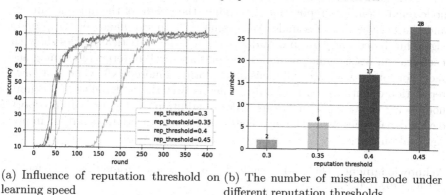

(a) Influence of reputation threshold on (b) The number of mistaken node under
learning speed   different reputation thresholds

Fig. 10. Influence of different proportions of malicious nodes

4.3 Impact of Reputation Threshold

In FedLyra, the strength of detection of malicious nodes can be adjusted by reputation threshold, i.e., a higher reputation threshold means that there is a greater possibility of judging a suspicious node with low reputation as a malicious node. We conducted experiments based on FashionMNIST to explore the impact of different reputation thresholds on the ability to protect against malicious nodes. The proportion of malicious nodes is fixed at 30% in the experiment. As shown in Fig. 10(a), the higher the reputation threshold, the faster FedLyra detects malicious nodes. For example, achieving 50% classification accuracy takes more than two hundred rounds with a threshold of 0.3, but less than fifty rounds when the threshold is 0.45. However, this does not mean that the higher the reputation threshold, the better the learning effect, because an excessive reputation threshold may lead to mistaking a large number of common nodes. Figure 10(b) shows the number of good nodes that are mistaken for malicious nodes under different reputation thresholds. It can be seen from the figure that the higher the reputation threshold, the greater the number of nodes that are misjudged, i.e., the probability of misjudgment continues to increase. Mistaking common nodes means inevitably losing a portion of the dataset, which in turn reduces model accuracy.

5   Conclusion

To improves the security and efficiency of federated learning under unstable edge networks, we propose FedLyra, a decentralized blockchain-based asynchronous federated learning architecture. FedLyra achieves trustworthiness and reliability through blockchain. To increase the system throughput and avoid the latency caused by synchronous communication, we adopt an asynchronous mechanism and the council-based consensus. We also propose a quantification mechanism for node reputation. The reputation determines the weight of the uploaded updates and the permissions of a node. We evaluate the performance of the proposed algorithm based on two types of datasets, and the statistical results show that FedLyra can resist malicious nodes and performs well in terms of learning accuracy. For future work, we will focus on exploring a more flexible and state-aware reputation quantification mechanism that reduces the probability of a common node being treated as a malicious node. In addition to this, we will incorporate device capabilities as a reference factor in council selection to further improve aggregation efficiency.

Acknowledgment. This work is supported by National Natural Science Foundation of China (62072049).

References

1. Ali, M.S., Vecchio, M., Pincheira, M., Dolui, K., Antonelli, F., Rehmani, M.H.: Applications of blockchains in the Internet of Things: a comprehensive survey. IEEE Commun. Surv. Tutor. **21**(2), 1676–1717 (2019)
2. Castro, M., Liskov, B.: Practical byzantine fault tolerance. In: Seltzer, M.I., Leach, P.J. (eds.) Proceedings of the Third USENIX Symposium on Operating Systems Design and Implementation (OSDI), New Orleans, Louisiana, USA, 22–25 February 1999, pp. 173–186. USENIX Association (1999)
3. Chen, M., Mao, B., Ma, T.: FedSA: a staleness-aware asynchronous Federated Learning algorithm with non-IID data. Future Gener. Comput. Syst. **120**, 1–12 (2021)
4. Chen, Y., Ning, Y., Slawski, M., Rangwala, H.: Asynchronous online federated learning for edge devices with non-IID data. In: 2020 IEEE International Conference on Big Data (Big Data), pp. 15–24 (2020)
5. Dong, S., Wang, P., Abbas, K.: A survey on deep learning and its applications. Comput. Sci. Rev. **40**, 100379 (2021)
6. Feng, L., Zhao, Y., Guo, S., Qiu, X., Li, W., Yu, P.: Blockchain-based asynchronous federated learning for Internet of Things. IEEE Trans. Comput. 1 (2021)

7. Jin, H., Yan, N., Mortazavi, M.: Simulating aggregation algorithms for empirical verification of resilient and adaptive federated learning. In: 2020 IEEE/ACM International Conference on Big Data Computing, Applications and Technologies (BDCAT), pp. 124–133 (2020)
8. Kang, J., Xiong, Z., Niyato, D., Xie, S., Zhang, J.: Incentive mechanism for reliable federated learning: a joint optimization approach to combining reputation and contract theory. IEEE Internet Things J. **6**(6), 10700–10714 (2019)
9. Khan, L.U., et al.: Federated learning for edge networks: resource optimization and incentive mechanism. IEEE Commun. Mag. **58**(10), 88–93 (2020)
10. Kim, H., Park, J., Bennis, M., Kim, S.L.: Blockchained on-device federated learning. IEEE Commun. Lett. **24**(6), 1279–1283 (2020)
11. Kingma, D.P., Ba, J.: Adam: a method for stochastic optimization. In: Bengio, Y., LeCun, Y. (eds.) 3rd International Conference on Learning Representations, ICLR 2015, San Diego, CA, USA, 7–9 May 2015, Conference Track Proceedings (2015). http://arxiv.org/abs/1412.6980
12. Krizhevsky, A., Hinton, G., et al.: Learning multiple layers of features from tiny images (2009)
13. Li, T., Sahu, A.K., Talwalkar, A., Smith, V.: Federated learning: challenges, methods, and future directions. IEEE Sig. Process. Mag. **37**(3), 50–60 (2020)
14. Li, T., Sahu, A.K., Zaheer, M., Sanjabi, M., Talwalkar, A., Smith, V.: Federated optimization in heterogeneous networks. In: Proceedings of Machine Learning and Systems 2020, MLSys 2020, Austin, TX, USA, 2–4 March 2020. mlsys.org (2020)
15. Li, Y., Chen, C., Liu, N., Huang, H., Zheng, Z., Yan, Q.: A blockchain-based decentralized federated learning framework with committee consensus. IEEE Netw. **35**(1), 234–241 (2021)
16. Liu, Y., Qu, Y., Xu, C., Hao, Z., Gu, B.: Blockchain-enabled asynchronous federated learning in edge computing. Sensors **21**(10), 3335 (2021)
17. Mao, Y., You, C., Zhang, J., Huang, K., Letaief, K.B.: A survey on mobile edge computing: the communication perspective. IEEE Commun. Surv. Tutor. **19**(4), 2322–2358 (2017)
18. McMahan, B., Moore, E., Ramage, D., Hampson, S., Aguera y Arcas, B.: Communication-efficient learning of deep networks from decentralized data. In: Proceedings of the 20th International Conference on Artificial Intelligence and Statistics. Proceedings of Machine Learning Research, vol. 54, pp. 1273–1282. PMLR, 20–22 April 2017
19. Reisizadeh, A., Mokhtari, A., Hassani, H., Jadbabaie, A., Pedarsani, R.: FedPAQ: a communication-efficient federated learning method with periodic averaging and quantization. In: Proceedings of the Twenty Third International Conference on Artificial Intelligence and Statistics. Proceedings of Machine Learning Research, vol. 108, pp. 2021–2031. PMLR, 26–28 August 2020
20. Tak, A., Cherkaoui, S.: Federated edge learning: design issues and challenges. IEEE Netw. **35**(2), 252–258 (2021)
21. Wang, X., Han, Y., Wang, C., Zhao, Q., Chen, X., Chen, M.: In-Edge AI: intelligentizing mobile edge computing, caching and communication by federated learning. IEEE Netw. **33**(5), 156–165 (2019)
22. Wu, M., Wang, K., Cai, X., Guo, S., Guo, M., Rong, C.: A comprehensive survey of blockchain: from theory to IoT applications and beyond. IEEE Internet Things J. **6**(5), 8114–8154 (2019)
23. Xiao, H., Rasul, K., Vollgraf, R.: Fashion-MNIST: a novel image dataset for benchmarking machine learning algorithms. CoRR abs/1708.07747 (2017). http://arxiv.org/abs/1708.07747

24. Xie, C., Koyejo, S., Gupta, I.: Asynchronous federated optimization. CoRR abs/1903.03934 (2019). http://arxiv.org/abs/1903.03934
25. Yaga, D., Mell, P., Roby, N., Scarfone, K.: Blockchain technology overview. arXiv preprint arXiv:1906.11078, October 2018
26. Zhou, Z., Chen, X., Li, E., Zeng, L., Luo, K., Zhang, J.: Edge intelligence: paving the last mile of artificial intelligence with edge computing. Proc. IEEE **107**(8), 1738–1762 (2019)

One-Time Anonymous Certificateless Signcryption Scheme Based on Blockchain

Yan Jin[1,2], Chunxiao Ye[1,2(✉)], Mengqing Yang[1,2], and Chunming Ye[1,2]

[1] College of Computer Science, Chongqing University, Chongqing, China
{jiny,yecx}@cqu.edu.cn
[2] Key Laboratory of CPS-DSC, MoE, Chongqing University, Chongqing, China
yangmengqing@pku.edu.cn

Abstract. The rapid increase of users in the blockchain makes it possible to exchange a large amount of data every moment. Since the information published on blockchain is recorded and cannot be tampered with, there is the problem of leaking the real identity of users under the big data clustering attack. Meanwhile, the existing key generation center (KGC) needs a secure channel to transmit partial private keys, which makes partial private keys depending on the channel of interaction and creates a private key security problem. In this paper, we propose a one-time anonymous certificateless signcryption (OTACLSC) scheme based on blockchain. We securely use the public channel to improve the security of the private key. By constructing a one-time pseudonym public key in the blockchain to achieve anti-identity leakage, the communication initiator constructs the pseudonym public key of both communication parties to avoid the reuse of the pseudonym public key. Then we prove the security of the scheme under the random oracle model and compare it with other schemes. Our scheme has less computation cost and shorter ciphertext length while maintaining more reliable security.

Keywords: Blockchain · Big data clustering attack · Certificateless signcryption · One-time pseudonym · Random oracle model

1 Introduction

As an emerging technology, blockchain has attracted extensive attention in the industry due to its decentralization, anonymity, tamper-proof, and other characteristics [25]. To ensure the security of communication, the communicating parties need to authenticate each other's identity and often need to go to verify the user's certificate through public key infrastructure (PKI). In order to simplify the certificate management process, Al-Riyami and Paterson [1] proposed the concept of certificateless public key cryptography on the basis of the identity-based encryption system (IBE) [20]. Based on the private key generator (PKG), the certificateless public key cryptosystem retains the process of incorporating user ID into the generation of public-private key pairs and uses a trusted third-party key generation center (KGC).

© ICST Institute for Computer Sciences, Social Informatics and Telecommunications Engineering 2022
Published by Springer Nature Switzerland AG 2022. All Rights Reserved
H. Gao et al. (Eds.): CollaborateCom 2022, LNICST 460, pp. 533–551, 2022.
https://doi.org/10.1007/978-3-031-24383-7_29

Using the certificateless algorithm, the generation of the public key requires a partial private key, and most certificateless schemes use a centralized KGC to generate the partial private key and send it to the user through a secure channel. There is no doubt that centralized KGC is convenient and available, but it cannot avoid the possibility of some common security flaws, such as man-in-the-middle attacks, and KGC compromised attacks. It is important to note that the use of secure channels makes the privacy of partial private keys dependent on secure channels. Once a secure channel is controlled by an attacker, the user's partial private key may be compromised, which is a serious security problem for both the cryptographic system and the communication system. In addition, maintaining a secure channel increases the complexity of communication systems and requires additional costs.

At the same time, blockchain technology, as a trust solution in the digital era, has a certain contradiction between its decentralized transparency and the reality of the required privacy. Posting transaction information in blockchain requires the use of user accounts, and data such as transactions are traceable and cannot be tampered with, which means vulnerability to big data clustering attacks. When we interact in the real world and the virtual world, the public key will be recorded and saved all the time, and the user's transaction records will be collected in large quantities, inevitably leaving traces that can be traced from transactions and other information to the real identity information [24]. The missing privacy protection is unacceptable in the real world, because not only individuals want to protect the privacy of their property information and other private information, but also any business or organization wants to keep its sensitive and valuable data confidential.

1.1 Related Work

Li et al. [13] built the certificateless scheme on the Internet of Things and divided it into the online/offline signcryption scheme. To reduce the tedious operations of online signcryption, the scheme eliminated all the tedious operations in the online stage and transferred them to the offline stage. To realize identity authentication on the chain, Fromknecht et al. [10] proposed the combination of PKI and blockchain. Under the characteristics of blockchain, Fromknecht et al. build a distributed PKI, which is responsible for managing the certificates disclosed by users on the chain. Based on the research of Fromknecht et al., Axon [4] proposed PKI privacy protection based on blockchain to reduce the risk of user privacy disclosure. The scheme uses online and offline double keys to protect user privacy. However, the solution does not solve the inherent problem of maintaining certificates at a high cost by building PKI on a blockchain. Therefore, Ao et al. [3] to solve the certificate management problem of PKI on the blockchain, constructed PKG on Ethereum, and constructed a blockchain-based IBE signature scheme to solve the certificate management problem. At the same time, the scheme combines PKG and smart contract on the blockchain to jointly undertake the key generation and applies the blockchain to the key generation process. Li et al. [14] considered that the disadvantage of certificateless cryptography is that verification of public key requires pre-broadcast, while blockchain provides a platform for sharing public information. This means that a user's public key can be shared via blockchain, enabling certificateless encryption in a blockchain-based Internet of Things system. Gervais et al. [11] then proposed a certificateless authenticated key agreement for wireless body area networks on the blockchain.

Tseng et al. [21] proposed an anonymous certificateless multi-receiver encryption scheme, which can verify the sender's identity while ensuring anonymity. Pang et al. [18] proposed an anonymous certificateless multi-message and multi-receiver signcryption scheme, which realized the anonymity of the receiver by the sender authorizing the decryptable receiver. Although the scheme protects the privacy of the receiver in ad-hoc networks, it does not consider the anonymity of the sender. Further, considering that the security of the partial private key depends on interactive channels, Pang et al. [17] proposed an anonymous certificateless multi-receiver signcryption scheme, which allows KGC to send a pseudo-partial private key to the user in the key extraction algorithm using only public channels. The specified user can extract the real partial private key from the pseudo-partial private key, while other users cannot. Mandal et al. [16] implemented secure access control over the Internet of Things through certificateless signcryption and communicated securely by establishing session keys. Guo et al. [12] proposed a controllable lightweight secure certificateless signature algorithm based on the federated blockchain security architecture of Hyperledger Fabric and edge computing. KGC saves all seeds for the user and restores the pseudonym and public key that belong to a particular ID. In low security, a single pseudonym and multiple keys are used. In high security, each pseudonym and key can only be used once. Although anonymity is guaranteed, KGC still maintains a list of pseudonyms required, and once KGC is in the hands of an attacker, the pseudonym list is also exposed. Cheng et al. [8] proposed a lightweight key negotiation mechanism using blockchain, certificateless encryption, and elliptic curve encryption, choosing the smart contract to act as KGC to provide session keys. Wang et al. [22] proposed a certificateless scheme using a smart contract on Ethereum to replace the role of KGC. Xu et al. [23] replaced the pseudonym form of user identity with a public key to achieve a certain certificateless anonymity and considered queries on blockchain to construct a hash table with user identity hash value and public key as key-value pairs.

1.2 Our Contribution

The main contributions of this paper are summarized as follows:

- We design a new anonymous certificateless signcryption scheme on blockchain for mitigating the aforementioned possible attacks and the interaction process does not use a secure channel.
- We design a one-time anonymous algorithm, which further disguises the public key based on the public key. The sender actively generates the pseudonym public keys of both communicating parties and does not need to maintain the list.

– We give anonymous authentication on blockchain and prove the security of the scheme through the random oracle model. Compared with other schemes, this scheme has better performance through experiments.

1.3   Organization

This paper is organized as follows. Section 2 gives the corresponding background, algorithm model, and security model of the one-time anonymous certificateless signcryption (OTACLSC) scheme. Section 3 presents a specific OTACLSC scheme. After that, Sect. 4 gives the security analysis of the scheme. Section 5 simulates the scheme and performs performance analysis. Finally, the paper is summarized in Sect. 6.

2   Preliminaries

2.1   Bilinear Mapping

Suppose there are two cyclic groups G_1, G_2, where G_1 is an additive group of prime order p, G_2 is a multiplicative group of prime order p, P is a random generator of G_1, and there exists a mapping $\hat{e} : G_1 \times G_1 \to G_2$, satisfying the following properties:

Bilinear: Any $P, Q \in G_1$, $a, b \in Z_p^*$, there is $\hat{e}(aP, bQ) = \hat{e}(P, Q)^{ab}$.
Nondegenerate: There is $P, Q \in G_1$, such that $\hat{e}(P, Q) \neq 1$.
Computable: Any $P, Q \in G_1$, $\hat{e}(P, Q)$ can be calculated effectively.

2.2   Hard Problems

The security of this paper depends on the difficulty of the following hard problems.

Definition 1. *Given groups G_1 and G_2 of the same prime order p, P is a generator of G_1, there exists the mapping $\hat{e} : G_1 \times G_1 \to G_2$. The q-bilinear Diffie-Hellman inversion (q-BDHI) problem is given $(P, \alpha P, \alpha^2 P, ..., \alpha^q P)$ to compute $\hat{e}(P, P)^{\frac{1}{\alpha}}$, where $\alpha \in Z_p^*$.*

Definition 2. *Given groups G_1 and G_2 of the same prime order p, P is a generator of G_1, there exists the mapping $\hat{e} : G_1 \times G_1 \to G_2$. The q-strong Diffie-Hellman (q-SDH) problem is given $(P, \alpha P, \alpha^2 P, ..., \alpha^q P)$ to compute $\hat{e}(w, \frac{1}{\alpha+w} P)$, where $\alpha \in Z_p^*$.*

2.3   Smart Contract

The smart contract is a computerized transaction protocol that can be verified digitally and automatically execute the terms of the contract and can conduct trusted transactions without a third party, without the need for an agency [9]. In this paper, the smart contract SC_{KGC} is used to generate keys instead of KGC and distribute them to the corresponding users, and any legitimate user can query the public parameters of this system. Meanwhile, the receiver can look up the passively generated pseudonym public key.

2.4 Algorithm Model

There are seven steps for our OTACLSC scheme.

Setup. The algorithm is run by smart contract SC_{KGC} on the blockchain system, inputs the security parameter k, generates the master secret key s and system parameter $params$. System parameters have been omitted in the following steps for simplicity.

Set Partial Private Key. The algorithm is run by smart contract SC_{KGC}, inputs a user's identity $ID \in \{0,1\}^*$ and a master secret key s, outputs a partial private key D_{ID}.

Set Public/Private Key. The algorithm is run by the user, inputs a partial private key D_{ID}, outputs public key PK_{ID}, private key SK_{ID}, and user identity tag M_{ID}.

Set Pseudonym Public Key. The algorithm is run by the user, inputs the public key PK_A of the sender and the public key PK_B of the receiver, and outputs the pseudonym public key PPK_A and PPK_B of both parties.

Signcryption. The algorithm is run by the user, inputs a message m, a sender's private key SK_A and identity tag M_A, and the pseudonym public key PPK_A of the sender and the pseudonym public key PPK_B of the receiver, and outputs a ciphertext δ.

Check. The algorithm is run by smart contract SC_{KGC}, inputs the pseudonym public key PPK_B submitted by the sender and the private key SK_B submitted by the receiver, and outputs the pseudonym public key PPK_B of the receiver.

Verification. The algorithm is run by the user, inputs the ciphertext δ, the sender's pseudonym public key PPK_A, and the receiver's pseudonym public key PPK_B and the private key SK_B. If the verification is successful, message m is output; otherwise, failure symbol $\perp$ is output.

2.5 Security Model

In this paper, we need to consider two types of adversaries [1]. Adversary $\Im_I$ does not possess the master secret key but can legally replace the pseudonym public key. $\Im_{II}$ knows the master secret key, but it cannot replace the user's pseudonym public key. In addition, a signcryption scheme should satisfy confidentiality (i.e. indistinguishability against adaptive chosen ciphertext attack) and unforgeability (i.e. existential unforgeability against adaptive chosen messages attack) [5].

Definition 3. *The OTACLSC scheme is IND-CCA2 secure if adversary $\Im$ does not have a polynomial probability time t has at least a non-negligible probability advantage $\epsilon \geq Adv^{IND-CCA2}(\Im)$ in the game.*

The first game (Game-I) is a confidentiality game played between adversary $\Im_I$ and challenger C.

Initial: Challenger C generates system parameters and sends them to adversary $\Im_I$.

Phase 1: Adversary $\Im_I$ performs adaptive queries.

- Partial private key queries: $\Im_I$ submits an ID to C, C generates partial private key D_{ID} and sends it to $\Im_I$.
- Private key queries: $\Im_I$ submits an ID to C, C generates private key SK_{ID} and sends it to $\Im_I$.
- Pseudonym public key queries: $\Im_I$ submits an ID to C, C generates pseudonym public key PPK_{ID} and sends it to $\Im_I$.
- Pseudonym public key replacement queries: $\Im_I$ can replace the pseudonym public key PPK_{ID} with a selected value, and save it as a new pseudonym public key from C.
- Signcryption queries: $\Im_I$ selects a message m, a sender's ID_i and a receiver's ID_j to send to C. C generates the sender's private key SK_i, pseudonym public key PPK_i and receiver's pseudonym public key PPK_j. Then, C generates the ciphertext δ and sends it to $\Im_I$.
- Unsigncryption queries: $\Im_I$ sends the ciphertext δ, a sender's ID_i and a receiver's ID_j to C. C generates the receiver's private key SK_j, pseudonym public key PPK_i and receiver's pseudonym public key PPK_j. Then, C generates the message m and sends it to $\Im_I$.

Challenge: $\Im_I$ decides when phase 1 ends. $\Im_I$ selects two message (m_0, m_1) of the same length, a sender's identity ID_A and a receiver's identity ID_B, and sends them to C, on which it wishes to be challenged. Among them, ID_B cannot be submitted to the private key query in phase 1. ID_B also cannot be used for both the partial private key query and the pseudonym public key replacement query. C chooses a random bit $\beta \in \{0, 1\}$ and generates the ciphertext δ^* from the *Signcryption* algorithm and sends it to $\Im_I$.

Phase 2: Adversary $\Im_I$ performs adaptive queries, as in phase 1. But $\Im_I$ cannot perform a private key query on the target identity ID_B. If the pseudonym public key PPK_B of the target identity ID_B has been replaced before the challenge phase, $\Im_I$ cannot query its partial private key. $\Im_I$ cannot ask an unsigncryption query on the target ciphertext δ^* unless the pseudonym public key PPK_A or PPK_B has been replaced after the challenge phase.

Guess: $\Im_I$ guesses β^*, if $\beta^* = \beta$, then game wins. $\Im_I$'s probability of winning this game is $Adv^{IND-CCA2-I}(\Im_I) = |2Pr[\beta^* = \beta] - 1|$.

The second game (Game-II) is a confidentiality game played between adversary $\Im_{II}$ and challenger C.

Adversary $\Im_{II}$ performs queries as in Game-I. Among them, there is no need to perform partial private key queries. Because $\Im_{II}$ can get master secret key s. $\Im_{II}$'s probability of winning is $Adv^{IND-CCA2-II}(\Im_{II}) = |2Pr[\beta^* = \beta] - 1|$.

Since the adversary knows the private keys of all senders, the Game-I and Game-II have the insider security in terms of confidentiality [2]. The insider security assures the forward security of the signcryption scheme. It means that if the sender's private key is disclosed, confidentiality is still maintained.

Definition 4. *The OTACLSC scheme is EUF-CMA secure if adversary $\Im$ does not have a polynomial probability time t has at least a non-negligible probability advantage ϵ in the game.*

The third game (Game-III) is an unforgeability game played between adversary $\Im_I$ and challenger C.

Adversary $\Im_I$ performs adaptive queries, as in the Game-I.

Forgery: $\Im_I$ outputs the ciphertext δ^*, a sender's identity ID_A and a receiver's identity ID_B. $\Im_I$ will win the game if the target ciphertext δ^* can be used to obtain the target message m^* by an unsigncryption query, $\Im_I$ cannot ask a private key query, both the partial private key query and the pseudonym public key replacement query for ID_A, and a signcryption query on the target message m^*. The advantage of $\Im_I$ is defined as the probability that it wins.

The fourth game (Game-IV) is an unforgeability game played between adversary $\Im_{II}$ and challenger C.

Adversary $\Im_{II}$ performs queries as in Game-II and Game-III.

In the Game-III and Game-IV, the receiver's private key SK_B is allowed to be known to the adversary. For unforgeability, the insider security can be obtained [2].

3 One-Time Anonymous Certificateless Signcryption Scheme

In this section, we assume that Alice is the sender A and Bob is the receiver B. In the following steps, they are abbreviated as A and B.

Setup. Input the security parameter k, select two cyclic groups $<G_1, G_2>$, where G_1 is the additive group of a large prime order $p > 2^k$, G_2 is the multiplicative group of the same prime order p, and there exists the mapping $\hat{e} : G_1 \times G_1 \to G_2$. P is a random generator in G_1, $g = \hat{e}(P, P)$. There are four hash functions $H_1 : \{0,1\}^* \to Z_p^*$, $H_2 : G_1 \to Z_p^*$, $H_3 : G_2 \to \{0,1\}^n$ and $H_4 : \{0,1\}^n \times G_2 \times G_1 \times G_2 \to Z_p^*$. Here n is the number of bits of a message to be sent. SC_{KGC} randomly selects the master secret key $s \in Z_p^*$, and set $P_{Pub} = sP$. Publish system parameters $params = <G_1, G_2, \hat{e}, n, p, P, P_{Pub}, g, H_1, H_2, H_3, H_4>$ on blockchain and secretly store the master secret key s.

Set Partial Private Key. The sender A inputs the identity ID_A used to construct $C_A = ID_A + ID_A P_{Pub}$ and $E_A = ID_A P$. Since the master secret key s is known only to SC_{KGC}, the sender can transmit the identity ID_A over the public channel. The smart contract SC_{KGC} is able to get the ID_A by means of $C_A - sE_A = ID_A + ID_A sP - sID_A P = ID_A$. Then, SC_{KGC} calculates

$D_A = sH_1(ID_A)$ and returns $CK_A = D_A + sE_A$ to A through the public channel, where D_A is the partial private key.

Set Public/Private Key. The sender A receives the CK_A and calculates the partial private key D_A by $CK_A - ID_A P_{Pub} = D_A + sE_A - ID_A sP = D_A + sID_A P - sID_A P = D_A$, and then confirms that the partial private key D_A is valid by whether the equation $\hat{e}(D_A, P) = \hat{e}(sH_1(ID_A), P) = \hat{e}(H_1(ID_A), sP) = \hat{e}(H_1(ID_A), P_{Pub})$ holds. If it holds, the partial private key D_A is correct.

The sender A generates $V_A = D_A + u_A$ and constructs the public key $PK_A = V_A P \in G_1$ according to the system parameters, where $u_A \in Z_p^*$. Then A randomly selects the secret value $x_A \in Z_p^*$, makes $Y_A = x_A + H_2(PK_A)$, generates user identity tag $M_A = g^{Y_A^{-1}} \in G_2$ and constructs private key $SK_A = Y_A^{-1} V_A^{-1} P$. The secret values u_A and x_A and the private key SK_A require local secret storage, while the public key PK_A and user identity tag M_A will be publicly published on blockchain.

Set Pseudonym Public Key. Input the public key PK_A of sender A and the public key PK_B of receiver B, and randomly select $\theta \in Z_p^*$ to generate the pseudonym public key $PPK_A = (\theta + H_2(\theta PK_B))PK_A$ of A and the pseudonym public key $PPK_B = (\theta + H_2(\theta PK_A))PK_B$ of B. The random number θ selected in the pseudonym public key is not public and does not need to be saved. A randomly generates the one-time pseudonym public key of the communication parties. The pseudonym public keys PPK_A and PPK_B are embedded in the sender and receiver of the transaction and published on blockchain.

Signcryption. The sender A randomly selects $\gamma \in Z_p^*$ and computes $\alpha = \gamma(\theta + H_2(\theta PK_A))$, $r = g^\alpha$ and $c = m \oplus H_3(r)$. Then get PPK_B to compute $T = \gamma PPK_B$ and $Z = (\theta + H_2(\theta PK_B))^{-1} SK_A + H_3(r)P$. A makes $h = H_4(m, M_A, PPK_B, r)$ and $S = (\alpha + h)(\theta + H_2(\theta PK_B))^{-1} V_A^{-1} P$. When publishing the ciphertext $\delta = (c, T, Z, S, t_1)$ on blockchain through the transaction, add the current timestamp t_1, where t_i is the timestamp.

Check. The sender A constructs $L_A = PPK_B + (\theta + H_2(\theta PK_A))P_{pub}$, $K_A = (\theta + H_2(\theta PK_A))P$, and submits $\{L_A, K_A, t_2\}$. Receiver B randomly selects $\vartheta, \tau \in Z_p^*$, generates $L_B = \vartheta Y_B + \tau P_{pub}$ and $K_B = \tau P$, and searches for the passively generated pseudonym public key PPK_B by submitting $\{L_B, K_B, \vartheta^{-1} SK_B, t_3\}$ to SC_{KGC}. SC_{KGC} verifies the timestamp $t_3 - t_2 < \triangle t_1$ and receives the input that meets the preset time threshold $\triangle t_1$. The pseudonym public key PPK_B can be transmitted over a public channel by way of $L_A - sK_A = PPK_B + (\theta + H_2(\theta PK_A))P_{pub} - (\theta + H_2(\theta PK_A))P_{pub} = PPK_B$. Similarly, the input submitted by receiver B can also be transmitted publicly according to $L_B - sK_B = \vartheta Y_B + \tau P_{pub} - \tau P_{pub} = \vartheta Y_B$. After calculating PPK_B and ϑY_B, determine if the equation holds by using Eq. 1.

$$\begin{aligned} \hat{e}(\vartheta Y_B \cdot PPK_B, \vartheta^{-1} SK_B) &= \hat{e}(Y_B(\theta + H_2(\theta PK_A))PK_B, SK_B) \\ &= \hat{e}(Y_B(\theta + H_2(\theta PK_A))V_B P, Y_B^{-1} V_B^{-1} P) \\ &= \hat{e}((\theta + H_2(\theta PK_A))P, P) \\ &= \hat{e}(K_A, P). \end{aligned} \tag{1}$$

If it holds, then the passively generated pseudonym public key PPK_B is found. Otherwise, the output is failure symbol $\perp$. After that, SC_{KGC} passes $PPK_B + sK_B$ through the public channel. Based on the random value τ, the receiver B can construct τP_{pub} and recover the pseudonym public key PPK_B according to $PPK_B + sK_B - \tau P_{pub} = PPK_B + sK_B - sK_B = PPK_B$.

Verification. The receiver B searches for the corresponding transaction information based on the obtained pseudonym public key PPK_B and retrieves the ciphertext δ. B verify whether $t_4 - t_1$ is within the time threshold $\triangle t_2$, where t_4 is the current timestamp. B can pass V_B^{-1} and T in the ciphertext δ to get r.

$$
\begin{aligned}
\hat{e}(T, V_B^{-1}P) &= \hat{e}(\gamma(\theta + H_2(\theta PK_A))V_B P, V_B^{-1}P) \\
&= \hat{e}(\gamma(\theta + H_2(\theta PK_A))P, P) \\
&= \hat{e}(\alpha P, P) \\
&= r.
\end{aligned}
\tag{2}
$$

After calculating the r, it can compute $m = c \oplus H_3(r)$. By using the pseudonym public key PPK_A of the sender A and the Z in the ciphertext δ, B can get the identity tag M_A of A.

$$
\begin{aligned}
\hat{e}(PPK_A, Z - H_3(r)P) &= \hat{e}((\theta + H_2(\theta PK_B))PK_A, \\
&\quad (\theta + H_2(\theta PK_B))^{-1}SK_A) \\
&= \hat{e}(V_A P, Y_A^{-1}V_A^{-1}P) \\
&= \hat{e}(P, Y_A^{-1}P) \\
&= M_A.
\end{aligned}
\tag{3}
$$

Then B obtains $h = H_4(m, M_A, PPK_B, r)$ and verifies whether $r = \hat{e}(PPK_A, S)g^{-h}$ holds according to Eq. 4.

$$
\begin{aligned}
\hat{e}(PPK_A, S)g^{-h} &= \hat{e}((\theta + H_2(\theta PK_B))PK_A, (\alpha + h) \\
&\quad (\theta + H_2(\theta PK_B))^{-1}V_A^{-1}P)g^{-h} \\
&= \hat{e}(V_A P, (\alpha + h)V_A^{-1}P)g^{-h} \\
&= \hat{e}(P, (\alpha + h)P)g^{-h} \\
&= g^{(\alpha + h)}g^{-h} \\
&= r.
\end{aligned}
\tag{4}
$$

If it holds, it means that the r calculated in Eq. 2 is correct, thus confirming that the message m is correct, and also detecting and confirming the identity tag M_A. Otherwise, the output is failure symbol $\perp$.

By implementing the above steps, the receiver B completes the OTACLSC verification process (Fig. 1).

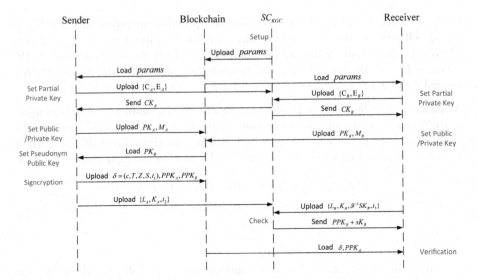

Fig. 1. One-time anonymous certificateless signcryption scheme process.

4   Security Analysis

This section presents the formal and informal security analysis of our scheme to show its resilience against various attacks.

4.1   Formal Security

In this subsection, we use the security model to prove the security of our OTA-CLSC scheme under the random oracle model.

Lemma 1. *Under the random oracle model, if there exists an adversary $\Im_I$ with a non-negligible probability advantage ϵ that wins the IND-CCA2-I security model game. Then C can solve the q-BDHI problem.*

Proof. Given a random instance $(P, \alpha P, \alpha^2 P, ..., \alpha^q P)$ of the q-BDHI problem, C solves the q-BDHI problem using $\Im_I$ and generates the following interaction procedure.

Initial: In Game-I, challenger C runs the *Setup* algorithm, selects the target $l \in \{1, .., q_{H_1}\}$, and generates $e_l \in Z_p^*$ and $w_1, .., w_{l-1}, w_{l+1}, w_q \in Z_p^*$ randomly. C sets $e_i = e_l - w_i$, $X = \alpha Q$, where $i \in \{1, .., l-1, l+1, q\}$, and generates elements $Q \in G_1$ such that there are q-1 pairs $(w_i, \frac{1}{\alpha+w_i}Q)$.

C chooses $c_0, .., c_{q-1} \in Z_p^*$ to expand $f(z) = \prod_{i=1, i\neq l}^{q}(z + w_i)$ into $f(z) = \sum_{j=0}^{q-1} c_j z^j$. Calculate the generating elements $Q = \sum_{j=0}^{q-1} c_j(\alpha^j P) = f(\alpha)P$ and $X = \sum_{j=1}^{q} c_{j-1}(\alpha^j P) = \alpha f(\alpha)P = \alpha Q$. For $(w_i, \frac{1}{\alpha+w_i}Q)$, this can be computed [7] by expanding $f_i(z) = \frac{f(z)}{z+w_i} = \sum_{j=0}^{q-2} d_j z^j$ into $\sum_{j=0}^{q-2} d_j(\alpha^j P) = f_i(\alpha)P = \frac{f(\alpha)}{\alpha+w_i}P = \frac{1}{\alpha+w_i}Q$.

Phase 1: Adversary $\Im_I$ sends a series of queries to C. C maintains the lists corresponding to the queries.

- H_1 queries: For the $H_1(ID_i)$ queries, C returns a result e_i and inserts (ID_i, e_i) in the list L_1.
- H_2 queries: These queries first check if the corresponding H_2 values are set for $H_2(\theta PK_i)$ and returns the value if it exists. Otherwise, C randomly selects $h_{2,i} \in Z_p^*$, sends it to $\Im_I$, and inserts $(\theta PK_i, h_{2,i})$ in the list L_2.
- H_3 queries: These queries first check if the corresponding H_3 values are set for $H_3(r_i)$ and returns the value if it exists. Otherwise, C randomly selects $h_{3,i} \in \{0,1\}^n$, sends it to $\Im_I$, and inserts $(r_i, h_{3,i})$ in the list L_3.
- H_4 queries: These queries first check if the corresponding H_4 values are set for $H_4(m_i, M_i, PPK_i, r_i)$ and returns the value if it exists. Otherwise, C randomly selects $h_{4,i} \in Z_p^*$, sends it to $\Im_I$. In response to the next phase of the queries, C queries $H_3(r_i)$, gets the ciphertext $c_i = m_i \oplus h_{3,i}$ and $\xi_i = r_i \hat{e}(Q, Q)^{h_{4,i}}$, and inserts $(m_i, M_i, PPK_i, r_i, h_{4,i}, c_i, \xi_i)$ in the list L_4.
- Partial private key queries: $\Im_I$ send the identity ID_i to C for partial private key queries, if the target identity $i = l$, then C fails and stops. Otherwise, C knows that $H_1(ID_i) = e_i$ and returns the partial private key se_i to $\Im_I$.
- Private key queries: $\Im_I$ send the identity ID_i to C for private key queries, if the target identity $i = l$, then C fails and stops. Otherwise, C knows the partial private key se_i. Then C checks if there is $(ID_i, PPK_i, u_i, x_i, \theta_i)$ in the list L_{fk}. If not, C randomly selects $u_i, x_i \in Z_p^*$, generates a new information in the list L_{fk} and saves it, and returns the private key $SK_i = (x_i + h_{2,i})^{-1}(se_i + u_i)^{-1}Q$.
- Pseudonym public key queries: $\Im_I$ sends the identity ID_i to C, C checks if there is $(ID_i, PPK_i, u_i, x_i, \theta)$ information in the list L_{fk}, and if it exists, returns the pseudonym public key. Otherwise C selects $\theta \in Z_p^*$ randomly, makes the pseudonym public key $PPK_i = (\theta + h_{2,i})PK_i$, where $PK_i = (se_i + u_i)Q$, and inserts $(ID_i, PPK_i, u_i, x_i, \theta)$ in the list L_{fk} and return the pseudonym public key.
- Pseudonym public key replacement queries: $\Im_I$ sends the replaced pseudonym public key PPK_i of the identity ID_i to C, C updates the list L_{fk} and reset the information $(ID_i, PPK_i, \perp, \perp, \perp)$ of the ID_i.
- Signcryption queries: $\Im_I$ sends the message m, the sender's ID_i and the receiver's ID_j to C. If the target identity $l \neq i$, then C knows the private key SK_i of the sender and returns the result according to the *Signcryption* algorithm. If the target identity $l = i$ but $l \neq j$, then C knows the private key SK_j of the receiver. C randomly selects $\eta, \theta, h \in Z_p^*$ and computes $S = \eta\theta^{-1}(se_j + u_j)^{-1}Q$, $T = \eta PPK_l - hPPK_j = \eta(\theta + h_{2,l})(se_l + u_l)Q - h(\theta + h_{2,j})(se_j + u_j)Q$, $r = \hat{e}(T, (se_j + u_j)^{-1}Q)$, and $Z = \theta^{-1}SK_j + H_3(r)Q$, where h is the value of $H_4(m, M_l, PPK_l, r)$. Finally, C outputs $c = m \oplus H_3(r)$ and sends the ciphertext $\delta = (c, T, Z, S)$ to $\Im_I$.
- Unsigncryption queries: $\Im_I$ sends the ciphertext $\delta = (c, T, Z, S)$, the sender's ID_i and the receiver's ID_j to C. If the target identity $l \neq j$, then C knows the private key SK_j of the receiver and returns the result according to the

Verification algorithm. If the target identity $l = j$ but $l \neq i$, then C knows the private key SK_i of the sender. For a valid ciphertext, $\log_{(se_i+u_i)^{-1}Q}(\theta S - h(se_i + u_i)^{-1}Q) = \log_{(\theta+h_{2,l})(se_l+u_l)Q}T$ can be calculated, where h is the value of $H_4(m, M_i, PPK_i, r)$. So the equation $\hat{e}(T, (se_i + u_i)^{-1}Q) = \hat{e}((\theta + h_{2,l})(se_l + u_l)Q, \theta S - h(se_i + u_i)^{-1}Q)$ holds. C computes $\xi = \hat{e}(S, (\theta + h_{2,i})(se_i + u_i)Q)$ and searches for $(m_i, M_i, PPK_i, r_i, h_{4,i}, c, \xi)$ in the list L_4. If it does not exist, then C rejects the ciphertext δ, otherwise, C computes whether $\frac{\hat{e}(T,(se_i+u_i)^{-1}Q)}{\hat{e}((\theta+h_{2,l})(se_l+u_l)Q,\theta S)} = \hat{e}((\theta + h_{2,l})(se_l + u_l)Q, (se_i + u_i)^{-1}Q)^{-h_{4,i}}$ holds. If holds, C returns the corresponding message m_i. Otherwise, C rejects the ciphertext δ.

Challenge: $\Im_I$ sends two message (m_0, m_1) of the same length, the sender's ID_A and the receiver's ID_B to C. If the target identity $ID_l \neq ID_B$, then C fails. Otherwise, C randomly selects $c^* \in \{0,1\}^n, \lambda \in Z_p^*, S^* \in G_1$, computes $T^* = -\lambda\theta Q - \lambda h_{2,B}Q$, and sends the ciphertext $\delta^* = (c^*, T^*, Z^*, S^*)$ to $\Im_I$. If we define $\rho = \frac{\lambda}{\alpha}$ and $u_l = -\alpha - se_l$, we can expand the equation as $T^* = -\lambda\theta Q - \lambda h_{2,B}Q = -\alpha\rho\theta Q - \alpha\rho h_{2,B}Q = (se_B + u_B)\rho\theta Q + (se_B + u_B)\rho h_{2,B}Q = \rho(\theta + h_{2,B})(se_B + u_B)Q = \rho PPK_B$.

Phase 2: Adversary $\Im_I$ performs adaptive queries as in phase 1. But $\Im_I$ cannot perform a private key query and a partial private key query on the target identity ID_B if the pseudonym public key PPK_B has been replaced. $\Im_I$ cannot ask an unsigncryption query on the target ciphertext δ^*.

Guess: $\Im_I$ submits the β^* to determine whether $\beta^* = \beta$ holds. If equal, $\Im_I$ wins the game and C can solve the q-BDHI problem.

C from the list L_3 to get $(r_i, h_{3,i})$ randomly or from the list L_4 to get $(m_i, M_i, PPK_i, r_i, h_{4,i}, c_i, \xi_i)$ randomly. The correct element is $r_i = \hat{e}(Q,Q)^\rho = \hat{e}(P,P)^{f(\alpha)^2\frac{\lambda}{\alpha}}$. Suppose $\xi^* = \hat{e}(P,P)^{\frac{1}{\alpha}}$, the q-BDHI problem can be solved [6] by equation $\hat{e}(Q,Q)^{\frac{1}{\alpha}} = \xi^{*(c_0^2)}\hat{e}(\sum_{j=0}^{q-2}c_{j+1}(\alpha^jP), c_0P)\hat{e}(Q, \sum_{j=0}^{q-2}c_{j+1}(\alpha^j)P)$.

In order to calculate the probability advantage of C, define the probability events. E_1: $\Im_I$ has not chosen to challenge the target identity ID_l as the receiver's identity. E_2: $\Im_I$ has asked a private key query on ID_l. E_3: $\Im_I$ replaces the pseudonym public key of the target identity ID_l and asks a partial private key query on ID_l before the challenge phase. E_4: C finds a conflict in the value of H_4 in the signcryption queries, and terminates the queries. E_5: C rejects a valid ciphertext in the unsigncryption queries, thus terminating the queries.

According to above analysis, we know that $Pr[\neg E_1] = \frac{1}{q_{H_1}}$, $Pr[E_4] = \frac{q_s(q_s+q_{H_4})}{2^k}$, and $Pr[E_5] = \frac{q_u}{2^k}$. Since the event E_1 contains the event E_2 and E_3, the probability that C not terminate the game is $Pr[\neg abort] = Pr[\neg E_1 \wedge \neg E_4 \wedge \neg E_5] \geq \frac{1}{q_{H_1}}(1 - \frac{q_s(q_s+q_{H_4})}{2^k})(1 - \frac{q_u}{2^k})$. Also, the probability that C obtains the record with the correct element from the list L_3 or list L_4 is $\frac{1}{q_{H_3}+2q_{H_4}}$. Therefore, the probability advantage is $\epsilon' \geq \frac{\epsilon}{q_{H_1}(q_{H_3}+2q_{H_4})}(1 - \frac{q_s(q_s+q_{H_4})}{2^k})(1 - \frac{q_u}{2^k})$. C takes time to complete the preparation phase as $O(q_{H_1}^2)$ point multiplication operations and time to complete the signcryption and unsigncryption queries as $O(q_s + q_u)$ bilinear pairing operations and $O(q_u q_{H_4})$ exponentiation operations.

Lemma 2. *Under the random oracle model, if there exists an adversary $\Im_{II}$ with a non-negligible probability advantage ϵ that wins the IND-CCA2-II security model game. Then C can solve the q-BDHI problem.*

Proof. Given a random instance $(P, \alpha P, \alpha^2 P, ..., \alpha^q P)$ of the q-BDHI problem, C solves the q-BDHI problem using $\Im_{II}$ and generates the following interaction procedure.

In Game-II, $\Im_{II}$ is similar to Game-I, expect pseudonym public key replacement queries.

Nonetheless, $\Im_{II}$ has the capability to steal the master key s and so has the possibility to crack the ciphertext of the target identity ID_l. When $\Im_{II}$ tries to crack a ciphertext, it must generate D_l beforehand, which is accessible to everyone via the smart contract SC_{KGC}. If successful, this means that 51% of the attacks are carried out in the blockchain system. That is, 51% of the attack requires $\frac{H_{\Im_{II}}}{H_t} \leq 51\%$, where $H_{\Im_{II}}$ denotes the available computational power of $\Im_{II}$ and H_t denotes the total computational power in the system. Due to the tamper-proof specification of smart contract and blockchain, it is almost impossible for $\Im_{II}$ to launch such an attack with sufficient hash power [22]. Therefore, the success probability ϵ' of adversary $\Im_{II}$ can be calculated as $\epsilon' \geq \frac{\epsilon}{q_{H_1}(q_{H_3} + 2q_{H_4})}(1 - \frac{q_s(q_s + q_{H_4})}{2^k})(1 - \frac{q_u}{2^k}) + P(\frac{H_{\Im_{II}}}{H_t} \leq 51\%)$, where $P(\frac{H_{\Im_{II}}}{H_t} \leq 51\%)$ is the probability of occurrence of a 51% attack performed by $\Im_{II}$. C takes time to complete the preparation phase as $O(q_{H_1}^2)$ point multiplication operations and time to complete the signcryption and unsigncryption queries as $O(q_s + q_u)$ bilinear pairing operations and $O(q_u q_{H_4})$ exponentiation operations.

Lemma 3. *Under the random oracle model, if there exists an adversary $\Im_I$ with a non-negligible probability advantage ϵ that wins the EUF-CMA-I security model game. Then C can solve the q-SDH problem.*

Proof. In Game-III, the proof is similar to the proof of Game-I, and its intermediate procedure will not be recapitulated. Using the forking lemma [19], assume that $\Im_I$ forges a ciphertext with probability $\epsilon' \geq \frac{10(q_s + 1)(q_s + q_{H_4})}{2^k}$, and then there exists time $t' \leq 120686 q_{H_1} \frac{t}{\epsilon}$ within which two valid ciphertext signatures (m, r, h_1, S_1), (m, r, h_2, S_2), where $h_1 \neq h_2$.

$\Im_I$ after inputting (X, ID_l) with sufficient time, two appropriate forged ciphertexts will be obtained (m_l, r, h_1, S_1), (m_l, r, h_2, S_2), where $h_1 \neq h_2$, but with common m_l and r. C recovers (ID_l, w_l) from the list L_1, where $w_l \neq w_1, .., w_{l-1}, w_{l+1}, w_q$ has a probability of at least $1 - \frac{q_{H_1}}{2^k}$.

If both forged ciphertexts satisfy the *Verification* algorithm, we can obtain the relation $\hat{e}(S_1, PPK)\hat{e}(Q, Q)^{-h_1} = \hat{e}(S_2, PPK)\hat{e}(Q, Q)^{-h_2}$, where $PPK = (\theta + H_2(\theta PK))(D + u)Q = (\theta + H_2(\theta PK))(w_l + \alpha)Q$, extracting the common part $\frac{1}{\theta + H_2(\theta PK)}$ of S_1 and S_2 and the relation becomes $\hat{e}(\frac{1}{\theta + H_2(\theta PK)}S_1', (\theta + H_2(\theta PK))(w_l + \alpha)Q)\hat{e}(Q, Q)^{-h_1} = \hat{e}(\frac{1}{\theta + H_2(\theta PK)}S_2', (\theta +$

$H_2(\theta PK))(w_l + \alpha)Q)\hat{e}(Q,Q)^{-h_2}$. The simplification gives $\hat{e}((h_1 - h_2)^{-1}(S_1' - S_2'), (w_l + \alpha)Q) = \hat{e}(Q,Q)$, hence $T_l = (h_1 - h_2)^{-1}(S_1' - S_2') = \frac{1}{w_l+\alpha}Q$.

Before returning the result (w_l, δ_l), use the long division expansion $f(z) = \gamma(z)(z + w_l) + \gamma_{-1}$ [7], where $\gamma(z) = \sum_{i=0}^{q-2} \gamma_i z^i$, $\gamma_{-1} \in Z_p^*$. Since $f(z) = \prod_{i=1}^{q-1}(z + w_i)$, which is not divisible by $(z + w_l)$, can be computed $\frac{f(z)}{z+w_l} = \frac{\gamma_{-1}}{z+w_l} + \sum_{i=0}^{q-2} \gamma_i z^i$. Finally, compute $\delta_l = \frac{1}{\gamma_{-1}}(T_l - \sum_{i=0}^{q-2} \gamma_i(\alpha^i P)) = \frac{1}{\gamma_{-1}}(\frac{f(\alpha)}{\alpha+w_l}P + \frac{\gamma_{-1}}{\alpha+w_l}P - \frac{f(\alpha)}{\alpha+w_l}P) = \frac{1}{\alpha+w_l}P$.

If $\Im_I$ may forge a ciphertext with probability $\epsilon' \geq \frac{10(q_s+1)(q_s+q_{H_4})}{2^k}$ in time t, then C can solve the q-SDH problem in the desired time $t' \leq 120686 q_{H_1} q_{H_4} \frac{t + O(q_s t_p)}{\epsilon'(1 - \frac{q_{H_1}}{2^k})} + O(q_{H_1}^2 t_m)$, where $O(q_{H_1}^2 t_m)$ is the time cost required for the point multiplication operation in the preparation phase.

Lemma 4. *Under the random oracle model, if there exists an adversary $\Im_{II}$ with a non-negligible probability advantage ϵ that wins the EUF-CMA-II security model game. Then C can solve the q-SDH problem.*

Proof. In Game-IV, the proof is similar to the proof of Game-II, and its intermediate procedure will not be recapitulated. Therefore, the success probability ϵ' of adversary $\Im_{II}$ can be calculated as $\epsilon' \geq \frac{10(q_s+1)(q_s+q_{H_4})}{2^k} + P(\frac{H_{\Im_{II}}}{H_t} \leq 51\%)$. C takes time to complete the signcryption queries as $O(q_s)$ bilinear pairing operations.

4.2   Informal Security

In this subsection, we will discuss some possible features of the scheme.

Anonymity: The purpose of anonymity is to hide the true identity, and various techniques are usually used to achieve this purpose. Assuming that an adversary captures the transmitted messages if the identity is not hidden, the adversary can easily know the true identity of the associated. Since we use the identity tag to indicate the origin of the pseudonym public key, the receiver can retrieve the corresponding sender's public key on the blockchain through the identity tag. Only the receiver can know the identity tag of the sender, but it is still not enough to know the true identity of the sender. Other users on the blockchain can only know that two anonymous users have made a transaction, but the real public keys of both are not known, only the pseudonym public keys of the transactions. Therefore, the OTACLSC scheme in this paper achieves anonymity.

KGC Compromised Attack: In the traditional anonymous certificateless scheme, there is always a centralized KGC. Although it is possible to build the KGC on the blockchain, there is a risk of the KGC being compromised, which can bring security vulnerabilities. To solve this problem, we use the smart contract instead of the original KGC. If there exists an adversary trying to control the whole blockchain system, this requires a 51% attack. From the perspective of the current blockchain system, this would undoubtedly spend a huge amount of cost, and it is unlikely that an adversary could obtain some secret values or even crack the blockchain system. Therefore, the OTACLSC scheme proposed in this paper can successfully defend against the KGC compromised attack.

Replay Attack: An adversary intercepts a received signature and resends it for spoofing purposes, most likely during the verification process. It is assumed that all signatures generated or transmitted by the sender can be intercepted by the adversary. If the actual timestamp is not used, the adversary can replay the received signature to the verifier to perform fake verification and gain the trust of the verifier. Therefore, in this paper, timestamps are added as an important element in the querying and signcryption process, and then each verifier needs to check the validity of the timestamp. Finally, the OTACLSC scheme in this paper can prevent potential replay attacks.

Man-in-the-Middle Attack: Most certificateless schemes assume that the user interacts with the KGC through a secure channel, thus ignoring the high probability of the man-in-the-middle attack. However, in a real-world environment, this type of attack occurs from time to time. To prevent an adversary from intercepting and altering all messages transmitted in this channel, we construct secure encryption with elliptic curves using a random value τ submitted by the receiver so that the pseudonym public key is transmitted implicitly. The returned pseudonym public key can be decrypted only by the receiver who knows the random value, i.e., $PPK_B + \tau sP$. Therefore, the OTACLSC scheme in this paper excludes man-in-the-middle attacks.

Forgery Attack: Based on the security definition mentioned in the previous subsection, we can know that the advantage of an adversary forging a valid signature is negligible. Since the receiver can correctly verify the result using the pseudonym public key provided by SC_{KGC} and the corresponding ciphertext, the OTACLSC scheme proposed in this paper is secure against forgery attacks.

Big Data Clustering Attack: The information of all transactions can be viewed on the blockchain, and the real information of users can be inferred from the transaction records. If only a single pseudonym is used, the adversary can infer the corresponding transaction rule by obtaining the user's transaction records, thus exposing the real information. To resist such attacks, we adopt the one-time pseudonym approach and do not repeatedly use a pseudonym to prevent adversaries from associating pseudonyms. Therefore, the OTACLSC scheme in this paper can resist the big data clustering attack.

5   Performance Analysis

In this paper, we compare the computation and communication cost of the anonymous certificateless signcryption scheme with those of Tseng et al. [21], Mandal et al. [16], and Xu et al. [23].

The experiments are based on Intel(R) Core(TM) i5-11400 CPU @ 2.60 GHz, 16.00 GB RAM and PBC library [15] on Windows 10. The results are shown in

Table 1. Where h denotes the hash function operation, mul denotes the point multiplication operation in G_1, exp denotes the exponentiation operation in G_2, and $pair$ denotes the bilinear pairing operation in G_1. $|m|$ denotes the length of the message, $|Z_p^*|$ denotes the length of the element in Z_p^*, $|G_1|$ denotes the length of the element in G_1, and $|G_2|$ denotes the length of the element in G_2.

Table 1. Performance comparison of certificateless signcryption schemes

Schemes	Signcryption/encryption	Unsigncryption/decryption	Ciphertext size
Tseng et al. [21]	$2h + 5mul + 2pair + 1exp$	$2h + 2mul + 2pair + 1exp$	$2\left|Z_p^*\right| + 3\left|G_1\right| + \left|G_2\right| = 363\ bytes$
Mandal et al. [16]	$12h + 11mul$	$9h + 3mul$	$1\left|m\right| + 3\left|Z_p^*\right| + 4\left|G_1\right| = 340\ bytes$
Xu et al. [23]	$3h + 3mul + 3pair$	$3h + 2mul + 1pair$	$1\left|m\right| + 1\left|Z_p^*\right| + 1\left|G_1\right| = 105\ bytes$
Ours	$2h + 4mul + 1exp$	$1h + 1mul + 3pair + 1exp$	$1\left|m\right| + 3\left|G_1\right| = 215\ bytes$

5.1 Computation Cost

To show the performance difference between the schemes more intuitively, the code can be reproduced according to the algorithm design in each literature, and the results are shown in Fig. 2. The experimental results are taken as the average value after 100 times of the same operation.

From Table 1 and Fig. 2, it can be seen that our scheme has less computation cost than the other schemes in the signcryption process, and although the schemes of Mandal et al. [16] and Xu et al. [23] are better than our scheme in the unsigncryption process, the overall computation cost is still the smallest in our scheme. Therefore, the computation cost of this paper's OTACLSC scheme is better than the above schemes.

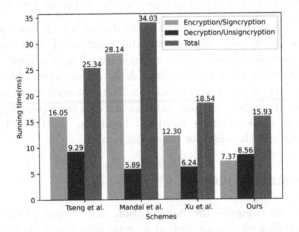

Fig. 2. Comparison of computation cost.

5.2 Communication Cost

For comparison, we assume that the message $|m|$ length is 160 bits, $\left|Z_p^*\right|$ length is 160 bits, $|G_1|$ length is 520 bits, and $|G_2|$ length is 1024 bits.

From Table 1, we can see that the ciphertext length used in our scheme is more advantageous than the schemes of Tseng et al. [21] and Mandal et al. [16], but longer than Xu et al. [23], because we add anonymity processing to protect our identity, while the scheme of Xu et al. [23] does not implement anonymity. The extra ciphertext length is acceptable considering the big data clustering attack. Therefore, the communication cost of the OTACLSC scheme in this paper is better than the above scheme.

5.3 Security Features Comparison

In this paper, we study the above security features and compare the anonymous certificateless signcryption scheme with other schemes in the literature, and the results are shown in Table 2.

Among the anonymity features, only Xu et al. [23] did not achieve anonymity. Due to the tamper-proof characteristic of blockchain, we use the smart contract to replace the function of KGC so that no one can falsify the data, not even the owner who issues the smart contract itself. At the same time, malicious nodes in the blockchain cannot access any private information of the smart contract, thus resisting the KGC compromise attack, which is not considered in other schemes. Considering the threat of the big data clustering attack, this paper uses a one-time pseudonym public key to circumvent the possible strong relationship between identity and public key, and can securely transmit relevant messages without passing through a secure channel, which is not reflected in other schemes. Therefore, the anonymous certificateless signcryption scheme in this paper can well solve the above attacks and achieve higher security.

Table 2. Comparison of security features

Features	Tseng et al. [21]	Mandal et al. [16]	Xu et al. [23]	Ours
Anonymity	Y	Y	N	Y
KGC compromised attack	N	N	N	Y
Replay attack	Y	Y	Y	Y
Man-in-the-middle attack	Y	Y	Y	Y
Forgery attack	Y	Y	Y	Y
Big data clustering attack	N	N	N	Y

Y: "a scheme is secure or it provides a functionality feature"; N: "a scheme is insecure or it does not provide a functionality feature".

6 Conclusion

In this paper, we propose a new OTACLSC scheme based on blockchain, which optimizes the computation cost and ciphertext length compared to other schemes and proves the security of this scheme under the random oracle model. This scheme is resistant to the possible attacks mentioned above and does not require a secure channel, so it requires less cost to maintain secure communication compared to other schemes. Due to the higher level of anonymity achieved, one does not have to worry about revealing one's identity in blockchain by the big data clustering attack. At the same time, this paper is one-time anonymity, which does not need to save the related data and reduces the overhead required to maintain the anonymity list. In the future, reducing the scheme cost and proposing more generalized anonymization methods will be the next research direction.

References

1. Al-Riyami, S.S., Paterson, K.G.: Certificateless public key cryptography. In: Laih, C.-S. (ed.) ASIACRYPT 2003. LNCS, vol. 2894, pp. 452–473. Springer, Heidelberg (2003). https://doi.org/10.1007/978-3-540-40061-5_29
2. An, J.H., Dodis, Y., Rabin, T.: On the security of joint signature and encryption. In: Knudsen, L.R. (ed.) EUROCRYPT 2002. LNCS, vol. 2332, pp. 83–107. Springer, Heidelberg (2002). https://doi.org/10.1007/3-540-46035-7_6
3. Ao, W., Fu, S., Zhang, C., Huang, Y., Xia, F.: A secure identity authentication scheme based on blockchain and identity-based cryptography. In: 2019 IEEE 2nd International Conference on Computer and Communication Engineering Technology (CCET), pp. 90–95. IEEE (2019)
4. Axon, L.: Privacy-awareness in blockchain-based PKI. CDT technical paper series **21**, 15 (2015)
5. Barbosa, M., Farshim, P.: Certificateless signcryption. In: Proceedings of the 2008 ACM Symposium on Information, Computer and Communications Security, pp. 369–372 (2008)
6. Barreto, P.S.L.M., Libert, B., McCullagh, N., Quisquater, J.-J.: Efficient and provably-secure identity-based signatures and signcryption from bilinear maps. In: Roy, B. (ed.) ASIACRYPT 2005. LNCS, vol. 3788, pp. 515–532. Springer, Heidelberg (2005). https://doi.org/10.1007/11593447_28
7. Boneh, D., Boyen, X.: Short signatures without random oracles. In: Cachin, C., Camenisch, J.L. (eds.) EUROCRYPT 2004. LNCS, vol. 3027, pp. 56–73. Springer, Heidelberg (2004). https://doi.org/10.1007/978-3-540-24676-3_4
8. Cheng, G., Chen, Y., Deng, S., Gao, H., Yin, J.: A blockchain-based mutual authentication scheme for collaborative edge computing. IEEE Trans. Comput. Soc. Syst. **9**(1), 146–158 (2021)
9. Clack, C.D., Bakshi, V.A., Braine, L.: Smart contract templates: essential requirements and design options. arXiv preprint arXiv:1612.04496 (2016)
10. Fromknecht, C., Velicanu, D., Yakoubov, S.: A decentralized public key infrastructure with identity retention. IACR Cryptology ePrint Archive 2014/803 (2014)
11. Gervais, M., Sun, L., Wang, K., Li, F.: Certificateless authenticated key agreement for decentralized WBANs. In: Shen, B., Wang, B., Han, J., Yu, Y. (eds.) FCS 2019. CCIS, vol. 1105, pp. 268–290. Springer, Singapore (2019). https://doi.org/10.1007/978-981-15-0818-9_18

12. Guo, X., Guo, Q., Liu, M., Wang, Y., Ma, Y., Yang, B.: A certificateless consortium blockchain for IoTs. In: 2020 IEEE 40th International Conference on Distributed Computing Systems (ICDCS), pp. 496–506. IEEE (2020)

13. Li, F., Han, Y., Jin, C.: Certificateless online/offline signcryption for the Internet of Things. Wireless Netw. **23**(1), 145–158 (2017). https://doi.org/10.1007/s11276-015-1145-3

14. Li, R., Song, T., Mei, B., Li, H., Cheng, X., Sun, L.: Blockchain for large-scale Internet of Things data storage and protection. IEEE Trans. Serv. Comput. **12**(5), 762–771 (2018)

15. Lynn, B.: PBC library: the pairing-based cryptography library (2013). https://crypto.stanford.edu/pbc/. Accessed 1 May 2022

16. Mandal, S., Bera, B., Sutrala, A.K., Das, A.K., Choo, K.K.R., Park, Y.: Certificateless-signcryption-based three-factor user access control scheme for IoT environment. IEEE Internet Things J. **7**(4), 3184–3197 (2020)

17. Pang, L., Kou, M., Wei, M., Li, H.: Anonymous certificateless multi-receiver signcryption scheme without secure channel. IEEE Access **7**, 84091–84106 (2019)

18. Pang, L., Wei, M., Li, H.: Efficient and anonymous certificateless multi-message and multi-receiver signcryption scheme based on ECC. IEEE Access **7**, 24511–24526 (2019)

19. Pointcheval, D., Stern, J.: Security arguments for digital signatures and blind signatures. J. Cryptol. **13**(3), 361–396 (2000). https://doi.org/10.1007/s001450010003

20. Shamir, A.: Identity-based cryptosystems and signature schemes. In: Blakley, G.R., Chaum, D. (eds.) CRYPTO 1984. LNCS, vol. 196, pp. 47–53. Springer, Heidelberg (1985). https://doi.org/10.1007/3-540-39568-7_5

21. Tseng, Y.F., Fan, C.I.: Provably CCA-secure anonymous multi-receiver certificateless authenticated encryption. J. Inf. Sci. Eng. **34**(6), 1517–1541 (2018)

22. Wang, W., Xu, H., Alazab, M., Gadekallu, T.R., Han, Z., Su, C.: Blockchain-based reliable and efficient certificateless signature for IIoT devices. IEEE Trans. Ind. Inform. **18**(10), 7059–7067 (2022)

23. Xu, G., Dong, J., Ma, C.: A certificateless encryption scheme based on blockchain. Peer-to-Peer Netw. Appl. **14**, 2952–2960 (2021). https://doi.org/10.1007/s12083-021-01147-w

24. Xu, S., Chen, X., He, Y.: EVchain: an anonymous blockchain-based system for charging-connected electric vehicles. Tsinghua Sci. Technol. **26**(6), 845–856 (2021)

25. Yuan, Y., Wang, F.: Current status and prospects of blockchain technology development. Acta Automatica Sinica **42**(4), 481–494 (2016)

Author Index

Printed in the United States
by Baker & Taylor Publisher Services

Printed in the United States
by Baker & Taylor Publisher Services